The Lucy Book

The Lucy Book

A Complete Guide to Her Five Decades on Television

GEOFFREY MARK FIDELMAN

BOOKS
RENAISSANCE BOOKS
Los Angeles

Library of Congress Cataloging-in-Publication Data
Fidelman, Geoffrey Mark.
The Lucy book / Geoffrey Mark Fidelman.
p. cm.
Includes index.
ISBN 1-58063-051-0 (pbk. : alk. paper)
1. Ball, Lucille, 1911– —Miscellanea. 2. Ball, Lucille, 1911– —Credits. I. Title.
PN2287.B16F54 1999
794.45'028'092—dc21 99-18747
CIP

10 9 8 7 6 5 4 3 2 1

Design by Lisa-Theresa Lenthall
Typeset by Jesus Arellano

Distributed by St. Martin's Press
Manufactured in the United States of America
First Edition

A Word from Lucie Arnaz and Desi Arnaz Jr.

This is quite a manuscript . . . or should we say MAMMOTH—script! It took over a week, reading every chance we got, to finish it. What a job! We are very impressed with the amount of research done. The TV-watching time alone must have put the author into bottle-bottom glasses. Lucy fans and radio and television scholars for decades will be indebted to Geoffrey for not only providing them with this wealth of comprehensive and detailed information, but, also, for making it such an enjoyable read.

This book is successful, in our minds, because the author sticks to the actual facts that have to do with the specific production of these programs and lets the reader in "behind the scenes" to little oddities. The trivia in the book makes for a great deal of fun. Great joy is brought through this book. This is a delightful tome.

This book is dedicated to all those millions of people (past, present, and future) whose lives were forever enriched when they turned on a television set and found joy in Lucille Ball's *Lucy*.

To Lucie Arnaz and Desi Arnaz Jr., who are both the fortunate and yet unwitting heirs to the tremendous legacy of their parents. May they both find serenity and peace in enjoying their own unique talents as the intelligent, charming, and generous people they are.

And to my extraordinary and beloved mother, my very own Viv, who always let me stay up late on Monday nights to watch *Lucy*, no matter what. See Mom, it was worth it!

Contents

Foreword

by
Steve Allen

Each generation chooses its own celebrities and heroes and is often remarkably ignorant about those of earlier periods. In my own youth, for example, while I was familiar with such esteemed names as Francis X. Bushman and Rudolph Valentino I had no serious interest in either the actors themselves or the films they had made. As we enter the twenty-first century we see that this same historic pattern continues, as it presumably always will. Today's twenty-year olds, although they are members of the most celebrity-obsessed generation in cultural history, simply do not care a great deal about many of the major television names of the 1950s. Jackie Gleason would now be of little interest to people were it not for the delightful *Honeymooners* sketches that were originally only one component of his comedy/variety shows. Fred Allen referred to his own work in radio and television as a "treadmill to oblivion." The same general pattern has presented itself as regards such other comedians of major importance as Milton Berle, Red Skelton, George Burns and Gracie Allen, and dozens of comic luminaries of lesser stature.

Lucille Ball is obviously an exception because she had the good fortune to perform in the sitcom structure, as a result of which to the present moment her programs are still being exhibited, and in many parts of the world. The specific reasons for Miss Ball's remarkable success and longevity are fully explored in the present volume by Mr. Fidelman.

Other books about the Lucy phenomenon have been written, and probably additional volumes will follow as new generations of cultural historians become fascinated by her. But it will be difficult to improve on the present work so far as the breadth of research is concerned.

For one thing the book includes . . . photographs that have not previously been published.

It is also important that the present volume provides one more opportunity to credit Lucille's highly talented coworkers, such as producer-writer Jess Oppenheimer, and the writing team of Bob Carroll Jr. and Madelyn Pugh, who worked for me before I left Hollywood for New York, which made it possible for them to move into Desi and Lucy's orbit. And speaking of Desi, he was far more than the good-looking Cuban gentleman who the public probably always thought of as little more than Lucille's straight man.

Everyone who enjoyed Lucille Ball's work will be fascinated by this *Lucy Book.*

Preface

This book chronicles the entire television career, season by season, of Lucille Ball. Starting with the 1947–48 season, every single prime time network appearance is covered, including her own five series (*I Love Lucy*, *The Lucille Ball-Desi Arnaz Show*, *The Lucy Show*, *Here's Lucy*, and *Life with Lucy*) and their network reruns, as well as Lucille's appearances on other situation comedies, dramas, game shows, talk shows, variety shows, and miscellaneous specials. Each show is broken down by cast members, crew, and plot, as well as original air date. Pertinent information about the great Ball's involvement with the show is discussed in detail, and critical analysis offered of her performances.

All shows listed are in color, *except* for those that carry the legend (b&w). If any shows are in *both* color and black and white, they will be indicated by the legend (color, b&w). ABC stands for the American Broadcasting Company, CBS for the Columbia Broadcasting System, FOX for Fox Television, HBO for Home Box Office, NBC for the National Broadcasting Company, and SYN for syndicated shows that were not on any of the networks of the time. All dates given are for the actual air dates of the shows, except where noted otherwise. The episode numbers of Lucille's series are for the order in which they aired, *not* for the order filmed. In some instances, certain listings have abbreviated cast and crew information due to lack of space or the limitations of best available information.

To differentiate the actress from the same-named characters she played, Lucille refers to Miss Ball, while Lucy refers to the character. In some cases, persons quoted refer to the actress as Lucy. Although it is no longer politically correct to refer to women as girls and men as boys, the Ricardos and the Mertzes will often be referred to in just such a manner in the synopses, because that is how they are referred to in the scripts. Ricky Ricardo will always be referred to as *Ricky*; for purposes of distinction, the offspring Ricky Ricardo Jr. will always be called *Little Ricky*. The plural of Arnaz is Arnazes, and that of Mertz is Mertzes; the possessive of Arnaz is Arnaz', and that of Mertz is Mertz'. Original *Lucy* writer Madelyn Pugh married twice during her long career, changing her last name first to Martin and then to Davis. These last names are reflected in the individual listings, but her quotes use her full name, Madelyn Pugh Martin Davis.

Adding spice to this already tasty stew are exclusive interviews with the performers and creative people who worked with Miss Ball over the many years. You will find an identifier in parentheses following their name, i.e., Jess Oppenheimer (producer). When you see "anonymous" before a quote, that person did not wish to have his/her identity revealed, but was happy to supply information "on the record."

I am grateful to those who shared their pertinent memories with me. There were some people interviewed whose recollections and observations were condensed or not used due to lack of space; my apologies. In some cases, I used the information provided without crediting a specific person, because it came from several different sources. Others refused to be interviewed. So be it.

There are additional entries of *some* of Lucille's more interesting syndicated and daytime appearances. Due to space consideration, it was infeasible to include every single nonnetwork, local, or daytime show Lucille Ball did over the decades. If this tome were any longer, it would have to be published with an intermission. If you have questions or comments, drop me a line in care of the publisher or E-mail me at WRITEGOOD@aol.com. I promise to answer everyone personally and update the book for the next edition.

—*Geoffrey Mark Fidelman*
Sherman Oaks, California

Acknowledgments

Very special thanks must be given to Lucie Arnaz and Desi Arnaz Jr. These fine people are besieged on a daily basis for information and use of their parents' names and likenesses. Lucie not only allowed me to interview her, but she contacted people on my behalf and donated photographs for this book. Without any doubt, her graciousness and generosity have made this a better book. Desi Jr. had not given an interview about his career in seventeen years when he opened up his professional life to me. His candor, willingness to discuss any subject relating to the work of his parents and that of himself, and support for this project are hugely appreciated. He is a brilliant and very special man.

It has been my very great pleasure and honor to personally interview the following very talented people for this book: Edie Adams, Steve Allen, Frank Alleter, Patty Andrews, Larry Anderson, William Asher, Lucille Ball, Kaye Ballard, Milton Berle, Dann Cahn, Jack Carter, Angela Cartwright, Tina Cole, Mike Connors, Carole Cook, Eliot Daniel, Irving Fein, Kathleen Freeman, Beverly Garland, Jimmy Garrett, Gale Gordon, Bert Granet, Pat Harrington Jr., Jerry Hausner, Jane Kean, Herbert Kenwith, Irma Kusely, Fernando Lamas, Ruta Lee, Ralph Levy, Barry Livingston, Stanley Livingston, Marjorie Lord, Sheila MacRae, Steve March, Dick Martin, Mary Martin, Jayne Meadows, Ethel Merman, Candy Moore, Gary Morton, Jay North, Cliff Norton, Gregg Oppenheimer, Larry Orenstein, Robert Pine, Marco Rizo, Robert Rockwell, William Schallert, Bob Schiller, Sherwood Schwartz, Jack Sheldon, Stuart Shostak, Doris Singleton, Michael Stern, Keith Thibodeaux, Maury Thompson, Clint Walker, Bob Weiskopf, Mary Wickes, William Windom, Alan Young.

There are many others who have preferred to remain anonymous. I thank them for their candor and will respect their wishes.

There are those who contributed in other ways to the book. My gratitude must be extended to: Wanda Clark, Kieth Dodge, Elisabeth Edwards, Tom Gilbert, Museum of Television and Radio (Jonathan Rosenthal—Research), Gail Newman, Bob Palmer, Barry Saltzman, Coyne Steven Sanders, David Schwartz, Lloyd Schwartz, Paul Seratt, Stuart Shostak, Marc Staenberg, Hans Svanoe, Fred Wostbrock.

This project has taken many years to complete. Along the way, I have faced good times and bad. There are people who have literally helped keep a roof over my head and food in my stomach. From the bottom of my heart, I thank the Lord for people like these: David Baker, Todd Bernstein, Jack and Roxanne Carter, Steve and Karen

Garren, Dwayne and Joan Hickman, Brad McClung, Sharon McClung, Carol McDonald, Bill Megalos, Paul Mendez, Don O'Neil, Gloria Orenstein, Paul and Rana Petersen, Mike Pinney, Howard Rogut, Tom Santoro, Tina Schiavone, Grady and Tina Sloan, Steve and Janel Whitney.

I can only hope I will have an opportunity to be as good to you fine people as you have been to me.

My great appreciation will always be extended to James Robert Parish. He not only fought to get this book published and provided tireless, expert editing advice, but he has been a true friend. I thank you, Jim.

Introduction

Why another book about Lucille Ball? Certainly reams have been written about her life (1911–1989), going into great detail about her stormy marriage to Desi Arnaz. Many biographies have proffered details down to the minutiae of the early life of Lucille Ball, her rise to stardom, and the tragedy of her personal life. Chapters have been published about the very active romantic life of Desi Arnaz. Such well-written books as *Desilu: The Story of Lucille Ball and Desi Arnaz* (1993) by Coyne Steven Sanders and Tom Gilbert have covered the ins and outs of the television empire built by la famille Arnaz that ended by almost destroying them. Yet, in my opinion, they all seemed to overlook a point.

From her television debut on a local Los Angeles show in 1947 until her television obituaries in 1989, Lucille Ball had the greatest career on television of anyone. Period! No one has ever been, nor probably will ever be, able to come close to the popularity, quality, or output of America's favorite redhead. Her approach to comedy, one that borrowed from all the great masters yet was uniquely her own, has yet to be critically analyzed and put into proper perspective.

The legacy of Lucille Ball lies not in her personal travails, but in her professional work, and the enormous effect it had (and still does) on the entire world. Discussing her television career is not simply a matter of "and then she did another show. . . ." Whenever popular culture greatly influences not only popular opinion and behavior, but an entire industry as well, there is much grist beneath the surface. Why was Lucille Ball, the performer, so beloved? How did she manage, literally overnight, to change her career and the world's perception of television in the early 1950s? How was she able to sustain her work for almost forty years, when five years is a long time to be a star on the tube? What made her funny? What was her comedic attitude? Above all, how did all of this alter as she got older? All of these intriguing questions are answered in this book.

One of the most interesting things in writing about Lucille Ball is that she is already one of the most written about persons of the twentieth century. Few other people have had more articles, books, or interviews printed about them; many incredibly inaccurate. She has graced more magazine covers, more TV talk shows, and more gossip columns than several top personalities put together. The face of Lucille Ball is the most recognized countenance on the planet Earth (this has actually been documented).

To wit: On a trip to the Far East in the middle 1950s, she and husband Desi Arnaz took a fishing trip to a stream high up in some mountain range. They boated and climbed for hours, looking for just the right place to make camp. At dusk, after a journey of over eight hours into the most isolated area imaginable, they stopped at a hut to ask directions. Out came a little old Asian woman and her daughter. The locals looked at the Western couple with the mild curiosity of people who do not receive many visitors. The woman looked perplexed for a moment; then a broad grin covered her face as she said, "Ah! I Rove Rucy!" and offered the Arnazes her full hospitality.

Many years after her death in 1989, the interest in Lucille Ball is as intense today as it ever was. I have been studying and researching this book for more than twenty-five years. As a member of the handful of outsiders who have been privileged to know the Arnaz family and who are referred to as experts on the subject of Lucille Ball, I have enjoyed the cooperation of Lucie Arnaz and Desi Arnaz Jr., who allowed me to interview them at length. They also opened networking doors that had been previously closed regarding the career of Lucille (and *Lucy*). Without dipping into the dross of her personal life (except where it affected her work), there are enough fascinating details of what happened onstage (and slightly backstage) to make even conscientious readers of the supermarket tabloids sit up and take notice.

So, this is a book for "Lucy" lovers, television addicts, couch potatoes, scholars, pop-culture freaks, people who enjoy reading, people who enjoy laughing, or practically anyone who has ever turned on a TV set.

Chapter One

A Brief History of How Lucille Ball Became Lucy

Lucille Ball is the female embodiment of the great American dream—the self-made millionaire. She was born on August 6, 1911, of lower middle-class parents in Celoron, New York. (The town is a suburb of Jamestown in the far western part of the state, ninety miles south of Buffalo and near the Pennsylvania border.) From the start, Lucille strove to be great in her work, and after years of slowly finding her way up the show business ladder, she struck the biggest load of pay dirt since the Forty-Niners found gold in California—the "Lucy" character. Yet, as Lucille herself often said, there was no great motivation on her part to succeed in a man's world, no great desire to own a movie studio and have great power, just her ongoing motivation to survive.

Having lost her father while still a toddler and living through the impermanence caused by a hard-drinking stepfather and less than nurturing step-grandparents, Lucille learned early to rely on herself for what she needed and wanted in life. A latch-key child decades before such situations became commonplace, she had too few memories of the attention and love upon which many children depend. What was instilled in her was a New England work ethic that drove her throughout her life. Only the ministrations of her wonderful but highly eccentric grandfather Fred Hunt, whom she called "Daddy," gave her the sense of childhood and wonder that she would later infuse into her work before the cameras.

The narrative of Lucille's rise through the ranks is very well known by now. Her mother DeDe was liberated long before that term was in use. She wisely perceived her daughter's talent for performing and her burning ambition, and allowed her offspring to act upon them. The younger Ball moved to New York in 1926 to be an aspiring actress living on her own at fifteen; then a debilitating illness (which some have called a car accident, some have termed rheumatoid arthritis, and others have labeled a botched abortion) left her unable to function for over a year (1929–30).

When she recovered, Lucille modeled for the famous couturier Hattie Carnegie. That exposure helped the aspiring model become the Chesterfield cigarette poster girl, which led to Lucille's first movie contract with famed independent producer Samuel Goldwyn and her first trip to Hollywood in 1933. Thereafter, she was never out of work until age forced her into semiretirement in 1980.

While she was working with Goldwyn, she was used as nothing more than a glamour girl in several Eddie Cantor musical comedy movies. There she met two actresses who became close friends for life—Ethel Merman and Ann Sothern. In the mid-1930s, Lucille gambled with her salary by taking a drop in pay to move to Columbia Pictures. There she was used mostly in their short-subject unit. While many writers have detailed her early career with the comedic Three Stooges, the truth is just one movie short was made, *Three Little Pigskins* (1934). When dropped by Columbia that year, she simply walked across the street in Hollywood to the RKO Studios and got herself a contract there. She sent for her family, and, one by one, her brother Fred, cousin Cleo (to whom she referred, and loved, as a sister), mother DeDe, and Grandpa Hunt joined Lucille to live in a small rented cottage in the heart of Hollywood.

Lucille's earliest screen efforts at RKO were in the glory days of Ginger Rogers, Fred Astaire, Katharine Hepburn, and Cary Grant, who reigned at the studio. Bit roles eventually led to bigger parts, and finally Ball starred over the title in a melodrama, *Panama Lady* (1939). From there, she should have become one of the major actresses at RKO, but short-sightedness, budget cuts, and the latest studio-takeover forced Lucille to reassess her position in that film company's roster. In 1943, she took her assets over to MGM, the Tiffany of film studios. There, after dying her hair that soon-to-be trademark shade of red, she again became a glamour girl, playing second leads and wearing expensive clothing onscreen. In the late 1940s, Ball got frustrated and returned to Columbia, where she made nice, little dramatic films.

Back in 1940, while still at RKO, Ball was summoned to costar in the movie musical *Too Many Girls*, where she was introduced to one toast of New York: Desi Arnaz. Young Arnaz, born to a prominent Cuban family in 1917, had been forced to flee to America during the Batista revolution in his homeland. His dark, incredibly sexy good looks, talent for music, and even greater knack for self-promotion made him a star of New York's cafe society. The sensual beat of his Conga lines packed them in at some of the top Big Apple night spots. Desi proceeded to squire many of the most sought after women in the city, including debutantes like Brenda Frasier and such stars as Betty Grable and Ethel Merman.

Notoriety brought the Broadway musical comedy composer-writer team of Richard Rodgers and Lorenz Hart into Desi's life. With veteran director George Abbott they were casting for their next stage musical, the aforementioned *Too Many Girls* (1939). Desi won the part of Manuelito, the college football player with the fractured English. He stopped the show nightly with his hard-driving, pelvic-thrusting Conga playing. When the show was acquired by RKO for a movie adaptation, Arnaz came along to reprise his role, and met Lucille (who was *not* a blonde at the time, as he erroneously stated in his 1976 autobiography). The chemistry formed between Ball and Arnaz was nothing short of atomic, and burned as long as they both lived. Ball (age twenty-nine) and Arnaz (age twenty-three) were wed in Greenwich, Connecticut, in 1940.

By the late 1940s, Lucille had been through the mill of Hollywood, battling studio heads, fighting her wandering but loving husband, and combating approaching middle age. She had made over sixty motion pictures, dozens of radio appearances, toured successfully in the play *Dream Girl*, and found herself totally independent of long-term studio support and control. She was starring on radio, and her latest picture (*Sorrowful Jones*, 1949) had been with Bob Hope and was the biggest moneymaker in which either had ever been cast. She also had a three-picture deal at Columbia that had one film remaining to be made. Fate intervened in the double guise of Columbia Studios' mogul Harry Cohn and of mother nature.

Lucille was offered a key part—the elephant girl—in the Paramount epic, *The Greatest Show On Earth* (1952), to be directed by Cecil B. DeMille. Although Cohn had no immediate work for Lucille at Columbia, it bothered him to have someone else in Hollywood use *his* talent for profit. He stalled and stalled about agreeing to the loanout, and finally Lucille found herself in a two-part predicament: She was offered what was called a "contract breaker," an awful script in which no one in their right mind would appear; and she was pregnant.

Her physical condition already precluded her accepting the taxing role of the elephant girl in *The Greatest Show on Earth*, which went to Gloria Grahame. Her anger at Harry Cohn provoked her second decision: She would make that screen turkey for him, end her relationship with Columbia, collect $100,000 for five days of work, and laugh all the way to the bank. She knew that such a quickie movie would have no impact on her career, because Columbia wouldn't widely release such a bomb. In fact, only later as a *Late Show* entry on television was the film (*The Magic Carpet*, 1950) ever really seen by the public, capitalizing on her success with *I Love Lucy*.

When DeMille learned what Ball had done, he turned to Desi Arnaz and said, "Congratulations. You're the first man in history to fuck his wife, Columbia Studios, Harry Cohn, Paramount Pictures, and Cecil B. DeMille all at the same time!"

Working as an independent, Miss Ball juggled a still-thriving movie career with her role as Liz Cooper in the CBS radio sitcom *My Favorite Husband* (1948–51), with Richard Denning as her on-the-mike spouse. While the first episodes of that series were less than spectacular, a new producer (Jess Oppenheimer) brought on two young writers to punch up the scripts: Bob Carroll Jr. and Madelyn Pugh—her future *Lucy* team. Jess was a brilliant man, a hilarious writer, and a savvy producer. He knew that Lucille flourished in front of a live audience, and her best performances came from situational comedy where she could react and clown. His contributions to the success of this radio series, and to Lucille's upcoming television career, cannot be stated strongly enough. She had the brilliant raw talent, *but* it was Jess who mined it, and then refined it for consumption. His one-of-a-kind sense of humor infiltrated the scripts and comic situations, and, to a degree, Miss Ball's performances.

Bob and Madelyn wrote very literate scripts, which not only allowed the characters to expand, but gave Lucille direction in the playing of her character. It was they who conjured up ideas that later became *Lucy* staples, and ensured that the jokes were realistic *and* funny so even the wilder shows could be believable to the listeners of *My Favorite Husband.* Lucille never stopped giving thanks to Bob and Madelyn for the brilliant work they did for her.

Lucille knew she was on to something with *My Favorite Husband*, and the better the radio scripts became, the more she allowed herself to perform them fully, as if on stage or in front of a camera and/or audience, instead of just reading them. While the on-air interaction between herself and costar Denning was never explosive, she developed a real chemistry with series regular Bea Benaderet that infused every scene they had together. Like Miss Ball, Bea played the scenes for full measure as if she were on a stage instead of a radio show. There was that same spontaneity with many of the character actors who regularly guested on the radio sitcom, including Doris Singleton, Frank Nelson, and Shirley Mitchell (if these names don't sound familiar now, they will in a few chapters).

My Favorite Husband was a very successful show, but it came along just as radio was beginning to lose its mass audience to television. In this transition period, many radio programs were either dropped, or transferred to the infant medium. From 1947 to 1949, Lucille did several small variety appearances on local television in both New York and Los Angeles, as well as some early live network appearances. Her earliest surviving appearance (on kinescope) was in January of 1950, guest-starring with her Latin lover husband on *The Ed Wynn Show* (1949–50).

Often, it has been written that Lucille Ball *had* to go into television because her movie career was finished. This is patent nonsense. Truthfully, Lucille would probably have had to graduate to character parts in movies like her show business friends (Ann Sothern, Ethel Merman, Martha Raye, and Eve Arden) did, had her great success in television not come along. By the 1960s, Lucille might have been playing some young actress' mother on a sitcom. But Fate extended yet another helping hand to Lucille.

When the time came to transfer *My Favorite Husband* to television, what emerged was, well, you know what. However, the transfer was not without a great deal of *sturm und drang* in the process.

Lucille thought television was a great idea for this radio series, but she had one proviso: She wanted Desi to replace Richard Denning in the role of her oncamera husband. CBS balked at the idea, claiming that no television viewer would ever believe girl-next-door Lucille as having a Latin husband. Besides, the network had several seasons of success with the radio show that gave the newly proposed property a built-in audience, and that audience would expect the entire cast, including Denning, Gale Gordon, and Bea Benaderet to be part of the new media format. Ironically, none of them made the initial transition with Lucille onto TV's *I Love Lucy.*

Lucille Ball

They said they wanted someone Amuriken *to play my husband. CBS didn't think anyone would believe we were married, but I told [CBS executive] Harry Ackerman, "But we* are *married." Desi and CBS head Bill Paley had their squabbles, but I always got along with Paley. Once [for example] Desi proved to them that they had made a million-dollar mistake in their budgeting. He had papers laid out end to end in hallways to back him up. After that, Bill Paley gained new respect for Desi. He never really bothered him again.*

To prove the public would accept the Arnazes as a believable couple (after all, they actually *were* a couple), they went on the road in a vaudeville act. Although most of the great vaudeville houses of the early part of the century had already been replaced by movie theatres, many of them still existed in larger cities. They became stage presentation houses, which featured a motion picture with a stage show offered between the screenings. Many of the variety artists of the day still made big money this way, appearing as many as six or seven times each day doing a twenty-minute act.

The Arnazes met with Jess, Madelyn, Bob, and Desi's friend, the clown Pepito Perez, to come up with an act they could do together. They finally settled on an act that featured Desi's singing of "Babalu," and three comedy sketches that eventually found their way onto *I Love Lucy*.

The first skit was the "professor" bit, with Lucille parading through the audience dressed in a shaggy set of men's formal tails carrying a bass fiddle. The interplay between the two as she interrupted Desi's act and tried to join the band, stopped the show every time. While much of this was actually lifted from the act comedian Professor Irwin Corey had been doing for years, the combination of writing, props, and performance fractured the audiences wherever they appeared. Props became a huge part of Lucille's comedy, and her deftness at handling them was second only to the screen masters: Charlie Chaplin and Buster Keaton. (Keaton actually coached Ball on the use of props when both were under contract to MGM in the 1940s.) The other highlight of Lucille and Desi's stage act was the number "Cuban Pete," which included Lucille's bumps and grinds as she sang the second chorus of the song in a skin-tight green sequined gown. More about both of these in later chapters.

Bob Palmer

(PUBLICITY MAN FOR THE PARAMOUNT THEATRE IN SAN FRANCISCO IN 1950)

The Arnazes were terrific—warm and enthusiastic. Despite good publicity, the stage show failed to attract big audiences, partly because of rainy weather. Lucille mostly stayed in her dressing room between shows, sipping red wine because she said she had to build up her blood. She complained of being queasy. On stage she was radiant and adorable. Desi and I had dinner together a few times at a little restaurant called Original Joe's. He talked about hoping to produce a movie starring him and Lucille, but said nothing about television. While Desi grew loud and testy during the run because he was unhappy with the publicity and attendance, Lucille was sensitive and cried a few times. Incidentally, no one *called her "Lucy." After they left town, I learned she was pregnant.*

With stunning reviews and offers to play their act all over the world, Lucille and Desi first took their series idea to the ABC television network. Jess Oppenheimer thought the fledgling company, then number four behind CBS, NBC, and DuMont, might be the place to launch the TV show. Just in case, he also wanted a place to fail before tackling CBS. ABC turned them down flat, a decision that Leonard Goldenson (then president of ABC) must have regretted for the rest of his life. Had the program that became *I Love Lucy* debuted on ABC, it most likely would have been the number one network right from the beginning.

CBS finally agreed that perhaps Desi wasn't so bad a choice after all to play Lucille's oncamera husband. A pilot, written by Oppenheimer, Pugh, and Carroll, was performed and kinescoped (a copy made by filming off of the closed-circuit television screen). This film was taken to New York and licensed by the company that handled the advertising for Philip Morris cigarettes. They bought time on CBS for a half-hour show starring the Arnazes that would debut in October of 1951.

Lucille gave birth to her daughter, Lucie, in July 1951, and Desi ended his radio show, *Your Tropical Trip* (1950–51), that August. All was well, until the network wondered when the couple were coming East to start rehearsing the show. *Coming East?*

It had never occurred to Lucille and Desi that their television series would *not* be done live from Hollywood. Both comedians Ed Wynn and Alan Young had done their TV shows from West Coast theatres. The now-nervous couple wondered why they couldn't do the same. The sponsors insisted that they wanted the program done live from New York, so the East Coast would get the better quality TV pictures and thus sell more cigarettes in those heavily populated markets. (In those days, there were no cables running from coast to coast. Everything was live, on film, or on kinescope, and the latter—which suffered from poor quality—was unacceptable to the sponsor.)

The next suggestion was to film the yet-untitled show in Hollywood like a movie. *The Life of Riley* (1949–50) had done that the previous season, and several low-budget TV dramas were doing the same. Jess Oppenheimer vetoed that notion, because he knew the quality of both Arnazes' performances would suffer without benefit of a live audience.

What to do, what to do? What if they filmed the show, so all stations could have a high-quality copy, but did it in front of a live audience with multiple cameras? Desi claimed that this then novel approach was his idea. *Truth or Consequences* (1950–58) was being done this way, as was *You Bet*

Your Life (1950–61). Besides, Cecil B. DeMille had been filming his theatrical movies with multiple cameras for years, on a sound stage.

No one in the industry believed it was possible to do a TV comedy this way, especially the physical type of fun projected by the writers in the early *I Love Lucy* scripts that were then being prepared. Many people later claimed to have solved all the problems inherent in this sort of filming. The fact is, solving the technical difficulties was a collaborative effort that involved the Arnazes, the writers Pugh and Carroll, producer Oppenheimer, director Marc Daniels, editor Dann Cahn and his assistant Bud Molin, cinematographer Karl Freund, sound engineer Cameron McCullough, production manager Al Simon, and art director Larry Cuneo.

Each played a significant role in making decisions, inventing ways of doing things better, and making arrangements and negotiations that brought *I Love Lucy* to fruition. Several of these people, including Desi, claim to have shouldered much of the responsibility. The truth is that this enterprise was so enormous, and done in such limited time, that everyone involved was collaboratively responsible, including Desi. The three (and later four and five) camera process of filming situation comedies was invented by a collaborative effort of some of the most talented, creative, and dedicated people ever brought together for one project in the history of show business. No one, not Desi, not Jess, not even Superman, could have husbanded *I Love Lucy* all alone.

Casting Fred and Ethel was also a problem. Bea Benaderet was not available to do more television, because she was already doing TV's *The George Burns and Gracie Allen Show* live every other week. (On radio, it was easy to do several different shows each week because there was minimal rehearsal, no blocking, and one read from a script. In television, this kind of multiple appearance each week was impossible.)

There was a different problem to overcome with the casting of crusty Fred Mertz. Although it has been stated for years that Gale Gordon was *not* available for the show because he was committed to doing the radio version of *Our Miss Brooks* (1948–55), this simply was not so. Gale could have easily read his part on radio and had plenty of time left to partake in the TV show. He was a much sought-after radio talent. The truth is that Gale Gordon wanted too much money to play the part, and the small budget of the first season simply would not allow him to be paid the salary he was asking. Thus, Gale Gordon was out of the running for the role of the cranky neighbor (though hardly out of Lucille's professional life, as we shall see).

There were several actors who wanted the part of Fred Mertz, including veteran character players Charley Grapewin, Charles Lane, and Charles Winninger. The dark horse was an ex-vaudevillian named Bill Frawley, who had been playing Irish wise-guys in movies since the early 1930s. Although Bill had already done some television, and was still winning small parts in movies, his heavy drinking habit had given him a less-than-savory reputation around Hollywood. He made an appointment with Desi, and promised that not once would his drinking interfere with his oncamera performance. Desi, who was always a supporter of the underdog, hired Frawley (after checking with Oppenheimer, who was, after all, the producer), and never regretted the casting choice for one moment.

Casting Ethel Mertz, however, was a lot stickier. Thought was given to Barbara Pepper, a longtime pal Lucille worked with when they were shapely Goldwyn Girls in the early 1930s. In fact, Lucille and Barbara made their first trip to Hollywood together in 1933. Pepper was talented, funny, and had the right sort of used-up look the character required. Unfortunately, the reason she was worn around the edges at age thirty-nine was that she, too, had a serious problem with alcohol. As much as Lucille cared for Barbara, it was decided to pass on her. Pepper later appeared on many episodes of *I Love Lucy* in small parts.

Another veteran entertainer, Mary Wickes, was also considered for the Ethel role. Wickes was already a friend of Lucille's, having met her in New York when they both did live television in the late 1940s. Lucille and Mary shared the same work ethic and devotion to their mothers. Mary, in fact, loved Lucie Arnaz like a godmother. Mary wisely turned down any thoughts of being Ethel, because she knew Lucille's perfectionist approach to her work would hurt their friendship, and because she could make much better money in the movies, live television, and on Broadway. Mary, too, would appear many times on Lucille's various television series and specials through the years.

It was director Marc Daniels who finally found Vivian Vance. Vance had been a Broadway success in musical comedy, at first understudying Ethel Merman and later becoming a stage star in her own right. She'd had a nervous breakdown in 1945, made a couple of small films, and was just getting back to playing before a live audience. Touring in John Van Druten's romantic comedy *The Voice of the Turtle*, she portrayed a bitchy other woman. Marc had known her, and went down to La Jolla, California, along with Desi and editor Dann Cahn to see her perform. Or Desi and producer Jess Oppenheimer went. Or Jess and Dann went. All depends on whom you believe. In retrospect, it is of no importance who went down to La Jolla. Vivian (who was reluctant and had to be talked into accepting the TV role) was hired on the spot, with no audition and without having first met Lucille.

Less than two weeks later, rehearsals began for the first episode of *I Love Lucy*. In the preceding weeks, appropriate studio space had been leased at General Service Studios in Hollywood, and then modified to fit the health codes for having a live audience. Proper flooring had been found at the loading dock of the May Company department store so the cameras could all move smoothly. Cinematographer Karl Freund devised an entirely new way to light the TV sound stage, so the actors and the set would be properly lit at any angle by any camera. Special lights were attached to the camera dollies to reflect up at Lucille and help mask her age. Makeup artist Hal King had a terrible time with the cosmetics, trying to make forty-year-old Lucille look twenty-eight and forty-two-year-old Vivian Vance look fifty, covering Desi's acne scars, making sixty-four-year-old Bill Frawley look healthy, and keeping them all looking well under the hot lights. Dann Cahn and Bud Molin literally invented a way to edit the film inexpensively while allowing all three angles of any scene to be viewed simultaneously, giving them the luxury to pick the best shot.

The actors found they really had to project their voices. Not only was it necessary for the studio audience to be able to hear the cast properly, but sound man Cameron McCullough couldn't let the microphone levels be too sensitive. There was always the danger of the sound equipment picking up the sounds of the cameras rolling, cables sliding, sets and furniture shifting, and crew members talking into their headsets. In later years, these obstacles were overcome, but Lucille continued to insist on everyone projecting their lines as if they were on a Broadway stage.

Meanwhile, Jess, Bob, and Madelyn were turning out the first four scripts for the show and director Marc Daniels was trying to figure out how to direct something no one had done before. Lucille and Desi were making all sorts of decisions, and getting used to their new daughter. A strict diet was thrust upon the Redhead so she could lose most of the considerable weight she had gained carrying Lucie. Hairstylist Roberta "Bert" French was creating hairstyles and colors for Lucille, Vivian, and Desi. She decided to cut Lucille's long hair chin length, dye it a darker red and tightly curl it. This would change drastically over the next several weeks. Vivian's hair was also red at first; it became bright yellow by the second week of filming. Everyone was *very* busy.

It was decided to take the basic *My Favorite Husband* character relationships (controlling husband, frustrated wife, older couple/best friends) and give them new names. Lucy and Larry Lopez had been the first thought, but had been rejected even before the pilot had been made because Jess felt that those names were too alliterate, so Lucy and Ricky Ricardo were born. The older couple were christened Fred and Ethel Mertz, their first names deriving from Lucille's brother Fred and her pal Ethel Merman. Mertz was the surname of a family Madelyn had known in her youth. These were the pivotal relationships around which the show was built. Many of the early *I Love Lucy* scripts were heavily based on episodes of radio's *My Favorite Husband.*

There was one other planned character, that of Jerry the agent, portrayed by middle-aged Jerry Hausner in the pilot and in later series episodes. Although Hausner could be amusing, the situations written never gave him much of a chance to be funny oncamera. As a result, his part became an occasional thing, and was eventually dropped in the third season (1953–54) under less-than-happy conditions.

As outlined, these were the circumstances that faced the cast and crew of *I Love Lucy*, named thusly so that Desi, the *I*, could have first billing. Now all these people had to face the first week of rehearsal and the approaching air date. For more on that, please see Chapter Three: 1951–52 Season.

Lucille continued to make movies during her early television years. *The Long, Long Trailer* (1954) and *The Facts of Life* (1960) were big hits for her; *Forever Darling* (1956) and *Critic's Choice* (1963) were not. Later, she had a sketch in the risqué *A Guide for the Married Man* (1967), and a starring role in her last movie blockbuster, *Yours, Mine and Ours* (1968). Her only Broadway excursion, the musical *Wildcat* (1960), provided her with a hit song ("Hey, Look Me Over"), as well as months of physical illness and mental despair as she tried to get over her failed marriage to Desi and cope with a musical comedy that was high on energy but too short on quality. The movie *Mame* (1974) was her last theatrical film; its initial failure began a series of depressions and personal crises from which Lucille never really recovered. Ironically, in more recent years *Mame* has become something of a cult classic, and can be widely seen on cable television and on video.

As the 1970s progressed, Lucille was forced out of her weekly television perch by an ungrateful CBS, whose network she practically single-handedly kept number one for twenty-three years. Although she continued to work, the deaths of her mother in 1977 and Vivian Vance in 1979 left Ball inconsolable. In the 1980s, coping with her son's drug problems and Desi Sr.'s incurable cancer left her too scattered to pay much attention to her diminished career. After she lost Desi in 1986, she lost most of the interest in her profession. When she passed away after heart surgery in April 1989, the entire world mourned fiercely.

A Fan

I was driving to work on the 405 freeway in Los Angeles during rush hour. Naturally, I had the radio on for company. When the disc jockey announced that Lucy had died, I slowed down and immediately began to cry. After about a minute, I realized that I had stopped completely on a very *busy highway. I immediately looked around, and saw that every car around me in both directions was stopped, and all of the passengers were shedding tears. We all sort of looked at one another, shared the moment, took a deep breath, and began to drive again.*

Lucille Ball just another television star? Hardly!

I Love Lucy was the first television show filmed in a movie studio in front of a live audience. It was the first sitcom to use three film cameras to capture all the action simultaneously. It was the first comedy show to use guest stars on a continuing basis. Above all, it was the first program to prominently feature a pregnant woman. Lucille also has several firsts to her very own credit: the first (and perhaps only) American female star to be smeared with the mark of Communism and have it recanted and apologized for; the first independent television producer to buy a major movie studio (RKO); the first woman vice president (and later president) of a major studio; the first woman to star in two top-five TV series back-to-back; the first woman to headline in three top-five TV series back-to-back. It is no wonder Lucille Ball is called, and always will be remembered as, the First Lady of Television!

Chapter Two

1947–51 Seasons

PANTOMIME QUIZ

(KTLA, LOS ANGELES, EXACT AIR DATE UNKNOWN, BUT NO LATER THAN DECEMBER, 1947), 30 MINUTES (B&W)

PRODUCED BY: Mike Stokey
DIRECTED BY: Phillipe DeLacey
CAST: Lucille Ball, Hans Conried, Jackie Coogan, Vincent Price, Adele Jergens

This show, one of the pioneer television efforts in Los Angeles, is a variation of the party game charades. Using two teams of four players, many Hollywood stars like Lucille appear on the early version of this show for the fun of it. It didn't harm their film careers because hardly anyone owned TV sets yet.

This long-running program was on network television for over nine years (on all four networks) starting in 1950, and resurfaced again as *Stump the Stars* in 1962. While it is not known how many episodes of the program Lucille actually did, or who the exact guests were on each such outing, the cast list above represents some of the people who were on air with Miss Ball. This is Lucille Ball's television debut.

THE TEXACO STAR THEATRE

(NBC, FEBRUARY 22, 1949), 60 MINUTES (B&W)

PRODUCED BY: Ed Cashman, Milton Berle
DIRECTED BY: Ed Lachman, Milton Berle
WRITTEN BY: Milton Berle, Selma Diamond, Nat Hiken, Buddy Arnold
CAST: Walter O'Keefe (guest host), Lucille Ball, the Ink Spots, the Mathis Duo, Paul Winchell and Jerry Mahoney

Lucille makes a guest appearance on the first season of this trailblazing variety hour. Unfortunately, the show's star (Milton Berle) is out sick this week, and Walter O'Keefe steps in for him. Without Berle's performance, this installment is very weak. Lucille has one short sketch with Winchell and Mahoney as she is cajoled into kissing the dummy. It is not even vaguely funny. She returns toward the end of the show as a contestant in a radio giveaway show, a sketch that foreshadows the kind of slapstick and parody that will be part and parcel of *I Love Lucy* in two years.

INSIDE U.S.A. WITH CHEVROLET

(CBS, NOVEMBER 24, 1949), 30 MINUTES (B&W)

PRODUCED BY: Arthur Schwartz
DIRECTED BY: Sherman Marks
WRITTEN BY: Sam Taylor, Terry Ryan, Harry Bailey
MUSIC BY: Jay Blackton
CAST: Peter Lind Hayes, Mary Healy, Lucille Ball, Mary Wickes, Sheila Bond

Inside U.S.A. had been a successful Broadway revue that was transferred to television. Peter Lind Hayes, very popular in early television (and who had costarred also with Desi Arnaz at the Copacabana nightclub), is showcased as a traveling minstrel. His observations about the United States and its people provide the show's comedy and music. His wife and frequent costar, Mary Healy, handles much of the music. Each week features a fairly big show business name, and Lucille does her turn in the late fall of 1949. Her standout moment is a sketch in which she plays a sleazy dancehall hostess, with Hayes as her intended victim. Ball also joins Hayes and Healy in singing "Louisiana Hayride."

Mary Wickes
(ACTOR)

Lucille and I met doing [this show] in New York. We immediately hit it off, because we both adored our mothers and we had the same approach to our work.

We didn't fool around . . . work always came first, and we were always giving our best right from the first read-through.

THE ED WYNN SHOW

(CBS, WEST COAST: DECEMBER 24, 1949, EAST COAST: JANUARY 7, 1950), 30 MINUTES (B&W)

PRODUCED BY: Harlan Thompson
DIRECTED BY: Ralph Levy
WRITTEN BY: Hal Kanter, Leo Solomon, Seaman Jacobs
MUSIC BY: Lud Gluskin
LUCILLE BALL'S GOWNS BY: Athena
CAST: Ed Wynn, Lucille Ball, Desi Arnaz, Patricia Morison

This is the first live television series to originate from Hollywood. A kinescope was made and shown in other parts of the country two weeks later, as there was no coaxial cable currently in use. Lucille and Desi take time off from their respective radio shows (*My Favorite Husband* 1948–51, *The Bob Hope Show* 1949–50) to appear.

The program opens with a typical Wynn monologue of bad puns and lisping delivery. Desi banters with Ed on a beach set. Handsome and extremely well dressed, Desi is already graying, without the benefit of the hair dye that became *de rigueur* in later years. The Cuban is presented as though he cannot speak English. Finally, Our Hero sings "The Straw Hat Song."

Lucille finally joins the under-rehearsed fun to give Desi his props for "Babalu." Looking thin but tired, her hair is long and pulled back at her shoulders, and her eyes have bags under them. (In the early days of television, the unsophisticated lighting was especially unflattering to women, and the makeup was embryonic in its development.) After plugs for their respective radio shows and more Wynn ad-libs (the Arnazes break up so much that Ed lisps, "Look at the way he's laughing—he should buy a ticket!"), the time comes for Lucille's sketch.

The skit is a sendup of 1920s vamp/spy silent movies. Lucille is dressed exactly as she one day would be for *I Love Lucy* when she vamps Tennessee Ernie Ford, down to the black wig and pearls. Even her slinky walk is the same, so this is one instance where Lucille will later borrow from herself. Both actors hold up cue cards as title cards for the "silent" theme. Desi occasionally breaks in on the scene trying to sing "Babalu," adding to the already funny sketch. Lucille even loses her wig, trying to keep a straight face as it keeps slipping off her head.

SHOW OF THE YEAR FOR CEREBRAL PALSY

(NBC, JUNE 10, 1950), 150 MINUTES (B&W)

PRODUCED BY: Irving Gray, Bill Gardner
DIRECTED BY: Arthur Knorr
ARNAZES' SKETCH WRITTEN BY:
Jess Oppenheimer, Madelyn Pugh, Bob Carroll Jr., Pepito Perez
MUSIC BY: Allen Roth
CAST: Milton Berle (host), Desi Arnaz, Lucille Ball, Mindy Carson, Jinx Falkenburg, Eddie Fisher, Jerry Lewis, Dean Martin, the Martin Brothers, Clem McCarthy, Tex McCrary, Robert Merrill, Jan Murray, Janis Paige, Jane Pickens, Verna Raymond, Sid Stone, George Tapps, Henny Youngman

Milton Berle created the term "telethon" in the late 1940s, so it is no surprise to find he hosted several of them in TV's early days. This is the first network show to benefit Cerebral Palsy and it airs live from New York on the fledgling NBC network. The Arnazes' contribution consists of an early version of their "Cuban Pete" duet, bantering with Berle, and a pitch for money for the charity.

THE STAR SPANGLED REVUE STARRING BOB HOPE

(NBC, SEPTEMBER 14, 1950), 60 MINUTES (B&W)

PRODUCED BY: Lee Morgan
DIRECTED BY: Hal Keith
WRITTEN BY: Marvin Fisher, Larry Gelbart, Mort Lachman, Larry Marks, Sy Rose, Norman Sullivan
MUSIC BY: Al Goodman
CHOREOGRAPHY BY: Jack Cole
CAST: Bob Hope (host), Lucille Ball, Bob Crosby, New York Mayor William O'Dwyer, Dinah Shore, Mary Wickes

This is the first television teaming of Ball and Hope. Lucille had originally been scheduled for Hope's second television outing the previous

Easter, but a filming commitment precluded her traveling to New York for the TV appearance. Until the coaxial cable is installed coast to coast to allow simultaneous live broadcasting everywhere, Hope's shows are produced in New York. Lucille does a sketch lampooning Los Angeles and featuring New York's mayor. She portrays a *female* mayor who finally does things the *right* way. Ball is the breadwinning mayoral wife and Hope is the frustrated house-husband, with Mary Wickes as their independently minded maid.

THE STORK CLUB

(CBS, MOST LIKELY LATE NOVEMBER, 1950), 15 MINUTES (B&W)

PRODUCED BY: Irving Mansfield, Sherman Billingsley
DIRECTED BY: Shelly Hull
CAST: Sherman Billingsley (host), Desi Arnaz, Lucille Ball, Betty Ann Grove, Peter Lind Hayes, Mary Healy

Sherman Billingsley was the owner of the Stork Club, one of Manhattan's swankiest night spots. For five seasons in the 1950s, Billingsley hosted a show from his famed club, seated at Table Fifty. The guests were usually celebrities in town having a good time, many of them personal friends of Billingsley. In exchange for a fifteen-minute chat, the guests enjoy a sumptuous meal, all the liquor they can drink, and a splendid floor show. All that and a chance to plug their latest project. For the Arnazes, it is an opportunity for each to promote their respective radio programs, their vaudeville show together, and a chance to remind CBS that they want to go into television themselves.

THE PETER LIND HAYES SHOW

(NBC, NOVEMBER 30, 1950), 30 MINUTES (B&W)

PRODUCED BY: Allen Ducovny
DIRECTED BY: Theodore Sills
MUSIC BY: Bert Farber
CAST: Desi Arnaz, Lucille Ball, Peter Lind Hayes, Mary Healy, Claude Stroud, Mary Wickes

Little is known about the Arnazes' visit to this live show. The action is largely set at a replica of the Hayes' suburban New York home. There, the guests sing, dance, or tell jokes. Mary Wickes, in her second appearance with Lucille, plays the maid. The show is called *The Peter and Mary Show* when Lucille and Desi visit, but will change a few weeks later to the title above.

THE "I LOVE LUCY" PILOT

(CBS, CLOSED CIRCUIT KINESCOPING, MARCH 2, 1951), 45 MINUTES (B&W)

PRODUCED BY: Jess Oppenheimer
DIRECTED BY: Ralph Levy
WRITTEN BY: Jess Oppenheimer, Madelyn Pugh, and Bob Carroll Jr.
CAST: Lucille Ball, Desi Arnaz, Jerry Hausner, Pepito (the Clown) Perez, the Desi Arnaz Orchestra

The characters of Lucy and Ricky Ricardo are introduced, living in a high-rise building in Manhattan. Ricky is a Latin bandleader, and Lucy is his ambitious wife. Lucy learns that Ricky is up for a big television audition, and she wants to be in the show. Eager to get ambitious Lucy out of the way, Ricky sends her on a bogus errand. When Pepito the Clown is injured on a bicycle rehearsing the show, Lucy replaces him at the audition.

This show is shot live at Studio A at the CBS studios located at Sunset and Gower in Hollywood. A kinescope is produced to show to prospective sponsors. Lucille looks much different from the Lucy Ricardo we will come to know. Her hair is shoulder-length and free-flowing; she is also five months pregnant and huge, despite loose-fitting clothing. Much of the dialog from this script will be used later for the *I Love Lucy* episode "The Audition" in the 1951–52 season. It will later be decided that four series regulars are enough for the sitcom, and Jerry Hausner's part as Ricky's agent will be switched from a recurring character to an occasional guest appearance.

Jerry Hausner

(ACTOR)

I was supposed to be on the show every week. It was all decided. Somehow, it all got changed after the show was sold. I never really got a chance to be funny and show what I could do.

Hausner, who died in 1996, will be bitter the rest of his life. His lines are given to Bill Frawley for "The

Audition," and in fact Jerry's planned recurring part as Ricky's confidant will be transferred to Fred Mertz' expanded role. Pepito's part is much the same as his later appearance on *I Love Lucy*. Lucille's professor bit is modified, as she is no longer in any condition to be rolling on her belly. Veteran live director Ralph Levy is brought in to helm the show.

Ralph Levy
(DIRECTOR)

I had worked with the Arnazes a few months earlier when we all did The Ed Wynn Show *together. I had enjoyed it, and was anxious to work with them again. Lucille was a total professional, giving 100 percent even though she was pregnant and not feeling too well. She needed very little direction. Desi did, but he took it with grace and gave a wonderful performance.*

The sets and costumes are very different in the pilot from the later shows, with a couple of unusual exceptions (the coat Lucille wears will show up repeatedly on *I Love Lucy*). The Ricardos both wear pajamas, as they will on later shows. Desi's rendition of "Cuban Cabby" demonstrates what a brilliant showman he is, and just how sexy he can be on a nightclub stage.

This kinescope was never intended for viewing by the public. It was made only to show network executives and prospective sponsors what the show might look like if it eventually became a series. The landmark pilot will eventually be aired on CBS after Ball's death in 1989, and will be made available on home video.

Chapter Three

1951–52 Season

I LOVE LUCY: THE FIRST SEASON

TECHNICAL REGULARS: Executive produced by Desi Arnaz (beginning with the episode "The Freezer"); produced by Jess Oppenheimer; directed by Marc Daniels (except where otherwise noted); written by Jess Oppenheimer, Bob Carroll Jr., Madelyn Pugh; makeup by Hal King; hairstyling by Bert French; music by Wilbur Hatch
CAST REGULARS: Lucille Ball (Lucy Ricardo); Desi Arnaz (Ricky Ricardo); Vivian Vance (Ethel Mertz); William Frawley (Fred Mertz)

I LOVE LUCY #1: "THE GIRLS WANT TO GO TO A NIGHTCLUB"

(CBS, OCTOBER 15, 1951), 30 MINUTES (B&W)
GUEST CAST: John Stephenson (announcer and commercials), Jay Jackson (middle commercial)

On the occasion of the Mertzes' eighteenth wedding anniversary, the girls want to attend a nightclub, while the boys prefer an evening at the fights. The quartet decides to celebrate separately, the men and the women. To teach the husbands a lesson, Lucy and Ethel appear in disguise (as hillbillies Euncy and her Maw) as Ricky's and Fred's dates for the evening.

HIGHLIGHTS & TRIVIA

This was not the initial regular series episode filmed, but was aired first because of the hilarious scene set in the Ricardos' apartment near the end.

Dann Cahn
(FILM EDITOR)

It has been said that we used this show first because of technical problems, but that really wasn't so. We had four shows in the can, working six days a week. CBS, Philip Morris, the Biow advertising agency, and the crew were all involved in deciding which show would be the first one. This switch almost murdered the editorial department, which consisted of my assistant Bud Molin and myself. We were already working fourteen-hour days, and switching the schedule really put us behind. We got a young USC film school apprentice named Gary Freund [not related to Karl] to help us out. Hal Hodge cut the negative, and Quinn Martin [future bigtime TV producer] quit his job at Universal to become our first music and sound effects editor. We got the final prints made in time by hours. In Los Angeles, there were two sound glitches. I thought Desi would have apoplexy. He had everything riding on this show. Luckily, the national reviews were sensational.

The show opens with little person Johnny, the Philip Morris mascot (played by forty-year-old Johnny Roventini), doing his famous yell, "Call for Philip Morris!" dressed as a hotel bellboy. Then, cartoon caricatures of Lucille and Desi appear—stick figures actually. Lucille's has a skirt on, and Desi's a bow tie. In one form or another, these cartoon figures would appear in the openings of the Ball-Arnaz TV shows until 1960. In this initial opening, the Lucy and Desi figures use vines to swing off a giant pack of cigarettes. This leads into an initial commercial done by John Stephenson on the Ricardo apartment set. It is unintentionally hysterical, with Stephenson peering into the camera with a sexual leer and asking, "May I ask you a personal question . . . do you inhale?"

Dann Cahn
(FILM EDITOR)

Today, this type of opening would easily be generated as computer effects, but in 1951, all of this had to be assembled every week on an optical printer using fine-grain masters [the commercials and cartoon bridges changed from week to week]. It was slow and complicated, and we had to do it on Saturdays. The original [printing company] didn't want to do this. Eventually, Darrell and Howard Anderson did the work, and the Howard Anderson Company worked with Desilu through Star Trek (1966–69). The original idea came right from the Biow Agency in New York.

Vivian's hair is now bleached a bright yellow (as opposed to the red of the first episode shot), and her makeup altered to make her look less attractive. Additionally, she has begun wearing housedresses. Viv's are purchased at Orbach's department store, and always altered to be intentionally slightly too small. Oncamera, she is not allowed to wear a girdle or any other foundation garments other than a bra and panties, and *these* too are a size too small. This gives the impression that Viv is stocky in the early shows, when she actually has a very trim figure. The point was to make Vance dowdy and frumpy in comparison to svelte Lucille Ball.

Maury Thompson

(SCRIPT CLERK)

In the beginning, before they got to know one another, Lucille gave Vivian a hard time. I mean a really hard time. One day, I pulled Viv aside and I said, "What are you going to do about her?" Vivian was very smart. She said, "Maury, if by any chance this thing actually becomes a hit and goes anywhere, I'm gonna learn to love that bitch!" I always wanted to tell Lucille what Vivian had said after Viv passed away, but I never did.

Desi sings "Guadalajara" in this one, which had been a semi-hit for him with his orchestra in the late 1940s. Also, listen to Lucille's voice in this episode. Most of the time, it is in its natural, lower register. Like Gracie Allen, Lucille would push her voice up an octave to sound younger and more innocent on camera.

Fans of the series are familiar with the cartoon heart logo, shown at the beginning, middle, and end of the program. However, in the original network run of the TV series, it does *not* exist. At the episode's middle commercial break, unlike the later syndicated reruns, there is no heart, but a pack of cigarettes and the cartoon figures of the stars to lead into the commercial. This will be true throughout the series. The famous heart opening will not be used until the show is sold to other countries, and Philip Morris is no longer the sponsor.

Notice, too, there are several closeup shots that do not seem to match the photographic quality of the rest of the show. (Often, these closeups had to be redone after the audience left the studio because of technical problems.) Unfortunately, these well-focused special shots stand out like a sore thumb and eventually it is decided to film them just like the rest of the show. The installment's ending scene, with the foursome at a boxing match, is shot in the sound stage's audience bleachers.

In the original script, there is an extra opening scene between Ricky and Fred, but it is cut due to time constraints. Also in the original teleplay, it is established that Fred and Ethel have been married twenty-four years, but this is later reduced to eighteen. There is a great deal of expository character dialog (referring mostly to manhood and Ethel's lack of looks) that is deleted. The closing credits, rolled over the ubiquitous pack of cigarettes, will later be used in the syndicated versions of the show rolling over the cartoon heart. They will be changed from white to black to look different.

Jess Oppenheimer

(PRODUCER/WRITER)

I think that line, "Ever since we said 'I do' there are so many things we don't" is one of the funniest lines in the entire series because it really talks about married life in a deep way.

I LOVE LUCY #2 : "BE A PAL"

(CBS, OCTOBER 22, 1951), 30 MINUTES (B&W)

GUEST CAST: Richard Reeves, Tony Michaels, John Stephenson (announcer and commercials)

Lucy feels that Ricky has grown tired of her. Ethel reads to her from *How to Keep the Honeymoon from Ending*, and it inspires Lucy to action. First, Lucy changes her appearance to become glamorous for Ricky; then she decides to be a pal, and play poker with Ricky and his buddies. Last, she tries to remind him of his Cuban roots by donning native costumes and props and singing "Mama Yo Quiero."

HIGHLIGHTS & TRIVIA

This is the first episode where Lucille wears anything tight fitting. Her sequined gown segment reveals that she has not yet lost all of the weight from her pregnancy. In fact, Vivian is thinner. Lucille has still not found the proper modulation for her voice and allows it to crack continually throughout the program.

The final scene, with Lucille doing an impression of Carmen Miranda, is a tour de force for the Redhead. Her timing is superb; in lesser hands the scene with Lucy lip-synching to a Miranda record that is greatly speeded up and then slowed down would be silly or embarrassing. Only through her great belief in what she is doing is the audience able to suspend their disbelief and enjoy the comedy ride. Not only has Lucy gotten permission from Miss Miranda to spoof her, but in the audience that night to see the routine are such celebrities as Sheila and Gordon MacRae, Jack and Mary Benny, Rosalind Russell, Van Johnson, Eve Arden, Ginger Rogers, and Miss Miranda.

It is revealed in this episode that Ricky has five brothers. They are never referred to again. This installment brings up an interesting point. Where does Lucy get the money to pay for the elaborate props and costumes used in this and subsequent shows?

Dann Cahn

(FILM EDITOR)

By and large, we had very few mistakes on filming night. The show was so well rehearsed that we didn't have glitches. Occasionally, we'd have to do a few pickups, which I would edit in later. Because our director was Marc Daniels from television and our producer was Jess Oppenheimer from radio, we didn't think in terms of motion picture techniques. We did not start and stop like a lot of shows did. We tried to do the entire show without having to redo scenes; then, we would go back and do inserts of things that needed fixing.

In the original script, it is obvious the writers have no idea what the actual set will look like, and structure the teleplay as if it is taking place on the set used in the pilot. There is also a tag scene in the kitchen, which has to be cut because the show runs longer than expected with laughter.

This show is based in part on the *My Favorite Husband* radio episode "Be Your Husband's Best Friend."

I LOVE LUCY #3 : "THE DIET"

(CBS, OCTOBER 29, 1951), 30 MINUTES (B&W)

GUEST CAST: Marco Rizo, John Stephenson (announcer)

Performer Joanne is quitting Ricky's show and Lucy wants the job, but Ricky stalls by telling her she is too fat. At the audition, Lucy tries on Joanne's dress and tears it at the seams. Undaunted, Lucy begins a strict diet and exercise regimen so she can fit into the size twelve dress.

HIGHLIGHTS & TRIVIA

This show establishes the premise of Lucy wanting to get into the act. It is also the first speaking part for Marco Rizo, the pianist for the Desi Arnaz Orchestra. He blows it, however, for if you listen closely, you can hear him refer to Ricky as Desi as he passes by. This is the one and only appearance of the Mertzes' dog Butch, a mutt. The "Cuban Pete" number is taken verbatim from Lucille and Desi's vaudeville act, the song itself coming from a movie of the same name that Desi did with the King Sisters in the 1940s. A photo of Lucille in the steam cabinet segment of the episode appeared in an early version of *TV Guide* when it was still a local New York magazine.

Everyone involved in the series is still getting into the swing of things. For example, cinematographer Karl Freund is still tinkering with the lighting, as there are frequently too many shadows on Lucille's face. Desi does not yet seem at ease with his part. Bert French is desperately trying fresh approaches with Lucille's hair because she hates the way she looks. Note the decorative ruffle bordering the Ricardos' headboard. It is soon discarded from the permanent bedroom set.

Dann Cahn

(FILM EDITOR)

Wilbur Hatch and the Desi Arnaz Orchestra were right there, on the set, playing all the transition music from cues just like a radio show. When we started to edit the shows, and for timing purposes we might need more or less music, we fixed it in the editing. It finally dawned on us that all of the musical cues could be recorded after the fact and dubbed in, like a movie. We kept the orchestra going for years, until we got so big that we had a music department. Besides, after Desi stopped doing numbers on the show regularly [around 1955], having them on the payroll was pointless.

Bob and Madelyn's script is very funny, full of alliteration and quirky one-liners. Even Lucille's delivery is delineated in the script so the Redhead knows exactly what the writers have in mind. This is the first episode in which Lucille utters her famous "spider" voice, that "*eeeuuuu*" sound as she purses her lips. The name comes from a radio commercial she did, playing Little Miss Muffet. When the commercial got to the part where the spider came down and sat down beside her, Lucille made that noise. Bob and Madelyn remembered it, and it became a trademark of the Lucy character. It became so well known that Gale Storm stole it for her sitcom radio and TV sitcom *My Little Margie* (1952–55), changing it to a gargling sound but using it in the same manner.

Lucille's fidgeting with her clothes during the plot-line audition to look more sexy is both hysterical and poignant. She is indeed still overweight, which makes the script even funnier. Within a few weeks, hard work and stress will make Lucille skinnier. This is the first use of the name McGillicuddy (and this is the way it is spelled in the scripts) as Lucy's maiden name. It was originally supposed to be Teitelbaum, but the writers decided that that might sound too Jewish.

This show is based in part on the *My Favorite Husband* radio episode entitled "Iris and Liz's Easter."

I LOVE LUCY #4 : "LUCY THINKS RICKY IS TRYING TO MURDER HER"

(CBS, NOVEMBER 5, 1951), 30 MINUTES (B&W)

GUEST CAST: Jerry Hausner, Hector and His Dogs, John Stephenson (announcer and commercials)

Lucy, an avid whodunit story reader, is enraptured by *The Mockingbird Murder Mystery*. The next day, Lucy's already over-imaginative suspicions are heightened when she overhears Ricky talking about getting rid of his girl singer, and she thinks he wants to get rid of *her*. Ricky (thinking Lucy is losing her sanity) slips her a sleeping powder, but before she falls asleep, Lucy and Ethel rush down to the club to confront Ricky.

HIGHLIGHTS & TRIVIA

This entry, the first episode actually shot, showcases important character elements that play in almost every future installment. Lucy's conniving mind is explained as an outgrowth of her love for mystery novels. Ricky's opening dialog tells the audience what he does for a living, where he does it (the Tropicana), and that his orchestra is held over at the club indefinitely. Fred's line, "Crazy for Lucy, or crazy for ordinary people?" sets up the premise that everyone thinks Lucy is a little wacky. In addition, the idea that the Mertzes are the Ricardos' landlords and best friends is fully established. The actors are still adjusting to their characters. The only role that seems solidified from the first word is Fred Mertz. The other three search and stretch over a period of weeks before their oncamera personalities are fully developed.

Lucille Ball

Bill Frawley was *Fred Mertz. Period.*

Dann Cahn

(FILM EDITOR)

The only real technical problems we had with this first show shot was that we used four cameras instead of three, and we had a slight sync problem. George Fox [film editor] was the one who came up with the idea for the three-headed moviola that we called the monster, but his sound syncing system never worked properly. We worked out a system with a clapper, fired Fox, and bought the machine from him after a small power struggle. The art director for the first few shows was Larry Cuneo. After a short while, there was no art director. So the set was in the hands of the prop men until Ralph Berger came in much later. The only other problem we had was in making Lucille happy with her closeups when we did the pickups of her on the settee after Ricky supposedly shot her. She was afraid that poor lighting would show off the lines in her neck, so we had to reassure her that the lighting would be done in a way to protect her looks.

The main set is not fully decorated as it will be for future episodes. This is the only appearance of the

Early-American settee in the Ricardos' living room; it will be replaced the following week by a love seat. None of the onstage windows have glass in them. The closets have no clothes in them. The backstairs off the kitchen, something common to older apartment buildings in Los Angeles, would *never* be found in a New York apartment. Neither would an electric oven or a garbage disposal. And that extra door in the kitchen, next to the upstage counter. What is it for? It is never opened or used for anything in the entire time the set is employed. If you watch closely, you can see one camera photographing another as Ricky writes at the desk. The filming of the middle commercial is done in the kitchen of the Ricardos' apartment set. The club set at the end is simply a curtain with the bandstand in front of it. This episode is shot in sequence without a break, just like a real stage show. It will be decided later that the studio audience can wait while costumes, sets, and makeup are changed, so the show will be later shot at a more leisurely pace.

Dann Cahn

(FILM EDITOR

The living room set was center stage. When the action moved to the Mertzes' apartment, that was usually done in front of the Ricardo bedroom set. Sometimes they just redressed the bedroom set; other times they brought the set in. When the Tropicana set was needed, it was built temporarily in front of the living room set so Desi's musical numbers could be center stage for the audience. Other minor sets were done over to the side, unless it was a large piece of action, in which case it, too, was done center stage.

The tag sequence at the finale, where Lucy is once again frightened and tosses her book out the window only to retrieve it because it is on a string, is cut soon after its original airing so we never see Lucy recovering the book in the reruns. A short scene on the back porch with the milkman was written but never filmed.

Vivian, with red hair and flattering makeup, looks her actual age (forty-two). For years, it was written that Vivian was actually a year younger than Lucille. Recently, it has been discovered that Vance was two years older than Ball. Vivian looking youthful *never* happens again. The plot idea that emotional wives should be controlled by slipping them a sleeping powder is so misogynistic and abusive that it could never be used in modern television.

Maury Thompson

(SCRIPT CLERK)

Right from the first day of rehearsal, everyone knew that this was going to be serious work. Bill and Vivian, Marc and Emily Daniels, Bob and Madelyn, Jess and I were there. Marc and Emily had brought Viv with them. Desi came in. Lucy arrived after everyone was seated at the read-through table. Her hair was up in a babushka, and she wore no makeup. She certainly didn't look like a movie star to me. Desi introduced Vivian to Lucy, and she said, "Hi! What part are you reading for?" Vivian was not made to feel at ease. Then Lucy started in, "You look just like me. Your hair is the same color as mine. You don't look like a landlady! You aren't right for this part. You aren't dumpy! You're an attractive woman!" So Desi asked her what she had in mind for the part. Lucy answered, "I want an old ragged bathrobe and fuzzy slippers with peroxide blond hair and curlers. That's what I want her to look like!" Viv looked her right in the eye and said, "You've got her! You should see me every morning. I look just like that." Lucille chuckled and began to look at Viv in a different light.

We went right to work. Once the scripts were opened, there were no social amenities. Willie Mae [the Arnazes' maid] had carried in a picnic basket with them. Around noon, Lucille pulled out the basket and began munching on fried chicken. There was enough there for twenty people. No one was offered a bite of food. After about fifteen minutes, Bill Frawley got peeved. "When do the peons *get to eat,?" he growled. "Didn't you already have lunch," she innocently inquired? "Hell no," he replied. "Nobody eats lunch at ten o'clock in the morning!" Lucille was all business right from the start. And that was the first day of* I Love Lucy.

Desi Arnaz

The chemistry which ignited at the first meeting of Lucille and Vivian and the rapport between, and understanding, [that] Bill and I had was somehow naturally transferred to the characters of Lucy and Ricky and Fred and Ethel. No one, including me, could have visualized that it would turn out so perfectly.

I LOVE LUCY #5: "THE QUIZ SHOW"

(CBS, NOVEMBER 12, 1951), 30 MINUTES (B&W)
GUEST CAST: Frank Nelson, John Emery, Phil Ober, Lee Millar, Hazel Pierce, John Stephenson (announcer and commercials)

When Ricky learns that Lucy is several months in arrears in paying the household bills, he takes over the budget and cancels her charge accounts. To cheer her up, Ethel takes Lucy to a radio show called *Females Are Fabulous* starring Freddie Fillmore. Lucy becomes a contestant, and Freddie offers her $1,000 if she will introduce an actor to Ricky that evening as her long-lost first husband.

HIGHLIGHTS & TRIVIA

The living room set shows several bottles of liquor on the pass-through counter. This uncharacteristic implication that the Ricardos are drinkers is played down in later episodes; usually they are confined to drinking wine and champagne. Listen for Lucy's arcane reference to her credit cards as her "charge-a-plates." This is the first time the show spoofs radio programs, but certainly not the last. Radio was still ahead of television in audience size, and series like the one satirized in this episode were common on both mediums. Notice that Lucille has her false eyelashes removed before the scene in which she is going to be squirted in the eyes with seltzer. The physical comedy in this scene is hardly true to life, as on radio no one would be able to see the action. Notice, too, the use of old-fashioned seltzer siphons, which rarely exist today.

Hazel Pierce, who is seen as Mrs. Peterson (the woman in bandages), was Lucille's TV stand-in and girl Friday in Ball's Beverly Hills home for many years. This is the first of many appearances for Frank Nelson, both as Freddie Fillmore and later as other characters. Phil Ober, as the radio actor, also makes his *Lucy* debut here. He was Vivian Vance's husband at the time. John Emery, as the bum, will also be seen again. Lucille liked to surround herself with talent she knew. The scene on the backstairs between Ethel and the vagrant displays an early version of the back porch. It will change from show to show to fit the plot needs. In this case, the bum walks off it as if it was on the first floor. Later episodes will reveal that the Mertzes live on the third floor. Desi's Spanish epithets are written in English and then translated into Spanish by Jess Oppenheimer's secretary, Mercedes Menzanares.

In the original script, the radio show *Females Are Fabulous* is called *Women Are Wonderful.* There is also a planned scene where Ethel is the first contestant on the radio show and doesn't win. This is cut due to time constraints.

Maury Thompson
(SCRIPT CLERK)

Vivian was excellent at seeing what might be wrong with a story. She was like a story detector, and wasn't shy about bringing up points that didn't seem right to her. Around this time, Lucille began to take notice that most often Vivian was right. Lucille realized she had in Vivian a lot more than she thought, and she began to trust Viv's comedic instincts. Miss Ball was smart enough to know that's what was needed, and she began to rely on Vivian more and more.

I LOVE LUCY #6: "THE AUDITION"

(CBS, NOVEMBER 19, 1951), 30 MINUTES (B&W)
GUEST CAST: Pat Moran, John Stephenson (announcer and commercials)

Lucy pesters Ricky to use her in his upcoming TV audition. When Buffo the Clown hurts himself on a bicycle at the audition rehearsal, Ricky sends him back to the Ricardos' apartment to rest. When Buffo demonstrates to Lucy what happened at the club, he hurts himself again and she takes his place.

HIGHLIGHTS & TRIVIA

The bit with Lucille as the Professor, written for her by Pepito the Clown, is again derived from the Arnazes' vaudeville tour. Honed to perfection by repeated performances over many months, Lucille is literally hysterical in this scene. Every movement, nuance, and gesture is flawless. The amount of talent it takes to perform and clown in this manner is extraordinary.

This episode is full of trivia. Desi sings his signature song "Babalu" for the first time on the series. The star-shaped decals above the Ricardos' bed are replaced with daisies starting with this episode. In the original version, the Ricardos' conversation in the bathroom is uncut, with Lucy holding up a pack of Philip Morris cigarettes to suggest how she might do the commercials for his show. (This minute of film is deleted from all subsequent showings, including the supposed uncut versions.) The basic plot of this installment, including most of the dialog, is taken directly from the original pilot the Arnazes shot the previous spring. In this version, all the lines originally assigned to Jerry the agent are delivered by Fred Mertz. Because Pepito the Clown is unavailable for the filming, the part is recast with Pat Moran and the clown character is renamed Buffo. The men playing the network executives are producer/writer Jess Oppenheimer and CBS vice president Harry Ackerman. Starting with this episode, the chair in the living room is reupholstered with material that matches the loveseat. By this episode, Lucy's poking fun at Ricky's English is actually written into the script, which disproves claims that it wasn't. Vivian Vance does *not* appear in this episode, and no one remembers why.

I LOVE LUCY #7: "THE SEANCE"

(CBS, NOVEMBER 26, 1951), 30 MINUTES (B&W)

GUEST CAST: Jay Novello, John Stephenson (announcer and commercials)

Lucy and Ethel's latest preoccupations are numerology and horoscopes. Lucy checks Ricky's horoscope, and advises him this is his day to say yes to everything. In actuality, it is a "no" day for Ricky. When a Mr. Merriweather calls for Ricky, Lucy rather rudely tells him no on Ricky's behalf, thinking he is the barber. When Lucy learns whom she told off, the couple rush to Merriweather's office to set things straight. They learn that Mr. Merriweather is also into the occult, so Lucy hosts a seance in his honor.

HIGHLIGHTS & TRIVIA

Still trying to explore the characters, this was one of the sillier plots of the first *I Love Lucy* season. Even the dialog is stilted. Starting here, an extra cushion (covered in the same material as the living room couch) is inserted under the love seat cushion whenever the script calls for Ricky to sit down. Desi had been troubled because when he sat down next to her on the set, Lucille looked taller. This cushion also made it easier for Desi to get up and down gracefully on his specially built shoes with their lifts. (While Desi was five feet eleven inches, in heels Lucille towered over him.) In this installment, it is revealed that Lucy's astrological sign is Taurus; Lucille is actually a Leo. It is also the first show to mention that Lucy dyes her hair. Jay Novello as Mr. Merriweather makes the first of many appearances with Lucille, proving he was an expert with comedic voices and accents. John Stephenson's commercials ("Did you know you inhale over 200 times a day?") are so ludicrous they are almost as funny as the show.

This show is based in part on the *My Favorite Husband* radio episode entitled "Numerology" in which Jay Novello played the same basic part. In the original script, Mr. Merriweather's name was Simpson.

I LOVE LUCY #8: "MEN ARE MESSY"

(CBS, DECEMBER 3, 1951), 30 MINUTES (B&W)

GUEST CAST: Kenny Morgan, Harry Shannon, Hazel "Sunny" Boyne, John Stephenson (announcer and commercials)

Lucy goes to great lengths to keep the apartment clean, but Ricky messes things up in a matter of moments. This infuriates Lucy, who divides the apartment in half, allowing Ricky his messy side. The next day, when Ricky asks Lucy to clean the *entire* apartment because a magazine photographer is coming by, she intends to teach him a lesson. Ricky arrives to find the place looking like a hillbilly farmhouse, with Lucy and Ethel in full regalia.

HIGHLIGHTS & TRIVIA

In the original broadcast version, a reference is made to the sponsor ("The cigarettes are on the line . . . I get Philip and you get Morris."). This piece of the show will be cut out for all subsequent airings, including the supposed uncut versions. Hairdresser Bert French is still struggling with Lucille's hairstyle to please the star. Kenny Morgan who appears oncamera is, in fact, the Arnazes' publicity agent, and married at that time to Lucille's cousin Cleo. "The Straw Hat Song" is another of Desi's stand-by offerings. Desi's interaction with the cleaning lady (Sunny Boynes) allows his natural charm to come to the surface, making Ricky Ricardo a more likeable character. Once again,

Lucille makes a good script wonderful. Her use of props, vocal inflections, and timing are superb.

This show is based on the *My Favorite Husband* radio episode entitled "George Is Messy."

I LOVE LUCY #9: "THE FUR COAT"

(CBS, DECEMBER 10, 1951), 30 MINUTES (B&W)

GUEST CAST: Ben Weldon, John Stephenson (announcer and commercials)

When Lucy comes home to find Ricky with an expensive fur coat, she assumes it is her anniversary present. Now guilty because he did not remember the occasion, Ricky obviously cannot take the gift back. An overjoyed Lucy wears the coat night and day, making it impossible to retrieve it. When Lucy learns the truth, she gets even with Ricky by cutting up a phony fur coat with scissors in front of the now-panicked Ricky.

HIGHLIGHTS & TRIVIA

Ricky makes reference to the date the Ricardos moved into the apartment building: August 6, 1948. While August 6 is Lucille's actual birthday, the year means that the Ricardos had been living there for a little more than three years. This will change drastically in later episodes. This episode marks the first appearance of Ricky's classic smoking jacket. Such attire had been out of style for years, but Desi single-handedly brings it back into popularity. In fact, a line of Ricky Ricardo smoking jackets will be marketed later in the season. Bert French again changes Lucille's hairstyle, trying to give her a softer, more feminine look. The incidental music used in the bedroom sequence is written by Eliot Daniel, who also wrote the theme music.

Eliot Daniel

(COMPOSER)

While Wilbur Hatch wrote most of the music coming in and out of scenes, I occasionally wrote some longer themes that were used on several shows. They could be lengthened or shortened as time was needed. Wilbur then arranged the pieces to fit the time constraints. Some folks don't realize that the music, although always credited to Wilbur, was sometimes created by myself or Desi's pianist and arranger, Marco Rizo.

Dann Cahn

(FILM EDITOR)

The ad agency provided us with the copy, but we filmed many of the commercials for them [some on the set of the series]. Desilu Productions got an extra fee for doing it, and it allowed members of the crew to make some extra money at the same time. So we shot right on the set, or used set pieces, to save money. After awhile, we began shooting commercials for other shows, too. This led to producing other shows, and before we knew it, Desilu was becoming a big-time studio.

Wedding anniversaries will become a recurring theme on the show. This is the only instance where Lucy claims not to know the actual date herself. Some years Ricky will know; some years he won't. It will depend on the plot demand. Strangely, the Mertzes have similar selective amnesia. One year they throw the Ricardos a party; the next they will have no idea when the date falls. There was an additional scene planned, where Ricky lights a fire and Fred turns up the heat to get Lucy to take off the fur coat (and in which she implies she is naked under it), but it was cut due to time constraints.

This show is based in part on the *My Favorite Husband* radio episode "Anniversary Presents."

I LOVE LUCY #10: "LUCY IS JEALOUS OF A GIRL DANCER"

(CBS, DECEMBER 17, 1951), 30 MINUTES (B&W)

GUEST CAST: Helen Silver, John Stephenson (announcer and commercials)

When an item in the *Daily Mirror* infers that Ricky is having an affair with Rosemary, his new club dancer, Lucy is furious. Ricky reassures her that the story is merely a publicity gimmick. Later, when Ricky accidentally tears a piece of Rosemary's lace costume, he absentmindedly puts it in his pocket where Lucy finds it. A suspicious Lucy joins the show to spy on the two.

HIGHLIGHTS & TRIVIA

The name of this episode was originally labeled ". . . Girl Singer" instead of ". . . Girl Dancer," but was crossed out and changed by hand in the scripts. The above title is the proper, official one; not the one listed in other sources. Notice that Lucille's dancing costume is not nearly as revealing as the other girls. Starting with this episode, Vivian's hair color is lightened several shades. Desi's performance of "Jezebel" is a rare instance of his singing a then-popular song made famous by someone else (in this case, Frankie Laine). He handles the number beautifully. So does Lucy, whose clowning as the phony dancing girl once again features her split-second timing. Lucy's making fun of Ricky's English ("All right, go ahead . . . 'splain!") is becoming a staple of the writing.

Madelyn Pugh Martin Davis
(WRITER)
We didn't start out writing lines that poked fun at Desi's English. Desi was very sensitive about the way he spoke. Off camera, he spoke much faster and with a thicker accent. After awhile, it became easier to work these things into the scripts, as long as we were careful to be sensitive to Desi's feelings.

Bob Carroll Jr.
(WRITER)
Strangely, the audience didn't like it if anyone else made fun of Ricky's English. They didn't laugh, and seemed to resent it. We could only get away with it when Lucy did it.

I LOVE LUCY #11: "DRAFTED"

(CBS, DECEMBER 24, 1951), 30 MINUTES (B&W)
GUEST CAST: Vernon Dent

Lucy reads a letter addressed to Ricky from the War Department and assumes he has been drafted. Actually, Ricky is scheduled to do a benefit at Fort Dix, New Jersey. When Ethel hears Fred is joining Ricky, the girls assume both boys (despite their age) are going into the army while Ricky and Fred jump to the conclusion that the girls are pregnant. The girls plan a surprise going-away party for the boys, and the guys set up a surprise baby shower for the girls—with the same guests invited to both occasions, which are scheduled at the same time.

HIGHLIGHTS & TRIVIA

When Lucy refers to Maurice Thompson as the commander sending Ricky his orders, the name was taken from script clerk and camera coordinator Maury Thompson. This is one of the only times a script infers that the characters of Fred and Ethel might actually be having a sex life. How else could Fred think she is pregnant? The idea of jumping to wild conclusions becomes a recurring theme in the series, as well as the early episodes of *The Lucy Show* (1962–68). The names on the guest list (Orsatti, Sedgwick, Buzzel, and Josephy) come from actual friends of the Arnazes. More and more often, names used in the show reflect real people, either behind the scenes or pals of Lucille and Desi. The crying jag (a favorite "Lucy" device that would repeatedly appear in every Ball series) is first evidenced here, displayed by both Ball and Vance in almost vocal harmony. It is becoming increasingly obvious how well the two women work together.

The middle commercial has a Christmas theme, with Lucille and Desi providing the voices to their cartoon look-alikes as they musically extol the virtues of giving cartons of Philip Morris cigarettes as Christmas gifts. At the end of the show, the Ricardos and the Mertzes are dressed as Santa Claus while they put their presents under the Ricardos' Christmas tree. There is no soundtrack reaction, as this bit was filmed after the studio audience had left. As the cast sings "Jingle Bells" and dances around the tree, another Santa (Vernon Dent) appears . . . the real one! Using a bit of magic, he disappears as the cast wishes the audience a Merry Christmas. A final scene, with the Ricardos and the Mertzes laughing together after the party, was written, but cut due to time constraints.

This installment is based in part on the *My Favorite Husband* radio episode "George Is Drafted—Liz's Baby."

I LOVE LUCY #12: "THE ADAGIO"

(CBS, DECEMBER 31, 1951), 30 MINUTES (B&W)
GUEST CAST: Shep Menken, John Stephenson (announcer and commercials)

When Lucy learns that Ricky desperately needs Apache dancers for his club, she hopes this is her big chance. Ethel introduces her to a professional French dancer (Shep Menken) who assumes that what Lucy wants is romance, because that is what he has been told about American women in general. When Ricky comes home and finds the Frenchman dangling out of the bedroom window, he assumes the worst. When the two men realize the truth, they teach Lucy a much-needed lesson.

HIGHLIGHTS & TRIVIA

Bert French tries yet more new hairstyles on both Lucille and Vivian to pacify the Redhead's growing discontent with her oncamera look. Ball's voice is cracked and raspy from the screaming she has to do throughout the episode. This is not one of the better shows. It is bogged down with a silly script and flat jokes, and the performances seem forced and under-rehearsed. This is the second time someone is at the Ricardo's bedroom window with a ladder. As the Ricardos are four flights up, this must be *some* ladder! In the original episode script, the finale is entirely different: Ricky gives a job to the French dancer in his club, and the two men practically beat Lucy up during the Apache dance to teach her a lesson.

I LOVE LUCY #13: "THE BENEFIT"

(CBS, JANUARY 7, 1952), 30 MINUTES (B&W)

GUEST CAST: Jay Jackson (announcer and commercials)

After an evening of cards and music, Ethel asks Lucy to get Ricky to perform at a benefit for her women's club (the Wednesday Afternoon Fine Arts League). Ricky agrees to do a duet with her, but "Auf Wiedersehen" is not what she has in mind. She and Ricky quarrel, so the Cuban sends Fred home from the club with a new routine for Lucy to practice. When she realizes that Ricky has taken all the jokes for himself, she double-crosses him by upstaging him during the performance.

HIGHLIGHTS & TRIVIA

This is the first show to establish Lucy's incredibly *un*-musical voice. It is very difficult to consistently hit the wrong notes the right way. Actually, Lucille can carry a tune and is as capable musically as many musical-comedy actresses. Lucille practices for hours to hit just the right notes and timbre. This bit is borrowed from the Arnazes' stage act, where the song used had been "Zing! Went the Strings of My Heart." It is also established that Ethel can play the piano. (In this episode, her playing is provided by house pianist Marco Rizo offstage, as is Desi's.) Viv's hair is once again lightened, this time to an almost white-yellow. It is unusual, given the context of later episodes, that Ethel is a member of a club to which Lucy does not also belong. The interplay between the girls is much more natural and indicative of how the female characters will mature in subsequent episodes. The scribes also establish that Ricky has a closet full of old costumes, which will come in very handy for future plot lines. Jay Jackson replaces John Stephenson as announcer with this entry.

This show is based on the radio episode of *My Favorite Husband* entitled "Charity Review," in which Richard Denning sang "We'll Build a Bungalow" with Lucille.

Vivian Vance

At one point, Lucille's agent wanted to have me fired, telling her that my eyes were bigger than hers. When I heard this, I told her that if I had her looks and talent, I'd keep me and fire the agent!

I LOVE LUCY #14: "THE AMATEUR HOUR"

(CBS, JANUARY 14, 1952), 30 MINUTES (B&W)

GUEST CAST: Gail Bonney, David Stollery, Sammy Ogg, Jay Jackson (announcer and commercials)

After buying an expensive dress on sale without Ricky's permission, Lucy is told she must pay for the garment. She answers an ad for a babysitting job paying $5.00 an hour. Her employer, Mrs. Hudson, neglects to tell Lucy that she is going to be in charge of twins. These devils make a shambles of Lucy's apartment and nerves, until Mrs. Hudson calls and asks Lucy to take her place with the twins at an amateur contest.

HIGHLIGHTS & TRIVIA

It should be noted that the boys playing the twins are not only *not* brothers, but aren't even related. This episode establishes the Ricardos' New York City address: 623 East 68th Street. If the fictitious address were literal, the building would be located in the middle of the East River. (The original address for the Mertzes' apartment building was going to be 323 West 54th Street.) Although

Lucille wears shin pads to protect herself from the kicks the youngsters give her, she ends up being badly bruised during the filming. Director Marc Daniels makes a mistake in his blocking of the kitchen scenes. He allows one of the youngsters to go in front of the breakfast counter to draw on the wall, which destroys the illusion of the "fourth" wall. Bill Frawley does not appear in this episode, although his laughter can be clearly heard on the soundtrack. When Ricky announces "Little Willie Mae" at the contest, the name is taken from the Arnazes' maid and their children's nanny, Willie Mae Barker. In the original script, there is a subplot of Fred not being able to play poker and win his spending money, so he too is in the amateur show and loses. This is cut from the final shooting script.

This show is based in part on the *My Favorite Husband* radio episode "Baby Sitting."

I LOVE LUCY #15: "LUCY PLAYS CUPID"

(CBS, JANUARY 21, 1952), 30 MINUTES (B&W)

GUEST CAST: Bea Benaderet, Edward Everett Horton, Jay Jackson (announcer and commercials)

Lucy's neighbor, old maid Miss Lewis (Bea Benaderet), is infatuated with Mr. Ritter (Edward Everett Horton), the grocer. Although Lucy has agreed to help Miss Lewis snare the old gentleman, Ricky forbids her to get involved. A determined Lucy disobeys him, delivering an invitation to Mr. Ritter for dinner. He misunderstands, thinking that Lucy is interested in him, so she must find some way to turn him off.

HIGHLIGHTS & TRIVIA

Bea Benaderet had played Lucille's best friend on radio's *My Favorite Husband.* Bea was only in her midforties when this TV episode was filmed, and Hal King's aging makeup is superb. The show is shot on one of the off-weeks when *The George Burns and Gracie Allen Show* is not being broadcast live, as Bea plays Blanche Morton on that series. Notice Ricky's spanking of Lucy. No television character today could possibly get away with physically abusing his wife in this manner. However, this spanking will occur again in later episodes. By the way, where does Lucy get the twenty-five children she has hidden in the bedroom? Also notice the not-so-subtle plug for the sponsor's product when Ricky phones Lucy. He pulls a cigarette out of a plastic mock-up of the Philip Morris "mascot," Johnny. Interestingly, the commercials for Philip Morris cigarettes are consistently boring and banal, and get worse each week. Neither Vivian Vance nor Bill Frawley appears in this installment. This show is based in part on the *My Favorite Husband* radio episode "Valentine's Day."

I LOVE LUCY #16: "LUCY'S FAKE ILLNESS"

(CBS, JANUARY 28, 1952), 30 MINUTES (B&W)

GUEST CAST: Hal March, Jay Jackson (announcer and commercials)

When Ricky advertises in *Variety* for new talent, Lucy and the Mertzes want to audition. While Ricky allows Fred and Ethel a chance, he refuses to give one to Lucy. When Ethel suggests that Lucy might get a complex if she is kept from doing what she really wants, Lucy consults a book and develops three symptoms: the personality of a famous actress, amnesia, and childlike behavior. Ricky is concerned until Fred overhears the truth and tells it to Ricky.

HIGHLIGHTS & TRIVIA

While Lucille's parody of stage, movie, and radio star Tallulah Bankhead is amusing, her later impersonation of her will be brilliant when the two work together in 1957 on the *Ford Lucille Ball-Desi Arnaz Show.* Hal March, a friend of the family, plays himself. An actor and a deft comedian, he will appear twice more with Lucille through the years. Hal will die much too young in 1970. In turn, his adopted son, Steve March, is a close friend of Desi Arnaz Jr. Ricky mentions that the Ricardos have been living in their apartment for five years, which ups the ante from the three years previously referenced. In the original script, the doctor is Lucy's lifelong physician, who is talked into teaching her a lesson to never fake an illness again. "Go-bloots," Lucy's diagnosed disease, and the "boo-shoo" bird carrier are the correct spellings for the now famous words. The song the band plays at the end is "I'll Be Glad When You're Dead, You Rascal You." This show is based in part on the *My Favorite Husband* radio episode "Liz Has the Flimjabs."

I LOVE LUCY #17: "LUCY WRITES A PLAY"

(CBS, FEBRUARY 4, 1952), 30 MINUTES (B&W)

GUEST CAST: Myra Marsh, Maury Thompson, Jay Jackson (announcer and commercials)

Lucy writes a play for a women's club competition. When Ricky refuses to take the lead role, she is stuck with Fred and must adapt the script accordingly. Later, Ricky agrees to do the play as a surprise to Lucy, but doesn't know she has rewritten it. The result is a *huge* comedy of errors.

HIGHLIGHTS & TRIVIA

This episode introduces the Wednesday Afternoon Fine Arts League, a group of women who will become increasingly important in future episodes. Otherwise, this is one of the weaker efforts of the first season. All of the actors seem to have trouble with their British accents. Maury Thompson plays the stage manager; in reality he is the show's script clerk and soon-to-be camera coordinator. Notice that while Lucille is rapidly losing weight, Desi is putting on pounds. He will battle with his weight problem the rest of his life. By the way, the writers seemed very fond of the poem "Hiawatha," as it is used not only here, but also several times in the future.

This entry is based in part on the *My Favorite Husband* radio episode "Liz's Radio Script."

I LOVE LUCY #18: "BREAKING THE LEASE"

(CBS, FEBRUARY 11, 1952), 30 MINUTES (B&W)

GUEST CAST: Bennett Green, Hazel Pierce, Barbara Pepper, Jay Jackson (announcer and commercials)

After an evening of singing around the piano until two o'clock in the morning, the Mertzes go home. When the Ricardos continue singing, the sleepy Mertzes complain. A fight ensues, prompting Lucy and Ricky to move. When the Mertzes expect them to pay off their lease, the Ricardos become undesirable tenants, hoping to be evicted.

HIGHLIGHTS & TRIVIA

Lucy and Ricky grappling with the bedroom window is a situation taken from real life. Lucille liked to sleep with the windows open, while Desi preferred to sleep warmly. Despite all of Bill Frawley's complaining about everyone's singing, and his self-appointment as an expert on harmony singing, he almost always sings off-key whenever the group harmonizes together. This is the first plot that pits the Ricardos against the Mertzes, and it is also the first appearance of Barbara Pepper. Barbara is fairly trim here, but soon will gain over 100 pounds. This is the first episode where the characters appear as we will see them for the remainder of the series. By now, the actors know their characters as well as the writers do. Watch Lucille's and Desi's reaction when Bill and Vivian enter with the chandelier on their heads.

Lucille Ball

When Bill and Viv entered with that thing on their head, Desi and I had to bite the insides of our cheeks to keep from laughing. Their expressions were priceless, and for all our concentration, we both broke up. Desi tried to cover it by pointing and coughing, but we both knew we blew it. God *they were funny!*

I LOVE LUCY #19: "THE BALLET"

(CBS, FEBRUARY 18, 1952), 30 MINUTES (B&W)

GUEST CAST: Mary Wickes, Frank Scanell, John Stephenson (announcer)

When Lucy hears that Ricky is mounting a cavalcade of show business at the club, she wants to participate. He tells her that the only parts available are for a ballet dancer or a pair of burlesque comics. Lucy disastrously tries to rehearse with a ballet troupe and a burlesque comic. When Ethel calls her at the last second to fill in for a no-show performer, pandemonium breaks loose.

HIGHLIGHTS & TRIVIA

The fact the Fred used to be in vaudeville is referenced here, although the name of his one-time partner (Ted Kurtz) will change in future episodes. Lucy claims to have studied ballet for four years in high school; this is the last time her ballet skills will be mentioned. Mary Wickes makes her debut here on a *Lucy* show, and it will not be her last. She is brilliant as the ballet teacher; not once does she allow Lucille to upstage her. If you look closely at Lucille in her ballet costume, you can see her legs are a mass of black and blue bruises from rehearsing. Although Lucille will later claim that getting her foot stuck in the barre is an accident, it is detailed in the script.

This is possibly the first time the classic burlesque sketch "Slowly I Turn" is presented on television; it will never be done as well. Bob and Madelyn work it into the show so smoothly, it seems fresh and unexpected. Vivian plays the piano herself, fumbling through "The Waltz of the Flowers." Desi looks tired here; the strain of mounting and acting in the series is beginning to tell. Nevertheless, his singing of "Martha" in two languages is excellent. Every once in awhile Desi will sing better than usual, and this is one of those times. For the record, this episode features Lucille's first pie in the face (as well as Desi's). In an unusual move, the middle commercial doesn't come until twenty minutes into the show. This is because the previous scene ran so well, the sponsors didn't want to interrupt the action. In the original script, the scene with Madame Lamond (Mary Wickes) is much longer. She phones Ricky to complain that Lucy is such a klutz, and they scheme to teach Lucy a lesson. When Lamond returns to the studio, Lucy is already stuck with her leg in the barre.

I LOVE LUCY #20: "THE YOUNG FANS"

(CBS, FEBRUARY 25, 1952), 30 MINUTES (B&W)

GUEST CAST: Richard Crenna, Janet Waldo, Jay Jackson (announcer and commercials)

When a teenage girl in the neighborhood gets a crush on Ricky, Lucy interferes by talking to her young boyfriend. Now he falls for Lucy, so the Ricardos scheme to scare off the infatuated youngsters.

HIGHLIGHTS & TRIVIA

Richard Crenna is on the Desilu lot to observe the three-camera TV filming process. He has been signed to play in the television version of *Our Miss Brooks* (1952–56), recreating his role from the radio version. He is already twenty-four years old, but will play a squeaky-voiced teenager for several more years. Janet Waldo will later play Lucy's sister on *The Lucy Show*, but will be known forever as the voice of Judy Jetson of the TV cartoon series *The Jetsons* (1962–63, 1985, 1987). This is the only first season episode directed by William Asher. Like Crenna, he is at the studio getting experience in the three-camera process before directing the early *Our Miss Brooks* shows.

It is revealed in this episode that Ricky Ricardo is thirty-five years old, the same age as Desi Arnaz. Desi is showing signs of being a sharp comedian in his own right. In the last scene, he matches Lucille laugh for laugh with a flair for broad comedy. His line, "Keep jiggling Peggy!" is oft repeated among aficionados of the show and collectors. Bert French finally settles on a hairstyle for Lucille, the classic bun that she will wear on camera until 1958. Vivian Vance and Bill Frawley do *not* appear in this episode.

This show is based in part on the *My Favorite Husband* radio episode "Liz Teaches the Samba."

Janet Waldo

(ACTOR)

I was terribly intimidated working with her [Lucille] because, well, she was Lucy, but she was marvelously professional. In rehearsals she was letter perfect, but I was shocked during the shoot. When the cameras started rolling in front of the live audience, she just "turned on"—she was so much bigger on camera than in rehearsal. I got the part because Madelyn called me and asked me if I would like to be on I Love Lucy. *I was thrilled to do it, but there was only one problem. I was* pregnant. *I was playing a teenager on radio on* Corliss Archer *at the time and didn't show too much, so we thought it was safe. Wardrobe covered me up so I didn't show at all. Lucy knew I was pregnant, and when we rehearsed the "keep jiggling Peggy" scene, she would say, "Janet, just cool it. Don't do it too much now. You don't want to miscarry!"*

I LOVE LUCY #21: "NEW NEIGHBORS"

(CBS, MARCH 3, 1952), 30 MINUTES (B&W)

GUEST CAST: Hayden Rorke, K. T. Stevens, Allen Jenkins, John Stephenson (announcer)

When new neighbors move into the building, Lucy's curiosity overwhelms her. She goes snooping and gets trapped in the new arrivals' apartment. She overhears a sinister, anti-American conversation that she thinks is real, but it is only from a script the neighbors, who are actors, are rehearsing. Lucy jumps to the wrong conclusions and mayhem ensues.

HIGHLIGHTS & TRIVIA

Beginning with this episode, the show's opening is changed. Johnny the Bellboy is still calling for Philip Morris, but now the cartoon characters are putting up a billboard on a highway, extolling the virtues of the tobacco product. This is the only time we see the living room windows to the Ricardos' apartment, as the girls lean out of one of them. Many of the jokes in this installment fall flat, without the usual hysterical audience reactions. Notice that the costume Lucille wears as the "chair" has a seat and back legs built into it to make it easier for her to sit and steady herself. The door to the Ricardos' apartment was cut out and rigged with a wire to pull away when the guns are fired to make it look as if a piece of the door has been blown away. In the original script, Lucy's middle name is Elenore, not Esmeralda as Ricky uses in the episode.

K. T. Stevens (the neighbor) was one of Vivian Vance's closest pals in real life. And, of course, Hayden Rorke will go on to television immortality as Dr. Bellows on *I Dream of Jeannie* (1965–70). The middle commercial features Robert Rockwell, who will be joining *Our Miss Brooks* when Desilu films it the following season.

Robert Rockwell

(ACTOR)

Until [the author] brought it to my attention, I had no memory of making those commercials. Back then, I just worked wherever they'd hire me. I am ashamed to say I did a lot of cigarette commercials in those days Who knew?

For the first time, Lucille and Desi do the final commercial themselves, live on film. With a few exceptions, they will continue this practice until 1960.

I LOVE LUCY #22: "FRED AND ETHEL FIGHT"

(CBS, MARCH 10, 1952), 30 MINUTES (B&W)

GUEST CAST: Hazel Pierce, John Stephenson (announcer)

After Fred and Ethel fight, he moves out of the building. Lucy schemes to get them together again by inviting them both to dinner without either one knowing the other one is coming. They reconcile, but now Lucy and Ricky argue about their last quarrel. Ricky leaves in a huff, so Lucy fakes an accident to win him back.

HIGHLIGHTS & TRIVIA

This episode is based on a real-life dinner party the Arnazes gave in 1944 that had similar odd circumstances. This show is filmed off-schedule on a Wednesday evening instead of Friday, to leave everyone free to be involved with the shooting of the *Our Miss Brooks* pilot that Saturday. In the drugstore scene, notice the huge poster of Johnny the Bellboy in the background as a sop to the sponsor. The middle commercial features Bud Collyer, who will live in television history as the host of *Beat the Clock* (1950–58) and *To Tell the Truth* (1956–67). The fact that Lucy uses henna rinse is first mentioned in this episode. Fred says that Ethel has gone home to her mother. By 1954, the story line will feature Ethel's father as a widower.

I LOVE LUCY #23: "THE MOUSTACHE"

(CBS, MARCH 17, 1952), 30 MINUTES (B&W)

GUEST CAST: John Brown, John Stephenson (announcer)

Ricky has grown a moustache to impress a Hollywood talent scout, hoping for a motion picture assignment. Lucy hates it, and in protest glues a phony beard to her face. Unfortunately, she uses cement glue and can't remove the beard.

HIGHLIGHTS & TRIVIA

The daisy decals above the Ricardos' bed have now disappeared. This whimsical entry infers for the first time that Ethel was also once in show business. Fred mentions that the last vaudeville date he played was in 1925. Notice Ricky's reference to being in the show *Too Many Girls*, which Desi had done on Broadway in 1939. John Brown (as the talent scout) had just finished six months playing Harry Morton on TV's *The George Burns and Gracie Allen Show.* The featured song, "I'll See You in C-U-B-A," was written by Irving Berlin.

This entry is based in part on the *My Favorite Husband* radio episode "Respective Moustaches."

I LOVE LUCY #24: "THE GOSSIP"

(CBS, MARCH 24, 1952), 30 MINUTES (B&W)

GUEST CAST: Richard Reeves, Bobby Jellison, John Stephenson (announcer)

When Ricky and Fred tire of Lucy and Ethel gossiping, the girls bet the boys they can hold off gossiping longer than the men. The prize: breakfast in bed for a month. To win the wager, the boys scheme to make the girls gossip. When the girls learn the truth, they get back at them.

HIGHLIGHTS & TRIVIA

This is the first of the many *I Love Lucy* shows whose plot line revolves around a bet. Bobby Jellison will appear as Bobby the Bellboy during the California episodes of the series in the 1954–55 season. The gold medallion Lucy wears in the first scene was a favorite piece of jewelry owned by Lucille; she will wear it on television as late as 1986. Every single thing Lucille does during her charades pantomime is detailed for her in the script. It truly was a great creative marriage between writers and a performer.

Madelyn Pugh Martin Davis

(WRITER)

When you write a script, you hope you can get sixty or seventy percent of what you write back from the actors in effort and performance. With Lucy, it was always one hundred and ten percent. That is why it was always such a joy to write for her.

This show has one of the few examples of Lucille doing a voice-over while she is "thinking," a device commonly used in soap operas. The ending commercial is changed, as the Arnazes now do it inside a cartoon heart.

This show is based in part on the *My Favorite Husband* radio episode "Gossip."

I LOVE LUCY #25: "PIONEER WOMEN"

(CBS, MARCH 31, 1952), 30 MINUTES (B&W)

GUEST CAST: Florence Bates, Ruth Perrott, John Stephenson (announcer)

Lucy and Ethel hope to join the Society Matrons' League, so they ask the boys for automatic dishwashers to avoid having dishpan hands. Ricky and Fred claim the girls have gotten soft, and could not possibly do the hard work their grandmothers did. Another bet ensues, seeing which sex better handles the rigors of life at the turn of the twentieth century.

HIGHLIGHTS & TRIVIA

This is a classic show, due to the memorable scene where Lucy and Ethel bake bread. The production staff had to find a bakery willing to make such a long loaf (it *is* real bread). There is an extra scene where Lucy and Ethel play with the dough that is cut out of the later syndicated rerun versions. This is one of the *Lucy* programs where the audience must suspend its disbelief for the sake of the comedy. For example, when the bread pops out of the oven, it is on a rack three times as long as the oven is deep! The actors so believe in what they are doing that the audience believes, too. The talent it takes to pull this off is extraordinary, and is a hallmark of the series. The scene on the back porch, where Ricky arrives on horseback, had to be ad-libbed due to a very uncooperative horse who refused to perform the scene as written. After the show is filmed, the entire audience is invited onstage to have a piece of that huge bread loaf with butter. Ruth Perrott is another veteran of the *My Favorite Husband* radio show asked to appear on *I Love Lucy*.

I LOVE LUCY #26: "THE MARRIAGE LICENSE"

(CBS, APRIL 7, 1952), 30 MINUTES (B&W)

GUEST CAST: Irving Bacon, Elizabeth Patterson, Jay Jackson (announcer)

When Lucy cleans out the living room desk, she finds her marriage license and discovers that Ricky's last name was misspelled as Bacardi. Lucy believes she is not legally married, and insists she and Ricky rewed. She drags him to the Byrum River Beagle Club in Connecticut so he can propose in the same spot he did the first time. They quarrel and return to the Eagle, a small town fleabag hotel.

HIGHLIGHTS & TRIVIA

This is the first television episode of any kind to have a home-viewing audience of ten million people. There weren't many television sets in use, and many areas of the country did not yet have TV stations. Lucille and Desi actually were married in

1940 at the Byrum River Beagle Club in Greenwich, Connecticut. Irving Bacon will be seen again as Ethel's father in 1954, and Elizabeth Patterson will join the cast in 1953 as Mrs. Trumbull. Both performers add a great deal of home-spun humor and warmth that enhance this entry. Notice Bacon's imitation of Johnny the Bellboy, yet another plug for the cigarette company sponsor. In real life, Desi Arnaz is related to the Bacardi rum business on his mother's side; his grandfather was a founder. The Arnazes do a new final commercial.

This show is based in part on two radio episodes of *My Favorite Husband*: "Marriage License" and "Anniversary."

I LOVE LUCY #27: "THE KLEPTOMANIAC"

(CBS, APRIL 14, 1952), 30 MINUTES (B&W)

GUEST CAST: Joseph Kearns, Jay Jackson (announcer)

Lucy is the chairperson of the club's bazaar, against Ricky's orders. She hides the club's treasury, as well as all of the items being auctioned at the upcoming bazaar. When Ricky finds the money in her purse and sees her hiding merchandise, he concludes she is a kleptomaniac, and hires a psychiatrist to help her. Lucy finds out about Ricky's plan, and teaches him a lesson.

HIGHLIGHTS & TRIVIA

Joseph Kearns is best known as Mr. Wilson on *Dennis the Menace* (1959–63). He will return to the show again in 1957. Lucille's split-second timing is evident again in the scene where she imitates a cuckoo clock. Lucille and Viv work so well together in the final scene, it is almost as if they are of one mind. Concerning Lucy's bit on her regression to childhood, the actress is imitating her close friend, movie star Ginger Rogers, who used that childlike voice to amuse friends at parties. Finally, where, oh *where*, do you suppose Lucy was able to get that elephant she has in the apartment?

I LOVE LUCY #28: "CUBAN PALS"

(CBS, APRIL 21, 1952), 30 MINUTES (B&W)

GUEST CAST: Alberto Morin, Rita Convy, Lita Baron, Jay Jackson (announcer)

Lucy finally meets some of Ricky's Cuban friends when he books them to perform at the Tropicana. When she is introduced to the youngest one, a sexy dancer, Lucy is extremely jealous, and schemes to take her place at the club.

HIGHLIGHTS & TRIVIA

This is the second episode where Lucy gets rid of a story line performer and it won't be the last. This show is notable for two reasons. First, it features Desi making a huge mistake when he acts as translator; he speaks English to the Cubans and then breaks up. Second, the filming of this episode would become a major plot theme in the movie *The Mambo Kings* (1992). In that film, the main characters are Cuban pals. Footage from this episode is used, with matching footage of the film's actors. Desi Arnaz Jr. hauntingly portrays his father in the film, which is full of historical errors concerning *I Love Lucy*.

This episode establishes Ricky has not been back to Cuba since he emigrated. Later, we will learn Lucy has never met her mother-in-law. Watch Desi's dancing during "The Lady in Red" number. "Similau" (sung by Ricky) was a minor hit for Desi; the arrangement is a wonderful showcase for his singing style. The original script included a tag scene with Ethel very angry at Lucy; she has received a telegram from Fred stating what a great time he and Cuban Rosita are having in Atlantic City. It was deleted from the script due to taste constraints of that time.

I LOVE LUCY #29: "THE FREEZER"

(CBS, APRIL 28, 1952), 30 MINUTES (B&W)

GUEST CAST: Frank Sully, Bennett Green, Fred Aldrich, Kay Wiley, Barbara Pepper, Hazel Pierce, John Stephenson (announcer)

Lucy and Ethel acquire a huge, walk-in freezer from Ethel's butcher uncle, who is retiring. They order two sides of beef, thinking they will be a little larger than sides of bacon. The enormous shipment of meat arrives, and the dumbfounded girls store it in the freezer. When the boys want to inspect the freezer, Lucy hides the meat in the furnace, and in the process gets locked in the freezer.

HIGHLIGHTS & TRIVIA

Once again, Lucille's total belief in what she is doing makes an unbelievable situation totally acceptable. (Obviously, people do not freeze meat the way Lucy does in this show.) This is a combination of exceptional character development in the writing, and genius talent in the performing. Lucille's spiel in the butcher shop ("tell you what I'm gonna do") is a parody of pitchman Sid Stone, the man who did the Texaco commercials on Milton Berle's TV program (1948–56). As this business is only partially written in the shooting script, it might actually be a case where Lucille has invented something during rehearsals that is incorporated into the show. Viv's hair is restyled for this outing; her hair will change styles, lengths, and colors several more times over the next year. This is the first time Desi is given credit as executive producer. It is done at Desi's request and against Jess Oppenheimer's better judgment. In later years, Jess will regret this decision as it sowed the seeds of friction between Desi and Jess, which led to Oppenheimer's departure from *I Love Lucy* in 1955.

ALL-STAR REVUE

(NBC, MAY 3, 1952), 60 MINUTES (B&W)

PRODUCED AND DIRECTED BY: Joseph Santley
WRITTEN BY: Artie Stander, Sid Dorfman
CAST: Ed Wynn (host), Lucille Ball, the Borden Twins, the Duncan Sisters, John K. M. McCaffery, the Whippoorwills, Ben Wrigley

Lucille does a second live variety turn with Ed Wynn, with the same hysterical results. Wynn seems to love the comedy concept of the reducing parlor for fat people, as he uses it frequently on his television programs. This time Lucille is caught in a slapstick melee with the zoftig Borden Twins, Rosalyn and Marilyn, who put her through the exercise wringer while sharing gym equipment. These same Borden Twins will play Teensy and Weensy on *I Love Lucy* in episode #112: "Tennessee Bound." Lucille and Ed also reprise the same spy sketch they did on their last joint TV appearance on December 24, 1949.

I LOVE LUCY #30: "LUCY DOES A TV COMMERCIAL"

(CBS, MAY 5, 1952), 30 MINUTES (B&W)

GUEST CAST: Ross Elliott, Jerry Hausner, Maury Thompson, Jay Jackson (announcer)

Ricky is to host a TV variety show, and Lucy wants to do the on-air commercials. After failing to win him over by staging a mock show inside their own television set, she arranges to replace the TV spokeswoman. Short on time, Ricky approves Lucy doing the commercial for Vitameatavegamin, which is twenty-three percent alcohol. After many rehearsals, Lucy gets inebriated.

HIGHLIGHTS & TRIVIA

This is it, the penultimate Lucille Ball performance! The scene of her rehearsing the commercial, and becoming progressively drunker, is a classic not only for television, but for classic comedy period! Lucille is perfect; there is not a wasted gesture or inflection. With each line and movement, she keeps topping herself in a never-ending crescendo of comedy.

The liquid in the Vitameatavegamin bottles is actually apple pectin. Vivian Vance does not appear in this episode, although in the original script all of Fred's lines were Ethel's. The original script had a tag scene where Lucy has a huge hangover, so Ethel goes to the store and buys her . . . you guessed it! It was not used due to time constraints.

Desi Arnaz

The scene where Ross Elliott and I had to watch her rehearse the commercial was so funny that both of us got sores from having to chew the inside of our cheeks to keep from laughing.

Jess Oppenheimer
(PRODUCER/WRITER)

I don't know of anyone who could have carried this scene off besides Lucille Ball. She had a huge amount of memorization, both lines and business. There were no cue cards back then. Probably only I would notice, but Lucille went up in her lines doing the Vitameatavegamin bit. She had to go back and change the lines around to make them come out right, but that only added to the humor.

Lucille Ball

While this may not be my favorite episode *per se, I think that Vitameatavegamin bit is the best thing I ever did. And one of the hardest. God, I was nervous! It really gratifies me to know the audience loves it so much, generation after generation.*

It is important to note that every line and piece of business Lucille does is written in the script. It cannot be emphasized often enough how much talent Jess, Bob, and Madelyn possess, and how much their efforts combined to make the series the success it becomes. The living room furniture is rearranged for this episode to film the scene with Lucille inside the television set. In the original show, there is extra footage of Lucille spoofing Johnny the Bellboy doing a Philip Morris commercial that is cut out of all rerun versions. Ross Elliott makes the first of several appearances with Lucille in this show; the last will be in 1974. Script clerk Maury Thompson plays himself in the show.

Maury Thompson

(SCRIPT CLERK)

Lucille insisted that I be made up and put in the scene, right in front of her. She was afraid she might blow her lines during the long bit, and so she had me right there with the script opened to subtly cue her in case she stumbled. It was worked out that if she fudged, I could cue her right on camera and it would seem reasonable that Lucy Ricardo might forget a line or two. That way, we wouldn't have to stop rolling and waste time and film.

I LOVE LUCY #31: "THE PUBLICITY AGENT"

(CBS, MAY 12, 1952), 30 MINUTES (B&W)

GUEST CAST: Peter Leeds, Bennett Green, Richard Reeves, Gil Herman, Jay Jackson (announcer)

Ricky is worried about his lack of publicity, so Lucy decides to handle it herself. Masquerading as the Maharincess of Franistan, she arranges a room at the Waldorf Astoria Hotel and a press conference/concert at the Tropicana. Ricky realizes that the Maharincess is really Lucy in disguise, and decides to teach her a lesson.

HIGHLIGHTS & TRIVIA

Lucille's performance is so over the top in this episode that it is easy to overlook just how good Vivian Vance is as the royal servant. Lucille is believable to a great extent because Vivian is excellent support. Desi wears specially-made shoes with six-inch platforms when he appears in the hotel room scene as the sadistic "Tiger." Perhaps because the set is so small, the blocking in the hotel room scene is awkward and appears under-rehearsed.

I LOVE LUCY #32: "LUCY GETS RICKY ON THE RADIO" [A.K.A. "MR. AND MRS. QUIZ"]

(CBS, MAY 19, 1952), 30 MINUTES (B&W)

GUEST CAST: Frank Nelson, Bobby Ellis, Roy Rowan, Jay Jackson (announcer)

When the Ricardos' television set breaks down and both couples are forced to listen to a radio quiz show, Lucy, Fred, and Ethel are amazed that Ricky knows all the answers. Lucy arranges for her and Ricky to appear on the quiz program, not knowing Ricky had been in the audience of the prerecorded show (which is why he knew the answers). To save face, Lucy schemes to get the answers to the questions she and Ricky will be asked, but the questions are all changed at the last minute.

HIGHLIGHTS & TRIVIA

There is extra footage in the scene in Freddie Fillmore's office that displays a Philip Morris poster. This footage is cut and the scene re-edited for all syndicated prints of the show. This is Frank Nelson's second appearance as Freddie Fillmore. Roy Rowan (appearing here as an actor) so impresses the staff that during the second *Lucy* season he becomes the show's announcer. With a couple of exceptions, Roy Rowan (who passed away in 1998) will announce every Lucille Ball TV show and special until 1981. Bud Collyer once again handles the middle commercial.

Dann Cahn

(FILM EDITOR)

They liked Roy Rowan so much that on top of being the announcer, he also began to do the audience warm-up for the show. He wasn't much of a comedian, but he'd do all the explaining and charm stuff. Then Desi would come out and tell a couple of jokes, and introduce Lucy, Bill, and Vivian.

Eliot Daniel

(COMPOSER)

The music behind the "movie" on television was another piece I wrote that was used on several episodes in different forms.

I LOVE LUCY #33: "LUCY'S SCHEDULE"

(CBS, MAY 12, 1952), 30 MINUTES (B&W)
GUEST CAST: Gale Gordon, Edith Meiser, Jay Jackson (announcer)

The Tropicana has a new owner, Mr. Littlefield, who is a stickler for punctuality. After the Ricardos are late to a Littlefield dinner party, Ricky puts Lucy on a schedule. All is well until Ethel and Mrs. Littlefield tell Lucy she is spoiling things for all womankind. The women scheme to teach the men a much-needed lesson.

HIGHLIGHTS & TRIVIA

This is the first television meeting of Lucille Ball and veteran character actor Gale Gordon, who here plays Mr. Littlefield. Their entire relationship is summed up with the look Lucy gives Mr. Littlefield when she takes away his radish. His frustration and her getting away with something (usually at his expense) will provide the plot lines for literally hundreds of their future shows together. Edith Meiser was a featured player when Vivian starred in the Broadway musical *Let's Face It* (1941) with Danny Kaye and Eve Arden. Lucyphiles seem to especially like the scene where Ethel pitches the biscuits to Lucy ("Ethel, let's have those biscuits!"). The writers wisely added in a career promotion for Ricky, making him the Tropicana's manager. In the future, this job advancement allows Ricky to perform at the club, and to produce the shows and supervise the employees.

This show is based in part on the *My Favorite Husband* radio episode "Time Budgeting."

I LOVE LUCY #34: "RICKY THINKS HE'S GETTING BALD"

(CBS, JUNE 2, 1952), 30 MINUTES (B&W)
GUEST CAST: Milton Parsons, Roy Rowan (announcer)

When Lucy notices a few wrinkle lines on her face, Ricky, in turn, becomes concerned about losing his hair. He becomes so obsessed with this touch of vanity, that Lucy tries to snap him back into reality.

HIGHLIGHTS & TRIVIA

Lucy's vanity table is moved center stage in the bedroom set to better showcase Desi's movements in the opening scene. This is one of the most reedited episodes of the series. After the filming, Jess Oppenheimer felt that the final scene, which was originally the bald men's party, wasn't funny enough for the climax. He had small sequences reshot so the bit where Lucy gives Ricky scalp treatments comes last. Dann Cahn does a brilliant job of editing so the scenes fit together almost seamlessly. Once again, Desi shows what a gifted comedian he is during the scalp treatment bit. Bill Frawley earns a huge laugh, just by wearing a toupee. Not only is this Roy Rowan's first episode as announcer, but Lucille and Desi film a new closing commercial for the series.

Dann Cahn

(FILM EDITOR)

It was around this time that Lucy spent a couple of weekends in the hospital. She was exhausted from all she had been through; having a baby, going right to work, then doing more than thirty episodes. Maybe it also had to do with her getting pregnant again. I don't know. I do know that this hospital stuff did not happen more than a couple of times.

I LOVE LUCY #35: "RICKY ASKS FOR A RAISE"

(CBS, JUNE 9, 1952), 30 MINUTES (B&W)
GUEST CAST: Gale Gordon, Edith Meiser, Maurice Marsac, Roy Rowan (announcer)

Lucy pesters Ricky to ask for a raise from Mr. Littlefield, and she tells the boss that Ricky has other, better-paying club offers. Mr. Littlefield fires him so as not to stand in his way, and hires Xavier Valdez to replace him. To save Ricky's job, Lucy and the Mertzes scheme to make Valdez look bad.

HIGHLIGHTS & TRIVIA

This is Gale Gordon's last *Lucy* appearance until 1958. The monicker of the quick-change artist mentioned, Hal King, is actually that of Lucille's makeup artist. He started working with Ball from the show's inception and will continue until his retirement in 1973. Maurice Marsac makes his debut here as the Tropicana maître d', garnering spontaneous applause for his scene at the reservations desk. Bill Frawley steals the episode by doing a very uncharacteristic scene in drag, wiggling his hips. This is the only show where we see the entry foyer of the Tropicana club. The final commercial features Lucille and Desi sitting on a trunk in their bedroom, wishing the audience a pleasant summer and inviting them to watch the show's summer replacement, *My Little Margie.*

It is during the rehearsals for this week's show that Lucille learns she is pregnant again.

Lucille Ball

At first, we kinda figured that this was it [because of her pregnancy]. We'd finish the season, and that would be the end of it. I felt terrible putting so many people out of work. But Jess had a better idea.

Jess Oppenheimer

(PRODUCER/WRITER)

When Desi told me the news, I said, "Great! Lucy Ricardo can have a baby, too! That'll give us all kinds of plot ideas for the second season!"

It is decided that five more shows will be filmed that spring to use for the new season. This will keep episodes featuring a pregnant Lucy to a minimum. These entries, broadcast out of order of filming, comprise the first shows of the second *I Love Lucy* season. These five weeks of filming also give Jess, Desi, the writers, the sponsor, and the network time to work out all the details of keeping the show on the air while Lucille is carrying the child.

Chapter Four

1952–53 Season

I LOVE LUCY: THE SECOND SEASON

TECHNICAL REGULARS: Executive produced by Desi Arnaz; produced by Jess Oppenheimer; directed by William Asher (except where otherwise noted); written by Jess Oppenheimer, Madelyn Pugh, Bob Carroll Jr.; makeup by Hal King; hairstyling by Bert French and Irma Kusely (during the pregnancy episodes); music by Wilbur Hatch
CAST REGULARS: Lucille Ball (Lucy Ricardo); Desi Arnaz (Ricky Ricardo); Vivian Vance (Ethel Mertz); William Frawley (Fred Mertz); Roy Rowan (Announcer)

I LOVE LUCY #36: "JOB SWITCHING"

(CBS, SEPTEMBER 15, 1952), 30 MINUTES (B&W)
GUEST CAST: Elvia Allman, Alvin Hurwitz, Amanda Milligan

When Lucy writes a check to the beauty parlor with an attached note asking the teller not to put it through until the following month, Ricky is fed up with Lucy's disregard for money. This leads to a battle of the sexes, where the girls must find jobs and the boys stay home to do the household chores.

HIGHLIGHTS & TRIVIA

This is probably the second most remembered episode in Lucille's entire TV career. Besides the very funny scene between Lucille and the candy dipper, the scene between Viv, Lucille, and Elvia Allman (as the supervisor) is hysterical. Originally, Amanda Milligan (an actual candy dipper at the Farmer's Market in Hollywood) had lines in her scene with Lucille, but they are cut because she is uncomfortable talking oncamera. Notice that Amanda's hitting Lucille's face with chocolate is used twice from different angles to elongate the laugh. In the next scene, from the moment Allman yells, "Let 'er roll," the laughs come harder and faster. Desi and Bill have equal time to convulse the audience in their domestic scenes. (In the process, Desi actually hurt himself falling on the overflowing pot of rice, badly bruising his ribs.) Parts of both candy scenes will be borrowed, word for word, for an episode of *Bewitched* entitled "Samantha's Power Failure," with Ron Masak taking Elvia Allman's role.

This *I Love Lucy* installment is based in part on the *My Favorite Husband* episode "Women's Rights, Part Two."

Dann Cahn
(FILM EDITOR)
Director Marc Daniels left the show because there was too much tension between himself and Lucy and Desi. Nothing personal, but in reference to control on the set. They remained friendly, and Marc eventually came back and directed some Star Treks *and some things for Lucy in the later years. Bill Asher worked better with Lucy than Marc did. He had been the first one asked to direct the series, but turned it down for other opportunities. It was Bill who originally recommended me to Jess. Around this time, James Paisley came on board as assistant director. This was most significant for the soundtrack, for like Lucille's mother DeDe, he had an unmistakable laugh. I can still hear it on the reruns of not only our show, but lots of others. Their two laughs were stolen off our soundtrack and used for years on other shows.*

Maury Thompson
(CAMERA COORDINATOR)
Marc Daniels was deaf in one ear, and often he wouldn't hear Lucille when she would talk to him. It

drove Lucille crazy, because she thought she was being ignored. When Bill Asher came on, I had the chance to become camera coordinator. Lucille had a fit, because she felt secure having me right there with her. So, I did the camera coordinating and covered the script job where she was concerned. We brought Adele Sliff in to be the script clerk.

William Asher

(DIRECTOR)

The second day of rehearsal, we had finished doing some blocking and then I had to look into some technical things. Lucy and the cast went off by themselves. When they came back and we started rehearsing again, everything was different and it was obvious that Lucy had redirected everything. I pulled her aside and said, "This is no way to start. There can only be one director, and that's me. If you want to direct, send me home and save yourself some money." I was shaken, and since I did not yet have an office of my own, I retreated into the nearest place I could find, which was the men's room. I took about a half an hour to get myself together and then went back to the stage. Desi was there waiting for me, fuming. After I explained to him what had happened, he agreed I was right. He spoke to Lucy, and then brought me back into her dressing room. She was crying, I was crying, and I said, "Why don't we get back to work?" She agreed, and we never had another problem like this again.

The series' opening credits change for the new season, with the cartoon characters of Lucille and Desi now riding an elevator up to a rooftop where an animated electric sign billboards the Philip Morris product. Although Roy Rowan continues to be the show's announcer, different people will now be used each week to appear in the commercials, so he will no longer be listed among the episode cast credits.

I LOVE LUCY #37: "THE SAXOPHONE"

(CBS, SEPTEMBER 22, 1952), 30 MINUTES (B&W)

DIRECTED BY: Marc Daniels

GUEST CAST: Herb Vigran, Charles Victor

Lucy learns that Ricky is embarking on a series of one-night stands, and only band members can go on the tour. Undaunted, she pulls out her old saxophone to join the band. Rejected, she schemes to make Ricky think it isn't safe to leave her alone at home.

HIGHLIGHTS & TRIVIA

Starting with this episode, Vivian's hair is gradually darkened to a honey brown. Although Lucy references Celoron High School, she actually attended Jamestown High School in upstate New York before going off to New York City to attend dramatic school. Herb Vigran makes his *Lucy* debut here; he will appear with the Redhead in several TV episodes through the late 1960s.

Maury Thompson

(CAMERA COORDINATOR)

When we first read through this script, Lucille said she had played the saxophone briefly as a kid. That's all that was required for the show. Yet, she couldn't leave it alone. Every day, when we weren't rehearsing the actual script, Lucille was blowing that damn saxophone. She was such a perfectionist, trying to play that thing, that she almost ruined the bit by becoming too good.

I LOVE LUCY #38: "THE ANNIVERSARY PRESENT"

(CBS, SEPTEMBER 29, 1952), 30 MINUTES (B&W)

DIRECTED BY: Marc Daniels

GUEST CAST: Gloria Blondell

Ricky wants to buy Lucy real pearls as a surprise gift for their eleventh wedding anniversary. He calls a neighbor's wife, Grace Foster, who works at Joseff's jewelry store, to obtain a discount. When he goes to her apartment to select the pearls, Lucy jumps to the conclusion they are having an affair.

HIGHLIGHTS & TRIVIA

This was the first episode filmed the previous spring and held back for fall airing. We finally meet Grace Foster (played by movie actress Joan Blondell's sister Gloria) who lives in the building's apartment 2A. Notice that Lucy gets real pearls in this episode. This fact will be ignored in the 1959 *The Westinghouse Lucille Ball-Desi Arnaz Show* episode "The Ricardos Go to Japan."

I LOVE LUCY #39: "THE HANDCUFFS"

(CBS, OCTOBER 6, 1952), 30 MINUTES (B&W)

DIRECTED BY: Marc Daniels

GUEST CAST: Paul Dubov, Will Wright
Veola Vonn

To keep Ricky at home with her, a desperate Lucy uses trick handcuffs on him that Fred provides. Unfortunately, she has borrowed the wrong pair, and the Ricardos are stuck in a pair of antique handcuffs they cannot unlock.

HIGHLIGHTS & TRIVIA

There is yet another new opening for the show, with the cartoon characters of Desi and Lucille now on a scaffolding in front of the package of cigarettes. The physical shtick with Lucy and Ricky in handcuffs was first worked out by scripters Bob and Madelyn, and then tried by director Marc Daniels and his wife Emily, before it was brought to the Arnazes.

Bob Carroll Jr.
(WRITER)

I always worked these things out with Madelyn first to make sure that the stunts were really doable, and doable by a woman. I figured if Madelyn could do them, Lucille wouldn't have any problem with them. I tried to take my coat off and could get one sleeve off, but found I had a lot of coat hanging off my other arm.

Madelyn Pugh Martin Davis
(WRITER)

This is one of those things where we wouldn't have thought to have the Ricardos try and take their clothes off if we hadn't tried it ourselves. It wouldn't have occurred to us otherwise.

The original script had Ricky dancing with the television hostess instead of singing for her, thus revealing Lucy behind him. It was changed during rehearsals because the blocking didn't work out. There is also an extra scene in the original script where Lucy takes Ricky to the beauty parlor with her, but it is cut from the final rendition. If the playoff music in the last scene sounds familiar, it should, as it will be used for TV's popular *The Bob Cummings Show* (1955–59). The closing commercial, done by the Arnazes, features a relaxed Lucille, rested from the summer break and hiding an already billowing figure.

This installment is based in part on the *My Favorite Husband* radio episode "Liz and George Handcuffed."

I LOVE LUCY #40: "THE OPERETTA"

(CBS, OCTOBER 13, 1952), 30 MINUTES (B&W)

DIRECTED BY: Marc Daniels
GUEST CAST: Myra Marsh

Lucy has been juggling the budgets of both her household and the treasury of the Wednesday Afternoon Fine Arts League, and now there is *no* money in either coffer. To produce an operetta as a fundraiser, Lucy unwisely relies on using postdated checks.

HIGHLIGHTS & TRIVIA

This episode is a marvelous showcase for Vivian, who has begun to let her dark roots grow out from under her bleached hair. Her rendition of "Lily of the Valley" shows the talent that led her to become a musical comedy star on Broadway. Note that with a tightfitting costume and dark wig, Vivian looks young and attractive. While all of the other music is done live, Desi's singing of "Prince Lancelot" is prerecorded because it is impossible for him to sing well and do the physical blocking the song requires. The lyrics to the specially conceived operetta are written by Oppenheimer, Carroll, and Pugh, while the music is by Eliot Daniel. The ongoing theme of Lucy being unable to sing is further magnified in this entry. This is Marc Daniels' last episode as director, and by the way, his favorite.

I LOVE LUCY: "THE QUIZ SHOW"

(CBS, OCTOBER 20, 1952), 30 MINUTES, (B&W)

This is a rerun of episode #5. When producer Jess Oppenheimer planned out the new season, it became obvious that Lucille could not possibly film enough episodes in advance to cover the time when she would be unavailable for the cameras. It finally dawns on him that the shows are on film and are available for rebroadcast. He decides to use several of these to pad out the season, and thus, single-handedly, invents the sitcom rerun. Believe it or not, it had never been done before on American television. Sometimes, new footage is shot and used as a flashback; other times, Roy Rowan will simply introduce the show as a much-asked-for repeat of a favorite episode, which is the case here.

I LOVE LUCY #41: "VACATION FROM MARRIAGE"

(CBS, OCTOBER 27, 1952), 30 MINUTES (B&W)

Lucy and Ethel decide that their marriages are stale, and they need a week away from the boys. All learn to regret the decision, but having too much pride, they try to trick the other sex into giving in first.

HIGHLIGHTS & TRIVIA

Lucille, only three months pregnant, is already beginning to show her condition. This is the only peek we ever have of the Mertzes' bedroom. It should be noted that they seem to sleep in double beds, because this view will be contradicted in the future. The roof scene is extremely well acted by Lucille and Viv, who emit great warmth while acting cold. The men, however, seem to have no fear of falling off the slanted roof of an apartment building, as they walk along the edges with a spring in their steps.

This show is based in part on the *My Favorite Husband* radio episode "Vacation from Marriage."

I LOVE LUCY: "LUCY THINKS RICKY IS TRYING TO MURDER HER"

(CBS, NOVEMBER 3, 1952), 30 MINUTES (B&W)

This is a rerun of episode #4. New footage is shot with Lucy bringing home paperback mystery books, which leads into a flashback of what happened the last time she read a mystery novel.

I LOVE LUCY #42: "THE COURTROOM"

(CBS, NOVEMBER 10, 1952), 30 MINUTES (B&W)

GUEST CAST: Moroni Olsen, Harry Bartell, Robert B. Williams

The Mertzes celebrate a happy twenty-fifth wedding anniversary, first having dinner with tenant Miss Lewis and then being surprised by the Ricardos with their gift of a television set. Things turn unhappy, however, when Ricky's mistuning makes the TV set blow up. In retaliation, Fred kicks in the picture tube of the Ricardos' set. Both couples sue one another, and have their day in court.

HIGHLIGHTS & TRIVIA

Desi really shines in the scene where he is moving the television set on his back down the stairs one step at a time. Note that just the previous season, the Mertzes had celebrated their eighteenth anniversary.

This show is based in part on the *My Favorite Husband* radio episode "Television."

STARS IN THE EYE

(CBS, NOVEMBER 11, 1952), 60 MINUTES (B&W)

PRODUCED AND DIRECTED BY: Ralph Levy
SCRIPT SUPERVISION BY: Sam Perrin
WRITTEN BY: George Balzer, Al Schwartz, Si Rose, Hugh Wedlock, Howard Snyder
ADDITIONAL DIALOG BY: the writers of *Amos 'N' Andy, The George Burns and Gracie Allen Show, I Love Lucy, Life with Luigi, Meet Millie,* and *My Friend Irma*
MUSIC BY: Lud Gluskin
CAST: Gracie Allen, Eddie Anderson, Eve Arden, Desi Arnaz, Lucille Ball, Jack Benny, Mel Blanc, Los Angeles Mayor Fletcher Bowrin, George Burns, Alvin Childress, Bob Crosby, Cass Daley, William Frawley, Gale Gordon, Florence Halop, Marvin Kaplan, Cathy Lewis, Art Linkletter, Gizelle McKenzie, Tim Moore, J. Carrol Naish, Alan Reed, the Sportsman's Quartet, Bob Sweeney, Vivian Vance, Elena Verdugo, California Governor Earl Warren, Spencer Williams Jr., Marie Wilson

This impressive listing of creative talents is brought together to celebrate the dedication of CBS Television City in Hollywood, located adjacent to the famous Farmer's Market. Previous to this, all live television emanating from Los Angeles was aired from makeshift locations, usually in the network radio buildings about town. This hour is an exercise in self-glorification, utilizing almost all of the CBS talent located on the West Coast. Gale Gordon and Bob Sweeney portray real-life CBS executives Hubbell Robinson and Harry Ackerman, whose big TV special is being threatened by the ego of Jack Benny. The script has Benny meddling everywhere, ruining costumes, sketches, songs, and angering everyone in the cast.

Lucille is seven months pregnant at the time, and has already retired from performing to await the birth of Desi Jr. on January 19th. This presented

CBS with a huge problem—how to feature their biggest star on a *live* television show when she is indisposed. She will not even travel to the new studio, choosing instead to watch the dedication on television from her Chatsworth ranch in the San Fernando Valley. Bob Carroll Jr. and Madelyn Pugh come to the rescue with a unique concept. During the filming of three different *I Love Lucy* episodes in the fall of 1952, an additional scene is shot featuring Benny as an interfering nudge, trying to get the Arnazes to appear at the CBS studio dedication. Desi appears as himself live on this entry, accompanied by his supposed Cuban attorney Jose Geisler (an inside joke referring to well-known lawyer Jerry Geisler), to sue Benny for ruining the filmings of *I Love Lucy*. A projector is set up, and three scenes with Lucille are shown.

The first bit is filmed the night of "Pregnant Women Are Unpredictable" (episode #46). In a phony scene from the end of the show, the cast (including Vivian and Bill) are shown in the Tropicana, where Lucille supposedly forgets her lines. Jack, in disguise, plays the waiter, and ruins the next take. The second bit is shot two weeks later during "Lucy Hires an English Tutor" (episode #48). This scene occurs on the couch in the Ricardos' apartment, where Benny surreptitiously steals a kiss while hiding behind the furniture. The third sequence is lensed the following week, in a bathroom set that is never used again. Benny gets drenched when he hides in the shower and Lucy turns on the water.

Historically, this footage is an archival wonder! It is the only existing example of the cast, in costume and on the set, breaking character. Also, the home audience gets to see the Ricardos' new furniture (and Lucy's new waistline) before these plot elements are even introduced on *I Love Lucy*.

I LOVE LUCY #43: "REDECORATING"

(CBS, NOVEMBER 17, 1952), 30 MINUTES (B&W)

GUEST CAST: Hans Conried, Margie Liszt, Florence Halop

After visiting a home show, Lucy and Ethel are convinced that they are going to win five new rooms of furniture because of 100 entries they made in a drawing. When they refuse to leave their apartments because they expect the winning phone call, the boys scheme to fool them away by letting them think they have won the contest.

HIGHLIGHTS & TRIVIA

This episode was written because the set had begun to look drab after so many segments being filmed on it. Lucille wanted to spruce up the set. It may also have been done at this time to take attention away from Ball's rapidly expanding waistline. The scene with Lucy and Ethel repapering the bedroom is obviously influenced by the comedy team of Laurel and Hardy, and foreshadows the kind of things the two women will do on *The Lucy Show*. Irma Kusely takes over doing Lucille's hair until after the baby is born.

Irma Kusely

(HAIRSTYLIST)

Lucy didn't want anyone but me touching her hair during her pregnancy, because she knew her hair got a little funky when she was large with Lucie. Even though I had my own babies at home to take care of, I agreed to come in for these couple of months.

This is the only reference to the Ricardos having a telephone party line. The name of Dan Jenkins the junk man comes from the *TV Guide* writer of the same name. If Lucy won five rooms of furniture, why are only two delivered in the next episode?

I LOVE LUCY #44: "RICKY LOSES HIS VOICE"

(CBS, NOVEMBER 24, 1952), 30 MINUTES (B&W)

GUEST CAST: Arthur Q. Bryan, Gertrude Astor, Helen Williams, Barbara Pepper, Hazel Pierce

Lucy is thrilled when the new furniture arrives, but Ricky is miserable because he has a bad virus. The doctor orders Ricky not to get out of bed until opening night of the new club show. Because the Tropicana's latest new owner, Mr. Chambers, will be out of town until opening night, Lucy stages the show herself.

HIGHLIGHTS & TRIVIA

The new furniture makes the set look more chic, and the Ricardos far more prosperous. Part of the purpose for changing the bedroom furniture is to please the network censors by making absolutely certain that Ricky and Lucy do not appear to be sleeping in the same bed now that she is pregnant. The Tropicana set has been redressed as well, giving the entire show a shiny new look. The opening scene, with Ricky and pianist Marco Rizo rehearsing a novelty song, is cut from most syndicated rerun versions of the episode. Arthur Q. Bryan, who plays Mr. Chambers, provided the voice of Elmer Fudd in the Bugs Bunny cartoons for more than twenty years. Audio from this episode will be used in the one woman show *Lily Tomlin on Broadway* (1977).

I LOVE LUCY #45: "LUCY IS ENCIENTE"

(CBS, DECEMBER 8, 1952), 30 MINUTES (B&W)

GUEST CAST: William Hamel, Richard Reeves

Lucy feels run down and goes to the doctor, only to learn she is finally pregnant after eleven years of marriage. Having dreamed of the day she'd tell her husband this kind of news, she wants the moment to be perfect. Unfortunately, fate intervenes.

HIGHLIGHTS & TRIVIA

This episode begins the story arc that will conclude the following April. As silly as it may seem today, "respectable" people didn't discuss pregnancy in public in 1952. There is great fear on everyone's part that the TV public will not accept these shows because of the maternity theme. A local priest, rabbi, and minister are brought in as consultants and assure producers et al. that there is nothing objectionable about these installments.

Desi Arnaz Jr.

I Love Lucy *was actually a very conservative show. I think the reason why it is still so popular is that it followed certain old-fashioned values. The genius of the show was that they didn't resort to things that were unbelievable or lewd. There is something very heartwarming that everybody feels in my parents' kind of humor. People like it when you don't offend them, and most people's essences are not vulgar. Lucy and Ricky could get flirtatious, but never vulgar. Shock and the lowest common denominator are not necessarily humor. Just because someone laughs, doesn't mean something is funny. Dad wanted to deal with the basic human emotions.*

By the way, "dawncey" is the correct spelling for the word that Lucy says her grandmother made up for feeling blah. Speaking of words, in the original script for this episode, the word pregnant is used *everywhere.* It is only later that network objections are made, and the word is banished from all *I Love Lucy* episodes. In the scene where Lucy practices telling Ricky about the forthcoming baby, the stage directions indicate the regard the writers have for their star: "She puts her arms around an imaginary neck. This will be facing her away from the cameras toward the back of the set, which is the way this particular scene should be played, considering that Lucy has more talent in the back of her neck than most performers have in their whole bodies." The original scene where Lucy tells Ricky about the baby at the nightclub has Ricky shouting, "What?" and then almost fainting. Lucy catches him, gives him a glass of water, and this leads into the baby song. As we all know, that is *not* the way the scene is shot.

Jess Oppenheimer

(PRODUCER/WRITER)

Lucy and Desi got to this point in acting out the script and then this strange thing happened: Suddenly they remembered their own real emotions when they discovered that at last they were going to be parents, and both of them began crying. We had to yell at Desi to keep going and do the baby song. Bill Asher thought the scene was ruined and had it reshot. When we saw both versions, we knew we had to go with the emotional one.

The dinner dress Lucy wears in the last scene will later be given to her protégée, actress Carole Cook, who will wear it for years. With Lucille's extra weight, it is easier to notice that she has a problem that makeup now can't hide—a droopy eyelid on her left eye. When she is fatigued or overweight, the lid partially closes over her eye. This is a key reason why *Lucy* always has a surprised look on her face . . . to keep that eye wide open.

I LOVE LUCY #46: "PREGNANT WOMEN ARE UNPREDICTABLE"

(CBS, DECEMBER 15, 1952), 30 MINUTES (B&W)

GUEST CAST: Bennett Green

Pregnancy makes Lucy emotional and moody. She can't decide on the proper name for the child. She feels that Ricky is only paying attention to her because of the baby. When he does focus on her, she feels he is ignoring the coming baby.

HIGHLIGHTS & TRIVIA

This episode is not all that funny, but it is a decently written character study of a youngish couple having their first child. Bennett Green, who plays a waiter, was Desi's stand-in on this series. Notice that Lucy does not smoke in the pregnancy episodes.

I LOVE LUCY #47: "LUCY'S SHOW BIZ SWAN SONG"

(CBS, DECEMBER 22, 1952), 30 MINUTES (B&W)

GUEST CAST: Pepito (the Clown) Perez, Jerry Hausner

Ricky is staging a Gay Nineties revue at the Tropicana. Although she is large with child, Lucy wants to participate. She talks Ethel into doing a duet of "By the Light of the Silvery Moon," with Ethel in drag and Lucy wearing a hoop skirt to hide her condition. Then she has a horrendous audition singing "Sweet Adeline." Finally, Ricky concedes and allows Fred and Ethel to join his barbershop quartet, but Lucy secretly takes the place of the fourth singer at the club.

HIGHLIGHTS & TRIVIA

Although other episodes might have had single moments that are funnier, it is this author's belief that this is the best overall segment in the entire Lucy mythos. From the very first, there isn't a wasted frame. Every scene is full of entertainment. Lucy's eyes when she hears there might be an opening at Ricky's club open wider than seems humanly possible. Watch Lucille in the hoop skirt. She nonchalantly pulls on a string fastened through the skirt to make her pantaloons drop on cue. Desi's mangling of an Irish brogue for the reprise of "Adeline" is a comic gem often overlooked.

When a rough cut of this episode is made, it proves to be too short, something that rarely happens on *I Love Lucy*. Desi's good friend Pepito the Clown again comes to the rescue. Exactly one month later, during the filming of "Lucy Becomes a Sculptress" (episode #50), Pepito's scene will be filmed and then edited into this installment. To further pad out the half hour, the Santa Claus sketch from the previous year's Christmas episode is tacked on to the end. This sketch is not included in any syndicated rerun prints, not even the uncut versions. Alfred Lyons, chairman of the board of Philip Morris and Company, does the final commercial himself. In it, he practically blackmails the audience (whom he claims now number thirty-two million) with the notion that if more cigarettes are not purchased, the show (which is seen by more people than any other entertainment in show business history) might not be on the air much longer.

Vivian Vance

Lucille had her own special dressing room right near the stage because of her condition. I had to run to my dressing room to make several quick changes for this episode. At one point, I almost didn't make it in time. Lucille growled at me, "You're late!" I turned to her and said, "I'd tell you to go fuck yourself, but I see that Desi has already handled that!" We had another problem with Bill Frawley. He insisted that he do the repeats in the "Sweet Adeline" number, and somehow it became my job to pull him aside and set him straight. I told him that Lucille was the star, and it would be funnier if she did them. He got loud with me, so I told him to shut up and that we had to do this thing the way we rehearsed it. He finally calmed down, but growled at me, "You know what she's going to sound like, don't you? Like putting a shovel full of shit on baked Alaska." Which was exactly what she was supposed *to sound like, but his ego couldn't see it that way.*

I LOVE LUCY #48: "LUCY HIRES AN ENGLISH TUTOR"

(CBS, DECEMBER 29, 1952), 30 MINUTES (B&W)

GUEST CAST: Hans Conried

Fearful that she is not properly educated to raise a child, Lucy hires a tutor to teach the Ricardos and the Mertzes to speak properly.

HIGHLIGHTS & TRIVIA

As stated in the plot line, there actually was a restaurant in New York that sold papaya juice milkshakes, located on 91st Street and Columbus Avenue. These references to an expectant mother's cravings add reality and texture to the situation that audiences adore. Hans Conried, as the tutor, returns in a much different role than before. Notice that he changes the tune of "Tippy Tippy Toe" each time he performs it.

I LOVE LUCY #49: "RICKY HAS LABOR PAINS"

(CBS, JANUARY 5, 1953), 30 MINUTES (B&W)

GUEST CAST: Louis D. Merrill, Jerry Hausner, Hazel Pierce

With the constant attention given to Lucy and the incipient baby, Ricky feels neglected and develops sympathetic physical symptoms of his own. Lucy has a physician examine him. The doctor suggests making Ricky the center of attention, so he is given a "Daddy" shower, or as Fred calls it, a "stag party." A stag party?

HIGHLIGHTS & TRIVIA

As with several of the pregnancy episodes, this show is enjoyable not so much because it is funny, but because it has overall warmth and humanity. Lucille and Desi are so obviously happy with what is going on in their private lives that it spills over into their performances. The final scene, the second of the cravings themes, has Lucy eating a hot fudge sundae with sardines. Mashed potatoes and gravy are substituted as look-alikes for the ice cream and hot fudge, but sardines are actually used, which Lucille loathes. As soon as director Bill Asher yells cut, she runs off stage and throws up.

This episode is based in part on the *My Favorite Husband* radio installment "The Christmas Stag."

I LOVE LUCY #50: "LUCY BECOMES A SCULPTRESS"

(CBS, JANUARY 12, 1953), 30 MINUTES (B&W)

GUEST CAST: Shep Menken, Leon Belasco, Paul Harvey

Fearing she won't be a good cultural influence on her forthcoming child, Lucy decides to become a sculptress. Ricky frowns on the enterprise, because it will cost too much money and the baby is due in only three weeks. They make a deal that if an art critic likes her work, he will support her art ambitions.

HIGHLIGHTS & TRIVIA

This is the weakest of the baby installments, both in plotting and in humor. The only truly funny moments occur at the finale, with Lucy pretending to be a bust of herself.

This show is based in part on the *My Favorite Husband* radio episode "Liz Becomes a Sculptress."

I LOVE LUCY #51: "LUCY GOES TO THE HOSPITAL"

(CBS, JANUARY 19, 1953), 30 MINUTES (B&W)

GUEST CAST: Charles Lane, Adele Longmire, Peggy Rea, Bennett Green, William Hamel, Ralph Montgomery, Barbara Pepper, Ruth Perrott, Hazel Pierce, James John Ganzer

At last, the time has come! Lucy Ricardo goes to the hospital to have her baby, Little Ricky.

HIGHLIGHTS & TRIVIA

Every word and movement the actors make in the "this is it!" scene is written in the original script. It is carefully rehearsed to be performed in precision, so the filmed panic moments are even funnier. The scene where Ricky is singing in his voodoo costume is shot the following week, because there is not enough space to have the Tropicana club set up on the sound stage due to the hospital scenery. This is Desi Arnaz' favorite episode. The Dr. Harris mentioned in the script derives from Lucille's physician, Joseph Harris. A higher percentage of the television viewing audience (ninety-two percent) watched this episode than any other *Lucy* show.

The end of the program features the following announcement: "Yes, there's a new baby, a wonderful baby at the Ricardos'. And we at Philip Morris rejoice in the blessed event. We know that all our millions of friends join with us in extending congratulations and good wishes to the Ricardos. May their lives together be filled with as much joy and laughter and carefree happiness as they have brought all of us week after week. To Lucy, to Ricky, and to the new baby: love and kisses from Philip Morris and from all America." The advertiser's wishes are sweet, but Lucy and Ricky are fictional characters. Why doesn't Philip Morris extend these good words to Lucille and Desi, who actually have a baby, Desi Arnaz Jr., born the morning this episode airs? It had been decided right from the beginning that the Ricardos' baby was going to be a boy, although this detail was kept secret. That the actual Arnaz offspring *is* a boy fueled a geyser of publicity said to be worth more than $50 million in advertising, contracts, and merchandising. Unfortunately, the line between fiction and reality will become too blurred, resulting in emotional problems for the Arnazes, Desi Jr., and Keith Thibodeaux (the actor who will play Little Ricky starting in 1956).

I LOVE LUCY #52: "SALES RESISTANCE"

(CBS, JANUARY 26, 1953), 30 MINUTES (B&W)

GUEST CAST: Sheldon Leonard, Verna Felton

Ricky, Fred, and Ethel reminisce about the time before the baby came when Lucy had problems with Harry Martin, the sales representative from the Handy Dandy company. Each time he sells Lucy something, she returns it and then ends up buying something more expensive because she has absolutely no sales resistance.

HIGHLIGHTS & TRIVIA

This series once again has new opening credits, with Desi Arnaz coming out from behind a curtain in a heart-shaped spotlight to announce the introduction of a new product, Philip Morris king-size cigarettes. He then leads the audience into the episode to find out "why I love Lucy." These next few shows, filmed in between "Ricky Loses His Voice" (episode #44) and "Lucy Is Enciente" (episode #45), fill out the schedule between the baby shows and Lucille's return to action in "No Children Allowed" (episode #57). This flashback technique, using a short scene that mentions Lucy and the baby before leading into an unaired episode, will be used on all the fill-in episodes until April 1953.

In this case, Ricky is singing a song into a tape recorder Lucy bought at the hospital because she has no sales resistance. This leads into a reminiscence of the last time Lucy was an easy prey for a salesman's pressure. "There's a Brand New Baby at Our House" is a song written by Desi and Eddie Maxwell to celebrate the birth of Lucie Arnaz in 1951. The lyrics used here are changed to reflect a boy instead of a girl. The recording of this song, along with the *I Love Lucy* theme, is released on Columbia Records at this time. Sheldon Leonard—who plays Harry Martin here—will produce and direct (along with a generous helping hand both financially and creatively from Desi Arnaz that is almost never acknowledged) *Make Room for Daddy* in the fall of 1953. Note that Ethel receives a new washing machine in this episode; this fact will be totally overlooked in a few months in the episode "Never Do Business with Friends" (episode #66). Instead of closing credits, announcer Roy Rowan mentions Arnaz' baby song record is now available in stores.

I LOVE LUCY #53: "INFERIORITY COMPLEX"

(CBS, FEBRUARY 2, 1953), 30 MINUTES (B&W)

GUEST CAST: Gerald Mohr

Ricky, Ethel, and Fred discuss giving Lucy plenty of attention in the hospital because she feels depressed. They reminisce about the time Lucy had an inferiority complex. Inadvertently, Ricky and the Mertzes put down Lucy's joke telling, singing, and card playing. Lucy gets so bad that Ricky seeks the help of yet another psychiatrist, whose unorthodox methods anger Ricky.

HIGHLIGHTS & TRIVIA

While the baby is not mentioned in the body of this entry, Lucy is obviously large with child and wearing maternity clothes. The scene with the psychiatrist outrageously flirting with a pregnant woman is one of the rare times *I Love Lucy* delves into humor that could be considered in bad taste. The character of the psychiatrist is named Henry Molin; the name comes from that of assistant film editor Henry "Bud" Molin, although the credit at the end of the show refers to the character as Dr. Stewart.

This show is based in part on the *My Favorite Husband* radio episode "Liz's Inferiority Complex."

I LOVE LUCY: "THE DIET"

(CBS, FEBRUARY 9, 1953), 30 MINUTES (B&W)

This is a rerun of episode #3, with new footage shot of Ricky and the Mertzes discussing Lucy's being at a gym to regain her figure.

I LOVE LUCY #54: "THE CLUB ELECTION"

(CBS, FEBRUARY 16, 1953), 30 MINUTES (B&W)

GUEST CAST: Jerry Hausner, Doris Singleton, Ida Moore, Margie Liszt, Hazel Pierce, Lurene Tuttle, Peggy Rea

While Lucy is out shopping for the baby, Ethel drops by to speak with her about the club elections. She and Ricky reminisce about the last time the group held elections, when Lucy and Ethel competed to win the presidency.

HIGHLIGHTS & TRIVIA

There is yet another fresh opening introduction for the show, with the cartoon characters now using animated spotlights to bring attention to the sponsor's product. Lucy wears tight fitting clothes in this episode, even though pregnant Lucille is already showing. Doris Singleton makes the first of many appearances as Caroline (originally called Lillian) Appleby, although Marion Strong (another club member) is not yet played by Shirley Mitchell. By the way, if there is no clubhouse, where are Lucy and Ethel putting up their campaign posters? Desi previously sang "The Cuban Cabby" on the show's pilot in 1951.

This show is based in part on the *My Favorite Husband* radio episode "Women's Club Election."

Doris Singleton

(ACTOR)

I started out as Lillian Appleby on the show, but then Lucy decided she didn't like that. She wanted me to use my own *name, but I didn't like* that. *So she said, "OK, you're Caroline Appleby and your husband's name is Charley." And my husband's name really is Charley. She said, "At least that I can remember!"*

I LOVE LUCY: "MEN ARE MESSY"

(CBS, FEBRUARY 23, 1953), 30 MINUTES (B&W)

This is a rerun of episode #8. Fresh footage is shot with Ricky bragging about a new magazine that has his picture in it. This leads to a discussion of his vanity, and a flashback to the last time he had his photograph in a magazine.

I LOVE LUCY: "THE AUDITION"

(CBS, MARCH 2, 1953), 30 MINUTES (B&W)

This is a rerun of episode #6. New footage is shot with Ricky, Fred, and Ethel bringing home musical instruments for the baby to play with and leads to a flashback of Lucy playing the cello.

I LOVE LUCY #55: "THE BLACK EYE"

(CBS, MARCH 9, 1953), 30 MINUTES (B&W)

GUEST CAST: Bennett Green

When Fred is bumped in the nose by Ethel opening a door, he fears it will lead to a black eye. This prompts the Mertzes and Ricky to recall the time when Lucy accidentally got a black eye from a thrown book, but no one believed her story.

HIGHLIGHTS & TRIVIA

There is yet another new *I Love Lucy* opening credit, this time with the cartoon characters drawing the product on an easel. Unfortunately, this is one of the more inferior scripts in the series.

It is based in part on the *My Favorite Husband* radio episode "The Misunderstanding of the Black Eye."

I LOVE LUCY: "THE GIRLS WANT TO GO TO A NIGHTCLUB"

(CBS, MARCH 16, 1953), 30 MINUTES (B&W)

This is a rerun of the first aired episode. New footage is shot of Ricky and Fred watching a boxing match on television. They end up missing a knockout and wish they could see the boxing match in person, which leads to a flashback of what happened the last time they wanted to go to the fights.

I LOVE LUCY: "THE SEANCE"

(CBS, MARCH 23, 1953), 30 MINUTES (B&W)

This is a rerun of episode #7. New footage is shot of Ricky and the Mertzes discussing Lucy purchasing a book on numerology, because she keeps changing the baby's name. This leads to a flashback of the last time Lucy became involved with numerology.

I LOVE LUCY #56: "LUCY CHANGES HER MIND"

(CBS, MARCH 30, 1953), 30 MINUTES (B&W)

GUEST CAST: Frank Nelson, Phil Arnold, John L. Hart, Sally Corner

Ethel notices, once again, that all the furniture has been rearranged in the Ricardos' living room. She wonders why Lucy changes her mind so often, and this leads to a reminiscence of when Ricky got furious at Lucy for not being able to make up her mind.

HIGHLIGHTS & TRIVIA

This show is based in part on the *My Favorite Husband* radio episode "Liz Changes Her Mind." The entire restaurant scene is taken from it verbatim, including Frank Nelson playing the same role he did on the parallel radio installment.

Bob Carroll Jr.

(WRITER)

The restaurant scene actually happened to us. Jess, Madelyn, and I were out to lunch one day. Madelyn ordered a ham sandwich, and then I ordered eggs. Madelyn thought that sounded good, so she changed her order to eggs as well. Then Jess ordered a steak, and Madelyn changed her mind again. We all looked at one another and realized we just acted out our next radio plot for My Favorite Husband.

I LOVE LUCY: "LUCY IS JEALOUS OF A GIRL DANCER"

(CBS, APRIL 6, 1953), 30 MINUTES (B&W)

This is a rerun of episode #10. New footage is shot with the Mertzes and Ricky reading the newspaper while Lucy is at the gym working to get back her figure. There is a blind item in the paper about a performer having an affair with a girl dancer, which leads to the flashback.

I LOVE LUCY: "LUCY'S FAKE ILLNESS"

(CBS, APRIL 13, 1953), 30 MINUTES (B&W)

This is a rerun of episode #16. New footage has Ethel asking Fred to clean out the building's furnace. He fakes an illness to avoid the job, which leads them to recall the last time Lucy pretended to be sick.

I LOVE LUCY #57: "NO CHILDREN ALLOWED"

(CBS, APRIL 20, 1953), 30 MINUTES (B&W)

GUEST CAST: Elizabeth Patterson, Richard and Ronald Simmons (hereafter referred to as the Simmons Twins), June Whitney, Charlotte Lawrence, Vivi Janiss, Peggy Rea, Margie Liszt, Kay Wiley, Jerry Hausner

Little Ricky's constant crying has elderly neighbor Mrs. Trumbull unnerved. All of the tenants in the Mertzes' building have signed a lease stating no children allowed, and she wants the baby quieted or the Ricardos evicted.

HIGHLIGHTS & TRIVIA

This is Lucille's first time before the Desilu cameras since she went into seclusion to have Desi Jr., and the first new full episode filmed in almost four months. Ball flubs several of her lines, calling for rare retakes of scenes. Lucille blames Desi for the gaffe, Arnaz blames her and in the ensuing fracas, she hits him hard in his back in protest. None of this is done in real anger, as Lucille is letting off steam from nervousness. Although Jerry Hausner often provides the sounds of the baby crying offstage (a trick he learned from Pepito), the oncamera crying of the baby in one scene is done on cue by the actual infant. With Bert French back as hairstylist, a new look is tried for Lucy Ricardo. It is totally abandoned the following week.

Elizabeth Patterson joins the cast as Mrs. Trumbull, Little Ricky's constant babysitter. Her character adds delightful old world charm, as well as a handy place to get Little Ricky out of the way. The baby has been a publicity boon to the show, but in short order it becomes apparent that the infant character is as much a curse as a blessing. Without a place to logically get him out of the storyline, he would have hampered the action in dozens of shows. Notice the headboard of the crib has copies of the cartoon characters that introduce each episode. Also, the piano has been moved back to its original position on the upstage wall. In the original script, Mrs. Trumbull's name is spelled Trimbull, and remains so in subsequent scripts for a few weeks. That is the way Vivian pronounces it in the show. It is also mentioned that she lives upstairs, which means the Mertzes' apartment building is at least five stories tall. The dress Lucille wears in the bridge scene will be copied in the 1980s by the Hamilton Collection to be worn on their porcelain doll of Lucy Ricardo.

I LOVE LUCY #58: "LUCY HIRES A MAID"

(CBS, APRIL 27, 1953), 30 MINUTES (B&W)

GUEST CAST: Verna Felton, Jerry Hausner

Lucy is absolutely exhausted, staying up day and night with the new baby. When she falls asleep in the middle of an evening with the Mertzes, Ricky hires a maid. Unfortunately, the one they employ is such a steamroller that she walks all over Lucy.

HIGHLIGHTS & TRIVIA

Even heavy makeup cannot disguise the fact that having a baby has taken its toll on Lucille. Although she has lost all of her pregnancy weight, her face is lined and her eyes are baggy. To capture both Arnazes in one shot, the middle night table in the bedroom set is removed, and the beds pushed together. Verna Felton is wonderful as the well-meaning but overbearing maid.

I LOVE LUCY #59: "THE INDIAN SHOW"

(CBS, MAY 4, 1953), 30 MINUTES (B&W)

GUEST CAST: The Simmons Twins, Jerry Hausner, Carol Richards, Richard Reeves, Frank Gerstle

When Ricky stages a club show centering on Native Americans, Lucy wants to join the festivities. Although Ricky hires Fred and Ethel to be in the production, he refuses to use Lucy. Insistent upon being in the entertainment, Lucy bribes the show's girl singer to let her take her place.

HIGHLIGHTS & TRIVIA

This show could never be made today, with its insensitive attitude toward Native Americans. Notice when Ethel scares Lucy, they dislodge the sofa cushions, yet in the next moment, they are sitting on the couch with cushions back in place. The musical number "Pass That Peacepipe" is one of the worst executed in the entire series; it is under-rehearsed, and both Frawley and Vance are forced to sing in Desi's key, which suits neither of the sidekicks. Conversely, "The Waters of the Minnetonka" is beautiful in its original presentation, and a laugh riot when Lucille repeats it. In the original script, instead of the song used, Ricky's duet with Juanita (the girl singer) was supposed to be "The Indian Love Call."

I LOVE LUCY #60: "LUCY'S LAST BIRTHDAY"

(CBS, MAY 11, 1953), 30 MINUTES (B&W)

GUEST CAST: Jerry Hausner, Elizabeth Patterson, William Hamel, Ransom Sherman, Byron Foulger, Barbara Pepper, the Simmons Twins

Lucy thinks that Ricky and the Mertzes have forgotten her birthday, while in actuality they have planned a lovely surprise party for her at the Tropicana. Dejected, she leaves the apartment and joins up with "The Friends of the Friendless" in Central Park. To get even with Ricky, she brings her new pals to the club.

HIGHLIGHTS & TRIVIA

Vivian, with a new, cute short haircut and loss of weight, actually looks younger than Lucille in this episode. When, at the club, Ricky introduces Pugh and Carroll as two of the greatest contortionists in America, the line gets a laugh. The savvy audience knows he is referring to writers Madelyn Pugh and Bob Carroll Jr. This is the only time the lyrics to the theme song, written by Harold Adamson, will be heard on the series.

I LOVE LUCY #61: "THE RICARDOS CHANGE APARTMENTS"

(CBS, MAY 18, 1953), 30 MINUTES (B&W)

GUEST CAST: Norma Varden, the Simmons Twins

Lucy decides their one bedroom apartment just isn't large enough now that they have a baby. When Ethel tells her that a neighbor's daughter has just married and they now have an empty bedroom, Lucy schemes to get them to trade apartments with the Ricardos. That way, Lucy gets her extra bedroom and she can stay in the Mertzes' apartment building.

HIGHLIGHTS & TRIVIA

The original script had an extra scene with Lucy, Fred, and Ethel having great difficulty moving the piano from apartment to apartment. Art director Ralph Berger must have been asleep at the switch. It is obvious that the new living room set is even smaller than the old one, and the furniture does not fit well. Once again Ricky's spanking of Lucy is disturbing, even in the context of humor. Starting with this episode, the ending commercials with the Arnazes are filmed in the costumes and sets of the following week's installment.

I LOVE LUCY #62: "LUCY IS A MATCHMAKER"

(CBS, MAY 25, 1953), 30 MINUTES (B&W)

GUEST CAST: Hal March, Doris Singleton, Peggy Rea, William Hamel, Phil Arnold, the Simmons Twins

At their afternoon of bridge, the girls decide they must marry off Sylvia Collins, who has been flirting with all of their husbands. When Eddie Grant, the nephew of an old pal of Fred's comes to town, the girls see their solution. The fly in the ointment is Ricky, who forbids Lucy to get involved. Naturally, she does anyway, and now Eddie thinks Lucy wants him for herself.

HIGHLIGHTS & TRIVIA

For the staid 1950s, there certainly are a lot of *I Love Lucy* episodes of suspected marital infidelity. In this episode, Little Ricky's room, which is peculiarly located off Lucy and Ricky's bedroom, is seen for the first time. However, Lucy and Ricky's new bedroom is not shown in this installment, as the set is being used as Eddie's hotel room.

This airing is based in part on the *My Favorite Husband* radio episode "Trying to Marry Off Peggy Martin."

I LOVE LUCY #63: "LUCY WANTS NEW FURNITURE"

(CBS, JUNE 1, 1953), 30 MINUTES (B&W)

GUEST CAST: the Simmons Twins

Lucy purchases new furniture on sale without Ricky's permission. Now she must buy it back from Ricky by economizing on luxuries, such as the beauty parlor and new clothes.

HIGHLIGHTS & TRIVIA

This is an excellent episode, springing from many of the themes the writers have established thus far. The dialog is crisp and clever; the exchange between Lucy and Ricky in the dinner sequence is particularly special. The old couch and coffee table were only, at the most, a year old per the story line. Is Lucy really that fickle? The answer is no in this case, as art director Ralph Berger is the one who is responsible. The old furniture doesn't fit well in the new living room set, as it interferes with smooth movement on the crowded set. This new arrangement is tried, but found to be awkward. Before long, the Ricardos will have even more new furniture. In fact, Lucy will have more new couches in eighteen months than most people have in a lifetime. Notice that when Lucy runs through the Mertzes' apartment, it is not their normal set but just a corner mock-up.

I LOVE LUCY #64: "THE CAMPING TRIP"

(CBS, JUNE 8, 1953), 30 MINUTES (B&W)

GUEST CAST: Doris Singleton, June Whitney

At yet another catty bridge session, the girls discuss how sooner or later in a marriage the couple becomes bored with one another. Not so, claims Lucy, who embarks on such clinging behavior with Ricky that it makes him uncomfortable. When Lucy insists on going along with Ricky and Fred on their upcoming summer camping trip, Ricky decides to teach her a lesson. Lucy learns about his scheme and double-crosses him with a plan of her own.

HIGHLIGHTS & TRIVIA

It is established in this episode that Ethel can drive, which will be contradicted on the series two years later. With Ricky, Ethel, and Lucy gone, the baby is left in Fred's care, which seems an unlikely solution.

Doris Singleton

(ACTOR)

Nobody ever played subtly on this series. We were big—we were character people. Lucy would say, "You are playing to the people at the top of the bleachers." You had *to project; you couldn't be cute.*

I LOVE LUCY #65: "RICKY AND FRED ARE TV FANS"

(CBS, JUNE 22, 1953), 30 MINUTES (B&W)

GUEST CAST: Larry Dobkin, Allen Jenkins, Frank Nelson, Roy Rowan

Lucy and Ethel are tired of their men ignoring them every week when the fights are on TV. In retaliation, they cut the antenna connection to the Ricardos' apartment. As a result, they are arrested and taken to the local police precinct.

HIGHLIGHTS & TRIVIA

The opening scene for this entry was reshot the following week during the filming of "Never Do Business with Friends." Lucy's phone number is given as Murray Hill 5-9975. This will change from time to time, as the scripters use phone numbers that New York Bell Telephone advises are not in service. Notice that the roof set is entirely different from the way it was in "Vacation from Marriage" (episode #41). In real life, Desi and Bill are inveterate boxing fans; Bill goes to the fights every week in Hollywood, and Desi watches them Wednesday nights on television.

I LOVE LUCY #66: "NEVER DO BUSINESS WITH FRIENDS"

(CBS, JUNE 29, 1953), 30 MINUTES (B&W)

GUEST CAST: Elizabeth Patterson, Herb Vigran

Lucy talks Ricky into buying her a new washer and dryer, so Fred wants to buy Lucy's old one for Ethel. Ricky is against it, fearful that it will harm their friendship. He is talked into it against his better judgment, and all is well *until* the machine breaks down.

HIGHLIGHTS & TRIVIA

Ethel just got a new washing machine in "Sales Resistance" (episode #52). She must be very hard on equipment! This is the only time that the Mertzes' kitchen is shown, and it proves to be huge compared to the Ricardos'. We learn that Ethel is from Albuquerque, New Mexico (Vivian was born in Cherryvale, Kansas, but lived in Albuquerque as a young woman), that the two couples now live right next door to one another, and that Mrs. Trumbull's first name is Mathilda. Note that the back porch setup is much different from the one shown in "Pioneer Women" (episode #25). Notice, too, that Lucille does not wear her false eyelashes in the Mertzes' kitchen scene, because she will be getting wet laundry in her face. Much of this sequence was shot after the studio audience left in one-camera pickups to allow closeups of laundry landing in exact spots on the cast regulars.

This TV season has been exceptionally long, filmed over an entire calendar year. Remember, the season started with the Ricardos in the old apartment, childless, two sets of furniture ago. The cast is very tired, and looks it. Vivian and Bill will take a much deserved rest (except for Vivian's appearance with Mel Ferrer in a summer stock version of the musical *Pal Joey* at the La Jolla Playhouse), but the Arnazes plunge right into making the MGM theatrical feature *The Long, Long Trailer* (1954)

Chapter Five

1953–54 Season

I LOVE LUCY: THE THIRD SEASON

TECHNICAL REGULARS: Executive produced by Desi Arnaz; produced by Jess Oppenheimer; directed by William Asher; written by Jess Oppenheimer, Madelyn Pugh, Bob Carroll Jr.; makeup by Hal King; hairstyling by Bert French; music by Wilbur Hatch
CAST REGULARS: Lucille Ball (Lucy Ricardo); Desi Arnaz (Ricky Ricardo); Vivian Vance (Ethel Mertz); William Frawley (Fred Mertz); Roy Rowan (Announcer)

I LOVE LUCY #67: "RICKY'S LIFE STORY"

(CBS, OCTOBER 5, 1953), 30 MINUTES (B&W)
GUEST CAST: Louis A. Nicoletti, Michael and Joseph Mayer (hereafter referred to as the Mayer Twins)

When Ricky has a photo spread in *Life* magazine, Lucy is furious that she has been cut out. Lucy pesters Ricky to let her join his club act so she won't be overlooked in the future. Fred advises Ricky to show her just how much hard work show business really is. As usual, Lucy learns about his plan and double-crosses him.

HIGHLIGHTS & TRIVIA

This episode was actually shot after "The Camping Trip" (episode #64), but was held back for the new season. The series has yet a new cartoon opening credits, with the figures carrying a giant cigarette. Lucy's athletic dancing in the episode proves how good Lucille actually is at Terpsichore when she puts her mind to it. This installment only received tepid reviews as a season opener (because it was compared with the classic second season opener "Job Switching"), which prompts Jess Oppenheimer to spruce up TV's number one show. The middle commercial is shot right in the sound stage bleachers (where the audience sat during filming), and is the only film available to show what an *I Love Lucy* audience actually looked like. Notice that Little Ricky is now a toddler, played alternately by Michael and Joseph Mayer. In the finale, Lucy wears the same flying belt (for her moments of suspension above the set) that she had used in the 1950 film *The Fuller Brush Girl.*

I LOVE LUCY #68: "THE GIRLS GO INTO BUSINESS"

(CBS, OCTOBER 12, 1953), 30 MINUTES (B&W)
GUEST CAST: Mabel Paige, Emory Parnell, Barbara Pepper, Kay Wiley

When Lucy learns that Mrs. Hansen is selling her dress shop, she cannot pass up the opportunity. She buys the business without Ricky's consent, but it soon is a bust. When Lucy has a chance to sell the shop and make a profit, she hatches a scheme.

HIGHLIGHTS & TRIVIA

This is the first episode filmed for the 1953–54 season, done after the Arnazes completed their filming of *The Long, Long Trailer* at MGM. Back in the 1930s, Lucille Ball had registered as a Communist to please her kookie grandfather, Fred Hunt. She never thought twice about it, until the House UnAmerican Activities Committee witch hunts of the late 1940s and early 1950s caught up with her. She was called to testify in private, and was totally vindicated. Nevertheless, powerful newspaper columnist Walter Winchell leaked the story to the public the week this TV episode was filmed. Desi, Jess Oppenheimer, CBS honcho Bill Paley, and Philip Morris head Alfred Lyons all went into overdrive with damage control. However, the final accounting that resolved the distressing fracas will not be printed until the day *after* the filming. At the shoot for episode #68, Desi tells their account of the facts to the studio audience, and then introduces Lucille.

Desi Arnaz

And now, I want you to meet my favorite wife—my favorite redhead—in fact, that's the only thing red about her and even that's *not legitimate—Lucille Ball.*

Dann Cahn

(FILM EDITOR)

When Desi introduced Lucy that night, the crowd went wild. I've never seen anything like that. Everyone was all choked up, but as soon as we all caught our breaths, we went right into the filming.

Lucille pushes too hard in the comedy, but it is understandable considering the stress under which she is performing. While Desi looks tanned and rested, Lucille's face shows the burden of her off-camera problem. It is not one of the better shows. In the middle commercial, the word "Shakespere" is a misspelling of the Bard's name. Notice that Lucille's hair will be much darker in the next several episodes, as a reaction to her being called a "Red." Lucille Ball is one of the few major stars tainted by the House UnAmerican Activities Committee investigations to walk away fully vindicated. Notice that new set decorator Ted Offenbecker has already eliminated the sectional part of the sofa from the living room set.

I LOVE LUCY #69: "LUCY AND ETHEL BUY THE SAME DRESS"

(CBS, OCTOBER 19, 1953), 30 MINUTES (B&W)

GUEST CAST: Shirley Mitchell, Doris Singleton, Ruth Perrott, Hazel Pierce, the Mayer Twins

The Wednesday Afternoon Fine Arts League has a chance to be showcased on a half-hour program special on Charley Appleby's local TV station. Lucy and Ethel buy new gowns for the occasion, but each has chosen the same dress. After agreeing that each will return the garment and buy another outfit, both women decide to wear "the" dress anyway.

HIGHLIGHTS & TRIVIA

By this point, the series has developed a fluidity and a feeling unmatched by any other TV sitcom of the time. Wilbur Hatch's music, Elois Jenssen's costumes, and Ted Offenbecker's set decoration provide the show with a slick uniqueness. There is a flavor about the show that is distinctly its own; and that includes the timing within the episode.

Dann Cahn

(FILM EDITOR)

The chemistry between those four people on stage was palpable. The audience reaction was right in tune with the performances. Desi always insisted that the timing not be tampered with in the editing. Sometimes we had to, because things would go so long we had to cut back the audience reactions. But we tried not to do that as much as possible.

Doris Singleton

(ACTOR)

Early on, Desi was trying to learn everything—lighting, camera angles, everything. He really wanted to know how to control the entire set. We had no cue cards, so we would write little notes on the palms of our hands to cue ourselves. If your palms got sweaty, you lost your cues!

Lucille Ball had sung the song "Friendship" in the MGM musical *DuBarry Was a Lady* (1943) and repeats it in this episode. Shirley Mitchell makes her first of three appearances as Lucy's fellow club member Marion Strong. Mitchell had been on numerous radio shows with Lucille.

Shirley Mitchell

(ACTOR)

On this series, you damn well better know how to wait for laughs. We lost more than a few that way. Lucy had this innate ability on the first day of rehearsal to sense that someone wasn't going to wait for their laughs. They'd suddenly disappear, never to be heard from again.

The dresses Ball and Vance wear are dreadful, purposely designed to be nothing more than long slips with tulle decorations geared to be ripped off. Beginning with this installment, Vivian's hair

is subtly lightened back to a dark blonde. When Fred refers to Ethel by her full name (Ethel Louise Mertz) with disdain, the middle name Louise is an inside joke referring to Frawley's despised ex-wife. Ethel's middle name will be twice more changed.
This installment is based in part on the *My Favorite Husband* radio episode "Liz Appears on Television."

I LOVE LUCY #70: "EQUAL RIGHTS"

(CBS, OCTOBER 26, 1953), 30 MINUTES (B&W)
GUEST CAST: Larry Dobkin, Fred Aldrich, Louis Nicoletti, Richard Reeves

A simple conversation leads to a heated discussion about women's rights. To make their point, when the two couples go out to dinner, the boys refuse to pay for the girls. Lucy and Ethel wash dishes to pay their bill, but still have the last laugh on Ricky and Fred.

HIGHLIGHTS & TRIVIA

If this installment was reshot today, the script would be just as effective; that's how timeless it is. More and more, this series is about the relationships of four people and not just an excuse to showcase physical comedy. Elois Jenssen, who joined the crew in this season, designs costumes that provide Lucy Ricardo with a much more sophisticated look, and Vivian's Ethel is given a lot more latitude to look attractive. Note the scene in the restaurant kitchen where Lucy blows up a paper bag. Lucille spent hours trying different types of bags, then spent more time rehearsing how to pop them to make exactly the right noise. This attention to small details makes every time she touches a prop a joy to behold. Also note Vivian's kiss to Bill. She personally dislikes her cantankerous coplayer so much she never even touches him with her lips.

This show is based in part on the *My Favorite Husband* radio episode "Women's Rights, Part One."

Dann Cahn
(FILM EDITOR)

Around this time, a piece of film was made that would be gold today. They wanted a backstage look at how the show was done. Billy Asher was too busy putting on the show every week to be involved, so Lucille's friend Eddie Sedgwick directed it. It shows everybody backstage, and what they did and how. We previewed the picture in Bakersfield, and then it disappeared.

I LOVE LUCY #71: "BABY PICTURES"

(CBS, NOVEMBER 2, 1953), 30 MINUTES (B&W)
GUEST CAST: Doris Singleton, Hy Averback, the Mayer Twins

Although the Ricardos have sworn not to bore others with pictures of Little Ricky, they can't help themselves when the Applebys brag about their own little Stevie. The next day, Lucy arrives at Caroline's unannounced and the two women escalate their feud, which jeopardizes Ricky's chances to host a variety show on Charley Appleby's TV station.

HIGHLIGHTS & TRIVIA

This episode introduces the character of Stevie Appleby, who is the same age as Little Ricky (approximately ten months old). Although he will be mentioned frequently, he only will be seen once more (in episode #166, "Lucy and Superman"). The interplay between Lucille and Doris (as Caroline Appleby) is hysterical.

Doris Singleton
(ACTOR)

The mother of the child playing Stevie told me that he had just gotten over the measles and was fussy. She advised me to hold him and play with him if he got antsy. I told Lucy this, and she said, "The hell you will. If he starts to act up, you drop him down out of camera frame and let go of him and they'll take him away!" The child reacted to one of my lines almost on cue, and we never had a moment of trouble with him.

Notice that Desi is totally out of breath from singing and dancing when he introduces Lucy and Stevie on the TV show within the episode.

I LOVE LUCY #72: "LUCY TELLS THE TRUTH"

(CBS, NOVEMBER 9, 1953), 30 MINUTES (B&W)
GUEST CAST: Doris Singleton, Shirley Mitchell, Charles Lane, Mario Siletti, Dorothy Lloyd, the Mayer Twins

When Lucy is caught concocting another lie, Ricky and the Mertzes bet her she can't tell the absolute truth for twenty-four hours. Things get sticky at bridge the next day, as Lucy not only tells the truth but admits to the others exactly what she thinks of them. To win the bet, Ricky takes Lucy to an open audition, knowing she will have to lie about her actual show business experience.

HIGHLIGHTS & TRIVIA

In the original script, the character of Marion Strong was called Harriet, and her cackling laugh wasn't put in until Shirley Mitchell was cast in the role. That laugh, and this episode, are very fondly remembered by *Lucy* aficionados.

Doris Singleton

(ACTOR)

Both Shirley and I had worked with Lucille on radio, so she knew our work. There was no question as to who was in charge on stage. We were there to learn our lines and work, work, work. There were no fun and games on the set. You had to perform, and perform well.

Shirley Mitchell

(ACTOR)

I loved playing this part, especially since people seem to remember it so well. We had no idea that these shows would still be being talked about, never mind being seen, after all these years. Lucy was a taskmaster; she was on top of everything. We rehearsed these things over and over until Lucille was comfortable that everything was just right. She was a perfectionist. Once Lucy worked with you, and felt she could relax with you, she treated you like a member of her family and was very protective of you both personally and professionally. She was very faithful to certain actors. She knew what she wanted, and if you could deliver it, she was extremely loyal. This is my favorite episode; I enjoyed doing this more than anything else in my entire career. I still sit and watch this show and die laughing.

The original ending of the story was totally different: Ricky has lied to the IRS, and Lucy gets even by telling the truth. Desi Arnaz had the plot line dropped, as he didn't want anyone to think that Ricky would cheat the U.S. government. The writers rewrote the ending at his request. The purpose behind Ethel and Ricky explaining things to Fred was that they were afraid the audience wouldn't follow the complicated plot. This is the episode where Dorothy Lloyd (as a woman auditioning) sings "Il Bacio" like a chicken. Many syndicated rerun prints leave this part out of the episode. Lucy claims to be thirty-three years old during the bridge game (Lucille Ball is actually forty-two at the time). Note that the Ricardos' apartment number is changed from 3B to 3D to accommodate the plot line joke at the audition.

This entry is based in part on the *My Favorite Husband* radio episode "Absolute Truth."

DINNER WITH THE PRESIDENT

(CBS, NOVEMBER 16, 1953), 60 MINUTES (B&W)

PRODUCED AND DIRECTED BY:
Richard Rodgers, Oscar Hammerstein II
I LOVE LUCY SKETCH WRITTEN BY:
Jess Oppenheimer, Madelyn Pugh, Bob Carroll Jr.
CAST: Walter Cronkite, Ben Grauer (hosts), Desi Arnaz, Lucille Ball, President Dwight D. Eisenhower, Eddie Fisher, William Frawley, Jane Froman, Oscar Hammerstein II, Rex Harrison, Helen Hayes, Ethel Merman, Lilli Palmer, Thelma Ritter, Jackie Robinson, Richard Rodgers, Vivian Vance, William Warfield
INTRODUCED IN THE AUDIENCE:
Bernard Baruch, David Goldenson, J. Edgar Hoover, Hubert Humphrey, William S. Paley, General David Sarnoff, Members of the U.S. Supreme Court

Douglas Edwards and the News and *The Perry Como Show* are preempted to bring the fortieth anniversary of the Anti-Defamation League of B'nai B'rith's awarding of the 1953 Democratic Legacy Medal to President Eisenhower. Broadcast live from the Hotel Mayflower in Washington, D.C., the star-studded evening is rife with iron curtain rhetoric and national backslapping at the supposed enlightened times of 1953.

The highlights of the hour are many. However, the two showstoppers involve Ethel Merman and the *I Love Lucy* cast. Merman wows the Washington brass with a medley of her hit songs. Then stage and screen star Rex Harrison introduces the Fab Four: "It seems there was an Irishman, a Cuban, a Welsh/Irish/English lass, and a redhead from Jamestown. And these people got together and decided to make people laugh. These four Americans, blending the gifts of many stocks, working together created the most successful TV show since, well, ancient Greece. That's why, we love Lucy!"

Vivian and Bill enter, singing the last four bars of "Carolina in the Morning," followed by Desi. All are wearing actual *Lucy* costumes to add to the illusion. When Lucille appears, the applause is loud and sustained. After dialog to set the scene, the cast does the entire "We'll Build a Bungalow" bit from "The Benefit" (episode #13). Also included is the complete Vance and Frawley version of "Carolina," delivered with a lot more enthusiasm on Bill's part than as originally performed in "Ricky Loses His Voice" (episode #44). Frawley belts out the number. He even laughs at Vivian's performance, causing his voice to crack.

Desi's and Lucille's song is also charged with energy. It is interesting to see these professionals performing the same comedy material in front of different audiences, for although the laughs come at the same places, the timing is different. Both Arnazes mug relentlessly, wringing every possible laugh out of the starchy attendees.

Vivian Vance

I had been Ethel Merman's understudy in two Broadway shows and rarely got to go on in her place. The night we did this show, I stood next to Merman backstage before she went on. I whispered in her ear, "This is the first time I've stood with you in the wings and didn't wish you'd drop dead!"

I LOVE LUCY #73: "THE FRENCH REVUE"

(CBS, NOVEMBER 16, 1953), 30 MINUTES (B&W)
GUEST CAST: Alberto Morin, Richard Reeves, Fred Aldrich, Louis Nicoletti, the Mayer Twins

After being embarrassed in a French restaurant by the couples' inability to order in French, Lucy arranges for the waiter to give her and Ethel French lessons in exchange for a singing audition with Ricky. Although displeased with Lucy's deception, Ricky agrees to hire the waiter and do a French revue at the club. However, he bans Lucy from entering the club (let alone getting into the act). Lucy bets him she will do so anyway and the war is on.

HIGHLIGHTS & TRIVIA

It is funny that when the cast imitates Maurice Chevalier, the only one who is a poor mimic is the French waiter Ricky hires for the revue. This bit will be lifted in toto for an episode of the Arnaz TV sitcom *The Mothers-in-Law* (1967–69), where scripters Carroll and Davis replace the Chevalier mimicry with that of Jimmy Durante, who was in real life Desi's close friend. The section of the episode, with Lucy in various disguises trying to crash the Tropicana, is not only a classic but archetypical *Lucy*. Gilda Radner will parody this exact scene many years later on TV's *Saturday Night Live*.

This installment is based in part on the *My Favorite Husband* radio episode "The French Lessons."

I LOVE LUCY #74: "REDECORATING THE MERTZES' APARTMENT"

(CBS, NOVEMBER 23, 1953), 30 MINUTES (B&W)
GUEST CAST: the Mayer Twins

Lucy is excited that Ricky is buying her a mink stole. However, Ricky is less than thrilled when Lucy hosts the women's club meeting in their apartment because Ethel is ashamed of her furnishings. Lucy decides to help the Mertzes redecorate their apartment, and absolute disaster follows.

HIGHLIGHTS & TRIVIA

This episode was written for two practical reasons. First, set decorator Ted Offenbecker was very unhappy with the Ricardos' furniture he inherited from art director Ralph Berger (who had previously been performing both tasks). Second, it was felt that it would be better if the Mertzes had a more attractive set in which to do scenes, so the action could occur more frequently out of the Ricardos' apartment. The new furniture does fit perfectly in both sets and will remain until 1957 when the *I Love Lucy* locale is shifted to Connecticut. Lucille makes a rare error in dialog that Desi cleverly covers. When she says, "paint the furniture and reupholster the old furniture," Desi repeats what she says and then tops her with, "I didn't hear you!"

I LOVE LUCY #75: "TOO MANY CROOKS"

(CBS, NOVEMBER 30, 1953), 30 MINUTES (B&W)

GUEST CAST: Elizabeth Patterson, Allen Jenkins, Alice Wills

At the same time as Fred's birthday, there is a rash of burglaries perpetrated by a woman crook. The Ricardos want to buy him a tailor-made tweed suit, so Lucy borrows an old one from the Mertzes' closet to get the proper measurements. Ethel learns of this and thinks Lucy is the female burglar. Lucy similarly thinks Ethel is the crook, and the shenanigans commence.

HIGHLIGHTS & TRIVIA

This is the only instance of Fred's birthday ever being mentioned on the series. It is also the only occasion we see the window with a fire escape in Lucy and Ricky's bedroom. Unfortunately, given the logistics of the apartment, the window either faces Little Ricky's room or the living room. The night this episode is aired, Desi gives Lucille a surprise anniversary party at the Mocambo nightclub in Hollywood. This incident will become the plot of one of the show's Hollywood entries in the following season.

I LOVE LUCY #76: "CHANGING THE BOYS' WARDROBE"

(CBS, DECEMBER 7, 1953), 30 MINUTES (B&W)

GUEST CAST: Oliver Blake, Jerry Hausner, Alberto Calderone, Lee Millar, Paul Power

Ricky and Fred insist on wearing comfortable old clothes to the movies, much to the consternation of the girls. Lucy and Ethel get rid of the boys' wardrobe by selling them to a used clothing store, thus forcing the men to wear newer ones. The boys catch on, retrieve their old favorites, and all is well, until Ricky is named one of the ten best-dressed men.

HIGHLIGHTS & TRIVIA

It is uncharacteristic for Ricky, who has always been a vain, fashion plate, to be sloppy in the story line. Again, new opening credits are used on the series, and they will continue to change as the sponsor (Philip Morris) continues to switch its advertising approach. Although this series is number one in television, Philip Morris' popularity in the cigarette field is slipping with each passing season and they are fighting back.

This installment is based in part on the *My Favorite Husband* radio episode "Husbands Are Sloppy Dressers."

I LOVE LUCY #77: "LUCY HAS HER EYES EXAMINED"

(CBS, DECEMBER 14, 1953), 30 MINUTES (B&W)

GUEST CAST: Arthur Walsh, Dayton Lummis, Shep Menken

Ricky brings home a theatrical producer (Dayton Lummis), who says he might be able to use Lucy in his latest show *if* she can jitterbug. Lucy gets "King Cat" Walsh (Arthur Walsh) to teach her, but at the same time she is concerned about Ricky's constant headaches. Lucy takes him to the eye doctor, but it is she who ends up with eyedrops that totally distort her vision.

HIGHLIGHTS & TRIVIA

Lucille's jitterbug is spirited and well performed. Note the energy and stamina required to repeat that dance twice within fifteen minutes; Lucille is no youngster at this point. Arthur Walsh was in real life a professional jitterbug dancer.

Vivian Vance:

Bill Frawley only learned his own lines in each script. Some weeks, he wasn't even clear what the plot was all about. Hal King was making me up one night, and Bill came over with a script in his hands with the title "Lucy Has Her Eyes Examined." He asked me if that was the script to next week's show. I was flabbergasted. I told him that we had been rehearsing that script all week and were starting to shoot it in fifteen minutes.

I LOVE LUCY #78: "RICKY'S OLD GIRLFRIEND"

(CBS, DECEMBER 21, 1953), 30 MINUTES (B&W)

GUEST CAST: Rosa Turich, Lillian Molieri, Jerry Hausner, the Mayer Twins

Fed up with listening to Lucy brag about her past boyfriends, Ricky makes up an old girlfriend he calls Carlotta Romero. Unfortunately, such a woman actually exists, knew Ricky in Cuba, and is now in town. Lucy gets *very* jealous.

HIGHLIGHTS & TRIVIA

The themes of adultery and seduction appear in this outing. No other American TV sitcom of this era has plot lines as sophisticated or as sexual as *I Love Lucy*, but they are always handled in good taste. The Christmas tag (with five Santa Clauses around the Christmas tree) from episode #11 ("Drafted") appears again at the end of this installment, even though the Ricardos are now in a different apartment.

I LOVE LUCY: "THE FREEZER"

(CBS, DECEMBER 28, 1953), 30 MINUTES (B&W)

This is a rerun of episode #29.

I LOVE LUCY: "THE GOSSIP"

(CBS, JANUARY 4, 1954), 30 MINUTES (B&W)

This is a rerun of episode #24.

I LOVE LUCY #79: "THE MILLION DOLLAR IDEA"

(CBS, JANUARY 11, 1954), 30 MINUTES (B&W)

GUEST CAST: Frank Nelson

Fred raves about Lucy's wonderful homemade salad dressing at dinner. Needing money desperately to pay household bills, Lucy and Ethel decide to bottle the dressing and sell it themselves. Although they arrange for free television advertising time at Charley Appleby's local TV station, Ricky figures out they are losing money on every jar.

HIGHLIGHTS & TRIVIA

The girls' two TV commercials for the salad dressing are not only very funny, but well-written satires on live commercials of the day. Notice that the Ricardos' living room coffee table is expandable into a dining table, eliminating the use of card tables on the set. Also note that Lucy gets sacks of mail orders *only hours* after being on television. Lucy refers to Ethel's middle name as Roberta (it had previously been mentioned as Louise in episode #69: "Lucy and Ethel Buy the Same Dress"). It will be changed once again to Mae in future episodes. This is the first of the *I Love Lucy* installments to be shown to the Armed Forces all over the world, courtesy of sponsor Philip Morris.

I LOVE LUCY #80: "RICKY MINDS THE BABY"

(CBS, JANUARY 18, 1954), 30 MINUTES (B&W)

GUEST CAST: the Mayer Twins

Ricky has a week's vacation from the club, and Lucy feels he should spend the time with Little Ricky. Ricky promises to take full charge of his son, but fails when he allows the boy to wander off while the Cuban is engrossed in a televised football game. Lucy schemes to teach him a lesson.

HIGHLIGHTS & TRIVIA

This episode was filmed *without* a live audience, because it was feared that the abundant use of the Mayer twins might cause delays and many retakes. The completed episode was later shown to an audience and their laughs were recorded for the broadcast. Desi's scene in the nursery reciting "Little Red Riding Hood" in Spanish to Little Ricky is a tour de force. Notice that he makes a mistake and begins to thank the wolf in Spanish, instead of thanking the hunter. Not having an audience is a wise decision; one of the Mayer boys begins to cry during Desi's recitation. Part of the sequence is filmed without a child in the crib, and part is shot with the other twin. This would have been impossible with an audience present. Once again, the length of the Mertzes' marriage is changed; this time they have been wed only twenty-three years.

Eliot Daniel

(COMPOSER)

The underscored music in the scene where Lucy is walking back and forth between the bedroom and the kitchen is something I wrote to be used again and again as "traveling" music.

I LOVE LUCY #81: "THE CHARM SCHOOL"

(CBS, JANUARY 25, 1954), 30 MINUTES (B&W)

Guest Cast: Natalie Schaefer, Tyler McVey, Vivi Janiss, Maury Hill, Eve Whitney Maxwell

At a party at the Ricardos', the men pay way too much attention to model Eve Whitney Maxwell (who plays herself). Lucy and Ethel decide they need to attend the same charm school as did Miss Whitney, to learn her secrets of allure.

HIGHLIGHTS & TRIVIA

The only thing wrong with this episode, and the others where Lucy wants some glamour, is that most men would give most anything for wives as beautiful as Lucille Ball. While the script tries to play down Ball's appeal, it fails. Natalie Schaefer (known to generations as Mrs. Howell on *Gilligan's Island*, 1964–67) may demonstrate a more sophisticated air as the charm school teacher, but Lucille's radiance is not to be denied.

I LOVE LUCY #82: "SENTIMENTAL ANNIVERSARY"

(CBS, FEBRUARY 1, 1954), 30 MINUTES (B&W)

GUEST CAST: Barbara Pepper, Hazel Pierce, Bennett Green, the Mayer Twins

Lucy wants to spend her wedding anniversary alone with Ricky in their apartment, but the Mertzes have other ideas. They have arranged a surprise party at the Ricardos', so Lucy and Ricky must hide in the closet to have their time alone.

HIGHLIGHTS & TRIVIA

Vivian Vance has a terrible cold the night of the shoot; it is impossible not to notice her stuffy nose and cough. The photographs used in the scene where the Ricardos reminisce come from the Arnazes' own photo album. The short scenes of Lucy and Ricky confined in the closet are filmed after the audience leaves. Instead of a closing commercial, the Arnazes film a public service announcement for the March of Dimes, urging each audience member to send in one dime to *I Love Lucy* to help stamp out polio.

I LOVE LUCY #83: "FAN MAGAZINE INTERVIEW"

(CBS, FEBRUARY 8, 1954), 30 MINUTES (B&W)

GUEST CAST: Joan Banks, Jerry Hausner, Kathryn Card, Elvia Allman, Hazel "Sonny" Boyne

An early-morning phone call from Ricky's agent, Jerry Hausner, informs the bleary-eyed Ricardos that magazine writer Eleanor Harris (Joan Banks) wants to follow Ricky through an average day, from morning to night. Later, Jerry tells Ricky he has mailed out postcards to all the women on the Tropicana's mailing list, inviting them to the club as Ricky's date as a publicity gimmick. Ricky takes one Jerry addressed twice to "Minnie Finch" as a sample, and puts it in his pocket. Later, Lucy finds it and assumes the worst, so she and Ethel go to Minnie's apartment to confront her.

HIGHLIGHTS & TRIVIA

This is not one of Bob and Madelyn's better scripts, but it is saved by the spectacular performances of Kathryn Card as Minnie Finch and Elvia Allman as her neighbor. Card will later play Mrs. McGillicuddy (Lucy's mother) in a totally different characterization, and Allman had last been seen yelling "Let 'er roll" on the "Job Switching" episode (#36).

This installment also sees the beginning of the breakdown in discipline on the set; its source is a matter of contention. While Desi Arnaz had always enjoyed having a few drinks, his alcoholism really begins to surface in his private life around this time. Jerry Hausner would blame this for what occurred the night of filming. Other sources say Hausner was bitter for not being a regular cast member and tried to use Desi as a scapegoat. Here's what happened. Desi had refused to make the phone connection "live" between himself and actor Jerry Hausner during their oncamera phone conversation. Hausner, positioned at the other end of the stage, couldn't hear Desi to get his proper cues. As a result, the scene needed several retakes. As soon as director Bill Asher yelled cut, Desi berated Jerry in language most fowl in front of the entire cast, crew, and studio audience.

Jerry Hausner

(ACTOR)

Desi was a drunk and Lucy was a control freak. Everybody thought it was so wonderful to be on the show, but they treated you like shit and paid you scale. I was supposed to be on every show, and was featured in the pilot. But Desi thought he was a big shot, and put his nose into everything. And there was no warmth from Lucy at all. They only cared about themselves.

After the way he embarrassed me, I could never look Desi in the eye again, and I never returned to the show.

Dann Cahn
(FILM EDITOR)
While Jerry's version is a little prejudiced, Desi did lose his temper that night. Desi rarely did that on the set, but occasionally, he would explode. He had a temper, but in this instance it had nothing to do with drinking but simply the pressures of the show. Jerry carried that ego hurt with him for the rest of his life. He was a disappointed, bitter, but very nice man.

Maury Thompson
(CAMERA COORDINATOR)
Much has been made of Desi's drinking in books. As far as his work was concerned, not once did alcohol interfere with his performance as Ricky Ricardo, or with his duties as an executive on the show. When it did, Desi sold the studio and retired. Professionally, he was a gentleman and very kind. If Desi was abusive to Jerry Hausner, I never saw it.

Hausner will, however, do small roles on other Desilu shows. Sadly, by the time of his death in the mid-1990s, Hausner's behavior wasn't much better than that of which he accused Desi. Much of what he said through the years about Lucille and Desi has to be taken with a grain of salt, as he was often inebriated himself.

THE TOAST OF THE TOWN: "THE MGM STORY"

(CBS, FEBRUARY 14, 1954), 60 MINUTES (B&W)
PRODUCED BY: Marlo Lewis, Ed Sullivan
DIRECTED BY: John Wray
CAST: Ed Sullivan (host), Desi Arnaz, Fred Astaire, Lucille Ball, Lionel Barrymore, Cyd Charisse, Johnny Green, William Holden, Van Johnson, Howard Keel, Gene Kelly, Ann Miller, Jane Powell, Debbie Reynolds, Lana Turner, Esther Williams

This salute to MGM's thirtieth anniversary is telecast from CBS Television City in Hollywood. The opening has a production number that features the entire cast, including Lucille and Desi, who are MGM alumni and are plugging their new film *The Long, Long Trailer*. The comic pair appear during the second half of the show in a combination movie plug and commercial. They sit in a Mercury convertible like the one they drive in the film (Mercury sponsors Sullivan's show), and offer Ed a Philip Morris cigarette. Crass commercialism!

I LOVE LUCY #84: "OIL WELLS"

(CBS, FEBRUARY 15, 1954), 30 MINUTES (B&W)
GUEST CAST: Harry Cheshire, Sandra Gould, Ken Christy

New tenants (Cheshire and Gould) from Texas move into the apartment building, claiming to be oil tycoons. Our friends all want a piece of the action and decide to invest. When a detective pal of Fred's comes looking for the tenants, they all fear they are being fleeced. Lucy schemes to retrieve their money.

HIGHLIGHTS & TRIVIA

Sandra Gould is known to generations of TV fans as Mrs. Kravitz in the color episodes of *Bewitched* (1964–72). The closing commercial featuring the Arnazes contains a generous plug for their new comedy feature, *The Long, Long Trailer* (1954).

WHAT'S MY LINE?

(CBS, FEBRUARY 21, 1954), 30 MINUTES (B&W)
EXECUTIVE PRODUCED BY: Gil Fates
PRODUCED BY: Mark Goodson, Bill Todman in association with the CBS Television Network
DIRECTED BY: Franklin Heller
CAST: John Daly (host)
PANELISTS: Dorothy Kilgallen, Steve Allen, Arlene Francis, Deborah Kerr
MYSTERY GUEST: Lucille Ball

The point of the program is to guess people's occupations. The final segment features a celebrity mystery guest, for whom the panel is blindfolded. Lucille is the mystery guest on this, the granddaddy of all TV panel shows. Answering the panel in the "Martian" dialect from the already filmed but yet unseen *I Love Lucy* episode "Lucy Is Envious" (# 89), there are laughs a-plenty for all concerned. Lucille is in New York (where this live show is broadcast) on a ten-day publicity tour as the spokesperson for the Heart Fund charity.

Lucille Ball

I was so nervous before the show started that I almost didn't have any voice left.

Steve Allen

(MEDIA GENIUS/TV PIONEER)

I had first worked with Lucille on radio doing My Favorite Husband. *I only had a small part then, but it was written by the same folks who wrote for my radio show, Bob and Madelyn.* Line *was totally legit, and they hired me for my type. As long as you were witty and urbane and got out two or three good laughs, you were a success. Much of the humor on this show came from the comedy of manners. That sort of comedy is gone today, along with manners. Television has become vulgarians entertaining barbarians. As far as that evening went, we really did have to gauge things just on the voices alone. On television, it seemed like Lucy was very far away from us, but in reality it was only about eight feet.*

I LOVE LUCY #85: "RICKY LOSES HIS TEMPER"

(CBS, FEBRUARY 22, 1954), 30 MINUTES (B&W)

GUEST CAST: Madge Blake, Byron Kane, Max Terhune

Lucy bets Ricky she can keep from buying a new hat longer than he can keep from losing his temper. Unfortunately, Lucy almost immediately buys a new hat, and must plot to make Ricky lose his temper as soon as possible.

HIGHLIGHTS & TRIVIA

Lucille displays split-second timing in her reactions in the final sequence, when the door buzzer rings just as she hangs up the phone. Notice Lucy Ricardo's pronunciation of tomato juice. Lucille Ball says it "tomahto," and catches herself in mid-sentence.

I LOVE LUCY #86: "HOME MOVIES"

(CBS, MARCH 1, 1954), 30 MINUTES (B&W)

GUEST CAST: Stanley Farrar

Ricky has become a bore showing home movies of the baby. When the Mertzes walk out on his latest screening, and Lucy falls asleep, he becomes furious. Unfortunately, Ricky is also making a filmed television pilot, and, out of anger, he refuses to let Lucy and the Mertzes participate. Naturally, Lucy makes a pilot of her own, and splices it into Ricky's.

HIGHLIGHTS & TRIVIA

This episode is shot without an audience due to the technical problems inherent in splicing together the various home movies. The finished installment is shown to an audience to record their laughs, which are then edited into the program. There is film in the projector shooting onto the screen, while the actual movies are later inserted optically into the screen standing in front of the fireplace. The projector in the Ricardos' kitchen comes from the home of producer Jess Oppenheimer; his son Gregg now has it in *his* home. Assistant film editor Bud Molin did an excellent job putting the pilot film together, the humor of which foreshadows programs like *Rowan & Martin's Laugh-In* (1967–72) by more than ten years. Lucy claims to have been in a Hollywood studio during the "western" sequence; in later episodes, she will claim her visit to Hollywood in 1954 is the first.

I LOVE LUCY #87: "BONUS BUCKS"

(CBS, MARCH 8, 1954), 30 MINUTES (B&W)

GUEST CAST: Tony Michaels, Don Garner, Frank Jacquet, Bennett Green, Patsy Moran, John Frank

A newspaper is running a prize contest based on serial numbers from dollar bills. Ricky finds a winning bill, and puts it in Lucy's purse so she can find it for herself. She mistakenly gives the dollar to the grocer, who hands it to Ethel in change. After fighting with Ethel over the currency and tearing it in half, Lucy sends her half to the laundry by error. Tribulations abound getting that bill back.

HIGHLIGHTS & TRIVIA

The audience laughter is so loud in the scene at the laundry that Desi keeps repeating "starch vat" over and over to ensure that the audience knows where Lucy is going. He knew that if they didn't, the final scene would make no sense. By the way, if Lucy has a washer and dryer (see episode #66), why is she sending pajamas out to the laundry?

I LOVE LUCY #88: "RICKY'S HAWAIIAN VACATION"

(CBS, MARCH 22, 1954), 30 MINUTES (B&W)

GUEST CAST: Frank Nelson

Ricky and the band are set to play a date in Hawaii, but he has no budget to take Lucy along. The Redhead schemes to appear on the *Be a Good Neighbor* TV show to win the trip for herself and the Mertzes.

HIGHLIGHTS & TRIVIA

The name, Cleo Morgan, mentioned on the Ricardos' blaring TV in the opening scene is taken from Lucille's cousin Cleo, who will one day produce *Here's Lucy*. This is Frank Nelson's third appearance as Freddie Fillmore. Lucille Ball and Vivian Vance will repeat the Hawaiian dance number almost exactly on *Here's Lucy* in the 1970–71 season. Notice that Lucille does *not* have on her false eyelashes in the final scene, knowing she will be doused with all sorts of liquids.

I LOVE LUCY #89: "LUCY IS ENVIOUS"

(CBS, MARCH 29, 1954), 30 MINUTES (B&W)

GUEST CAST: Mary Jane Croft, Herb Vigran, Dick Elliot, Kay Wiley, Louis A. Nicoletti

Wealthy old schoolmate Cynthia Harcourt (Mary Jane Croft) is in town raising money for charity. When Lucy learns that their mutual friend Anita "gave six," she pledges five, only to discover that the "five" means "five hundred" dollars. To earn the money and save face, Lucy is prompted by Ethel to answer a newspaper ad for girls who are brave.

HIGHLIGHTS & TRIVIA

This is producer-writer Jess Oppenheimer's least favorite episode. He feels it is unbelievable that Lucy and Ethel would climb up to the top of the Empire State Building for *any* amount of money. For trivia fans, the actual wording in the script for Lucy's "Martian" dialect does read "moo-moo." This is Mary Jane Croft's first TV experience with Lucille Ball. Fans know this certainly is not her last, as she will work with Lucille as a regular cast member on *I Love Lucy*, *The Lucy Show*, and *Here's Lucy*.

Mary Jane Croft

(ACTOR)

Unlike ladies such as Doris Singleton and Shirley Mitchell, I did not work with Lucy in radio. My husband Elliot Lewis was a director and producer in radio and television, and perhaps that's where the writers heard of me. They wanted someone very haughty and grand for this episode, and I guess she liked what I did. There was no way I could have known I'd be working with her again. She was in control of what went on during the rehearsal process, although not as much as she would be in later years. To this day, whenever I see something really unusual or peculiar, I say to myself, "It's a moo-moo."

Actually, Mary Jane is incorrect. She did play a small part on *My Favorite Husband*, and was a known entity to both the writers and to Lucille.

I LOVE LUCY #90: "LUCY WRITES A NOVEL"

(CBS, APRIL 5, 1954), 30 MINUTES (B&W)

GUEST CAST: Pierre Watkin, Dayton Lummis, Bennett Green

Hoping to duplicate another housewife's success as a novelist, Lucy writes a *roman à clef* that is a little too close to reality as far as Ricky and the Mertzes are concerned. Although they try to destroy her work, she sends carbon copies to publishers, and one wants to buy it. Unfortunately, it is all a mistake and Lucy is broken-hearted, until another firm shows an interest in her writing.

HIGHLIGHTS & TRIVIA

This installment is not big on physical comedy, but is very funny due to clever one-liners and situational humor. Dorrance and Company, the publisher referred to in the plot, was then an actual publishing firm in Philadelphia. The theme of this episode is very close to "Lucy Writes a Play" (episode #11). Ricky's statement that he came to this country by plane to Miami from Havana will be contradicted in 1957 in the *Lucille Ball-Desi Arnaz Show* #1: "Lucy Takes a Cruise to Havana." This is the only time in the entire run of the series when we see the Ricardos actually having a fire in the living room fireplace.

I LOVE LUCY #91: "LUCY'S CLUB DANCE"

(CBS, APRIL 12, 1954), 30 MINUTES (B&W)
GUEST CAST: Doris Singleton, Shirley Mitchell

The Wednesday Afternoon Fine Arts League once again needs money, so the girls form an all-girl orchestra and plan a dance. When, under great pressure, Ricky agrees to give the girls much-needed musical advice, Marion Strong (who is in charge of the publicity) plants a newspaper item that Ricky has formed his own all-girl orchestra. To save face, Ricky enlists members of his own band to dress in drag and be ringers at the dance.

HIGHLIGHTS & TRIVIA
In this, the last of Shirley Mitchell's three appearances as Marion Strong, we learn that Marion's husband's name is Bill. For reasons unknown, this is one of Desi Arnaz' least favorite episodes. While the finale featuring his band members in drag is funny, none of them enjoyed doing it. Art director Ralph Berger makes an error in the newsstand set by placing Roseland Ballroom behind the stand. The actual Roseland is located on the west side of Manhattan, completely across town from where the Ricardos live and where their neighborhood newsstand would be located.

I LOVE LUCY #92: "THE BLACK WIG"

(CBS, APRIL 19, 1954), 30 MINUTES (B&W)
GUEST CAST: Eve McVeagh, Douglas Evans, Louis A. Nicoletti, Bennett Green

At the beauty parlor, Lucy bemoans the fact that Ricky won't let her have one of the new Italian haircuts, so her stylist Roberta (Eve McVeagh) lets Lucy try on a wig. Convinced that she looks like a different person, Lucy schemes to trap Ricky to see how he would react to a little flirting. After being tipped off by the salon's manager, Ricky pretends to be fooled by her, which infuriates Lucy. She enlists Ethel's aid, Ricky gets Fred's help, and the battle of the sexes is on.

HIGHLIGHTS & TRIVIA
The name of Roberta for Lucy's hairdresser is taken from Bert French, the *I Love Lucy* hairstylist whose never-used actual first name is Roberta. The set of the finale is a redressed version of the diner in the episode of the same name, which was filmed first but aired just after this one. Around the time of this entry, Lucille and Desi threw Vivian a surprise party called "This Is Your Life, Vivian Roberta Jones." Dozens of people attended the soiree, which took three months to plan.

This show is based in part on the *My Favorite Husband* radio episode "Hair Dyed."

I LOVE LUCY #93: "THE DINER"

(CBS, APRIL 26, 1954), 30 MINUTES (B&W)
GUEST CAST: James Burke, Fred Sherman, Don Garner, Marco Rizo, Nick Escalante, Alberto Calderone, Joe Miller, the Mayer Twins

Ricky is disgusted with show business, and wants to invest in a normal occupation. Fred decides to join him, and the foursome buy a diner. Ego problems abound, and soon the eatery is in a shambles.

HIGHLIGHTS & TRIVIA
This episode contains the largest pie fight ever undertaken on this TV show; it is one of the best ever filmed for television on *any* series. The emphasis on Ricky's Cuban background, and the series' New York locale, add an ethnic flavor that is missing in Miss Ball's later TV efforts.

I LOVE LUCY #94: "TENNESSEE ERNIE VISITS"

(CBS, MAY 3, 1954), 30 MINUTES (B&W)
GUEST CAST: Tennessee Ernie Ford

Lucy's mother gives permission for someone she doesn't even know to stay with the Ricardos. Ernie Ford is a country guy, well meaning, but innocent of big city ways. When he turns into a huge pain for his hosts, Lucy tries to get rid of him as soon as possible.

HIGHLIGHTS & TRIVIA
It is in this episode that Lucille lifts, in toto (costume and all), her vamp bit from *The Ed Wynn Show* TV appearance in 1949. While Lucy's mother, Mrs. McGillicuddy, has been mentioned

before, this episode begins to define her wacky character in preparation of meeting her in person next season. The name of Pauline Lopus, referred to in Mrs. McGillicuddy's letter, is taken from a childhood friend from Lucille Ball's hometown of Celoron, New York. This episode and the one that follows help to propel Ernie Ford from a slightly known country artist to actual national stardom. The writers' use of the southern, country vernacular is brilliant, even surprising Ford, who had no input in the script.

I LOVE LUCY #95: "TENNESSEE ERNIE HANGS ON"

(CBS, MAY 10, 1954), 30 MINUTES (B&W)

GUEST CAST: Tennessee Ernie Ford, Richard Reeves

Ernie Ford is still at the Ricardos', becoming the house guest from hell. More schemes fail to get rid of him, but if the Ricardos and the Mertzes agree to appear with him on a country television show, he'll leave of his own accord.

HIGHLIGHTS & TRIVIA

In the original script, Mrs. Trumbull joins Ernie's efforts to raise money on behalf of the Ricardos, and gives Lucy five dollars of her own. These two "Ernie" shows are the most popular installments of the 1953–54 season, which encourages producer Jess Oppenheimer to begin the regular use of guest stars when there is an appropriate script. These entries also inspire the entire "California" batch of shows the following season.

I LOVE LUCY #96: "THE GOLF GAME"

(CBS, MAY 17, 1954), 30 MINUTES (B&W)

GUEST CAST: Jimmy Demaret, Louis A. Nicoletti, George Pirrone

Ricky and Fred have become golf enthusiasts, and neglect the girls. Figuring if you can't beat them, join them, the girls want to learn to play golf so they can join the boys. Ricky and Fred teach the girls ridiculous golfing rules to discourage them, which almost works *until* they meet golf legend Jimmy Demaret.

HIGHLIGHTS & TRIVIA

This episode boasts new opening credits, now featuring the "snap-open" Philip Morris cigarette pack. In real life, Desi Arnaz was an inveterate golfer. Lucille's voice is a bit gruff and hoarse in this entry; it will get even worse in the next one.

I LOVE LUCY #97: "THE SUBLEASE"

(CBS, MAY 24, 1954), 30 MINUTES (B&W)

GUEST CAST: Jay Novello, Virginia Brissac, the Mayer Twins

Lucy and Ricky are going to Maine for the summer, where Ricky has a hotel booking. The Ricardos decide to sublease their apartment, eventually working it out with the Mertzes. An extremely nervous man who has just finished being the witness at a murder case moves in just as Ricky finds out that his Maine booking has been canceled. The Ricardos can't make the new tenant leave because he has a lease, so Lucy attempts to make him leave of his own accord.

HIGHLIGHTS & TRIVIA

Lucille is clearly tired and hoarse in this installment, and will take a month off from work before filming four episodes that will be used for the following season. Ricky tells everyone that, now with the Maine booking canceled, they will be spending the summer in Del Mar, California. While that is actually where the Arnazes do spend their summer, the Ricardos will claim to never have been in California before when they hit Hollywood in the next season. The cigarette brand "Parliament" is introduced to the public in the closing commercial.

I LOVE LUCY: "CUBAN PALS"

(CBS, MAY 31, 1954), 30 MINUTES (B&W)

This is a rerun of episode #28, introduced by Roy Rowan.

I LOVE LUCY: "PIONEER WOMEN"

(CBS, JUNE 7, 1954), 30 MINUTES (B&W)

This is a rerun of episode #25, introduced by Roy Rowan.

I LOVE LUCY: "THE KLEPTOMANIAC"

(CBS, JUNE 14, 1954), 30 MINUTES (B&W)

This is a rerun of episode #27, introduced by Roy Rowan.

I LOVE LUCY: "THE MARRIAGE LICENSE"

(CBS, JUNE 21, 1954), 30 MINUTES (B&W)

This is a rerun of episode #26, introduced by Roy Rowan.

I LOVE LUCY: "JOB SWITCHING"

(CBS, JUNE 28, 1954), 30 MINUTES (B&W)

This is a rerun of episode #36, introduced by Roy Rowan.

LUCY'S COMPETITION ON THE OTHER TV NETWORKS

Listed below are the attempts by the other television networks to beat *I Love Lucy* in the ratings during the time period that *Lucy* aired on Mondays from 9:00 to 9:30 P.M. The shows detailed are the ones that began each season opposite *I Love Lucy*'s time slot.

SEASON	*NETWORK*	*PROGRAM*
1951	ABC	*Curtain Up* (1951)
	DUMONT	*Wrestling from Columbia Park* (1948–52)
1952	NBC	*Lights Out* (1949–52)
	ABC	*All-Star News* (1952–53)
	DUMONT	*Guide Right* (1952–53)
1953	NBC	*Hollywood Opening Night* (1951–53)
	ABC	*Junior Press Conference* (1953–54)
	DUMONT	*Boxing from Eastern Parkway* (1952–54)
1954	NBC	*RCA Victor Show Starring Dennis Day* (1953–54)
	ABC	*Junior Press Conference* (1953–56)
	DUMONT	*Boxing from St. Nicholas Arena* (1954–56)
1955	NBC	*Medic* (1954–56)
	ABC	*The Dotty Mack Show* (1953–56)
1956	NBC	*Medic* (1954–56)
	ABC	*Life Is Worth Living* (1952–57)

Chapter Six

1954–55 Season

I LOVE LUCY: THE FOURTH SEASON

TECHNICAL REGULARS: Executive produced by Desi Arnaz; produced by Jess Oppenheimer; directed by William Asher; written by Jess Oppenheimer, Madelyn Pugh, Bob Carroll Jr.; makeup by Hal King; hairstyling by Bert French; music by Wilbur Hatch
CAST REGULARS: Lucille Ball (Lucy Ricardo); Desi Arnaz (Ricky Ricardo); Vivian Vance (Ethel Mertz); William Frawley (Fred Mertz); Roy Rowan (announcer)

THE TOAST OF THE TOWN

(CBS, OCTOBER 3, 1954), 60 MINUTES (B&W)
PRODUCED BY: Marlo Lewis, Ed Sullivan
DIRECTED BY: John Wray
COMEDY MATERIAL FOR THE ARNAZES BY: Jess Oppenheimer, Bob Carroll Jr., Madelyn Pugh
MISS BALL'S GOWNS BY: Elois Jenssen
CAST: Ed Sullivan (host), Lucille Ball Desi Arnaz, Vivian Vance, William Frawley

Ed Sullivan turns his entire program into a salute to Lucille Ball and Desi Arnaz. This is done as a kickoff for the fourth TV season of *I Love Lucy*. The first segment features a sketch by Arnaz and Ball playing themselves at home in California, being visited by Ed Sullivan. This is the first time since *I Love Lucy* began that Lucille calls her husband "Desi" in a comedy sketch. The bit is hilarious, and even includes a cameo by Philip Morris' Johnny the Bellboy, jumping out of a cigarette box when Ed asks for a smoke. Vance (referred to on TV by Ball as "Viv" for the first time) and Frawley appear in the opening sequence, singing a song ("Hullabaloo") that was (despite the dialog in the scene) never featured on *I Love Lucy*. Desi is hoarse and perspiring fiercely; Sullivan later reveals that Arnaz has the flu and a high fever, but insisted on performing anyway. When Sullivan asks to see the *I Love Lucy* pilot, what is actually screened is the "Professor" bit from "The Audition" (episode #6) of *I Love Lucy*.

After screening moments from Arnaz and Ball motion pictures, and a mandatory performance of "Babalu" by Desi, the Arnazes are "roasted" by a panel, which includes baseball star Dusty Rhodes, Philip Morris executive Harry Chesley, actor John Hodiak, lyricist and MGM executive Howard Dietz, INS (International News Service) correspondent Don Dixon, and toastmaster Tex O'Roarke. Although the first few speakers are so long-winded that most of the other panel members do not get to talk, the highlight is the heartfelt, tearful words by Desi Arnaz: "You know . . . we came to this country and we didn't have a cent in our pockets . . . from [starting out in my first job] cleaning canary cages to this night in New York is a long ways, and I don't think that any other country in the world would give you that opportunity. I want to say thank you, thank you, America!"

I LOVE LUCY #98: "THE BUSINESS MANAGER"

(CBS, OCTOBER 4, 1954), 30 MINUTES (B&W)
GUEST CAST: Charles Lane, Elizabeth Patterson

The Ricardos' finances are in such bad shape that Ricky hires a business manager who puts Lucy on a strict budget, cutting off all charge accounts except at the food market. To create spending cash, Lucy begins to take orders for groceries from her friends, then charging them to the store. When Ricky finds a wad of dough in Lucy's purse and sees a pad with the scribblings of her orders, he jumps to the conclusions that she is in the stock market.

HIGHLIGHTS & TRIVIA

The new season has a fresh opening credits sequence, with the cartoon Arnazes playing on a teeter-totter as they open a pack of the sponsor's tobacco product. This is the third of the episodes filmed the previous June and held for the fall. The name of the business manager, Andrew Hickox (Charles Lane), comes from the Arnazes' actual business manager of the same name. In the original script, the actual stock Ricky thinks Lucy has invested in was left blank. Hundreds of names and abbreviations were tried to come up with a plausible grocery product that would sound like a stock abbreviation; the actual one used (Can All Pet) didn't surface until the day of the filming. Beginning with this episode, the Ricardos' kitchen table and chairs often will disappear and reappear from scene to scene, depending on the physical needs of the sequence. Starting with this installment, the Arnazes no longer appear in the final Philip Morris product commercial.

I LOVE LUCY #99: "MERTZ AND KURTZ"

(CBS, OCTOBER 11, 1954), 30 MINUTES (B&W)
GUEST CAST: Charles Winninger
Stephen Wooten

Fred's old vaudeville partner Barney Kurtz comes to town, and the Mertzes pretend to be well-to-do. Barney has been very successful, and his only trouble seems to be finding time to see his young grandson. When the Mertzes admit that they are not as financially solvent as they pretended, and have sent for Barney's grandson as a surprise, Barney then admits that he, too, has been pretending and is actually broke.

HIGHLIGHTS & TRIVIA

This is the last of the episodes filmed the previous June. The entire cast seems to have trouble with the lyrics to "By the Beautiful Sea." Charles Winninger (as Barney Kurtz) was originally a candidate to play Fred Mertz. The character's name was originally referred to as Ted Kurtz in the early *I Love Lucy* episodes. Desi Arnaz worked out with weights before the shoot to make his biceps pop when he flexed them during the "They Go Wild Over Me" musical number. The Arnazes filmed a public service spot for the Community Chest on the finale set of "Ricky's Screen Test" (episode #104), aired at the end of this installment.

I LOVE LUCY #100: "LUCY CRIES WOLF"

(CBS, OCTOBER 18, 1954), 30 MINUTES (B&W)
GUEST CAST: Beppy DeVries, Fred Aldrich,
Louis A. Nicoletti

Paranoid Lucy reads a newspaper article about a woman whose husband did not come to her defense during a robbery and wonders how Ricky would react under similar circumstances. She calls him in a phony panic, then waits out on the ledge of the building to see his reaction.

HIGHLIGHTS & TRIVIA

This was the first filmed episode shot the previous June for the new season. Lucille's voice is still raspy from exhaustion. Notice that the Italian lustres, always kept on either end of the piano, have been replaced by matching hurricane lamps to give Lucille easier access to the window and ledge. Vivian Vance has gained a great deal of weight during the summer vacation. Her marriage to Phil Ober is in trouble, and she is almost fifteen pounds heavier. It shows as she now goes through her paces as Ethel Mertz.

I LOVE LUCY #101: "THE MATCHMAKER"

(CBS, OCTOBER 25, 1954), 30 MINUTES (B&W)
GUEST CAST: Sarah Selby, Milton Frome,
Bennett Green, the Mayer Twins

Lucy once again indulges in matchmaking, this time between friends Dorothy and Sam. When all of her planned meddling goes awry, she and Ricky have a huge fight, causing him to walk out on her.

HIGHLIGHTS & TRIVIA

This is the second of the shows filmed the previous June. Vivian's hair is once again cut short, and it is the last time she will wear short hair on this series.

I LOVE LUCY #102: "MR. AND MRS. TV SHOW"

(CBS NON-NETWORK AFFILIATES, NOVEMBER 1, 1954), 30 MINUTES (B&W)

GUEST CAST: John Litel, Lee Millar

When Lucy has lunch at the 21 Club, she runs into a big advertising executive and talks him into building a morning television show around herself and Ricky. Although Ricky wants none of it, the ad agency talks him into it. Ricky lies to Lucy, saying it was his idea all along, but Lucy learns of his deception and is inspired to teach him a lesson.

HIGHLIGHTS & TRIVIA

This is the fourth show held over from the previous June. Lee Millar, who plays the young advertising executive, is the son of actress Verna Felton, who did many radio shows with Lucille Ball as well as two episodes of this series in 1953. Notice that Bill Frawley sings the wrong lyrics to the Phipps commercial jingle the second time they are done. Imagine Lucy Ricardo affording lunch at the expensive 21 Club. The restaurant was mentioned because Desi Arnaz had been served free meals there during his early days in New York.

A curious thing happened to this episode. Originally scheduled for November 1, 1954, on the full CBS network, the Republican party bought the half hour of time to show a filmed campaign commercial. While the CBS owned and operated stations, as well as many of its affiliates, air the Republican program, there are many other stations that are not actually part of the network that carry *I Love Lucy*. (In the 1950s, many smaller stations shared time among the various networks.) Those outlets actually air this episode as scheduled. The rest of the country will see it the following spring, while these stations will be fed a rerun.

I LOVE LUCY #103: "RICKY'S MOVIE OFFER"

(CBS, NOVEMBER 8, 1954), 30 MINUTES (B&W)

GUEST CAST: Frank Nelson, James Dobson, Elizabeth Patterson, the Mayer Twins

When Ricky lets it be known that a Hollywood talent scout is coming to the house to discuss a possible picture deal, everyone in the neighborhood schemes to get an audition.

HIGHLIGHTS & TRIVIA

This is the first episode filmed especially for the new season. The Ricardos and Mertzes in California story arc begins with this installment and will continue through the beginning of the next season (1955–56). The new story line injects an excitement, enthusiasm, and sense of anticipation missing in the series since Little Ricky was born in the 1952–53 season. *I Love Lucy* is the first sitcom to use such an extended continuing story line. Once again credit must be given to producer Jess Oppenheimer for his innovative thinking and foresight. Lucille's imitation of Marilyn Monroe generates spontaneous applause from the studio audience.

I LOVE LUCY #104: "RICKY'S SCREEN TEST"

(CBS, NOVEMBER 15, 1954), 30 MINUTES (B&W)

GUEST CAST: Clinton Sundberg, Ray Kellogg, Louis A. Nicoletti, Alan Ray, the Mayer Twins

It's time for Ricky to actually make his screen test. Because Lucy has been helping him with his lines all along, she is asked to participate as well. However, her idea of helping out includes hogging the spotlight and being discovered herself.

HIGHLIGHTS & TRIVIA

The opening scene, with Lucy cajoling Little Ricky into dancing and performing, is cut from most syndication rerun prints. The finale, encompassing Ricky's actual screen test, is written with a comedic device for which the writers are well known: first playing a scene straight, and then burlesquing it with each repeated sequence. The bit with Lucy reacting to the clapper will be reused almost verbatim in 1977 for the CBS TV special *Lucy Calls the President*.

I LOVE LUCY #105: "LUCY'S MOTHER-IN-LAW"

(CBS, NOVEMBER 22, 1954), 30 MINUTES (B&W)

GUEST CAST: Fortunio Bonanova, Virginia Barbour, Mary Emery, Pilar Arcos, Rodolfo Hoyos, Bennett Green, the Mayer Twins

Ricky's mother finally makes the trip from Cuba to meet her son's wife and child. Wanting to make a good impression on the señora, Lucy enlists the aid of a Spanish-speaking mentalist, whose hidden microphone and receiver allow her to converse with Mamacita in Spanish.

HIGHLIGHTS & TRIVIA

The writers try to use Desi's mistake in the "Cuban Pals" episode (#28) as a comedy device in the translation scene between Lucy and Ricky's mother; it fails miserably because it is impossible to accurately repeat what was a charming error. Notice the plug for the sponsor's product when Lucy offers her Spanish-speaking guests a "Philip(e) Morris(a)." Listen for the "uh-oh" during this scene; it is Lucille's mother DeDe Ball uttering this loud reaction. She will do it often throughout the series, and it will be heard on countless other sitcoms that rented the *I Love Lucy* soundtrack as their canned laughter. In the original script, Desi's pianist Marco Rizo was supposed to be the one in the kitchen giving Lucy translations. It is decided to expand the role of the Professor (Fortunio Bonanova) from the opening scene instead, and Marco is not used.

I LOVE LUCY #106: "ETHEL'S BIRTHDAY"

(CBS, NOVEMBER 29, 1954), 30 MINUTES (B&W)
GUEST CAST: Richard D. Kean, Mary Lansing

Fred asks Lucy to buy a present on his behalf for Ethel's birthday, because the ones he purchases Ethel never likes. When Ethel finds the present Lucy bought and opens it, she hates it and insults Fred's taste in gifts. The girls get into a huge argument, and Ethel refuses to go with the Ricardos to the theatre, which is *their* present to her.

HIGHLIGHTS & TRIVIA

This episode is a special favorite among *Lucy* fans. Although it contains no great physical comedy, the argument between Lucy and Ethel is so sharp it is memorable. The finale, with the girls not speaking to one another and then making up, is wacky and then very sentimental. Such warmth is as much a hallmark of *I Love Lucy* as is the physical comedy.

I LOVE LUCY #107: "RICKY'S CONTRACT"

(CBS, DECEMBER 6, 1954), 30 MINUTES (B&W)

Ricky is in a terrible funk, waiting to hear from Hollywood about the results of his screen test. No amount of cheering up can keep his mind off the test. Fred writes a phony message telling Ricky he got the job, but he and Ethel think better of it. Unfortunately, Ethel forgets to destroy the note before Lucy finds it and tells Ricky false good news.

HIGHLIGHTS & TRIVIA

After two non-California themed episodes, the story line gathers momentum with this entry. In the original script, there is a full scene of Lucy, Fred, and Ethel doing their rendition of *The Shooting of Dan McGraw* to distract Ricky. It is cut due to time constraints. Instead, Desi once again sings "I'll See You in C-U-B-A," as he did in episode #23, "The Moustache."

I LOVE LUCY #108: "GETTING READY"

(CBS, DECEMBER 13, 1954), 30 MINUTES (B&W)

After deliberating between air, train, and bus travel, Lucy decides that the only sensible way to get to California is by car. That decision opens the door to two others: With an empty back seat, why not take along the Mertzes, and what kind of car to get? Fred takes matters in hand and comes home with a Cadillac convertible . . . from the roaring Twenties.

HIGHLIGHTS & TRIVIA

This is the first of a two-part story. While it is established that the Ricardos will be in Hollywood for one month, that will eventually be changed to almost ten months in the plot line. Having the Mertzes come along is a necessity for the series, but it does bring up an anomaly. It is true that traveling in the back seat saves the Mertzes the price of travel tickets, but what about food and motel costs? And what about the price of their Beverly Hills accommodation hotel once they reach the West Coast? It is totally out of character for Fred to spend *that* kind of money. A still of the foursome in the antique Cadillac will be used as the network's publicity "card" for the *Lucy-Desi Comedy Hour* in 1962.

I LOVE LUCY: "THE CAMPING TRIP"

(CBS, DECEMBER 20, 1954), 30 MINUTES (B&W)

This is a rerun of episode #64.

I LOVE LUCY: "VACATION FROM MARRIAGE"

(CBS, DECEMBER 27, 1954), 30 MINUTES (B&W)

This is a rerun of episode #41.

I LOVE LUCY #109: "LUCY LEARNS TO DRIVE"

(CBS, JANUARY 3, 1955), 30 MINUTES (B&W)

Although still stuck with Fred's old Cadillac, Ricky buys a new Pontiac convertible for the trek. Lucy immediately begins a crusade to learn to drive, and a reluctant Ricky agrees as long as the car is first insured. Ricky teaches Lucy, Lucy teaches Ethel, the two cars lock bumpers, and Ricky is glad he didn't rely on Lucy to insure the cars.

HIGHLIGHTS & TRIVIA

This is a continuation of episode #108, "Getting Ready." Starting with this installment, Proctor and Gamble joins Philip Morris as alternate weekly sponsors of *I Love Lucy,* promoting the brand new laundry detergent "Cheer." The tobacco company had lost so much of its market share that they do not want to put all of their advertising dollars into this series any longer. To initiate this new arrangement, this entry begins with Desi Arnaz emerging from behind a curtain and announcing the new sponsor.

Although Ethel claims she doesn't know how to drive, she had no problem handling the lodge station wagon back in episode #64, "The Camping Trip," which was coincidentally rerun two weeks previously. The Pontiac used in this and subsequent episodes is one of several donated to Desilu in exchange for the inherent publicity. The special effects department does a good job with the "collision" of the two cars; they are specially wired to come together and break in a certain fashion. The motor is never actually turned on in either vehicle.

I LOVE LUCY #110: "CALIFORNIA, HERE WE COME"

(CBS, JANUARY 10, 1955), 30 MINUTES (B&W)
GUEST CAST: Elizabeth Patterson, Kathryn Card, the Mayer Twins

As the day for departure approaches, Mrs. McGillicuddy (Lucy's mother) arrives unannounced to join the caravan to California. Ricky gets furious and says things in anger that are overheard by Ethel. Everybody becomes infuriated with everybody else. After the air clears, it is decided that Mrs. McGillicuddy and Little Ricky will fly to the West Coast (after the others are settled there), all extra baggage is sent by rail, and the Ricardos and the Mertzes drive off in comfort.

HIGHLIGHTS & TRIVIA

Kathryn Card joins the cast as Mrs. McGillicuddy, a part she will play occasionally until 1959. Card was last seen on this series in a much different part for episode #83: "Fan Magazine Interview." Her scatterbrained, Gracie Allen-like character adds an extra dimension to the program, and helps explain why Lucy is the way she is. A still from the finale, with the foursome singing "California Here I Come," is one of the most reproduced photographs from the entire series. The piece of film of the Pontiac being driven toward and across the George Washington Bridge is the first location filming done by the Desilu crew.

Dann Cahn

(FILM EDITOR)

It was me driving across the George Washington Bridge. They had Pontiacs stationed all over the country for me, in New York, in Tennessee, and other places.

I LOVE LUCY #111: "FIRST STOP"

(CBS, JANUARY 17, 1955), 30 MINUTES (B&W)
GUEST CAST: Olin Howlin

Typical of many long-distance drivers, Ricky won't stop until he feels he has made enough mileage for the day. When he finally calls a halt, it is at a broken-down diner and motel. Although the foursome tries to find better accommodations, they are stuck spending the night at the inferior lodging.

HIGHLIGHTS & TRIVIA

Although the episode is titled "First Stop," it is physically impossible to leave Manhattan later than four in the morning and be in Ohio before dark. The entire motel sequence, with the bed moving each time a train rambles by, is a favorite among fans. Notice that Fred and Ethel claim to have a bed just like it at home; yet in "Vacation from Marriage" (episode #41), the Mertzes have double beds.

I LOVE LUCY #112: "TENNESSEE BOUND"

(CBS, JANUARY 24, 1955), 30 MINUTES (B&W)

GUEST CAST: Tennessee Ernie Ford, Will Wright, Rosalyn and Marilyn Borden, Aaron Spelling

Caught in a small-town speed trap, the Ricardos and the Mertzes are brought before the local sheriff. Lucy's indignation gets her arrested and all seems lost until they remember they are in Bent Fork, Tennessee, the hometown of folksy Cousin Ernie.

HIGHLIGHTS & TRIVIA

Ernie Ford makes another guest appearance after his big two-parter the previous spring. The Borden Twins gain TV immortality as Teensy and Weensy, the sheriff's chubby offspring. The ladies worked with Lucille in 1952 on Ed Wynn's *All Star Revue* previous to this filming. They will act on other Desilu shows, commercials, and spend their later years entertaining on cruise ships. The bit player who is the gas station attendant in the opening scene is mighty observant. He learns all he can about television, and becomes the most successful producer in American TV history: Aaron Spelling. Spelling later will coproduce Miss Ball's final series, *Life with Lucy* (1986). Note that a fourth camera, on a boom, is used to film much of the square dance.

I LOVE LUCY #113: "ETHEL'S HOME TOWN"

(CBS, JANUARY 31, 1955), 30 MINUTES (B&W)

GUEST CAST: Irving Bacon, Chick Chandler, Kathryn Card, the Mayer Twins

Arriving in Ethel's hometown of Albuquerque, everyone expects a sweet family reunion. What they find is a town braced for the return of Ethel Mae Potter Mertz, incipient movie star. When Ethel's ego gets totally out of hand, Lucy, Ricky, and Fred decide to burst her bubble.

HIGHLIGHTS & TRIVIA

There is a brief phone call scene at the beginning of the episode between Mrs. McGillicuddy and the cast that is cut from most syndicated rerun versions. Irving Bacon (Ethel's father) had appeared in episode #26 ("The Marriage License") as the justice of the peace. He is in reality only eight years older than Vivian Vance, and almost two decades younger than Bill Frawley. This episode finally establishes Ethel's middle name as Mae, and her maiden name as Potter. The finale is hysterical, with Lucy, Ricky, and Fred upstaging Ethel at every turn during her one-woman show. And while Ethel is less than fair to her comrades, the audience gets a vicarious thrill seeing middle-aged, frumpy Ethel finally having her moment in the spotlight.

I LOVE LUCY #114: "L.A. AT LAST"

(CBS, FEBRUARY 7, 1955), 30 MINUTES (B&W)

GUEST CAST: William Holden, Eve Arden, Bobby Jellison, Harry Bartell, Dayton Lummis, Dani Sue Nolan, Alan Ray

The Ricardos and the Mertzes finally arrive in Hollywood, staying at the Beverly Palms Hotel. Immediately, Ricky leaves for the movie studio without Lucy, so she and the Mertzes head for the famous Brown Derby restaurant. There, they have a run-in with William Holden, who also happens to be Ricky's guest when he returns later from MGM.

HIGHLIGHTS & TRIVIA

The set for the Ricardos' hotel suite is huge and sumptuous compared to their New York apartment. While they claim to be in Beverly Hills, the view from their balcony clearly places them geographically in the heart of Hollywood. This installment introduces Bobby Jellison as Bobby the Bellboy. His character will recur throughout the California episodes. Actress Dani Sue Nolan (the studio secretary) is married at the time to *I Love Lucy* director Bill Asher.

Lucille Ball

That moment when I buttered my hand . . . [the author] found something I actually ad-libbed on the set.

Madelyn Pugh Martin Davis

(WRITER)

In her later years, when she'd get on talk shows, sometimes Lucy would tell stories that weren't always accurate. I think she liked to believe things happened this way, but more often than not the things she claimed to ad-lib were right there in the script. For instance, if Lucy's nose had really caught on fire by accident, there would have been forty-two firemen on the set immediately.

Madelyn is right. Lucille buttering the back of her hand is definitely in the original script. However, what Lucille *does* actually ad-lib is dunking her nose in the coffee. It had always been in the script that Lucy would light her nose on fire. That was *not* spontaneous, despite what others have written or said. The script calls for her to pull off the putty nose and dunk it in the coffee. Taking her whole head and dunking her nose right in the coffee cup was something Lucille tried on filming night.

I LOVE LUCY #115: "DON JUAN AND THE STARLETS"

(CBS, FEBRUARY 14, 1955), 30 MINUTES (B&W)

GUEST CAST: Ross Elliott, Dolores Donlon Beverly E. Thompson, Shirlee Tigge, Maggie Magennis, Iva Shepard

Because Ricky's movie assignment casts him as a Latin lover, the studio's publicity ignores the fact that he is married. What makes Lucy even angrier is all of the beautiful women with whom he is photographed. When Ricky returns late one night and leaves very early the next morning for the studio, Lucy concludes that he stayed out all night.

HIGHLIGHTS & TRIVIA

This is probably the weakest of all the California episodes; the comedy is not well motivated. It really isn't all that funny that Lucy thinks Ricky is cheating on her. Ross Elliott, here as Ricky's publicity agent, had last been seen as the man directing Lucy's Vitameatavegamin commercial (see episode #30) .

I LOVE LUCY #116: "LUCY GETS IN PICTURES"

(CBS, FEBRUARY 21, 1955), 30 MINUTES (B&W)

GUEST CAST: Lou Krugman, Onna Conners, Bobby Jellison, Louis A. Nicoletti

With Ricky busy at the studio, and Fred, Ethel, and Bobby the Bellboy landing small parts in other movies, Lucy is desperate to get some work in films like the others. After eating a glutton's feast at Schwab's drug store hoping to be discovered like Lana Turner supposedly had been, Ricky takes pity on her and arranges for a small chorus girl role in a film. However, Lucy has other ideas.

HIGHLIGHTS & TRIVIA

Lucille's grace and athleticism serve her well in the last scene, where she wears the oversized headdress on the sound stage set. Lucille shows much prowess handling it. Even at this early point in her lengthy television career, Lucille Ball looks a bit old to play a chorine, especially when she stands next to young women. Notice that Ricky refers to Lucy's friend as *Lillian* Appleby instead of Caroline. During the warmup for the show, house pianist Marco Rizo plays "Lucy's Mambo," a new song he has written for his employers. Lou Krugman (as the movie director) impresses Lucille sufficiently that she continues to hire him for TV parts well into the 1960s.

I LOVE LUCY #117: "THE FASHION SHOW"

(CBS, FEBRUARY 28, 1955), 30 MINUTES (B&W)

GUEST CAST: Don Loper, Sheila MacRae, Amzie Strickland, Brenda Marshall Holden, Jeanne Martin, Frances Heflin, Marylin Tucker, Sue Carol Ladd, Mona Carlson

Lucy decides she must have a fashionable Don Loper dress, just like all of the other ritzy ladies in Beverly Hills. She visits his salon and buys a $500 dress. To get Ricky's sympathy so he will pay for the purchase, she lies out in the sun to get a sunburn. Lucy gets "fried to a crisp," then learns that if she wears a tweed suit in a Loper charity fashion show, she'll be given her outfit for free.

HIGHLIGHTS & TRIVIA

Beginning with this episode, before the first scene of each installment, the cartoon characters of Lucille and Desi are featured posing on a wooden tree, regardless of the show's sponsor. Vivian Vance's hair is now noticeably lightened; it will become and remain a light blonde until 1963. Makeup artist Hal King's work (still unbilled at the time as the credits only read Makeup by Max Factor) is extremely effective in making Lucy look sunburned—one can almost feel her pain just by watching.

Sheila MacRae

(ACTOR/SINGER/WRITER)

It was because of Lucy that I got into this part of show business. I had been doing Shakespeare in my native country of England, and continued it in stock as a young girl. That led to a scholarship at the Radio City school, where I met Jeff Chandler, Jack Carter, and my future husband Gordon MacRae. I became a wife, and didn't work again until this show. Lucy had this show written for me. I had just had a miscarriage, and was in a deep depression. Lucy and Desi and Gordy and I were very close friends. She was very concerned about my mental condition, and figured it would be good for me to have something to do. Lucy was always trying to mother everybody. And she was so skillful; a wonderful farceur and a wonderful satirist. Lucy told me to be "snobby" for the show; she thought I dressed like what a Hollywood star's wife would *dress like.*

Don Loper was probably one of the first gay men to just be themselves on television and not care. The fashion sequence was originally much longer, including my introduction of Don, but was cut in rehearsals because Lucy was so funny with the sunburn bit that it took up all the time. She was so real. You could feel *the sunburn. And two of the ladies [in the celebrity fashion show] were drunk the night we filmed. No matter where I go, at no matter what hour, somebody starts throwing lines at me from this show. It never fails.*

I LOVE LUCY: "THE COURTROOM"

(CBS, MARCH 7, 1955), 30 MINUTES (B&W)

This is a rerun of episode #42.

I LOVE LUCY #118: "THE HEDDA HOPPER STORY"

(CBS, MARCH 14, 1955), 30 MINUTES (B&W)

GUEST CAST: Hedda Hopper, Hy Averback, Bobby Jellison, Kathryn Card, John Hart, the Mayer Twins

Mrs. McGillicuddy finally arrives with Little Ricky, but the Ricardos have more pressing concerns. A new publicity agent concocts a kooky stunt for Ricky to save Lucy from drowning in a pool where gossip columnist Hedda Hopper will just happen to be. All goes wrong, and when the Ricardos return to their suite dripping wet, who should they meet but Mrs. McGillicuddy's new friend—Hedda Hopper.

HIGHLIGHTS & TRIVIA

Notice Ricky's explanation of the time change between New York and Los Angeles. He actually *is* wrong and Mrs. McGillicuddy is right. This is the first of four times that Hedda Hopper and Lucille Ball will work together on TV between now and 1960. They are close friends. A new cigarette brand, Marlboro, is introduced to the public in the final commercial, and the Arnazes close the show by doing a public service announcement for the Olympic Games.

I LOVE LUCY #119: "DON JUAN IS SHELVED"

(CBS, MARCH 21, 1955), 30 MINUTES (B&W)

GUEST CAST: Kathryn Card, Phil Ober, Bobby Jellison, Jody Drew

Variety prints that Ricky's movie is being shelved, so Lucy takes matters in her own hands. She knows MGM studio head Dory Schary is meeting Ricky at the hotel, so she hires someone to play a Broadway producer to make Schary jealous. Whom does she hire? Dore Schary, naturally.

HIGHLIGHTS & TRIVIA

Dore Schary, MGM production chief, had originally been cast to play himself. He backed out, much to the betterment of the show, as he was not a dynamic personality. Vivian Vance's husband at the time, Phil Ober, plays the part instead. Once *Don Juan* gets shelved, we are never told the name of the movie Ricky eventually makes instead.

Bob Carroll Jr.
(WRITER)
We didn't come up with a new movie name because we didn't want to create a whole new set of circumstances. We were tired, and it was easier for us this way.

I LOVE LUCY #120: "BULLFIGHT DANCE"

(CBS, MARCH 28, 1955), 30 MINUTES (B&W)
GUEST CAST: Ross Elliott, Ray Kellogg

Two separate events intertwine: Ricky is doing a television benefit for the Heart Fund, and Lucy is asked by *Photoplay* magazine to write, "What It's Really Like to Be Married to Ricky Ricardo." Using the article as blackmail, Lucy wrangles a part in the TV fundraiser, singing a duet with Ricky. When she fails at that, Ricky finds the perfect part for her: playing a bull.

HIGHLIGHTS & TRIVIA
In real life, the Arnazes were spokespeople for the Heart Fund for several years. Notice that Ricky calls the pianist "Marco"; did the Ricky Ricardo Orchestra also come to California? There are technical problems with the finale; much of it is reshot with one camera after the studio audience departs.

I LOVE LUCY #121: "HOLLYWOOD ANNIVERSARY"

(CBS, APRIL 4, 1955), 30 MINUTES (B&W)
GUEST CAST: Kathryn Card, Bobby Jellison, Ross Elliott, the Mayer Twins

When Ricky once again forgets the date of their wedding anniversary and then lies about it to cover up his behavior, Lucy is furious. She will not attend the party he is hosting for her at the famed Mocambo nightclub, preferring instead to go to the club with her mother and Bobby the Bellboy.

HIGHLIGHTS & TRIVIA
Beginning with this episode, Lilt Home Permanents becomes the alternate weekly sponsor with Philip Morris cigarettes. Movie star Janet Blair appears in the middle commercial as the Lilt spokesperson. This plot is inspired by the actual party Desi gave for Lucille at the Mocambo on their previous wedding anniversary.

I LOVE LUCY

(CBS, APRIL 11, 1955)

"Mr. and Mrs. TV Show" is rerun on network affiliates, while "Ricky Loses His Voice" is rerun on nonnetwork affiliates.

New footage of the cast reminiscing in Hollywood leads to the flashbacks to these episodes in the TV markets where they had not been aired before.

I LOVE LUCY #122: "THE STAR UPSTAIRS"

(CBS, APRIL 18, 1955), 30 MINUTES (B&W)
GUEST CAST: Cornel Wilde, Bobby Jellison

Lucy reads that movie star Cornel Wilde is hiding out in Beverly Hills to get a rest and tricks Bobby the Bellboy into admitting that Wilde is in their hotel. She persuades Bobby to sneak her into Wilde's suite, where she gets trapped.

HIGHLIGHTS & TRIVIA
Van Johnson was the first choice to play the part, but had other obligations. Cornel Wilde (as the celebrity upstairs) is probably better remembered by many fans for this TV appearance than for most of the movies he made or directed. Notice the bandage on Lucy's face after she falls out of the upstairs balcony; this is a rare example where Lucille Ball actually is injured doing physical comedy. Vivian is hysterical in her scene where she tries to keep Ricky from seeing Lucy dangling off the balcony above.

Madelyn Pugh Davis Martin
(WRITER)
Whenever Lucy did a physical stunt, we'd pan to Vivian's reactions, which always made the scenes twice as funny. Viv was brilliant in this one. When she saw Lucy going by and falling below, she was a marvel.

THE SUNDAY LUCY SHOW

(CBS, APRIL–OCTOBER 1955), 30 MINUTES (B&W)

This is a collection of *I Love Lucy* programs, beginning with "The Ballet" (episode #19). Because so many home viewers requested to see the early episodes as they did not have sets when they originally aired, CBS and the Arnazes reran these shows in the late afternoon on Sundays.

I LOVE LUCY #123: "IN PALM SPRINGS"

(CBS, APRIL 25, 1955), 30 MINUTES (B&W)

GUEST CAST: Rock Hudson, Kathryn Card

Once again, the Ricardos and the Mertzes are getting on one another's nerves and feel that a temporary separation is necessary. The women go to Palm Springs for a week, where they sit in the rain missing their husbands. When the sun finally shines, the girls meet Rock Hudson at poolside.

HIGHLIGHTS & TRIVIA

This is the first episode that reveals there is a kitchenette in the Ricardos' hotel suite. Of the annoying habits shown, only Ethel's had been seen previously. When Rock Hudson refers to Adele Sliff in his scene, the name derives from the *I Love Lucy* script clerk. Notice that the lamps in the Ricardos' living room keep changing styles and disappearing from episode to episode, depending on the plot needs.

I LOVE LUCY #124: "THE DANCING STAR"

(CBS, MAY 2, 1955), 30 MINUTES (B&W)

GUEST CAST: Van Johnson, Doris Singleton, Marco Rizo

Lucy has been writing letters back east, boasting of her new friendships with big movie stars. When Caroline Appleby visits Hollywood on her way to Hawaii, Lucy must back up her claims. Van Johnson is doing his act in the hotel's nightclub, so Lucy schemes to be seen with him to satisfy Caroline.

HIGHLIGHTS & TRIVIA

This is the first of a two-part story, although it is filmed second. The first choice for the dancing star had been Ray Bolger, but he was replaced when Van Johnson became available. When Lucille fumbles her line, "I danced with Van," watch how her stomach contracts in laughter. She is clearly breaking up and turning her face away upstage to hide it. Desi covers her mistake and her laughing by ad-libbing, "Vance with Dance? What is that?" These are the only installments in which Caroline Appleby wears glasses. The last scene in the show has an odd feel to it, because both Lucille and Van receive strong recognition applause from the audience, as if they are being seen for the first time.

Maury Thompson

(CAMERA COORDINATOR)

Cam McCullough was responsible for that. He was in charge of the sound. Sometimes he'd get excited, and his foot would go down on the pedal that picked up audience reactions. When he saw Van, his foot went all the way down, and what was a slight applause sounds like an ovation.

I LOVE LUCY #125: "HARPO MARX"

(CBS, MAY 9, 1955), 30 MINUTES (B&W)

GUEST CAST: Harpo Marx, Doris Singleton

Caroline Appleby postpones her Hawaiian vacation to attend Lucy's open house at her hotel suite, which is supposed to feature movie stars aplenty. While Lucy plans to fool the nearsighted Caroline with masks of stars (the girls have stolen Caroline's glasses), Ricky and Fred encounter Harpo Marx (one of the famed Marx Brothers comedians) and persuade him to visit the suite as a surprise.

Maury Thompson

(CAMERA COORDINATOR)

Lucille adored Harpo, but like several other comedians she worked with through the years, he never did anything the same way twice. That was deadly for this episode, because she had to be his mirror image. This is one occasion where we had to reshoot a scene over and over again after the audience left. Then Dann Cahn had to piece it together in editing to look like one continuous performance. He did an excellent job, because most people never dreamed it wasn't done all at once in front of the audience.

Doris Singleton

(ACTOR)

This episode was so much fun to do. Lucille was very excited at the prospect of working with Harpo, and was really on her toes. There was a party on the set after the audience left. Harpo played and Vivian sang. It was lovely.

Harpo Marx

(ACTOR)

I hadn't worked for awhile before this show, because I'd had a heart attack. My doctor advised me against it, but I really wanted to do it. Lucille loved to rehearse, but I had done *this stuff for thirty-five years. I had a great time. Right after the show, I had another heart attack.*

I LOVE LUCY #126: "RICKY NEEDS AN AGENT"

(CBS, MAY 16, 1955), 30 MINUTES (B&W)

GUEST CAST: Parley Baer, Helen Kleeb

Ricky is disheartened just doing publicity while the studio decides what to do with him. Lucy goes to the studio pretending to be his agent and hoping to get some action. She gets action all right—she gets him released from his movie contract.

HIGHLIGHTS & TRIVIA

Ricky's problems being cast in an MGM motion picture mirror the same problems Desi Arnaz had encountered when *he* was at Metro-Goldwyn-Mayer in the early 1940s. Desi gives a bravura performance in the "anger" scene, completely trashing the hotel suite. The bric-a-brac is made from special materials that crumbles easily, and sound effects are later added to give the impression of glass and china breaking. Notice that Lucy makes reference to the time they had been handcuffed together for forty-eight hours; actually, it had only been twenty-four hours.

I LOVE LUCY: "NEVER DO BUSINESS WITH FRIENDS"

(CBS, MAY 23, 1955), 30 MINUTES (B&W)

This is a rerun of episode #66.

I LOVE LUCY #127: "THE TOUR"

(CBS, MAY 30, 1955), 30 MINUTES (B&W)

GUEST CAST: Richard Widmark, Juney Ellis, Benny Rubin, Audrey Betz, Barbara Pepper

When Ricky bans Lucy from a luncheon he is having with big screen star Richard Widmark, she and Ethel take a bus tour of movie stars' homes. When they reach Widmark's house, they pick a grapefruit from his backyard. The tour bus leaves without them, and Lucy is trapped in Widmark's abode just as the owner arrives with Ricky.

HIGHLIGHTS & TRIVIA

The Beverly Hills house that Lucy and Ethel are shown walking toward when they get off the tour bus is actually the Arnazes' on Roxbury Drive. Although it has been reported elsewhere that the end of this show has a tag scene, with Lucy and Ricky telling the audience they'd be back in thirteen weeks and to enjoy *The Whiting Girls* (their summer replacement), a viewing of the original film reveals no such tag sequence.

Madelyn Pugh Martin Davis

(WRITER)

Bob and I took the tour of the movie stars' homes just to see how it went. The big event of the trip was seeing Pat O'Brien come out in his bathrobe to get the mail.

Lucille Ball

This episode came back to haunt me. Many years later, after I had been married to Gary [Morton], some people actually came to our house and climbed over the wall. When we asked what they were doing, they told us that since I [meaning Lucy Ricardo] had done it, they thought it was OK, too!

I LOVE LUCY: "LUCY'S SCHEDULE"

(CBS, JUNE 6, 1955), 30 MINUTES (B&W)

This is a rerun of episode #33.

I LOVE LUCY: "RICKY THINKS HE'S GETTING BALD"

(CBS, JUNE 13, 1955), 30 MINUTES (B&W)

This is a rerun of episode #34.

I LOVE LUCY: "RICKY ASKS FOR A RAISE"

(CBS, JUNE 20, 1955), 30 MINUTES (B&W)

This is a rerun of episode #35.

I LOVE LUCY: "THE HANDCUFFS"

(CBS, JUNE 27, 1955), 30 MINUTES (B&W)

This is a rerun of episode #39.

Chapter Seven

1955–56 Season

I LOVE LUCY: THE FIFTH SEASON

TECHNICAL REGULARS: Executive produced by Desi Arnaz; produced by Jess Oppenheimer; directed by James V. Kern; written by Jess Oppenheimer, Madelyn Pugh, Bob Carroll Jr., Bob Schiller, Bob Weiskopf; makeup by Hal King; hairstyling by Irma Kusely; music by Wilbur Hatch
CAST REGULARS: Lucille Ball (Lucy Ricardo); Desi Arnaz (Ricky Ricardo); Vivian Vance (Ethel Mertz); William Frawley (Fred Mertz); Roy Rowan (Announcer)

THE LUCY SHOW

(CBS, OCTOBER 1955–APRIL 1956), 30 MINUTES (B&W)

No, this is *not* a misprint *nor* Miss Ball's classic 1960s sitcom. The reruns of *I Love Lucy* on Sundays had done so well for CBS that they decide to add this extra night of *I Love Lucy* reruns on Saturdays in the very early evening. New graphics are made to reflect the change of title and sponsor.

WHAT'S MY LINE?

(CBS, OCTOBER 2, 1955), 30 MINUTES (B&W)
EXECUTIVE PRODUCED BY: Gil Fates
PRODUCED BY: Mark Goodson, Bill Todman in association with the CBS Television Network
DIRECTED BY: Franklin Heller
CAST: John Daly (host)
PANELISTS: Dorothy Kilgallen, Robert Q. Lewis, Arlene Francis, Bennett Cerf
MYSTERY GUESTS: Lucille Ball, Desi Arnaz

The panel guesses that the mystery guest has something to do with *I Love Lucy* and might be Lucille or Desi, but it takes veteran participant Arlene Francis to figure out that it is both of them.

John Daly
(HOST)
They [the Arnazes] are both, to put it into one or two words, very *nice people, and they always have been.*

I LOVE LUCY #128: "LUCY VISITS GRAUMAN'S"

(CBS, OCTOBER 3, 1955), 30 MINUTES (B&W)
GUEST CAST: Gege Pearson, Hal Gerard, Ben Numis, Clarence Straight, the Mayer Twins

While on a routine sightseeing trip to Grauman's [now Mann's] Chinese Theatre on Hollywood Boulevard, Lucy discovers that John Wayne's cement footprints in the forecourt are loose. She steals them as a souvenir. When Ricky demands that she return them, Lucy accidentally drops them and they break into a million pieces.

HIGHLIGHTS & TRIVIA
This is the first of a two-part story. The episode opens with Desi coming out from behind a curtain to announce that General Foods (Sanka Coffee) and Proctor and Gamble (Lilt Home Permanents) will now be sponsoring the series. Philip Morris has decided to concentrate more on print ads. This is the first installment written by Bob Schiller and Bob Weiskopf.

Bob Schiller
(WRITER)
I had just finished being fired off The Red Buttons Show *[1952–55], the first in a long line of writers Buttons fired because he had to take money out of the writers' budget. Bob and I were both handled by the same agent at the William Morris Agency. He had*

been moving out to Los Angeles from Westport, Connecticut, (now you know why the Ricardos moved there *in 1957) to write some Danny Thomas shows. Bob had gotten lonely working alone and was looking for a partner.*

Bob Weiskopf
(WRITER)

I am almost five years older than Bob is, so my career got started earlier. He was one of a large group of writers who came out of the Army after the war. I had worked on radio for several big names, and had become a writing partner of Paul Henning's [creator of The Beverly Hillbillies, *1962–71,* Petticoat Junction, *1963–70, and* Green Acres *1965–71]. My wife was Japanese, and she was put into an internment camp during the war. Besides ruining my marriage, it forced Paul and I to end our working partnership. In the interim, I lived with Jess Oppenheimer, who was single at that time. After the war, my wife and I moved to New York until the time Bob and I met. Bob and I were hired by Artie Stander as staff writers for* It's Always Jan *(1955–56), but after one script, we couldn't get any of our story lines cleared. We went to our agent's office at [William] Morris to complain, and there was Jess Oppenheimer. He hired us on the spot for* I Love Lucy.

Bob Schiller
(WRITER)

Jess was a very organized guy. We would all get locked in a room until we came up with a story. Rarely did it take more than a day. Madelyn would type down the notes. Bob and I would write a first draft of a script, and then it was given to Bob Carroll Jr. and Madelyn for editing and reworking. We never lost a script. There was never anyone who wrote a script besides the five of us. Carroll and Pugh had written every script for four seasons. That would be unheard of today, where there are armies of writers on every sitcom.

This is the episode where Irma Kusely takes over as Lucille's on-the-set hairstylist.

Irma Kusely
(HAIRSTYLIST)

I met Lucille when she was doing publicity at MGM. I did her hair for some photo shoots, and then I was assigned to be the hairdresser for the film Without Love *[1945]. I did both her hair and Katharine Hepburn's hair. Lucy and I became friends. I didn't come on to* I Love Lucy *in the beginning because I had just had my children and didn't want to work every day. From this point forward, Lucille's hair was consistently the same color for the rest of her career, because I used the same formula. It was the same for Vivian. Previous to this, Viv's hair was all kinds of colors. I gave her a formula, and she took it to her personal hairdresser in Pacific Palisades. I never colored Vivian's hair. I dyed Lucille's hair every two weeks, gave her a permanent every month or so, and put her hair in curlers before the dress rehearsals. Then, right before the show, she came to me and I combed it out. Sometimes, I put a net on the bun to keep it in place when she had physical things to so.*

This is the first episode directed by James V. Kern.

Maury Thompson
(CAMERA COORDINATOR)

After three seasons with Bill Asher, Lucille felt she needed someone new to play off directorially. His successor, Jim Kern, was a pushover, and never stood up to Lucille. He didn't last very long.

Bob Schiller
(WRITER)

Jimmy Kern was a nice man, but he was not a very good director. He was originally a singer, and after our show he worked exclusively in one-camera shows. Jim was not a creative man the way Bill Asher and Marc Daniels were. I think Desi thought that anything Jim lacked, he could handle himself. Desi was a very capable director, and Lucille was the most exacting actress I ever knew. Desi knew how to handle Lucille, and relieved her of all responsibilities except acting. She trusted him completely. He was charming, and handled people for her. In the beginning, he couldn't remember my name. He kept referring to me as Bob Fisher. So we got big cards made, and they all had Schiller written on them. We got people in the bleachers to hold them up. Desi laughed at this a lot.

With Kern at the helm, the camera angles are now awkward. Sometimes, Lucille is filmed badly. Kern seems to have trouble capturing the physical comedy in the three-camera process. In the scene in the Mertzes' hotel room, notice that while Lucy's foot is in cement, she lets it dangle completely off the chaise she is lying on. The weight of real cement would have snapped her foot off. In reality, most of what passed for cement was styrofoam, with a harder substance substituted for the closeup of Ricky smashing it. Well-respected costume designer Edward Stephenson replaces Elois Jenssen with this outing as Lucille allowed a minor salary dispute to come between herself and Jenssen's designs. (Elois made Lucille look feminine, chic, and youthful. Eddie makes her look more matronly and stiff. He will continue as Ball's designer well into the 1960s.) Makeup artist Hal King finally gets onscreen acknowledgement with this episode. There have not been this many firsts in an *I Love Lucy* episode since the show's debut season.

I LOVE LUCY #129: "LUCY AND JOHN WAYNE"

(CBS, OCTOBER 10, 1955), 30 MINUTES (B&W)

GUEST CAST: John Wayne, Ralph Volkie, Louis A. Nicoletti, the Mayer Twins

To salvage his film career after Lucy's Grauman's Theatre fiasco, Ricky contacts John Wayne to ask him to make new footprints for the theatre's forecourt. Wayne graciously complies, and continues to do so over and over as each successive set of footprints is somehow ruined.

HIGHLIGHTS & TRIVIA

This is the second of two parts. Wayne agreed to this appearance to publicize his new action movie, *Blood Alley* (1955). Even though he does not appear in the first installment, he and his picture are discussed enough there to ensure top value. The new Schiller-Weiskopf scripts fit seamlessly into the series' format. Notice Lucy's reference to her hairstylist Irma; the name is taken from show stylist Irma Kusely. The scene where Little Ricky plays in the wet cement has to be reshot after the studio audience goes home. The little Mayer boy playing the part doesn't want to ruin his new shoes and has to be promised new ones to get him to play in the cement.

Bob Schiller

(WRITER)

Using guest stars helped the show because it gave us another element to write about. There are only so many perspectives you can show about four people, but each time we had a guest star it stirred up the mix and gave us something new.

Bob Carroll Jr.

(WRITER)

There was nothing Lucy wouldn't do, and there was nothing Desi wouldn't pay for. These guest stars were very expensive. Once, we got the idea to use Brigitte Bardot, so Desi immediately got on the phone to her agent. It didn't work out, but he tried.

Madelyn Pugh Martin Davis

(WRITER)

Desi's cooperation gave us the feeling like there was nothing we couldn't write.

I LOVE LUCY #130: "LUCY AND THE DUMMY"

(CBS, OCTOBER 17, 1955), 30 MINUTES (B&W)

GUEST CAST: Lee Millar

Although MGM asks Ricky to perform at a studio party, he already has plans to go deep-sea fishing. Lucy accepts on his behalf, wrangling an invitation for herself as his partner. Using a plastic bust of Ricky's head obtained from the studio, she constructs a dummy of Ricky and dances with it at the party. All goes wrong, but the front office offers her a contract as a comedian.

HIGHLIGHTS & TRIVIA

Notice that the model head of Ricky looks more like Fernando Lamas than Desi Arnaz. An entire scene from this episode is missing from all subsequent rerun prints. The show came up too short, so Desi Arnaz called movie producer Samuel Goldwyn, asking for footage of his latest film to preview on the series. Neither Arnaz nor Goldwyn spoke English very clearly, but Goldwyn politely agreed to whatever Desi requested. He then dispatched his secretary to phone Desilu, to figure out what the two moguls had agreed to. Out of all of this came a clip from *Guys and Dolls* (1955) featuring Frank Sinatra, which was inserted into the TV program just before Lucy does her dance at the studio. The day after the broadcast, Sinatra was besieged by people telling him they had seen him on *I Love Lucy*. The crooner had no idea what they were talking about.

I LOVE LUCY #131: "RICKY SELLS THE CAR"

(CBS, OCTOBER 24, 1955), 30 MINUTES (B&W)
GUEST CAST: Bennett Green, Donald L. Brodie

With his movie completed, Ricky sells the car and buys the family train tickets to get home to New York, but forgets to include the Mertzes. Thinking he has forsaken them, the Mertzes buy and wreck a motorcycle trying to get back to New York on their own. Certain Ricky will make good and buy the extra train tickets, Lucy gives theirs to the Mertzes.

HIGHLIGHTS & TRIVIA

With the new sponsors, the openings of the series keep changing, depending on which product is being highlighted that week (such as Post Toasties, Sanka, Fluffo Shortening, Lilt, etc.). This installment features one of the few routines on *I Love Lucy* that goes nowhere: the bit about Fred buying pool cue tips when Lucy asked for Q-tips.

Bob Weiskopf
(WRITER)

The funny thing about this script was that when Desi had originally read it, he hated it and pulled Jess aside to complain, wondering if the new writers were any good. Jess had to explain to him that this show had been written exclusively by Bob and Madelyn, the only one they did once we came on board. That made our stock soar in Desi's eyes. They had become the senior story editors, releasing Jess to concentrate on his other producing chores. We all sat together and came up with the concepts; then Bob Schiller and I wrote the first draft alone. Bob Carroll and Madelyn then edited our draft, and returned it to us for a rewrite. Any further writing after that was done by them and Jess. This episode was rewritten into the form that got shot, but it still wasn't a very funny show.

Bob Schiller
(WRITER)

There was never any contention between the five of us writers. No one was keeping track of who wrote what. It was a collaborative effort, and we all treated it as such.

Notice in the motorcycle scene, that the sound of crashes comes *before* the cycle is actually out of sight, and that some of Fred's dialog is looped (re-recorded) and doesn't match his lip movements. The Mertzes' hotel room is different from the one we saw in episode #128: "Lucy Visits Grauman's." The name Ralph Berger (the man to whom Ricky sells his car) comes from the name of the series art director.

I LOVE LUCY #132: "THE GREAT TRAIN ROBBERY"

(CBS, OCTOBER 31, 1955), 30 MINUTES (B&W)
GUEST CAST: Frank Nelson, Kathryn Card, Lou Krugman, Harry Bartell, Joseph Crehan, Sam McDaniel, Louis A. Nicoletti, Hazel "Sunny" Boyne, Saul Gross, Hubie Kerns, Evelyn Finley, Lila Finn, Gil Perkins, Hazel Pierce, the Mayer Twins

After a mix-up with train compartments, Lucy is questioned by a detective about a possible jewel thief on board. Her imagination running wild, Lucy suspects the man (a jewelry salesman) occupying the adjoining compartment. The real thief overhears her telling Ethel about the salesman, and she is accidentally trapped into helping the thief steal the gems.

HIGHLIGHTS & TRIVIA

Notice that Lucille is the only one of the cast simulating walking on a moving train. This installment is a favorite among *Lucy* devotees, especially for the scenes with Fred and Ethel emerging from the dining car with food all over them. The original broadcast version has scenes of the Mertzes entering and being seated in the diner that are cut from all subsequent rerun versions of the episode. The train car where Lucy continually pulls the emergency break is built on springs to capture the actual movement of a train being stopped.

Jess Oppenheimer
(PRODUCER/HEAD WRITER)

We actually constructed the set, which represented the entire interior of a Pullman car, from one end to the other, and mounted it on huge springs. At the appropriate moment, a very large, coiled spring was released. Its power shot the entire set forward about four feet, literally sending the actors to their knees.

I LOVE LUCY #133: "HOMECOMING"

(CBS, NOVEMBER 7, 1955), 30 MINUTES (B&W)
GUEST CAST: Elizabeth Patterson, Elvia Allman, Eva June Mayer, Roy Schallert, Charlotte Lawrence, Barbara Pepper, Bennett Green, Hazel Pierce, the Mayer Twins

When the two couples finally arrive back in Manhattan to 623 East 68th Street, everyone treats Ricky like a big celebrity, infuriating Lucy. That is until a magazine reporter visits, and reminds Lucy how many other women would like to be Ricky's wife. Lucy becomes one of Ricky's fawning fans, until he teaches her a lesson.

HIGHLIGHTS & TRIVIA

The issue of Ricky's fame and how it might affect the other characters is an interesting theme, which is handled adroitly.

I LOVE LUCY #134: "FACE TO FACE" A.K.A "THE RICARDOS ARE INTERVIEWED"

(CBS, NOVEMBER 14, 1955), 30 MINUTES (B&W)
GUEST CAST: John Galludet, Elliot Reid, Monty Masters, Bennett Green

Ricky has a new agent, who has wrangled an appearance for the Ricardos on *Face to Face*, a television show to be shot in their apartment. The agent suggests that the Ricardos move to nicer digs, which insults the Mertzes. Then the mishaps begin, ending with both couples fighting on nationwide television.

HIGHLIGHTS & TRIVIA

This is a parody of the popular interview program *Person to Person* (1953–61) starring Edward R. Murrow. Actor Elliot Reid, as the TV host, cannot actually see the cast when he interviews them. The visuals are optically inserted later. John Galludet (the Agent) is Frawley's closest friend in real life, and will be a pallbearer at Frawley's funeral in 1966.

I LOVE LUCY: "THE BLACK WIG"

(CBS, NOVEMBER 21, 1955), 30 MINUTES (B&W)

This is a rerun of episode #92. New footage is shot where the gang comes home from a movie, and this time Lucy imagines herself to be Sadie Thompson, which leads to the flashback to the original episode. Note that these reruns with new footage do not cut anything out of the original episodes, but out of the commercial time.

I LOVE LUCY #135: "LUCY GOES TO THE RODEO"

(CBS, NOVEMBER 28, 1955), 30 MINUTES (B&W),
GUEST CAST: John Galludet, Dub Taylor, Doye O'Dell

At the same time Fred decides to stage a western show at his lodge, Ricky finds out that the radio show he thought he was booked for is actually a rodeo. Stuck for talent, he reluctantly hires Lucy and the Mertzes.

HIGHLIGHTS & TRIVIA

Notice Desi's singing of "Texas Pete." During the song, his gun belt falls off. This stops the filming, but the bit is thought to be so humorous that the song is reshot, with Desi purposely making the belt drop. Lightning does not strike twice, and what was funny and spontaneous the first time doesn't really work the second time. Actor Doye O'Dell (the rodeo M.C.) was actually the host of a local Los Angeles program with a western theme. This episode is a welcome change of pace for the series.

I LOVE LUCY #136: "NURSERY SCHOOL"

(CBS, DECEMBER 5, 1955), 30 MINUTES (B&W)
GUEST CAST: Olan Soule, Howard Hoffman, Iva Shepard, Maxine Semon, Alan Ray, Robert Brubaker, the Mayer Twins

After Lucy reluctantly agrees to send Little Ricky to nursery school, he develops tonsillitis, requiring an operation. Against hospital rules, over-protective Lucy insists on being in the hospital with him.

HIGHLIGHTS & TRIVIA

This is actually the last *I Love Lucy* episode in the original format (the Ricardos and the Mertzes in their apartments having marital tribulations) as conceived by writer/producer Jess Oppenheimer. The European shows fill up the rest of the season;

the following season (the first without Oppenheimer) will feature an older Little Ricky as part of the regular cast and the move to Connecticut.

I LOVE LUCY #137: "RICKY'S EUROPEAN BOOKING"

(CBS, DECEMBER 12, 1955), 30 MINUTES (B&W)
GUEST CAST: Harry Antrim, Barney Phillips, Dorothea Wolbert, Hazel Pierce, Louis A. Nicoletti, the Pied Pipers

When Lucy learns that Ricky has been booked on a European tour with Fred as his band manager, she is desperate to go along. Ricky says the girls can go if they pay their own way, so Lucy and Ethel concoct a scheme to raise the needed $3,000.

HIGHLIGHTS & TRIVIA

This installment begins the European story arc that will last the rest of the season. There is a not-so-subtle plug for the Arnazes' upcoming film *Forever Darling* (1956) when Ricky is shown recording the title song with the harmonizing group, the Pied Pipers. The reason for the plot line involving taking a ship to Europe is financial: Desilu has made a deal with American Export Lines. In exchange for publicizing one of its ships (the U.S.S. *Constitution*), the company pays $12,000 toward set costs, donating such items as uniforms, deck chairs, and life preservers, and provides technical assistance to the Desilu crew.

Bob Schiller
(WRITER)

There is a great deal of similarity between writing a weekly show and sexual intercourse. You are never certain that you are going to be able to get it up. There began to become a sense of, "My God, we are running out of ideas!" That's why we took the show to Europe, and later to Connecticut.

Bob Weiskopf
(WRITER)

I tend to disagree that we were concerned, because any writer of a weekly show gets concerned about what to do next week. Somehow, we always came up with something. It was easy for us to write the shows, because the characters were already established before we got there; we didn't have to create them or the way they spoke.

I LOVE LUCY #138: "PASSPORTS"

(CBS, DECEMBER 19, 1955), 30 MINUTES (B&W)
GUEST CAST: Sheila Bromley, Robert Forrest, Sam Hearn, Marco Rizo

In applying for her passport, Lucy learns that the Jamestown Hall of Records does not have her birth certificate. She seeks out affidavits from people who were present when she was born, but runs into one problem after another. Desperate to go abroad even if she has to stow away, Lucy accidentally gets locked in a steamer trunk.

HIGHLIGHTS & TRIVIA

Lucille Ball, a closet claustrophobic, has a terrible time being locked in the trunk. She suffers a panic attack during the filming. When Lucy almost faints when she gets out of the trunk, Lucille is in reality ready to pass out. Lucy Ricardo claims to have been born in 1921 in West Jamestown (a place that does not exist), some ten years after Lucille Ball was born. Notice that pianist Marco Rizo once again calls Ricky "Desi."

This entry is based in part on the *My Favorite Husband* radio episode "The Passports."

I LOVE LUCY: "LUCY'S CLUB DANCE"

(CBS, DECEMBER 26, 1955), 30 MINUTES (B&W)

This is a rerun of episode #91. New footage is shot of the Wednesday Afternoon Fine Arts League's exhausting its treasury to send Lucy bon voyage flowers. This problem leads to a reminiscence of the last time the club had to raise money, and the repeat episode.

I LOVE LUCY #139: "STATEN ISLAND FERRY"

(CBS, JANUARY 2, 1956), 30 MINUTES (B&W)
GUEST CAST: Charles Lane, Stanley Farrar

Fred admits that he gets seasick and now refuses to go to Europe, until Lucy offers to take him on the Staten Island ferry to show him that he'll have no problem if he uses seasick pills. Unfortunately, it is Lucy who falls ill, and the fistful of pills she takes make her so groggy that when she has to go for her passport, she can barely keep her eyes open.

Bob Weiskopf

(WRITER)

Bill Frawley was an unusual actor. Most actors count their lines and complain they haven't enough to do. Frawley would come over and ask us, "How many pages do I have this week?" In an episode like this one where he had a lot, he'd say, "Geez, can't you cut it down a little?" He just wanted to get out as early as possible and begin his drinking at Musso and Frank's [a well-known Hollywood restaurant still in existence].

Bob Schiller

(WRITER)

Bill [Frawley] was also a bigot, which, when you have a Cuban boss and three Jewish writers, is not a good thing to be.

I LOVE LUCY: "BABY PICTURES"

(CBS, JANUARY 9, 1956), 30 MINUTES (B&W)

This is a rerun of episode #71. New footage is shot of Lucy picking out pictures of Little Ricky to take along on the trip. That leads to a reminiscence of the first time they took baby pictures, and the repeat episode.

I LOVE LUCY #140: "BON VOYAGE"

(CBS, JANUARY 16, 1956), 30 MINUTES (B&W)

GUEST CAST: Kathryn Card, Elizabeth Patterson, the Mayer Twins, Tyler McVey, Ken Christy, Jack Albertson, Frank Gerstle, Bennett Green, Bob Carroll Jr.

After checking into their stateroom aboard ship, Lucy just has to go back down to the dock to hug Little Ricky one more time. Her skirt gets caught in a bicycle and she misses the boat. Desperate to get on board, Lucy hires a helicopter to fly out to the boat and drop her on the deck.

HIGHLIGHTS & TRIVIA

The names (Bill, Dani, and Jerry Asher) on the card for Lucy's flowers refer to the show's former director Bill Asher and his wife and child. The man Ethel talks to on the deck is writer Bob Carroll Jr. Notice veteran actor Jack Albertson in a small part as the helicopter clerk. This appearance was two decades before his success on the TV sitcom *Chico and the Man* (1974–78). While having Lucy delivered to the boat by helicopter is humorous, it is also illegal and—like so many things on *I Love Lucy*—could never have happened in real life. This episode has a special tag, featuring Lucy and Ricky on board listening to Ricky's new recording of "Forever Darling." The sequence would be dropped from later reruns of the installment.

Dann Cahn

(FILM EDITOR)

This was one of the most expensive technical things we did in the studio. We had a mock-up helicopter, process shots—even had the entire ship hull set moving. Plus all of the footage of the ship moving and the helicopter flying. It came off beautifully because we had a great crew. We used a friend of my wife's to double for Lucy in the helicopter shots. She looked just like her and copied Lucy's mannerisms. When I got the film back and showed it to Mrs. Arnaz, she couldn't believe it wasn't her.

Jess Oppenheimer

(PRODUCER/HEAD WRITER)

The scene in which Lucy was lowered from a helicopter to the deck of a ship left us breathing a sigh of relief when it came to a successful conclusion. She didn't tell us until afterwards, but early in her career Lucy had fallen in a similar situation, and broken some vertebrae in her back.

I LOVE LUCY #141: "LUCY'S SECOND HONEYMOON"

(CBS, JANUARY 23, 1956), 30 MINUTES (B&W)

GUEST CAST: Tyler McVey, Louis A. Nicoletti, Virginia Barbour, Harvey Grant, Herbert Lytton, Paula Winslow, Marco Rizo

Lucy's frustration with Ricky's busy schedule (which makes it almost impossible for him to spend any time with her) is heightened by the Mertzes' sudden preoccupation with romance. Feeling left out, Lucy schemes to keep Ricky in their stateroom for an evening of togetherness. Like most of her schemes, it backfires.

HIGHLIGHTS & TRIVIA

While this episode has its cute moments, the funniest parts are the exchanges between Fred and Ethel on their "second honeymoon." This is the second instance during the series when it is inferred that the Mertzes might actually be enjoying a sex life.

I LOVE LUCY #142: "LUCY MEETS THE QUEEN"

(CBS, JANUARY 30, 1956), 30 MINUTES (B&W)
GUEST CAST: Sam Edwards, Robert Shafter, Nancy Kulp, Betty Scott, Patti Nestor

Ricky is invited to do a command performance for the Queen of England, and learns that the only way for Lucy to meet the Monarch is for Lucy to be in the show. Sympathetically, he allows Lucy to do a dance number. Unfortunately, rehearsing her curtsey for the Queen gives Lucy a bad leg cramp, and she limps through her paces.

HIGHLIGHTS & TRIVIA

Television fans will recognize Nancy Kulp (the maid) from her stint as Miss Jane Hathaway on the hugely successful *The Beverly Hillbillies* (1962–71). The entire scene with Lucy teasing the Queen's guard will be borrowed by Ethel Merman for her 1960 special *Ethel Merman on Broadway*. Choreographer Jack Baker was a favorite of Ball's, and will work with her well into the 1970s.

THE ED SULLIVAN SHOW

(CBS, FEBRUARY 5, 1956), 60 MINUTES (B&W)
PRODUCED BY: Marlo Lewis, Ed Sullivan
DIRECTED BY: John Wray
ARNAZES' COMEDY MATERIAL BY: Bob Schiller, Bob Weiskopf
CAST: Ed Sullivan (host), the Ames Brothers, Desi Arnaz, Lucille Ball, Oscar Hammerstein II, Bill Johnson, Ricky and Velvel, Richard Rodgers, Judy Tyler, Orson Welles

The Arnazes open the show (playing themselves) with a skit featuring Sullivan and a generous clip from the Arnazes' new feature film *Forever Darling*. The skit receives little audience reaction, and the film clip bombs. After the first commercial, Desi is reintroduced, along with the Ames Brothers (who also recorded the theme from the Arnaz-Ball picture for their own label). Lucille tags along as the fifth Ames Brother, Irving, finally garnering some laughter. It is an unusual move to have competing vocalists sing the same song together. However, because Desi owns the music rights to the song, it is all money in his pocket. At the end of the music, Lucille is presented with the *Radio and TV Mirror* trophy as the best comedienne on television, as well as recognition for her work for the Heart Fund.

Bob Schiller
(WRITER)

Orson Welles was on the show as well. When Lucille and Desi were on with Ed, I saw him staring intently at her. I asked him what he was staring at, and he said, "I'm staring at the greatest actress in the world today." He had great respect for Lucille.

I LOVE LUCY #143: "THE FOX HUNT"

(CBS, FEBRUARY 6, 1956), 30 MINUTES (B&W)
GUEST CAST: Walter Kingsford, Hillary Brooke, Trevor Ward

Although Lucy wrangles an invitation to a real English manor, she is less than pleased to find that the owner is the father of a young actress who has her sights set on Ricky. When a fox hunt is arranged, Lucy proves to be a poor rider and almost breaks her neck.

HIGHLIGHTS & TRIVIA

The opening scene, with Ricky and Lucy arguing over the party they had just attended, is deleted from most syndication rerun prints. The fox hunt sequence is so close to the one Ball will do in the 1974 musical film *Mame* (including the costume) it is almost eerie. Lucy's nemesis in this episode, Hillary Brooke, made an acting career playing haughty society dames with a slightly British accent. The actress was actually born in Brooklyn. There is a tag at the end of the show with the Arnazes imploring viewers to see their new film *Forever Darling* at movie theatres.

I'VE GOT A SECRET

(CBS, FEBRUARY 9, 1956), 30 MINUTES (B&W)
EXECUTIVE PRODUCED BY: Gil Fates
PRODUCED BY: Allan Sheman
DIRECTED BY: Frank Satenstein

CAST: Garry Moore (host); Panel: Bill Cullen, Jayne Meadows, Henry Morgan, Lucille Ball
GUEST: Desi Arnaz

What could have been another in a series of triumphant television appearances is almost a disaster when Lucille appears as a panelist on this game show. Although quite humorous in her prepared comedy bit with Moore at the top of the program, once she sits down Ball seems as if she has taken stupid pills. She acts as if she is unfamiliar with the game, or perhaps has never even seen it before. Henry Morgan has to coach her on what to ask, and has to define the word "tangible" for her as she doesn't know what it means.

If this is a planned act, it falls flat. If Lucille is really this ignorant of the game, she should never attempt playing it.

Lucie Arnaz

My father never wanted my mother to appear out of the "Lucy" character on television, because he knew the audience would be disappointed.

Desi must have agreed to this one against his better judgment, because *Forever Darling* (their then-current motion picture) desperately needs plugging to boost sagging box-office receipts. It is, in fact, the only reason for the appearance. Desi comes out as the celebrity with the secret, which leads to another ridiculous moment. The panel is asked to leave the stage, whereupon Desi explains that because Lucy had always fooled him so often on their show, he is going to fool her with the secret "I love Lucy." Not only that, but the panel members (except for Lucille) are in on the gag. When Lucille asks, "Is it pink and furry?," the entire enterprise reaches a new low in taste, although Ball asks the remark in innocence.

Steve Allen

(MEDIA GENIUS/TV PIONEER)

Quite often, the secret wasn't really legit. The idea was just to get the celebrities on the show, and have some urbane banter with them. Lucy should never have been on a show like this. She was a brilliant situational comedian, but she was the first to admit she was not a great wit. That wasn't her talent. She was not an extemporaneous speaker, and both she and Desi knew that.

It was well known that *Secret* was the least honest of the panel shows, and that most of the celebrity guests had secrets written for them just to get them on the popular program. In the midst of all this, the show has on perhaps its best guest: a man who, as a small child, witnessed the assassination of Abraham Lincoln!

MGM PARADE

(ABC, FEBRUARY 10, 1956), 30 MINUTES (B&W)

EXECUTIVE PRODUCED BY: Leslie Petersen
CAST: George Murphy (host), Desi Arnaz, Lucille Ball

Mr. and Mrs. Arnaz appear on this program, which salutes the rich history of the MGM Studios and plug its current output, as well as publicize their current film, *Forever Darling*. Lucille and Desi appear in typical *I Love Lucy* costumes while Murphy interviews them; then a clip from their movie is shown. This program was MGM's first stab at television production.

I LOVE LUCY: "LUCY HAS HER EYES EXAMINED"

(CBS, FEBRUARY 13, 1956), 30 MINUTES (B&W)

This is a rerun of episode #77. Ricky once again is experiencing headaches due to his eyes, and the cast remembers the last time this happened, which leads into the rerun.

I LOVE LUCY #144: "LUCY GOES TO SCOTLAND"

(CBS, FEBRUARY 20, 1956), 30 MINUTES (B&W)

GUEST CAST: Larry Orenstein, John Gustafson, John Hynd, Robert E. Hamlin, Ann Ellen Walker, Norma Zimmer, Betty Noyes, Dick Byron, Chuck Schrouder, Betty Allen

Ricky says there just isn't any time for Lucy to visit Scotland, the home of her ancestors. That night, imaginative Lucy has a musical dream in which she visits the land of Kildoonan and all of her Scottish relatives, as well as a two-headed dragon who wants to devour her.

Larry Orenstein

(ACTOR/WRITER/LYRICIST)

Bob Schiller came to me and said they wanted to do an all musical half hour. They had the story outlined, with spots suggesting where songs might go. The writers wanted me to work with their house composer Eliot Daniel, who thankfully turned out to be a lovely, affable guy. I was assigned to do the lyrics. I sat down with the script and came up with six situations that called for songs, including one for a mayor character. I bounced my ideas off of Eliot, who liked them and then wrote the music.

I was aware that Desi had a limited range vocally; his musical talent was as a showman. Surprisingly, Lucy had more basic vocal ability than Desi did, but we didn't have time to work with her to stretch her voice. She had a theatrical gift for music, and could make a song come to life. Lucy is a wonderful example of someone who delivered the essence of the material and could cut right to the heart of the song. Bill and Vivian were hampered by being in that two-headed dragon costume and not having very long to rehearse in it. There was also the problem that they sang in different keys, and Vivian had to adjust to Bill's. The production values in this show bothered me greatly. There was not enough rehearsal for anyone musically. I was amazed at the lack of musical direction on the show. Eliot wrote some pieces of incidental music, which Wilbur Hatch arranged. Wilbur wrote other music. Marco Rizo also wrote and arranged music, but never got proper credit. And Wilbur always conducted. Yet, no one seemed in charge. They had a beat-up upright piano and drums offstage that were not properly miked. I assumed that this would provide a "scratch" track, which would later be sweetened by a full orchestra to make it work. I was horrified at the raw sound. I spoke with Eliot and Jimmy Kern, but no one seemed to have the authority to do anything.

James V. Kern

(DIRECTOR)

I told Larry that I had learned one thing as director of this show. When you are directing the man who owns the cameras, you are not really the director.

Larry Orenstein

(ACTOR/WRITER/LYRICIST)

Lucy was very good to work with and very supportive. That sword dance was mostly her working with choreographer Jack Baker. She was flexible and responsive. Desi was not too happy with me butting in about the music track. And we had a problem with the dragon's dinner song. It was written to have a light, ironic Noël Coward feeling in the verse, then some sadness in the chorus. Desi never really learned the song, and as we got to the end of the verse, he yelled, "OK, this is where the chorus comes in!" I was stunned that he had misunderstood a simple musical term, that he thought the *chorus of the song was meant to be sung by* a *chorus. I said to him, "If I had written refrain instead of chorus, would you have stopped singing altogether?" He was not amused. And the chorus ended up singing it.*

I got hooked into playing the mayor because when I auditioned the songs for everyone, Desi said, "That's great, and you're gonna play the mayor. No one's ever gonna sing that song better than you!" So I then became a part of the cast. Eliot worked with all of us to learn the songs.

I LOVE LUCY #145: "PARIS AT LAST"

(CBS, FEBRUARY 27, 1956), 30 MINUTES (B&W)

GUEST CAST: Larry Dobkin, Shep Menken, Maurice Marsac, Rolfe Sedan, Fritz Feld, Trevor Ward, Ramsey Hill, John Mylong, Vincent Padula, Hazel Pierce, Bob Carroll Jr.

On a Parisian street, Lucy is offered an exchange of francs for dollars much better than the American Express office will provide. After paying the lunch bill at a cafe, she is arrested for counterfeiting, as the money is phony.

HIGHLIGHTS & TRIVIA

Shep Menken (the painter) was already an *I Love Lucy* veteran, having made two previous appearances in character parts. Likewise for Larry Dobkin (the counterfeiter) and Maurice Marsac (the waiter). The man Lucy toasts at the cafe is writer Bob Carroll Jr. The highlight of this installment is the translation scene in the Parisian police station, from French to German to Spanish to English. The writers obviously have disdain for Paris, depicting its citizens as con artists, counterfeiters, and snobs. The episode ends with a filmed tag by the Arnazes plugging the Heart Fund.

I LOVE LUCY #146: "LUCY MEETS CHARLES BOYER"

(CBS, MARCH 5, 1956), 30 MINUTES (B&W)

GUEST CAST: Charles Boyer, Jack Chefe

Ricky encounters movie matinee idol Charles Boyer, who is lunching at the same cafe as the Ricardos and the Mertzes. Warning him of all the trouble Lucy causes when she meets film stars, he advises Boyer to deny that he *is* Boyer, to keep Lucy away. The plan backfires when Lucy, who thinks Ricky is jealous of Boyer, hires Boyer, who she believes is someone else, to play Boyer and cure Ricky of his jealousy.

HIGHLIGHTS & TRIVIA

Although the plot line calls for the foursome to be in Europe for only three weeks, dialog in this installment reveals that they will be overseas much longer than anticipated. Boyer does the series to promote his own TV show, *Four Star Playhouse* (1952–56); the episode was originally written with Maurice Chevalier in mind. Boyer was very vain about his clothing. He wouldn't wear Desilu-provided wardrobe and he wouldn't allow his *own* clothing to be ruined. Disappearing ink had to be used for his shirt, and the overcoat he ripped belonged to Desi Arnaz. Although the prop department goes to great lengths to obtain a copy of the Parisian *Herald Tribune* for Boyer to read, the wine on Lucy's table is California's *Paul Masson*. This episode will be rewritten and used in 1964 for *The Lucy Show*, with Ethel Merman taking Boyer's part.

I LOVE LUCY: "CHANGING THE BOYS' WARDROBE"

(CBS, MARCH 12, 1956), 30 MINUTES (B&W)

This is a rerun of episode #76. New footage is shot in which Ricky wants to dress casually because he has to wear a dinner jacket every night. This leads to a reminiscence of the last time the boys didn't want to get dressed up, and into the repeat segment.

THE EIGHTH ANNUAL EMMY AWARDS

(NBC, MARCH 17, 1956), 90 MINUTES (B&W)

PRODUCED BY: William Kayden, Herb Braverman
DIRECTED BY: William Bennington, Richard Schneider
WRITTEN BY: Hal Goldman, Larry Klein, Glen Wheaton
HOSTS: Art Linkletter, John Daly
PRESENTERS: Bob Cummings, Jimmy Durante, George Gobel, Phil Silvers, Sam Levenson, Hal March

Lucille Ball wins the award for Best Actress in a Continuing Performance. It is her first televised win, and the last time she will win an Emmy until 1967.

I LOVE LUCY #147: "LUCY GETS A PARIS GOWN"

(CBS, MARCH 19, 1956), 30 MINUTES (B&W)
GUEST CAST: John Bleifer

Lucy wants an original Paris gown, and (with Ethel's assistance) goes on a phony hunger strike to get one. Ricky and Fred learn of the deception, and present the ladies with gifts of ludicrously phony gowns.

HIGHLIGHTS & TRIVIA

Notice the supposed "French" creations by designer Edward Stephenson; toned down versions of the styles will become popular in the 1960s and will be worn by Lucille Ball.

I LOVE LUCY #148: "LUCY IN THE SWISS ALPS"

(CBS, MARCH 26, 1956), 30 MINUTES (B&W)
GUEST CAST: Torben Meyer

After Fred mistakenly routes the band to the wrong city, Lucy suggests a mountain climb to get Ricky's mind off the problem. The Ricardos and the Mertzes make it up the mountain, but get stuck in a cabin during an avalanche.

HIGHLIGHTS & TRIVIA

Although the local band Fred finds is of German extraction, the city (Lucerne) they are in is in *the French*-speaking part of Switzerland. These European-set shows are very expensive to produce, as each episode requires fresh sets, special effects, new costumes, and several extras.

I LOVE LUCY: "TOO MANY CROOKS"

(CBS, APRIL 2, 1956), 30 MINUTES (B&W)

This is a rerun of episode #75. New footage is shot of Lucy in Switzerland not being able to find her wedding rings and thinking they have been stolen. This leads to a reminiscence of her jumping to conclusions about a theft in the past, and into the repeat installment.

I LOVE LUCY #149: "LUCY GETS HOMESICK"

(CBS, APRIL 9, 1956), 30 MINUTES (B&W)
GUEST CAST: Vincent Padula, Bart Bradley [Braverman], Ida Smeraldo, Kathryn Card, Kathleen Mozalo, the Mayer Twins

The Ricardos and the Mertzes arrive in Florence on the day of Little Ricky's birthday. Sentimental Lucy not only wants to telephone her son, but wants to have a party for him in absentia.

HIGHLIGHTS & TRIVIA
The child actor who plays the Italian shoeshine boy grows up to be Bart Braverman, an actor familiar to TV audiences of the late 1970s and the 1980s. These are the last appearances of Kathryn Card and the Mayer Twins on *I Love Lucy*. The boys retire from show business, and Card will play Mrs. McGillicuddy one more time in 1959 on *The Lucille Ball-Desi Arnaz Show* #12: "Lucy Goes to Japan."

I LOVE LUCY #150: "LUCY'S ITALIAN MOVIE"

(CBS, APRIL 16, 1956), 30 MINUTES (B&W)
GUEST CAST: Franco Corsaro, Saverio Lo Medico, Teresa Tirelli, Ernesto Molinari, Rosa Barbato

When an Italian movie producer tells Lucy he wants her in his new film, *Grapola Pungente*, Lucy takes the translation, "bitter grapes" literally. She soaks up local color at a nearby vineyard.

HIGHLIGHTS & TRIVIA
This installment contains probably the third most favorite comedy bit Ball did on *I Love Lucy*, after Vitameatavegamin (episode #30) and the chocolate factory (episode #36).

Bob Schiller
(WRITER)
The grape vat scene was shot in one long take. It was even musically scored that way. It was a command decision from Jess to cut it in half and insert the hotel scene in between. Originally, the script had called for Lucy to drop an earring into the vat. While she was stumbling to look for it, the other woman was supposed to push her. But they felt that the earring was too small to be seen."

Bob Weiskopf
(WRITER)
Lucille pretty much performed the scene the way it was in the script, which was pages of black stuff, just direction. She added wonderful little touches, little nuances of her own that really added to the physical comedy. This was my favorite episode.

Irma Kusely
(HAIRSTYLIST)
For the scene where she has to appear purple from the grapes, we used a water-based lilac coloring. Lucille's skin was very sensitive, and I was concerned about what to use on her hair because we were already perming and coloring it.

Lucille Ball
We did not rehearse with the grapes, and I didn't know what to expect. Stepping on those grapes was like stepping on eyeballs. That woman in the vat with me [Teresa Tirelli] didn't understand what was going on, and she took the fight seriously. All the action was supposed to take place from the waist up so the camera could see it. Instead, she took me down and held my head under the squashed grape juice. She was like a wrestler. I almost drowned!"

The local grape industry happily supplies the needed fruit, with the proviso that somewhere in the script a mention is made that wine is no longer made by grape stomping. The crew took home all the extra fruit; otherwise it would have spoiled and soured over the weekend.

I LOVE LUCY #151: "LUCY'S BICYCLE TRIP"

(CBS, APRIL 23, 1956), 30 MINUTES (B&W)
GUEST CAST: Mario Siletti, Francis Ravel, Felix Romano, Henry dar Boggia

Stubborn Lucy insists the two couples travel by bicycle from Italy to the French Riviera. A misunderstanding about the location of her passport almost keeps Lucy a prisoner in Italy.

HIGHLIGHTS & TRIVIA

This is the weakest of all the European episodes. It is unthinkable that Fred and Ethel (let alone the Ricardos) can ride thirty-five miles on a bicycle. The plot device of Lucy losing her passport over and over becomes annoying rather than humorous. Honey was used on Lucille's face to get the goat to lick her in the barn scene.

Lucille Ball

It really is too bad you couldn't see it on television, but I really got that cow to squirt milk! I made a big stream in the air, but I don't think the lights caught it properly. I had to practice to get the milking just right. And you haven't lived until you've milked a cow with your bare hands!

Madelyn Pugh Martin Davis

(WRITER)

That was the mangiest cow I have ever seen. I went down on the set and Lucy said, "You wrote it; you *milk it!"*

I LOVE LUCY: "THE GOLF GAME"

(CBS, APRIL 30, 1956), 30 MINUTES (B&W)

This is a rerun of episode #96. New footage is shot of Ricky and Fred in Nice swinging golf clubs, and Lucy complaining she didn't come to Europe to be a golf widow. That dialog leads into the rerun.

I LOVE LUCY #152: "LUCY GOES TO MONTE CARLO"

(CBS, MAY 7, 1956), 30 MINUTES (B&W)

GUEST CAST: John Mylong, Gordon Clark, Jacques Villon, Louis A. Nicoletti, Bob Carroll Jr.

While the two couples are in Monte Carlo, Ricky forbids Lucy to go into the casino. Disobeying her husband, the Redhead ends up winning a fortune and must hide the loot from Ricky.

HIGHLIGHTS & TRIVIA

This is another tepid episode. It is illogical that Lucy would think Ricky would be angry because she wins a great deal of money. The man in the fez at the casino is Lucy scribe Bob Carroll Jr. Notice Vivian Vance's costumes. The actress had been insisting on more flattering oncamera wardrobe, and is now allowed to wear fancier gowns, furs, and jewelry when the plot calls for it.

I LOVE LUCY #153: "RETURN HOME FROM EUROPE"

(CBS, MAY 14, 1956), 30 MINUTES (B&W)

GUEST CAST: Mary Jane Croft, Mildred Law, Frank Nelson, Ray Kellogg, Bennett Green

Lucy insists on bringing her mother in New York a huge hunk of Italian cheese, even though the Ricardos are already over limits with the weight of their airline luggage. Thinking that infants travel on airplanes free, Lucy disguises the cheese as a baby. When she learns that she must also pay for a baby, Lucy hides the cheese.

HIGHLIGHTS & TRIVIA

This is the last episode Jess Oppenheimer produces. He leaves the series to become an executive at NBC.

Bob Carroll Jr.

(WRITER)

I got the cheese idea when I was coming back from Europe and this little Italian man had this huge twenty pound wheel of cheese. The customs official chopped it into bits thinking he was smuggling jewels.

Dann Cahn

(FILM EDITOR)

After this show was filmed, Lucy and Desi gave a going away party for Jess at their home in Beverly Hills. Jess handed out little award statues he called "Oppies" to the cast, Bob and Madelyn, me, Karl Freund, and a few other people. I walked out with Desi and Jess to Jess' car, and Desi said, "Please stay Jess and make it work." But Jess could not bend to Desi being the total boss. After this, the show changed. Jess had a spark that was missed. A lot of the flavor of the show came from Jess Oppenheimer.

Mary Jane Croft

(ACTOR)

It was not fun and games on the set. Lucy took her work very *seriously. I had a hard time keeping a straight face, sitting next to her in the airplane set. When she took a swig of the baby formula, I had to look away. I really loved doing this episode.*

Frank Nelson and Mary Jane Croft will return next season (1956–57) to play the ongoing characters of Ralph and Betty Ramsey in the Connecticut episodes.

I LOVE LUCY: "FAN MAGAZINE INTERVIEW"

(CBS, MAY 21, 1956), 30 MINUTES (B&W)

This is a rerun of episode #83.

I LOVE LUCY: "SENTIMENTAL ANNIVERSARY"

(CBS, MAY 28, 1956), 30 MINUTES (B&W)

This is a rerun of episode #82.

I LOVE LUCY: "EQUAL RIGHTS"

(CBS, JUNE 4, 1956), 30 MINUTES (B&W)

This is a rerun of episode #70.

I LOVE LUCY: "BONUS BUCKS"

(CBS, JUNE 11, 1956), 30 MINUTES (B&W)

This is a rerun of episode #87.

I LOVE LUCY: "TENNESSEE ERNIE VISITS"

(CBS, JUNE 18, 1956), 30 MINUTES (B&W)

This is a rerun of episode #94.

THE ED SULLIVAN SHOW

(CBS, JUNE 24, 1956), 60 MINUTES (B&W)

PRODUCED BY: Marlo Lewis, Ed Sullivan
DIRECTED BY: John Wray
CAST: Ed Sullivan (host), Abbott and Costello, Eddie Albert, Pier Angeli, Louis Armstrong, Desi Arnaz, Lucille Ball, Harry Belafonte, Ernest Borgnine, Marlon Brando, Teresa Brewer, Red Buttons, Eddie Cantor, Marge and Gower Champion, Jeanne Crain, John Daly, Walt Disney, Howard Duff, Jinx Falkenberg, Ruth Gordon, Susan Hayward, Tab Hunter, Klauson's Bears, Burt Lancaster, Sam Levenson, Margo, James Mason, Virginia Mayo, Tex McCrary, Margaret Meade, Ethel Merman, Michael O'Shea, Jack Paar, Gregory Peck, Walter Pidgeon, Ronald Reagan, Phil Silvers and the cast from his TV show, Red Skelton, Kate Smith, Robert Stack, Robert Wagner, Richard Widmark, Shelley Winters, Natalie Wood

The reason for this star-studded telecast is twofold. First, it is in celebration of Ed's eighth anniversary on his weekly television show; second, it is meant to knock off the competition, the debut of Steve Allen's variety hour on NBC. Allen's lineup includes Kim Novak, the Will Mastin Trio featuring Sammy Davis Jr., Wally Cox, Dane Clark, Vincent Price, and Bambi Lynn and Rod Alexander. Allen's excellent show will run for four years against Sullivan, but in the end Ed will prevail. Lucille and Desi host a remote segment from Hollywood, featuring a bevy of stars who do nothing more than wish Ed a happy anniversary.

I LOVE LUCY: "TENNESSEE ERNIE HANGS ON"

(CBS, JUNE 25, 1956), 30 MINUTES (B&W)

This is a rerun of episode #95. This entry has a tag at the end, with the Arnazes saying goodbye to the audience until the fall.

Chapter Eight

1956–57 Season

I LOVE LUCY: THE SIXTH SEASON

TECHNICAL REGULARS: Produced by Desi Arnaz; directed by James V. Kern, William Asher (all episodes after #168: "Lucy Wants to Move to the Country"); written by Madelyn Martin (Madelyn Pugh had married Quinn Martin over the summer), Bob Carroll Jr., Bob Schiller, Bob Weiskopf; makeup by Hal King; hairstyling by Irma Kusely; music by Wilbur Hatch
CAST REGULARS: Lucille Ball (Lucy Ricardo); Desi Arnaz (Ricky Ricardo); Vivian Vance (Ethel Mertz); William Frawley (Fred Mertz); Keith Thibodeaux a.k.a. Richard Keith (Little Ricky); Roy Rowan (announcer)

THE ED SULLIVAN SHOW

(CBS, SEPTEMBER 30, 1956), 60 MINUTES (B&W)
PRODUCED BY: Marlo Lewis, Ed Sullivan
DIRECTED BY: John Wray
CAST: Ed Sullivan (host), Lucille Ball, Desi Arnaz, Vivian Vance, William Frawley, Gizelle McKenzie, Dick Shawn, Joyce Grenfell, the Swedish Glen Club, Rollano and Lily Yokov, Sal Maglic, Yogi Berra, the Milwaukee Braves, Dr. Albert Jorgensen and the Stockholm Gosskor, President Dwight D. Eisenhower

The *Lucy* cast appears in a live remote pickup from Hollywood in a sketch written for them by Bob Schiller and Bob Weiskopf. Desi mentions *I Love Lucy* going to New Orleans, as well as featuring guests Jack Benny and Maurice Chevalier; none of this ever takes place.

Bob Weiskopf
(WRITER)
We wrote a very funny skit for this show. Lucy overhears Desi trying to call Ed Sullivan long distance. He asks the operator to place the call to Ed, person to person. Lucy thinks Desi is calling Ed Murrow on the television show, Person to Person. *When they get on television, Lucy thinks she's going to meet Murrow, and gets disappointed with Sullivan. "You're not Edward R. Murrow," she cried.*

I LOVE LUCY #154: LUCY AND BOB HOPE

(CBS, OCTOBER 1, 1956), 30 MINUTES (B&W)
GUEST CAST: Bob Hope, Lou Krugman, Peter Leeds, Dick Elliot, Maxine Semon, Henry Kulke, Ralph Sanford, Bennett Green

Ricky buys a controlling interest in the Tropicana club and renames it the Club Babalu. Bob Hope has agreed to perform at the opening, but Ricky keeps that information from Lucy so she will not interfere. Lucy, fearing Hope won't do the club show because of her bad reputation with celebrities, seeks him out at Yankee Stadium to convince him to do the show.

HIGHLIGHTS & TRIVIA
This is the first *I Love Lucy* episode not produced by Jess Oppenheimer. Desi hurts his back rehearsing this show and requires medical attention. As a result, the filming is postponed from its usual Thursday evening to the following Tuesday night. Even so, Desi is very stiff physically in the finale due to the pain from his injury. Bob Hope reads his lines off cue cards, the first time they are used on this series. Robert de Grasse replaces Karl Freund as director of photography, as Freund returns to feature films. It takes de Grasse several episodes to become acclimated, but finally he gets up to

speed. Beginning with this installment, there are new final graphics incorporated with the sponsor's logo. When *I Love Lucy* is sold to CBS for daytime reruns, new graphics are made to replace these. It is on these CBS-made graphics that Desi Arnaz' name is misspelled "Dezi" one of the times it appears. It is not that way on the original broadcasts. Keith's first moments on the sitcom as Little Ricky in the first scene earns a hand from the studio audience. This scene is cut from most syndication rerun prints.

Keith Thibodeaux
(ACTOR/MUSICIAN)
In the beginning, it was my Dad who gave me my line readings. It is he that you see me looking off stage at in many of the early shows. Later, Desi and Lucy usually gave me direction. Of all the shows I did, I felt I was the cutest in this episode. I didn't have the tension and strain I had in other episodes.

Larry Orenstein
(ACTOR/WRITER/LYRICIST)
They came to me and said they needed a baseball song to wrap up the show, but left it wide open. The writers were very good about not boxing you in. I had envisioned the song as a kind of a "Take Me Out to the Ballgame." The part where Lucy searches for her note was added by her writers; it was not a part of the song as written. There was also a lot more to the song that they didn't do.

Irma Kusely
(HAIRSTYLIST)
When we started this season, I had a big fight with Desi that I wanted my name in the episode credits. Otherwise, all this work was a big waste of energy. I wanted to do it for those who came after me. Hairdressers had never been credited on television before. Lucille also began wearing her hair longer at this time. She fancied that she looked more feminine in bedroom scenes if it could hang a little looser. I also think she was trying to look younger for Desi away from the set.

Dann Cahn
(FILM EDITOR)
All the time that Jess was with the show, he was responsible for the final cut and look of the show. He was a great producer. For the first five years, Desi never got into that stuff. Lucy might ask why her close-up wasn't longer or that sort of thing, but Jess was the man in charge. Now, Desi began to do these things instead. Desi knew what he was doing, but he wasn't as professional as Jess was. There were a lot of clashes in personality that weren't there with Jess. And at the same time, Desi began to build his empire, so his focus wasn't just on I Love Lucy.

I LOVE LUCY #155: "LITTLE RICKY LEARNS TO PLAY THE DRUMS"

(CBS, OCTOBER 8, 1956), 30 MINUTES (B&W)
GUEST CAST: Elizabeth Patterson

Little Ricky exhibits talent for percussion, and starts drumming incessantly night and day. The Ricardos and the Mertzes feud over the noise until they find Little Ricky missing.

HIGHLIGHTS & TRIVIA

This is a very funny installment; it has been a long time since the show had a good Ricardos vs. the Mertzes fight. Notice in the bathroom scene that although Lucy has taken off her false eyelashes to wash her face, when she emerges into the living room they have magically reappeared. This was necessary to accommodate the sequence, and is often done in TV shows. Although this episode is aired first (and comes first in the story line), "Little Ricky Gets Stage Fright" (episode #157) was filmed earlier. This is Elizabeth Patterson's final appearance as Mathilda Trumbull.

Keith Thibodeaux
(ACTOR/MUSICIAN)
In the beginning, I think my line readings were terrible. But I was only a little guy, and my father wasn't helping things any by directing me. Desi Arnaz was a great guy, and he began to coach me a little. I think as long as Desi was in the picture, my best interests were (for the most part) being looked after. Although I don't think that getting no billing at all, as Richard Keith or as Keith Thibodeaux, was in my best interest. All the other kids on shows got billing, except me.

I LOVE LUCY #156: "LUCY MEETS ORSON WELLES"

(CBS, OCTOBER 15, 1956), 30 MINUTES (B&W)
GUEST CAST: Orson Welles, Ellen Corby, Lou Krugman, Ray Kellogg, Jack Rice, Fred Aldrich, Hazel Pierce, Bennett Green

Ricky agrees to send Lucy to Florida to keep her away from the legendary Orson Welles, who has agreed to do a benefit at the club doing magic and wants Lucy as his magician's assistant. The Redhead runs into Welles at Macy's department store and learns of the deception. She okays assisting Orson, but is convinced he will really be performing Shakespeare and plans to do some of her own.

HIGHLIGHTS & TRIVIA

This episode, more than any other, reflects the transition the series is going through without the talents of Jess Oppenheimer and Karl Freund. As a result, many shots have to be redone after the studio audience departs and some of the comedy pacing is off. These technical problems will smooth out as everyone adjusts. Although it is uncertain if this is done intentionally, the characters of Lucy and Ricky seem to age a few years since the end of the previous season. Lucy is no longer the wide-eyed young housewife and is instead a married woman and mother bordering on middle age. Ricky (and Desi) has gained weight, and has a much more mature look about him. This series is now about two middle-aged couples and a growing child. While the difference is subtle, it adds an extra dimension to the performances. TV fans will recognize Ellen Corby as Grandma in the long-running *The Waltons* (1972–81).

Bob Schiller

(WRITER)

Orson Welles surprised me. He began supposedly quoting Shakespeare while Lucy was levitated, but it wasn't the way Shakespeare wrote it and nobody knew the difference.

Dann Cahn

(FILM EDITOR)

This was one of my favorite episodes for personal reasons. I worked with Orson when I was in my early twenties, and I had come a long way in ten years. Orson's scene with Lucy in the club was hysterical. That show led to our doing one of the greatest things ever made for television, The Fountain of Youth. *Here's a piece of trivia. There was an extra scene filmed with Bill and Vivian in Shakespearean costumes, but we had to cut it out completely because the show ran too long.*

THE BOB HOPE CHEVY SHOW

(NBC, OCTOBER 18, 1956), 60 MINUTES (B&W)

PRODUCED BY: Jack Hope
DIRECTED BY: Jack Shea
WRITTEN BY: John Rapp and Lester White, Mort Lachman and Bill Larkin, Charles Lee
CAST: Bob Hope (host), Desi Arnaz, Lucille Ball, James Cagney, Diana Dors, William Frawley, the Hollywood Deb-Stars, Don Larsen, Vivian Vance

This is the first NBC-TV appearance by the Arnazes, who are reciprocating with Hope for his prior stint on *I Love Lucy*. Their contribution is a skit set in the Ricardos' New York apartment, with Bob Hope playing Ricky, Desi Arnaz playing Fred, and Bill Frawley portraying a tenant. Things go immediately awry, when the seal with which Lucille is working refuses to cooperate and holds up the main action for almost a minute. The set is almost an exact duplicate of the original, down to the furniture and knickknacks, with the addition of two extra closets needed to assist the plot line. Lucille gets a chance to repeat her "seal" bit from the "Professor" sketch (this time the musical instrument is called a gramazouzaxylophonovitch), and Hope reprises some jokes stolen from his appearance on *I Love Lucy*. While the skit is funny, especially the insider remarks poking fun at the character switches, there is no motivation behind the humor. It is never an easy matter to write an *I Love Lucy* script, a truth future writers will come to learn the hard way.

Bob Schiller

(WRITER)

Lucille and Desi were very disappointed in this show. Jack Benny used to have the same problem. Whenever he'd guest on someone else's show, all they would write for him were jokes about being miserly. Hope's writers wrote this as their perception of an I Love Lucy *show. They didn't know how to write for the characters. The day after the Hope show, we [the writers] were summoned onto the set and sat down in the bleachers. Then, the Arnazes entered with the entire studio—literally, over 100 people—for "Writers Appreciation Day." They said they never realized how well we did our jobs. Jess had taught Desi to appreciate writers.*

I LOVE LUCY #157: "LITTLE RICKY GETS STAGE FRIGHT"

(CBS, OCTOBER 22, 1956), 30 MINUTES (B&W)

GUEST CAST: Howard McNear, Marjorie Bennett, Laurie Blaine, Diana Van Fossen, Jeffrey Woodruff, Larry Gleason, Robert Norman, Buddy Noble, Earl Robie

Little Ricky gets stage fright at a music school recital, and refuses to play the drums again due to the humiliation. Big Ricky invites the music students to all play at the Club Babalu, hoping to cure his son of his fears.

HIGHLIGHTS & TRIVIA

The scene between Ricky and his son in the bedroom is more reminiscent of *Father Knows Best* (1954–61) than this series. Although it is well written and performed, it doesn't really fit the format.

Keith Thibodeaux

(ACTOR/MUSICIAN)

Most of the time, I totally understood the humor of the situation. Rarely did I have to have something explained to me. This episode was an easy one for me.

Bob Weiskopf

(WRITER)

I guess Jess had spies on the set reporting back to him. Now our first few shows without him were a little rocky, but by the time we did this one, it was smooth sailing. He calls me one day and says, "I hear things aren't going very well on the set." I told him that if he had wanted to see the show sink without him, he left three seasons too late. By now the show was running under its own power.

I LOVE LUCY #158: "VISITOR FROM ITALY"

(CBS, OCTOBER 29, 1956), 30 MINUTES (B&W)

GUEST CAST: Jay Novello, Eduardo Ciannelli, James Flavin, Aldo Formica, Peter Brocco, Louis A. Nicoletti

Gondolier Mario Orsatti arrives on the Ricardos' doorstep unannounced, accepting a misunderstood invitation received when they were all in Venice. Mario is seeking his brother, who has left a note that leads Lucy to believe he has gone to San Francisco. Lucy schemes to get Mario the needed money for the trip, but disaster follows.

HIGHLIGHTS & TRIVIA

Jay Novello makes his third appearance on a *Lucy* show, this time as Mario, the gondolier. Notice the way this episode shows pizza being made, with the dough being pushed through a machine to flatten it. While this is common in Los Angeles pizza restaurants of the era, it would never be found in a real New York pizzeria. When Lucille throws the pizza dough over her head, she finds she has to suck out an air hole in the dough immediately because she has trouble breathing.

I LOVE LUCY #159: "OFF TO FLORIDA"

(CBS, NOVEMBER 12, 1956), 30 MINUTES (B&W)

GUEST CAST: Elsa Lanchester, Strother Martin

Lucy loses her train tickets to Florida, so she and Ethel spend the little bit of money they have by sharing a car ride south with a very peculiar woman whom they become convinced is an axe murderer.

HIGHLIGHTS & TRIVIA

Although mention was made of Lucy going to Florida in episode #156 ("Lucy Meets Orson Welles"), she never actually went. Three weeks later, Ricky now has a booking that sends them all there anyway. This is a great installment, aided by an excellent guest cast playing characters rather than themselves. Lanchester is an old family friend, and Martin will one day be known for his dramatic screen roles.

I LOVE LUCY #160: "DEEP SEA FISHING"

(CBS, NOVEMBER 19, 1956), 30 MINUTES (B&W)

GUEST CAST: James Hayward, Billy McLean

To pay for expensive new clothes, Lucy and Ethel bet Ricky and Fred that they can catch a bigger fish on their next fishing excursion. Both the boys and the girls decide to win the bet unfairly by buying a huge tuna and claiming to have caught it.

HIGHLIGHTS & TRIVIA

The oversized fish used in this episode are real. They were purchased at Fisherman's Wharf in San Francisco, and then flown down to Hollywood in children's-sized coffins packed with ice.

Dann Cahn

(FILM EDITOR)

I went down and scouted locations in Miami Beach. I stayed at the Eden Roc Hotel. That establishing shot, with the sign on the beach [Eden Roc Hotel], that sign was made by me just for that shot.

I LOVE LUCY #161: "DESERT ISLAND"

(CBS, NOVEMBER 26, 1956), 30 MINUTES (B&W)

GUEST CAST: Claude Akins, Joi Lansing, Jil Jarmyn

When Ricky is asked to appear in a film documentary on Miami Beach, Lucy and Ethel get jealous of the bathing beauties with whom the boys spend time. To ensure that the boys are unavailable to judge a beauty contest, the girls arrange a boat excursion guaranteed to run out of gas. The quintet end up marooned on a desert island.

HIGHLIGHTS & TRIVIA

Notice that Lucille is beginning to have trouble pushing her voice up into Lucy's girlish soprano. A throatiness becomes evident in this episode that will continue for the rest of her career, deepening every season. There is a controversy over the possible origins of this throat problem that will be discussed later in this book.

Keith Thibodeaux

(ACTOR/MUSICIAN)

Claude Akins [playing himself in this installment] was really a nice guy, but I remember he had really *bad breath. The long shots with us in the water were all done by stand-ins. The rest of it was done on fairly expensive sets on the lot. I also remember watching the chemistry between Joi Lansing and Desi, and Lucy's reaction. Even at my age, I knew this couldn't be good.*

Dann Cahn

(FILM EDITOR)

We did a lot of rear projection work on this episode, which was not filmed in front of a live audience. Lucy and Desi gave a party on that island set after the show was filmed. They had a luau.

I LOVE LUCY #162: "THE RICARDOS VISIT CUBA"

(CBS, DECEMBER 3, 1956), 30 MINUTES (B&W)

GUEST CAST: Mary Emory, George Trevino, Nacho Galindo, Angelo Didio, Barbara Logan, Eddie LeBaron, Lillian Molieri, Rodolfo Hoyos Jr., Manuel Paris, Amapola Del Vando, Abel Franco

The Ricardos and the Mertzes fly from Florida to Havana for a Ricardo family reunion and for Ricky to appear at the Hotel Nacionale. Lucy makes a complete fool of herself in front of Uncle Alberto (George Trevino), the Ricardo family patriarch. She only makes things worse when she tries to make amends to him.

HIGHLIGHTS & TRIVIA

Lucille is brilliant in the tobacco shop scene; her timing is impeccable. At this point in her TV career, she is able to do her physical comedy as well as she ever could. What has changed is the smoothness with which the script writers are able to motivate and incorporate comedy segments into the episode plot lines. Mary Emory repeats her role as Ricky's mother.

Keith Thibodeaux

(ACTOR/MUSICIAN)

I worked really hard trying to get "Babalu" perfectly. I couldn't really get those little [dance] kicks Desi did right. And if you see the show, I didn't get the part where I am supposed to look up correctly. I did it too early; I didn't wait for the crescendo of the number the way Desi did it. Also the song was not in my key, and I was squeaking to follow along on the singing. I was truly embarrassed after we finished that number and Lucy kissed me. But then again, I always felt embarrassed in those clinches. I was very shy, and couldn't understand why I was getting all that attention.

I LOVE LUCY #163: "LITTLE RICKY'S SCHOOL PAGEANT"

(CBS, DECEMBER 17, 1956), 30 MINUTES (B&W)

GUEST CAST: Candy Rogers Schoenberger

Little Ricky gets the lead in the P.T.A. show, *The Enchanted Forest.* Lucy, Ricky, Fred, and Ethel all have parts in the production, which is a good thing because Little Ricky can't remember all of his lines.

HIGHLIGHTS & TRIVIA

If Little Ricky is in kindergarten (his first year in school), how does Lucy know who appeared in the pageant the year before? A great deal of *The Enchanted Forest* is refilmed after the audience leaves because of all the children and technical aspects involved. Pepito Perez, in association with Joanne Dancing Academies, provides the staging, choreography, and settings for the children's show.

I LOVE LUCY #164: "THE I LOVE LUCY CHRISTMAS SHOW"

(CBS, DECEMBER 24, 1956), 30 MINUTES (B&W)

PRODUCED BY: Jess Oppenheimer, Desi Arnaz
DIRECTED BY: William Asher, James V. Kern
WRITTEN BY: Jess Oppenheimer, Madelyn Martin, Bob Carroll Jr., Bob Schiller, Bob Weiskopf
GUEST CAST: Cameron Grant

Trimming the holiday tree on Christmas Eve brings back happy memories for the Ricardos and the Mertzes of the events leading up to Little Ricky's birth. Christmas morning, Little Ricky delights in opening his presents, while the adults all dress up like Santa Claus to surprise him.

HIGHLIGHTS & TRIVIA

This is the *first ever* retrospective episode for a sitcom, a common practice with TV series today. Included are flashback scenes of Lucy telling Ricky she is pregnant (episode #45), the barbershop quartet (episode #47), and the cast taking Lucy to the hospital to have Little Ricky (episode #51). The last scene, with five Santa Clauses, is a rewritten version of the one that appeared in the holiday installments during the first three seasons of the series (with Cameron Grant replacing Vernon Dent as St. Nick). Contrary to what has been reported elsewhere, this is *not* originally a special; it is just another episode of the series. The new scenes are all filmed in one day without a studio audience present. This episode will be repeated twice by CBS after Lucille Ball's death as a special, both in black and white and in a colorized version (see Chapter Forty-Two: Loose Change).

Lucille Ball

This episode wasn't sold into syndication with the rest of the shows, because CBS thought no one would want to see a Christmas show at the wrong time of the year. Who knew? There is something eerie and spooky about this show. I don't know what it is, but it makes me a little nervous and I do not enjoy watching it.

I LOVE LUCY #165: "LUCY AND THE LOVING CUP"

(CBS, JANUARY 7, 1957), 30 MINUTES (B&W)

GUEST CAST: Johnny Longdon, Hazel Longdon, Robert Foulk, Jesslyn Fax, Byron Kane, Lester Dorr, Phil Tead, Sandra Gould, Florence Ann Shawn, William L. Erwin

Ricky is to present jockey Johnny Longdon with a trophy for being the most successful jockey in history. Lucy buys a new hat for the occasion, which Ricky loathes so much that he claims she'd look better with the trophy on her head. Lucy tries it on for spite and finds that she cannot get it off.

HIGHLIGHTS & TRIVIA

Notice that Ethel is still insisting to be married twenty-five years, several years after first claiming the same matrimonial time span. This episode is a "feeler" for Desi Arnaz, an inveterate horse racing fan who optioned the screen rights to Longdon's life story earlier in the year. However, the motion picture biography is never made.

There are actually tiny holes in the decorative flowering of the metallic loving cup so claustrophobic Lucille can see where she is going and not feel ill at ease. Great care is taken by the crew so the subway has the proper signs for an east-side Manhattan train headed toward Brooklyn. This is the last time we see the Club Babalu/Tropicana set on the series. Ball and Arnaz, who have not appeared in any of the final segment commercials during the 1955–56 season, do the end-of-show Lilt commercial in this entry.

I LOVE LUCY #166: "LUCY AND SUPERMAN"

(CBS, JANUARY 14, 1957), 30 MINUTES (B&W)

GUEST CAST: George Reeves, Doris Singleton, Madge Blake, George O'Hanlon, Ralph Dumke, Steven Kay

When Lucy and Caroline Appleby clash over the same date to hold their respective sons' birthday parties, Lucy promises to get television's Superman to make an appearance. Caroline begrudgingly relents, but Lucy finds out the actor isn't available. Naturally, she decides to play Superman herself and almost gets herself killed . . . until the real Superman saves her.

HIGHLIGHTS & TRIVIA

This is Doris Singleton's final appearance as Caroline Appleby, who to be noted, has a new apartment and furniture. Notice that the sheer curtains have been removed from the Ricardos' living room window to create easier access to the ledge (which has changed since episode #100: "Lucy Cries Wolf"). Madge Blake, who plays the prospective tenant, is best known for her work as Aunt Harriet on TV's *Batman* (1966–68). Lucille and Desi do the final commercial for Sanka, cleverly parodying the ad campaign that has been used previously on the series.

Bob Schiller

(WRITER)

In those days, we had agents pitching guest stars to us. One guy offered George Reeves. We thought it might be a good idea, so we took a couple of weeks to come up with a premise and then gave the go-ahead.

Si Simonson

(SPECIAL EFFECTS MAN ON TV'S THE ADVENTURES OF SUPERMAN

George wouldn't go without me, so Jimmy Kern and I worked out all the details between us. His entrance through the pass-through was pretty standard stuff . . . George [Reeves] just held onto a bar and swung himself in. They imported special casters for the piano so he could move it as if he had super-strength. Although [the Lucy *episode] carried a copyright credit for the Superman character, strangely George didn't get any billing for playing the part.*

Keith Thibodeaux

(ACTOR/MUSICIAN)

Although I don't think this was my best performance, this was my favorite episode. Like everyone else at that time, I grew up watching Superman on television. I really thought George [Reeves] was *Superman, and was thrilled when he picked me up and asked me if I wanted to go flying with him.*

Lucie Arnaz

I think the reason George didn't get credit is that kids believed in Superman, and Mom and Dad honored that. I know that for Desi, Keith, and I, that week, it was like Superman was really there on the set.

I LOVE LUCY #167: "LITTLE RICKY GETS A DOG"

(CBS, JANUARY 21, 1957), 30 MINUTES (B&W)

GUEST CAST: John Emery, June Foray

Little Ricky brings home a puppy, adding to the already crowded Ricardo menagerie. When a new tenant threatens to move out because his lease calls for no pets in the building, Lucy is forced to hide the canine.

HIGHLIGHTS & TRIVIA

This is the last aired episode directed by James V. Kern. June Foray, the queen of female voice-over artists, gets hoarse providing the voice of the yelping puppy, which has to be done live to match the dog's actions. Notice the Ricardos' bedroom. Where there used to be a window next to Ricky's bed, there is now a wall lamp. Desilu has changed filming locations, and somebody is "asleep at the switch" when they rebuild the set. John Emery is a *Lucy* veteran from the first season, when he played the bum in episode #5: "The Quiz Show." In an unusual move, Desi appears in the end commercial *without* Lucille.

Keith Thibodeaux

(ACTOR/MUSICIAN)

I fell in love with that little dog. I was too young to understand that he was a trained, professional dog. When I wanted to take him home with me, it had to be explained to me that he belonged to the trainer. When Lucy, a real dog lover, heard me complaining, she admonished my father to get me one of my own.

I LOVE LUCY #168: "LUCY WANTS TO MOVE TO THE COUNTRY"

(CBS, JANUARY 28, 1957)

GUEST CAST: Frank Wilcox, Eleanor Audley

While visiting the Munsons in Connecticut, Lucy falls in love with an Early American house for sale and wants to move there. While Ethel's tearful reactions convince Lucy she cannot move, Ricky has already bought the house as an anniversary present. Now Lucy has to convince the owners to return the deposit.

HIGHLIGHTS & TRIVIA

It is decided to relocate the Ricardos to the country to provide fresh plot avenues. The move is handled gradually over several episodes, to make a graceful transition and to milk the story potential. Most sitcoms today would toss off a move in less than ten minutes, but the writers were wise enough to anchor their comedy in recognizable reality. The scene in the Connecticut house, with Lucy and the Mertzes pretending to be criminals, is hysterical, but very tiring for the cast. Try holding your hands up as long as they do. It hurts. William Asher returns as director, and handles those chores for the rest of the season. The Arnazes once again do the closing commercial, and will do so for the remainder of the TV year.

Bob Weiskopf

(WRITER)

The idea for the Ricardos moving to Westport, Connecticut, came from my own time living there.

Bob Schiller

(WRITER)

As writers, we were concerned with the eventual layout of the Connecticut set. It was huge compared to the apartment. There was a tremendous crossover from the front door to the main part of the set. So we suggested putting in the Dutch door by the dining room to give the house an extra entrance.

I LOVE LUCY #169: "LUCY HATES TO LEAVE"

(CBS, FEBRUARY 4, 1957), 30 MINUTES (B&W)

Guest Cast: Gene Reynolds, Mary Ellen Kaye

Fred rents the Ricardos' apartment to newlyweds, who also agree to buy all of the Ricardos' furniture. All the Ricardos have to do is move out a couple of days early and stay with the Mertzes. All is well, until sentimental Lucy buys back all of her old furniture piece by piece.

HIGHLIGHTS & TRIVIA

Notice that the wall lamp by Ricky's bed has now been replaced by a framed painting. Gene Reynolds (a former child actor), who plays the young married man, will become one of TV's busiest directors. Many of the old times Lucy and Ethel reminisce about actually happened in the Ricardos' former apartment upstairs during the first two seasons (1951–53) of the show.

I LOVE LUCY #170: "LUCY MISSES THE MERTZES"

(CBS, FEBRUARY 11, 1957), 30 MINUTES (B&W)

GUEST CAST: Tristam Coffin, Jesse Kirkpatrick, Robert Bice, Gary Gray

The Ricardos have moved to Westport, and immediately pine for the Mertzes who are back in New York feeling the same way about the Ricardos. Both couples decide to surprise the other with a visit. Bad timing and miscommunication lead the Ricardos home to Connecticut, where they think they have burglars—the Mertzes!

HIGHLIGHTS & TRIVIA

The opening scene, with the Ricardos and the Mertzes saying goodbye, shows what wonderful actors the cast are, able to make viewers both laugh and cry. Notice the Ricardos' new bedroom set, complete with fireplace. We won't see it again until 1958 ("Lucy Makes Room for Danny," hour-long episode #7), when the fireplace will have mysteriously disappeared. Fred takes a bite of an apple out of the fruit basket, but when the Ricardos notice and a closeup is shown (filmed and inserted later), it is an orange.

I LOVE LUCY #171: "LUCY GETS CHUMMY WITH THE NEIGHBORS"

(CBS, FEBRUARY 18, 1957), 30 MINUTES (B&W)

GUEST CAST: Mary Jane Croft, Frank Nelson, Parley Baer, Ray Ferrell

Lucy becomes friendly with next-door neighbors Ralph and Betty Ramsey. Betty recommends Lucy to a furniture dealer offering a huge discount. Embarrassed to admit that she can only afford to spend $500, Lucy ends up by buying a houseful of expensive new stuff.

HIGHLIGHTS & TRIVIA

This is the last of the new furniture plots. Although the decor shown at the end of the episode will change with the next outing, the style will remain the same. Desi Arnaz came up with the idea for using two couches back-to-back in the living room. This installment introduces neighbors Ralph (Frank Nelson) and Betty (Mary Jane Croft) Ramsey. Although Betty will be seen quite often, Ralph is featured in only one more episode. Vivian Vance films a Schaeffer pen commercial as Ethel on the Mertzes' set this week, although it will not be seen on *I Love Lucy*.

Bob Weiskopf

(WRITER)

The Ramseys were introduced because my own neighbors in Westport had been Ralph and Betty Ramsey.

Keith Thibodeaux

(ACTOR/MUSICIAN)

The scene where Bruce Ramsey [Ray Ferrell] and I have a fight was one of the times when Desi took me aside and explained what he wanted. I pretty much knew about half of what was expected before I got to the studio, but he filled in the rest. There wasn't huge amounts of rehearsal for me because of my age.

Mary Jane Croft

(ACTOR)

I didn't see Desi very much during the week. He had a huge business to run. He'd run on the set, rehearse his lines, and then he'd be off running somewhere else. Frank Nelson was an absolute joy. I worked with him a lot in radio. I always seemed to play his wife. He was funny and fun, and very quiet actually. Frank was a fabulous talent.

I LOVE LUCY #172: "LUCY RAISES CHICKENS"

(CBS, MARCH 4, 1957), 30 MINUTES (B&W)

GUEST CAST: Mary Jane Croft, Mary Alan Hokenson, Tyler McVey

The cost of living in the country is much higher than the Ricardos expected, so Lucy suggests they raise chickens for profit. The plan sounds even better when the Mertzes offer to move into the guest house and go into business with them. The project falls apart when Lucy finds her house full of baby chicks.

HIGHLIGHTS & TRIVIA

This episode begins with Desi stepping out from behind a curtain, explaining that he has agreed to preview the newest Ford car. A two-minute commercial follows the announcement, with Lucille and Desi discussing on the phone the Ford's new retractable hardtop. The plot device of raising chickens is necessary to get the Mertzes to Connecticut and continue the well-established next-door neighbor format on the series. If you observe carefully in the new house set, you can see the washer and dryer partially visible behind the door leading from the dining room into the kitchen. Yet, in the kitchen set there is another washer and dryer revealed behind the door leading to the back porch. Notice when Little Ricky enters the living room from outside. A man's arm can plainly be seen opening the door and pushing him in.

Irma Kusely

(HAIRSTYLIST)

For a few of the Connecticut episodes, we experimented with not doing Lucille's hair so formally and just pinning it up, perhaps like a woman living in the country would. She liked it quite a bit, but the sponsors didn't, and after a few episodes, we went back to the old way.

Madelyn Pugh Martin Davis

(WRITER)

When Lucy and Desi lived in Chatsworth [in the San Fernando Valley, north of Los Angeles], they raised chickens. They were the oldest chickens in the world, because [Lucy] didn't have the heart to kill them. One day, Lucy got up and did her impression of her old chickens. We remembered it, and used it in this episode.

I LOVE LUCY #173: "LUCY DOES THE TANGO"

(CBS, MARCH 11, 1957), 30 MINUTES (B&W)

GUEST CAST: Ray Ferrell

The Ricardos and the Mertzes trade in their baby chicks for full-grown chickens, hoping for immediate profits. However, the hens don't lay eggs, and Ricky threatens to quit the chicken business, which would force the Mertzes back to New York. Lucy and Ethel start sneaking store-bought eggs concealed on their bodies out to the hen house. Just then, Ricky announces he wants to rehearse a tango with Lucy for the P.T.A. show.

HIGHLIGHTS & TRIVIA

The bit with the eggs at the end of the episode is the longest laugh Lucille ever earns in her television career and has to be cut back in the aired version. Ball and Vance never rehearse with the raw eggs until the actual filming, so their reactions can be genuine. Notice the Mertzes' furnishings in the guest house. Ethel must have convinced cheap Fred into buying brand new items, because none of the Mertzes' old stuff is there.

Bob Schiller
(WRITER)

No matter what we wrote for the scene with the eggs, Lucille did it better than we could have imagined it. That bit with the eggs dripping down her leg was not in the script.

Bob Weiskopf
(WRITER)

And that bit where Frawley opens the door and hits Viv in the ass, cracking the eggs, was the topper. And [director] Bill Asher thought this whole thing wouldn't work.

Bob Schiller
(WRITER)

I was never sure if Bill [Asher] meant the part with Viv, or the whole [egg] thing. When Bill came back to the show, he thought he was replacing Jess [Oppenheimer] and not just Jimmy Kern. Bill got into more things than a director normally would. In later years, he denied ever having doubted that the [egg] scene would work. It must have been embarrassing to him as a director not to have had faith in the show's biggest laugh.

THE NINTH ANNUAL EMMY AWARDS

(NBC, MARCH 16, 1957), 90 MINUTES (B&W)
EXECUTIVE PRODUCED BY: William Kayden
PRODUCED BY: Elliott Lewis
DIRECTED BY: William Bennington
CONTINUITY BY: Carrol Carrol
MUSIC BY: Gordon Jenkins

Sponsored by RCA Whirlpool, and Oldsmobile, the annual awards dinner show is broadcast live from Desilu Studios. Even the credits are done in the syndicated *I Love Lucy* style. Roy Rowan, long time announcer for the Arnazes, does the same chores for this show.

Desi is one of the hosts for the program. Dressed in tails and trying to look sophisticated, the Cuban does not do well this night. Having had too much to drink, Desi sweats profusely, constantly wiping his face with a handkerchief. This is the only time in his career where his drinking interferes with a television performance. Usually Arnaz, despite personal problems, was completely professional. However, this evening his manner is forced and overdone. When his jokes, written by Bob Schiller and Bob Weiskopf, receive little audience response, he simply gives an embarrassed laugh and mops his brow some more. He can't stand still, and the cameras must follow him all over the stage. His accent is even thicker than it is on *I Love Lucy*, which makes it even more difficult to understand what he is saying.

Danny Thomas saves the evening by giving Desi the kind of salute that rarely occurs while he is alive. "We were fortunate to have Desi as a boss for the [*Make Room for*] *Daddy* [1953] pilot. He laughed so hard on the soundtrack that we sold the pilot in forty-eight hours," offered Thomas. Lucille sits with Vivian, Bill Asher, and actor Bob Cummings. Although nominated, along with Edie Adams, Gracie Allen, and Ann Sothern for best comedienne, Ball loses her Emmy bid to Nanette Fabray (*Caesar's Hour*, 1954–57).

I LOVE LUCY #174: "RAGTIME BAND"

(CBS, MARCH 18, 1957), 30 MINUTES (B&W)

Once again, Lucy offers Ricky's services as a performer for a charity event without asking him first. After all her efforts to convince him to do it fail, she uses Little Ricky and the Mertzes to form their own band. Their rehearsals are such a disaster, that Ricky takes pity and performs with the group.

HIGHLIGHTS & TRIVIA

Notice that when Ricky gets home, the grandfather clock on the Ricardos' living room set still shows noon; someone forgot to reset it. Lucy claims she can only play "Sweet Sue" on the saxophone, while previous episodes have established "Glow Worm" as her masterpiece. Ethel seems to have musical amnesia as well, as she has always been able to play piano and read music in previous installments. This time around she only knows how to play "She'll Be Coming 'Round the Mountain." These details fall through the cracks because series scribes Schiller and Weiskopf don't know the full history of the *I Love Lucy* show, and Martin and Carroll don't make the necessary corrections.

Keith Thibodeaux

(ACTOR/MUSICIAN)

We had surprisingly little musical rehearsal for the scene where the group is supposed to sound bad. I just did what I normally did, and [Lucy, Bill, and Viv] just messed up on purpose. We had it worked out in less than twenty minutes. For the calypso number, Desi's percussionist taught me some new licks [on the bongos] and it came pretty easily.

I LOVE LUCY #175: "LUCY'S NIGHT IN TOWN"

(CBS, MARCH 25, 1957), 30 MINUTES (B&W)

GUEST CAST: Joseph Kearns, Gladys Hurlbut, Doris Packer, John Eldredge, Louis A. Nicoletti, Jody Warner, Roy Lazarus, Susan Johnson, John Henson, Alan J. Gilbert, Shorty Lang, Art Lund, Paul Power

Lucy orders four tickets to the Broadway hit musical, *The Most Happy Fella*. At dinner in New York, Lucy realizes her tickets were for the matinee. Ricky manages to get two more tickets for the evening performance, but the Ricardos and the Mertzes sharing two seats leads to disaster.

HIGHLIGHTS & TRIVIA

Desilu Music is a major backer for the Broadway musical *The Most Happy Fella*, featured in this episode, which had opened the previous year and would run for 676 performances. Fred claims to be carrying $500 after collecting the monthly rents for the apartment building (which he still owns). There are at least nine apartments in the building, so Fred is either charging fifty dollars per month, or many tenants are late with the rent. Joseph Kearns had last appeared on this series in episode #27: "The Kleptomaniac."

I LOVE LUCY #176: "HOUSEWARMING"

(CBS, APRIL 1, 1957), 30 MINUTES (B&W)

GUEST CAST: Mary Jane Croft, Ray Ferrell

Ethel feels left out of Lucy's new friendship with Betty Ramsey, so Lucy arranges a luncheon to make pals of her two friends. Realizing that their families knew one another in Albuquerque, Ethel and Betty warm up to one another. Now Lucy feels left out, until she thinks the girls are planning a surprise housewarming for her and Ricky.

HIGHLIGHTS & TRIVIA

The installation of an at-home intercom system in this entry is a clever plot device, and will be used in future episodes as well. There is a great deal of chemistry between Lucille, Vivian, and Mary Jane. It is a shame *I Love Lucy* will end before those possibilities are more fully explored.

Bob Schiller

(WRITER)

When we were rehearsing the show, Vivian came up with the ad lib, "I've had sufficient!" At the time, I complimented her on her creativity. She never corrected me. It wasn't until I met [the author of this book] that I found out she was stealing a line Bob and Madelyn had written for her in the first season.

Mary Jane Croft

(ACTOR)

It was so much fun sitting at that dining room table doing the luncheon scene with those two actresses. They gave you so much to play with.

I LOVE LUCY #177: "BUILDING A BAR-B-QUE"

(CBS, APRIL 8, 1957), 30 MINUTES (B&W)

Lucy wants Ricky to build a backyard brick barbeque while he is on vacation. He puts it off, so she and Ethel pretend to start the project to get Ricky and Fred motivated. Unfortunately, Lucy loses her wedding ring in the process.

HIGHLIGHTS & TRIVIA

Viewers should note the bathrobe Ethel wears in the night scene. Twelve years later, Ann-Margret will wear that same terrycloth robe when she guests on *Here's Lucy*.

I LOVE LUCY #178: "COUNTRY CLUB DANCE"

(CBS, APRIL 22, 1957), 30 MINUTES (B&W)

GUEST CAST: Barbara Eden, Mary Jane Croft, Frank Nelson, Tristam Coffin, Ruth Brady

The Munsons' sexpot houseguest has Ricky, Fred, and Ralph giddy with testosterone. Lucy, Ethel, and Betty fight fire with fire and glamorize themselves for a country club dance.

HIGHLIGHTS & TRIVIA

This installment is a reworking of episode #81: "The Charm School." It is the only time an *I Love Lucy* script is recycled to produce another one. Ralph Ramsey appears here for the second and last time. Barbara Eden, as young Diana, is making her sitcom debut here; she is twenty-two. The exposure will lead to her own syndicated sitcom, *How to Marry a Millionaire* (1957–59) and later *I Dream of Jeannie* (1965–70). Notice Ethel's hairstyle in the second act; that is how Vance actually wore it in real life at the time. While Lucille still has the figure and beauty to pull off the glamour look, the one thing she (and Desi) can no longer fake is the youth. Eden is a full generation younger than the rest of the cast.

Mary Jane Croft

(ACTOR)

Lucy could hardly move in that blue taffeta dress. She would literally have to crawl around because it was so tight.

I LOVE LUCY #179: "LUCY RAISES TULIPS"

(CBS, APRIL 29, 1957), 30 MINUTES (B&W)

GUEST CAST: Mary Jane Croft, Peter Brocco, Eleanor Audley

Lucy and Betty are rivals in a gardening contest, with both gardens featuring tulips. Lucy accidentally mows through Betty's flower bed, and replaces her destroyed tulips with wax ones. Ricky has a similar accident, and now both gardeners have wax blooms.

HIGHLIGHTS & TRIVIA

Notice Lucy's scene on the runaway lawn mower. The film is speeded up and the sound is overdubbed to give the impression that she is moving much faster than she is. Lucille makes the second of her "entrances after danger" in this episode. This shtick, entering all messed up and shaken after an unseen physical stunt, is a late addition to Lucille's repertoire of physical bits, and will follow her well into *Here's Lucy* (1968–74) after other trademarks have been discarded.

I LOVE LUCY #180: "THE RICARDOS DEDICATE A STATUE"

(CBS, MAY 6, 1957), 30 MINUTES (B&W)

GUEST CAST: Desi Arnaz Jr.

Lucy is in charge of the festivities for Westport's "Yankee Doodle Day," which includes the unveiling of a commemorative minuteman statue. When Little Ricky's dog runs away and Lucy hops in the car to go after him, she destroys the statue. Guess who takes its place?

HIGHLIGHTS & TRIVIA

This is the last episode of *I Love Lucy*. Three months later, Desilu will begin filming the first of the hour-long shows based on this format. The name of the statue maker, Silvestri, is the actual name of the company that makes the minuteman statue used in this installment. Desi Arnaz Jr. is featured in the last scene, standing in front of Vivian Vance. The girl with him is not Lucie Arnaz, as has been reported elsewhere. This is Desi Jr.'s *only* appearance on *I Love Lucy*.

Bob Schiller

(WRITER)

This episode was terrible, just dreadful. It was never really planned that this was going to be the last season of half hour shows. But Desi began to take on so much responsibility with all these other shows he was

producing that he needed more time. He just didn't have the time to play Ricky Ricardo every week.

Desi Arnaz Jr.

I have a vague memory of doing this show. We were always there [on the set] anyway, and being with Mom and Dad just seemed natural.

Keith Thibodeaux

(ACTOR/MUSICIAN)

As a surprise to me, I was given my own new dressing room during the filming of the show. I still had the clown makeup on from the first scene when Lucy and Desi took me to see it. I was just thrilled. It made me feel like I belonged.

I LOVE LUCY

(CBS, SEPTEMBER 1957—SEPTEMBER 1959),
30 MINUTES (B&W)

With the show no longer in weekly production, CBS purchases the rights to the show from Desilu Studios and reruns them in prime time for two seasons. New graphics are made to reflect the new weekly sponsors. After this prime-time run, the show moves to CBS daytime, where it will be rerun until 1967 and then go into syndication and cable . . . forever. The show will not air in June of 1958.

Chapter Nine

1957–58 Season

THE LUCILLE BALL-DESI ARNAZ SHOW: THE SEVENTH SEASON OF THE I LOVE LUCY FORMAT

TECHNICAL REGULARS: Executive produced by Desi Arnaz; produced by Bert Granet; directed by Jerry Thorpe; written by Madelyn Martin, Bob Carroll Jr., Bob Schiller, Bob Weiskopf; makeup by Hal King; hairstyling by Irma Kusely; music by Wilbur Hatch

CAST REGULARS: Lucille Ball (Lucy Ricardo); Desi Arnaz (Ricky Ricardo); Vivian Vance (Ethel Mertz);William Frawley (Fred Mertz); Keith Thibodeaux (Little Ricky); Roy Rowan (announcer)

THE FORD LUCILLE BALL-DESI ARNAZ SHOW #1: "LUCY TAKES A CRUISE TO HAVANA"

(CBS, NOVEMBER 6, 1957), 75 MINUTES (B&W)

GUEST CAST: Ann Sothern, Rudy Vallee, Cesar Romero, Hedda Hopper, Frank Nelson, George Trevino, Nestor Paiva, Joaquin del Rio, Vincent Padula, Louis A. Nicoletti, Barrie Chase

Movie columnist Hedda Hopper interviews the Ricardos and the Mertzes in Connecticut. The two couples reminisce about how Lucy and Ricky first met. It seems that Lucy McGillicuddy and her friend Suzy McNamara were on a cruise to Havana, as were Fred and Ethel Mertz (who were celebrating their tenth wedding anniversary). Also aboard is radio star Rudy Vallee. In Cuba, Lucy was fixed up with Ricky Ricardo, and the two fell in love. When at a café, Lucy tried to convince Vallee to hire Ricky and take him to New York; her aggressiveness started a riot. Lucy and Suzy ended up drunk and in jail, and almost missed their boat.

HIGHLIGHTS & TRIVIA

When the Arnazes decided to call it quits after six hugely successful seasons of *I Love Lucy*, they planned to continue the format in hour-long specials on the CBS network. The Ford Motor Company agreed to finance five of them for the 1957–58 season, although Desi had originally wanted to produce twelve shows. The show is *not* titled *The Lucy-Desi Comedy Hour;* that name will be used for summertime network (and syndicated) repeats of these hour shows. A new cartoon opening, as well as a modernized arrangement of the *I Love Lucy* show theme, are created, as no expense is spared on this first outing. The cast is huge, the production numbers sumptuous, and the plot full of entertaining twists and turns. In fact, Desi Arnaz decides it can't be done justice in only sixty minutes. *The U.S. Steel Hour* (1953–63) is the program that is scheduled to follow this one, and it is not doing well in the ratings. Desi contacts the sponsor, and asks to "borrow" fifteen minutes out of the program's schedule for that evening. He guarantees that if U.S. Steel puts on a forty-five minute show that evening, preceded by the Ball-Arnaz hour, it will receive its highest ratings ever. He is right, and Desi puts on the only show in CBS history that is scheduled to run for seventy-five minutes.

"Lucy Takes a Cruise to Havana" does spectacularly well in the ratings, but is not a creative success. Overproduced and poorly paced, it suffers from a lack of involvement by Vivian Vance and Bill Frawley. There is little chemistry between stuffy Rudy Vallee and anybody else. This is the first comedy episode to have crossover characters from another TV sitcom; in this case Ann Sothern as Suzie McNamara from her successful series *Private Secretary* (1953–57). Cesar Romero is charming as

Ricky's pal Carlos, but his interplay with Ann Sothern is not convincing. Note that the Mertzes are celebrating their tenth anniversary *second* honeymoon, not their honeymoon as has been reported elsewhere. This plot line places the Mertz wedding in 1930, contradicting all previous mentions of the length of their marriage. Barrie Chase, Fred Astaire's dancing partner in three upcoming television specials, is a chorus girl in the opening number. The Arnazes do the closing Ford commercial.

Maury Thompson
(CAMERA COORDINATOR)
If the show seemed over-produced, or not quite on the mark, remember we weren't quite sure what we were doing. The long format was new to all of us, including the writers. We learned as we went along. It took time to analyze the format.

Bert Granet
(PRODUCER)
I had worked with Lucille when she was a young starlet at RKO [in the 1930s]. I wrote a few comedy pictures for her. And then I had no contact with Lucy for years. In the meantime, picture work had become scarce for me, so I started working in television. I worked for Loretta Young, producing her program and the anthology series that replaced her when she became ill. Then my agent took me to Desilu. I had never met Desi Arnaz before. He put me on Those Whiting Girls, *and then on a Walter Winchell pilot. After that, he put my office right next to his and put me on these [Lucy-Desi] shows. The biggest contribution I made to the shows was to do nothing. Everything was set long before I got there. I'm not even certain why Desi felt he needed another producer on these shows besides himself, except he was so busy running the studio as well. Eventually, I began to handle a lot of that, too. I think I was an appealing personality for Desi because I didn't have a big ego and was not concerned with my own publicity. We worked very well together. This first one was an hour and fifteen minutes, which was unheard of. No one had done that before.*

Bob Schiller
(WRITER)
The hour shows were much tougher to write. First of all, we lost the week to week continuity of both plotting and having the actors in character. Secondly, the shorter shows usually built on one large comedy scene, where these shows had to have two or three to sustain the humor. These shows were never as successful as the shorter ones, despite larger budgets and longer rehearsal time.

Bob Weiskopf
(WRITER)
Rudy Vallee was a pain in the ass.

Dann Cahn
(FILM EDITOR)
I went down to Havana and shot second unit stuff for this episode. We were there a week before [Fidel] Castro took over the city. I used doubles in the carriage scenes. The rest of the show was done in front of an audience. Jerry Thorpe had been the assistant director on The Long, Long Trailer *(1954). He was a very intelligent man. Desi brought him in on the television show as the first assistant director, then associate producer on* Forever Darling *(1956). He became a director on the sitcom* December Bride *(1954–61). Jerry stayed on with the studio after Desi left (1962) to help run it, but he stopped directing the shows after two seasons. He and Lucy ended badly; they did not part amicably.*

Madelyn Pugh Martin Davis
(WRITER)
In this episode, Lucy was wearing a white pleated skirt and flat shoes. While she certainly wasn't fat, I didn't think it flattered her. I told Desi, and he just turned around and said, "Honey, Madelyn thinks that you look fat in that outfit." I never went through him *again!*

Bob Weiskopf
(WRITER)
Whenever you criticized her wardrobe, Lucille's stock answer was, "Well, that's all I've got!" Like she couldn't afford anything else.

THE FORD LUCILLE BALL-DESI ARNAZ SHOW #2: "THE CELEBRITY NEXT DOOR"

(CBS, DECEMBER 3, 1957), 60 MINUTES (B&W)

GUEST CAST: Tallulah Bankhead, Elvia Allman, Richard Deacon, Phyllis Kennedy

As with the last special, the show has a cold opening with Desi coming out from behind a curtain.

He thanks the viewing audience at home for their terrific response to the first show, and then Lucille interrupts him for a word about the sponsor (Ford). Then the animated opening begins: "Ford, and your Ford dealers, bring you the *new* Lucille Ball-Desi Arnaz Show. . . ."

The actual episode starts with Lucy and Ethel looking through binoculars at the new neighbor moving in next door, Tallulah Bankhead, who soon comes to the Ricardos' front door to ask to use the phone. Lucy embarrasses herself in front of the stage and film star, and then invites her for dinner. With Fred and Ethel pretending to be her butler and maid, the evening is a disaster. Later, Winslow, Bankhead's new butler, borrows the Ricardos' paint sprayer. Lucy shows Winslow how to use it, and in the process splatters paint all over Bankhead as she enters the garage. Lucy goes by Tallulah's the next day to apologize, and is caught in a recently painted chair. Lucy insists that Bankhead got her paint wet on purpose, and the war is on.

HIGHLIGHTS & TRIVIA

This is one of the great episodes. It is also one of the most infamous. The installment was originally conceived for Bette Davis, but she begged off due to ill health. The Arnazes have great trouble with Tallulah on the set, and wish they could have waited for Davis. Bankhead is drunk during most of the extended two-week rehearsal period, which greatly angers Ball, a stickler for professional rehearsals. Lucille and Desi are so nervous about Tallulah's condition, they are afraid Bankhead won't make it through the filming. She fools them all, and turns in such a bravura comedic performance that Lucille flubs her lines and a scene has to be reshot. Vivian steals the show playing Ethel Mae, the maid. Her timing and delivery are so sharp that three times the studio audience breaks into spontaneous applause.

Bob Schiller
(WRITER)

We later found out that this was something Tallulah liked to do, especially if there was another major actress involved. She would purposely act up during rehearsals to throw the other woman off-balance, then be letter-perfect for the actual show.

Tallulah Bankhead
(ACTOR)

I've got not even one picayune derogatory thing to say about those wonderful people. Of course, I did *have pneumonia at the time. And someone nearly blinded me one day at rehearsals with hairspray. But Lucy? She's* divine *to work with! And Desi? He's brilliant. He has a temper, however. But that's because* he's *fat. It worries him. . . . I broke a tooth. I broke the cap they put on the tooth. I broke my nails. I had pneumonia.*

Irma Kusely
(HAIRSTYLIST)

Tallulah was either so drunk or stoned during the rehearsal process that we were dreading the shooting night. I thought I was going to be there all night, never getting home. Yet, as soon as she appeared in front of the audience, everything went like clockwork. It was amazing. And that was Tallulah's own hair, not a wig. I didn't [have to work with her], thank goodness, but it was hers.

Bob Schiller
(WRITER)

Tallulah was drunk the entire time. She would remove her panties for no reason. She kept calling Vivian "Cunty." At one script conference in her bungalow at the Beverly Hills Hotel, she was an hour late. She then breezed into the room, saying, "Hello, Dahling! I've just gotten over triple pneumonia!" Triple pneumonia—in all three *lungs. She was full of herself.*

Lucille Ball

We babied Tallulah to make sure she'd make it. Desi and I drove her home to our house, made sure she ate something and got bathed. Then we took her back to her hotel. This went on every day. Finally we got to the show day, and it struck me. I thought to myself, "I don't know what the hell I am doing!" I learned something from that, and never allowed myself to get that distracted again. I don't like watching this episode. It reminds me how I allowed Bankhead to mop up the floor with us.

Bert Granet
(PRODUCER)

At night, we would all meet back in Desi's office [on the studio lot] to discuss the day's work. Everybody, that is, but Tallulah. We didn't want her. She had borrowed a sweater from Lucy, and used that as an excuse to crash the meeting. She comes in, "Lucy, dahling, I wanted to return your sweater." She took it off and threw it at Lucy. Whereupon Vivian piped up, "If you ever decide to throw your pants away, I'll take 'em." Tallulah dropped her pants and gave them to Vivian. Of course, she was wearing nothing underneath them. Everyone got hysterical, except poor Madelyn, ever the lady, who got so embarrassed she didn't know where to hide.

This is also a show of firsts, lasts, and trivia. It is the last time Lucille appears in her trademark bun hairstyle. It is the last mention of neighbor Betty Ramsey. It is the first time the new dining room furniture is used in the Ricardos' living room set (with no explanation). In the dinner scene, Lucy wears the same dress that she wore in episode #82 "Sentimental Anniversary." Ethel mentions she and Fred have been married for twenty-eight years, yet in the previous special their wedding year is established as 1930. Ethel says she saw *Lifeboat* (1944) in her home town of Albuquerque, New Mexico, but Ethel had already been married to Fred for fourteen years in 1944, the year the Alfred Hitchcock movie was released. In the play (*The Queen's Lament*) within the episode, Ethel serves a mandarin orange sauce. Mandarin, in medieval times? Finally, Tallulah's kitchen door has an opening, but no window glass, for the cord from the blind clearly swings back and forth through it.

THE FORD LUCILLE BALL-DESI ARNAZ SHOW #3: "LUCY HUNTS URANIUM"

(CBS, JANUARY 3, 1958), 60 MINUTES (B&W)

GUEST CAST: Fred MacMurray, June Haver, Charles Lane, Maxine Semon, Bobby Jellison, Norman Leavitt, William Fawcett, Paul Powers, Richard King, Rick Warrick, Louis A. Nicoletti

The Ricardos and the Mertzes go to Las Vegas, where Ricky is booked to entertain at the Sands Hotel. Lucy wants to hunt for uranium while in the desert, much against Ricky's wishes. On the train across country they meet movie star Fred MacMurray, who also is scheduled to stay in the same Las Vegas hotel. Later, MacMurray is concerned about telling his wife, actress June Haver, that he has lost money gambling, because she is very frugal. (In real life, MacMurray was a hugely rich tightwad.) Fred Mertz has bought Little Ricky a gag newspaper with a phony headline, so Lucy gets the idea to make one of her own touting the idea of uranium hunting. The paper is found and misunderstood, causing a rush into the desert by everyone to be the first to find the lucrative radioactive rocks.

HIGHLIGHTS & TRIVIA

Beginning with this episode, Lucille wears new, short, red wigs (she actually wears four different ones). There is only a brief mention of her new hairstyle in the first scene, and never will it be mentioned that she is not wearing her own hair. She has, however, begun to gain weight while Vivian has begun losing it. Inactivity, middle age, and stress will continue to add extra pounds on Lucille for the rest of the 1950s. There is zero oncamera chemistry between Ball and MacMurray, who only have one scene alone together. Bobby Jellison, who played Bobby the Bellboy on the California episodes of *I Love Lucy* during the 1954–55 season, once again plays a bellboy. MacMurray's real-life wife, June Haver, plays herself. During the desert location shoot, done in the Mojave desert, the crew has a problem maneuvering one of the cars to come to a skidding stop in the needed manner. Frustrated by the time and money wasted, Desi gets in the car and does the stunt himself—perfectly. Although he receives crew applause for his effort, it is soon discovered there is no film in the camera. Arnaz blows his top while the cast gets hysterical. Tennessee Ernie Ford did the commercials for Ford, except for the last one featuring the Arnazes.

Irma Kusely

(HAIRSTYLIST)

That "bun" hairstyle was Lucille's idea. Neither Bert French nor I ever liked it. I kept asking Lucille to let me cut it and give her a more modern look. She resisted, because Desi liked long hair. Finally, I proposed the idea of her using a wig, just to see what it would look like. I bleached the hair all around her hairline so none of it would show through, and ordered a stylish, short wig. From this point forward (with a couple of exceptions), every time you saw Lucille Ball in public, she was wearing a wig ordered and styled by me. The wigs gave me an opportunity to bandage her skull and help smooth out the wrinkles. I made little braids in special places, then pin curls with the rest of her hair. Then I had a hose stocking cap I used, covered by a skull bandage. I made it very tight, making both her head and face a smooth surface. Then I put the wig on, made an eighth of an inch shorter than her own hair, matching her own hair line. Eventually, Lucille cut her own hair as well. Although the process could sometimes be painful, I made it as comfortable for her as possible. After awhile, she hardly knew the difference.

Lucille Ball

I didn't like the "clamps" at first. I felt like I couldn't move my face, and that it hampered my comedy. But there was no denying how much better I looked on film. Irma was right.

Bert Granet

(PRODUCER)

This show was an experiment that never was totally successful. There is a big difference between shooting a show in front of a live audience like a stage play, and shooting a movie comedy. Totally different techniques are used. This show tried to do a little of both, and succeeded at neither. Jerry Thorpe wasn't experienced enough as a movie comedy director to make it work. And Madelyn and the Bobs weren't screenwriters. But we were running out of ideas for the format, and this was something different.

Lucille Ball

*Fred MacMurray was a nice enough guy, but a complete square to work with. I didn't think he was funny, and kept working with him on that telephone scene to his wife. He just couldn't get it. I guess I was wrong, though. He was on for eleven seasons with his own show [*My Three Sons, *1960–72]. But not my kind of comedy.*

Bob Schiller

(WRITER)

This show was inspired by [the Humphrey Bogart movie] The Treasure of the Sierra Madre *[1948]. We really loved the scene out in the desert where they are all suspicious of one another.*

THE FORD LUCILLE BALL-DESI ARNAZ SHOW #4: "LUCY WINS A RACEHORSE"

(CBS, FEBRUARY 3, 1958), 60 MINUTES (B&W)

GUEST CAST: Betty Grable, Harry James, Norman Leavitt, James Burke, Joe Hernandez, James Burton, Sid Melton

Little Ricky has his heart set on having a horse, so Lucy enters a breakfast food contest to win one. She enters repeatedly, and, lo and behold, wins a horse (Whirling Jet). All is well until Harry James, Ricky's latest costar at the Club Babalu, tells him how expensive it is to keep one. Lucy, Betty Grable, and Ethel scheme to harness race the horse themselves to pay for his upkeep, but because the horse is in love with Lucy, she becomes his driver.

HIGHLIGHTS & TRIVIA

Neither Lucille nor Desi look particularly well in this episode. A special chair was built for the den to hold the horse's weight when he "sits down" for publicity pictures. While everyone involved with this installment who was interviewed insists there is a live audience at the filming, the timing and sound of the studio audience laughter suggests that the response is either totally canned or heavily sweetened. There is a mechanical feeling to the show, more of a movie than a live TV show. There is a great deal of process shooting and second unit work, and a lot of it does not match up very well. All of this dampens the humor. Most of the spontaneity, a hallmark of the series, is lost in this outing. Tony, the stunt horse, is so well trained that all one has to do is whisper the word "action" in his ear, and he is ready to go through his paces. This show is a reunion of sorts. Lucille and Harry James were teamed in the movie musical *Best Foot Forward* (1943), while Betty and Desi had dated in New York in the late 1930s. "The Bayamo" was written by Arthur Hamilton. Note that Little Ricky's best friend is now referred to as Billy Thompson, not Billy Ramsey.

Bert Granet

(PRODUCER)

There were some funny moments in this one, and again we shot on location at the [Santa Anita] race track. But the format began to exhaust itself. [The production number] "The Bayamo" was done to a prerecorded track with the actors lip-synching onstage. Again, they were trying to marry movie techniques with theatre techniques, and the result was not terrific.

Irma Kusely

(HAIRSTYLIST)

A funny thing happened right around this time. I had this little cell I worked in on the lot, and Desi used to come up to get his hair dyed black. He had gotten gray

very young (as did Desi Jr.), and I had to dye his whole head to make it one consistent color. One day he comes up to my little area wearing his favorite gabardine golf shirt. I asked him to take it off, because I didn't want to stain it. Well, in those days he was like a whirling dervish, running from set to set, answering calls, and he didn't want to have to pull his shirt on over the goop on his head if he had to leave suddenly. Mind you, he didn't care if he ran around the studio with the goop; he just didn't want to do it shirtless. Well, he lunged forward to answer a phone, and this big splotch of dye got on his shirt. He got very upset, yelling, "My lucky shirt, my lucky golf shirt!" I just said, "Don't worry, I'll get it out after we finish your hair!" I got together with the wardrobe girl Della Fox, and we figured the only way out of it was to cut the stain out and have the shirt re-weaved by the tailors on the lot. I went down on the set, and Desi asked me if I had gotten the spot out. I held up the shirt, putting my fist through the hole I had made, and said, "I sure did!" Well, he got so furious you've never seen anything like it before in your life with his language, cursing me in Spanish. Lucille fell on the floor laughing, holding her sides. Naturally, it was no problem to fix the shirt.

Keith Thibodeaux

(ACTOR/MUSICIAN)

I had almost nothing to do with that horse when I was not in a scene with him. He was kept away from me and most of the cast when he was not being used.

LOVE OF LIFE

(CBS, APRIL 14, 1958), 15 MINUTES (B&W)

GUEST APPEARANCE: Lucille Ball, Desi Arnaz

Love of Life (1951–80)? That's right! The Arnazes make an appearance at the end of this daytime drama to promote that night's Sun Valley episode of their show. It is done live and has, sadly, been lost to the ages.

THE FORD LUCILLE BALL-DESI ARNAZ SHOW #5: "LUCY GOES TO SUN VALLEY"

(CBS, APRIL 14, 1958), 60 MINUTES (B&W)

GUEST CAST: Fernando Lamas

Lucy and Ricky plan a romantic vacation to Sun Valley, Idaho, but Ricky cancels when a TV commitment interferes. A furious Lucy goes anyway, taking Ethel with her and leaving the three boys at home. At the lodge, the girls encounter movie star Fernando Lamas. Lucy convinces Lamas to help her make Ricky jealous, but the plan falls apart when Ricky and Fred show up to surprise the girls.

HIGHLIGHTS & TRIVIA

This is a very taxing installment for all concerned. Hours are spent with Lucille on the skating rink ice on location in Sun Valley, where the still agile Ball undertakes almost all of her own stunts. Much of the location filming is done very early in the morning, so as not to interfere with the guests at the resort lodge. Luckily for Ball and the show's producers a stunt double is used for the skiing scenes, as the stunt person unfortunately breaks her leg filming the scene where Lucy is at the top of the mountain. All of these hour shows for 1957–58 will be rerun again during the next two seasons as part of the *Westinghouse Desilu Playhouse*. This episode will be shown again on Christmas Eve, 1958, with new footage of the Ricardos in their Connecticut home reminiscing about Sun Valley, and Little Ricky reciting a Christmas poem. None of the new scenes appear in any reruns after 1960. This is the third TV special that combines location filming with the usual in-studio, live audience work. Ball uses a plethora of differently styled wigs in this entry, practically one for each outfit she wears. Bill Frawley sings the old standby, "Melancholy Baby," in one scene; he has every right to do so, as he introduced the song when he was a vaudevillian in the 1920s!

Desi Arnaz Jr.

One of the first professional things I remember doing was the closing Ford commercial in this show. We were actually on those big round sleighs going over bumps [with his sister Lucie in Sun Valley as Lucille and Desi extol the virtues of Ford automobiles].

Fernando Lamas

(ACTOR)

*I had just finished doing a terrible show on Broadway [*Happy Hunting, *1956] with Ethel Merman and was happy to get away to Sun Valley. Desi was very gracious to me during this shoot. You know, he spoke with a much thicker accent offstage than he did* *onstage. The funniest thing was that when he spoke Spanish, his Cuban accent was so thick, and he spoke it so quickly, that I rarely understood him. I always had to ask him to repeat what he said in English. And he always said the same sorts of things on those shows in Spanish. He was afraid that if he varied the words, he might end up saying something dirty.*

THE ED SULLIVAN SHOW

(CBS, JUNE 22, 1958), 60 MINUTES (B&W)

PRODUCED BY: Marlo Lewis, Ed Sullivan
DIRECTED BY: John Wray
GUEST CAST: Lucille Ball, Desi Arnaz, and a host of other performers, including Fred Astaire, Jack Benny, Victor Borge, Perry Como, Jackie Gleason, Helen Hayes, Audrey Hepburn, Tony Martin, Elvis Presley, Ethel Waters, Ed Wynn

This is Ed's tenth anniversary program, and *all* of the celebrities appear via kinescope clips from the decade of Sullivan's Sunday night variety hour.

Lucille performs her "professor" character at a Navy benefit show in San Francisco, 1950. COURTESY OF BOB PALMER.

The *I Love Lucy* writers: Jess Oppenheimer, Bob Weiskopf, Madelyn Pugh, Bob Schiller, and Bob Carroll Jr., 1956. COURTESY OF BOB SCHILLER.

Lucille, Vivian, Jess, and Desi at a backstage party, 1954. COURTESY OF GREGG OPPENHEIMER.

Bill Frawley, Lucille Ball, Jess Oppenheimer, Vivian Vance, and Desi Arnaz at farewell party for Jess, 1956.
COURTESY OF MAURY THOMPSON.

Bob Schiller, Bob Carroll Jr., Lucille Ball, Desi Arnaz, Madelyn Pugh, and Bob Weiskopf during filming of "Lucy Goes to Sun Valley," 1958. COURTESY OF BOB SCHILLER.

Maury Thompson, Desi Arnaz, Lucille Ball, and Hedda Hopper relax backstage during filming of "K.O. Kitty," 1958. COURTESY OF MAURY THOMPSON.

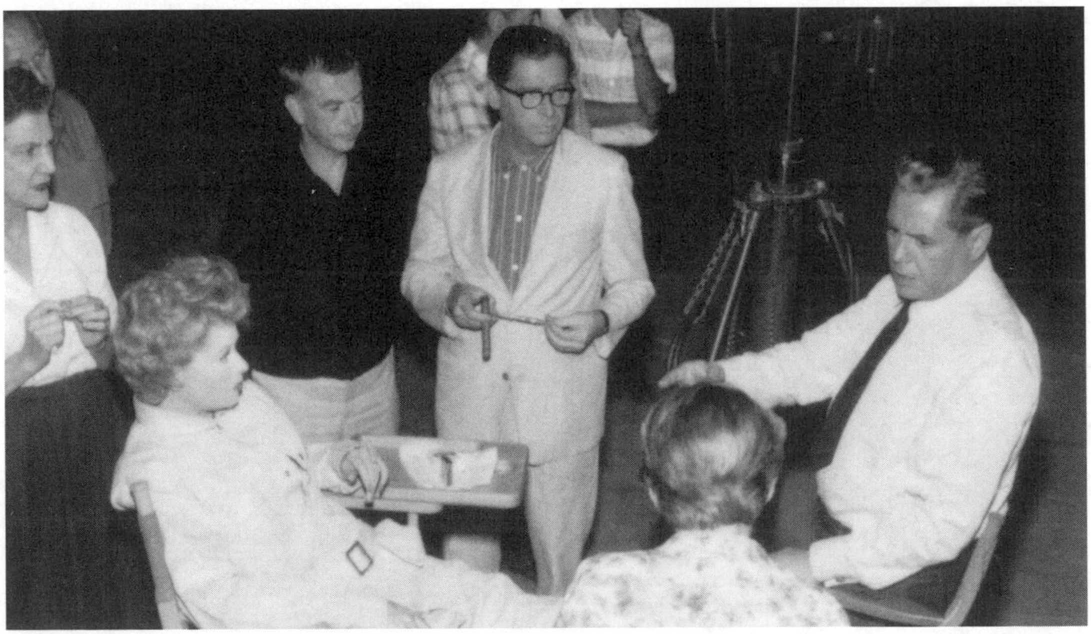

Elvia Allman, Lucille Ball, Maury Thompson, Milton Berle, and Desi Arnaz take a break during the filming of "Milton Berle Hides Out at the Ricardos," 1959. COURTESY OF MAURY THOMPSON.

Bob Schiller and Lucille Ball share a laugh during the filming of *The Desilu Revue,* 1959. COURTESY OF BOB SCHILLER.

Glamorous Lucille Ball strikes a publicity pose during the filming of "Lucy Meets Danny Kaye," 1964.
COURTESY OF MICHAEL STERN.

Maury Thompson (left) and Tommy Thompson (right) are literally in a gag photo on the set of "Lucy and the Golden Greek," 1965. COURTESY OF MAURY THOMPSON.

Lucille Ball as Charlie Chaplin with Maury Thompson on the set of "Lucy Meets Mickey Rooney," 1965. COURTESY OF MAURY THOMPSON.

(Clockwise) Gale Gordon, Lucille Ball, Desi Arnaz Jr., and Lucie Arnaz in Ball's backyard, 1968.
COURTESY OF DESILU, TOO, LLC.

Lucille Ball attempts the watusi with Desi Arnaz Jr. on the set of "Lucy's Birthday," 1968. COURTESY OF DESILU, TOO, LLC.

Celebrating Lucie Arnaz's seventeenth birthday, 1968. COURTESY OF DESILU, TOO, LLC.

Lucie Arnaz has a laugh with brother Desi Jr. on the set of *Here's Lucy*, 1968. COURTESY OF DESILU, TOO, LLC.

Lucie Arnaz stuns Gale Gordon in a tour de force performance during "Lucy Protects Her Job," 1969.
COURTESY OF DESILU, TOO, LLC.

Chapter Ten

1958–59 Season

THE LUCILLE BALL-DESI ARNAZ SHOW: THE EIGHTH SEASON OF THE I LOVE LUCY FORMAT

TECHNICAL REGULARS: Executive produced by Desi Arnaz; produced by Bert Granet; directed by Jerry Thorpe; makeup by Hal King; hairstyling by Irma Kusely; music by Wilbur Hatch
CAST REGULARS: Lucille Ball (Lucy Ricardo); Desi Arnaz (Ricky Ricardo); Vivian Vance (Ethel Mertz); William Frawley (Fred Mertz); Keith Thibodeaux (Little Ricky); Roy Rowan (announcer)

LUCY BUYS WESTINGHOUSE

(PRODUCED FOR WESTINGHOUSE DEALERS, JULY 1958), 45 MINUTES (B&W)
PRODUCED AND DIRECTED BY: Desi Arnaz
WRITTEN BY: Bob Carroll Jr., Madelyn Pugh Martin, Bob Schiller, Bob Weiskopf
CAST: Lucille Ball, Desi Arnaz, Vivian Vance, William Frawley, Ross Elliott

This, trivia fans, is a never-aired-on-television film that was produced for the Westinghouse dealers to get them excited about the forthcoming commercial tie-ins with *The Westinghouse Desilu Playhouse*, which will premiere in October, hosted by Desi Arnaz. Filmed with no studio audience, this one-camera show is done at different locales on the Desilu lot. The opening sequence is actually shot in Desi's executive office. The plot revolves around Lucy Arnaz (the only time she is ever called *that* on television) wanting to buy all the goodies she sees in her Westinghouse catalogue for her new dressing room at Desilu Studios. Desi keeps stalling her, not wanting her to spend so much money. Naturally, Lucy schemes to get what she wants, with the cooperation of the local Westinghouse dealer, played by Ross Elliott.

Viv and Bill play themselves as Lucy's costars and coconspirators. The line between reality and fantasy is generously blurred as all the actors, although called by their real names, behave like their *I Love Lucy* counterparts. They visit the sets to both the debut *Playhouse* episode *Bernadette* (starring Pier Angeli) and the upcoming Lucy-Desi hour with Maurice Chevalier. There is also a look at the Desilu prop department (where the original model for *King Kong* is shown), as well as makeup and wardrobe. The highlight of the promotional film is an aerial tour of all three Desilu Studios (two in Hollywood, one in Culver City) by helicopter.

THE WESTINGHOUSE DESILU PLAYHOUSE PRESENTS THE LUCILLE BALL-DESI ARNAZ SHOW #6: "LUCY GOES TO MEXICO"

(CBS, OCTOBER 6, 1958), 60 MINUTES (B&W)
WRITTEN BY: Bob Schiller, Bob Weiskopf, Everett Freeman
GUEST CAST: Desi Arnaz (host), Maurice Chevalier, Alan Costello, Charles Lane, Addison Richards, Chalo Chacan

Ricky is performing in San Diego for the Navy, along with legendary French entertainer Maurice Chevalier. Lucy and Ethel want to go into Mexico to buy souvenirs, but end up getting into trouble with the border authorities. When Ricky, Fred, and Chevalier join them in Tijuana, they land in legal trouble that can only be remedied by the American Consul, who is at the bullfights.

HIGHLIGHTS & TRIVIA

This is the first episode of the new anthology series. Each week, Desi hosts this hour-long program, which features westerns, dramas, comedies, and musical shows. Lucille appears in a short scene at the end of each week's installment, which leads into the final commercial. The Westinghouse commercials all feature Betty Furness as spokesperson. The series will run for two seasons, until it is canceled in the spring of 1960. All of the remaining Lucy-Desi shows appear as part of this series, instead of as specials. Only the installments starring Lucille will be discussed in this book.

Bert Granet
(PRODUCER)

Desi and I went to New York, and he made a speech I wrote that not only played up Desilu, but knocked Lew Wasserman, who was also making a pitch for MCA (Universal, actually) to do a show with Westinghouse. The reason it sold was because of Lucy and Desi. Nobody really needed another [TV] anthology series. But, two important pilots came out of this series. One was The Untouchables, *which I produced, and the other was* The Twilight Zone.

Bob Schiller
(WRITER)

We used to call Bert "No, No, Gran-et" because he never liked anything we wrote. Desi had sold an enormous bill of goods to Westinghouse, promising them thirty-nine hours of original programming for two years. He did a wonderful sales job . . . he went and visited their main warehouse, and promised them it would be empty in six months if they sponsored the shows. Then he came back to us. He said, "Boys, I have a problem. I don't remember why I sold them on this idea that Lucy would appear every week, because she won't."

Bob Weiskopf
(WRITER)

An employee who shall go nameless let Desi down. He came to us looking for an idea to save the deal. I had remembered that George Jessel made a whole career out of making humorous phone calls to his mother. So we wrote tag scenes where Lucy called Desi and reviewed the show she had just seen at home, like the rest of the audience. It gave Mrs. Arnaz something to do every week without having to be in the shows. To thank us he gave us each a sports car. Desi was a sport.

Bob Schiller
(WRITER)

[Desi Arnaz] gave me a Jaguar, and it was like a sick wife, always in the hospital. About three years later, after he left the studio, I went down to Palm Springs to play golf with him. He asked if this was the car he had given me, and if I had liked it. I said, "You son of a bitch, if you hadn't given me this car I'd be a rich man today!"

Bert Granet
(PRODUCER)

In my opinion, every comedy show reaches a point where it has outwritten itself. So you do the best you can to keep the thing afloat. That's where I Love Lucy *was at this point. Of these hour-long shows, five or six of them are really memorable. The rest are probably better left forgotten. In this case, Chevalier was a personal friend of mine. He'd been given a hard time for rumors that he had been a Nazi sympathizer during World War II. Actually, he had been gassed during the First World War, and had been a German prisoner. He really appreciated the patriotic theme of the show. Maurice was a joy to work with.*

Keith Thibodeaux
(ACTOR/MUSICIAN)

I remember we shot very late to finish up this show. It was not usual for us to go so long into the night to finish something up. For this show, the music was done live [actually, only Keith's music is live; Arnaz and Chevalier lip-synch]. I sang "Valentina" and played the drums right there. There was no audience for this show, because so much of it was filmed on location and there were so many sets. Actually, we didn't shoot anything on the aircraft carrier, just some establishing shots. Chevalier was a gracious man, and he was like a grandfather. We had kinship between us because we are both French. I think he respected kids if they did their jobs in a professional way. He was even tempered and a pleasure to work with.

Bob Schiller
(WRITER)

Chevalier had been one of Desi's heroes. Desi always fancied himself as the Cuban Chevalier. Maurice spent most of his time on the set asleep. He was an old man by this point. I want to clear up inaccuracies about the credits to this show. Everett Freeman is listed as a writer on this show. This is the only episode where another writer is so credited. This is what really happened. Bob and Madelyn temporarily quit the series, so Desi called us and asked us if we wanted some help. We asked him to let us think about it. We had done some work with Everett Freeman on That's My Boy *[1954–59] before* I Love Lucy. *Everett was at this time doing* Bachelor Father *[1957–62]. We called Everett and he came over. We knocked ideas around for awhile, then Everett got up and said, "You guys don't need me!" He left. We finished the story, we wrote the script, and by the end of the show Bob and Madelyn returned to the studio. The next thing we know, Everett wants top credit. He didn't deserve* any *credit, but he wanted* top *credit [he didn't get it].*

Bob Weiskopf

(WRITER)

We used one of my favorite actors in this episode, Charley Lane. I just loved him. We used him wherever we could.

THE WESTINGHOUSE DESILU PLAYHOUSE: "K. O. KITTY"

(CBS, NOVEMBER 17, 1958), 60 MINUTES (B&W)

EXECUTIVE PRODUCED BY: Bert Granet, Desi Arnaz in charge of production
PRODUCED BY: Quinn Martin
DIRECTED BY: Jerry Thorpe
WRITTEN BY: Madelyn Martin, Bob Carroll Jr.
BASED ON A STORY BY: Quinn Martin, Madelyn Martin, Bob Carroll Jr.
CAST: Desi Arnaz (host), Lucille Ball, Harry Cheshire, William Lundigan, Sid Melton, Aldo Ray, Roy Rowan, Jesse White

Kitty Winslow is a woman who has not married because her attorney boyfriend won't wed until he is a partner in his firm. Meanwhile, Kitty gets an inheritance from her Uncle Charley: a gold watch, a diamond stickpin, and a washed-up boxer name Harold. Out of sentiment for her uncle's memory, Kitty becomes Harold's trainer and manager.

HIGHLIGHTS & TRIVIA

Lucille looks pretty but overweight in this one-camera shot episode, which is shown with a canned laugh track. Her costuming, makeup, wig, and deeper voice make her appear as if she is Lucy Carmichael, the part she will start playing in 1962 on *The Lucy Show*. There are elements in the script of several *I Love Lucy* episodes. Lucille's interaction with Bill Lundigan (as her lawyer beau) shows what *I Love Lucy* might have been like with Richard Denning (her costar from radio's *My Favorite Husband*, 1947–51) and not Desi Arnaz: boring! The name of Harold's opponent, Tommy Thompson, is taken from the Desilu production assistant of the same name, who will later produce several seasons of *The Lucy Show* and *Here's Lucy*. The basic plot of this story will turn up again, this time in the Barbra Streisand-Ryan O'Neal comedy *The Main Event* (1979). The plot contrivance of a boxer needing to hear music in order to win is itself borrowed from *Punch Drunks* (1934), a Three Stooges short.

Bert Granet

(PRODUCER)

This was not a great show. I thought it was kind of stock and pat. I just didn't like the idea of the show. We could have done better for Lucy.

THE WESTINGHOUSE DESILU PLAYHOUSE PRESENTS THE LUCILLE BALL-DESI ARNAZ SHOW #7: "LUCY MAKES ROOM FOR DANNY"

(CBS, DECEMBER 1, 1958), 60 MINUTES (B&W)

WRITTEN BY: Bob Weiskopf, Bob Schiller
GUEST CAST: Danny Thomas, Marjorie Lord, Rusty Hamer, Angela Cartwright, Gale Gordon, Jess Kirkpatrick

Lucy and Ricky are going to California where Ricky is to shoot a movie. They rent their Connecticut house to the Williams family (the characters from the hit TV sitcom *The Danny Thomas Show*, 1953–64). At the last minute, the picture is shelved, so the Ricardos move in with the Mertzes. Lucy's interference with the Williams household while they are in her home leads to all three couples arguing, and suing one another in court, whose judge is played by Gale Gordon.

HIGHLIGHTS & TRIVIA

This is undoubtedly the best of the hour-long shows. Even the closing commercial for Westinghouse, featuring Lucille, Desi, and Betty Furness, is humorous in its writing and execution.

Bert Granet

(PRODUCER)

This episode got me the Producer's Guild Award. I'm going to make a confession. Those writers really produced these shows. They had been with Lucy for years, came up with the concept, and were really the driving force. Madelyn and the three Bobs. They should have gotten the award.

Bob Schiller

(WRITER)

I think that this is the best of the hour-long shows. It is superb, because it kept building on itself. Each scene got progressively funnier and funnier.

Marjorie Lord

(ACTOR)

I had first met Lucille through [actor] Helen Parrish, who took me to her house in Chatsworth [in the San Fernando Valley]. But that was before I Love Lucy. *After she started television, I'd see her quite often on the lot. In fact, we quite often got our hair done together. Lucy's hairdresser Irma even did my hair for a season [1960–61] while Lucy was on Broadway. I loved doing this show. While Danny was* always *king of the roost, when he was with Lucille he was a pussycat. He had great respect for her, and he knew he was going to be a part of a great show. Lucy was top gun on the set, but Desi was the business man. He really was the brains, and she was the first one to tell you that. Desi knew what was good for Lucy. The writers were very talented men, and they knew our head writer Artie Stander very well. They made a very fair melding of both our shows, being true to each set of characters. It was very well done, and very funny. When we shot the show, I was fighting some severe dental problems, but that was the only bad part of the shoot. I loved the scene where I caught Lucy and Danny in the bedroom.*

You know, Lucy was very serious about her work. There was no horsing around on her set. Danny was very serious too, but on our set things were played a little more loosely. Lucy rehearsed harder than anyone I have ever seen. Sometimes I felt we rehearsed a little too much. I liked to be a little freer in my work. We had two weeks to put this show together, and we worked hard. Desi seemed to have a retentive memory. He'd just come in from meetings and he knew everybody's *lines. He didn't need to rehearse that much.*

There wasn't much of a conflict with the direction. Although Lucy, Danny, and Desi all liked to be in charge, Jerry Thorpe really did direct the show. There was no dissention, because most of the direction was in the script, which was so well done. We all had our moments to shine, and everyone was so darn good in it. Vivian Vance and I went way back together. We had been in summer stock together, and did a play in San Francisco and we lived together. Bill Frawley played my father in a movie at Universal, so I knew everybody very well.

I don't think Vivian was very happy doing this show by this point. Her performances were still excellent as always, but she wanted to be doing other things. I also don't think she was a very happy lady at this point, either. Vivian was so identified with Lucy that she really didn't get a lot of other work, and her marriage to Phil Ober was a disaster. It's funny, because Vivian always wanted to be very glamorous and I don't think she ever appreciated how good she was in this show. I was allowed to be glamorous, because that gave contrast to Danny. I also wasn't a comic, but an actress who did comedy.

Lucy was very generous with me as far as how I looked. She wanted me to look my best, and there was no sense of jealousy. There were times when Lucy would be very preoccupied. You'd say hello to her and she wouldn't even acknowledge you. Other times, she'd ask about your kids and how you were and she'd really open up. So I figured, this girl has a lot of responsibilities and it's nothing I should take personally. When we did the snow scenes, that was real snow they brought in. The fake stuff wouldn't have melted that way it did. The scenes looked natural and played well. Gale Gordon was great, not only for Lucy but for every show he did. He was a very private man, and went off by himself when we were not rehearsing or shooting. Lucy and I were talking between shots, and she said, "No matter how extreme the scene is, inside you've got *to believe it!" That was the basis for her comedy. There were tender moments in this show and ours, and it made the comedy even funnier. The children all got along fine in this show, which was good because Rusty could be* very *difficult. He was very spoiled by Danny and his own mother. They always made him the center of attention, and he sometimes acted out if he wasn't. He and little Angela did not get along. And Angela sometimes enjoyed herself so much, we'd have to do retakes where she wouldn't be smiling and giggling.*

Angela Cartwright

(ACTOR)

I was with my familiar people, so doing this didn't seem strange at all. I liked Keith, and we went to school together on the lot. Rusty could be very annoying sometimes. He'd trip me, and things like that. He came from a broken home, and had been acting since he was little like I had. We were not very close. I loved working with Gale Gordon. He was lovely to me, both on this show and on ours.

Keith Thibodeaux

(ACTOR/MUSICIAN)

To me, this was the funniest show I was on. That scene between Gale Gordon and Lucy when she smashes that snowball in his face just cracked me up.

THE DANNY THOMAS SHOW: "LUCY UPSETS THE WILLIAMS HOUSEHOLD"

(CBS, JANUARY 5, 1959), 30 MINUTES (B&W)

EXECUTIVE PRODUCED BY: Louis F. Edelman
PRODUCED AND DIRECTED BY: Sheldon Leonard
WRITTEN BY: Arthur Stander, Sid Dorfman
CAST: Danny Thomas, Marjorie Lord, Lucille Ball, Desi Arnaz, Angela Cartwright, Sandra Wright

When Ricky and Danny Williams appear together in a nightclub, Danny suggests that Ricky and Lucy move in with him and his wife Kathy in Manhattan. This is so Kathy's calming and sensible influence can rub off on Lucy. Unfortunately, just the opposite occurs, leading to an all-out war between the men and the women.

HIGHLIGHTS & TRIVIA

This episode does not work nearly as well as the hour-long show they all did together. The writing is not nearly as strong, and it is obvious Lucille misses her own creative team. The characters of Lucy and Ricky are not true; they say and do things that would *never* happen on their own series. By this point, Lucy Ricardo is a responsible mother and a pillar of her community. She would never leave her son in Westport while she stays in New York for weeks. She is a fine housekeeper and cook. The idea that Lucy only *now* cooks and knits is absurd. The show is plotted so Lucy and Ricky have only one tender moment together, and that one is both forced and phony. Lucille has gained significant weight in the interim and looks matronly.

Marjorie Lord

(ACTOR)

I had a very different function as Danny's wife than Lucy had as Ricky's wife. I was there to give Danny some class and some sex appeal, where Ricky's character already had those things. There was a chemistry between Danny and me right from our very first scene together. When Kathy stood up to Danny, it was funny because it was a little out of character, and you knew she had to be really angry to do it. It was different between Lucy and Ricky. Kathy was always impeccably dressed and never looked ridiculous. Lucy was able to take a pie in her face and still be believable and feminine. That scene where Lucy and I go shopping had to be rehearsed over and over and over. She liked to rehearse a lot.

Lucy had gained a lot of weight around this time out of unhappiness [due to her faltering marriage], and eventually she began to eat her main meal in the middle of the day to lose weight. Whatever was going on in their private lives, they never let it show in their performances. She loved him, and he was always looking out for what was best for Lucy. Professionally, they were very good for each other. She was very careful about the lighting and cameras, and I think she felt the pressure of being on someone else's show and wanting to be good. Sheldon Leonard was very respectful of her, and he kowtows to no one. *We were used to having major stars on our show, but Lucy was special.*

Angela Cartwright

(ACTOR)

Danny was always redoing scripts, trying to make things sound more natural. Lucy and he seemed to work very similarly that way. They both knew exactly what they wanted. I was very protected from any of the stress on the set, so my memories are really only of the show night. Remember, I was only six years old.

THE WESTINGHOUSE DESILU PLAYHOUSE PRESENTS THE LUCILLE BALL-DESI ARNAZ SHOW #8: "LUCY GOES TO ALASKA"

(CBS, FEBRUARY 9, 1959), 60 MINUTES (B&W)

WRITTEN BY: Bob Weiskopf, Bob Schiller

SCRIPT CONSULTING BY: Madelyn Martin, Bob Carroll Jr.
"POOR EVERYBODY ELSE" BY: Arthur Hamilton
GUEST CAST: Red Skelton, Sid Melton, William Newell, Hugh Sanders, Iron Eyes Cody, Charlie Stevens, Jess Kirkpatrick

Fred buys a piece of land, sight unseen, in Alaska (newly made the forty-ninth state of the United States), and cuts Ricky in on the real estate deal. The Ricardos and the Mertzes fly to Nome to inspect their investment, but find they are a day early for their hotel reservations. Red Skelton is staying at the same hotel, and offers the foursome one of the rooms in his suite. The two couples conclude the land they bought is worthless, so Lucy tries to sell it to Skelton to save her friendship with the Mertzes.

HIGHLIGHTS & TRIVIA

With each succeeding hour show, the episodes seem more diluted from the original *I Love Lucy* concept in almost every aspect. Vivian especially seems out of character, as though she is auditioning for her role as Vivian Bagley on the upcoming *The Lucy Show*. There are, however, two excellent scenes in this offering. One is the bedroom sequence, with Lucy wrestling with a hammock for a good night's sleep. Ball's timing is still impeccable. The other is a "Freddie the Freeloader" sketch with Ball and Skelton, which is top-drawer. It is a shame that these two clowns (who had starred together in the 1943 MGM musical film *DuBarry Was a Lady*) never work together again, but their disparate approaches to comedy do not gel. Most of the installment is filmed in front of a live audience, but there is a great deal of "sweetening" that gives the feeling of canned laughter. Like all of the location, second-unit, or audience-free filming, many of these scenes do not match up with the lighting, costuming, and hairstyling of the rest of the sound stage scenes (especially Lucille's wigs, as no two are exactly the same).

Sherwood Schwartz

(WRITER/PRODUCER ON THE RED SKELTON SHOW)

I do not envy the writers on this [Lucy] *show. Red Skelton hated writers. Hated writers. He* hated *to admit that he needed them so much. But Red was brilliant. And he didn't do the same thing twice, so actors learned to follow along with him.*

Bert Granet

(PRODUCER)

Lucy was a stickler for rehearsals. She loved to work. Red used to just throw things in, or throw them away. It worked for him, but Lucy couldn't stand that. She liked everything worked through and set. She was a very hard worker and earned every dollar she made. Eventually, she ended up showing Red how to do the Freddy the Freeloader sketch [a character he had done for years] so that he could follow a set pattern.

Dann Cahn

(FILM EDITOR)

These shows began to be less like television shows and more like movies. The fourth wall was built up as we used studio audiences less and less.

THE PHIL SILVERS SHOW: "BILKO'S APE MAN"

(CBS, MARCH 18, 1959), 30 MINUTES (B&W)

PRODUCED BY: Edward J. Montagne
DIRECTED BY: Aaron Ruben, Al DeCaprio
WRITTEN BY: Arnie Rosen, Coleman Jacoby
CAST: Phil Silvers, Lucille Ball, Harvey Lembeck, Maurice Gosfield, Allan Melvin, Bernie Fein, Maurice Brenner, Terry Carter, Herbie Faye, Mickey Freeman, Jack Healy, Billy Sands, Kenneth Vaughn, Joe E. Ross, Beatrice Pons, John Alexander, Fred Harrick, Edith King, Hope Sansbury

Sergeant Bilko is annoyed when a new recruit, who has the physique of Tarzan, is used to whip the platoon into physical shape. Bilko sees dollar signs when he enters him in a movie studio competition to find a *new* Tarzan; the first prize is $100,000. To ensure winning, the recruit is entered in the Mr. Universe contest.

HIGHLIGHTS & TRIVIA

Lucille Ball plays a cameo role as a woman Bilko hires to faint when she sees his muscular recruit. She has almost no lines, and is totally unbilled. Ball does this as a personal favor to Silvers, whose TV series (1955–59) is floundering in the ratings.

THE WESTINGHOUSE DESILU PLAYHOUSE PRESENTS THE LUCILLE BALL-DESI ARNAZ SHOW #9: "LUCY WANTS A CAREER"

(CBS, APRIL 13, 1959), 60 MINUTES (B&W)
WRITTEN BY: Bob Weiskopf, Bob Schiller
SCRIPT CONSULTING BY: Madelyn Martin, Bob Carroll Jr.
GUEST CAST: Paul Douglas, Pierre Watkin, Doris Packer, Joi Lansing, Sue Casey, Lorraine Crawford, Lari Thomas, Sam Hearn, Louis A. Nicoletti

After eighteen years of marriage, Lucy is sick of being just a housewife. When she learns that actor Paul Douglas will be hosting a new morning TV program, Lucy auditions and actually gets hired. After a rocky start, she is finally the huge show business success she always said she wanted to be, but finds that she misses her family, friends, and being just a housewife. Unfortunately, she has an iron-clad contract and cannot break it.

HIGHLIGHTS & TRIVIA

Because of the requirements of the audition scene, Ball is forced to wear her own hair during much of the episode. She looks a great deal more natural, and more like Lucy Ricardo. After several location episodes, it is a pleasure to see Lucy back in her home, doing domestic things. These scenes, and those between Ricky and Lucy in the train station, are the last believable sentimental moments in the series. Those train scenes are based on the Arnazes' early marriage, where their conflicting schedules forced them to meet for a few stolen moments while traveling. Although the Arnaz marriage has, by this time, totally unraveled, Lucille and Desi are still living together and being affectionate toward each other. That affection shows through in their joint scenes. Although there had previously been a little sexual tension between Desi and actress Joi Lansing on the set (in the 1956 *I Love Lucy* episode #161, "Desert Island"), by this point it no longer matters, and Lansing is a welcome addition to the cast.

The writers have come up with a novel plot idea, finally allowing Lucy to be a success and having Ricky recognize her talent. Unfortunately, this also kills any future plots about Lucy wanting to get into the act. Ball is hilarious in the scene where she is drugged on sleeping pills; her concentration is still keen and the audience reactions keep her on her toes. This is the last of the installments filmed in front of the usual studio audience. It is also the last of the really good shows; the last four decline greatly in quality. By this point, the entire regular cast is involved in the final Westinghouse commercial, which at times is as long as three minutes and presented in a sketch format.

THE WESTINGHOUSE DESILU PLAYHOUSE PRESENTS THE LUCILLE BALL-DESI ARNAZ SHOW #10: "LUCY'S SUMMER VACATION"

(CBS, JUNE 8, 1959), 60 MINUTES (B&W)
WRITTEN BY: Bob Weiskopf, Bob Schiller
SCRIPT CONSULTING BY: Madelyn Martin, Bob Carroll Jr.
GUEST CAST: Ida Lupino, Howard Duff, William Fawcett, Carelton Young, Karen Norris

Booking agent Harry Bailey offers the Ricardos his mountain lodge in Vermont for a summer vacation. Unfortunately, the absent-minded Bailey has also offered his digs to married movie stars Howard Duff and Ida Lupino for the same week. The Ricardos and the Duffs decide to share the accommodations. Unfortunately, the men spend all their time together, leaving the ladies romanceless and maneuvering for time with their spouses.

HIGHLIGHTS & TRIVIA

This is the *only* episode of the entire *I Love Lucy* format that is actually bad. The lack of the Mertzes, who are written out of the installment in the first scene, reduces the onscreen chemistry by half. Desi looks bloated and tired. Ida Lupino seems like a fish out of water with the broad comedy required of her. Lucille desperately misses the interaction with the live audience. The only good comedy moment is the rowboat scene. Unfortunately, it is poorly shot and edited, and it never builds to its proper crescendo. While next season's efforts will be better, it is at this point that the entries lose any tie they had to the classic series. Without producer Jess Oppenheimer, cinematographer Karl Freund, a live audience, weekly continuity, youthful and eager performers, and new story line directions, the series just barely treads water.

Bert Granet

(PRODUCER)

This is the first of the hour-long shows that was filmed completely without a live audience. It was mostly a matter of economics. It was cheaper to use less people, less cameras, less lighting. "Vacation" was the worst of the shows. They were running out of gas and the comedy was forced. Also, Lupino and Duff were no longer major stars. The Westinghouse contract had many restrictions as to who the Arnazes could barter appearances with because of sponsor conflicts. That precluded a lot of talent from working on the show. Also, sometimes there wasn't enough money for the people you wanted. The most we ever paid was $10,000 [per star], and that was for the stars of the dramatic episodes of the Playhouse. *When you have a format that is getting moldy, writers who are exhausted, stars who are barely speaking to one another, and second-rate guest stars, you have at best a mediocre show.*

Keith Thibodeaux

(ACTOR/MUSICIAN)

On a show like this, where I only had a small part, I did my scenes and went home. I didn't hang around the set when I wasn't needed, although I could have. I was welcome to. But I had schooling and drum rehearsing to look after. Its just as well, since this episode really wasn't very good.

Dann Cahn

(FILM EDITOR)

It was at this point that the show began to lose some of its flavor. No matter how well we knew the characters and the audience's reactions to them, we could not artificially recreate that relationship. Filling in holes, assuming where laughs would come and for how long, knowing when to cut away . . . all of these things were only good guesses. Then you do a show where two of the main characters [Fred and Ethel] hardly appear. It is no wonder no one cares for this episode.

Bob Weiskopf

(WRITER)

This was not our finest hour. There was only one really funny line in the script. Not even a whole scene, just a line.

Chapter Eleven

1959–60 Season

THE LUCILLE BALL-DESI ARNAZ SHOW: THE NINTH SEASON OF THE I LOVE LUCY FORMAT

TECHNICAL REGULARS: Executive produced by Desi Arnaz; produced by Bert Granet; directed by Desi Arnaz; written by Bob Schiller, Bob Weiskopf; script consulting by Madelyn Martin, Bob Carroll Jr.; makeup by Hal King; hairstyling by Irma Kusely; music by Wilbur Hatch

CAST REGULARS: Lucille Ball (Lucy Ricardo); Desi Arnaz (Ricky Ricardo); Vivian Vance (Ethel Mertz); William Frawley (Fred Mertz); Keith Thibodeaux (Little Ricky); Roy Rowan (announcer)

THE WESTINGHOUSE DESILU PLAYHOUSE PRESENTS THE LUCILLE BALL-DESI ARNAZ SHOW #11: "MILTON BERLE HIDES OUT AT THE RICARDOS"

(CBS, SEPTEMBER 25, 1959), 60 MINUTES (B&W)

GUEST CAST: Milton Berle, Larry Keating, Elvia Allman, Sid Melton, Frank Mitchell, Walter Pietila, Herman Snyder

Lucy wants comedy legend Milton Berle (who has recently published a book) to be in the P.T.A. show. She offers him the solitude of the Ricardo home to finish his next book in exchange for doing the school event. The fly in the ointment is keeping Berle's presence a secret from Ricky, and Ricky's true identity a secret from Berle.

HIGHLIGHTS & TRIVIA

This installment is stiff, badly edited, and overdirected. Most of the heavy-duty physical comedy is done by doubles. Although the premise is excellent, and the script is superior, the execution falls flat. The comedy plods along; Ball's usual impeccable timing seems distracted. Even Vance acts as if she is underwater. The only player who is at the top of his form is Berle, whose super energy makes everyone else look tired. Although Desi can be a talented director, there isn't a trace of nuance or subtlety to be found in this outing. The cast is no longer creating anything; it is as if they are parodying themselves. What could have been the best scene, with Lucille and Berle in the crane-carried bucket high above the street, is made silly by the extensive use of stunt doubles, bad trick photography, and piecemeal filming. Originally, there was much more to the show, including a long sequence set in Central Park with Lucy, Ricky, and Milton chasing after pages of Berle's manuscript that blow away in the wind. However, that and other moments were cut from the script due to time constraints.

Bert Granet

(PRODUCER)

At this point, [director] Jerry Thorpe left the show. Lucy thought Jerry was throwing too much emphasis and attention onto the guests and not enough to Lucy. Jerry was very bitter. He was very talented, and esoteric about some things. Desi took over as director. He was a great man to work for, because he took responsibility. If something went wrong, he would say, "Amigo, we *blew it!" not, "Amigo,* you *blew it!" You found very few bosses like that. I began to take on more responsibility because Desi was traveling a lot at this time. That western sketch at the end of the show was embarrassing. I wanted to cut it off and throw it away. It was like a high-school play.*

Maury Thompson

(CAMERA COORDINATOR)

Jerry Thorpe was like a schoolteacher. If Lucille questioned the smallest thing, he'd say, "OK, take ten

everybody." He'd sit down, light up his pipe, cross his legs, and say, "OK, you asked a question, Mrs. Arnaz, now I'm going to tell you." You could not treat Lucille like that . . . it wasn't appropriate. He was always slapping her on the wrist and being condescending to her.

Milton Berle
(PERFORMER/LEGEND)

I couldn't get over what a marvelous director Desi was. He knew everything about his operation. He was in total control. He reminded me of me! I was so impressed, I asked him to direct one of my specials for NBC, and we shot it using his format at Desilu. This was a funny show, except for that awful musical thing at the end. Here's a piece of television trivia: It was not Desi in that horse's outfit. They got a dancer to fill in, so he could just direct the scene. I've been told we filmed without an audience, but I remember there being people there laughing. Maybe they brought in a small group just to give us some timing.

Bob Schiller
(WRITER)

We brought in an audience for some of the scenes, and did the "bucket" scene and the musical number without one.

Keith Thibodeaux
(ACTOR/MUSICIAN)

We prerecorded that western number at Glen-Glenn Sound, which was located adjacent to the studio. All of that stuff was done by lip-synching. It was Jack Baker inside of that horse outfit.

THE ANN SOTHERN SHOW: "THE LUCY STORY"

(CBS, OCTOBER 5, 1959), 30 MINUTES (B&W)

EXECUTIVE PRODUCED BY: Desi Arnaz
PRODUCED BY: Devery Freeman
DIRECTED BY: James V. Kern
WRITTEN BY: Leonard Gershe
SCRIPT CONSULTING BY: Bill Manhoff
CAST: Ann Sothern, Lucille Ball, Don Porter, Ann Tyrell, Jack Mullaney

Lucy is angry because Ricky has postponed going away for the weekend for the tenth time. She checks into the Bartley Hotel in New York, where her old pal Katy O'Connor is the assistant manager. Katy schemes to get Lucy back with Ricky, Lucy plots to fix Katy up with her boss Mr. Devery (Don Porter), and Devery maneuvers to teach Katy a lesson.

HIGHLIGHTS & TRIVIA

This episode might have been very funny if Lucille wasn't playing Lucy Ricardo. She is totally out of character. Ball and Sothern, both in their late forties, look beautiful but plump. The one-camera method allows the best possible angles and lighting, but hinders the flow of the comedy. It is a shame that at this point in her career, Lucille totally abandons live audiences, so vital to her style of performing. The two ladies perform an excellent drugged bit, something they will do several times in their television visits together. Lucy Ricardo has also met Sothern's former television series character, Suzie McNamara (see *The Lucille Ball-Desi Arnaz Show* #1, "Lucy Takes a Cruise to Havana"). Lucille and Ann, friends for decades, work very well together, and will do quite a bit of work together in the 1960s on *The Lucy Show*.

THE SUNDAY SHOWCASE: "THE MILTON BERLE SPECIAL"

(NBC, NOVEMBER 1, 1959), 60 MINUTES (B&W)

EXECUTIVE PRODUCED BY: Milton Berle
PRODUCED BY: Irving Starr
DIRECTED BY: Desi Arnaz
WRITTEN BY: Lou Derman, Arthur Julian, Bob Schiller, Bob Weiskopf
CAST: Desi Arnaz, Lucille Ball, Stephen Bekassy, Milton Berle, Ruth Berle, Marion Colby, Lloyd Corrigan, Cyril Delvanti, Nancy Kulp, George Macready, Mike Mazurki, Leslie Sheldon

Milton Berle and Ricky are performing at the El Rancho Hotel in Las Vegas. Milton forgets his wedding anniversary, so Lucy talks him into buying the rare Winthrop diamond ring as a gift for his angry wife. Lucy tries on the ring, and it gets stuck on her finger. Jewel thieves try to kidnap Milton and Lucy, and the merry chase is on.

HIGHLIGHTS & TRIVIA

There is no live audience for this show, and the laugh machine on the soundtrack is used extensively and badly. It isn't that this special doesn't have humorous moments, but they are too few and far between. Desi looks haggard. Lucille appears almost matronly in the wedding gown sequence. The name of the jeweler, Jacques Marcel, is the same as that of the French couturier in the *I Love Lucy* episode "Lucy Gets a Paris Gown" (episode #147). A syndicated version of this special will be released shortly after Lucille's death in 1989, retitled "Milton Loves Lucy." A few of the nonessential scenes will be deleted, and a new introduction, filmed by Berle, will be incorporated into this version.

Bob Weiskopf

(WRITER)

Milton and I got into a shouting match during the filming of this show. He had overheard something I said to his brother about the shtick Milton was using in the way he walked. Berle got very angry and said, "If you want someone to walk regularly, we can hire a $30 actor!" I immediately replied, "If you want someone to write old shtick, we can hire a $30 writer!" We were like two little boys. Desi finally had to throw me off the set. "Amigo," he apologized, "I don't like to do this to you, but I've gotta direct the show with this man!"

Bob Schiller

(WRITER)

When we originally wrote this script, I truly thought it was very clever. I saw it recently and I was very disappointed in it. I was appalled. I loved the concept of the story, which was kind of like the Beatles movie Help! *[1966]. Lucy and Desi looked terrible [due to stress], and the whole thing came across very heavy-handed. Once again, we hired outside writers to work with us. Artie Julian had a huge ego, which made writing this show somewhat less than pleasant.*

Milton Berle

(PERFORMER/LEGEND)

Desi never got the credit he so richly deserved. He knew what he was doing at all times, which made me trust him. And when it comes to my comedy, I trust almost no one. I really enjoyed doing this show. It was a nice change of pace from the variety specials I was doing. Lucille and I always got along very well. I had dated her when she first got to Hollywood [in the early 1930s] and nobody knew who she was. There was always a special bond between us that I have never discussed in public. It is private, and maybe someday I'll let [the author] write about it. Besides our personal relationship, I think she was the funniest woman of the twentieth century.

THE WESTINGHOUSE DESILU PLAYHOUSE PRESENTS THE LUCILLE BALL-DESI ARNAZ SHOW #12: "THE RICARDOS GO TO JAPAN"

(CBS, NOVEMBER 27, 1959), 60 MINUTES (B&W)

GUEST CAST: Bob Cummings, Kathryn Card, Teru Shimada, Linda Wong, Sondi Sodasi, May Lee

The Ricardos and the Mertzes fly to Japan, and Lucy is determined to buy herself a real pearl necklace, which is much less expensive if purchased there. Next-door hotel neighbor, movie star Bob Cummings, arranges the purchase for Lucy despite Ricky's objections. When the Redhead is forced to return them, she mistakenly gives Cummings her phony pearls. To save Cummings from embarrassment, she follows him to a geisha house to make the switch.

HIGHLIGHTS & TRIVIA

This is another instance where this could have been a great episode but for the lack of a live audience and the lackluster performances. Vivian inaugurates wearing her hair in a French twist with this installment, losing any resemblance to the Ethel Mertz we once knew. The comedy timing is clumsy and slow-paced. Lucy Ricardo *got* real pearls back in *I Love Lucy* episode #38: "The Anniversary Present," making the entire plot of this episode moot. This is the last appearance of Kathryn Card as Mrs. McGillicuddy, Lucy's mother.

Keith Thibodeaux

(ACTOR/MUSICIAN)

This was my only chance to meet and work with Kathryn Card. She was a kind lady, and I wish I could have gotten to know her better. Doing these shows without a live audience was easier for me because there was less pressure. If I made a mistake, we easily did retakes.

Carole Cook

(ACTOR/FAMILY FRIEND)

This is one of the few shows where Lucy and Desi's private life interfered with the work. She was so upset about the impending divorce, all she could do was cry. When she wore that geisha makeup, her eyes looked even more red in contrast to the white makeup. She took a lot of her anger out on Vivian, and gave her a bad time. Viv probably didn't like it, but she understood because her *marriage to Phil Ober was ending, too.*

Dann Cahn

(FILM EDITOR)

Things were pretty bad backstage on this one. Lucy and Desi were out of control, and it is very hard to do comedy when people are so unhappy. The set was very tense, and there were a lot of retakes. It was very sad.

Bob Weiskopf

(WRITER)

Vivian was really unhappy about playing Ethel Mertz by this point. She had a harder time getting into character, and in fact acted more like Vivian Bagley [of The Lucy Show*] than Ethel Mertz.*

THE WESTINGHOUSE DESILU PLAYHOUSE: "THE DESILU REVUE"

(CBS, DECEMBER 25, 1959), 60 MINUTES (B&W)

PRODUCED BY: Lucille Ball
DIRECTED BY: Claudio Guzman
WRITTEN BY: Bob Schiller, Bob Weiskopf
MUSIC BY: Walter Kent, Walton Farrer
CAST: Desi Arnaz, Lucille Ball, John Bromfield, Spring Byington, Rory Calhoun, William Demarest, William Frawley, Hedda Hopper, Lassie, George Murphy, Hugh O'Brian, Ann Sothern, Danny Thomas, Vivian Vance
ASPIRING PERFORMERS: Jerry Antes, Majel Barrett, Bob Barron, Janice Carroll, Carole Cook, Georgine Darcy, Dick Kallman, Marilyn Lovell, Fran Martin, Gary Menteer, Johnny O'Neill, Bob Osborne, Roger Perry, Howie Storm, Mark Tobin, Mark Trevis

It is Christmastime, and gossip columnist Hedda Hopper visits the Desilu studios. Fledgling producer Lucille Ball is working with a group of young performers, and introduces them to Hedda. They all reminisce about the trials and tribulations of putting on the Desilu Revue, featuring those young hopefuls of the Desilu Workshop.

HIGHLIGHTS & TRIVIA

Lucille does have a great eye for talent. Majel Barrett will best be known as Nurse Chapel on *Star Trek* (1966–69), and the wife of *Star Trek* creator Gene Roddenberry. Bob Osborne will become a *Hollywood Reporter* columnist, as well as the host of *Turner Classic Movies* on the Turner Cable television network. Roger Perry will appear in scores of television episodes as a guest star. Dick Kallman will have his own series, *Hank* (1965–66). One member of the workshop became so successful early on that he left the group before this entry: Ken Berry. At the time, it seemed as though the breakout discovery was Carole Cook, who here sings a smashing "I'm Only Happy When I'm Singing the Blues." Carole will later play in movies for Disney, the lead in the Australian company of *Hello, Dolly!*, star on Broadway, and appear in dozens of television shows, including *The Lucy Show* and *Here's Lucy*.

Carole Cook

(ACTOR/FAMILY FRIEND)

I had known Dick Kallman, and he had seen me perform in New York at a club called Number One Fifth Avenue. Dick landed out in Hollywood and became a member of the Desilu Workshop. That was fate step number one. Lucille had started this group to give her something to do while her marriage was falling apart. Other than the occasional hour long show, she was between gigs. This workshop was done in the same little theatre where Lela Rogers [Ginger Rogers' mother] had given a similar workshop for the young contract players at RKO. Lucille had been in several plays there supervised by Lela. Anyway, Dick's background was in musical theatre, and he was pushing Lucille to put on a revue. I don't think any of the players were under contract to Desilu, but they were each paid around $50 a week to keep them going. Lucille complained that she didn't have a strong musical comedienne to be in the show, and that's when Dick remembered me, little Mildred Cook. That was fate step number two. I was out on tour in Kismet *in Warren, Ohio, and they got a hold of me through the front desk man at my apartment building, who had happened to be a chorus boy in all the Rodgers and Hart musicals. He liked me, and tracked me down until he found where I was and told them. That was fate step number three. I get called to the phone, "Lucille Ball calling for Mildred Cook," and I said, "No shit!" Indeed, it was Dick and Lucille calling. They flew me out to Los Angeles and we just talked. I was lucky. She liked whatever I was, and liked hearing the stories of my family in Texas. I came from a Southern Baptist background; my grandmother still thinks I'm in Los Angeles doing missionary work.*

Anyway, they had me do a screen test. For some unknown reason, they had me use an old I Love Lucy *script. Desi Arnaz even did the test with me. Then Desilu put me under contract. I never really went back to New York. Lucille had me living in the pool house of her mansion in Beverly Hills. She was even the matron of honor when I married [actor] Tom Troupe.*

To get back to the show, we did it as a live show in the little theatre for about six weeks. It only held about 150 people. Then the decision was made to transfer the show to television for Westinghouse. We had a choreographer [Jack Baker], Paul Davis was the director, and Desi helped out, but Lucille was absolutely in charge. Wilbur Hatch was in charge of the music. Hedda Hopper wrote that Desi came in after a trip to Europe and in fifteen minutes had the show running like clockwork. She was there, and had no reason to lie, but I never saw that. The show was filmed almost exactly the way we had rehearsed it. There was no major redoing of the actual performances. Perhaps Desi's contribution was on the technical side, with the cameras and everything. Lucille was always with us, a real mother hen. The show was shot on a sound stage with no audience with one or two cameras like a movie. Only the musical numbers were used for the television show. There were very funny sketches we did that were not used. Bob Osborne and I did the old Nancy Walker–Bert Lahr sketch about a woman who has like twenty children.

It was funny, because Lucille really didn't know that much about putting on a live show, but she did very well. I think it was therapy for her. She was very angry about her relationship with Desi, but she never allowed anyone to put him down. She always insisted that he was the brains behind everything. Lucille never wanted to be a star, but she wanted to be constantly working. By the way, it was Lucille who renamed me Carole after her friend [the late movie star] Carole Lombard. Lucille gave me tons of her old clothes, and I wore one of her pregnancy dresses in that show. I wore that dress until you could see through it! She also allowed me to use the same recipe for my hair color that she used.

Maury Thompson

(CAMERA COORDINATOR)

At the first rehearsals, things were not going so well. The show was deadly dull, and they hadn't come up with a way to fix it. Carole Cook was sitting up on a ladder, and out of nowhere she yells, "Who do you have to fuck to get out of this thing?" Well, let me tell you there was silence. *Finally, Lucille let out a scream of laughter. She never expected anything like that to come out of a newcomer who had been sent for. After that, Lucille Ball accepted anything that came out of Carole Cook!*

Irma Kusely

(HAIRSTYLIST)

By this point, Lucille was gaining weight and wanted another change in her hairstyle to look chic. This was the year of the chignon, so I had a wig made and then styled it for her. She wore it for several shows, until the fad changed again.

Bert Granet

(PRODUCER)

Lucy did everything for this show. She chose the people, directed, produced, and renovated the theatre. That theatre is now part of the Paramount commissary.

HEDDA HOPPER'S HOLLYWOOD

(NBC, JANUARY 10, 1960), 60 MINUTES (B&W)

PRODUCED BY: Michael Abbott
DIRECTED BY: William Corrigan
WRITTEN BY: Sumner Locke Elliot
CAST: Hedda Hopper (host), Lucille Ball, Stephen Boyd, Francis X. Bushman, John Cassavetes, Gary Cooper, Ricardo Cortez, Bob Cummings, Marion Davies, Walt Disney, Janet Gaynor, Bob Hope, Hope Lange, Harold Lloyd, Jody McCrea, Liza Minnelli, Don Murray, Ramon Novarro, Anthony Perkins, Debbie Reynolds, Teddy Rooney, James Stewart, Venetia Stevenson, Gloria Swanson

A myriad of vintage and contemporary guest stars appear as Hedda pressures some of the legendary greats to make her TV special shine with talent. Produced on film and video tape, Lucille's segment finds her in a dark suit with a fox collar, wearing four strands of pearls and a wig in a long French twist. Standing outside of her Desilu Workshop with some of her Playhouse students, she is overweight, puffy, and overly made-up. Briefly discussing her plans with Hopper for the Playhouse (and mentioning Desi several times), she then drives off in her electric cart to attend to her studio duties.

BUICK ELECTRA PLAYHOUSE: "THE SNOWS OF KILIMANJARO"

(CBS, MARCH 25, 1960), 60 MINUTES (B&W)

Lucille appears at the end of the show to promote the following week's *Westinghouse Desilu Playhouse*, "Lucy Meets the Moustache." The *Playhouse* is aired on alternate weeks with the *Buick* show. She appears on film in one costume from the upcoming show, obviously done at the same time as the yet unaired Ernie Kovacs episode.

THE WESTINGHOUSE DESILU PLAYHOUSE PRESENTS THE LUCILLE BALL-DESI ARNAZ SHOW #13: "LUCY MEETS THE MOUSTACHE"

(CBS, APRIL 1, 1960)

GUEST CAST: Ernie Kovacs, Edie Adams, Paul Dubov, Norman Leavitt, Louis A. Nicoletti, Dick Kallman

Ricky is depressed because he hasn't gotten any movie or television offers lately. Meanwhile, Little Ricky has become friendly with Kippy Kovacs, daughter of comedian Ernie Kovacs. Lucy invites Ernie and his wife Edie to the house to induce Kovacs into hiring Ricky, but only manages to get a TV gig for *Little* Ricky. After infuriating Kovacs by barging into his house to make a pitch for Ricky, Lucy disguises herself as the Kovacs' chauffeur Krandall to have a chance to apologize.

HIGHLIGHTS & TRIVIA

This is the last episode of the *I Love Lucy* format. The original concept created by Jess Oppenheimer has completely played itself out after nine years. If the Arnazes were not facing such dire personal troubles, and had a desire to continue, the format would have had to be changed to give the writers new focus. Bill Frawley was getting old and having trouble with his lines; he would read from cue cards during his years (1960–65) on his next series, *My Three Sons* (1960–71). Vivian was chafing at the bit to do more glamorous acting assignments. Lucille and Desi were decidedly middle-aged and tired. Above all, Ball and Arnaz were finally divorcing, making it impossible for them to play Lucy and Ricky any longer. At the end of this season, *The Westinghouse Desilu Playhouse* will be canceled, putting Desi Arnaz out of a job as host and producer. At the time, Desi is vilified in the press, while Lucille is made to look like a long-suffering martyr. This brand of media attention affects both of their careers. Arnaz chooses to retreat from the public eye, while Ball plunges into movie work (*The Facts of Life*, 1960) and a Broadway musical, *Wildcat*. It is widely assumed both of their television careers are finished. Time will tell a much different story.

Bert Granet

(PRODUCER)

By this point, Lucy and Desi were barely speaking to one another. The entire enterprise had begun to disintegrate. Morale hardly existed.

Edie Adams

(ACTOR/SINGER)

I had no idea there was going to be a problem with this show. Ernie and I were newly moved to California, and we hadn't heard any of the gossip. We were only concerned with what we were going to do and wear. My first call [at the studio] was before lunch, and I showed up with my usual long page boy hairstyle. Lucille looked at me, and then huddled with Irma Kusely in a corner. Irma came over to me and said, "I'm sorry, but we're going to have to redo your hair. Miss Ball doesn't like your hair." No one had ever complained about my hair before, but I decided to acquiesce. Ernie then asked Lucy to lunch and left me there to get my head soaked. I was furious. Desi came over and apologized. "She's just in one of those moods," he said. So Irma redid my hair, and she put it in a chignon just like Lucy's. I looked terrible. When they came back from lunch, Lucy took one look at me, huddled with Irma again, and again Irma tells me she has to redo my hair. Again I got soaked and rolled, and my hair came out exactly the way it was when I walked in. All of this for one shot at four in the afternoon.

Irma Kusely

(HAIRSTYLIST)

Everything Edie said is true. Lucille was so unhappy and distraught. It was not because Lucille was a bitch, but because she was stressed out.

Edie Adams

(ACTOR/SINGER)

Desi directed the show. He was charming and brilliant. After five minutes with him you knew that he *knew*

what was funny and what was not. He was a marvelous director because he knew how to set things up for the comedy. He was a hands-on floor director, as opposed to someone who just sat up in the booth and talked over a microphone. Lucy was another story. I just couldn't seem to please her. If I concentrated on learning my blocking, she'd say, "Stop! That's no way to read that line!" So, I'd do it full out as I were on Broadway, and she'd say, "Stop! You're not in your light!" Of course, the lights weren't on *yet, but she knew where the lights were* going to be. *So it went, back and forth. And not just with me, but with all of the cast and crew.*

Once it became obvious that this was an unusual situation because of the pending divorce, I just decided to go along with it and just get through it. Both Ernie and I stayed out of it and just did our jobs. Bill and Vivian were the same way. They were almost on autopilot. Ernie and I weren't sitcom people, we were sketch comedians. The only thing I really enjoyed doing was my song, "That's All." Things were very strained with Desi and Lucy. He could be three feet away from her, but he'd ask someone else to repeat his directions to her. Then she would respond the same way, asking some intermediary to repeat her curses at Desi. The language flew fast and furiously. This went on with every shot for the entire show. Everybody was walking around on glass. The show was written so that Lucy and Desi had as few moments together on camera as possible. The Arnazes were both so obviously unhappy, and the comedy seemed forced because of it. Lucy would just start crying, or would be holding back tears. She was so troubled. Everyone knew we had *to get the show in the can because we knew it was over and none of us were coming back to that set.*

Keith Thibodeaux
(ACTOR/MUSICIAN)

We really *shot into the night to finish this one. The next day, my Dad told me that I was out of a job because they were going to get a divorce. It was a shock to me. As far as I knew, we were coming back for more shows. I had known there were problems, because the tension between Lucy and Desi on the set was very noticeable. The rehearsal process was business as usual, but between them it was different.*

THE DINAH SHORE CHEVY SHOW

(NBC, APRIL 3, 1960), 60 MINUTES
PRODUCED BY: Bob Finkel
DIRECTED BY: Dean Whitmore, Bob Finkel
WRITTEN BY: Charles Isaacs, Carl Reiner
CAST: Dinah Shore (host), "Little Ricky's Combo" featuring Desi Arnaz Jr. and Keith Thibodeaux, Vic Damone, Betty Grable

Keith comes out and does banter written by Carl Reiner. He bemoans the fact that no more *I Love Lucy* shows will be made, and audiences will always think of him as being seven years old. Although Keith is actually ten at the time (three years are stripped off his age to make him the same age as Desi Jr.), more prophetic words are never said. This is Desi Jr.'s first TV variety show appearance. He is poised and charming. The two boys play their hearts out, with Keith banging on a set of drums and Desi hitting a Conga drum. They stop the show with "Babalu." This is the only time Desi Jr. will appear on television in connection with *I Love Lucy* (except for his cameos in 1957 and 1958), and the last major performance by Keith, who will be relegated to bit parts on different Desilu filmed series over the next few years.

Desi Arnaz Jr.

Keith and I had a Dixieland band, and we used to rehearse at the studios. Either I would play the Conga and percussion and Keith the drum set, or we'd switch. We had eight other kids on brass and percussion, and a twelve-year-old girl singer. This was our first job, and it was a lot of fun. We disbanded this group a few years later and started a rock and roll band, previous to my being in Dino, Desi, and Billy.

Keith Thibodeaux
(ACTOR/MUSICIAN)

It was neat, because they had the big band behind us, and we had our Dixieland thing in front of them. The night the show was aired (it was taped in Burbank), Lucy invited me to come over to her house in Beverly Hills and we all sat in her living room together and watched it. We thought it was terrible.

Desi Arnaz
(IN 1960)

Even if we don't do any more hour-long shows, [Keith Thibodeaux] is such a talented young guy, and we have him under contract, that there will be plenty for him to do.

Keith Thibodeaux

(ACTOR/MUSICIAN)

But there wasn't plenty for me to do. I was so identified as Little Ricky that parts were few and far between. I really didn't want to be an actor. My whole heart wasn't in it. And no one at Desilu was paying any attention to my musical career. Music was changing, and Dixieland was out. After Desi left the studio, I was pretty much forgotten about professionally, although I was still very close to Desi Jr.

LUCY IN CONNECTICUT

(CBS, JUNE 3–SEPTEMBER 25, 1960), 30 MINUTES (B&W)

This is a collection of reruns from *I Love Lucy* episodes all dealing with the Ricardos and the Mertzes in Connecticut that were originally aired in the spring of 1957. New cartoon graphics are made for the new opening and closing credits and different sponsors.

I LOVE LUCY EPISODES IN WHICH LUCY ACTUALLY DOES GET INTO RICKY'S ENTERTAINMENT ACT

(IN CHRONOLOGICAL ORDER)

"The Diet" (episode #3, 10/29/51)
"The Audition" (episode #6, 11/19/51)
"Lucy Is Jealous of a Girl Dancer" (episode #10, 12/17/51)
"The Benefit" (episode #13, 1/7/52)
"The Ballet" (episode #19, 2/18/52)
"Cuban Pals" (episode #28, 4/21/52)
"Lucy Does a TV Commercial" (episode #30, 5/5/52)
"Ricky Loses His Voice" (episode #44, 11/29/52)
"Lucy's Show Biz Swan Song" (episode #47, 12/22/52)
"The Indian Show" (episode #59, 5/4/53)
"Ricky's Life Story" (episode #67, 10/5/53)
"The French Revue" (episode #73, 11/16/53)
"Lucy Meets the Queen" (episode #142, 1/30/56)
"Lucy and Bob Hope" (episode #154, 10/1/56)
"Lucy Meets Orson Welles" (episode #156, 10/15/56)
"Ragtime Band" (episode #174, 3/18/57)

Chapter Twelve

1960–61 Season

THE GARRY MOORE SHOW

(CBS, SEPTEMBER 25, 1960), 60 MINUTES (B&W)

EXECUTIVE PRODUCED BY: Bob Banner
PRODUCED BY: Joe Hamilton
DIRECTED BY: Dave Geisel
WRITTEN BY: Vincent Bogert, Neil Simon, Coleman Jacoby
CAST: Garry Moore (host), Lucille Ball, Carol Burnett, Eydie Gorme, Alan King, Durward Kirby, Marion Lorne

Lucille is invited to participate on this installment to inaugurate a new regular feature on the program: "Somebody Goofed." She shows outtakes from her latest movie *The Facts of Life* (1960), and is so caught up in the clip that she sees that she actually breaks up oncamera.

ELEANOR ROOSEVELT'S DIAMOND JUBILEE PLUS ONE

(NBC, OCTOBER 7, 1960), 60 MINUTES (B&W)

PRODUCED BY: Michael Abbott
DIRECTED BY: Dick Schneider
WRITTEN BY: Reginald Rose
CAST: Bob Hope (host), Lucille Ball, Jack Benny, General Omar Bradley, George Burns, Carol Channing, Nat King Cole, Irene Dunne, Jimmy Durante, Mahalia Jackson, Senator John Kennedy, Mary Martin, Paul Newman, Vice President Richard Nixon, Richard Rodgers, Simone Signoret, Joanne Woodward

Bob Hope hosts this celebration from New York on the former First Lady's seventy-sixth birthday and for the benefit of the Eleanor Roosevelt Cancer Research Foundation. Lucille does nothing more than lend her name, charm, and beauty to the festivities and does not actually perform any comedy.

WHAT'S MY LINE?

(CBS, JANUARY 1, 1961), 30 MINUTES (B&W)

EXECUTIVE PRODUCED BY: Gil Fates
PRODUCED BY: the CBS Television Network in association with Mark Goodson and Bill Todman
DIRECTED BY: Franklin Heller
CAST: John Daly (host)
PANELISTS: Bennett Cerf, Arlene Francis, Dorothy Kilgallen
MYSTERY GUEST: Lucille Ball

Lucille's purpose for this visit is to plug *Wildcat*, her Broadway musical. She looks thin and tired, and her voice is hoarse.

I'VE GOT A SECRET

(CBS, FEBRUARY 15, 1961), 30 MINUTES (B&W)

EXECUTIVE PRODUCED BY: Gil Fates
PRODUCED BY: Chester Feldman
DIRECTED BY: Franklin Heller
CAST: Garry Moore (host), Lucille Ball, Johnny Carson, Betsy Palmer, Henry Morgan, Bess Myerson

Lucille appears on this panel show to promote her stage musical *Wildcat.* She wears her hair in the old Lucy Ricardo bun, although not curly, but teased.

THE BOB HOPE BUICK SPORTS SHOW

(NBC, FEBRUARY 15, 1961), 60 MINUTES (B&W)

EXECUTIVE PRODUCED BY: Bob Hope
PRODUCED BY: Jack Hope
DIRECTED BY: Jack Shea
WRITTEN BY: Mort Lachman, Bill Larkin, Lester White, John Rapp, Charles Lee
WRITING CONSULTANT: Norman Sullivan
ADDITIONAL MATERIAL BY: Gig Henry
CAST: Bob Hope (host), Dana Andrews, Lucille Ball, Julie London, Jayne Mansfield,

Dean Martin, Ronald Reagan, Ginger Rogers, Jane Russell, Tuesday Weld, Esther Williams, Jane Wyman

A comical awards show with sports editors selecting the best and brawniest of 1960 in eleven categories. The winners receive gold statuettes. Lucille does her turn with boxing champion Floyd Patterson.

THE ED SULLIVAN SHOW

(CBS, FEBRUARY 19, 1961), 60 MINUTES (B&W)

PRODUCED BY: Robert Precht
DIRECTED BY: John Wray
CAST: Ed Sullivan (host), Lucille Ball, Leon Bibb, the Bill Black Combo, Jack Carter, the National Guard, H.M.S. *Park Royal Seamen*, Rowan and Martin, Paula Stewart, Wayne and Shuster, Justise Wilson

Lucille, returning to her Broadway musical *Wildcat* after being ill, performs her hit number "Hey, Look Me Over" with costar Paula Stewart. The Redhead, looking still run down, hits her head on the undercarriage of the car as she makes her scene entrance from underneath it, almost causing her to pass out.

Ed Sullivan

(HOST/COLUMNIST)

I have had every big star come on my stage through the years. Looking back, I have to say that the most beloved star by the American public was Lucille Ball. No one else has captured the hearts of the people out there the way Miss Lucille did, and probably nobody ever will again.

LUCY GOES TO BROADWAY

(UNPRODUCED, STORY OUTLINE SUBMITTED MARCH 10, 1961), 60 MINUTES

PLANNED PRODUCER AND DIRECTOR: Desi Arnaz
WRITTEN BY: Madelyn Martin, Bob Carroll Jr.
PROJECTED CAST: Keith Andes, Desi Arnaz, Desi Arnaz Jr., Lucie Arnaz, Lucille Ball, William Frawley, Bob Hope, Hedda Hopper, Michael Kidd, Ethel Merman, Paula Stewart, Don Tompkins, Vivian Vance

This special is written as a way to capitalize on Lucille's current Broadway success and keep her on television at the same time. Had it been filmed, it might have been the finest thing Ball had ever done.

The plot revolves around the different reminiscences of Vivian Vance, Ethel Merman, and Bob Hope as they recall their contributions toward getting Lucy onto the stage in *Wildcat*. Lucy and Viv are in New York sharing a hotel suite while both are up for consideration for the lead in the musical. Both ladies play up to Bob Hope, who, it is rumored, is a major investor in the show. When Viv is offered the lead in a drama, she withdraws from consideration and helps Lucy get prepared. Lucy arranges for Ethel Merman to give her singing lessons so she can project onstage. Bill Frawley, who is in town doing personal appearances, happens to be staying at the hotel as well and comes up to complain about all the noise. Lucy goes into rehearsals, where the whole cast helps her get ready. Finally, opening night is a huge success, and Desi greets his ex-wife at Sardi's with their children to congratulate her.

Many of the bits from this outline will be used on *The Lucy Show* during its first two seasons. This would have been the only television reunion between Vivian and Bill, and between Lucille and Desi. It also would have been the only time Lucie and Desi Jr. appeared with both of their parents at the same time. The special is canceled because Lucille is ill and exhausted from the stresses in her life, and it is decided not to push her into anything else. What a pity that circumstances prevented the special from being made.

THE ED SULLIVAN SHOW

(CBS, JUNE 11, 1961), 60 MINUTES (B&W)

PRODUCED BY: Bob Precht
DIRECTED BY: John Wray
CAST: Ed Sullivan (host)

Lucille Ball takes a bow from the audience.

Chapter Thirteen

1961–62 Season

I LOVE LUCY

(CBS, SEPTEMBER 1961), 30 MINUTES (B&W)

For four weeks, CBS airs reruns of this series to fill a scheduling gap. This is the last prime-time airing of the series in a regular time slot.

TWELVE STAR SALUTE TO THE FEDERATION OF JEWISH PHILANTHROPIES

(ABC, DECEMBER 9, 1961), 60 MINUTES (B&W)

PRODUCED BY: Hi Brown
CAST: Danny Kaye (host), Anna Maria Alberghetti, Lucille Ball, Benny Goodman, Morton Gould, Charlton Heston, Eartha Kitt, Tony Martin, Mitch Miller, Jan Pierce, Edward G. Robinson

This is a salute to the great charitable work of the FJP. There are songs and comedy, but mostly testimonials to the fine deeds of this organization. Lucille looks wan and slightly overweight, adding little of her usual verve to the proceedings.

THE GOOD YEARS

(CBS, JANUARY 12, 1962), 60 MINUTES (B&W)

PRODUCED BY: Leland Hayward, Marshall Jamison
DIRECTED BY: Franklin Shaffner
BASED ON THE BOOK BY: Walter Lord
ADAPTED BY: A. J. Russell
MUSICAL SUPERVISION AND CHORAL ARRANGEMENTS BY: Jay Blackton
CAST: Lucille Ball, Henry Fonda, Margaret Hamilton, Mort Sahl

This is the first full-out television effort La Ball has attempted since ending her career as Lucy Ricardo almost twenty-one months earlier. Videotaped in New York in November of 1961 immediately after her wedding to comedian Gary Morton, her honeymoon is postponed to make her available for the two-week combination rehearsal and taping schedule. Lucille still has her Manhattan apartment, but has been bicoastal since ill health forced her to walk away from the Broadway musical *Wildcat*.

Appearing in this special is an unusual decision for the Redhead to make. To begin with, there is no audience involved, and Lucille had discovered long ago that she was not nearly as effective just playing to cameras. Second, the script requires the services of a woman of that certain age (in other words, over thirty-five but not showing how much) who can sing and dance. Lucille's specific gifts are not called for; any good musical comedienne would do. Mary Martin would have been the perfect choice. Broadway producer Leland Hayward had been producing high-quality TV specials since the early 1950s. It is most likely that Martin *was* the first choice, as she had appeared in several of Hayward's productions and is, in fact, a close friend. However, two variables swing the pendulum in La Ball's favor.

To begin with, Mary Martin is busy doing eight shows a week on Broadway in *The Sound of Music* and cannot undertake the project. Second, the leading man is Henry Fonda. Fonda and Ball have been close ever since they first appeared together in RKO's *The Big Street* (1942).

The special is a retrospective, with sketches and blackouts, of the early part of the twentieth century, from 1900 to 1913. Lucille's first appearances are in a series of blackout skits: at first, she expects the amorous advances of her suitor as she reaches to turn out the light; then, in the second one, she hangs onto a phony branch in a takeoff of *The Perils of Pauline*; and, finally, she is a prohibitionist who wields an axe in a bar. Lucille's first musical number has her sitting in a vine-covered swing singing "(Swing Me) Just a Little Bit Higher."

Next, Fonda and Ball duet on "Tell Me Pretty Maiden" as vaudeville players. They follow this with a suffragette piece with Lucille as the leader and a parlor scene with Lucille as the mother viewing a stereopticon.

One major sketch of the hour occurs in a courtroom set, where Lucille plays a woman arrested for disorderly conduct for singing in public "Everybody's Doin' It" and "The Turkey Trot." The Redhead is not shown in the most flattering light and is clearly overweight. She will lose more than fifteen pounds before beginning her new series in the coming months. The best part of the special is a sketch between Lucille and Henry that is a direct steal from the long-running Broadway comedy hit, *Life with Father* (1939).

Irma Kusely

(HAIRSTYLIST)

This was a dreadful show. Both Fonda and Lucille hated it. Lucille did not look well. She was still battling weight. Few people know it, but she was not a candidate for plastic surgery due to her skin type. She literally had very thin skin which bruised easily. Surgery was out of the question, and she never had it done, despite what anyone says.

THE FIFTEENTH ANNUAL EMMY AWARDS

(NBC, MAY 22, 1962), 120 MINUTES (B&W)

HOSTED BY: Bob Newhart (Los Angeles), David Brinkley (Washington, D.C.), and Johnny Carson (New York)

The highlight of the trophy show is a wonderful parody by Edie Adams of Marilyn Monroe singing the Gershwins' hit song, "S'Wonderful." Lucille wears a chiffon gown and a necklace of pearls and diamonds as she presents the Comedy Writing Award to Carl Reiner for *The Dick Van Dyke Show* and the Comedy Directing Award to Nat Hiken for *Car 54, Where Are You?* Sporting a very teased wig and heavy makeup, Lucille looks (and sounds) about as young and glamorous as she ever has.

THE ED SULLIVAN SHOW

(CBS, JUNE 24, 1962), 60 MINUTES (B&W)

PRODUCED BY: Bob Precht

DIRECTED BY: Tim Kiley

CAST: Ed Sullivan (host), Steve Allen, Lucille Ball, Jack Benny, Ray Bloch, Teresa Brewer, Red Buttons, Johnny Carson, Jack Carter, Bing Crosby, George Gobel, Will Jordan, Jerry Lewis, Ted Mack, Katherine and Arthur Murray, Phil Silvers, Kate Smith

This show is subtitled "Stars of TV's Great Variety Shows Salute the All-Time Great Variety and Its Star Ed Sullivan" for the occasion of Ed's fourteenth anniversary on television. In a change of pace, Ed sits in the audience while the stars perform for him. Wishing Ed congratulations in a nonhumorous short speech, Lucille looks beautiful in her *Critic's Choice* (1963) wig, wearing a velvet top with a fur collar. The camera pans back, to reveal she is sitting on an elephant, which takes her offstage.

THE LUCY-DESI COMEDY HOUR

(CBS, JULY-SEPTEMBER, 1962), 60 MINUTES (B&W)

The thirteen hour-long specials that Lucille and Desi made for Ford and Westinghouse are rerun as a summer replacement series. New opening and closing graphics are created to incorporate the new name and sponsorship. This same series in the same format will be used four more times between now and 1967. There is heavy on-air promotion of the forthcoming *The Lucy Show*, with Lucille doing voice-overs during the closing credits reminding folks to tune in come October to her new CBS-TV sitcom.

Chapter Fourteen

1962–63 Season

THE LUCY SHOW: THE FIRST SEASON

TECHNICAL REGULARS: Executive produced by Desi Arnaz (episodes #1-8 only), Elliot Lewis; produced and directed by Jack Donohue; written by Madelyn Martin, Bob Carroll Jr., Bob Schiller, Bob Weiskopf; makeup by Hal King; hairstyling by Irma Kusely; music by Wilbur Hatch
CAST REGULARS: Lucille Ball (Lucy Carmichael); Vivian Vance (Vivian Bagley); Candy Moore (Chris Carmichael); Jimmy Garrett (Jerry Carmichael); Ralph Hart (Sherman Bagley); Roy Rowan (announcer)

OPENING NIGHT

(CBS, SEPTEMBER 24, 1962), 60 MINUTES (B&W)
PRODUCED BY: Burt Shevelove
DIRECTED BY: Sidney Smith
WRITTEN BY: Larry Gelbart
ANNOUNCED BY: Don Wilson
MUSIC COMPOSED AND CONDUCTED BY: Paul Weston
CAST: Lucille Ball, Jack Benny, Andy Griffith, Garry Moore, Danny Thomas

A series of sketches and blackout skits featuring some of CBS' top stars, this special is used to kick-off the 1962 fall season. The taped show opens with a series of instant TV sketches: Andy and Garry as stars of "Saddle Sore," Lucille conducting a TV exercise session, and Andy and Danny analyzing the news à la Chet Huntley and David Brinkley. Lucille is shown the types of suitors she may encounter on her new TV series. This is a touchy subject, as no one is quite sure how audiences will react to seeing their beloved *Lucy* with men other than *Ricky*. All five performers recall what they were doing twenty years earlier. The show ends with a series of dramatic readings done in a tongue-in-cheek style.

THE LUCY SHOW #1: "LUCY WAITS UP FOR CHRIS"

(CBS, OCTOBER 1, 1962), 30 MINUTES (B&W)
GUEST CAST: Tom Lowell

When Lucy waits up for her daughter Chris to return from a date, the fourteen-year-old girl is mightily embarrassed. Lucy promises never to do it again, but can't help herself. To not be discovered, Lucy accidentally locks herself out of the house and has to enter by the only means available: a trampoline.

HIGHLIGHTS & TRIVIA

Faced with huge changes in the television industry and Desi Arnaz' inability to produce new programs that the networks will buy, Lucille Ball is prevailed upon to come back to TV to save Desilu, the studio she helped to create. Vivian Vance has no desire to return to work with Lucille, but is offered enough salary to make commuting to Hollywood from her home in Connecticut worthwhile. Desilu owns the rights to a book called *Life without George* (1960) by Irene Kampen, and claims to be basing this new half-hour series on that property. While some of the incidentals from the book are used (two divorced women living together with their children), the program is really based on the Lucy Ricardo character created by Jess Oppenheimer.

Gary Morton
(PRODUCTION CONSULTANT)

[Agent] Don Sharpe got involved with procuring the book Life without George *for Desilu. However, they digressed from the original theme of the book. The concept for* The Lucy Show *was never really ironed out*

from the beginning. There was no master plan. The writers developed it as they wrote it. Jess Oppenheimer was a brilliant man, a child prodigy. Bob [Carroll Jr.] and Madelyn [Pugh Martin Davis] were excellent writers, but didn't have the talent for planning that Jess had.

It is never intended for this program to go beyond one TV season; it is meant to be a stop-gap measure for the beleaguered studio. Desilu uses the sale of this series as leverage to force the CBS network to invest in and air other upcoming Desilu products. Ball will use these tactics as long as she owns the studio.

While in the original book both women are divorcees, it is decided to make Lucy Carmichael a widow. It is felt that fans will not empathize with a Lucy who divorced Ricky, even though this is a *new* character. Vivian Vance plays American TV sitcom's first divorced woman (Vivian Bagley) who is a focal character. Somehow it is thought more acceptable that Ethel might have divorced Fred. Lucy and Viv share a house with Lucy's son Jerry (Jimmy Garrett), daughter Chris (Candy Moore), and Viv's son Sherman (Ralph Hart).

While the first several draft scripts do carry the title *The Lucille Ball Show*, contrary to what has been reported elsewhere this name is *never* used on the air, and the series is *always* called *The Lucy Show*. Also, several episodes firmly place Danfield in New York State, just north of New Rochelle. Many books state that the town was located in Connecticut, but this is not so. (There *is* a Danfield in Connecticut, but it is not *The Lucy Show*'s town.) This premiere episode is very funny, but has a strange look. It is a little unnerving for the audience to see Lucille and Vivian playing other characters. While Viv was always supposed to be middle aged playing Ethel Mertz, now both dames are unmistakably past forty. Their oncamera relationship is different, as Lucy no longer always has the upper hand. Vivian is very careful to play Vivian Bagley very differently from Ethel Mertz. Unfortunately, in so doing she loses some of Ethel's warmth and humility. Vivian Bagley is a lot more arrogant, vain, and proud than Ethel Mertz ever was. No one who views this series ever truly believes that Sherman is her son, as there is no real chemistry between Vivian and Ralph Hart, a talented, clean-cut dancer who plays the nine-year-old.

Candy Moore
(ACTOR)

There was no time for Vivian [Vance] and Ralph [Hart] to work on their onscreen relationship. Vivian never had children of her own, and maybe she found it difficult to relate to Ralph as her son on the show. Rehearsals were mostly for technical issues. Vivian was very polite and kind, but on a surface level. I never really got to know her, or have any deep personal exchanges with her. But her character was perfect for Lucy, as a support for her.

Vivian had lost weight since her *I Love Lucy* days, and also changed her hair and had a face lift. Lucille fluctuates between wearing wigs and her own hair in the first half of this season; she reverts back to wigs full-time after that. The wardrobe for Lucy Carmichael is neither chic nor particularly flattering. Most episodes have Lucy in a pair of slacks and an oversized, button-down blouse. The basic set is a lower-middle-class two-story home, with an old-fashioned kitchen and living room downstairs, four bedrooms and a bathroom upstairs, and a basement. The furnishings are comfortable but not expensive.

Lucille easily infuses warmth into her role as Lucy Carmichael, although she pushes much too hard in this first installment. Whenever nervous, Lucille plays her comedy with too much force. That happened in the first episode of *I Love Lucy*, and it will happen again. Nonetheless, it is great to see Ball playing in front of a studio audience again, something she really hasn't done on TV since 1958. To make the visual transition from one series to the next a little easier, cartoon characters are again used for the show's opening, with one of Vivian replacing that of Desi. The children tapped to play the oncamera kids all do quite well. As Lucy's son, Jimmy Garrett is a great little comedy actor. Almost every time he opens his mouth, the audience is laughing. Unfortunately, none of the characters of this series are truly dimensional or ever allowed to grow.

Two additional characters (next-door neighbor and boyfriend Harry Connors, played by Dick Martin, and banker Mr. Barnsdahl, played by Charles Lane) will be introduced in the next few episodes, but both will be written out of the show by the following spring. As with the early *I Love Lucy* installments, there are many inserted closeups of Lucille that do not match the rest of the show's shots. Director Jack Donohue is making the same mistake that Marc Daniels did in his first outings: trying to make Ball look as beautiful as possible without regard to the overall visuals of the show.

Carole Cook

(ACTOR/FAMILY FRIEND)

Lucille could be very superstitious. She liked the letters "ar" together. That's part of the reason for the name "Carmichael," as it was for "Carter" and "Barker." I reminded her once that she had done pretty well with the name Lucille Ball, but she said, "Yeah, but I didn't do really *well until my name was ARnaz and RicARdo."*

Dick Martin

(ACTOR/COMEDIAN)

When I first came on the set, I thought that Viv looked like an old woman. Lu looked young and sprightly. I had no idea that Viv wasn't a lot *older than Lu. This show had a lot of complicated shots, because they had to shoot Vivian through a frame to get shots of her looking down, then they had to shoot from the audience's perspective up. Viv's closeups were not done at the same time; if you look closely I don't even think her makeup and hair match up. Lucille's shots on the trampoline were done by her, although they were all done as pickups after the audience left. She was very athletic.*

Dann Cahn

(FILM EDITOR)

Elliot Lewis [the producer] had been a radio actor. He was very big on Jack Benny, *doing all sorts of crazy voices when Mel Blanc wasn't around. He was also a regular on the Phil Harris-Alice Faye radio show in the 1940s. When television came around, he became a director and a producer. Being Mary Jane Croft's husband, it was only natural that he'd drift over to Desilu. After he left* I Love Lucy, *he produced* The Mothers-in-Law *[1967–69] for Desi. Then he directed several episodes of* Petticoat Junction *[1963–70]. He was a very nice man. His first wife was the actor Cathy Lewis.*

Bob Schiller

(WRITER)

The reason they bought the book Life without George *and the reason they claimed the show was based on the book was so that they wouldn't have to pay Jess Oppenheimer for the use of the characters he created. Jess later sued, and won, because our contracts stated that the character of Lucy Carmichael was to be based on Lucy Ricardo.*

Candy Moore

(ACTOR)

They had been testing girls for about six months to play the part of Lucy's daughter, and although I was working steadily in episodic television, I was never sent up for an interview. Then [Elliot Lewis] remembered me from a pilot I had done (Time Out for Ginger) *and thought I might have the qualities Lucy was looking for. So I got this call to come in the next day to audition for Lucy. That was on a Thursday. I was very excited because I loved* I Love Lucy *and really admired her. So I went in on Friday and read for her, and she just enjoyed the whole experience of reading with me. She told me right then and there that I was hired, and we started rehearsing the following Monday. It was the easiest job I ever got.*

I was a little scared that the first episode revolved around me, but I had already been used to being a featured player, so I knew I could handle it. This script (like all the scripts) was contrived around enabling Lucy to have one, stunning, centerpiece of comedy. Every episode built to that centerpiece. My contract called for my appearing on seven out of every thirteen episodes filmed, and in the beginning it usually ended up being nine or ten. Looking at the show now, I look about eighteen, but I was only thirteen or fourteen. I was wearing a lot of makeup. You know Hal King, the makeup artist, really was *an artist. He took his time with us and made sure that we looked just right. We were heavily made up, but he made us look natural.*

Everyone on the show was extremely nice to us, with the exception of [director] Jack Donohue. I don't think he liked children at all, and he had no way of relating to us. That caused him to be awkward with us. Jack wasn't the kind of director who helped me figure out what I was doing, or what my motivation might be for a scene. He was concerned with where we were standing and how the cameras were capturing us. I never worked with the man on a one-on-one level to help me find my character, which is what I think a good director does. He handled the technical part, but frankly I missed the creative part of the work. While I was very *grateful to be on the series, I was very unhappy with the part of Chris. She was a plastic teenager, and I wanted to make her more real. They kept her pretty much as a cardboard character. As an actor, I like to be vivacious. Not always happy, but vivacious. Chris had no colors. They wanted to keep her on one note. I felt awkward and frustrated because of it.*

Jimmy Garrett

(ACTOR)

I had done a lot of television already before the audition for The Lucy Show. *Literally every kid actor in town was brought in to read for the part of Jerry Carmichael. I've always said it was lucky that Ronny Howard was already working on* The Andy Griffith Show *[1960–68], or I might not have gotten the part. By the end of the audition, they had let everyone go except myself, Ralph Hart, and Deborah Walley. Candy Moore wasn't even a part of this process. We thought for sure that Deborah had gotten the part, but when we came back on Monday morning for the reading of the first script, there was Candy!*

For the scene where Lucy is jumping outside of Viv's window, two grips had her on a platform and raised and lowered her to look like she was jumping. For the scenes done outside the house on the trampoline, Lucy was hooked up to wires and a harness.

Gary Morton

(LUCILLE BALL'S HUSBAND AND PRODUCTION CONSULTANT)

Lucy was adamant about not *bringing in "the husband" to do work. She didn't want comparisons between Desi and me, or to have people think I was getting a free ride. She started by having me read scripts to see what my comedy point of view was. Once she got a taste of where I was coming from comedically, she gradually brought me in to work on* The Lucy Show.

THE LUCY SHOW #2: "LUCY DIGS UP A DATE"

(CBS, OCTOBER 8, 1962), 30 MINUTES (B&W)

GUEST CAST: Dick Martin, William Windom, Don Briggs, Robert Rockwell, James Gonzales, Gene O'Donnell, Vito Scotti, Bob Stephenson, Ralph Faulkner, Victor Paul

Lucy and Viv are tired of the same old dates on Saturday nights. When Jerry's handsome math teacher Mr. Taylor (William Windom) shows up at the door, Lucy just has to know if he is single. After maneuvering to get his wallet, checking his driver's license, and returning the wallet all without his knowledge, Lucy discovers she has forgotten to put the license back in the wallet and must now find a way to return it.

HIGHLIGHTS & TRIVIA

It is never fully explained to any satisfaction why Lucy Carmichael, a woman with great beauty, charm, and some money in the bank, is so desperate to find a date. In the early 1960s television, such desperate women were usually thought to be tramps (see any soap opera) or recipients of comic pathos (think of Rose Marie on *The Dick Van Dyke Show*). Lucy is neither one of those, and this aspect of her character is never very appealing. In later years, the Lucy character will be almost sexless. This episode introduces Dick Martin as next-door neighbor, and sometimes date, Harry Connors.

Dick Martin

(ACTOR/COMEDIAN)

Dan Rowan and I were working a club in Hollywood called The Crescendo, *and [syndicated columnist] Walter Winchell brought Lucille to see us. We then went to Sparks, Nevada, where I got a call from Desi with this idea. He asked for our schedule; in those days we were booked for awhile, then we'd have a couple of weeks off. He said, "I'll work with your schedule." The first one had to be done immediately, so he sent a twin-engine Cessna for me, flew me into Burbank, had a car take me to Desilu to work, then sent me back to Nevada to work. Anyway, I guess they figured that Lucille and Vivian needed to have boyfriends. I also did the warm-ups for the shows I was on. Neither Desi nor Gary [Morton] did them when I was there. After I left, Gary started doing them. He was a stand-up comic, and very personable.*

Candy Moore

(ACTOR)

Both Desi Jr. and Keith Thibodeaux [Little Ricky from I Love Lucy*] played in the band that entertained at the filmings, during the warm-up and between scenes. They were such talented musicians! It was fantastic! It was so heartwarming to see a kid following in his parents' footsteps, but doing it in his own way with his own style.*

William Windom

(ACTOR)

I came out to California in 1961, and found myself working almost immediately. My agent simply told me to report to Desilu for work. There was never an audition. Much later I was told that Lucy almost fired me after the first couple of readings. She never said a word to me at the time. I'm glad she didn't—it might have undermined my confidence. The point of the show was not for me to be funny; I was the guy at the beach flexing his muscles. The part was totally straight. Why did they hire me? Beats me. Who knows what led to my being asked to do this show? There was nothing on paper that called for me to be even slightly humorous. The week was pleasant but not memorable. Lucy had been such a feminine beauty, so cute. I was a little surprised how much makeup she wore. There was also a toughness about her that I wasn't expecting. Many women in show business get this leatheriness about them—Roz Russell, for example. As they get older, they begin to lose their femininity out of having to constantly put up barriers.

Robert Rockwell

(ACTOR)

I never understood the casting of this episode. Bill Windom and I should have switched parts. I was known for playing muscular but kind of square guys in a comedy way, while Bill was more of a straight actor (and a very talented one). Lucy certainly was familiar with my work from all the years of Our Miss Brooks *(1952–56).*

THE LUCY SHOW #3: "LUCY IS A REFEREE"

(CBS, OCTOBER 15, 1962), 30 MINUTES (B&W)

GUEST CAST: Dick Martin, Dennis Rush, Desi Arnaz Jr.

To please Jerry, Lucy becomes the referee of his YMCA football team. She learns all the signals, but cannot help interfering in her son's behalf. To save face, she offers to take both teams to a pro football game, but a blizzard interferes.

HIGHLIGHTS & TRIVIA

Lucille is brilliant in the scene where she is rehearsing the football signals with Dick Martin. Her intensity, concentration, and belief in her comedy turns a funny idea into a tour de force. While the full installment does not keep to this level of humor, it certainly has its great moments.

Dick Martin

(ACTOR/COMEDIAN)

Desi was at every reading, wearing a big straw hat and smoking a thin Cuban cigar. He never wrote down a word. When it was over, he'd give notes right off the top of his head, going through the entire script from memory. He was brilliant, and an incredible director. Although Jack Donohue was the [official] director on the show, it was also directed by Lucille and Desi. That was their system, and it obviously worked. Lucille was uncanny. She could be looking me right in the eye, and without turning her head say, "Camera three you are off your mark." And by God, he was! Then I guess the shit hit the fan, and after a few shows, Desi was no longer there.

Desi Arnaz Jr.

It may seem as though I am taking particular pleasure in whacking my mother on the behind with that pillow, but the truth is that they were trick pillows. Problem was, they weren't working, so we had to really knock them around to make the feathers fly.

Candy Moore

(ACTOR)

Jimmy Garrett was a warm, loving, funny, *little boy. There wasn't a mean bone in his body. I loved going to school with Jimmy. Mrs. Hainey was our main teacher, and she had wonderful show business stories to tell. Although we were each in different grades, we were given separate work to do and did it independently.*

THE LUCY SHOW #4: "LUCY MISPLACES $2,000"

(CBS, OCTOBER 22, 1962), 30 MINUTES (B&W)

GUEST CAST: Dick Martin, Charles Lane, Reta Shaw, Katie Sweet, Murvyn Vye, Sandra Gould, Tom McDonough

Lucy and her banker Mr. Barnsdahl have a falling out, so Lucy closes her account. Instead of a check for $20, she is given one for $2,000. Lucy cashes it and hides the money in a candy box to teach the banker a lesson. Unfortunately, the youngsters take the candy to a carnival, and everyone frantically tries to recapture the bills.

HIGHLIGHTS & TRIVIA

One of the best efforts of the first season, this installment is funny from beginning to end. It is rife with sitcom favorites, including Reta Shaw as the fat lady (uncharacteristic for her, as she almost never allowed her size to be a point of derision) and Sandra Gould as the bank clerk. And then there is that elephant.

Dick Martin

(ACTOR/COMEDIAN)

I had worked with Bertha the Elephant in Reno, and I learned that all Indian elephants are taught the same things. They brought this elephant in on Tuesday, so the cast and crew could get used to it being around. Lucille was terrified of this huge beast. I just walked up and said, "trunk up," and up went the elephant's trunk. Lucille thought I was from Mars! It raised its leg for me and let me pet it. That show was so much fun.

Madelyn Pugh Martin Davis

(WRITER)

Lucy was afraid to work with that elephant. We had a meeting about it, because the whole end of the show depended upon it. While we were wondering what to do, we got a call from Vivian on the set, and she said, "Don't worry, she'll do it! I told her if she didn't want to do the thing with the elephant, I'd *do it. She's ready to do it* herself, *now!"*

The basic plot of this entry was adapted for a children's book that was published around this time by Whitman Press called *Lucy and the Madcap Mystery* by Cole Fannin. Interestingly enough, the other plot in the book will become the basis for the first two parts of a four-part *Here's Lucy* episode in 1969. The episode here introduces Charles Lane as banker Mr. Barnsdahl. Although Lane is a veteran of many *Lucy* appearances, he is not a success on this series (Lane has trouble remembering his lines) and before long his character will be written out. Notice the built-in bookcase where Lucy hides the candy box; it mysteriously disappears from the set two weeks later.

THE BOB HOPE SHOW

(NBC, OCTOBER 24, 1962), 60 MINUTES (B&W)
PRODUCED BY: Jack Hope
DIRECTED BY: Jack Shea
WRITTEN BY: Mort Lachman, Bill Larkin, John Rapp, Lester White, Charles Lee, Gig Henry
CAST: Bob Hope (host), Lucille Ball, Bing Crosby, Juliet Prowse

Lucille's main contribution is in a sketch casting her as a lady district attorney in love with an underworld syndicate boss. She looks especially lovely. She and Bob also show outtakes from *Critic's Choice* (1963), their most recent film together. Ball is not in the longest sketch, a parody of *Bonanza* (1959–73), but does join the cast for the finale singing of "Thanks for the Memory."

THE LUCY SHOW #5: "LUCY BUYS A SHEEP"

(CBS, OCTOBER 29, 1962), 30 MINUTES (B&W)
CAST: Charles Lane, Parley Baer, Eddie Quillan

Left with no one to tend the lawn, Lucy buys a sheep named Clementine to take care of the grass. Unfortunately, weather and circumstances make Clementine an unwelcome house guest, and Lucy sneaks her back to the farm. Only then is she offered $200 for Clementine to appear in a blanket ad.

HIGHLIGHTS & TRIVIA

This is the only episode of *The Lucy Show*, in all six seasons, where we see Lucy Carmichael's bedroom. In fact, the original script places that entire scene in the kitchen and not in her bedroom. Lucille spends a great deal of time rehearsing with that sheep, ensuring that she not only wrings every drop of humor out of the situation, but that the animals are handled in a humane manner. When Lucy and Viv do their *a capella* duet in the sheep pen, it is not only humorous but heartwarming. They actually sound good together. The opening scene from this episode was used as the audition scene for the children. In the original script, and in the scripts for the first few weeks, Lucy's daughter Chris is called Linda.

Bob Schiller

(WRITER)

Jimmy Garrett [as Lucy's eight-year-old son] was a cute kid, and Candy Moore was beautiful; both were talented . . . but they came across so dull . . . real white-bread kids. This series had no ethnic flavor to it at all, the way I Love Lucy *did.*

Jimmy Garrett

(ACTOR)

We kids got each week's script the Friday before the first Monday reading, while the adults didn't get theirs until Monday. This gave us a chance to digest the show and hopefully memorize it. I generally knew all my lines before I came to the studio on Monday. There were cue cards for the adults if they perhaps got lost and needed a reminder, but us kids never were allowed to use them. They were afraid we'd start to read them during our performances. As far as the delivery of my lines, that was a combination of input from [director] Jack Donohue, Lucy, and sometimes Vivian, and my mother, who was my manager and coach. Vivian used to say that I got all the "Fred Mertz" lines in the script, and that, according to her, "I did them better than that old poop."

Stanley Livingston

(ACTOR)

We shot My Three Sons *(1960–72) on the sound stage right next door, and we would often go and watch rehearsals or filmings if we had a break.* The Lucy Show *was so different from our show because it was done live in front of an audience, and there was this rehearsal process. There were no restrictions to our coming on* The Lucy Show *set and observing. On our show, we just learned our lines and then shot a scene. I often wondered how it would have impacted our show if we had done it Lucy's way. She was like a female Charlie Chaplin. They'd rehearse, and funny accidents would come out of it that would be wonderful for the show.*

It is always a thing for child actors: What do you do when you are not actually in front of the cameras? You try and find kid things to do, and we often played with Ralph Hart and Jimmy Garrett next door. There was a really smooth area right in front of our stages, and an extra area next door that wasn't being used that had a nice steep ramp, so several of us would go skateboarding there. We did this for about six months with Jimmy and Ralph, until one of them took a bad spill and got hurt. Lucy found out, and needless to say, that *was the end of skateboarding at Desilu Studios. Soon, basketball was also eliminated.*

Jimmy Garrett

(ACTOR)

The funny thing is, it was Vivian *who bought Ralph and I our skateboards. I wonder if Lucy knew that!*

THE LUCY SHOW #6: "LUCY BECOMES AN ASTRONAUT"

(CBS, NOVEMBER 5, 1962), 30 MINUTES (B&W)

GUEST CAST: Dick Martin, Alix Talton, Nancy Kulp

Former Navy Waves Lucy and Viv volunteer to take a special test for women in space. The publicity goes to Lucy's head, so Viv and Harry scheme to bring her down to earth and teach her a lesson.

HIGHLIGHTS & TRIVIA

Writers Schiller and Weiskopf very cleverly begin introducing a "back story" for the characters of Lucy and Viv. We now know that they met in the Waves during World War II, and have been close friends ever since. Filling in this kind of information gives the characters a sense of reality needed to balance the unreality of the comedy, something that will be sorely missing from the series in the future. There are several references in the original script to Lucy missing out on a celebrity party with Ethel Merman, and to Lucy's imitation of Merman singing "I Got Rhythm" that are not in the final version. For trivia fans, it is Lucille who has the claustrophobia in real life, not Vivian (as revealed in the "isolation" scene). While Lucille Ball will never appear in the closing commercials for alternate sponsors Lever Brothers and General Foods, Vivian and the rest of the cast get to make extra money each week by pitching soap and pudding.

Candy Moore

(ACTOR)

I got to be in a lot of the commercials we did for The Lucy Show. *I had done a lot of commercials previous to being on the series, and one commercial generally took a whole day to shoot. We did these things for Jell-O and Dove soap on Thursday nights after the filming of the episodes. I don't think they took longer than a half an hour each to shoot! I was paid extra money, but it wasn't a lot of fun.*

Dick Martin

(ACTOR/COMEDIAN)

[Director] Jack Donohue knew Lu's needs and what was right for her. He was good, but not as strong a director as, say, a John Rich. Lucille knew every light and camera. She owned them. And in what is basically a one-set show, there are only so many options

physically. I can't fault Lu for taking charge. She was that type. I am such a fan of directors. But at that time, I didn't know much about television. Now I have realized that with a sitcom, it is ninety-nine percent casting. The rest is the writing."

Gary Morton

(PRODUCTION CONSULTANT)

We all loved Jack Donohue as a director. Lucille had worked with him at MGM when he was a choreographer. He made her laugh, which was important. He knew how to work the three-camera system. Later on, some of the directors didn't do so well with that system. They didn't last long. Elliot Lewis was a wonderful man, very bright. He and Lucy got along very well. Bob Carroll Jr. and Madelyn [Pugh Martin] Davis are very talented, but they don't ever seem to mention the contributions made by Jess Oppenheimer or Bob Schiller and Bob Weiskopf. It was Schiller and Weiskopf who were actually writing the scripts on the first couple of seasons of The Lucy Show. *Bob and Madelyn were head writers, who made changes, tightened up the scripts, and made each show sound as if it came from one voice. Lucille said they became producers when they ran out of ideas as writers.*

THE DANNY KAYE SHOW

(NBC, NOVEMBER 11, 1962), 60 MIN (COLOR)

PRODUCED BY: Jess Oppenheimer
DIRECTED BY: Greg Garrison
WRITTEN BY: Herbert Baker, Ernest Chambers, Sylvia Fine
CAST: Danny Kaye (host), Lucille Ball, Hollis Morrison, Roger Til.

This is Lucille's first variety show appearance since Ed Sullivan's show in June, 1962. It is also the first occasion her red hair is shown on TV in full color, this time muted to a deeper red from her usual flaming orange. Lucille looks thinner and younger than she has in years, wearing a stylish wig and extremely heavy makeup. She seems healthy, glamorous, and happy, but her voice!

When last heard on *I Love Lucy*, her throat uttered the noises associated with Lucy Ricardo, that girlish soprano that gave the character so much of its charm. Now, the timbre is rougher, and the voice has dropped a full octave in its delivery. She can no longer push her voice to the upper end. Occasionally, her voice has a slight rasp. In context, at this moment in time, it seems as if Lucille is simply tired. In hindsight, Lucille had already seriously hurt her voice. Screaming at the top of her lungs on Broadway in *Wildcat*, smoking three packs of cigarettes a day (she always claimed she didn't inhale), and having what became more than an occasional drink has damaged her throat beyond repair. Polyps have already developed, and surgery eventually has to be performed.

Lucie Arnaz

I think my mother got a hold of some voice teacher and he gave her some really bad advice! Had she seen someone better, she might have saved her voice from getting so gruff.

Anonymous

Lucy abused her voice terribly. She smoked like a chimney, and had a big taste for scotch. She was by no means an alcoholic or anything, but she enjoyed drinking. Scotch really wears at the vocal chords. Also, trying to sound *young all the time put incredible pressure on her throat. She wasn't using her diaphragm properly, and foolishly no one ever taught her* how. *Even at this point, her voice might have been saved. But no one had the guts to pull her aside and tell her the damage she was doing to herself. She was surrounded by men with no balls.*

Ball agrees to do this guest appearance to promote *The Lucy Show* and to substantiate she is a musical performer. It is a wise move. She is in top form, proving the interval since *Wildcat* has not dulled her comedy sense. The opening features Lucille as a chorus girl while Danny sings "The Glory Hallelujah Twist," and she keeps in step with trained dancers half her age. One sketch has Lucille and Danny parodying the then-popular one man or woman show, as done by Judy Garland, Carol Channing, and Marlene Dietrich. Lucille goes through her musical paces like a trouper, singing snatches of "Swanee," "Diamonds Are a Girl's Best Friend," and "Falling in Love Again." Lucille is not parodying her *own* singing; she is presented as a musical performer. Although her speaking voice reveals signs of wear, her recent Broadway and musical TV experience shows in her ease with the musical moments, especially in her duet with Kaye of "You're Just in Love." Working in a freer environment than a sitcom also allows Lucille to try satire. Through the years, both on her own shows and guest appearances, she shines when allowed to do parody and lampoon.

The best moments of the show involve the two redheads and their dining experiences. A first date in a French restaurant features the pair getting successively drunker as they eat their fare served in an intoxicating wine sauce. While Lucille's drunk bit had been honed to perfection performing the Vitameatavegamin routine (on *I Love Lucy* episode #30: "Lucy Does a TV Commercial"), she brings something new to this sketch that often is missing when she tries it in other venues. A visit to a Japanese restaurant (then brand new in this country) has the tight-skirted Lucille trying to sit down at the low Japanese tables and handle chopsticks. Both skits are hysterical! Had Lucille chosen the variety format instead of the sitcom format for her return to television, there is no doubt she could have been just as successful. Lucille receives a hefty $100,000 for her appearance on Danny Kaye's showcase.

Gregg Oppenheimer

(WRITER/SON OF PRODUCER JESS OPPENHEIMER)

This was the first time my father was reunited with Lucille creatively since he left I Love Lucy *in 1956. The show was nominated as show of the year at the Emmy Awards, but lost to a documentary called* The Tunnel, *which was about a group of people trying to tunnel out of East Berlin. How can you possibly compare the two shows?*

THE LUCY SHOW #7: "LUCY IS A KANGAROO FOR A DAY"

(CBS, NOVEMBER 12, 1962), 30 MINUTES (B&W)

GUEST CAST: Charles Lane, Majel Barrett, Norman Leavitt, Sid Gould, John McGiver

Lucy needs money to buy her son a bicycle for his birthday, so Mr. Barnsdahl arranges for her to be a temporary secretary in Manhattan. Her unfamiliarity with modern, electric equipment soon turns the office into a shambles. As a last chance, she is sent on an errand to deliver contracts. With extra time, she goes to pick out the bicycle, but destroys her suit in the process and has to borrow a kangaroo costume to make her delivery.

HIGHLIGHTS & TRIVIA

Again, the show is brilliant because the writers give a sound *reason* for Lucy's ineptness. It is not because she is stupid or scatterbrained that she fails as a secretary; it is because she is not familiar with such things as electric pencil sharpeners, intercoms, and electric typewriters. As long as the story has a basis in reality, Lucille's clowning is hilarious. In later years, her character's inability to perform even the simplest of office tasks is grating and annoying because it is impossible to like anyone that inept. Notice Majel Barrett as the secretary Lucy replaces. A veteran of Lucille's Desilu Workshop, she will soon gain television immortality as Nurse Chapel on *Star Trek* (1966–69). The entire bit where Lucy's knitted suit unravels is taken from the script outline for *Lucy Goes to Broadway* (1961), which was never produced. This is the first appearance of Sid Gould (the waiter). He is Gary Morton's cousin, and becomes a staple of Lucille's shows for the next fifteen years. While he never has a large part, almost every waiter, bell captain, or bit character on Ball's series will be played by Sid.

Irma Kusely

(HAIRSTYLIST)

Sid Gould was a pain in the ass. He thought he was so funny, and he made me bilious. He was Gary Morton's cousin, so they used him in tiny parts as often as they could. Later, they also used his wife, Vanda Barra.

Jimmy Garrett

(ACTOR)

The first time I made my entrance on the bicycle, the assistant was supposed to hold me up and then give me a little shove out the door [from the pantry]. I ended up crashing into the door frame and we had to retake the whole thing.

THE LUCY SHOW #8: "LUCY, THE MUSIC LOVER"

(CBS, NOVEMBER 19, 1962), 30 MINUTES (B&W)

GUEST CAST: Mary Jane Croft, Frank Aletter, Susan Oakes, Richard Gittings

Lucy accepts Audrey Simmons' offer to arrange a blind date for her because Audrey knows so many eligible bachelors. The man (Frank Aletter) is a doctor and an avid classical music fan and violinist, so Lucy feigns interest to please him. When he meets Vivian, he is taken with her sincere interest in the music, and Lucy gets so mad she accidentally smashes his fingers in the piano lid. All of this occurs, of course, just before his charity music recital.

HIGHLIGHTS & TRIVIA

This is Mary Jane Croft's debut playing Audrey Simmons. The character is very close to that of her Betty Ramsey on *I Love Lucy*, but it will be phased out by the third season. Mary Jane will, of course, return when the show's locale is moved from New York to California in 1965.

Frank Aletter

(ACTOR)

My agent sent me in for an interview. I didn't read. Lucy was sitting behind a desk, and all the writers were there. We chatted for a minute, then Lucy asked me to stand up and stand back. I stood up, and she came out from behind the desk and stood next to me. She said, "Can you get elevators?" meaning lifts in my shoes to make me taller. I said, "For you, my dear, definitely!" That was when I bought my first pair of shoes that had risers in them that added two inches. To this day, whenever I refer to them, I call them my "Lucy shoes."

The first thing she did was explain the plot to me, and told me that they had done this physical bit before. She took me to a screening room and ran the old "Handcuffs" episode from I Love Lucy *to show me what she and Desi had done. In the actual shoot, I was surprised to find that Lucy had taped to the keyboard of the piano, hidden from the audience, all the key sentences that she was having a hard time with. She was not yet relying on cue cards. In the concert box scene, we rehearsed Lucy going to sleep. At one point, she falls behind me. With her head on the chair, she booms up at me, "We do not do triple takes on this show without my permission!" In the final scene, while we filmed, Lucy was constantly whispering direction in my ear. In fact, she bit my ear! I have heard Lucy was difficult, but I found her to be a delight. Actually, I found Vivian to be the pain in the ass, not Lucy. When Dick Martin left the show, they wanted to bring me in again as her ongoing boyfriend. After this episode, I went under contract to NBC to do a pilot through Jess Oppenheimer, and because of it I couldn't do* The Lucy Show. *The pilot never sold, and I really missed out.*

Ralph Hart

(ACTOR)

I loved being able to dance on this show. [Director] Jack Donohue had been a dance choreographer, and on Tuesdays and Wednesdays when we had a little extra time, he would take me to the pavement outside the stage and teach me soft-shoe routines. The funny thing is, after all that training, I can't dance at all *today!*

Candy Moore

(ACTOR)

Ralph Hart was a very talented kid who was very full of imagination. He was sweet, nice, and a fabulous dancer—a hard-working kid who would do anything asked of him. Like Jimmy [Garrett]. They never had tantrums, or emotional disorders; they were happy and glad to be working. But Ralph was very introverted, which is unusual for a child actor. I never saw him enjoying that he was such a good looking kid.

THE LUCY SHOW #9: "LUCY PUTS UP A TV ANTENNA"

(CBS, NOVEMBER 26, 1962), 30 MINUTES (B&W)

GUEST CAST: Del Moore, Lloyd Corrigan, Chuck Roberson, Hubie Kerns

When Lucy's TV set doesn't work, she discovers that the antenna has blown off the roof. Refusing to spend extra money, she talks Viv into helping her replace it themselves.

HIGHLIGHTS & TRIVIA

The bit on the roof is yet another classic TV moment for the two ladies, each brilliant in her execution of the dialog and physical humor. It is as funny as anything they did together on *I Love Lucy*. There is a very expensive matte shot that is used when Lucy and Viv are on the roof. The women do their comedy in front of a blue screen, and the whole town behind them is optically edited in later. The plot line also establishes a home repair theme that will be used extensively on the show during its first two seasons. The scene in the TV repair shop is greatly edited, and was much longer when filmed. In it, Lucy holds up a cardboard TV screen to show the repairman how her screen looks by contorting her face. A color still from this sequence will be used as part of the show's opening credits for the next season. The end of the episode, where Viv lights a fire that billows smoke up to Lucy stuck in the chimney, brings up a question. *What* fireplace? There is no fireplace in *this* set as there was in every other *Lucy* set.

THE LUCY SHOW #10: "VIVIAN SUES LUCY"

(CBS, DECEMBER 3, 1962), 30 MINUTES (B&W)
GUEST CAST: Charles Lane

When Viv falls and hurts her ankle on a carelessly left toy, Lucy is in a pickle. She neglected to renew her liability insurance, and now fears Viv will sue her. Lucy waits on Viv endlessly, while Viv gives Lucy a hard time for even thinking she would sue her.

HIGHLIGHTS & TRIVIA

Vivian's antipathy towards her ex-husband is even funnier because everyone watching is thinking of Fred Mertz as the one she hates so much. Notice that Viv's bedroom is much changed from the last time we saw it in the first episode. This room will continue to change almost every time it is used, a lack of continuity that was unheard of on *I Love Lucy*. This is the last aired appearance of Charles Lane as Mr. Barnsdahl.

Bob Schiller
(WRITER)

Charley [Lane] was a great guy, and one of [Bob] Weiskopf's favorite actors, but he began to have serious trouble remembering his lines. He wasn't good on live shows. I don't think he ever worked in front of a live audience again. We couldn't afford to stop continuously for retakes, so he was written out. Also, there wasn't good chemistry between Charley and Lucy. He always came off as just being mean, and it wasn't funny. Gale Gordon became available after Dennis the Menace *(1959–63) went off the air, and we brought him in to play Mr. Mooney.*

Ralph Hart
(ACTOR)

They [the writers] would give me silver dollars for an extra good performance. [In this episode], Vivian changed her line reading from "mess and clutter" to "mess and junk." The crew feared I'd give my original line response, but I changed it to fit Viv's line. That was a two-silver-dollar night for me!

THE LUCY SHOW #11: "LUCY BUILDS A RUMPUS ROOM"

(CBS, DECEMBER 10, 1962), 30 MINUTES (B&W)
GUEST CAST: Dick Martin, Don Briggs, Chris Warfield, Jim Boles

When Lucy and Viv both invite dates over for a home-cooked meal, they decide everyone should go out rather than argue as to who will have the use of the house. Unfortunately, both girls double-cross the other with plans to actually stay home. It is finally decided that the only long-term answer is to build separate areas to entertain dates, but Lucy wants to do the project herself.

Dick Martin
(ACTOR/COMEDIAN)

This was a difficult special effect to do [having a load of coal delivered through the basement window by a chute on top of Lucille and Vivian]. They brought the coal in, and when the cloud of dust was raised, they cut. Lu and Viv were then made up to look as if they were full of coal dust, and we explained to the audience what had happened right before my entrance. Of course, the girls were never in any danger. Then prop coal was put all around them. The whole pile probably didn't weight two pounds. I enjoyed doing my reactions in this scene, because my character was able to find the situation funny the same way the audience did.

THE LUCY SHOW #12: "LUCY AND HER ELECTRIC MATTRESS"

(CBS, DECEMBER 17, 1962), 30 MINUTES (B&W)

Viv complains bitterly about the state of her mattress before taking a short trip out of town. While she is away, Lucy treats her to a newly decorated room and vibrating bed. The bed doesn't work properly and Lucy returns it. When Viv comes home unexpectedly with no place to sleep, the girls use their sons' bunk beds.

HIGHLIGHTS & TRIVIA

This is a *Lucy* classic. The entire episode is well paced, with two major block comedy scenes (those scenes that rely mostly on physical or slapstick comedy with little or no dialog). The writing is sharp, and the acting even sharper. References to Viv's Uncle Ned, Viv's claustrophobia, Viv's compulsive eating, and Viv's complaining expand on the character and make her more human and likeable to the viewer. Although Vivian Vance is a solid actor, at times it appears she has trouble getting into the character of Viv unless she is in the middle of the action. She sometimes displays a detachment that ruins any sense of warmth or playfulness. Lucille's stilt-walking in this entry is a genius turn of comedy that ranks with the best of the physical comedians. The laughter and applause are so sustained that they had to be cut down in the final print due to time constraints. Not all of what Lucille does with the stilts is in the script. This is an example of Lucille Ball actually creating a scene as she rehearses it, figuring out what works and what doesn't. Much of the second half of the show is different from the original script.

Bob Weiskopf
(WRITER)

This was one of those times when we got an idea, went to Lucy and said, "Have you ever walked on stilts?" When she told us she'd done it briefly as a child and then again for publicity pictures when she was a starlet, we said, "Stop! That's all we wanted to know!"

Dick Martin
(ACTOR/COMEDIAN)

I wasn't in this episode, but I was there that week and did the warm-up. Lu rehearsed for hours with those stilts. For hours. *She was a workaholic and a perfectionist. She loved to rehearse. Lucille was the antithesis of a Dean Martin. She was just like Carol Burnett.*

Jimmy Garrett
(ACTOR)

Lucy worked so much with those stilts that she became an expert. In fact, she got so *good that she had to tone down what she was doing in order to make it appear as if she was struggling with them. Whatever she tried to do, Lucy had so much talent and usually got so good at it that she would have to temper her performance or she would look* too *good.*

THE LUCY SHOW #13: "TOGETHER FOR CHRISTMAS"

(CBS, DECEMBER 24, 1962), 30 MINUTES (B&W)
GUEST CAST: Joel Mell, Tom Lowell

For the first time, the Carmichaels and the Bagleys will be spending Christmas together. Unfortunately, differences in family traditions cause Lucy and Viv to fight, almost ruining the holiday for the children.

HIGHLIGHTS & TRIVIA

This is actually a very insightful script. No one on TV had effectively addressed the idea that families from different backgrounds celebrate Christmas *very* differently. The cultural and traditional disparities of Americans were almost always homogenized in any holiday show produced by Hollywood. And again, even more background is given here on the Carmichael and Bagley families, including the fact that *this* Lucy also comes from Jamestown, New York, and that her mother is still alive.

Jimmy Garrett
(ACTOR)

We really were like a family. Ralph was a great kid. Because we were at a point where age made a big difference, Ralph hung out more with Desi Jr. and Keith Thibodeaux [Little Ricky] than with me because I was a few years younger. Candy Moore was my "big sis." She was always very loving and kind and warm and made me feel very special. She's the closest thing I'm ever going to have to a real sister.

THE LUCY SHOW #14: "CHRIS' NEW YEAR'S EVE PARTY"

(CBS, DECEMBER 31, 1962), 30 MINUTES (B&W)
GUEST CAST: Dick Martin, Don Briggs, Tom Lowell, James Gonzales

Chris exacts a promise from Lucy that she can throw a New Year's Eve party without Lucy's interference. Lucy and Viv take the boys to the Elm Tree Inn to stay out of Chris' way. After a sweet but dull dinner with the boys, Viv's boyfriend Eddie drops by to tell them that the party is a disaster and Chris needs their help.

HIGHLIGHTS & TRIVIA

The "silent movie sketch" is nothing but a long stretch of physical comedy without dialog. Every single move Lucille makes is written in the script. Ball is brilliant at making this sort of material come alive, but only when it is completely supported by what is on the paper. Ah, the innocence of 1962. Can you imagine a television show today where teenaged boys and girls do not know what to do together when there are *no* parents around?

Dick Martin

(ACTOR/COMEDIAN)

Lucy was marvelous as [Charlie] Chaplin. She rehearsed on her own incessantly, and we rehearsed quite a bit together. Remember, that was all done in only four days. I have a picture from that show hanging in my office. I was in nightclubs, doing two shows a night, at the same time I was doing this episode. It was a long *week.*

Candy Moore

(ACTOR)

This was my favorite episode of The Lucy Show. *It was a thrill to see it happening before your very eyes—Lucille Ball becoming Charlie Chaplin—layer upon layer upon layer. I never saw magic like that unfold in front of my eyes and it gave me a sense of Lucy as a transcendental artist who was also a magician! She rehearsed with such focus. The woman had extraordinary powers of concentration. She could do in three hours what it would take someone else three days to accomplish. Lucy would zoom in on her objective and strip away anything extraneous to her mission. She would envision something in her mind with such power that you could see it emerge out of her. Between [the] first reading Monday morning and show time Thursday night, Lucille Ball* became *Charlie Chaplin. I defy anyone else to do that!*

Jimmy Garrett

(ACTOR)

I did not like that costume I wore, coming down the steps as baby New Year one bit! A top hat, a diaper, black socks and shoes. I was very *embarrassed! It was Marl Young who played ragtime piano while they did the Chaplin sketch, but it was something that was dubbed in later. There was no piano music while we actually shot the scene.*

THE LUCY SHOW #15: "LUCY'S SISTER PAYS A VISIT"

(CBS, JANUARY 7, 1963), 30 MINUTES (B&W)

GUEST CAST: Dick Martin, Janet Waldo, Peter Marshall

Lucy's sister Marge visits after leaving her new groom Hughie. Lucy restores harmony when Hughie arrives, but talks the young couple into having the big wedding they missed by eloping. The nuptials are planned for the next day, with disastrous results.

HIGHLIGHTS & TRIVIA

There actually is an upholstered armchair called a *fauteuil,* which Lucy supposedly gave to her sister as a wedding gift. There is a reference in the original script to Jack and Paula Carter being almost like family; comedian Jack Carter and his then-wife Paula Stewart are indeed close friends of Ball and her spouse, comedian Gary Morton. Lucille's drunk bit is trotted out again in this outing, this time with Viv matching her hiccup for hiccup. It is very similar to the scene Lucille did with Ann Sothern in the first *Lucy-Desi* hour show in 1957. It is a shame that the writers never use any of Lucy's relatives again in the series. For example, it would have been interesting to have Lucy's sister be an occasional character, or Lucy's mother from Jamestown or Viv's Uncle Ned. Actually Lucille had an Uncle Ned in real life, Ned Orcitt. Janet Waldo last appeared on *I Love Lucy* all the way back in 1952 as the love-struck teenager with a crush on Ricky. Peter Marshall will be forever known as the host on the long-running game show *The Hollywood Squares* (1968–79).

Janet Waldo

(ACTOR)

I was doing the voice of Judy Jetson on The Jetsons *[1962–63, 1985, 1987] at the same time as we were doing this. . . . You know, Peter [Marshall] gets very nervous before he performs. When it came time for his first scene, he couldn't be found. He was in the bathroom throwing up!*

[Director] Jack Donohue kept having me do my first entrance over and over. I couldn't figure out what I was doing wrong or what I wasn't doing that he wanted. Finally, Lucy pulled me aside and said, "He wants you to bawl like me!" I did it her way, and that's exactly *what he wanted.*

Peter Marshall

(ACTOR)

We rehearsed this episode during the Cuban Missile Crisis. I'll never forget it. I was so worried about what would happen to my children if something happened. The production company seemed oblivious to what was going on. Only Janet Waldo seemed sympathetic. I had another problem with the rehearsal process. [Director] Jack Donohue would direct me, then Lucy would change my line reading. While they discussed it, Vivian Vance would pull me aside and tell me how my line should really *be read. I really got fed up, and I said in a loud voice, "I really don't give a shit* how *I read this line. Do I take direction from you, Miss Ball, you, Miss Vance, or you, Mr. Donohue?" Lucille Ball went apeshit! She said, "Do it any way you want!" After the filming, Lucille knocked on my dressing room door and told me my performance was terrific. The production company offered me a job as a regular at $750 a week (which was a lot of money back then), but I didn't want to put up with that crap.*

Lucille was still a great looking woman at this point in her life. No one could pull herself together like Lucille Ball, even in her later years. I knew series regular Dick Martin very well. In fact, my partner Tommy Noonan and I introduced Dick to his *partner Dan Rowan!*

THE LUCY SHOW #16: "LUCY AND VIV ARE VOLUNTEER FIREMEN"

(CBS, JANUARY 14, 1963), 30 MINUTES (B&W)

GUEST CAST: Pat McVey, Carole Cook

Lucy's letter-writing campaign for a Danfield fire department leads to her becoming the captain of an all-women volunteer brigade. Lucy and Viv practice and practice, making sure they are ready for their first call to duty. When the alarm finally rings, the girls accidentally set the firehouse on fire.

HIGHLIGHTS & TRIVIA

This is a wonderful outing, very reminiscent of Lucy and Ethel's old adventures. The timing of the scene with the panicked girls putting on their uniforms is perfect. Lucille wears only her own hair in this one to accommodate the fire hat. The name of the politician Lucy writes to is John Dodds, which also happens to be the name of Vance's new husband. There is an extra scene at the end with Lucy and Viv back at the house that is cut from the script due to time constraints. The scene in the firehouse is a wonderful showcase for Carole Cook.

Carole Cook

(ACTOR/FAMILY FRIEND)

As well as I knew her, there was a cutoff when she was working. Work was work, and there was a focus and a professionalism. Some people called it a toughness. But when you put on a show in four days, week after week, there is no time to waste. I just accepted that about her. In this episode, I did a stunt that Lucille did not want to do. I came down that fire pole because Lucille was afraid to. It was very high up, and it was scary. She got up there, looked at it, and said no. Lucille felt that if she got hurt doing something, it would throw everyone out of work. She only did the stunts that she felt comfortable with. That was very professional thinking. She changed it in rehearsals. This was the only stunt she said she would do when it was written that she later changed her mind about. The scene where Lucille and Vivian were putting on their uniforms was rehearsed moment to moment. Lucille worked meticulously with every detail. Everything was worked out—choreographed. And she and Viv worked so well together that they could do it this way. Everything was on the paper. Certainly, if they found something funny to do in rehearsal they added it in, but it was mostly there to begin with. She always gave her writers credit for that. Naturally, her execution was brilliant. But nothing was impromptu.

THE LUCY SHOW #17: "LUCY BECOMES A REPORTER"

(CBS, JANUARY 21, 1963), 30 MINUTES (B&W)

GUEST CAST: John Vivyan, Roscoe Karns, Bobs Watson, Emlen Davies

Lucy gets a temporary job on a newspaper and messes everything up. When she learns that an old flame of Viv's is now a famous financier, she disguises herself as Viv to get an interview and save her job.

HIGHLIGHTS & TRIVIA

This was probably the weakest of the first season shows. Lucy is shown as scatterbrained, and it never really is funny.

Stanley Livingston

(ACTOR)

Although they were no longer working together, Bill Frawley [now costarring in My Three Sons, *1960–65] was still carrying on a feud with Vivian Vance. I was Bill's puppet because I just idolized him. I never knew either of my grandfathers, so he became a surrogate one for me. Bill would have me help him pull dirty tricks on Vivian. He'd see her walking on the [Desilu] lot, or they'd be rehearsing a scene, and he'd say, "Come on, we've got to pull something on her!" One time, we got two whole boxes full of empty film cans, which make a lot of noise. I had one and he had the other. We snuck into the doorway of their sound stage, and Bill said, "When I say now, throw your box and run like hell!" We waited for Lucy to finish her dialog, and as soon as he heard Vivian saying, "Well, hi Lucy," he growled, "Now!," and about twenty-five of these things went crashing down. Bill said, "That'll fix that old bitch!" and we'd go running back to our stage. Vivian would sometimes let him have it verbally, but Bill always instigated it. The nicest thing I remember him calling her was a douche bag. I got the feeling that two of them almost enjoyed the battle, that it wasn't pure hatred but something they liked doing, like a game.*

THE LUCY SHOW #18: "LUCY AND VIV PUT IN A SHOWER"

(CBS, JANUARY 28, 1963), 30 MINUTES (B&W)

GUEST CAST: Dick Martin, Don Briggs, Stafford Repp

Although she can't afford to install an extra bathroom, Lucy decides that an extra shower is needed to meet the needs of five people. Her friend Harry gets out of the installation job by hiring a plumber and telling Lucy it is free. Lucy is such a persistent meddler that the plumber quits, leaving Lucy and Viv to finish the task.

HIGHLIGHTS & TRIVIA

This episode is a classic, ranking with almost anything Lucille had done in the past. There was so much laughter, and the scene ran so long, that it had to be edited down to fit the time slot. The final scene (with the girls stuck in the shower as the water continually rises) was almost a physical disaster for Lucille.

Dick Martin

(ACTOR/COMEDIAN)

There was no dress rehearsal for this episode because of the water involved. I don't remember Lucille and Viv even having a chance to work with the water before they were in front of the audience.

Bob Schiller

(WRITER)

Actually, in this case the dress rehearsal was done the day before. The girls did get a chance to work in the water, but not twice on the same day. That would have been too much for them to do.

Irma Kusely

(HAIRSTYLIST)

This was one of the few episodes where, because of the physical stunt involved, we had to use Lucille's own hair. We matched the wigs to be the exact color of her hair, so no one would ever be able to tell the difference. And [makeup artist] Hal King pulled off her false eyelashes before the scene got too involved.

Lucille Ball

This was the most dangerous stunt I ever did. When I went down to the bottom of the shower, I couldn't get up again. There I was in front of a studio audience trying to be funny, and I thought I was going to drown. I swallowed a lot of water. Luckily, I was wearing my own hair. Viv realized I was in trouble, and pulled me up by the roots of my hair. To give me a chance to catch my breath, she began to do all of our dialog, doing my lines as questions. She had great theatre training, and she knew how to cover for me. The distressed look on my face was real. When they got us out of the shower, I went to grab for a microphone to say goodnight to the audience [the final scene was shot after the audience left to give Ball a chance to recover and dry off]. Gary [Morton] screamed at me not to touch it, for fear I would electrocute myself. Believe me, I was all wet! I don't think the audience ever knew the difference. They continued to scream with laughter.

THE LUCY SHOW #19: "LUCY'S BARBERSHOP QUARTET"

(CBS, FEBRUARY 4, 1963), 30 MINUTES (B&W)

GUEST CAST: Hans Conried, Carole Cook, Dorothy Konrad, Alan Ray

Lucy is very hurt that she is left out of the Volunteer Firemen's barbershop quartet. When one lady in the singing group moves, Lucy wants to replace her, despite her tiny voice. She seeks the aid of voice teacher Dr. Gitterman, and learns to sing out until she gets stage fright just before a show.

HIGHLIGHTS & TRIVIA

Lucille loved working with Hans Conried, who plays the voice teacher. The entire voice lesson scene will be repeated the following season, with Lucy as the teacher and Ethel Merman as the nonplussed pupil.

Carole Cook

(ACTOR/FAMILY FRIEND)

Lucille was very enamored of doing these musical comedy things. I always found it very interesting that she did, because she had no background in it.

THE LUCY SHOW #20: "LUCY AND VIV BECOME TYCOONS"

(CBS, FEBRUARY 11, 1963), 30 MINUTES (B&W)

GUEST CAST: Don Briggs, Bern Hoffman

Vivian's boyfriend Eddie goes crazy for her homemade caramel corn, so the three decide to go into business together. Things go well until the police investigate rumors of someone operating a business in a residential zone.

HIGHLIGHTS & TRIVIA

This is another episode where Lucille wears her own hair. Hairstylist Irma Kusely and Ball keep experimenting with coiffure styles and wigs to come up with the right look for Lucy Carmichael. Whenever she wears her own hair she looks more natural, although she looks younger with the wigs. During the filming of this entry, an extra scene is shot for the BBC. In it, the cast sits around the dining room table discussing the fact that the show is now being aired in England, and the kids complain that they will have to eat all their vegetables on two continents.

Carole Cook

(ACTOR/FAMILY FRIEND)

Things have been written that after Desi left the studio, the show became different, but I disagree. Lucille was still surrounded by the same people who had been with her for years. The only real difference was that now she was put in the position of being responsible for the studio, which she hated. I don't remember her taking time away from rehearsals to do studio work. She was forced to deal directly with people, where before Desi would take care of it for her. Now, when the writers and directors and producers all changed a few years later, that was a different story.

THE LUCY SHOW #21: "NO MORE DOUBLE DATES"

(CBS, FEBRUARY 18, 1963), 30 MINUTES (B&W)

GUEST CAST: Dick Martin, Don Briggs, Leon Belasco, Rolfe Sedan, Louis A. Nicoletti, Alan Ray

Every time Lucy, Viv, and their dates get together, there is an argument about where to go and what to do. Lucy and Harry decide they'd like to spend a Saturday night alone, so they make up a story about having tickets to see a Broadway show. After they escape Viv and Eddie (who insist on putting them on the train to New York), they go to a new restaurant where they run into, of course, Viv and Eddie!

Dick Martin

(ACTOR/COMEDIAN)

This is the one show where they really tried to push the romance. I tell you that it was just marvelous to work with her. It was a joy. Lu was a great low comedienne. Very few women can do low comedy. That scene where she is hiding under the table and eating is priceless. This episode is probably the one that most resembles I Love Lucy *because of the relationship of the two couples.*

THE LUCY SHOW (NO NUMBER): "LUCY AND VIV FIGHT OVER HARRY"

(UNPRODUCED)

Yes, fans, there is a script written for the first season that is not filmed. In this one, Viv and Eddie quarrel and break up due to Eddie's lack of attention to Viv. Lucy has a similar mis-encounter with Harry, so Harry asks Viv out instead. The two become an item, much to Lucy's consternation. She schemes to make Harry jealous and get him back by pretending to have a romantic, intimate date—with a tackling dummy!

The script is actually very funny, although technically difficult because it calls for split-screen work and silhouette filming that would be totally new to the series. While these details might have been worked out, the main reason the episode isn't shot is that it would have firmly established Lucy and Harry as having deep feelings for one another. It has already been decided to phase out Harry's character (Dick Martin was not available every week, and Lucille did not want a steady boyfriend for her character), so this outing would have been at cross-purposes with the show's long range plans. The script also has some unusually adult moments, with intimations that perhaps Lucy might be sexually seduced by this "man."

Jimmy Garrett

(ACTOR)

During rehearsals, they would cover the carpeting in the audience bleachers with cardboard. On Monday of this week, I fell in the bleachers and cracked my ankle. It didn't require a cast, but it got taped up and I was limping around. By Wednesday, Lucy just wasn't feeling right about the show, and with her bad feelings and my limping, it was decided to shelve the episode. We were all sent home and it never got produced.

THE LUCY SHOW #22: "LUCY AND VIV LEARN JUDO"

(CBS, FEBRUARY 25, 1963), 30 MINUTES (B&W)

GUEST CAST: Dick Martin, Henry Kulky, Ed Parker

After a rash of burglaries in the neighborhood makes the girls feel unsafe, they learn judo for self-protection. The entire thing backfires when they teach it to their sons, who boisterously use it on one another.

HIGHLIGHTS & TRIVIA

This is the last episode aired featuring Dick Martin.

Dick Martin

(ACTOR/COMEDIAN)

The ladies were like a Laurel and Hardy team, and after about eleven episodes, they realized they didn't need me. I had been signed for, and got paid for, thirteen. Dan and I were getting booked more and more, so it worked out just fine. They should have kept some sort of romantic interest on the show for Lu to play up her femininity. For years, all I could remember about this episode was working with Ed Parker, who was wonderful at martial arts, and that someone got thrown over the couch. Then [the author] reminded me that it was me! No wonder I couldn't remember!

Bob Schiller

(WRITER)

There was a problem with Lucy not having some sort of romantic interest. We used to call the show "The Dyke Van Dick" show because all you had were these two women. But it was decided to pretty much keep Lucy dateless, and I think that was a mistake.

THE LUCY SHOW #23: "LUCY IS A SODA JERK" A.K.A. "LUCY IS A DRUM MAJORETTE"

(CBS, MARCH 4, 1963), 30 MINUTES (B&W)

GUEST CAST: Paul Hartman, Lucie Arnaz

When Chris comes home with the news she has been chosen to be a drum majorette in a parade and that her uniform will cost forty dollars, Lucy tells her she can't afford it. Chris gets a job at the ice cream shop to pay for it, but the owner won't let her off to be in the parade. Lucy and Viv take her place at the shop, with predictable misadventures.

HIGHLIGHTS & TRIVIA

The script develops beautifully, with each succeeding scene building until Lucy is literally prancing through drums of ice cream. The moments with Lucy and Viv musically chanting the list of ice cream flavors are charming. Lucille is especially energetic in this installment, because it is the first time she is working with her twelve-year-old daughter Lucie.

Lucie Arnaz

This was my big debut as an actor. I remember putting up my hair in a pony tail and cutting bangs across the top of my head in order to look as old as Candy Moore. I look at the episode now and scream. I also got to do the Jell-O commercial.

Candy Moore

(ACTOR)

I just adored working with Lucie Arnaz. She was sweet and kind, and I just enjoyed playing scenes with her so much. We were still young enough to enjoy playing. Lucie was also a very empathetic person. We could share our real feelings with no defenses. She wasn't given any special treatment on the set, but all of us kids were treated with kind and loving regard by Lucy. We were all treated like special people.

I had learned to twirl a baton when I was eight, but hadn't done it since then. I was surprised how quickly it came back to me [for this episode]. It is very hard to twirl in front of a live audience like that, because you can't control how sweaty your hands get. I used to sweat a lot on the series because it was so hot under all those lights, and I was always wearing sweaters and wool skirts. I knew that if I dropped that baton and we had to do a retake, [director] Jack Donohue would kill *me!*

Jimmy Garrett

(ACTOR)

Lucie Arnaz was talented, and you could tell that she was trying to learn what was going on. She was right there learning everything she could. She wanted to do it right, she wanted to impress her mom, and she wanted to be the best she could be. I knew Lucie was going to be the success she has become because she wanted *it. She was a very sweet girl.*

My mother coached both Lucy and Candy on how to use the batons. My mother had been a championship baton twirler. Nobody knew until I decided to brag about my mom to the assistant director. They asked her to do it, and she was a little nervous, but she did it.

THE LUCY SHOW #24: "LUCY DRIVES A DUMP TRUCK"

(CBS, MARCH 11, 1963), 30 MINUTES (B&W)

GUEST CAST: Mary Jane Croft, Carole Cook, Dorothy Konrad, Richard Reeves, Ben Weldon

After promising the ladies of the Volunteer Fire Department that the town council will pay for their already purchased new uniforms, the girls find that they will be stuck for the cost themselves. They want to relieve Lucy as captain, until she comes up with the idea of selling newspapers for salvage. Everything goes wrong, and Lucy and Viv end up trucking the papers to another town themselves.

HIGHLIGHTS & TRIVIA

Episodes where Viv has the upper hand with Lucy are never as funny as the other way around. It almost seems out of character for Lucy to allow anyone else to control the moment. Richard Reeves returns to the *Lucy* family after appearing in dozens of episodes in the 1950s. This is a difficult episode to shoot, because of the use of the truck and the piles of recycled newspapers.

Carole Cook

(ACTOR/FAMILY FRIEND)

I think the directors who worked with Lucille had to make an adjustment, or they didn't last very long. Jack [Donohue] did because he collaborated with her and included her in the process. Lucille knew every aspect of the filmings better than anyone. She would impose herself on the director and crew, but she was almost always right.

THE LUCY SHOW #25: "LUCY VISITS THE WHITE HOUSE"

(CBS, MARCH 25, 1963), 30 MINUTES (B&W)

GUEST CAST: Elliot Reid, Frank Nelson, Alan Reed, Pat Colby, Duncan McLeod, Desi Arnaz Jr.

After Lucy calls President Kennedy to tell him of the sugar cube replica of the White House the local cub scout troup made, they are all invited to Washington, D.C., to present it to him. The miniature gets destroyed soon after they board the train, so Lucy and Viv connive to get more sugar cubes and rebuild it themselves.

HIGHLIGHTS & TRIVIA

There is a basic flaw with this installment. Lucy's horse ride, neck and neck with the train, is badly produced and totally unbelievable. There is no basis in reality for the comedy, which always makes Ball's pranks fall flat. Longtime *Lucy* veteran Frank Nelson makes his final appearance with Ball here, playing the same basic character (the railroad conductor) he did back in 1954 on *I Love Lucy*. Elliot Reid portrayed interviewer Ed Warren in the *I Love Lucy* episode "Face to Face" (# 134) in 1955, and Alan Reed is best known for providing the voice of Fred Flintstone on the TV cartoon series *The Flintstones* (1960–66).

Desi Arnaz Jr

Being in the show was no big deal. I was there every week anyway. I grew up at the studio, hanging from the rafters with Keith [Thibodeaux], lunching with the crew. The only direction I was given as a cub scout was to speak up. *It was very important to my mother that everything be heard clearly. As for me, put me in a uniform and I was a happy boy.*

THE LUCY SHOW #26: "LUCY AND VIV TAKE UP CHEMISTRY"

(CBS, APRIL 1, 1963), 30 MINUTES (B&W)

GUEST CAST: Lou Krugman

Lucy and Viv decide to update their education, so they enroll in an adult education course in chemistry. Lucy gets carried away with herself, so Viv and the professor decide to teach her a lesson.

HIGHLIGHTS & TRIVIA

More and more, Lucy is presented as scatterbrained instead of crafty. Also, the offerings with Viv plotting against Lucy never ring true.

THE LUCY SHOW #27: "LUCY IS A CHAPERON"

(CBS, APRIL 8, 1963), 30 MINUTES (B&W)

GUEST CAST: Hanley Stafford, Don Grady, Eddie Hodges, Lucie Arnaz, Charlotte Lawrence, Karen Balkin, Patty Gerrity

The only way Chris and her classmates can spend a week at the beach is if Lucy and Viv act as chaperones. The ladies agree, but decide to act as teenagers themselves to fit in.

HIGHLIGHTS & TRIVIA

The scene with Lucy and Viv singing "Big Girls Don't Cry" is extremely funny and topical. Don Grady (Robbie on *My Three Sons*, 1960–72) is given an excellent showcase here for his good looks and musical talent.

Candy Moore

(ACTOR)

This was my least favorite episode of The Lucy Show. *I just felt the whole plot was so corny! It was like a bad "beach" movie. Don Grady is such a lovely person. He and I went to the Emmy Awards together.*

THE LUCY SHOW #28: "LUCY AND THE LITTLE LEAGUE"

(CBS, APRIL 15, 1963), 30 MINUTES (B&W)

GUEST CAST: Desi Arnaz Jr., William Schallert, Mary Jane Croft, Herb Vigran

Athletic stage mothers Lucy and Viv become so overwhelmed with their sons doing well in little league baseball, they drive the boys to distraction and end up being tossed out of the ballpark.

William Schallert

(ACTOR)

I had just been through several years of working nonstop in all sorts of shows. This show came along just as I had finished doing [The Many Loves of] Dobie Gillis *[1959–63] and frankly I needed the work. Most of these shows had been one or two camera shows with no audience. I had gotten used to working a certain way. When we began rehearsals, Lucille pulled me aside and said, "Listen, buddy, you'd better speak up if you expect the folks to hear you." I guess she told me!*

Jimmy Garrett

(ACTOR)

This episode is one of the very few times we actually had to stop a filming in front of the audience. When Lucy was hiding in that trash can and was supposed to be peeking out of the slot, she got her finger caught in it. They had to stop the cameras and help her; then we resumed immediately.

I almost always wore my own clothes, which were coordinated by wardrobe mistress Della Fox. Whenever we had a show like this one, which required a baseball uniform or anything special, Della provided it for us.

A BOB HOPE SPECIAL

(NBC, APRIL 16, 1963), 60 MINUTES (B&W)

PRODUCED BY: Jack Hope

DIRECTED BY: Jack Shea

WRITTEN BY: Mort Lachman, Bill Larkin, John Rapp, Lester White, Charles Lee, Gig Henry
CAST: Bob Hope (host), Lucille Ball, Dean Martin, Martha Raye

Ball's appearance here sets the pace for all of her future visits to Hope's specials: looking glamorous, reading stale jokes from cue cards with Hope, and perhaps doing a corny sketch near the end.

THE LUCY SHOW #29: "LUCY AND THE RUNAWAY BUTTERFLY"

(CBS, APRIL 22, 1963), 30 MINUTES (B&W)

GUEST CAST: Philip Carey, Mary Wickes, Ellen Corby, Benny Rubin, Carl Benton Reid

Jerry has to get a rare white butterfly for his school project, and Lucy promises to help him. After accidentally letting it go, she upsets a fancy date and a courtroom trial trying to recapture it.

HIGHLIGHTS & TRIVIA

Poor Lucy never seems to have any luck with men. This entry capitalizes on Lucille's ability to be funny and feminine simultaneously.

Jimmy Garrett

(ACTOR)

There was no actual butterfly on the set. We had to swing at the air, and a butterfly was optically inserted later.

THE LUCY SHOW #30: "LUCY BUYS A BOAT"

(CBS, APRIL 29, 1963), 30 MINUTES (B&W)

Lucy decides that instead of going to the lake for a summer vacation, the family should buy a boat she sees advertised. Although it needs a huge amount of work, they fix it up. When Lucy and Viv put it into the water, it breaks its mooring and drifts out onto the lake. To add insult to injury, the boat springs several leaks.

HIGHLIGHTS & TRIVIA

The finale of this episode has one of the last really great physical comedy scenes between Lucille and Vivian. The set for the inside of the boat is built on a platform slightly above floor level. When they need the boat to rock, stagehands simply lift one side of the platform, and then the other. The "panic" bit always does well for the two ladies, but it will hardly be used in the future.

THE ED SULLIVAN SHOW

(CBS, MAY 5, 1963), 60 MINUTES (B&W)

PRODUCED BY: Bob Precht; directed by Tim Kiley
CAST: Ed Sullivan (host), Lucille Ball, Bob de Voye Trio, Dick Contino, Ella Fitzgerald, Four West, Bob Hope, Grant Johannasen, Kalani and the Kids from Tahiti, Jackie Mason, Kaye Stevens

When Sullivan is introduced at the top of the show, it is Bob Hope who comes out. He then introduces Lucille, who comes out looking glamorous in velvet and fur. Their only purpose is to promote the opening of their new screen comedy *Critic's Choice*, both of them reading badly off of cue cards.

Ed Sullivan

(HOST/COLUMNIST)

Of all the shows I did on television, the greatest opening act I ever had was Lucille Ball and Bob Hope. How can you possibly top that?

THE LUCY-DESI COMEDY HOUR

(CBS, JUNE-SEPTEMBER, 1963), 60 MINUTES (B&W)

The thirteen hour-long specials that Lucille and Desi did for Ford and Westinghouse from 1957–60 are rerun as a summer replacement series. Fresh opening and closing graphics are created to accommodate the new show title and sponsorship.

Chapter Fifteen

1963–64 Season

THE LUCY SHOW: THE SECOND SEASON

TECHNICAL REGULARS: Executive produced by Elliot Lewis; produced and directed by Jack Donohue; written by Madelyn Martin, Bob Carroll Jr., Bob Schiller, Bob Weiskopf (except where otherwise noted); makeup by Hal King; hairstyling by Irma Kusely; music by Wilbur Hatch
CAST REGULARS: Lucille Ball (Lucy Carmichael); Vivian Vance (Vivian Bagley); Gale Gordon (Theodore J. Mooney); Candy Moore (Chris Carmichael); Jimmy Garrett (Jerry Carmichael); Ralph Hart (Sherman Bagley); Roy Rowan (announcer)

OPENING NIGHT

(CBS, SEPTEMBER 23, 1963), 60 MINUTES (B&W)
EXECUTIVE PRODUCED BY: Leland Hayward
PRODUCED BY: Marshall Jamison
DIRECTED BY: Norman Abbott
WRITTEN BY: Goodman Ace, Selma Diamond, Jay Burton, Frank Peppiatt, John Aylesworth
CAST: Lucille Ball, Jack Benny, Andy Griffith, Don Knotts, Garry Moore, Phil Silvers, Danny Thomas

To kick off a new season of programs, starring the names listed above and all sponsored by General Foods, a second annual special is produced. This time there is a theme, as *Variety* (fictionally) publishes an article that relates how one General Foods' star will be dropped with the addition of Phil Silvers to the roster. All of the stars fantasize how life would be like if they didn't have their shows. Lucille's main contribution comes in a sketch where she tries to induce Silvers to film his new series (*The New Phil Silvers Show*, 1963–64) at Desilu Studios.

PASSWORD

(CBS, SEPTEMBER 26, 1963), 30 MINUTES (B&W)
EXECUTIVE PRODUCED BY: Bob Stewart
PRODUCED BY: Frank Wayne
DIRECTED BY: Lou Tedesco
CAST: Allen Ludden (host), Lucille Ball, Gary Morton

This is the Redhead's first time playing *Password*, a game where two teams (made up of a celebrity and a noncelebrity) try to get one another to guess a word by offering one-word clues. This is the first onscreen pairing of Ball and Morton since their marriage in 1961. Lucille so enjoys it that she begins playing the game at home with family and friends.

THE LUCY SHOW #31: "LUCY PLAYS CLEOPATRA"

(CBS, SEPTEMBER 30, 1963), 30 MINUTES (B&W)
GUEST CAST: Hans Conried, Mary Jane Croft, Mary Wickes, Sid Gould, Gretchen Houser, Patricia Tribble

When Professor Gitterman puts on an amateur production of *Cleopatra*, Lucy and Viv both want the lead. A compromise is made, with Lucy as Cleo and Viv as Marc Antony! The girls continuously upstage one another, ruining the show and infuriating Gitterman.

HIGHLIGHTS & TRIVIA

Although it had originally been planned as a one-season TV series, Ball is so happy to be back in her

TV arena that she decides to continue her show for a second year. Starting with this episode, there are new opening credits for the show. The cartoon characters that had been part of the opening of all of Lucille Ball's past television seasons are retired. In their place are color stills of scenes from past episodes intermingled with publicity stills. It is decided to shoot the series in color from this point forward, although the episodes are broadcast in black and white because the CBS network does not yet have a policy of airing sitcoms in color. Desilu Studio feels the use of color film will enhance the price of the series when it later goes into syndication. The only adjustment to the use of color is in the makeup, with both stars sporting blue eye shadow, and their hairstyles. Viv's hair is darkened slightly and restyled to give her a more youthful appearance as she has gained weight during the hiatus between seasons. The set is still beige, and most of the costumes are in the muted shades necessary to photograph well in black and white. This episode is a poor choice as a season opener. The comedy is belabored and hackneyed, giving an excellent cast very little with which to work.

Jimmy Garrett

(ACTOR)

When we started shooting in color, they began using this strange, orange makeup on us. It had to be thick enough to look good on a black-and-white TV set but look natural in color.

THE LUCY SHOW #32: "KIDDIE PARTIES, INC."

(CBS, OCTOBER 7, 1963), 30 MINUTES (B&W)

GUEST CAST: Lyle Talbot, Ronnie Dapo, Jimmy Gaines, Sid Gould

Lucy and Viv bemoan the rising cost of all the birthday parties they host and their kids attend. They decide they can make a profit by throwing parties themselves. Unfortunately, everything they plan for their first party goes wrong, until Lucy grabs a handful of helium balloons and floats away.

HIGHLIGHTS & TRIVIA

Each scene in this fun installment gives Lucille a chance to shine, and her ascension (by wires) holding the helium balloons is extremely well handled. Ball makes one of her classic "after the fact" entrances, disheveled and in shock after her off-camera balloon ride.

THE LUCY SHOW #33: "LUCY AND VIV PLAY SOFTBALL"

(CBS, OCTOBER 14, 1963), 30 MINUTES (B&W)

GUEST CAST: William Schallert, Mary Jane Croft, Mary Wickes, Karen Norris, Herb Vigran

Lucy and Viv participate in a post-season charity softball game. Mr. Cresant, the team manager, doesn't put Lucy with the top squad because she plays so badly. When another teammate faints, Lucy is substituted and inadvertently becomes the heroine.

HIGHLIGHTS & TRIVIA

For Lucy to wear the baseball uniform and cap, her wig had to be removed. In the scene at the ballpark, with Lucy in the outfield, her hair is darker and much longer. That is because it is her own hair, which Ball wore chin length in private life. Guest actor William Schallert (as Mr. Cresant) has been called the busiest man in television, having appeared on more series (as a guest star or a regular) than any actor in history.

William Schallert

(ACTOR)

Although Jack [Donohue] was the director, it seems to me that he was mostly concerned with Lucy. It was [associate producer] Tommy Thompson, a very nice man, who put the rest of us through our paces.

Maury Thompson

(CAMERA COORDINATOR)

Every once in awhile, Lucille would get very mean to Viv. When they were rehearsing the bit of choosing up sides with the bat, Miss Ball kept throwing the bat to Viv in such a way that she couldn't catch it. This went on and on, with Lucille berating her more and more each time. Finally, Viv yelled, "I could catch it right if you threw it right!" Lucille just stormed off the set, and Viv came over to my desk by the bleachers. "Why, Maury,?" she cried, "why Maury does she do this to me?" I really didn't want to get into the middle of this, and besides it was [director] Jack Donohue's job to handle problems like this. But I loved Viv, so I called over [prop man] Kenny Wescott, and I said, "Now they put tapes on bats sometimes, don't they? Why don't we tape the bat at the exact place Viv should catch it, so no matter how Lucy throws it, she'll know where to grab it?" So we did that, and Viv rehearsed a few times with Kenny and everything was fine. Lucille came back to the set and said, "Now where were we?" as if nothing had taken place.

THE LUCY SHOW #34: "LUCY GETS LOCKED IN THE VAULT"

(CBS, OCTOBER 21, 1963), 30 MINUTES (B&W)

GUEST CAST: Ellen Corby, Barry Livingston, Sid Gould

When Lucy goes to the Danfield Bank to plead for money, she finds her trustee Mr. Barnsdahl has been replaced by Mr. Mooney. Mooney orders her to economize, so Lucy decides to give her kids do-it-yourself haircuts. She first disastrously practices on one of son Jerry's new friends, who turns out to be Mooney's son. When she goes to the bank to apologize, she inadvertently locks herself and Mooney in the vault.

HIGHLIGHTS & TRIVIA

This episode, the first of a two-part story, introduces Gale Gordon as Theodore J. Mooney, the new trustee of Lucy's money and manager of the bank. By this point, Gordon already had a long association with Ball, working with her as far back as 1947 on radio. The writers wisely set up the relationship between Lucy and Mooney by giving him a reason to dislike her beyond his just being mean. These character motivations, almost always found in the scripts written by Lucille's original writing team, are almost never found when others script the episodes. In later years, Mooney's conservative, middle-aged, stuffy characterization will be replaced by that of a screaming, short-tempered miser.

Dick Martin

(ACTOR/COMEDIAN)

I know I am in the minority when I say that I didn't appreciate Gale Gordon's work on this show. I think they made a mistake. Desi was funny, and Bill and Vivian were funny, and the relationship of the four of them was funny. I think this series would have been better served if they would have kept someone doing a part like mine (although not necessarily me) going on. It would have given them so many more ways to go. All you were left with was the two girls, and how many things can go wrong in that house until you start writing shows where one of them buys the wrong nail polish and the other one schemes to return it? Gale didn't broaden the horizons. How many different ways could she ask him for money? They became boxed in. There was *no relationship between Viv and Gale on the show, and the Mr. Mooney character wasn't very likeable. And they began writing the Lucy character as being stupid. That was another mistake. Lucy Ricardo was crafty and intelligent. And feminine! Lucy Carmichael was dumb and tacky.*

Sheila MacRae

(ACTOR/SINGER/WRITER)

Gale Gordon brought something to this part that you don't get on television anymore: a distinctive voice. He could be funny simply by talking, even if what he had to say wasn't particularly amusing. That also became his downfall, because they relied too much on his delivery and didn't give him the material to work with. Gale was a real professional who cared.

Robert Rockwell

(ACTOR)

Gale basically played the same sort of bombastic character he'd done for us on [radio and TV in] Our Miss Brooks. *However, I don't think he was as well written for here, especially in the later years. Bombastic is funny if something motivates it. In the later years, they showed him being that way for no reason at all. Gale was a lovely, quiet man who always did his best no matter what he was given to do.*

Maury Thompson

(CAMERA COORDINATOR)

I loved Gale, and laughed at everything he did, but he had a problem. When you are at full tilt right from the beginning, you have no where to build to—nowhere to go. This first week, he came over and asked me how he was doing. I told him the truth. He said, "You know, other people have told me that. But I can't seem to help myself. I'll try to temper it." But he couldn't. Perhaps that's why he never won an award for his work.

Kathleen Freeman

(ACTOR)

Gale was absolutely brilliant with Lucille. He was one of the funniest American men ever to do this genre of comedy. We have almost nobody like him anymore.

Candy Moore

(ACTOR)

In all the time we worked together on The Lucy Show, *I don't remember [Gale Gordon and I] ever even saying hello or goodbye to one another. It was like I was invisible. I don't know if it was that he didn't like children, or that our characters had nothing to do with one another. He was a talented, hard-working man, but he had* nothing *to do with me.*

Bob Schiller

(WRITER)

These shows could not be the classics that I Love Lucy *were because you don't have the same protagonists and antagonists. A husband is a funny authority figure. A banker, although certainly an authority figure, doesn't have any of the warmth, humor, or sex of a husband.*

Mary Jane Croft

(ACTOR)

The big change, of course, was Gale. Their relationship was wonderful. He had such power. She kind of relaxed around Gale because she knew he was so strong.

Barry Livingston

(ACTOR)

I had to put on that awful wig for Lucy to cut my hair, and it didn't go right, so I had to go backstage and put another *wig on and we had to do it all over again, still in front of the audience. It was very uncomfortable for me. The only other strong memory about this week was getting to go to the studio school with Jimmy Garrett and Ralph Hart. Of course, we always saw Lucille riding all around the studio on her golf cart, her hair up in a scarf and a cigarette dangling from her mouth. She was there morning, noon, and night, and practically lived in her bungalow.*

THE LUCY SHOW #35: "LUCY AND THE SAFE CRACKER"

(CBS, OCTOBER 28, 1963), 30 MINUTES (B&W)
GUEST CAST: Jay Novello, Ellen Corby, William Woodson, James Flavin, Louis A. Nicoletti, Karen Norris

After Lucy and Mr. Mooney accidentally get locked in the bank vault, she locks him back in when she demonstrates how she made the initial mistake. Desperate to get him out, she talks Mr. Bundy, the owner of a candy store located near the bank (and a former safecracker), into assisting. Unfortunately, Bundy decides to go back to a life of crime, and ties the ladies up in his store so he can now rob the bank.

HIGHLIGHTS & TRIVIA

This is the second of the two parts. There is a very funny physical bit, where Lucy and Viv (tied up) try to feed themselves from the candy counter. Viv pushes Lucy into the candy, and she ends up with the chocolates smashed not only onto her face but also her bust! This would have been tasteless in lesser hands. Gale Gordon's performance is evenly paced and controlled in much of this, his first season. He will eventually perform over-the-top in almost every episode.

THE LUCY SHOW #36: "LUCY GOES DUCK HUNTING"

(CBS, NOVEMBER 7, 1963), 30 MINUTES (B&W)
GUEST CAST: Keith Andes, Donald Briggs, Gordon Jones, Sid Gould, Alan Ray

Lucy lies to her handsome new boyfriend (Keith Andes) that she is an experienced duck hunter, so off they go to shoot ducks. It doesn't take long for Lucy to mess everything up, but in the process they learn she does the world's best duck call.

HIGHLIGHTS & TRIVIA

Keith Andes had been Lucille's costar in her Broadway show *Wildcat* (1960). Handsome and very muscular, he also possessed a booming baritone singing voice. Once again, Lucy wears her own, longer hair in the scenes where she dons the hunter's cap. This is a very funny installment.

THE LUCY SHOW #37: "LUCY AND THE BANK SCANDAL"

(CBS, NOVEMBER 11, 1963), 30 MINUTES (B&W)
GUEST CAST: James Flavin, Eddie Applegate

When Chris comes home with Bob Mooney (Mr. Mooney's teenaged son), Lucy learns of all the expensive items Mr. Mooney has just purchased. Viv then comes home with the news that the bank's books don't balance. The girls jump to the conclusion that Mr. Mooney is an embezzler, and investigate—with disastrous results.

HIGHLIGHTS & TRIVIA

While jumping to conclusions had always been a part of the *I Love Lucy* format, here in *The Lucy Show* it is totally unmotivated. We do not know Mr. Mooney well enough oncamera to know if he could be a crook or not, which make Lucy's suspicions a lot less funny.

Candy Moore

(ACTOR)

Eddie Applegate [Bob Mooney] was very *polite and easy to work with. It was a shame, but we really never got to know one another because he was cast on* The Patty Duke Show *[1963–66] right after this and we never had a chance to work together again on this series.*

THE LUCY SHOW #38: "LUCY DECIDES TO REDECORATE"

(CBS, NOVEMBER 18, 1963), 30 MINUTES (B&W)

Feeling that her home is looking a little shabby, Lucy cooks up a scheme to get it redecorated. While Mr. Mooney allows some small upgrades, Lucy goes overboard and manages to almost destroy the house.

HIGHLIGHTS & TRIVIA

Much of the dialog in the first scene is an inside joke. Lucille has recently done some print ads for carpeting and linoleum wearing a yellow chiffon gown, implying one can wear such an outfit to install the flooring. Vivian's line referring to not being able to help Lucy paint the couch because her yellow chiffon gown is at the cleaners is a gentle jibe by the writers at their boss. Notice that although in every episode of the series until now the stairs are carpeted, for the purposes of the plot, they are now bare floors. This is the last of the "Lucy wants to redecorate" themes used on a Ball TV sitcom. The final scene is shot without an audience several weeks later, after the cast and crew take a break from filming. The newly decorated set will change after this installment because it is found to be too "busy" with props for blocking purposes. It is never fully explained how, if Lucy's trust fund is always strained, she can afford to pay for what amounts to a remodeled house. The kitchen set, which had been old-fashioned in style, is now updated and modernized.

Jimmy Garrett

(ACTOR)

That was actually quite a special effect to do in front of a live audience, having a car crash through a wall. [Prop man] Kenny Wescott and studio special effects guy Joe Lombardi rigged that. It was actually only half a car, pulled through the wall on wires.

THE LUCY SHOW #39: "LUCY PUTS OUT A FIRE AT THE BANK"

(CBS, DECEMBER 2, 1963), 30 MINUTES (B&W)

GUEST CAST: Alan Hale, Mary Wickes, Mary Jane Croft, Erwin Charone, Sid Gould, James Gonzales

When the Danfield municipal finance committee doesn't want to renew the Volunteer Fire Department's appropriation because of all the mistakes it has made, Lucy arranges to have them professionally trained. Lucy realizes that something dramatic might further change the committee's mind, so she schemes to save the bank from a fire.

HIGHLIGHTS & TRIVIA

Like the second season opener, this one isn't funny enough. There is no easy explanation for this state of affairs, because the cast and crew have not changed.

THE LUCY SHOW #40: "LUCY AND THE MILITARY ACADEMY"

(CBS, DECEMBER 9, 1963), 30 MINUTES (B&W)

WRITTEN BY: Bob Carroll Jr., Madelyn Martin, Iz Elinson, Fred S. Fox

GUEST CAST: Leon Ames, Jackie Coogan, Stephen Talbot, Lee Aaker, Sid Gould

Lucy's son, Jerry, is sent off to military school, and Lucy is heartbroken. She tries to visit him before visitor's day, but is rebuffed. She sneaks onto the grounds disguised as a cadet, and gets into all sorts of mischief.

HIGHLIGHTS & TRIVIA

Jerry will eventually be sent off to military school permanently when the series moves its locale to Los Angeles in 1965. Child actor Stephen Talbot (who, along with Lee Aaker, plays a cadet) is the son of veteran actor Lyle Talbot, who appears several times on Lucille Ball programs. This is Jimmy Garrett's favorite episode of *The Lucy Show*.

Lee Aaker

(ACTOR)

Lucille and Jackie Coogan [the drill Sergeant] were definitely running the show. They collaborated on all the little bits they did together, and worked out some of the business for the cadets to do. It was very much a group effort . . . everyone throwing in ideas to make it funnier.

THE GREATEST SHOW ON EARTH: "LADY IN LIMBO"

(ABC, DECEMBER 10, 1963), 60 MINUTES (B&W)

PRODUCED BY: Stanley Colbert
DIRECTED BY: Don Richardson
WRITTEN BY: Tom and Frank Waldman
CAST: Lucille Ball, Roger C. Carmel, Stuart Erwin, Billy Mumy, Jack Palance

Working to perfect her act and win an exchange appearance in Russia, horse trainer Kate Reynolds has no time for friends. That is until she becomes a temporary mother to an animal trainer's orphaned son.

HIGHLIGHTS & TRIVIA

Desilu produces this circus-set series (1963–64), its only network show on the air at that time besides *The Lucy Show* and the game program *You Don't Say* (1963–69). Its ratings are plummeting, so it is decided that Lucille will make her dramatic television debut in a piece of stunt casting that goes awry. The show is universally panned, with Lucille doing the same kind of scenery chewing she did in her RKO days when she was given inferior screen material to perform.

THE LUCY SHOW #41: "LUCY'S COLLEGE REUNION"

(CBS, DECEMBER 16, 1963), 30 MINUTES (B&W)

WRITTEN BY: Bob Carroll Jr., Madelyn Martin, Tom Koch
GUEST CAST: Roland Winters, Lyle Talbot, Carole Cook, Sid Gould, Florence MacMichael, Tina Cole

Lucy and Viv attend Lucy's college reunion so they can show Chris the campus. They become involved with the traditional stealing of the founder's statue, which is usually ignored. This year, however, the Dean is cracking down, and Lucy and Viv scheme to make things right.

HIGHLIGHTS & TRIVIA

We learn in this installment that Lucy's maiden name was Taylor, and that she is a college graduate. These facts will change in later years.

Tina Cole

(ACTOR)

The only thing that I really remember about this show is being so in awe of being with Lucy. I just had a little part [as a coed], and I grew up in a show business family [the King Family], but being with her just floored me. Candy [Moore] was very sweet and a pleasure to work with.

Lucille Ball

I hated doing this episode because I had to cut off all my nails to play that damn ukulele!

THE LUCY SHOW #42: "THE LOOPHOLE IN THE LEASE"

(CBS, DECEMBER 23, 1963), 30 MINUTES (B&W)

When a leak caused by Viv's son Sherman causes Lucy to ask Viv to pay for the repairs (as per her lease), Viv finds out that her agreement allows her to use her rent payments as a deposit to take over the house. Mr. Mooney and Lucy are frantic, and decide that the only solution is to steal Viv's lease before she can act on it.

HIGHLIGHTS & TRIVIA

This is probably the best of the Lucy vs. Viv episodes on *The Lucy Show*. Very similar in theme to "Vivian Sues Lucy" (episode #10), the final scene where Lucy and Mooney sneak into Viv's bedroom while she feigns sleep is hysterical.

PASSWORD

(CBS, DECEMBER 26, 1963), 30 MINUTES (B&W)
EXECUTIVE PRODUCED BY: Bob Stewart
PRODUCED BY: Frank Wayne
DIRECTED BY: Lou Tedesco
CAST: Allen Ludden (host), Lucille Ball, Gary Morton

This is the second time the real-life married couple of Ball and Morton are presented to the TV public as husband and wife. They wisely choose a game format where there are no real performances, and no interviews involved. Lucille is a nervous player; Gary is handsome, charming, and amusingly "cheats" at the game.

THE LUCY SHOW #43: "LUCY CONDUCTS THE SYMPHONY"

(CBS, DECEMBER 30, 1963), 30 MINUTES (B&W)
GUEST CAST: Wally Cox, Jack Donohue, Leon Belasco

Viv's cousin Harold (Wally Cox), a symphony percussionist, comes to visit. He is so nervous about an upcoming concert that Lucy hypnotizes him into relaxing. She does so well that she can't wake him up, and must take his place.

HIGHLIGHTS & TRIVIA

Wally Cox actually has a small part. The bulk of the show features Ball's silent performance as Harold's concert replacement. She is perfection personified. This performance is as good as anything Lucille has ever done, but for some reason is usually overlooked in discussions of her work. Director Jack Donohue plays the indignant symphony conductor.

Jimmy Garrett
(ACTOR)

Wally Cox was really nothing like that mousy, "Mr. Peepers" character he always portrayed. On our set he was lively and had quite a bit of energy. He made his living out of being the nerd, but he really wasn't like that. It was really Wilbur Hatch, our musical director, who conducted that symphony orchestra out of camera range.

THE LUCY SHOW (NO NUMBER): "LUCY PLAYS BASKETBALL"

(NEVER PRODUCED)
GUEST CAST: Mary Jane Croft, Mary Wickes

Yes, fans, another unproduced *Lucy Show* script. Mooney sponsors an all-girl basketball team comprised mostly of ladies from the Volunteer Fire Department. The team is so inept that Mooney wants to withdraw sponsorship rather than embarrass the bank. Lucy elicits a promise from him that *if* they win the next game, the sponsorship will continue. When she breaks training, Lucy is taken off the team, but still gets into the big game and helps her team win.

HIGHLIGHTS & TRIVIA

This would have been a very physical TV episode, with stunt people and special effects abounding. It is very well written, although it seems to be a revamped version of *The Lucy Show* episode #24 ("Lucy Drives a Dump Truck"), with Viv removing Lucy as captain of the team and punishing her for ruining the uniforms. Lucille has misgivings about filming this script, but can't pinpoint her negative reaction to it.

Lucie Arnaz

It often happened in later years when I was on the show that scripts were written and then rejected. It was very unusual, however, to have a script go into rehearsal and not be produced.

THE LUCY SHOW #44: "LUCY PLAYS FLORENCE NIGHTENGALE"

(CBS, JANUARY 6, 1964), 30 MINUTES (B&W)
WRITTEN BY: Bob Carroll Jr., Madelyn Martin, Fred S. Fox, Iz Elinson
GUEST CAST: Kathleen Freeman, Paula Winslowe, Bernie Kopell, Karen Norris, Sid Gould

Lucy needs money to buy daughter Chris a dress for her first formal dance. When she learns that Mr. Mooney is in the hospital with a broken leg, she uses her status as a candy striper to visit his room and get him to sign a check. Naturally, she turns the entire hospital upside down.

HIGHLIGHTS & TRIVIA

It is a hallmark of this second season that many of the shows are built around comedy scenes not necessarily rooted in motivation. The writers have already begun running out of viable things for these characters to do. Without developing the characters further, or adding new story elements, many of these segments have a sameness about them.

Kathleen Freeman

(ACTOR)

If you are lucky enough to get a few good parts, and you are good at what you do and love doing it, then you will work in this business. I had done The Donna Reed Show *[1958–66], some Jerry Lewis movies, and worked on the Desilu lot on other sitcoms. So I had worked for awhile before working for Lucy, and we had known one another just from being in the same industry and in the same town. I don't really remember if I had to read for this first part, but I do know that once I did the show and she felt comfortable with me, I kept being asked back.*

I liked Miss Ball a great deal. We had the same outlook on our profession. This outlook is hard to describe, which is unusual because we are in a profession based on language, and yet a discussion of it is almost unlanguageable. She was a great comedian because she was fearless, and that's what that takes. She was willing to be in danger all the time; in danger of losing her personal dignity, in danger of her vulnerability to everybody else's opinion, and of the foolishness that can get you in trouble with people who are not on the same wavelength. They can dislike you a lot, and deeply, and for a long time. And she was a woman in control at a time when it was not considered proper. A man is in control; a woman is a bossy control-freak. A man is aggressive and knows what he wants; a woman is a bitch. Things really haven't changed much, but it is being tolerated a little better today because there are more women doing things.

There was also a confusion between the woman and the part she played on television. Lucille had to know what she wanted or it wouldn't have worked. If she had actually been *that character, there wouldn't have been any [character to play]. In the shows, everything was in her way; her friends, physical objects, circumstances, even herself. That's where the comedy stems from. [But the real woman] couldn't be that way, or there wouldn't have been any show. The* Lucy *character had to be the center of the hurricane, but Lucille Ball had to* control *the hurricane or she would not have had a career. If Lucille Ball had not been a major* achiever *(and I wish people would see her from this perspective instead of from a negative one), then we would not have all this joy she left behind for us in her work.*

THE LUCY SHOW #45: "LUCY GOES TO ART CLASS"

(CBS, JANUARY 13, 1964), 30 MINUTES (B&W)

GUEST CAST: Robert Alda, John Carradine, Howard Caine

After meeting a handsome bachelor (Robert Alda) in an art store, Lucy and Viv take an art class to be near him. When Viv wrangles a date with him, Lucy schemes to ruin it and, in the process, makes a fool of herself.

HIGHLIGHTS & TRIVIA

This is the first *Lucy* appearance for stage, screen, and TV veteran Robert Alda. He becomes a near-regular over the years, showing up when the plot calls for a good-looking older man.

THE LUCY SHOW #46: "CHRIS GOES STEADY"

(CBS, JANUARY 20, 1964), 30 MINUTES (B&W)

GUEST CAST: Michael J. Pollard

When Lucy learns that daughter Chris and Mr. Mooney's son Ted (renamed and recast) are going steady, she overreacts and gets Mr. Mooney to help her use reverse psychology to break them up. Chris figures out her mother's scheme, and teaches her a lesson.

HIGHLIGHTS & TRIVIA

Eddie Applegate is busy on *The Patty Duke Show* (1963–66), so his part as Mr. Mooney's teenaged son is given now to Michael J. Pollard. Pollard seems like he is on another planet, and will never be used again on *The Lucy Show.* The entire scene with Lucy and Mr. Mooney in the tree house will be reused more than twenty years later (in 1986) for the seventh episode (unaired) of *Life with Lucy.*

THE LUCY SHOW #47: "LUCY TAKES UP GOLF"

(CBS, JANUARY 27, 1964), 30 MINUTES (B&W)

WRITTEN BY: Bob Carroll Jr., Madelyn Martin, Fred S. Fox, Iz Elinson

GUEST CAST: Gary Morton, Jimmy Demaret, F. G. "Bo" Winninger, Robert J. Wilke, Roy Rowan

Lucy dates yet another athlete, this time golfer Gary (Gary Morton). She takes lessons to keep up with him, but she remains a terrible golfer. Gary is to play in a tournament with professionals (Demaret and Winninger), and Lucy ends up being Gary's partner. Her playing so unnerves the pros, that she and Gary end up winning.

HIGHLIGHTS & TRIVIA

This episode is based in part on the *I Love Lucy* episode "The Golf Game" (# 96). Even that installment's guest star Jimmy Demaret is used again. This is Gary Morton's first appearance on a *Lucy* installment. It is discussed making him a permanent part of the cast as Lucy's boyfriend, but it never happens.

THE LUCY SHOW #48: "LUCY TEACHES ETHEL MERMAN TO SING" A.K.A. "LUCY MEETS THE MERM"

(CBS, FEBRUARY 3, 1964), 30 MINUTES (B&W)

GUEST CAST: Ethel Merman

Broadway legend Ethel Merman moves to Danfield, but does so *incognito* (as Agnes Schmidlapp) at the suggestion of Mr. Mooney so she can buy a house without paying inflated prices. Lucy, who has promised her son Jerry she can deliver Ethel Merman to perform for his Cub Scouts charity, meets "Mrs. Schmidlapp" and decides to teach her how to sing like the Merm to pass her off as the star and save face with her son.

HIGHLIGHTS & TRIVIA

This show, the first of a two-part story, is a reunion of sorts. Lucille was a Goldwyn Girl in Hollywood movie musicals of the mid-1930s featuring Ethel Merman. They have remained friends ever since. Vivian was Merman's understudy in *Anything Goes* (1934) on Broadway, and they, too, are good pals. The warmth between all three ladies is evident on the screen. There is tremendous *esprit de corps* between them. These two episodes have a very strange history. Merman was hired by Lucille to do a TV sitcom pilot called *Maggie Brown* (1963). When the comedy fails to sell to CBS, Merman is given this assignment as a consolation prize. It is originally written as only a one-part installment. The end of the segment was supposed to feature Ethel singing a solo, and that was going to be it. The original script reads that way. Then it was altered in the second draft to be a duet between Merman and Ball of "You're the Top," with Ethel belting the lyrics and Lucy acting out the actions.

However, the singing lesson scene is so funny, and Lucille and Viv have so much fun working with Merman, that the show is expanded into a two-parter. A second, follow-up script is written, but not immediately shot. Merman has a prior commitment to make her Las Vegas debut, so four weeks go by before she is available again. To give the now two-parter continuity, the last scene of the first show is rewritten and reshot on the same night the continuation episode is filmed. Unfortunately, someone is asleep at the continuity switch. In the intervening weeks, Lucille has begun wearing a totally different wig, Vivian has taken a holiday in the sun and is tanned, and Ethel has changed the color of her hair from dark brown to auburn. When the new scene is spliced into the old show, none of this matches. There is no onscreen explanation as to why the cast looks totally different. Notice, too, that Lucille has trouble making the phonograph work. They have to stop the filming to get the instrument going properly. This mishap is a rarity for Lucille working oncamera with a prop.

Bob Schiller

(WRITER)

Almost no one knows it, but this is actually a reworking of the I Love Lucy *episode "Lucy Meets Charles Boyer" (#146). The dialog is very different, but the basic plot is the same.*

Bob Weiskopf

(WRITER)

Television writer Nat Hiken used to summer in Westport [Connecticut] when I lived there. When he wanted to rent a house, he'd give a different name because in those days his was very recognizable. He

didn't want to get fleeced. We thought it would be even funnier with someone like Merman, whose face and voice were so totally unique. Ethel gave us the name Agnes. Actors often like to give writers names because it makes them feel like they are contributing to the script.

Maury Thompson
(CAMERA COORDINATOR)

Merman was great to work with, and Lucille left her totally alone. She had great respect for Ethel. The only technical problem was that Ethel was so used to being told exactly where to walk on a Broadway stage, we had to make marks for every step she was to take. I said, "Ethel, dear, walk wherever it feels natural. We'll cover you somehow."

Candy Moore
(ACTOR)

The only times I remember Lucille Ball acting deferential to someone was when Ethel Merman was on the set, and when Danny Kaye was on the set. Ethel wanted to take over my dressing room because it was a trailer, but my mother got into it with her, telling her it wasn't fair to displace someone just because Merman was a star. I was so embarrassed that I avoided Ethel all week whenever I could!

THE LUCY SHOW #49: "ETHEL MERMAN AND THE CUB SCOUTS SHOW"

(CBS, FEBRUARY 10, 1964), 30 MINUTES (B&W)
GUEST CAST: Ethel Merman

Ethel Merman, who is staying with Lucy and Viv, is starring in the Cub Scouts revue while Lucy and Viv sew the costumes. Lucy is resentful and teary at the situation, causing the sentimental Merman to include both ladies and Mr. Mooney in the show.

HIGHLIGHTS & TRIVIA

Everyone is in rare form for this outing. Like the old days on *I Love Lucy*, there is barely a wasted movement or line of dialog. The old themes of wanting to get into the act and jumping to conclusions reappear. Vivian's sardonic reading of her lines is pure Ethel Mertz. Lucille, surrounded by two powerhouses, pulls out all the stops to ensure she is not upstaged. Merman, herself a veteran of doing broad comedy in front of a live audience, really shines. She works in the same manner as Lucille, doing a full-out performance right from the first rehearsal. Merman's rendition of "Everything's Coming Up Roses" (from her Broadway hit musical *Gypsy*) is electrifying. Although the music is prerecorded, Merman sings the song live.

Jimmy Garrett
(ACTOR)

I had a habit that after I shot my scenes, I used to sneak up behind the audience bleachers and come under them to watch the filming. Lucy didn't like it very much. When Ethel was going to sing, I snuck out to watch as usual. Lucy came and stood behind me with her hands on my shoulders. Lucy said to me, "Watch closely, because you'll never see a better performer!"

Irma Kusely
(HAIRSTYLIST)

In her personal life, Lucille liked to do her own hair. That led to one funny story with Merman.

Ethel Merman
(BROADWAY LEGEND)

After the filming of the show, Lucy and Viv and I decided to get together for a hen party at Lucy's house in Beverly Hills. She sent Gary and the children away, and just the three of us got together. She pulled out some old scotch, and the three of us got progressively snockered. Then Lucy decided she wanted to do our hair. She had a little mock beauty parlor thing in the back of the house. Viv and I were drunk enough to let her. My God *what we ended up looking like . . . we were hysterical with laughter! I never let Lucy touch my hair again! The next day, Lucille threw a bridal shower for me, as I was about to make my disaster with Ernie Borgnine.*

THE LUCY SHOW #50: "LUCY AND VIV OPEN A RESTAURANT"

(CBS, FEBRUARY 17, 1964), 30 MINUTES (B&W)
GUEST CAST: Jack Albertson, Kathleen Freeman, Alan Hewitt, Benny Rubin, Jay Ose, Sid Gould

Lucy talks Viv into investing her nest egg in a local restaurant that is for sale. No matter how they redecorate the place, it is a total flop. Finally, Mr. Mooney learns a highway will be built nearby, and now offers to become a partner. Unfortunately, the blasting for the highway shakes the building and ruins any chance for a partnership.

HIGHLIGHTS & TRIVIA

Like many of these final episodes written by the original scripters, energy or costume changes are substituted for solid plot development. It's not that the show isn't funny; it just adds nothing to the *Lucy* mythos. A top-notch supporting cast is mostly wasted.

THE LUCY SHOW #51: "LUCY TAKES A JOB AT THE BANK"

(CBS, FEBRUARY 24, 1964), 30 MINUTES (B&W)

GUEST CAST: Mary Jane Croft, Kathleen Freeman, Carole Cook

When Jerry needs a new tuba, cash-poor Lucy talks Mr. Mooney into giving her a job at the bank. All she has to do is hand out toasters to people opening new accounts, but she has no success. Lucy talks her friend Audrey Simmons (Mary Jane Croft) into withdrawing her money and then redepositing it again to stimulate business; Audrey's gossip spreads a rumor that the bank is failing and starts a run on the financial institution.

HIGHLIGHTS & TRIVIA

The premise here is very funny and rises to a highly humorous crescendo. It is unusual for this series to utilize short, quickly cut scenes. However, its use here is exceptional, and adds much to the comedy.

Mary Jane Croft

(ACTOR)

I loved doing The Lucy Show *because it was like doing a play. I was doing both* The Lucy Show *and* The Adventures of Ozzie and Harriet *(1952–66) at the same time and it was like night and day. The* Ozzie and Harriet *set was so boring. You'd just stand in front of a camera, say your lines, and get off.*

THE LUCY SHOW #52: "VIV MOVES OUT"

(CBS, MARCH 2, 1964), 30 MINUTES (B&W)

WRITTEN BY: Bob Carroll Jr., Madelyn Martin, Iz Elinson, Fred S. Fox

GUEST CAST: Roberta Sherwood, Jerry Lanning

After yet another argument, Viv and her son Sherman move out. Mr. Mooney makes Lucy take in another boarder, entertainer Roberta Schaeffer and her son Bob. Their constant rehearsing drives Lucy crazy. Meanwhile, Viv wants to move back in. The girls and Mr. Mooney help the Schaeffers' get a booking so they will move out.

HIGHLIGHTS & TRIVIA

This is another very funny episode. Roberta Sherwood is a well-known nightclub singer, and this series is a great showcase for her. Jerry Lanning, Sherwood's real-life son, has been appearing on other Desilu sitcoms that spotlight his good looks and booming baritone. In 1962, Desilu produced a sitcom pilot with Gale Gordon and Sherwood playing husband and wife, with Lanning as their singing son. It did not sell. It is this episode that brings pianist Marl Young into the *Lucy* fold; he will eventually take over the music supervision chores when Wilbur Hatch passes away in 1969.

THE LUCY SHOW #53: "LUCY IS HER OWN LAWYER"

(CBS, MARCH 9, 1964), 30 MINUTES (B&W)

GUEST CAST: James Westerfield, John McGiver, Joe Mell, Lord Nelson (the dog)

Lucy complains when Mr. Mooney's barking sheepdog Nelson keeps her up all night. He tells her to sue him, and she does. After making a shambles of the court procedures, she finally makes her point by cross-examining Nelson.

HIGHLIGHTS & TRIVIA

It is out of character for Mr. Mooney, who has been shown to be a pillar of the community, to be insensitive to keeping his neighbors awake all night. Unfortunately, any sense of continuity in his oncamera character will be lost after this season.

THE LUCY SHOW #54: "LUCY MEETS A MILLIONAIRE"

(CBS, MARCH 16, 1964), 30 MINUTES (B&W)

GUEST CAST: Cesare Danova, Jay Novello

Lucy's date with a handsome Italian millionaire turns into a fiasco. He doesn't speak English; Mr.

Mooney's translations embarrass her, and she accidentally dumps pasta in her date's lap. When Lucy tries to get her escort's other tuxedo from the cleaners, disaster follows, with Lucy ending up in a vat of green dye.

HIGHLIGHTS & TRIVIA

Cesare Danova is a charming and handsome romantic foil for Lucille. Notice many of the new plots feature less and less of Vivian, who is unhappy with her role on the series. She is tired of commuting to Hollywood from her Connecticut home just to play secondary parts. Jay Novello (seen here as the owner of the Italian restaurant) is an old friend from the *I Love Lucy* years. However, this is his last *Lucy* appearance.

Irma Kusely

(HAIRSTYLIST)

Strangely enough, the green dye at the end didn't ruin my wigs, but it did great harm to Lucille's skin. They used a cake coloring to achieve the effect, and it bled right into her skin and caused a major irritation.

THE LUCY SHOW #55: "LUCY GOES INTO POLITICS"

(CBS, MARCH 23, 1964), 30 MINUTES (B&W)

GUEST CAST: J. Pat O'Malley, Howard Caine, Sid Gould

Mr. Mooney is running for city comptroller, so Lucy and Viv volunteer for his campaign. After ruining a huge campaign poster, Lucy and Viv mess up the entertainment for Mooney's rally and must handle it themselves.

HIGHLIGHTS & TRIVIA

The scene with Lucy and Viv putting up the billboard of Mooney is hysterical, and very reminiscent of the type of motivated but wacky comedy the duo did so well in the past.

THE LUCY SHOW #56: "LUCY AND THE SCOUT TRIP"

(CBS, MARCH 30, 1964), 30 MINUTES (B&W)

GUEST CAST: Desi Arnaz Jr., Barry Livingston

When one of the fathers cancels out of a Cub Scout trip, Lucy and Viv show up to take his place. They mess up every event planned, which will ruin the scouts' chances of winning a free trip to the World's Fair in New York. Lucy, Viv, and Mr. Mooney later get lost, and the scouts' ingenuity in finding them helps win them their World's Fair trek.

HIGHLIGHTS & TRIVIA

Note that the "Indian" outfit and wig that she wears in this installment is the same one she wore on *I Love Lucy* in "The Indian Show" (episode #59).

THE LUCILLE BALL COMEDY HOUR: "MR. AND MRS."

(CBS, APRIL 18, 1964), 60 MINUTES (B&W AND COLOR)

EXECUTIVE PRODUCED BY: Jess Oppenheimer
PRODUCED BY: Edward H. Feldman
DIRECTED BY: Jack Donohue
WRITTEN BY: Richard Powell
BASED ON A PLAY BY: Sherwood Schwartz
SPECIAL MATERIAL BY: Arthur Julian
CAST: Lucille Ball, John Banner, John Dehner, Rudy Dolan, Stanley Farrar, Gale Gordon, Sid Gould, Bob Hope, Danny Klega, William Lanteau, Joseph Mell, Sally Mills, Eddie Ryder, Max Showalter, Jack Weston

Lucille Ball, studio head, is in trouble with the bank that holds the mortgage on the studio. She must convince Bob Hope to appear in a television special with her (to prove she is the proper corporate image), so she follows him all over the world. He agrees to do the special, which is the story of a couple who pretend to be man and wife to make a television series successful.

HIGHLIGHTS & TRIVIA

Lucille and Gale look and sound great in the bookend segments to the story. Without having to scream out their dialog to an audience, they are able to give controlled performances. The predicament of Lucille Ball, actor, fighting with outsiders over control of her studio (fictionalized for this special) is exactly what Lucille is experiencing in her own life at the time. Jess Oppenheimer's fine production hand is visible everywhere. The pace, timing, and production values are all first-rate. The show within the show is funny and witty. Lucille looks like a million dollars in her Edith Head creations. Both Hope and Ball read from cue cards, but they handle it well. Hope actually has some superior comedy moments. The supporting cast is superb, extremely well cast. It has been rumored that Lucille is looking to this special as the prototype for a new series to replace *The Lucy Show*. If it was, the idea was quickly abandoned. This special is originally aired in black and white, but will be shown in color when it is rerun.

Sherwood Schwartz
(WRITER/PRODUCER)

Mr. and Mrs. *was a play about a young man and a young woman who go to be interviewed to play the Mr. and Mrs. for a new television show. They just met that day, but the person interviewing them thought they were married. So they were hired on that basis. And they had to live together to keep up the charade. When they find other people to marry, they have to first get a phony divorce. The play never got to Broadway. It was produced in a suburb of Chicago, and then toured in summer theatre. It originally starred Jackie Coogan as the agent, Marilyn Maxwell in the Lucy part, and Steve Dunne in Hope's role. Anyway, after the play failed I tried to turn it into a motion picture, and Lucy's agent got a hold of it. Now here comes the tricky part. I was told that this story was, coincidentally, also the story of Lucy and Desi. I was told, however true this is, that they were never really married in 1940 like they said they were. And that when they sought a divorce in 1944, it was so that they could reunite and eventually get legally married. So Lucy glomed on to this property because it struck a nerve with her. [Author's note: There are dozens of pictures and documents to prove that Lucille and Desi were, in fact, always married as they claimed.]*

The show had to be rewritten to fit Lucy's hour-long format. I had nothing to do with the rewriting, and I didn't much like it. At least they managed to keep the basic story. I was there the day they shot it. There was no live audience, although they did use three cameras for the play within a play segment. The reactions were dubbed in later. Lucy was a magic person. She was like Judy Garland. Her sum was greater than all of her individual parts. She was striking looking, and usually those kind of women can't be funny. Edith Head did her costumes, and she was just beautiful. She did not look like a woman in her fifties. And she was able to look pregnant and still be funny.

THE LUCY SHOW #57: "LUCY IS A PROCESS SERVER"

(CBS, APRIL 20, 1964), 30 MINUTES (B&W)

GUEST CAST: Keith Thibodeaux, Stafford Repp, Lee Millar, Carole Cook, Jose Betancourt, Dick Kindelon

Lucy is distressed because she has no money for a summer vacation. She gets a job at an attorney's office and must serve Mr. Mooney with a subpoena. She tracks him to a train station and then to the ship he is taking for a cruise. While the subpoena proves not to be bad news, Lucy ends up on the ship, which will not make another stop for twenty-eight days.

HIGHLIGHTS & TRIVIA

If you watch carefully, you can spot Keith Thibodeaux (Little Ricky) in the train station. This is his first *Lucy* appearance since 1960; it is also his last.

THE LUCY SHOW #58: "LUCY ENTERS A BAKING CONTEST"

(CBS, APRIL 27, 1964), 30 MINUTES (B&W)

GUEST CAST: Mary Jane Croft, Kathleen Freeman, Carole Cook, Dorothy Konrad

When Viv ridicules Lucy's efforts at baking, Lucy enters a pie-baking contest to prove Viv wrong. One after another, Lucy and her friends switch the two ladies' entries in the contest. The result? A pie-throwing melee.

HIGHLIGHTS & TRIVIA

This is the final *Lucy Show* written by original writers Bob Carroll Jr. and Madelyn Martin. Lucille is very unhappy with the script when it is first delivered to her. Rather than discuss solutions, Ball offers a frustrated epithet that leads the writers to believe that their services are no longer required. They clean out their offices, which then angers Ball (who had never intended to fire them at all). They feel betrayed, she feels betrayed, and a sixteen-year working relationship is torn apart because of poorly chosen words and other misunderstandings. Bob and Madelyn will not write for Ball again until 1970. That no one steps in to salvage the relationship is part of what is wrong with the series. There is no one who will stand up to Lucille and tell her she is wrong except for Vivian, and *that* is causing problems between the two ladies.

Lucille moves swiftly and hires ex-Jack Benny scribe Milt Josefsberg to supervise the series' writing for its third season. She also promotes Jack Donohue, producer/director, giving him greater production responsibilities.

Bob Schiller

(WRITER)

After this season, we pretty much left Lucy to take a lucrative offer with a variety show. We were not too happy working with Lucy by this point. She was a pain in the ass. She really didn't know scripts, that was Desi's forte. He was a charmer. He could tell you he hated your script and make you feel good about it. Lucy would say your script's OK, and you'd hate her for it.

Bob Weiskopf

(WRITER)

We had been there a long time and Desi was gone. Desi was our man; he liked us and we liked him.

Kathleen Freeman

(ACTOR)

Mary Jane Croft was a lovely lady, and a very settling influence for Lucille. Whenever the "pie" of the show seemed like it might start to crumble for whatever reasons, Mary Jane always seemed to be able to pat the "crust" back into place.

PASSWORD

(CBS, MAY 7, 1964), 30 MINUTES (B&W)

EXECUTIVE PRODUCED BY: Bob Stewart
PRODUCED BY: Frank Wayne
DIRECTED BY: Lou Tedesco
CAST: Allen Ludden (host), Lucille Ball, Gary Morton, Lucie Arnaz, Desi Arnaz Jr.

This is the first occasion for the Arnaz offspring to appear as themselves on television, and the first time the four are presented as a family. By now, Lucille and Gary have been married about two-and-a-half years, and this program reveals just how much she is trying to place her past well behind her.

The Mortons have been playing the *Password* game at home, as Lucille's penchant for playing games has already taken hold in her private life. Offcamera, such friends as Mary Wickes and Carole Cook are invited over for *Password* evenings, and often the children join in.

Lucie Arnaz

In my mother's house, to play you had to be good.

Everyone is obviously trying to put their best feet forward. Eleven-year-old Desi Jr. is relaxed and seems comfortable, but Lucie (who is not quite thirteen) is quite another matter. With short curly hair and braces, she could be anyone's gawky sister, just entering puberty. It's *just* that she is doing this in front of millions of people.

Lucie Arnaz

I had no sense of who I was.

It certainly shows, and she mugs all over the place, animated beyond need. Mostly, it seemed like she is trying to copy hyperactive Carol Burnett.

Lucie Arnaz

I can't even watch the tapes of that show, it makes me sick. I was trying to copy-cat comics. It's sad. I was trying too hard. I want to go to that little girl to say, 'You don't have to do this!' I wanted to be like Mom and Gary—snap my fingers to the music and have snappy patter.

It's hard to imagine that the beautiful, talented, and charming woman Lucie will become has such a hard time with this show. Part of the problem is that her brother is already a charmer.

Lucie Arnaz

My brother had visible talent. I couldn't see what my talents could be. I felt like, "Why do you want me? I'm just her daughter." I had no self-esteem. Desi had more experience in front of people. He was more advanced.

Desi Arnaz Jr.

This is one of my favorite experiences of all time. I loved doing this show. I think Lucie was at an awkward age. I was more comfortable as a person in front of an audience. My sister hadn't had as much experience doing that sort of thing. The real Lucie wasn't coming through. You should have seen her in her school plays. She was brilliant. I was a little nervous about getting the answers right, but the game was easy and we were with Mom and Gary. And Allen Ludden was very good at what he did. He was funny, interesting, urbane, and real.

Another problem is the obvious discomfort in the family unit. Although everyone is acclimated to Gary's role in Lucille's life, even Allen Ludden stumbles as he refers to Gary as "Dad," or to the Mortons as "your parents." And then there is the differing attitudes toward the money. The kids play for charity (obviously picked by Lucille as they can't remember it when asked) until the last round, when the kids get a quarter each per point. "They can keep that *little* bit of money," decided Lucille, but to the kids it is not insignificant.

Lucie Arnaz

We thought it was fun *to win a quarter. My mother never gave us money. I got fifty cents a week until I was fifteen. The money was a huge big deal to us.*

THE LUCY-DESI COMEDY HOUR

(CBS, JUNE-SEPTEMBER, 1964), 60 MINUTES (B&W)

The thirteen hour-long specials that Lucille and Desi did for sponsors Ford and Westinghouse from 1957–60 are rerun as a summer replacement series. New opening and closing graphics are created for the shows.

TOP TEN EPISODES OF I LOVE LUCY

(RANKED IN ORDER OF PREFERENCE BY THE AUTHOR)

"Job Switching" (episode #36, 9/15/52)
"The Operetta" (episode #40, 10/13/52)
"Lucy Does a TV Commercial" (episode #30, 5/5/52)
"Lucy Is Enceinte" (episode #45, 12/8/52)
"Lucy Goes to the Hospital" (episode #51, 1/19/53)
"L.A. at Last" (episode #114, 2/7/55)
"Lucy Tells the Truth" (episode #72, 11/9/53)
"Harpo Marx" (episode #125, 5/9/55)
"Lucy Does the Tango" (episode #173, 3/11/57)
"Lucy's Show Biz Swan Song" (episode #47, 12/22/52)

TOP TEN EPISODES OF THE LUCY SHOW

(RANKED IN ORDER OF PREFERENCE BY THE AUTHOR)

"Lucy and Viv Put in a Shower" (episode #18, 1/28/63)
"Lucy Teaches Ethel Merman to Sing" (episode #48, 2/3/64)
"Lucy and Her Electric Mattress" (episode #12, 2/17/62)
"No More Double Dates" (episode #21, 2/18/63)
"Vivian Sues Lucy" (episode #10, 12/3/62)
"Lucy Is a Kangaroo for a Day" (episode #7, 11/12/62)
"Lucy and Viv Are Volunteer Firemen" (episode #16, 1/14/63)
"Lucy Meets the Berles" (episode #133, 9/11/67)
"Lucy Gets Jack Benny's Account" (episode #138, 10/16/67)
"Lucy and the Countess Have a Horse Guest" (episode #90, 10/25/65)

TOP TEN EPISODES OF HERE'S LUCY

(RANKED IN ORDER OF PREFERENCE BY THE AUTHOR)

"Lucy Visits Jack Benny" (episode #2, 9/30/68)
"Lucy and Ann-Margret" (episode #44, 2/2/70)
"With Viv As a Friend, Who Needs an Enemy" (episode #95, 2/14/72)
"Lucy Is N.G. as an R.N." (episode #137, 1/21/74)
"Lucy Meets the Burtons" (episode #49, 9/14/70)
"Lucy the Crusader" (episode #53, 10/12/70)
"Lucy Runs the Rapids" (episode #28, 10/13/69)
"Lucy and Jack Benny's Biography" (episode #59, 11/23/70)
"Lucy and the Used Car Dealer" (episode #33, 11/17/69)
"Lucy and Art Linkletter" (episode #99, 1/10/66)

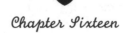

Chapter Sixteen

1964–65 Season

THE LUCY SHOW: THE THIRD SEASON

TECHNICAL REGULARS: Produced and directed by Jack Donohue; script consultant: Milt Josefsberg; makeup by Hal King; hairstyling by Irma Kusely; music by Wilbur Hatch
CAST REGULARS: Lucille Ball (Lucy Carmichael); Vivian Vance (Vivian Bagley); Gale Gordon (Theodore J. Mooney); Candy Moore (Chris Carmichael); Jimmy Garrett (Jerry Carmichael); Ralph Hart (Sherman Bagley); Roy Rowan (announcer)

THE LUCY SHOW #59: "LUCY AND THE GOOD SKATE"

(CBS, SEPTEMBER 21, 1964), 30 MINUTES (B&W)
WRITTEN BY: Jerry Belson, Garry Marshall
GUEST CAST: Charles Drake, Glenn Turnbull, Ray Kellogg, Sid Gould

Lucy feels she hasn't been spending enough quality time with teenaged daughter Chris. Despite the fact Lucy hasn't been roller skating in years, she joins Chris in an afternoon of skating fun. When she returns home, she discovers her feet are so swollen she can't remove her skates and must wear them to the formal dance at the country club that evening.

HIGHLIGHTS & TRIVIA
Both producer Elliot Lewis and the writing staff are replaced beginning with this episode. Different writers will be used for all *Lucy* TV installments from this point forward. There will never again be a permanent staff of writers that work on every episode.

Bob Schiller
(WRITER)
Milt Josefsberg was absolutely the wrong man to take over the show. He was not a situation writer; he was a joke writer. Stories were not his strong point. With Lucy, you needed a believable plot to make the unbelievable comedy work. He brought in all his old cronies, who were all old radio [one-line joke] writers.

Maury Thompson
(CAMERA COORDINATOR)
Elliot Lewis was not at all vociferous. You hardly knew he was there. He would sit in during the first reading of the script, and then he would disappear. I never remember him sitting on the set or having any influence with things. I cannot remember one decision he made. I loved Elliot; he was a very nice man, and we socialized together. But he was hardly missed when Jack took over as producer as well as being director. Lucille was very nervous for quite awhile after the original writing staff left. Sometimes she'd be in the middle of a script reading and ask distastefully, "Who wrote *this?" She hired great writers like Josefsberg and Garry Marshall who wrote great things for other people. But they never seemed to capture the right formula for successful* Lucy *scripts.*

Candy Moore
(ACTOR)
Elliot Lewis was so elegant and quiet. He had such gentility that I think he was overlooked in this business. He wasn't loud, just hardworking. He did his job without making a noise, making sure that everything was looked after and that everyone was happy, especially the [CBS] network. Elliot was a wonderful diplomat. Even at the first read-throughs his presence was felt without being overbearing. However, the driver of the car was Lucy. It didn't matter who showed up or didn't show up for the ride, the show was going forward on her talent, her vision, and her

power. Everyone else was either her support or her embellishment.

In my mind, this is the point when the show began to fall apart. Without our original writers, we lost whatever identity we had as a show and as characters. The new writers who came in couldn't capture the magic of the show. We now had no cohesiveness. We started getting scripts that weren't true to our family unit. Tensions developed because everybody started feeling it. It was very unnerving. We lost our support system. You couldn't put your finger on it. The scripts weren't as funny. There was this void underneath us, and we were all resisting falling into it.

There is a fresh opening for the new season, with clips from both the black-and-white and color episodes strung together. The discrepancy doesn't matter at this point, as the series is still telecast in black and white.

PASSWORD

(CBS, SEPTEMBER 24, 1964), 30 MINUTES (B&W)
EXECUTIVE PRODUCED BY: Bob Stewart
PRODUCED BY: Frank Wayne
DIRECTED BY: Mike Gargiulio, Lou Tedesco
CAST: Allen Ludden (host), Lucille Ball, Gary Morton, Vivian Vance, Peter Lawford

The men play a lot better than the women this time out. Lucille and Vivian seem stumped at some very simple words, and come across as being at odds with one another. Peter Lawford had been at MGM with Lucille during her last days at that studio in the 1940s.

THE LUCY SHOW #60: "LUCY AND THE PLUMBER"

(CBS, SEPTEMBER 28, 1964), 30 MINUTES (B&W)
WRITTEN BY: Milt Josefsberg, Bob O'Brien
GUEST CAST: Jack Benny, Bob Hope, Willard Waterman

Lucy's kitchen plumbing goes amuck, and Mr. Mooney approves her getting a plumber. The workman who shows up is a dead ringer for Jack Benny, whose life in plumbing and music has been ruined by the resemblance. Lucy, who had previously gotten a merchant on a local TV talent show with disastrous results, schemes to do better for the plumber.

HIGHLIGHTS & TRIVIA

This is the first of the episodes that do not feature Vivian Vance. Part of the healing process between the ladies is that Viv gets several weeks off during the season where she is not required to travel to California from her East Coast home. Ball has Roy Rowan's voice-over, "Costarring Vivian Vance," erased from the opening on the weeks Vance doesn't appear. Ball and Jack Benny work very well together, and are in fact real-life next-door neighbors in Beverly Hills. Lucille ends up owing both Benny and Hope appearances on their shows in return for their contributions to this one.

Jimmy Garrett
(ACTOR)

Whatever tensions there might have been between Lucy and Vivian, they handled it very professionally. I was never aware of any problems between them. This first week that Viv wasn't on the show, it was explained to us that she had been working with Lucy for a very long time and that she was tired. We were also told that Vivian's home was in Connecticut with her husband, and that she was starting a project of renovating a barn into a house.

Jack Benny was a pleasure to be around. Quite often, guest actors sort of stayed to themselves during the week, but Jack was out and around and very accessible. It was also Lucy's birthday that week, so we had cake and refreshments on the set. One day, my mother and I went to the Desilu commissary for lunch. In walked Jack Benny and his entourage. After a few minutes, he waved and came over to our table. He stood behind an empty chair and chatted with us. And chatted with us. For a long time. Then he went back to his own table. My mother said, "I wonder if he wanted us to ask him to sit down and join us. Nah, he's a big star!" So we go back to the set, and Jack Benny is a little late. We're all standing there, and he walks in. "Everybody gather around, I want to make an announcement," he said. "Some *of the people on this show are very unfriendly.* Some *people have a nice man stand at their table to talk, and they don't even invite him to sit down. Now, I know I'm cheap, but it's not like I was going to stick them with the check!" My mother and I just died. He was a very sweet man. Bob Hope just showed up about a half hour before we started filming. He had not been there all week. They put him in makeup and costume, and he and Lucy traded crony talk in the green room between scenes. I wasn't even introduced to him.*

THE JACK BENNY PROGRAM: "THE LUCILLE BALL SHOW"

(NBC, OCTOBER 2, 1964), 30 MINUTES (B&W)
EXECUTIVE PRODUCED BY: Irving Fein
PRODUCED AND DIRECTED BY: Norman Abbott
WRITTEN BY: Sam Perrin, George Balzer, Al Gordon, Hal Goldman
CAST: Jack Benny (host), Lucille Ball, Dennis Day, Elisabeth Fraser, Hoke Howell, Arte Johnson, Ned Miller, Don Wilson, Mary Young

This episode is a payback for Jack Benny's appearance on *The Lucy Show* the previous week. Lucille makes her entrance at the top of the show wearing her professor costume from her old vaudeville act, exchanging banter with Benny. The bulk of the installment is a sketch featuring Benny as Paul Revere and Ball as his long-suffering wife. Lucille handles the sketch comedy superbly. Scribes Sam Perrin and George Balzer will pen several *Here's Lucy* TV scripts in the future.

THE LUCY SHOW #61: "LUCY AND THE WINTER SPORTS"

(CBS, OCTOBER 5, 1964), 30 MINUTES (B&W)
WRITTEN BY: Ray Singer, Dick Chevillat
GUEST CAST: Keith Andes

Lucy once again wants to please her muscular boyfriend (Keith Andes), who is a sports nut. After bragging how good she is at winter sports, he arranges a skiing weekend. When Mr. Mooney's skiing lessons end in catastrophe, Lucy schemes to teach herself.

HIGHLIGHTS & TRIVIA

This is one of the better offerings by the new writers, because the comedy has a solid foundation in the plot. The major comedy sequence finds Lucy skiing down a makeshift track off her roof and sailing into the air.

THE LUCY SHOW #62: "LUCY GETS AMNESIA"

(CBS, OCTOBER 12, 1964), 30 MINUTES (B&W)
WRITTEN BY: Leonard Gershe
GUEST CAST: Fifi D'Orsay, Max Showalter

After buying a poor-quality fur coat for $100, Lucy must ask Mr. Mooney for the money. She finds she must see his temporary replacement, who turns out to be an old flame from her teenage years. When she can't remember him or the pet name she once called him, she feigns amnesia rather than lose the hoped-for reimbursement for the coat.

HIGHLIGHTS & TRIVIA

Although these installments begin to suffer in quality, Lucille looks younger and sounds better than she has in quite awhile.

CHRYSLER PRESENTS A BOB HOPE COMEDY SPECIAL: "HAVE GIRLS, WILL TRAVEL"

(NBC, OCTOBER 16, 1964), 60 MINUTES
PRODUCED BY: Mort Lachman
DIRECTED BY: Fred De Cordova
WRITTEN BY: Alex Gottlieb, Robert Hammer
CAST: Bob Hope (host), Lucille Ball, Jack Benny, Bruce Cabot, Rod Cameron, Rhonda Fleming, Marilyn Maxwell, Burt Mustin, Aldo Ray, Jill St. John, Sonny Tufts

A filmed special that is actually an hour-long sitcom rip-off of *Paleface* (the Bob Hope-Jane Russell western comedy from 1948) with a laugh track. Lucille does a cameo (as does Jack Benny) in the last minute of the show as Bob's fiancée, Emily. She has no lines, but simply exits a stagecoach in full costume, makeup, and wig.

THE LUCY SHOW #63: "LUCY AND THE GREAT BANK ROBBERY"

(CBS, OCTOBER 19, 1964), 30 MINUTES (B&W)
WRITTEN BY: Bob Schiller, Bob Weiskopf
GUEST CAST: John Williams, Lloyd Corrigan

Lucy and Viv rent a room to people seeking hard-to-find lodgings due to the New York World's Fair. Unfortunately, their boarders prove to be bank robbers who hide their loot in Lucy's mattress where she later finds it.

HIGHLIGHTS & TRIVIA

A superior show, due mostly to the fact that it is written by two of her original writers.

THE LUCY SHOW #64: "LUCY, THE CAMP COOK"

(CBS, OCTOBER 26, 1964), 30 MINUTES (B&W)

WRITTEN BY: Bob Schiller, Bob Weiskopf
GUEST CAST: Harvey Korman, Madge Blake

The boys have gone away to summer camp, but Lucy and Viv can't afford for them to stay there an extra two weeks. When the camp cook quits, the ladies offer to take over to pay for the boys' extended stay. Naturally, the girls destroy the kitchen.

HIGHLIGHTS & TRIVIA

Comedian Harvey Korman (seen here as the camp counselor) is a favorite of Lucille's, and she will use him quite a bit whenever he can get free time from Danny Kaye's TV variety show (1963–67), on which he is a regular.

Bob Schiller
(WRITER)

We came in and did a few scripts as a favor to Lucy and Milt. They needed some overlap in creativity, so we provided it.

THE LUCY SHOW #65: "LUCY, THE METER MAID"

(CBS, NOVEMBER 2, 1964), 30 MINUTES (B&W)

WRITTEN BY: Bob O'Brien, Vic McLeod
GUEST CAST: Parley Baer, Joe Mell

Lucy takes her new job as a meter maid way too seriously and gets drunk with power. She cites Viv for a plethora of offenses and takes her to traffic court. The poor judge gets frustrated trying to keep order between the arguing females.

HIGHLIGHTS & TRIVIA

Although most of the Lucy vs. Viv plot line shows are annoying, this one is so well acted that it is quite satisfying.

THE DANNY KAYE SHOW

(CBS, NOVEMBER 4, 1964), 60 MINUTES

PRODUCED BY: Perry Lafferty
DIRECTED BY: Robert Scheerer
WRITTEN BY: Sheldon Keller, Gary Belkin, Ernest Chambers, Larry Tucker, Paul Mazursky, Billy Barnes, Ron Friedman, Mel Tolkin
CAST: Danny Kaye (host), Lucille Ball, Red Callendar, John Gary

Lucille's appearance here is in exchange for Kaye's participation on *The Lucy Show* (episode #73) that will be aired in December. The opening sketch is done à la Mike Nichols and Elaine May, just Lucille and Danny sitting on stools with no props, scenery, or costumes as they enact a couple trying to fire a maid. It isn't very funny, but it is different from anything Ball has done before on TV. In a musical moment called "The Balloonists," Lucille and Danny perform what is certainly one of the most joyous production numbers of Ball's entire career: "We Believe in Blowing Balloons." Wearing an uncharacteristic long wig with a braid and an outfit that shows off her legs, Lucille is beautiful and energetic as she and Danny pop an entire studio full of balloons in time to the music.

The most unique moments come in an extended sketch when the two Redheads portray actors who are forced to play all the roles in a melodrama because a blizzard has kept everyone else home. Not only do they have a delightful romp changing costumes, but when the sketch is over, they show parts of it again from a backstage camera, recalling what they went through to get in and out of costume, makeup, and wigs.

THE LUCY SHOW #66: "LUCY MAKES A PINCH"

(CBS, NOVEMBER 9, 1964), 30 MINUTES (B&W)

WRITTEN BY: Bob O'Brien, Vic McLeod
GUEST CAST: Jack Kelly, Alan Carney, Jack Searl, John Harmon

As part of her work with the police department, Lucy is used as a decoy in the local lover's lane to catch a thief. After spoiling the stakeout, Lucy talks Viv into dressing as a man to help her redeem herself in a stakeout of their own.

HIGHLIGHTS & TRIVIA

It is never really explained how Lucy moved from being a meter maid to being a member of the police department, or when she took any professional training. This might have been a good plot point for the show, having wacky Lucy hold a responsible job with Danfield's finest. However, the whole thing is dropped with no explanation.

PASSWORD

(CBS, NOVEMBER 12, 1964), 30 MINUTES (B&W)

EXECUTIVE PRODUCED BY: Bob Stewart
PRODUCED BY: Frank Wayne
DIRECTED BY: Mike Gargiulio, Lou Tedesco
CAST: Allen Ludden (host), Lucille Ball, Gary Morton, Lucie Arnaz, Desi Arnaz Jr.

Much has changed since the family last appeared on this series earlier in the year. Lucie is now a poised, beautiful young lady. Desi Jr. is about to become a real-life rock star with his group Dino, Desi, and Billy.

THE LUCY SHOW #67: "LUCY BECOMES A FATHER"

(CBS, NOVEMBER 16, 1964), 30 MINUTES (B&W)

WRITTEN BY: Iz Elinson, Fred S. Fox
GUEST CAST: Cliff Norton

Lucy wants to accompany her boy Jerry on a father and son trip. Although she talks the other dads into it, they scheme to make things so tough on her that she will leave of her own accord.

Cliff Norton

(ACTOR/COMEDIAN)

I had done a Desilu pilot with [director] Jack Donohue that starred Jackie Coogan, Soupy Sales, Donald O'Connor, and I. It was a great pilot, and Lucille hoped it could be used as a replacement for The Lucy Show, *because she wanted to quit. She wanted to fill an hour with this series and* Many Happy Returns *(1964–65). CBS wouldn't buy ours because they wanted her.* Returns *just died, even though it aired right after* The Lucy Show *on Monday nights. So although [the pilot] didn't sell, Jack and Lucille knew my work. Jack called me, and I was hired for this episode without an interview or an audition. Because there was a real bear on the set, we got instructions from the trainer not to pet him or feed him, and just to leave the bear to him. The bear was very securely leashed, and everyone did what the trainer suggested. I didn't want the bear angry at* me. *People like me did these shows for the challenge, not for the money. I was usually paid about $1,500 for doing a show with Lucille, which is peanuts compared to what people get today.*

Gale Gordon was a thorough, 100% professional. He knew every second what he was doing. Lucille could get awfully tough with him sometimes, but he had duck feathers and just let everything roll off his back. She never rattled him. He'd let her go on, and then he'd just say, "So, Lucy, shall we continue?" This was not the best script. I think sometimes Lucille could be creatively selfish. She would see things in the script that were for other people, or weren't out and out funny but more about character, and she would just cut it out of the script. Lucille felt, and perhaps rightly so, that the focus needed to be on her.

THE LUCY SHOW #68: "LUCY'S CONTACT LENSES"

(CBS, NOVEMBER 23, 1964), 30 MINUTES (B&W)

WRITTEN BY: Bob Schiller, Bob Weiskopf
GUEST CAST: Teddy Eccles

Lucy is too vain to wear much-needed glasses, so she gets contact lenses. After baking and icing a chocolate cake for a charity sale at the bank, Lucy realizes that one of her lenses has dropped into the pastry. She and Viv figure out that Mrs. Mooney bought her cake and they sneak into the Mooney home with a new cake to make a switch.

HIGHLIGHTS & TRIVIA

This is a superior episode. Every scene is funny and the ladies work beautifully together as in years gone by.

THE LUCY SHOW #69: "LUCY GETS HER MAID"

(CBS, NOVEMBER 30, 1964), 30 MINUTES (B&W)

WRITTEN BY: Bob O'Brien
GUEST CAST: Kathleen Freeman, Norma Varden

Lucy gets jealous of the sophisticated ladies of the Danfield Art Society (which she and Viv want to join) because they all have maids. Determined not to be bested, Lucy goes to work *as* a maid for another society matron to pay for one of her own. Unfortunately, her first big project is to serve dinner to the Danfield Art Society.

HIGHLIGHTS & TRIVIA

Norma Varden last appeared with Lucille and Viv on TV (in 1953, in *I Love Lucy* episode #61, "The Ricardos Change Apartments") as Mrs. Benson, the woman in apartment 3B who switched apartments with Lucy Ricardo.

Kathleen Freeman

(ACTOR)

I had a ball doing this one. It had a very bad plot, but it was basic Lucy: *Loveable, scatterbrained girl gets herself into deep [trouble] and then gets herself out of it again by her wits. But Lucille was fearless. If there was something she was asked to do, and it was going to be funny, she'd do it. There was no, "Let's get six guys in and see if this will be safe." If she was told it would be funny, she'd try it. However, if she didn't think something was funny immediately, she'd challenge it. The original writers (Bob and Madelyn) were brilliant with her in this manner. They knew how to explain it to her and make her feel confident [in the writing]. The later writers were not as successful. Lucille felt that as much as the dough might be kneaded, if it was not going to rise, then she was going to throw it out. You can't make someone as talented as Lucille Ball slave through a lull in a script because a writer isn't able to convey why something is funny.*

[Director] Jack Donohue worked beautifully with Lucille. He treated her like a treasure, and he understood her. Lucille and Vivian were magical together. Vivian Vance could be a little "peppery." I don't really know how much outside work she was doing or how she felt about doing this series. Certainly, Vivian's work with Lucille all through the years is what made her known to the public. Sometimes, Vivian liked to establish her own influence. Lucille might say, "Go around the couch on the left and then face me." Then Vivian would pull you aside, and say, "You know, if you went around the couch on the right side and then faced the audience it would be a lot funnier." When this happened, I would go to Jack Donohue, because they were going to both be on my case no matter which way I did it. Invariably, he would say, "Do what Lucille wants; that's OK." Norma Varden [the woman for whom Lucy is a maid] was also magical. Like many character actors, she was very malleable and could fit herself into any situation on a show."

THE LUCY SHOW #70: "LUCY GETS THE BIRD"

(CBS, DECEMBER 7, 1964), 30 MINUTES (B&W)

WRITTEN BY: Jerry Belson, Garry Marshall
GUEST CAST: Tim Herbert, John "Red" Fox, Ginny Tyler

Lucy and Viv birdsit for Mr. Mooney's parakeet, Greenback. After accidentally letting the bird fly away and failing to recapture it, the girls buy another bird and pass it off as Greenback.

HIGHLIGHTS & TRIVIA

Mr. Mooney seems to have no end of pets and hobbies. Besides his sheepdog, we have seen, or will see, Mooney collect stamps and coins, enjoy skiing, singing, and dancing. Soon we will discover he is a wine connoisseur. Although he is never given billing, Mel Blanc provides the voice of the bird, as well as many other offstage voices for this series.

THE LUCY SHOW #71: "LUCY THE COIN COLLECTOR"

(CBS, DECEMBER 14, 1964), 30 MINUTES (B&W)

WRITTEN BY: David Braverman, Bob Marcus
GUEST CAST: Ray Kellogg, Sid Gould, Nonya Andre, Bill Maeder, James Gonzales

After Lucy's son Jerry finds a penny worth fifty cents, Lucy and Viv comb through thousands of coins gotten at the bank until they find one worth $16.50. On the way home, Lucy drops the valuable penny down a storm drain. The two ladies don worker's uniforms to retrieve their coin without suspicion.

HIGHLIGHTS & TRIVIA

We have to wade through a pretty dull episode to get to the final scene, where Lucille and Vivian are brilliant together searching the storm drain for a valuable penny. What makes the scene work so well is Vivian, who has dropped the haughtiness of her character's personna to be Lucy's pal. Anytime Vivian's oncamera characterization of Vivian Bagley is more Ethel Mertz, the scenes definitely play better.

THE LUCY SHOW #72: "LUCY AND THE MISSING STAMP"

(CBS, DECEMBER 21, 1964), 30 MINUTES (B&W)

WRITTEN BY: Ray Singer, Dick Chevillat
GUEST CAST: Mabel Albertson, Nestor Paiva, Herb Vigran, Robert S. Carson, Flip Mark, Karl Lukas, Sid Gould

Lucy, a floundering vacuum cleaner salesperson, accidentally vacuums up a rare stamp of Mr. Mooney's worth $3,000. She realizes she has left the stamp at her next stop, when she emptied the dirt bag. The stamp was taken by the lady of the house and used, and now Lucy must get it back before the stamp is canceled at the post office.

HIGHLIGHTS & TRIVIA

More and more, this series lacks character continuity. One week Lucy is a cop, the next week she is a salesperson with no explanation for the sudden job shift. In addition, it is unlikely that laid-back Viv would be a better salesperson than sparkling Lucy. Tiring of her look, Ball begins using new wigs around this time in an effort to appear younger and more chic.

THE LUCY SHOW #73: "LUCY MEETS DANNY KAYE"

(CBS, DECEMBER 28, 1964), 30 MINUTES (B&W)

WRITTEN BY: Bob Schiller, Bob Weiskopf
GUEST CAST: Danny Kaye, Leon Belasco, Ray Kellogg

Lucy makes yet another ridiculous promise to her children, this time that she will get tickets to a Danny Kaye television show. She hunts Kaye down at a restaurant and then follows him to his hotel in a relentless pursuit for tickets. Finally, Danny arranges for the Carmichaels to be extras on his program.

Bob Schiller

(WRITER)

We happened to have a couple of weeks off from the show we were working on, and Milt Josefsberg called us. He said Danny Kaye was going to be a guest on the show, and that we were the only ones to write it.

Bob Weiskopf

(WRITER)

We did a couple of scripts that year after we all had left. This was done as a favor to Lucy, to help make the transition smooth. So we wrote the script and submitted it. We had lunch at the commissary, and at the next table are Lucy and Milt Josefsberg. He is telling her the plot of the show we wrote, and she is laughing uproariously. The next thing we know, we are summoned to meet Miss Ball in her dressing room. We walk in, and the only words out of her mouth were, "So what else have you got?" I asked her, "What do you mean, what else have we got? You were just laughing at our idea at lunch!" "Well," she said, "I changed my mind." So we went home and tried to come up with something, and we couldn't. We called her and told her that. The next morning, we were once again told to appear in her dressing room. We walked in, and she points a finger at me and said, "Because of you, I lost a night's sleep!" I pointed right back at her, and said, "Because of you, I've lost a lot *of nights' sleep!" She said she'd talked to Gary and some other people, and if we all believed in the show, she'd do it. I have to give her credit for that. Once she decided to do it, she did it all out; she didn't dog it.*

Bob Schiller

(WRITER)

That "Scarbidia" comedy bit Danny did was not written by us. It was an old piece his wife Sylvia Fine had written for him.

Candy Moore

(ACTOR)

Lucy gave Danny Kaye full reign to do whatever he wanted this week. Other than Ethel Merman, I never saw her defer to anyone *like she did with Danny. I think she was a little in awe of him.*

Maury Thompson

(CAMERA COORDINATOR)

When Danny guested on our show, he gifted Lucille with a beautiful Asian, jeweled jewelry box. Just gorgeous. She gave him an extra large tin of popcorn. Danny was so upset at the slight, he said he'd never work with her again. And they had been very good friends. The popcorn was Gary Morton's idea.

Lucie Arnaz

This is so unfair. I am sure my mother was just unprepared and never expected Danny to give her something like that. She probably gave him what she had on hand. Believe me, she made up for it later and they were friends for years!

PASSWORD

(CBS, JANUARY 7, 1965), 30 MINUTES (B&W)

EXECUTIVE PRODUCED BY: Bob Stewart
PRODUCED BY: Frank Wayne
DIRECTED BY: Mike Gargiulio, Lou Tedesco
CAST: Allen Ludden (host), Lucille Ball, Gary Morton

This series is becoming the perfect guest appearance for Lucille. She gets to play a game (her favorite thing to do besides performing), appear with her husband Gary, look beautiful, plug her TV series, and not have to learn any lines or set blocking.

THE LUCY SHOW #74: "LUCY AND THE CERAMIC CAT"

(CBS, JANUARY 11, 1965), 30 MINUTES (B&W)

WRITTEN BY: Ray Singer, Dick Chevillat
GUEST CAST: Larry Dean, John "Red" Fox, Sid Gould, Gail Bonney, Karen Norris

When Lucy and Viv are asked to keep Mrs. Mooney's surprise birthday present (a ceramic cat), naturally they manage to break it. The only other such cat in town is in a store window, and Lucy insists on getting it.

HIGHLIGHTS & TRIVIA

Another superior third season installment. This is the only time in this series Lucy Carmichael utters Lucy Ricardo's famous "spider" (exclamatory) sound, made after she realizes she has broken Mrs. Mooney's gift. The scene with Ball and the "mechanical man" in the store window is very well done. The Redhead rehearses this bit for hours to ensure the timing is exactly right.

THE LUCY SHOW #75: "LUCY GOES TO VEGAS"

(CBS, JANUARY 18, 1965), 30 MINUTES (B&W)

WRITTEN BY: Bob O'Brien
GUEST CAST: Jim Davis, Sid Gould, Jimmy Ames, Louis A. Nicoletti, Carole Cook

Viv has won a trip to Las Vegas for two, but she and Lucy aren't having any fun. With no money to gamble or to take in the club shows, the girls disguise themselves as a wealthy gambling addict and her companion to get the royal (free) treatment.

HIGHLIGHTS & TRIVIA

It is a shame that this installment is not aired in color, because Ball's jade green gown is spectacular. While this is a very entertaining episode, had there been someone with the big picture in mind regarding this episode we might have seen Lucy entering the contest, the girls traveling to Las Vegas, and perhaps another segment of them together in Nevada. This sort of story arc would have been common in earlier times, when the same writers wrote all of the scripts and Desi Arnaz or Jess Oppenheimer was in charge of production.

THE LUCY SHOW #76: "LUCY AND THE MONSTERS"

(CBS, JANUARY 25, 1965), 30 MINUTES (B&W)

WRITTEN BY: Jerry Belson, Garry Marshall
STORY BY: Maury Thompson, Art Thompson
GUEST CAST: George Barrows, Robert H. Burns, Jan Arvan, Shep Sanders, Sid Haig, James Gonzales

After seeing a scary movie, Lucy has a horrific nightmare in which she and Viv visit a haunted house and are changed into witches.

HIGHLIGHTS & TRIVIA

A true change-of-pace episode, it is surprising this is not the Halloween installment of the series. All of the cast spend a great deal of time in makeup, so this one is not filmed in front of a studio audience. Lucy uses the name "Sassafrassa" in the dream sequence; this is actually the name she gave an imaginary friend when she was a child in Celoron, New York.

THE LUCY SHOW #77: "LUCY AND THE COUNTESS"

(CBS, FEBRUARY 1, 1965), 30 MINUTES (B&W)

WRITTEN BY: Leonard Gershe
GUEST CAST: Ann Sothern, Carole Cook, Sid Gould, James Gonzales

Lucy's childhood friend, Rosie Harrigan, is now the broke and widowed Countess Framboise. She comes to stay with Lucy while Viv is out of town, and Mr. Mooney is greatly impressed with her. They wrangle an invitation to a wine-tasting party, hoping for great food and drink, and end up getting sloshed.

HIGHLIGHTS & TRIVIA

To fill in the blanks for some of the weeks Vivian does not appear, Ball's close friend Ann Sothern is written into the show. In this one, Ball and Sothern (as Rosie Harrigan) repeat the same drunk bit they had done on both *The Ford Lucille Ball-Desi Arnaz Show #1* ("Lucy Takes a Cruise to Havana") in 1957 and *The Ann Sothern Show* in 1959.

Notice that by this time, there are no shows that really feature any of the children. It is almost as if the writers have forgotten they exist. Although they all have contracts calling for them to be paid for ten out of every thirteen episodes filmed, they are barely seen.

THE LUCY SHOW #78: "MY FAIR LUCY"

(CBS, FEBRUARY 8, 1965), 30 MINUTES (B&W)
WRITTEN BY: Jerry Belson, Garry Marshall
GUEST CAST: Ann Sothern, Reta Shaw, Byron Foulger, John "Red" Fox, Bobby Jellison, Carole Cook

To gain income, Rosie decides to open a charm school in Danfield. She approaches the wealthy Dunbars for backing, promising to turn a disguised Lucy (as scrubwoman Liza Lumpwhomper) into a real lady. The Dunbars throw a party to debut the Countess' work, but Lucy mistakenly eats caviar (to which she is allergic) and disaster ensues.

HIGHLIGHTS & TRIVIA

The blockbuster film *My Fair Lady* (1964) has just been released. Many sitcoms are doing parodies of the screen musical, but this is among the best. Lucille is wonderful as the scrubwoman, then a vision of loveliness in the final sequence. Notice Ann Sothern in that last scene. When Lucy arrives, Sothern's Rosie is wearing a black gown covered by a green coat trimmed with fur. Later in the scene, she is wearing the same dress, but now carries a black satin stole instead of wearing the coat. Go figure!

Herbert Kenwith
(DIRECTOR)

Ann Sothern was an extremely well-trained film actress. She took direction well, and always gave the director exactly what he wanted. She was very personable and professional. Lucille and Ann were friends, so their episodes together went very well. Ann did as she was told, and was happy to do it. The only trouble Lucille had with Ann was that Ann was sensitive about her weight, and always wanted to stand behind a chair, or wear a long coat or stole, to cover her size. And sometimes Lucille didn't want her to do that. But there was no conflict between them.

THE LUCY SHOW #79: "LUCY AND THE COUNTESS LOSE WEIGHT"

(CBS, FEBRUARY 15, 1965), 30 MINUTES (B&W)
WRITTEN BY: Jerry Belson, Garry Marshall
GUEST CAST: Ann Sothern, Norman Leavitt, Carole Cook

Mr. Mooney has made a bad investment in a fat farm, and promises Lucy and Rosie money if they will take the weight-reducing course for publicity. The girls hate the regimen, and almost ruin everything for Mooney.

HIGHLIGHTS & TRIVIA

This is the least appealing of the Countess shows with Ann Sothern. It is not entertaining to see a still beautiful but overweight Ann Sothern in a sweatsuit complaining about doing exercise.

THE LUCY SHOW #80: "LUCY AND THE OLD MANSION"

(CBS, MARCH 1, 1965), 30 MINUTES (B&W)
WRITTEN BY: Ray Singer, Dick Chevillat
GUEST CAST: Ann Sothern, Lester Matthews, Maida Severn

Viv returns home just in time to help the Countess with a problem. European friends are arriving, and Rosie borrows a dilapidated mansion from the bank as a front. It is in drastic need of repairs, and the three girls paint, wallpaper, reupholster, and fix the place so it looks presentable. The Countess' friends arrive, but all the handiwork begins to fall apart.

Ann Sothern

(ACTOR)

Lucille could be very vulnerable. But if she didn't respect you, she could be very tough. This is the only one of the Lucy Shows *I did with Vivian. There was a lot of tension that week because Vivian was leaving the show.*

WHAT'S MY LINE?

(CBS, MARCH 7, 1965), 30 MINUTES (B&W)

EXECUTIVE PRODUCED BY: Gil Fates
PRODUCED BY: the CBS Television Network in association with Mark Goodson and Bill Todman
DIRECTED BY: Franklin Heller
CAST: John Daly (host)
PANELISTS: Arlene Francis, Dorothy Kilgallen, Bennett Cerf
MYSTERY GUEST: Lucille Ball

Lucille is in New York for her annual talks with CBS executives. She looks beautiful, and once again stumps the panel!

I'VE GOT A SECRET

(CBS, MARCH 8, 1965), 30 MINUTES (B&W)

PRODUCED BY: Chester Feldman
DIRECTED BY: Franklin Heller
CAST: Steve Allen (host), Lucille Ball (Guest)
PANELITSTS: Bill Cullen, Betsy Palmer, Henry Morgan, Bess Myerson

What is Lucille's big secret? Her series, *The Lucy Show,* will begin broadcasting in color in September.

THE LUCY SHOW #81: "LUCY AND ARTHUR GODFREY"

(CBS, MARCH 8, 1965), 30 MINUTES (B&W)

WRITTEN BY: Fred S. Fox, Iz Elinson
GUEST CAST: Arthur Godfrey, Max Showalter, Carole Cook, Stanley Farrar, Clyde Howdy

Lucy and Viv travel to Virginia to convince media veteran Arthur Godfrey ("The Old Redhead") to appear in Danfield's town founders' play. Godfrey agrees, and the ladies, Mooney, and Godfrey do the show.

HIGHLIGHTS & TRIVIA

Arthur Godfrey had been a huge television star in the 1950s, but by this time was semi-retired. His arrogance, combined with rumors of strong anti-Semitism, had made him almost *personna non grata* in show business. Lucille didn't care. She liked him, and thought that his work was solid, and that it was being ignored. This is an excellent installment, with fine performances by Lucille and Vivian to songs written by guest star Max Showalter.

Carole Cook

(ACTOR/FAMILY FRIEND)

There were always people watching us rehearsing these shows. I came through the swinging doors [playing a saloon girl in the town founders' show] and did my speech. Lucille stopped me because she said I lost heart. She said, "You go out there and come back in again and I don't want to see you lose heart while you are doing your lines!" I turned around and walked to the swinging doors. As I exited, I turned to look all around and said, "Someday, I'm going to own all of this!" This was a line that Lucille had supposedly said one day after getting a talking to at RKO. I waited and heard silence, so I just kept walking. I thought maybe I should just keep walking. Then the silence was broken by her laugh. Everybody joined in. I had taken a chance, but had felt the need to cover my humiliation.

THE LUCY SHOW #82: "LUCY AND THE BEAUTY DOCTOR"

(CBS, MARCH 22, 1965), 30 MINUTES (B&W)

WRITTEN BY: Bob O'Brien, Iz Elinson, Fred S. Fox
GUEST CAST: Dick Patterson, Tommy Farrell, Steven Geray, Sid Gould, Carole Cook

Lucy lies to Mr. Mooney to wheedle money to go to a beauty specialist. A *Candid Camera*-type TV show has taken over the specialist's salon, and captures Lucy on film. Fearful of Mooney seeing her on TV, Lucy schemes to retrieve the footage before it airs.

HIGHLIGHTS & TRIVIA

This is a silly and pallid effort compared to the one that precedes it.

THE LUCY SHOW #83: "LUCY THE STOCKHOLDER"

(CBS, MARCH 29, 1965), 30 MINUTES (B&W)
WRITTEN BY: Ray Singer, Dick Chevillat
GUEST CAST: Elliot Reid, Harvey Korman, Carole Cook, Sid Gould

After Lucy buys a share of stock in the Danfield Bank, she feels it is her job to help Mr. Mooney land the account of a wealthy psychiatrist who specializes in hypnosis. Visiting the doctor, Lucy, Viv, and Mr. Mooney end up pretending to be hypnotized, acting as children.

HIGHLIGHTS & TRIVIA

This is the last episode where Lucy, Viv, and Mr. Mooney all have a chance to be funny together. The supporting cast are all *Lucy Show* regulars, and the installment is very satisfying.

THE LUCY SHOW #84: "LUCY AND THE DISC JOCKEY"

(CBS, APRIL 12, 1965), 30 MINUTES (B&W)
WRITTEN BY: Garry Marshall, Jerry Belson
GUEST CAST: Pat Harrington Jr.

Lucy wins a contest, and becomes disc jockey for a day at a local radio station. It does not take long before the station is in a shambles.

HIGHLIGHTS & TRIVIA

Notice the kitchen set is remodeled to accommodate the older refrigerator and the blocking required for the scene where it falls apart. This is the last aired episode of the current format. Vivian has decided to leave the show unless she gets more creative control. Lucille's advisors warn her that if Vivian gets what she wants, she will in fact become her partner. It is decided not to meet Vivian's demands, and Vance leaves the series. This is a decision Lucille will regret for the rest of her life. Without Vivian aboard, Lucille truly toys with the idea of ending the program.

Anonymous

I think there was some sort of outside agenda interfering between Lucille and Vivian. Lucille was sold this bill of goods about how Viv wanted to be partners or nothing, and was told it in not a very nice manner. Lucille came to me crying that day, wondering why Vivian would do that to her. She felt very hurt and totally betrayed. I have since heard that Vivian's intentions were simply to become better paid, help make the show return to its former level of quality, and have the stories revolve more around her if she was going to keep commuting to the set from Connecticut. She found it exhausting, and her marriage to John Dodds was in trouble because he was bisexual and seeing men when she wasn't around. Although they sort of hashed this out, I don't think the two women ever discussed these things together in detail. It was all done through agents and executives. If they had, I bet they could have agreed upon something and Viv would have returned. As it stood, each felt the other had let her down.

Gary Morton

(PRODUCTION CONSULTANT)

Vivian Vance had a home in Connecticut and was married to John Dodds. She was tired. *Doing our shows, week in and week out, could be grueling. We only had four days from the first reading to get a show filmed in front of a live audience. There was a real love relationship between Viv and Lucy. And Viv was a great script doctor. Lucy missed working with Viv. It took a lot of convincing to get Lucille to continue.* She *finally realized that she was the star, and could carry the show on her own.*

Ralph Hart

(ACTOR)

When I found out that the format was changing, I was crushed. Finding out that I was to be removed from these people who had become my family was devastating to me.

Candy Moore

(ACTOR)

My agent called my house, and it was my father who gave me the news that we weren't coming back. I was shocked! I had no idea this was a possibility. We were on a hit show.

Maury Thompson

(CAMERA COORDINATOR)

Most people don't know it, but [associate producer] Tommy Thompson [no relation] and I are responsible for the continuation of The Lucy Show. *I went to Tommy and told him that we were in the driver's seat. This was the opportunity of a lifetime. We met at my house, and decided that if we could get Lucy Carmichael out to California, it might work as a premise. So we came up with the idea that the kids are in a private school in California, and Lucy comes out to visit them. While she is there, she has to go to the bank, and runs into Mr. Mooney, who has been transferred. Then we wrote little story blocks, with Lucy wearing pretty California clothes and driving a sports car, or Lucy having dinner with celebrities like Dean Martin and John Wayne. When we were done, I called Lucille's secretary Wanda Clark, and asked to make an appointment to see her. Wanda told me she was going to be at the studio the next day having her hair done by Irma Kusely. The next day, we went to Irma's little area on the lot. Lucille greeted us by saying, "I understand you want to see me. Tell me what you want to say now, because I haven't any time for you." I insisted that she give me five uninterrupted minutes before she left. She began to read what we put together, and began giggling. "Who wrote this shit?" she demanded. I told her we did. She said, "I like it. I really think it's a good format. You can direct it, can't you? And Tommy can produce it. You both know how things work. Nothing would change.*

She picked up the phone and said, "Get me Bill Paley in New York." I don't know who she actually spoke to, although it could have been Paley himself. "Hello? This is Lucy," she shouted. "We're going on in the fall." We walked out, and I turned to Tommy and said, "Do you know how lucky we are, to be at the right place at the right time? There are probably a thousand guys out there who can direct this thing better than I can, and produce better than you can." And that's the true story of how the show continued. One director, one producer, and most shows were filmed in less than ninety minutes. Today you have thirty producers, and they shoot until four in the morning.

Pat Harrington Jr.

(ACTOR)

I had no idea when we filmed this one that it would be shown last. Although it wasn't a large part, I wanted to do it because it meant working with Lucille Ball. I had been a regular with Steve Allen and Danny Thomas, but I wanted to learn more on my own. I wanted to be a sitcom actor and she was the best. . . .

THE LUCY-DESI COMEDY HOUR

(CBS, JUNE-SEPTEMBER, 1965), 60 MINUTES (B&W)

The thirteen hour-long specials that Lucille and Desi did for Ford and Westinghouse are rerun yet again as a summer replacement series.

WHAT'S MY LINE?

(CBS, JULY 25, 1965), 30 MINUTES (B&W)

EXECUTIVE PRODUCED BY: Gil Fates
PRODUCED BY: the CBS Television Network in association with Mark Goodson and Bill Todman
DIRECTED BY: Franklin Heller
CAST: John Daly (host)
PANELISTS: Arlene Francis, Dorothy Kilgallen, Bennett Cerf
MYSTERY GUEST: Lucille Ball

The Redhead once again manages to fool the panel, who cannot figure out who she is.

PASSWORD

(CBS, AUGUST 26, 1965), 30 MINUTES (B&W)

EXECUTIVE PRODUCED BY: Bob Stewart
PRODUCED BY: Frank Wayne
DIRECTED BY: Mike Gargiulio, Lou Tedesco
CAST: Allen Ludden (host), Lucille Ball, Gary Morton, Lucie Arnaz, Desi Arnaz Jr.

The Arnaz offspring are growing into personable, talented, and very good looking teenagers right before our eyes. Desi Jr. is already a major musical star from his work with Dino, Desi, and Billy.

THE MOST FAMOUS VISITORS TO LUCYLAND

Ann-Margret—*Here's Lucy* #44

Tallulah Bankhead—*The Lucille Ball-Desi Arnaz Show* #2

Jack Benny—*The Lucy Show* #60, *The Lucy Show* #100, *The Lucy Show* #138, *Here's Lucy* #2, *Here's Lucy* #59, *Here's Lucy* #70, *Here's Lucy* #81

Milton Berle—*The Lucille Ball-Desi Arnaz Show* #11, *The Lucy Show* #96, *The Lucy Show* #133, *Here's Lucy* #33, *Here's Lucy* #140

Charles Boyer—*I Love Lucy* #146

Carol Burnett—*The Lucy Show* #117-118, *The Lucy Show* #146-147, *Here's Lucy* #17, *Here's Lucy* #48, *Here's Lucy* #71

George Burns—*The Lucy Show* #111

Richard Burton—*Here's Lucy* #49

Sid Caesar—*The Lucy Show* #155

Johnny Carson—*Here's Lucy* #35

Jack Carter—*The Lucy Show* #144

Maurice Chevalier—*The Lucille Ball-Desi Arnaz Show* #6

Mike Connors—*Here's Lucy* #76

Joan Crawford—*The Lucy Show* #154

Sammy Davis Jr.—*Here's Lucy* #51

Tennessee Ernie Ford—*I Love Lucy* #94-95, *I Love Lucy* #112, *The Lucy Show* #131, *Here's Lucy* #23

Jackie Gleason—*Here's Lucy* #2

Betty Grable—*The Lucille Ball-Desi Arnaz Show* #4

Buddy Hackett—*The Lucy Show* #151

Helen Hayes—*Here's Lucy* #89

William Holden—*I Love Lucy* #114

Bob Hope—*I Love Lucy* #154, *The Lucy Show* #60

Rock Hudson—*I Love Lucy* #123

Van Johnson—*I Love Lucy* #124, *Here's Lucy* #11

Danny Kaye—*The Lucy Show* #73

Ernie Kovacs—*The Lucille Ball-Desi Arnaz Show* #13

Liberace—*Here's Lucy* #40

Ida Lupino—*The Lucille Ball-Desi Arnaz Show* #10

Fred MacMurray—*The Lucille Ball-Desi Arnaz Show* #3

Dean Martin—*The Lucy Show* #105

Harpo Marx—*I Love Lucy* #125

Ethel Merman—*The Lucy Show* #48-49

Wayne Newton—*The Lucy Show* #98, *Here's Lucy* #9, *Here's Lucy* #46

Vincent Price—*Here's Lucy* #58

Tony Randall—*Here's Lucy* #54

Ginger Rogers—*Here's Lucy* #84

Mickey Rooney—*The Lucy Show* #102

Dinah Shore—*Here's Lucy* #79

Phil Silvers—*The Lucy Show* #123

Red Skelton—*The Lucille Ball-Desi Arnaz Show* #8

Elizabeth Taylor—*Here's Lucy* #49

Danny Thomas—*The Lucille Ball-Desi Arnaz Show* #7, *The Lucy Show* #91, *Here's Lucy* #121

John Wayne—*I Love Lucy* #129, *The Lucy Show* #120

Orson Welles—*I Love Lucy* #156

Chapter Seventeen

1965–66 Season

THE LUCY SHOW: THE FOURTH SEASON

TECHNICAL REGULARS: Produced by Tommy Thompson; directed by Maury Thompson; script supervised by Milt Josefsberg; makeup by Hal King; hairstyling by Irma Kusely; music by Wilbur Hatch
CAST REGULARS: Lucille Ball (Lucy Carmichael); Gale Gordon (Theodore J. Mooney); Mary Jane Croft (Mary Jane Lewis); Roy Rowan (announcer)

THE LUCY SHOW #85: "LUCY AT MARINELAND"

(CBS, SEPTEMBER 13, 1965), 30 MINUTES
WRITTEN BY: Bob O'Brien
GUEST CAST: Jimmy Garrett, Jimmy Piersall, Harvey Korman, Teddy Eccles, Robert S. Carson, Sid Gould, Larry Clark, Richard M. Williams, DeDe Ball, Lucie Arnaz, Desi Arnaz Jr.

Lucy has left Danfield, New York, and moved to Hollywood, transferring her trust fund to the Westland Bank there. By great coincidence, Mr. Mooney has been transferred to Hollywood and is once again the trustee for her money. Lucy's daughter Chris is in college and her son Jerry is being enrolled in a military academy. Unfortunately, the school is going to Marineland for Jimmy Piersall Day and Jerry can't go because he is not yet an official student, so Lucy talks Mr. Mooney into taking her and Jerry anyway.

HIGHLIGHTS & TRIVIA

A new opening, featuring a kaleidoscope of *The Lucy Show* scenes from previous seasons, is used this year. This is the first *The Lucy Show* featuring the voice-over, "Costarring Gale Gordon." When the series goes into syndication, some of the releases of the first three seasons will feature this opening in black and white or color, with Vivian's name cut in instead of Gale's.

Done without an audience because of the location work, this is *one strange episode* (for many reasons). For one thing, Lucille's mother, DeDe Ball, is actually seen by the TV audience. She has no lines and is just seen in the bleachers at Marineland behind Lucille as are Lucie and Desi Jr. Then, it is amazing that the writers cannot concoct a better plot line transition for the Lucy character. Episodes could have been written about Viv's wedding (which happened, presumably before the Carmichaels left for California, and which explains why Vivian Vance is no longer seen on the series in any regular manner), Chris' entering college, or the tribulations of getting to Los Angeles from Danfield. Instead, all of these concepts are thrown away in a few careless sentences like, "We just moved here from back east," or "I wonder how Viv likes her new husband."

Bob Schiller

(WRITER)

These were bad writing decisions. Unfortunately, you had two people in charge who shouldn't have been. One was Milt Josefsberg and the other was Lucille Ball. Lucy's area was performing, not producing and script supervising.

Bob Weiskopf

(WRITER)

I don't want to sound mean, but where was Lucy in all of this? Why didn't she demand better writing for herself? She certainly was in charge. Given the same writers, directors, and actors, if Desi or Jess [Oppenheimer] had been there, this would have been handled much more smoothly and with greater humor.

Candy Moore
(ACTOR)
I later found out from Oscar Katz [one of the Desilu Studio's vice presidents] the reason why the transition was handled this way. It was all about money. If you go into a network with the same series but a radically changed format, the contracts allow for greater financial renegotiation. By dropping all of us at once, Desilu was able to get a lot more money out of CBS for the continuation of The Lucy Show.

Gary Morton
(PRODUCTION CONSULTANT)
The development of the Lucy *character, once the locale of the series was moved to Hollywood, just happened. There was no planning or thought to shaping it. We had Milt Josefsberg in charge of the writing, and he hired all sorts of writers to get scripts for us. But the* Lucy *character changed a little bit depending on who was writing* that *week's script.*

Additionally, the premise seems silly that Lucy and Mr. Mooney would end up in the same place together. By the way, this is as good a spot as any to correct misinformation that has been included in reference books for years. The Lucy character does *not* move to San Francisco, but to Hollywood. Over and over, shows revolving around the concept of her being new to Hollywood, around her selling maps to movie stars' homes, or being at one studio or another place her firmly in L.A. Yet, in many published sources, the Golden Gate city is listed as Lucy Carmichael's second home.

Maury Thompson
(DIRECTOR)
I almost wet my pants when I found out that the first show I was going to direct was this one. It was a very difficult day of shooting. We were out of our element, and everything was different from what we were used to.

The actual filming at Marineland (which was located about twenty-two miles south and east of Los Angeles on the Palos Verdes Peninsula, and which is no longer in existence) is torture for Lucille. To begin with, it is windy and unseasonably cool that day. It wreaks havoc with her wigs and makeup. It also makes for very cold water, because those fish pools are not heated. While Lucille wears a wet suit under her pants outfit most of the time, her scenes in the raft are filmed without it. She is very frightened of the water and of the dolphins, which weigh between 250 and 300 pounds each. Scenes that last only seconds take hours to film, as only one camera can be used at any given time. Frustrated by the experience, Lucille becomes very brusque with the crew, growling orders and losing patience every few minutes. The dolphins are not cooperative, and the filming disintegrates into a mess. It is only through persistence, professionalism, and genius editing that the installment ever gets into shape for airing. Lucille will not risk location shooting again for more than three years. This is the first *Lucy Show* episode aired in color.

Jimmy Garrett
(ACTOR)
Lucy was very frustrated by this episode. Remember, she was used to controlling everything in her own little environment. Here, almost everything was out *of her control, and she had to deal with these large, powerful animals on their terms. That crying you see at the end was the real thing. She was* not *happy. We were there for more than one day, because shooting was so laborious. All of [baseball player] Jimmy Piersal's scenes were shot there right on location as well.*

THE STEVE LAWRENCE SHOW

(CBS, SEPTEMBER 13, 1965), 60 MINUTES
PRODUCED BY: George Schlatter
DIRECTED BY: Jay Chicon
STAGED BY: Ernest Flatt
WRITTEN BY: Tony Webster, Sydney Zelinka, Saul Turtletaub, Gary Belkin, Mel Diamond
CAST: Steve Lawrence (host), Lucille Ball, Charles Nelson Reilly, Johnny Olson (announcer)

Lucille is Lawrence's only guest on his variety program debut. The opening number is taped in New York's Shubert Alley, as Steve helps Ball on the back of an elephant and they ride and sing into the theatre. Lucille is brought onstage with cheerleaders, marching bands entering from the audience, and a chorus line of dancers and singers. She does a comedy entrance, straddling two chorus boys' shoulders and then swinging from a suspended chandelier. She is dazzling in a designer gown, looking much more glamorous than she is allowed to on her own series. Her second sketch appearance has her showing outtakes from her own TV series, with Lucille in the pool with the porpoises at Marineland. In her musical moment, she and Steve duet "Hey, Look Me Over" (from her 1960 Broadway musical *Wildcat*) wearing top hat and tails. It is excellent, with the song's key lowered in places to suit Ball's voice.

THE ED SULLIVAN SHOW

(CBS, SEPTEMBER 19, 1965), 60 MINUTES

PRODUCED BY: Bob Precht
DIRECTED BY: Tim Kiley
CAST: Ed Sullivan (host); Lucille Ball; Polly Bergen; Dino, Desi, and Billy; the Moro Landis Dancers; Sandler and Young; Red Skelton

This is Ed Sullivan's first color episode, broadcast from CBS Television City in Hollywood. Lucille Ball, wearing her own hair and a black suit, takes a long bow from the audience because her son, Desi Arnaz Jr. (sporting bleached blond hair), is appearing on the program with his group, Dino, Desi, and Billy.

THE LUCY SHOW #86: "LUCY AND THE GOLDEN GREEK"

(CBS, SEPTEMBER 20, 1965), 30 MINUTES

WRITTEN BY: Garry Marshall, Jerry Belson
GUEST CAST: Howard Morris, Robert Fortier, Joe De Santis, Sid Gould

Lucy meets her new neighbor, Mary Jane Lewis, who arranges a blind date for her. He turns out to be a half a head shorter than she, and painfully shy. All that changes when they go to a Greek restaurant, where the music intoxicates her escort and he becomes a tiger.

HIGHLIGHTS & TRIVIA

This episode establishes Lucy's new apartment, and life without her children. Mary Jane Croft (as Mary Jane Lewis) is once again a regular cast member, playing the mousy-voiced character for which fans have come to know her. The plot is thin and Morris' humor very unmotivated. Notice the kitchen in Lucy's apartment. Its design will change from episode to episode, depending on the plot needs.

Mary Jane Croft

(ACTOR)

People always ask me how come I spoke so differently as Mary Jane after playing Betty Ramsey. The answer is simple. [From an acting standpoint] the more money you have, the more dignified you sound. It just evolved through the situations [written] that I had silly lines to read so I started using a silly voice. Also, when I talked that way, it really made Lucy laugh.

Jimmy Garrett

(ACTOR)

When Viv left, Mary Jane Croft took on a lot of what would have been Viv's responsibility on the show. She did an admirable job under less than easy circumstances, because nobody could replace Vivian Vance. She was a lovely lady, and that voice was something I loved listening to!

THE LUCY SHOW #87: "LUCY IN THE MUSIC WORLD"

(CBS, SEPTEMBER 27, 1965), 30 MINUTES

WRITTEN BY: Bob O'Brien
GUEST CAST: Mel Torme, Lou Krugman, Reb Foster

In need of money, Lucy takes a temporary job as secretary to Mr. Miller, the president of a large recording company. Coincidentally, Lucy's neighbor Mel Tinker is a songwriter who needs a contract. When he is rejected because the current fad is rock and roll music, Lucy arranges for him and her to perform his now revamped numbers on the youth-oriented television program *Wing Ding*.

HIGHLIGHTS & TRIVIA

This is the first excellent offering of the new format. Torme (as the songwriter) and Ball have a remarkable oncamera chemistry, and his character will be brought back again. The show-within-a-show parody of then current programs such as *Hullabaloo* (1965–66) is superb, with top-notch performances by all concerned. Mel writes special musical material that is both satirical and very funny. Lucille assumes almost total control of this installment.

Maury Thompson

(DIRECTOR)

Tommy Thompson is the nicest guy in the world, and a very close friend. But he, too, was a pushover for Lucille. He was afraid to stand up to her, so he never really made a decision on his own.

THE LUCY SHOW #88: "LUCY AND JOAN"

(CBS, OCTOBER 11, 1965), 30 MINUTES

WRITTEN BY: Iz Elinson, Fred S. Fox, Bob O'Brien

GUEST CAST: Joan Blondell, Keith Andes, William Fawcett, Queenie Smith

Lucy meets two more of her neighbors: Ethel Mertz like Joan and studly Keith. The girls become pals, and contrive to get Lucy and Keith together romantically.

HIGHLIGHTS & TRIVIA

This is another well-crafted episode. Although Lucy and Joan are very compatible onscreen, off-camera Lucille and veteran screen star Joan Blondell do *not* get along at all. Keith Andes has already made several *Lucy Show* appearances as a different romantic interest for Lucy back in Danfield and, as noted before, had been her Broadway leading man in the musical *Wildcat* (1960).

Maury Thompson

(DIRECTOR)

Lucille was intimidated by Joan Blondell, because she was so strong. Blondell was going to be considered as a replacement for Vivian, but it never got far. Joan showed up in an awful dress to wear in the show that made her look like a streetwalker. Lucille approved it and dismissed Joan. I tried to broach the subject, but Lucille cut me off. "Stick with the money," she said. "Forget about her, just make sure that I *look good!" I said, "Honey, I want the* whole show *to look good. That way,* you'll *look better."*

THE LUCY SHOW #89: "LUCY THE STUNT MAN"

(CBS, OCTOBER 18, 1965)

WRITTEN BY: Edmund Beloin, Henry Garson

GUEST CAST: Joan Blondell, Don McGowan, Lou Krugman, Eddie Quillan, Burt Douglas, Chuck Hicks

When Mr. Mooney refuses to advance Lucy the money for a fur coat that is on sale, she is desperate to raise the needed cash. Lucy's pal Joan and her stuntman boyfriend visit and he hurts his back. Joan convinces Lucy to take his place on a movie set and earn the needed money.

HIGHLIGHTS & TRIVIA

This is the first of the "Iron Man Carmichael" shows, one of the few fresh continuing themes introduced in the new format. Lucille is excellent in her stuntman paces, but the obvious pains taken in rehearsal to ensure the star does not harm herself while doing the stunts prevent any sense of spontaneity.

Herbert Kenwith

(DIRECTOR)

Joan Blondell was a friend of mine. Although I was there on the set (to offer moral support), we pretended not to know one another. While they were rehearsing together, Lucille said, "I thought you were a comedienne. Can't you turn any of those lines to be funny?" And Blondell said, "If that were written in that vein I could do it, but these are straight lines. There is nothing I can do except feed you *the lines." But Lucille couldn't accept that. During the filming, Lucille and Joan did their scene together. As it ended and [director Maury Thompson] yelled, "cut," Lucille pulled an imaginary chain in the air as if flushing an old-fashioned toilet. Blondell had turned away, but caught the end of it. "What does* that *mean?" she demanded. Lucille said, "It means that stunk!" Joan looked her right in the eye and said, "Fuck you, Lucille Ball!" and left. The studio audience was stunned. You didn't hear words like that in those days. Blondell never came back.*

Maury Thompson

(DIRECTOR)

Around this time, Gary Morton comes to me and says, "Take those steps out from in front of the door [to the apartment]. Lucy doesn't like them and she wants

them out." This surprised me, because we had already filmed several shows with them in, and Lucille never said a word about it. I tried to stall Gary by telling him how much manpower and money it would take to redo the set. Just then, Lucille walked in. "What's going on here?" she bellowed, "why is everybody standing around?" I asked if she disliked the steps, and told her what Gary had said. She looked at me, then turned to Gary and said, "Gary, go out and buy a car, but get outta here." Gary just hung his head and left. She never asked any more questions; she knew what Gary had tried to do. Lucille wanted him to be another Desi, but he just couldn't cut it.

THE LUCY SHOW #90: "LUCY AND THE COUNTESS HAVE A HORSE GUEST"

(CBS, OCTOBER 25, 1965), 30 MINUTES

WRITTEN BY: Garry Marshall, Jerry Belson
GUEST CAST: Ann Sothern, William Frawley, Bill Quinn, Herb Vigran

Lucy's old pal, Rosie the Countess, arrives on her doorstep with lots of luggage and no money. Her only asset is a pregnant racing horse, and the girls get Mr. Mooney to finance the mare's care (on Lucy's terrace) until the foal is born.

HIGHLIGHTS & TRIVIA

This is a very special episode. Lucille acts more like Lucy Ricardo than she has in years! Her new longer wig is very youthful. The interplay between Ball and Sothern has an ease missing with all of the Vivian replacement wannabes. Then, of course, there is the overwhelming moment when Bill Frawley does his cameo as the track maintenance man. The audience reaction is loud and long. From the gleam in her eye, it is obvious that Lucille is very pleased to share the stage with her costar one last time.

Maury Thompson
(DIRECTOR)

I called Ann Sothern "The Princess" because she always wanted to be treated like royalty. You had to pamper Ann to get a good show out of her. Despite what has been written, Lucille and Ann were very close friends, and on the set there was always girl talk between them. They could talk anyway they wanted to one another, and no one took offense. Ann was being considered as Vivian Vance's replacement, but she had the same problem Viv did. She wanted to be Lucille's equal partner, not just an underbilled costar. Lucille was also very happy to have Bill Frawley on the set that week. She just loved working with him. But he and Viv just didn't get along, so this was the only chance to bring him back before he passed away in 1966.

Irma Kusely
(HAIRSTYLIST)

Lucy decided she wanted to try a new look, something more youthful looking. So I had several long wigs made and styled them in a flip, which was the height of fashion at the time. Lucy wore them a few times in shows, then went back to the old wigs. I think someone at the network said something about not liking the new look, and that's all the excuse she needed to go back to her old familiar look.

THE LUCY SHOW #91: "LUCY HELPS DANNY THOMAS"

(CBS, NOVEMBER 1, 1965), 30 MINUTES

WRITTEN BY: Bob O'Brien
GUEST CAST: Danny Thomas, Dick Patterson, Mickey Manners, Sid Gould

Lucy is so often short on money she convinces Mr. Mooney that working for him part-time at the bank might be a good source of added revenue and a good influence on her. To test her, Mooney has Lucy deliver an envelope to a television studio. In short order, she becomes a chorus girl on a Danny Thomas TV special.

HIGHLIGHTS & TRIVIA

This episode has many things wrong with it! To begin with, it establishes that Lucy now works for Mr. Mooney *part-time*. Yet, in a few weeks she will be working for him *full-time*, and behaving as if this has always been their relationship, boss and employee. In fact, any further mention of her trust fund is totally forgotten. At this point, *The Lucy Show* really does become a different series. The setup is awkward, and the follow-through in future weeks is nebulous at best.

Second, it has middle-aged Lucy competing with young girls for a job in a chorus line, and winning. When Danny Thomas calls her "young lady," one almost winces. The original *Lucy* writers always kept Lucy Carmichael's age unknown, but youthful *within* reason. The new series regime treats her as if she is now a young lady about town. This destroys the character's credibility. Also, when Lucy Carmichael was a lousy secretary in the first season, it was because she was unfamiliar with the electric office machinery. Her failure was funny because it wasn't her fault. Now, she is written as being stupid and incompetent. This is a *serious* plotting error in judgment.

Lastly, the entire bit about Lucy having trouble with a heavy headdress is stolen from the 1955 *I Love Lucy* episode "Lucy Gets into Pictures" (#116). It is not nearly as well done here. Notice Mr. Mooney's office. It will change constantly over the next few months, getting larger and more luxurious each week until its layout is frozen in the next season.

Maury Thompson

This was a tough week. Danny [Thomas] wanted to direct everything, and so did Lucille. We had a lot of careful choreography in the musical number, with Lucy hooking Danny's nose on an umbrella. We ended up having to fake it, with him playing along as if he were actually hooked. Lucille did not enjoy working with Danny as much when Desi wasn't around, because Danny never tried to take over when he was there.

THE LUCY SHOW #92: "LUCY HELPS THE COUNTESS"

(CBS, NOVEMBER 8, 1965), 30 MINUTES
WRITTEN BY: Edmund Beloin, Henry Garson
GUEST CAST: Ann Sothern, Karen Norris

The Countess has taken up real estate sales, so Lucy attempts to get Mr. Mooney to rent an apartment in an ultra-modern building Rosie the Countess represents. The trio find themselves automatically locked into the apartment for the weekend, with no food and no way out.

HIGHLIGHTS & TRIVIA

This episode is stolen from the earlier episode "Lucy Gets Locked in the Vault" (#34), and again no credit is given to the original writers. The installment is amusing, and no more. Karen Norris often appears on this series and its successor in parts calling for efficient, attractive women. It is never explained where the Countess has been in the weeks since episode #90, "Lucy and the Countess Have a Horse Guest."

THE LUCY SHOW #93: "LUCY AND THE SLEEPING BEAUTY"

(CBS, NOVEMBER 15, 1965), 30 MINUTES
WRITTEN BY: Jerry Belson, Garry Marshall
GUEST CAST: Clint Walker, Leopold Kress, Sid Gould, Mary Wickes

When she meets Mr. Mooney at a construction site the bank is financing, Lucy literally falls into the incredibly muscular arms of Frank the builder. She invites him to her apartment for a date, but when he arrives Frank is totally exhausted from overwork. Due to his commando training, he is afraid to take a nap because if he is awakened suddenly, he is geared to attack.

HIGHLIGHTS & TRIVIA

Hulking Clint Walker, like Keith Andes, is an excellent studly foil for Lucy's femininity. In fact, extremely masculine men are now needed to point up Lucille's feminine side, which is not as obvious as it once was. Although thirty-nine year-old Walker is much younger than she, the couple make the teaming work.

Clint Walker

(ACTOR)

I was thrilled to be asked to do this show. It was an opportunity to show that I could do comedy, and it was a privilege to work with Lucy. I had done a Jack Benny show, so the [live] audience didn't frighten me. She and her people were so good at putting things together that the special effects just fell into place. Everything was carefully rigged on the sofa, and, of course, the post was made of breakable balsa wood. I was really afraid that I might hurt her, because I must have weighed more than twice what she did. She rehearsed everything so it was just right. Maury Thompson seemed to be in control of the situation, and occasionally Lucy would make some small suggestions about what I was doing.

THE LUCY SHOW #94: "LUCY THE UNDERCOVER AGENT"

(CBS, NOVEMBER 22, 1965), 30 MINUTES
WRITTEN BY: Bob O'Brien

GUEST CAST: Ann Sothern, Jack Cassidy, Parley Baer, James Dobson, Sid Gould

After viewing the latest James Bond film, Lucy, Mr. Mooney, and the Countess let their imaginations go wild when at dinner they encounter two suspicious-looking men. Our heroes scheme to trap these seeming spies, only later to find the shoe is actually on the other foot.

HIGHLIGHTS & TRIVIA

Every sitcom seems to be parodying the highly popular James Bond movie series fad, and this one is no exception. Lucille's impersonation of Carol Channing in her *Hello, Dolly!* costume is extremely well executed. Someone should have reminded Ann Sothern that America's enemies at this time are the Russians, *not* the Germans, as she responds to Jack Cassidy with a resounding *"ja vold"* instead of *"da."* The Countess shows are all filmed in succession, but for some reason are aired only sporadically, which prevents any sense of continuity among them.

A SALUTE TO STAN LAUREL

(CBS, NOVEMBER 23, 1965), 60 MINUTES

PRODUCED BY: Henry Jaffe, Seymour Burns
DIRECTED BY: Seymour Burns
WRITTEN BY: Charles Isaacs, Hugh Wedlock Jr., Allan Mannings
MUSIC BY: David Rose
CHOREOGRAPHY BY: James Starbuck
CHORAL DIRECTOR: Johnny Mann
CAST: Dick Van Dyke (host), Lucille Ball, Fred Gwynne, Danny Kaye, Buster Keaton, Harvey Korman, Tina Louise, Audrey Meadows, Bob Newhart, Gregory Peck, Cesar Romero, Phil Silvers

A tribute to the recently-deceased comedic screen great, Stan Laurel (1890–1965), is a benefit for the Motion Picture Relief Fund. Lucille and Buster do a silent sketch on a park bench, with the two clowns wrestling over an oversized newspaper, until policeman Harvey Korman breaks up the fun. This represents the only episode Ball and Keaton (who were both under contract to MGM in the mid-1940s) worked together in front of a camera.

THE LUCY SHOW #95: "LUCY AND THE RETURN OF IRON MAN"

(CBS, NOVEMBER 29, 1965), 30 MINUTES

WRITTEN BY: Edmund Beloin, Henry Garson
GUEST CAST: Ross Elliott, Saul Gorss, Sid Gould

Lucy and Mary Jane run into Mr. Mooney at the horse races (he had previously admonished Lucy not to go). Upon seeing a prominent client, Mooney ducks out, giving Lucy winning tickets that she mistakenly tears up. To pay him back, Lucy again takes on the identity of rugged stuntman Iron Man Carmichael.

HIGHLIGHTS & TRIVIA

As with the earlier "Iron Man" effort, the episode is very funny, but the physical humor is *so* choreographed that it dampens the fun. Ross Elliott returns to the *Lucy* fold as the director, looking amazingly the same as he had ten years before on *I Love Lucy*. Notice Mr. Mooney's hysterics in Lucy's apartment. These tirades, funny at first, have already become annoying. Mr. Mooney used to be a man of dignity, but now he seems to be nothing more than a screaming hysteric who is obsessed with money. This one-dimensional characterization lends nothing to the series.

THE LUCY SHOW #96: "LUCY SAVES MILTON BERLE"

(CBS, DECEMBER 6, 1965), 30 MINUTES

WRITTEN BY: Garry Marshall, Jerry Belson
GUEST CAST: Milton Berle, Ned Glass, Charles Cantor, Eleanor Audley

Lucy, Mary Jane, and Mr. Mooney do volunteer work in a soup kitchen where Milton Berle has chosen to go *incognito* to learn about bums for an upcoming movie role. Lucy takes Berle home with her to rehabilitate him, thinking he is Berle's impoverished twin brother Arthur.

HIGHLIGHTS & TRIVIA

As in years past, Lucille and Berle work very well together. Because both perform over-the-top, they compliment one another. Unfortunately for continuity purposes, two seasons later Lucy Carmichael will again meet Milton Berle for the *first* time!

Maury Thompson
(DIRECTOR)
Milton was a professional, but he always had this entourage with him, including his brother Jack and [longtime writer] Buddy Arnold. Now Jack could never keep his mouth shut, and he was forever telling dirty jokes. Lucille hated *off-color humor, especially when she was trying to work. I was forever having to say, "Jack, please not now. We're working. Save it for after lunch." Anything to just shut him up.*

A DANNY THOMAS SPECIAL: "THE WONDERFUL WORLD OF BURLESQUE"

(NBC, DECEMBER 8, 1965), 60 MINUTES
PRODUCED AND DIRECTED BY: Alan Handley
WRITTEN BY: Hugh Wedlock Jr., Allan Mannings
COMEDY CONSULTANT: Herbie Faye
CHOREOGRAPHY BY: Jack Bunch
MUSIC BY: Frank DeVol
CAST: Danny Thomas (host), Lucille Ball, Jimmy Durante, Shirley Jones, Sheldon Leonard, Jerry Lewis

This is a payback for Danny's visit to *The Lucy Show* earlier in the season. Lucille has two contributions to this TV salute to vaudeville. As a stripper, she sings "Poor Butterfly" (voice dubbed by Carole Cook) before she goes aloft on wires. Later, she joins Danny and Jerry in a very funny spoof of the 1920s Broadway melodrama hit *White Cargo* as the tempestuous native girl Tandelayo.

There would be two more of these special salutes to burlesque hosted by Thomas, one in 1966 and one in 1967. It has been erroneously reported elsewhere that Lucille also appeared on the second one. She did not.

THE LUCY SHOW #97: "LUCY THE CHOIRMASTER"

(CBS, DECEMBER 13, 1965), 30 MINUTES
WRITTEN BY: Bob O'Brien, Lila Garrett, Bernie Kahn
GUEST CAST: Jimmy Garrett, Lloyd Corrigan, Sid Gould, Michael Blake, Robert Roter, Teddy Eccles, Theodore Miller, the St. Charles Boys Choir

It is Christmastime in sunny California, and Lucy wants the fellow students from son Jerry's military academy to sing carols at the bank as boys did back in Danfield, New York. She not only gets her way, but persuades Mr. Mooney to become the group's bass singer.

HIGHLIGHTS & TRIVIA
This is the last appearance by Jimmy Garrett as Jerry Carmichael. To not use him occasionally, or even mention daughter Chris, is a mistake. This series needs an occasional change of pace, and without Vivian or the kids as the story line participants, Lucy Carmichael relies weekly on guest stars to keep her from being boxed in by Mr. Mooney's office and that particular plot line format. Although shown out of sequence, this is the 100th shot episode of this series.

Jimmy Garrett
(ACTOR)
My agent called and told my mother than this would be my last episode. Mom handled it great, and told me that we were now going to go on to other things. I actually sang with that choir that week. We rehearsed our song right on the set.

THE LUCY SHOW #98: "LUCY DISCOVERS WAYNE NEWTON"

(CBS, DECEMBER 27, 1965), 30 MINUTES
WRITTEN BY: Bob O'Brien
GUEST CAST: Wayne Newton, Gary Morton

Lucy loses Mr. Mooney's beloved sheepdog Nelson, but thankfully honest farm boy Wayne finds him and phones Lucy. When she comes to retrieve the dog, she discovers that Wayne is a talented singer and musician. She contrives to get the boy a recording contract with Mr. Morton, the head of a record company.

HIGHLIGHTS & TRIVIA
This is one of the best installments of the 1965–66 season. Young Wayne Newton, although already a known entity as a fast rising singer of pop songs, is literally catapulted into stardom by this appearance. His talent, charming shyness, and easy ability to generate a laugh make him a superb guest star.

Maury Thompson

(DIRECTOR)

This was a wonderful episode. Wayne was a great, young guy with amazing talent. His brother [Jerry] was also on the show, and he, too, was talented and very *friendly. That little goat who took the cookie out of Lucy's hand was so cute . . . he did it right on cue. Gary Morton's mother was in this one, and I had to keep reminding her that she was just background, an atmosphere player.*

THE LUCY SHOW #99: "LUCY THE RAIN GODDESS"

(CBS, JANUARY 3, 1966), 30 MINUTES

WRITTEN BY: Brad Radnitz, Bruce Howard

GUEST CAST: Willard Waterman, Douglas Fowley, Larry Blake, Alan Reed Jr., Jamie Farr, Marc Cavell

Lucy follows Mr. Mooney to a Native American-themed hotel because he has left without signing important bank papers. While there, some local natives confuse her for their rain goddess, and press Lucy into a tribal rain dance. The only problem is that if she does not succeed, she and Mr. Mooney will be harmed.

HIGHLIGHTS & TRIVIA

In retrospect, this episode might appear somewhat bigoted, a little insensitive, and in fact just badly written. While Lucille tries hard to be funny, there is little in the script to support her. The two "modern" braves are played by future *M*A*S*H* (1972–83) performer Jamie Farr and Alan Reed Jr., the son of the voice of TV's Fred Flintstone.

THE LUCY SHOW #100: "LUCY AND ART LINKLETTER"

(CBS, JANUARY 10, 1966), 30 MINUTES

WRITTEN BY: Iz Elinson, Fred S. Fox

GUEST CAST: Art Linkletter, Doris Singleton, Jerome Cowan, Roy Rowan, George Barrows, Sid Gould, Ray Kellogg, Jack Searl, Barbara Perry

Lucy is a contestant on *The Art Linkletter Show*, and promises to remain completely silent for twenty-four hours to win $100. Linkletter assigns Helen Cosgrove (Doris Singleton) to chaperone Lucy to ensure she is faithful to her promise. Mr. Mooney, unaware of the reason for Lucy's silence, concludes she has an emotional problem and tries to shock her out of it.

HIGHLIGHTS & TRIVIA

If for no other reason, this installment is recommended for the return of beautiful Doris Singleton to the *Lucy* players. Missing in action since the 1956 *I Love Lucy* episode "Lucy and Superman (#166)," she is a welcome addition. Looking better (and blonder) than she ever had on the original series, the age difference between Lucille and the much younger Doris is now obvious. Lucille trades this guest shot for one on Linkletter's daytime series *Art Linkletter's House Party*. On it, she does a very funny recreation of an old-time radio show sound effects person.

Maury Thompson

(DIRECTOR)

Lucille really liked Art Linkletter personally, so this was a most pleasant week of work. He never caused any problems and handled himself professionally. We also got to use lovely Doris Singleton again. Lucille loved Doris' voice, how she used it and how she projected to the audience.

THE LUCY SHOW #101: "LUCY BAGS A BARGAIN"

(CBS, JANUARY 17, 1966), 30 MINUTES

WRITTEN BY: Henry Taylor, Howard Ostroff

GUEST CAST: Jonathan Hole, Sid Gould, Barbara Morrison, Bennett Green, Barbara Perry, Natalie Masters, Elvia Allman, Amzie Strickland, Joel Marston, Donald Foster

Lucy puts a deposit on a dinette set during a big department store sale, beating out an infuriated socialite. When Lucy realizes that the furniture is more expensive than she thought, she takes a job at the store to pay for it.

HIGHLIGHTS & TRIVIA

This is a very athletic outing for Ball, as most of the humor is physical. Again, the block comedy scenes find her being physically manipulated or working with a prop, as opposed to something she is actually performing on her own.

THE LUCY SHOW #102: "LUCY MEETS MICKEY ROONEY"

(CBS, JANUARY 24, 1966), 30 MINUTES

WRITTEN BY: Allan Mannings, Hugh Wedlock Jr.
GUEST CAST: Mickey Rooney, Dorothy Konrad, Steven Marlo, Jack Perkins, Fred Krone, Harvey Parry, George Barrows, Sid Gould

Movie star Mickey Rooney asks Mr. Mooney for bank financing for his acting school. Lucy and Mooney are so impressed they both seek Rooney's training themselves.

HIGHLIGHTS & TRIVIA

The plot line theme of celebrities just walking into Mr. Mooney's office is already becoming tiresome. Seemingly every star in Los Angeles visits the banker sooner or later. The high point of this installment is the Chaplin sketch Ball does with Rooney, reminiscent of the one she had done with Vivian Vance in 1962's episode #14, "Chris' New Year's Eve Party."

Maury Thompson
(DIRECTOR)

In between the second and third acts [of the episode], we had to kill time while Lucille put on her Chaplin make-up. Gary Morton went over to the vegetable stand we had set up for the set, picked up a sizeable cucumber, unzipped his fly and put it in his trousers. When Lucille came out and saw what he had done, she simply turned on her heels and walked away. She was angry, and she knew that kind of horsing around wasn't going to help the comedy that was going to follow.

THE LUCY SHOW #103: "LUCY AND THE SOAP OPERA"

(CBS, JANUARY 31, 1966), 30 MINUTES

WRITTEN BY: Edmund Beloin, Henry Garson
GUEST CAST: Jan Murray, John Howard, Jane Kean, John Alvin, Sid Gould, Bennett Green

Lucy's neighbor (John Howard) stars in her favorite TV daytime drama, but fears his acting job may be over if the plot line finds him guilty of a crime. The Redhead decides to pester the writer of the show (Jan Murray) to find out the outcome of the oncamera trial and then try to change his mind if it goes against her actor pal.

HIGHLIGHTS & TRIVIA

Miss Ball's characterization of a Japanese gardener is plain offensive. This is one of the worst installments of the season.

Jane Kean
(ACTOR/SINGER)

Paula Stewart was originally supposed to play my part [the beautiful juror], but something happened and I was brought in instead. Lucy and I had been friends since the 1940s. We had a tough time rehearsing this show, because Lucy just unnerved [comedian] Jan Murray. She expected a performance right from the beginning. Some people don't work that way, they have to sort of work their way into it. She said, "I can't tell what you're going to do Jan!" And he said, "I'm not there yet. I don't know what *I'm going to do." Well, Lucy just had to* know. *Even with props, she worked with them right from the beginning. Jan was so nervous, he ended up giving Lucy nothing to work with.*

THE LUCY SHOW #104: "LUCY GOES TO A HOLLYWOOD PREMIERE"

(CBS, FEBRUARY 7, 1966), 30 MINUTES

WRITTEN BY: Edmund Beloin, Henry Garson
GUEST CAST: Edward G. Robinson, Kirk Douglas, Vince Edwards, Reta Shaw, Johnny Grant, Bert Freed, Flip Mark, Eva Pearson, Robert Foulk, Ken Delo

Yet another apartment neighbor (Reta Shaw) has to move back east, so Lucy takes over her "maps to the movie stars' home" stand to be a real part of show business. When the neighbor's son drops off his theatre usher's uniform for Lucy to return for him, she wears it herself and attends her first Hollywood premiere.

HIGHLIGHTS & TRIVIA

This mediocre effort is made exciting by the cameo appearances of several major stars. The theme of Lucy in drag is once again evident, and handled well this time.

Maury Thompson
(DIRECTOR)

It was easy to get all those stars to do this episode, because they were all friends or admirers of Lucille's.

And they were all such good sports and a pleasure to work with. It was a lousy set . . . it looked so hokey.

THE DEAN MARTIN SHOW

(NBC, FEBRUARY 10, 1966), 60 MINUTES

PRODUCED AND DIRECTED BY: Greg Garrison
WRITTEN AND CO-PRODUCED BY: Paul W. Keyes
WRITTEN BY: Harry Crane
CAST: Dean Martin (host), Lucille Ball, Bill Cosby, Ken Lane, Big Tiny Little and His Wild Ones, Rowan and Martin, Kate Smith

For some reason, Lucille Ball just loves working with Dean Martin, and it really shows in this guest outing by the Redhead. Her first sketch has Ball planted in the studio audience as little old farm lady Emma Frump, whom Martin pulls onstage to trade old vaudeville jokes. Later in the evening, Dean and a beautifully gowned Lucille (wearing a sexy two-piece powder blue evening dress with silver jet) banter about how relaxed his show is, and how much he enjoys working with her. The finale of the show has Martin and Kate Smith singing a medley of turn-of-the-century tunes, with Lucille as a perky chorus girl dancing in the line and acting out the lyrics. It is a very funny bit, and Ball carries off her terpsichorean chores with aplomb.

THE LUCY SHOW #105: "LUCY DATES DEAN MARTIN"

(CBS, FEBRUARY 14, 1966), 30 MINUTES

WRITTEN BY: Bob O'Brien
GUEST CAST: Dean Martin, Tommy Farrell, Sid Gould

Mary Jane arranges for Dean Martin's stunt double to take Lucy to a fancy Hollywood charity ball and auction. When the double (called Eddie Feldman for the purposes of this episode) has to work and cannot make it, Dean goes on the date for him instead so Lucy won't be disappointed.

HIGHLIGHTS & TRIVIA

Lucille once again wears one of the longer wigs, which gives her a much more feminine look. Martin was in Hawaii just previous to the filming of this episode, and doesn't show up for the rehearsal on Monday. Or Tuesday. While Ball would normally have "castrated" any other star for this sort of behavior, this time she is (for reasons unknown) forgiving and remains enchanted by Martin when he does appear.

Maury Thompson
(DIRECTOR)

This was Lucille's favorite episode of all time, but I don't know why. In real life, Edward Feldman was a film producer.

Gary Morton
(PRODUCTION CONSULTANT)

This episode is Lucy's favorite show ever, and even I *am not certain why. The only thing she said at the time was that she loved working with Dean Martin, and that the script had a* Sabrina *quality to it that really appealed to her. She also loved that jewelled jacket she got to wear in the last scene.*

THE LUCY SHOW #106: "LUCY AND BOB CRANE"

(CBS, FEBRUARY 21, 1966), 30 MINUTES

WRITTEN BY: Edmund Beloin, Henry Gerson
GUEST CAST: Bob Crane, John Banner, Oscar Beregi, Larry Dean, Sid Gould

TV star Bob Crane comes into the bank as a new client and is captivated by Lucy's femininity. He takes her to dinner, where they encounter Mr. Mooney and the director of Crane's new picture. The film requires a good stuntman, so Mooney blackmails Lucy into becoming "Iron Man" Carmichael again.

HIGHLIGHTS & TRIVIA

This is the last of the "Iron Man" shows. While these excursions are always a little forced, they have at least provided Lucille with motivated comedy and continuity. Bob Crane of *Hogan's Heroes* (1965–71) is totally miscast as a romantic interest for Lucy. He is neither tall nor muscular enough, and the eighteen year age difference between them is disturbing. Watch for John Banner's cameo in his Sergeant Schultz character from *Hogan's Heroes.*

Maury Thompson
(DIRECTOR)

I didn't even know who Bob Crane was, *never mind what he could do. I never understood why an entire episode was built around nothing, except perhaps that Lucille had a piece of Bing Crosby Productions, which produced* Hogan's Heroes.

THE LUCY SHOW #107: "LUCY THE ROBOT"

(CBS, FEBRUARY 28, 1966), 30 MINUTES

WRITTEN BY: Jerry Belson, Garry Marshall

GUEST CAST: Jay North, Vito Scotti, Dorothy Konrad, Larry Dean, Sid Gould

Lucy has two problems. Her neighbor is a genius inventor in need of financing, and Mr. Mooney's bratty nephew has scared away six babysitters. The answer to both problems? A mechanical babysitter invented by Lucy's friend.

HIGHLIGHTS & TRIVIA

Rehearsal scenes from this episode will be used in a CBS special regarding the state of modern television, hosted by Arthur Godfrey.

Jay North

(ACTOR)

It was great to work with Gale again [they had costarred on TV's Dennis the Menace *in 1962–63]. He seemed genuinely pleased to see me. Lucy was very nice to me, and was gentle in her guidance with what I was supposed to do. They were really sort of trading in on my* Dennis the Menace *character, only this kid got to be an out and out evil menace. I enjoyed that!*

THE LUCY SHOW #108: "LUCY AND CLINT WALKER"

(CBS, MARCH 7, 1966), 30 MINUTES

WRITTEN BY: Jerry Belson, Garry Marshall

GUEST CAST: Clint Walker, Sid Gould

Lucy decides to knit a red sweater for her construction worker boyfriend Frank's birthday. Unfortunately, he hates the color red, and her efforts produce an unwearable garment.

HIGHLIGHTS & TRIVIA

The second of two installments featuring the mountainous Clint Walker, it is too bad he is too major a star to become a regular. His physical appearance is a good balance for Ball's hyperactivity, and they work well together.

Clint Walker

(ACTOR)

That was actually me playing the harmonica in the picnic scene. I was going through a divorce at the time of this second show, so I don't remember as much about it. I know a lot of the plot had to do with my being such a big, good looking guy. You know, I never thought too much in terms of being a sex symbol. It all lies in the eyes of the beholder. I was flattered that they wanted me to do another appearance. I considered myself to be very fortunate to be working with her caliber of performer. The whole enterprise was very well coordinated. Lucy was always very businesslike . . . she wanted a good show. That was primary in her mind, giving it the best that she had. Occasionally, she'd make some funny little remark, but it was always complimentary and in good taste. She was totally prepared when she went in front of the cameras. By the way, I have a twin sister named Lucille.

THE LUCY SHOW #109: "LUCY, THE GUN MOLL"

(CBS, MARCH 14, 1966), 30 MINUTES

WRITTEN BY: Bob O'Brien

GUEST CAST: Robert Stack, Bruce Gordon, Steve London

The FBI asks Lucy to help trap a gangster because she is a dead ringer for his girlfriend, performer Rusty Martin.

HIGHLIGHTS & TRIVIA

This is a classic episode! Occasionally this series produces an installment that is well-written, well-produced, funny, and brilliantly played. Stack and Gordon had been the costars of the Desilu-produced *The Untouchables* (1959–63), and, in fact, this entire offering is an homage to that series. Lucille gets to sing "My Heart Belongs to Daddy" and perform her standard chorus girl characterization. The name Rusty Martin is a wink to Mary Martin, the star who has introduced "Daddy" on Broadway.

Mary Martin

(BROADWAY LEGEND)

A lot was made in the press of Lucy singing my song and doing an impression of me. I was out of the

country at the time, but it amazed me how many calls and letters I got about this show. I eventually saw it in reruns, and while Miss Ball was wonderful, she certainly wasn't doing an impression of me!

Robert Stack

(ACTOR)

It was a delight to do this show. In the beginning, Lucy started to pull me around and direct me, but I turned to her and said, "Do you know anyone who knows more about playing this part than I *do?" She looked at me and started to laugh, and from that moment on she left me alone.*

THE LUCY SHOW #110: "LUCY THE SUPERWOMAN"

(CBS, MARCH 21, 1966), 30 MINUTES

WRITTEN BY: Elroy Schwartz
GUEST CAST: Robert F. Simon, Joel Marston, Robert S. Carson, Parley Baer, Herb Vigran, John Perry, Sid Gould, Jack Perkins

When a new computer is accidentally dropped on Mr. Mooney's foot, Lucy amazes everyone by lifting the one-ton machine. Doctors discover that she has a "stuck" adrenal gland, and she becomes an instant celebrity.

HIGHLIGHTS & TRIVIA

While the plot is actually inventive, the execution suffers. Lucille's stunts are so cartoon-like that they even have to be done after the audience leaves and inserted into the show later.

LUCY'S FAVORITE CHARACTER ACTORS

Lucille Ball loved to surround herself with actors that she trusted and with whom she felt comfortable. She used them time and again to populate the unique world of her television characters in her five TV series and specials. Some had very small parts, or were only on camera for atmosphere:

John "Red" Fox
Sid Gould
Bennett Green
Ray Kellogg
Lee Millar
Louis Nicoletti
Barbara Pepper
Hazel Pierce
Marco Riz
Richard Reeves
Roy Rowan
Phil Vandervort
Karen Norris

Others could be counted on to play major parts, assuming a variety of characters over the years. Their performances (listed in descending order by number of appearances) gave the various *Lucy* TV shows depth and continuity. *Lucy* lovers everywhere are indebted to these talented players:

Mary Jane Croft	Jack Collins
Vanda Barra	William Lanteau
Carole Cook	Hans Conried
Mary Wickes	Reta Shaw
Doris Singleton	Sandra Gould
Frank Nelson	Kathleen Freeman
Charles Lane	Cliff Norton
Parley Baer	Elliot Reid
Bobby Jellison	Ross Elliott
Roy Roberts	Herb Vigran
Elvia Allman	Herbie Faye
Jerry Hausner	Shirley Mitchell

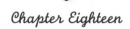

Chapter Eighteen

1966–67 Season

THE LUCY SHOW: THE FIFTH SEASON

TECHNICAL REGULARS: Executive produced by Bob O'Brien; produced by Tommy Thompson; directed by Maury Thompson; script supervised by Milt Josefsberg; makeup by Hal King; hairstyling by Irma Kusely; music by Wilbur Hatch

CAST REGULARS: Lucille Ball (Lucy Carmichael); Gale Gordon (Theodore J. Mooney); Mary Jane Croft (Mary Jane Lewis); Roy Rowan (announcer)

THE MILTON BERLE SHOW

(ABC, SEPTEMBER 9, 1966), 60 MINUTES

EXECUTIVE PRODUCED BY: Nick Vanoff, William Harbach

PRODUCED BY: Stan Harris

DIRECTED BY: Mark Goode

WRITTEN BY: Buddy Arnold, Stan Burns, Mike Marmer, Stanley Davis, Marvin Worth, Howard Leeds, Hal Goodman, Larry Klein

CAST: Milton Berle (host), Lucille Ball, Irving Benson, the Dan Blocker Singers, Bill Dana, Richard Harris, Bobby Rydell

After almost a decade, Mr. Television returned to a weekly series, this time on ABC. In exchange for an appearance on *The Lucy Show*, Lucille is Milton's first big name guest. She appears twice, first as a bungling illusionist's assistant, and then as an overbearing hostess on a supersonic plane, with Berle as the meek passenger. Although the program is very well produced and is funny, America does not take this series to its heart, and it is soon canceled.

THE LUCY SHOW #111: "LUCY AND GEORGE BURNS"

(CBS, SEPTEMBER 12, 1966), 30 MINUTES

WRITTEN BY: Bob O'Brien

GUEST CAST: George Burns, Sid Gould, Joan Carey (voice only), Jack Benny (voice only)

George Burns visits Mr. Mooney at the bank to get his dividend statements and meets wacky Lucy. He is so taken with her, he grooms her to be the new girl in his nightclub act. After a sensational opening, Lucy must decide to either go into show business or stay with Mr. Mooney.

HIGHLIGHTS & TRIVIA

This is a wonderful fifth-season opener! The cast is in fine fettle, the show is funny, and there is great chemistry between Ball and Burns. Although the Lucy character seems to be getting more stupid with each passing season, at least here it is not grating or forced.

Maury Thompson

(DIRECTOR)

Although the kaleidoscope opening [credits shots] of the previous season was effective, I always felt that since not one of those scenes was actually going to be in the show, the audience might feel cheated. We had made it a policy to change the opening every season anyway, so I went to Gary and said, "We need something new, something fresh besides using clips. How about if we get a little Lucy puppet, and animate it to open a classy curtain on the show?" "Oh, no, " he said, "no puppets. Lucy would never like that. Besides, it would be much too expensive to put together. We have to stay within the budget." So, they did this jack-in-the-box thing that looked awful. We used it exactly once, and then went back to the kaleidoscope with a new musical arrangement. Later, Gary [took] my idea for the puppet to use as the opening for every episode of Here's

Lucy. *As for the show itself, George Burns could do no wrong. He was wonderful with her, and she was excellent doing those old Gracie Allen routines.*

George Burns

(ACTOR/COMEDIAN)

There's nothing Lucy can't do. She is not only a great comedienne and a great actor, but she knows where the lights belong, where the camera should be, she knows about directing, editing, timing . . . and there isn't anything that you can do that she can't do better.

THE LUCY SHOW #112: "LUCY AND THE SUBMARINE"

(CBS, SEPTEMBER 19, 1966), 30 MINUTES

WRITTEN BY: Perry Grant, Dick Bensfield
GUEST CAST: Roy Roberts, Robert S. Carson, Steven Marlo, Eddie Ryder

Mr. Mooney, running late for his two-week naval reserve tour, forgets to sign some vital papers. Lucy follows him onto the submarine on which he is stationed, but before she can leave, the sub submerges!

HIGHLIGHTS & TRIVIA

"Lucy in drag" is a major theme in these later years. Whether playing a stuntman, military man, or doorman, the lowered eyes, hoarse voice, and physical discomfort are basically the same. The only problem is the repetitious nature of these shows, and the fact that Lucille's normal speaking voice is getting so low it is hard to distinguish it from her "manly" voice.

THE LUCY SHOW #113: "LUCY THE BEAN QUEEN"

(CBS, SEPTEMBER 26, 1966), 30 MINUTES

WRITTEN BY: Phil Leslie
GUEST CAST: Ed Begley, Sid Gould

Lucy wants new apartment furniture, but Mr. Mooney won't lend her the needed $1,500. Seeing an advertisement that guarantees double your money back if Bailey's Baked Beans aren't the best you've ever tasted, Lucy and Mary Jane go about Los Angeles buying cases of beans and returning them for double their money.

HIGHLIGHTS & TRIVIA

This episode is superior for several reasons. First of all, any installment that utilizes veteran actor Ed Begley has to be good. Second, it revives the notion that the Lucy character is clever and conniving, *not* stupid. Third, when Lucy refuses the refund check because the beans *are* better than her mother's, it reinforces the notion that Lucy is indeed a moral person, and a likeable one at that. Lucille spends much rehearsal time working with the forklift to ensure she can maneuver it on the proverbial dime if necessary.

A BOB HOPE SPECIAL

(NBC, SEPTEMBER 28, 1966), 60 MINUTES

PRODUCED BY: Jack Hope
DIRECTED BY: Jack Shea
WRITTEN BY: Mort Lachman, Bill Larkin, John Rapp, Lester White, Charles Lee, Gig Henry
CAST: Bob Hope (host), Lucille Ball, Madeleine Carroll, Joan Caulfield, Joan Collins, Jerry Colonna, Arlene Dahl, Phyllis Diller, Anita Ekberg, Rhonda Fleming, Joan Fontaine, Signe Hasso, Hedy Lamarr, Dorothy Lamour, Peter Leeds, Paul Lynde, Marilyn Maxwell, Virginia Mayo, Vera Miles, Ken Murray, Janis Paige, Jane Russell

This is clearly a misogynistic special poking fun at the fairer sex, utilizing a bevy of Hope's leading ladies from his movies. In one sketch, Hope parodies the search for an actor to portray Scarlett O'Hara in the motion picture *Gone with the Wind*. At one point, Lucille peddles in on a tandem bicycle with walrus-moustached comedian Jerry Colonna bringing up the rear. In a moment that actually parallels her own experience many years earlier, Lucille declares that she wants to be considered for the key part. In a desire to demonstrate her ability to emote, she "chews" the scenery trying to be dramatic. For a finish, she pulls the prop telephone cord out of the wall. Dorothy Lamour comes out, followed by all of the women in the cast. The payoff of the sketch occurs when Hope chooses Phyllis Diller as Scarlett and they all sing "Thanks for the Memory." Much ado about nothing!

THE LUCY SHOW #114: "LUCY AND PAUL WINCHELL"

(CBS, OCTOBER 3, 1966), 30 MINUTES
WRITTEN BY: Milt Josefsberg, Ray Singer
GUEST CAST: Paul Winchell, Sid Gould (voice only), Joan Carey (voice only)

When Mr. Mooney needs a star to entertain at the bank employees' show, Lucy saves the day by persuading ventriloquist Paul Winchell to appear. Unfortunately, Paul assigns Lucy with bringing his dummies to the show, and Lucy leaves them in the cab. Now Lucy must substitute for Tessie, one of the dummies.

HIGHLIGHTS & TRIVIA

In later years, Lucille is intent on gaining more young TV viewers, and the booking of Paul Winchell is done for this reason. Winchell is the host of a very successful children's TV program in Los Angeles, and had been an early star on live television. The charming interplay between Winchell and his "friends," and their interchanges with Lucy, makes for a classic episode.

THE LUCY SHOW #115: "LUCY AND THE RING A DING DING"

(CBS, OCTOBER 10, 1966), 30 MINUTES
WRITTEN BY: Milt Josefsberg, Ray Singer
GUEST CAST: Don Beddoe, Ray Kellogg, Lucie Arnaz

When Mr. Mooney buys his wife Irma a huge diamond ring, Lucy must try it on. Naturally, it gets stuck. Mooney gives her a tranquilizer to relax her fingers, and now must take an almost unconscious Lucy home to recover the piece of jewelry.

HIGHLIGHTS & TRIVIA

We have seen this plot before, and we will certainly see it again. The idea is stolen from the 1959 Milton Berle special Lucille and Desi had done where Lucy gets Mrs. Berle's ring stuck on her finger. It will be used again on *Here's Lucy* in 1970, when Lucy gets attached to Elizabeth Taylor's big ring. What makes this offering stand out is Lucille's smart portrayal of a woman sedated by pills. She had done it before in 1959 for the hour-long Lucy-Desi episode "Lucy Wants a Career," and she is just as successful here. By this time, the writers are often recycling old plots and past characterizations, even though they themselves are not the scribes who had written the original material.

I'VE GOT A SECRET

(CBS, OCTOBER 17, 1966), 30 MINUTES
PRODUCED BY: Chester Feldman
DIRECTED BY: Franklin Heller
CAST: Steve Allen (host)
PANELISTS: Bill Cullen, Betsy Palmer, Henry Morgan, Bess Myerson
GUEST: Lucille Ball

This is Ball's final appearance on this panel show. Her secret is that she has a TV special on the following week.

THE LUCY SHOW #116: "LUCY GOES TO LONDON"

(CBS, OCTOBER 17, 1966), 30 MINUTES
WRITTEN BY: Bob O'Brien
BASED ON AN IDEA BY: Bob Carroll Jr., Madelyn Pugh
GUEST CAST: Walter Burke, Romo Vincent, Pat Priest, James Wellman, Maury Thompson, Ben Wrigley

Lucy earns a free trip to London by writing a winning dog food limerick, and finds herself on the same plane from Los Angeles to New York as Mr. Mooney.

HIGHLIGHTS & TRIVIA

This episode is the precursor to the hour-long special the following week. Much of this installment had originally been written by Bob Carroll Jr. and Madelyn Pugh in 1960 for a Desilu pilot that never sold. Lucille and/or Desi often performed brief bits in these pilots to help bring attention to them. In this pilot, Lucille and Gale had a small scene as first class passengers on an airline, with Lucille's character never having flown before. Much of the dialog on the *Lucy Show* entry between Lucy and Mr. Mooney is taken from this earlier effort, and Bob and Madelyn are given story credit. It is not as well done as the original scene, as Lucille cannot (as Lucy Carmichael) play the part with the same chicness and elan of the obviously wealthy woman she had earlier portrayed in the pilot.

Maury Thompson

(DIRECTOR)

Lucille cast me in this one as the guy who sits near her on the plane and he gets to take her picture. It was unbearably hot on the set, and I could feel the sweat just rolling down my ass. I kept ad-libbing things while we filmed, and it really broke up the crew. Bob O'Brien came up to me after the show and said, 'Maury, that was just what I had in mind when I wrote the script!

A LUCILLE BALL SPECIAL: "LUCY IN LONDON"

(CBS, OCTOBER 24, 1966), 60 MINUTES

EXECUTIVE PRODUCED BY: Lucille Ball
PRODUCED AND DIRECTED BY: Steve Binder
WRITTEN BY: Pat McCormick, Ron Friedman
CO-PRODUCED AND CHOREOGRAPHED BY: David Winters
EXECUTIVE IN CHARGE OF PRODUCTION: Cleo Smith
MUSIC BY: Irwin Kostel
THE SONG "LUCY IN LONDON" BY: Phil Spector
CAST: Lucille Ball, John Blanshard, Jenny Counsell, the Dave Clark Five, Dennis Gilmore, Wilfrid Hyde-White, Robert Morley, Edna Morris, Anthony Newley, Bonnie Paul, James Robertson-Justice, John Stone, Frank Thornton, Peter Wyngarde

Lucy Carmichael has won a jingle contest and the prize is an all-expense-paid trip to London for one day. Her tour guide talks Lucy into dropping her list of standards sights to see and to put herself in his hands. He takes her around in his motorcycle and sidecar, and she gets a whirlwind peek at London.

HIGHLIGHTS & TRIVIA

This special is actually a nice change of pace for Lucille. Filmed like a movie with one camera and done almost totally on location, there is no laugh track. The show is cute and whimsical, although hardly a laugh fest. Both Britisher Newley and the English group, the Dave Clark Five, are at the height of their popularity, and are the most in-vogue performers Lucille has employed in years. The song "Lucy in London" is presented as a veritable music video, with the Redhead bewigged and wearing the latest in mod fashions. It is extremely well executed.

Irma Kusely

(HAIRSTYLIST)

We used about fifteen different wigs for this show, both for the mod sequence and just to keep Lucy's hair together in the London weather.

The scene where Lucille and Tony Newley punt in the Thames River is badly edited, with the voice track not matching the actors' mouths and the action not making much sense. Throughout the special, Lucille looks old because it is impossible to control the lighting and camera angles on location shooting. There is a marked difference in the scenes shot indoors. The entire Madame Tussaud's sequence is silly and also badly edited. It is reminiscent of a cartoon as opposed to live action. In contrast, the scene where Lucille plays Kate in a scene from *The Taming of the Shrew* is quite funny and extremely well paced. Above all, the last act, with Lucille and Newley in a theatre, makes the entire hour worthwhile. Newley is dazzling with his singing, and Lucille is charming and uncharacteristically vulnerable in her pantomime and song. The ending has a sweetness and warmth missing from her weekly TV series. As a whole, the special is not exceptional, but has several wonderful moments. As an experiment, it is very successful.

Gary Morton

(PRODUCTION CONSULTANT)

We loved being in England for Lucy in London. *We were able to hire some wonderful British actors. Lucy loved nepotism; she loved her cousin Cleo like a sister, so she just went to Cleo and said, "Let's get to work!" As it turned out, Cleo worked very hard, did a wonderful job, and ended up being the producer for most of the* Here's Lucy *episodes.*

THE LUCY SHOW #117: "LUCY GETS A ROOMMATE"

(CBS, OCTOBER 31, 1966), 30 MINUTES

WRITTEN BY: Bob O'Brien, Elroy Schwartz
GUEST CAST: Carol Burnett, Don Germano, Al Torre, Dino Natali, Atillo Risso

Mr. Mooney tells Lucy (again) that she must economize, so Lucy advertises for a roommate. She is very pleased that librarian Carol Bradford (Carol Burnett) moves in, but is less than overjoyed at the newcomer's personal habits and incredible shyness. Lucy and Mary Jane scheme to nudge Carol out of her emotional shell.

HIGHLIGHTS & TRIVIA

This is the first joint video gig for the two unnatural redheads, the first of many over the following six years. There is an obvious affection between them, something this series has been badly lacking ever since the departure of Vivian Vance. Lucille had been an early booster of Burnett's, and considers her a protégée.

Maury Thompson
(DIRECTOR)

Carol was perfect. When she did the striptease, I had to tell Carol every step to take. She was not a dancer and knew it, and was happy to have the help. Lucille loved Carol, and protected her. She always wanted to make sure Carol was shown to her best advantage.

THE LUCY SHOW #118: "LUCY AND CAROL IN PALM SPRINGS"

(CBS, NOVEMBER 7, 1966), 30 MINUTES
WRITTEN BY: Bob O'Brien, Elroy Schwartz
GUEST CAST: Carol Burnett, Dan Rowan, Gary Morton, Dom Germano, Al Torre, Dino Natali, Atillo Risso, William Woodson, Jonathan Hole, Sid Gould

Lucy's roommate Carol is the vocalist with the Vagabonds, and gets booked for a golf tournament in Palm Springs. When Mr. Mooney won't let Lucy join Carol, she fakes illness to get the time off from the bank. The duo have a swell time in the desert flirting with the golfers, until who should show up on the scene but Mr. Mooney.

HIGHLIGHTS & TRIVIA

Comedian Dan Rowan makes an unusual guest appearance without partner Dick Martin, who had played Harry Connors in the first season (1962–63) of *The Lucy Show*. Lucille and Dan had once had a brief real-life romance, and their fondness for one another shines through oncamera. The finale is typical of the musical efforts by this series: well executed but plastic in its presentation, with prerecorded music and a smattering of lip-synching.

THE LUCY SHOW #119: "LUCY GETS CAUGHT IN THE DRAFT"

(CBS, NOVEMBER 14, 1966), 30 MINUTES
WRITTEN BY: Milt Josefsberg, Ray Singer
GUEST CAST: Clark Howett, Harry Hickox, Ben Gage, Sid Gould, Herb Vigran, Jim Nabors (cameo)

Lucy receives a draft notice intended for Lou C. Carmichael, and no matter what she says, the Marines won't discharge her until official orders arrive. She is forced to submit to boot camp, until the mistake is finally rectified.

HIGHLIGHTS & TRIVIA

There is a huge continuity mistake in the first scene. Lucy receives a letter from her son, the first time he has been mentioned this season. Unfortunately, Lucy calls him *Jimmy* instead of *Jerry*. When Lucille saw the original script, she complained that the wrong name had been put in. The crew reminded her that *Jimmy* Garrett was the actor who played *Jerry* Carmichael, but she insisted she was right and had the scene filmed her way. This is one of the rare times that Lucille should have listened, but it also points out part of the problem with this TV series. Lucille no longer trusts anybody but herself, and the people around her are too afraid for their jobs to stand up to her. There are many installments of *The Lucy Show* that might have been greatly improved if they had confronted "The Boss."

Jim Nabors makes a cameo appearance at the end, playing his Gomer Pyle TV sitcom character (1964–70). This is actually a very funny excursion, as are many of the story line efforts that get Lucy out of the bank setting.

THE LUCY SHOW #120: "LUCY AND JOHN WAYNE"

(CBS, NOVEMBER 21, 1966), 30 MINUTES
WRITTEN BY: Bob O'Brien
GUEST CAST: John Wayne, Joseph Ruskin, Morgan Woodward, Bryan O'Byrne, Kay Stewart, Joyce Perry

Mary Jane invites Lucy to lunch at the movie studio where she works, and there Lucy bumps into John Wayne. Later, Mary Jane arranges for Lucy to visit a set where Wayne is filming, and she wreaks total havoc on the sound stage.

HIGHLIGHTS & TRIVIA

This is a classic episode. It has been more than a decade since Wayne guested on *I Love Lucy* (episode #129, "Lucy and John Wayne"), but the interplay between the two is still fine. While the Lucy character these days is pushy and grating, in this case it is well modulated and hysterically funny.

Maury Thompson
(DIRECTOR)

Lucille wanted to make sure that no one made any waves while John Wayne was on the show. There was this big barroom brawl in one scene, and I didn't know anything about how to stage a barroom brawl. I was learning as I was going along. I think John realized this was not my forte, and he said, "Well, son, let me give you a little advice here on how to do this." Immediately, Lucille nervously yelled, "Maury, let John do it, let John do it." Her confidence in me was staggering. *So, I stepped back and let him do it. In less than ten minutes, he had it all working perfectly. Except for the bit with the ketchup capsule. We had to go back and pick that up after the audience left.*

THE LUCY SHOW #121: "LUCY AND PAT COLLINS"

(CBS, NOVEMBER 28, 1966), 30 MINUTES
WRITTEN BY: Milt Josefsberg, Ray Singer
GUEST CAST: Pat Collins, Patricia Cutts, Joan Swift, Dr. L. Kenneally, Mrs. L. Kenneally, Denise Purcell, George Kates

Mr. Mooney is suffering terribly from insomnia, so Lucy takes him to a nightclub to see Pat Collins, the "hip hypnotist." Pat makes Lucy and Mr. Mooney two of her subjects and she hypnotizes them on stage, and then leaves Mooney with a post-hypnotic suggestion to cure his insomnia.

HIGHLIGHTS & TRIVIA

The plot of this entry is quite forced, but it does allow Lucille and Gale to do superior clowning with Collins, who is a major club star at this point.

Maury Thompson
(DIRECTOR)

I hated *this episode. I didn't like the premise at all! It was ridiculous for Lucy to act hypnotized. Everyone knew she was acting; it was not part of the natural action of the show. This was just an excuse to get Lucille and Gale to do shtick together, but it had no motivation. During the dress rehearsal, Kenny Wescott, our props man, sat in on the panel with Pat Collins. At one point, she turns to him and says, "You are going to see the saddest thing you've ever seen." Well, he started in to bawl, and I looked at him out of the corner of my eye because I thought he was kidding. He wasn't! He had really gone under. Kenny's not an actor at all. When it was over, he just ran off. He was so embarrassed, but he was still under. Pat sent for someone to bring him back so she could clap her hands at him.* Then *he came out of it.*

THE LUCY SHOW #122: "LUCY AND THE MONKEY" A.K.A. "MOONEY THE MONKEY"

(CBS, DECEMBER 5, 1966), 30 MINUTES
WRITTEN BY: Sam Locke, Joel Rapp
GUEST CAST: Hal March, Lew Parker, Janos Prohaska

When overworked Lucy becomes exhausted, Mary Jane warns her to lighten up or, according to Mary Jane, she will start hallucinating. When comedian Bob Bailey (Hal March) leaves his trained chimp in Mr. Mooney's office, Lucy thinks she is seeing things and that Mr. Mooney has turned into a monkey.

HIGHLIGHTS & TRIVIA

This episode is just dreadful. To begin with, it shows Lucy as an efficient, overworked secretary, which totally goes against the Lucy Carmichael persona. Second, the idea that Lucy thinks the monkey is Mr. Mooney is ludicrous, poorly motivated, and weak in execution. This is the last guest appearance by close family friend Hal March (1920–1970).

THE LUCY SHOW #123: "LUCY AND PHIL SILVERS"

(CBS, DECEMBER 12, 1966), 30 MINUTES
WRITTEN BY: Milt Josefsberg, Ray Singer
GUEST CAST: Phil Silvers, Rosemary Eliot, Tol Avery

The bank hires efficiency expert Oliver Kasten (Phil Silvers), who not only takes over Mr. Mooney's office and responsibilities at the bank, but Lucy as well.

HIGHLIGHTS & TRIVIA

This hilarious offering is basically an excuse for bombastic comedian Phil Silvers to do his patented "take over" bit. Once again, Lucy is shown as being competent in her job, but this time it is believable because she has been motivated by the dynamic Kasten. The final scene, with Lucy putting toy horses together on an assembly line, would be a scream if it did not remind one of the perfection of Lucy and Ethel on that chocolate factory assembly line back in the 1952 *I Love Lucy* episode, #36, "Job Switching." With that kind of comparison, it comes up short.

Maury Thompson

(DIRECTOR)

Phil was the kind of performer who never did the same thing twice, and that really bugged her.

Lucille puts up with Silvers' lack of consistency because she knows he is fighting a huge compulsive gambling problem, and needs both the money and the TV exposure. Lucille is often very sentimental in casting people from television's golden age, especially when she admires their talent.

Mary Jane Croft

(ACTOR)

Stars would come on the show and she would make them so *nervous. She was just being herself, but she was such a powerhouse. They were in awe of her. They'd come over to me and ask, "How do you* do *this?"*

THE LUCY SHOW #124: "LUCY'S SUBSTITUTE SECRETARY"

(CBS, JANUARY 2, 1967), 30 MINUTES

WRITTEN BY: Bob O'Brien
STORY BY: Bob O'Brien, Vic McLeod
GUEST CAST: Ruta Lee, Barbara Morrison, Roy Roberts

Lucy gets yet another vacation, this time scheduled for Lake Arrowhead, California. Her office replacement, Audrey Fields (Ruta Lee), is a curvaceous schemer who wants to take over permanently. Lucy stays in town, donning a variety of disguises to snoop on Audrey and ruin her plans at the bank.

HIGHLIGHTS & TRIVIA

This episode introduces Roy Roberts as Mr. Cheever, Mr. Mooney's boss. This is a wise move, for it cuts down on Mooney's venom and better motivates his desire for perfection and cost-cutting. Although not billed in the opening credits (Mary Jane Croft never receives such billing either), Roberts will become a de facto regular cast member next season (1967–68). Ruta Lee is wonderful as the office snake-in-the grass. The plot allows Lucille several costume changes and characterizations; the best is her mod decorator disguise.

Ruta Lee

(ACTOR)

I had met Lucy years earlier with Desi and had spent the day with her at the [horse-racing] track at Del Mar. She took an interest in me because I was this tiny little slip of a girl with this big deep voice, much like hers. By the time we did this episode, Lucy had been watching me develop, and asked for me to be on the show. I did not have to audition. She was tough to work with, but not at all uncomfortable being with a younger, pretty woman. They let me control my own makeup, hair, and wardrobe. She'd get disturbed with things and sort of pushed people and things around, so you had to just roll with it. She changed her mind a lot, and could be very demanding. Lucy was quite capable of yelling, "No, no, no, that's not how you do it; this *is the way to do it!" If you were frail, you didn't last. But she was so marvelous at what she did, and she was usually right. That stuff got worse as she got older. At this point, she was still having fun in her work. I laughed a lot on the set, and she thought I was a good dame. Gale Gordon was a wonderful, fine gentleman, and Lucy adored him.*

THE LUCY SHOW #125: "VIV VISITS LUCY"

(CBS, JANUARY 9, 1967), 30 MINUTES

WRITTEN BY: Bob O'Brien
GUEST CAST: Vivian Vance, Chet Stratton, Jerry Rush, Steven Marlo, Ray Kellogg, John "Red" Fox, Ralph Maurer, Charles Britt, Tony Barro, Les Brown Jr.

Longtime pal Viv (now named Vivian Bunson since her series character's marriage) finally makes her first visit to California to see former roommate Lucy. Lucy and Viv begin to gossip about old acquaintances, and Viv reveals that Herbie Walton, son of old friends, is now an unwashed hippie hanging out on the Sunset Strip. Lucy and Viv scheme to get him back into his former, conventional lifestyle.

HIGHLIGHTS & TRIVIA

This is Viv's first visit to *The Lucy Show* since she quit in early 1965. Whatever acrimony there was between the two personalities has been settled, and Lucille and Vivian resume a friendship that is actually healthier than it had ever been because they are *not* constantly working together. It is a little unnerving to see the two talents together again, because it points up how much the two have aged in just two years. Now in their middle fifties, Lucille is looking tired and Vivian is puffy. The episode itself, however, is a clever parody on mainstream impressions of the hippie life on the anti-establishment Sunset Strip. The final sequence is very well done, with the two old warhorses working together like clockwork. The actor playing Herbie is the son of famed bandleader Les Brown.

CAROL + 2

(CBS, JANUARY 15, 1967), 60 MINUTES

PRODUCED BY: Bob Banner, Nat Hiken
DIRECTED BY: Marc Breaux
WRITTEN BY: Nat Hiken
MUSIC BY: Harry Zimmerman
CAST: Carol Burnett (host), Lucille Ball, Zero Mostel

This is one of two TV specials that serve as models for Carol's long-running CBS network variety series (1967–78). Lucille barters with Carol, exchanging this appearance for the two-part *Lucy Show* stint by Carol. The show is also a reunion, of sorts, between Lucille and Zero. The two had been together in the MGM movie musical *DuBarry Was a Lady* (1943). While they seem genuinely pleased to be in each other's company, the show does not allow for any interplay between the two except for minor introductions of sketches. All of the interaction is between Carol and Lucille or Carol and Zero.

Lucille appears in two very funny pieces with Carol. The first is called "Goodbye, Baby." Lucille and Carol play sisters spending the afternoon together with Carol's new baby. As the three walk along to help Lucille catch her bus for her first vacation to Florida, Carol won't let Lucille go until the infant says goodbye. The machinations the two go through until the baby finally utters the crucial words is the basis for a truly enjoyable sketch. The second, and more memorable piece, has the two ladies as charwomen in the executive offices of a movie studio. The humorous juxtaposition of these cleaning women discussing multi-million dollar deals starts them into one of the best musical numbers in which Lucille is ever involved: "Chutzpah!" Using the Yiddish word for courage and guts, the two sing, strut, dance, jump, and have a good old time destroying the office in which they clean (which features a picture of Vivian Vance on the wall). This interlude has been used several times on retrospective specials throughout the years. This sketch is also important as it contains what are perhaps Lucille's last real close-ups on television. As the show is videotaped instead of filmed, it is impossible in the technology of the 1960s to hide the bags under Lucille's eyes, or to disguise just how much makeup it requires to make Lucille look like "Lucy." The obvious age difference between the two women is distracting, as they look more like mother and daughter than contemporaries.

Carol Burnett

(ACTOR)

I first met Lucille Ball when she came to see me in a play in New York. I was very nervous, but thought I hid it well. She came backstage and spent an hour with me, calming me down. I couldn't fool her. *When CBS announced my special, the first phone call I got was from Lucy. "When do you want me?" was her greeting. She was always very supportive of me.*

THE LUCY SHOW #126: "LUCY THE BABY SITTER"

(CBS, JANUARY 16, 1967), 30 MINUTES

WRITTEN BY: Milt Josefsberg, Ray Singer
GUEST CAST: Mary Wickes, the Marquis Chimps, Elvia Allman, Sid Gould, Jonathan Hole, Joyce Baker

Lucy and Mr. Mooney argue about her efficiency, leading Lucy to seek another job where she will be more appreciated. She tries an employment agency, and inadvertently ends up babysitting a family of chimps.

HIGHLIGHTS & TRIVIA

This is an important episode in the Lucy mythos. Not because it is clever and funny (it isn't), but because it introduces a concept that will later prove very important. The firm Lucy visits is the Unique Employment Agency, whose motto is "Unusual Jobs for Unusual People." The following year, this premise will be at the heart of the plot gimmick used for the creation of the *Here's Lucy* series.

There is also another of the animal mishaps during the making of this entry that plagues many of these episodes. An elephant used on the set goes wild and pushes Mary Wickes into one of the prop trees. The trainer has to hit the elephant with a club to get it away from Mary, who injures her arm in the melee. Lucille quickly scoops up the baby chimps in her arms for protection (both hers and theirs). This is Elvia Allman's final appearance on one of Lucille's shows. She was first on *I Love Lucy* in 1952, playing the candy factory supervisor who yelled, "Let 'er roll!," in episode #36, "Job Switching."

THE LUCY SHOW #127: "MAIN STREET, U.S.A."

(CBS, JANUARY 23, 1967), 30 MINUTES

WRITTEN BY: Bob O'Brien

GUEST CAST: Mel Torme, John Bubbles, Paul Winchell, Hal Smith, Carole Cook, Barry Kelley, Burt Mustin, Jackie Minty, Louis A. Nicoletti

The bank sends Lucy and Mr. Mooney to Bancroft, a small town where the financial institution is bankrolling a new freeway. Lucy's neighbor Mel Tinker is in town, and he and the townsfolk convince Lucy and Mooney that the freeway project will ruin the gentle little town.

HIGHLIGHTS & TRIVIA

In this first part of a two-part episode, Torme makes his second appearance as Mel Tinker (see also *The Lucy Show*, episode #87, "Lucy in the Music World"). This is a delightful romp for all, and a welcome change of pace for the series. Paul Winchell, a guest star just a few months previously, is now a character actor in this one as the aging owner of the soda shop. Dancer John Bubbles is not only charming, but the first billed African-American guest star on a Lucille Ball series. With little fanfare, Ball has her show become integrated both in front of and behind the cameras. The offering is rife with song and dance, the former written by Torme and the latter choreographed by Jack Baker. This is a very difficult shoot.

Carole Cook

(ACTOR/FAMILY FRIEND)

We rehearsed these two shows a lot. *The rehearsal hours were extended, and we'd be running the musical numbers while the stand-ins did the dialog for the cameras.*

Maury Thompson

(DIRECTOR)

These two shows were a directing nightmare. We were working on sets we were not accustomed to, with large groups of people, marching bands, prerecorded music, choreography . . . and no room to do any of it. I felt the shows were just so darn corny. Mel Torme did a great job with the music. And of course, we had to use Louis Nicoletti. Desi had known him in New York in the Thirties when he was struggling to put his band together. He always wanted to make certain that Louis had an extra paycheck. Even after Gary [Morton] came in and most of the people from the Desi days were banished, Lucille felt a loyalty to him. He was like a piece of furniture, a fixture on the set.

THE LUCY SHOW #128: "LUCY PUTS MAIN STREET ON THE MAP"

(CBS, JANUARY 30, 1967), 30 MINUTES

WRITTEN BY: Bob O'Brien

GUEST CAST: Mel Torme, Paul Winchell, Carole Cook, John Bubbles, Dan Rowan, Roy Barcroft, Burt Mustin, Hal Smith

Lucy, Mr. Mooney, and Mel Tinker plan to bring Bancroft's freeway problem to the attention of the world. They stage a rally, then fake a shootout at the bank to get press and television coverage.

HIGHLIGHTS & TRIVIA

This second of two parts holds up almost as well as the first part, with even more wonderful music by Mel Torme, including a reprise of the rousing "Main Street, U.S.A." Dan Rowan once again makes a solo guest appearance as the TV reporter.

Maury Thompson

(DIRECTOR)

This thing was a headache. Rickles never stops. You never knew when he was kidding and when he wasn't, and you can't do that with Lucille. There was no time to be a clown, except when you were supposed to be. She didn't like working with him.

THE LUCY SHOW #129: "LUCY MEETS THE LAW"

(CBS, FEBRUARY 13, 1967), 30 MINUTES

WRITTEN BY: Alan J. Levitt

GUEST CAST: Claude Akins, Iris Adrian, Ken Lynch, Joe Perry, Byron Foulger, Jody Gilbert

When a redheaded female jewel thief slips stolen loot into Lucy's purse, Our Girl is arrested and jailed. She is forced to deal with a couple of tough cookies behind bars until the real thief is finally caught.

HIGHLIGHTS & TRIVIA

The "Lucy in jail" theme is one that will reappear more and more often in later years, usually with good results. Akins had been on *I Love Lucy* in 1956 (episode #161, "Desert Island").

THE LUCY SHOW #130: "LUCY THE FIGHT MANAGER"

(CBS, FEBRUARY 20, 1967), 30 MINUTES

WRITTEN BY: Les Roberts, Ronald Axe

GUEST CAST: Don Rickles, Cliff Norton, Lewis Charles, Stanley Adams

When Mr. Mooney won't loan ex-pugilist Eddie Rickles the money to open a flower shop, Lucy offers to manage him as a fighter to raise the money.

HIGHLIGHTS & TRIVIA

Shades of *K. O. Kitty* (the 1958 installment of *The Desilu Playhouse* starring Lucille as a woman who coaches a prize fighter)! Lucy has been down this road before, although the results this time are tepid. Lucy taking people into her home to help them is a common theme on *The Lucy Show*. In real life, no one would allow total strangers to be guests in their home as often as Lucy Carmichael does. Ascerbic standup comic Rickles is making quite a name for himself as a sitcom guest star at this time.

THE LUCY SHOW #131: "LUCY AND TENNESSEE ERNIE FORD"

(CBS, FEBRUARY 27, 1967), 30 MINUTES

WRITTEN BY: Bob O'Brien

GUEST CAST: Tennessee Ernie Ford, Carole Cook, Roy Roberts, the Back Porch Majority, Robert Easton, Joan Swift, William O'Connell, Roy Rowan, Bert May, Sid Gould

Mr. Mooney is in a slump acquiring new accounts for the bank, so to help save his job, Lucy targets nouveau-riche country singer Homer Higgins (Tennessee Ernie Ford) as a potential customer. Scheming Lucy talks Mooney and Mr. Cheever into having a barn dance at the bank to make the country boy feel really at home.

HIGHLIGHTS & TRIVIA

This is Ernie Ford's first visit to a *Lucy* show since his appearances on *I Love Lucy* in 1954 and 1955 (episodes #94, "Tennessee Ernie Visits"; #95, "Tennessee Ernie Hangs On"; and #112, "Tennessee Bound"). The script steals generously from TV's *The Beverly Hillbillies* (1962–71), and from Ernie's earlier guest shots with Lucille. Carole Cook has one of her biggest guest-starring roles as Ernie's wife Effie. This is Maury Thompson's last work with Lucille Ball, and the final episode filmed for the 1966–67 season.

Carole Cook

(ACTOR/FAMILY FRIEND)

I loved doing this episode. Ernie was a lot of fun to work with. Jack Baker did the choreography, and I had know him since the Desilu Revue *(1959). I also loved that wig I wore, with the pigtails and the curls.*

Maury Thompson

(DIRECTOR)

Ernie Ford was a very nice guy, and a pleasure to work with. [Lucille] liked working with him because it allowed her to do hillbilly things, too. This was the last thing I did with Lucille. In the big dance sequence at the bank, I had to use all three cameras to cover the action. Lucille, Gale, and someone else were standing over to the side by the curtain. This confused me, so I cut the action. I told Lucille that her standing there was going to be a distraction for the audience, and that I either needed to photograph her there as part of the action, or she needed to stand somewhere else. She refused to do either each time we rehearsed it. Finally, I got so angry at her for not taking my direction that I started to scream at her, "Either get out of the shot or let me take your picture. One or the other!" She turned on her heels and walked away. During the filming, she was not in that spot, because she knew I was right.

After the show, I went backstage to see her in her dressing room. She was in her bathrobe, and she turned to me and said, "Well, we got a good show, didn't we honey?" She reacted like nothing had happened. I started to cry, with tears running down my face. She noticed, and said, "What are you crying about?" I knew I had reached the turning point. I was getting ready to go away on my vacation. I called my agent and told him that I wanted more money to come back the next season, because she was getting difficult to deal with. I instructed him not to go to her at this point but to wait, because I knew she was in a bad mood. Instead, he went the next day. Tommy Thompson went to Lucille with my agent's request. He later told me that her response was, "He wants more money? Fuck him! Give me the phone." She called Jack Donohue, asked if he was busy for the coming season, and when he said no, she said, "Well, you are now!"

THE LUCY SHOW #132: "LUCY MEETS SHELDON LEONARD"

(CBS, MARCH 6, 1967), 30 MINUTES

WRITTEN BY: Milt Josefsberg, Ray Singer
GUEST CAST: Sheldon Leonard, George Sawaya, Fred Stromsoe, Harvey Parry

Ex-movie gangster and current television producer Sheldon Leonard arranges with Mr. Mooney to shoot a scene for a TV pilot in the bank after hours. Not recognizing the producer and overhearing him talk about "shooting at the bank," Lucy jumps to the conclusion that he must be a bank robber. She schemes with Mary Jane to capture him.

HIGHLIGHTS & TRIVIA

This is actually a very Lucy and Ethel script. Many of Mary Jane's lines are written as if they should be coming out of Vivian's mouth. Sheldon Leonard is renting a lot of space on the Desilu lot, as he is the producer of such current studio-made shows as *I Spy, Gomer Pyle*, and *The Andy Griffith Show*.

THE NINETEENTH ANNUAL EMMY AWARDS

(ABC, JUNE 4, 1967), 120 MINUTES

PRODUCED AND DIRECTED BY: Dick Dunlap, Sid Smith
WRITTEN BY: Martin Ragaway, Jerome Bredoux, Harry Crane, Garry Marshall
HOSTS: Joey Bishop, Hugh Downs

In a surprise win, Lucille Ball gets the nod as Outstanding Actress in a Leading Role in a Comedy Series. Her competition in this category is Elizabeth Montgomery and Agnes Moorehead for *Bewitched* and Marlo Thomas for *That Girl*. She is visibly moved, holding back tears, as she chokes out, "The last time you gave me one of these, I thought it was because I had a baby!" Actually, Lucille won last in 1956 for the 1955–56 season as Best Actress in a Continuing Performance.

THE LUCY-DESI COMEDY HOUR

(CBS, JULY-AUGUST, 1967), 60 MINUTES (B&W)

The thirteen hour-long specials that Lucille and Desi did for Ford and Westinghouse years ago are rerun as a summer replacement series for the last time. The same opening and closing graphics are used as in previous summers. These shows now go into syndication, usually shown on the same stations that air daily reruns of *I Love Lucy*.

Chapter Nineteen

1967–68 Season

THE LUCY SHOW: THE SIXTH SEASON

TECHNICAL REGULARS: Executive produced by Bob O'Brien; produced by Tommy Thompson; directed by Jack Donohue; script supervision by Milt Josefsberg; makeup by Hal King; hairstyling by Irma Kusely; music by Wilbur Hatch

CAST REGULARS: Lucille Ball (Lucy Carmichael); Gale Gordon (Theodore J. Mooney); Roy Roberts (Mr. Cheever); Mary Jane Croft (Mary Jane Lewis); Roy Rowan (announcer)

THE LUCY SHOW #133: "LUCY MEETS THE BERLES"

(CBS, SEPTEMBER 11, 1967), 30 MINUTES

WRITTEN BY: Bob O'Brien

GUEST CAST: Milton Berle, Ruta Lee, Ruth Berle

Mr. Mooney joyfully allows Lucy time off from the bank to be a temporary secretary to an important client, Milton Berle. When Lucy overhears Milton discussing a love scene with Ruta Lee, she thinks the two are having an affair and it leads to a series of misunderstandings and comic repercussions.

HIGHLIGHTS & TRIVIA

Lucy Carmichael has already met Milton Berle in the 1965–66 season (episode #96, "Lucy Saves Milton Berle"), and logically the two should not be strangers now to one another. In earlier times, more attention would have been paid to Lucy already having met Berle on this TV series and such gaffes would have been avoided in the scripting of the episode.

Milton Berle

(COMEDY LEGEND)

We never rehearsed with that salad on my head, because it was too messy. So the night of the filming, we were very surprised by what happened. The salad dripped down my face and onto my glasses, and kept dripping. I was afraid to move, because the more I did, the more it dripped. The audience was hysterical. I was aware we were eating up time, and that we had to finish the dialog. Both Lucy and I started yelling at one another to get the audience's attention. We got screams. And dear Ruta. Lucy had her introduction written into the script as "that big movie star, Ruta Lee." I think she was trying to build Ruta up, because Ruta was never a movie star. I don't know if she ever did a picture. She was and is a wonderful television actor and a great beauty. To this day, whenever I see her (and we are dear friends), I point and yell, "There's that big movie star, Ruta Lee!"

Ruta Lee

(ACTOR)

We all started laughing so hard when that Thousand Island dressing came dribbling down his [Milton Berle's] glasses and he used his fingers as windshield wipers that I practically peed in my pants. That laugh went on forever. I was enchanted to be working with Lucy and Milton in the same show, and Ruth [Berle] and I got along famously. She [Lucille] had a reputation for being [difficult], but she [was a trouper and had a lot of fun] on this set. That big intro Lucy gave me was very sweet. I guess she figured that a lot of the audience wouldn't know who I was. Elizabeth Taylor I ain't. To this day, Milton kids me about it. He also gets melancholy about this episode, because I believe this is the only time he and Ruth [who died days before Lucille Ball in 1989] performed together on film [actually, she had appeared with Lucille and Desi on Berle's 1959 TV special].

THE LUCY SHOW #134: "LUCY GETS TRAPPED"

(CBS, SEPTEMBER 18, 1967), 30 MINUTES
WRITTEN BY: Milt Josefsberg, Ray Singer
GUEST CAST: William Lanteau, Bartlett Robinson, Joan Swift

Lucy feigns illness to take time off from the bank and attend a huge department store sale. When she wins all sorts of prizes as the store's ten millionth customer, her picture ends up in the newspaper, making Mr. Mooney very angry.

HIGHLIGHTS & TRIVIA

William Lanteau is a marvelous light comedian, and will appear in many *Lucy* episodes well into the 1970s. Like Ray Kellogg, he becomes one of the newer *Lucy* players used repeatedly on the program. Lucy scheming to get out of work is already becoming a tired plot device; by the time of the *Here's Lucy* years, it seems to be resurrected almost monthly.

THE LUCY SHOW #135: "LUCY AND THE FRENCH MOVIE STAR"

(CBS, SEPTEMBER 25, 1967), 30 MINUTES
WRITTEN BY: Ray Singer
GUEST CAST: Jacques Bergerac

When a sexy French movie star client asks Mr. Mooney to recommend someone to help him dictate a letter of agreement, Lucy chomps at the bit to be sent. Under pressure, Mooney agrees, but Lucy becomes quite inebriated when the sex symbol plies her with champagne and, in the process, she almost loses her job.

HIGHLIGHTS & TRIVIA

Lucille is almost sixteen years older than Bergerac, a handsome man in his late thirties. It seems the writers have not yet adjusted the scripts to Lucille's age. Her drunk bit is by now old hat, and Lucille adds nothing new here.

THE MOTHERS-IN-LAW

(NBC, 1967– 69), 30 MINUTES
EXECUTIVE PRODUCED BY: Desi Arnaz
PRODUCED BY: Elliot Lewis
DIRECTED BY: Desi Arnaz, Maury Thompson, Elliot Lewis, and others
WRITTEN BY: Bob Carroll Jr., Madelyn Davis
MUSIC BY: Wilbur Hatch
CAST: Eve Arden, Kaye Ballard, Herbert Rudley, Roger C. Carmel, Richard Deacon, Jerry Fogel, Debbie Watson

Lucille Ball never appears in this series, but it is written and produced *as if* she does. Ex-husband Desi Arnaz is the driving force behind this amusing series about two frustrated, meddling mothers-in-law. The entire crew is Desilu people; in fact, the only people missing from the old days are Lucille and Vivian. The scripts are written as if they are still there.

Maury Thompson
(DIRECTOR)

Eve Arden was a lady. *By this time, I am sorry to say that Desi's disease had gotten out of control. He hardly knew what was going on around him. Eve didn't know how to deal with Desi's condition, but she never raised her voice or made a fuss. When it got to the point where she felt uncomfortable, she said, "Desi, darling, I'm really tired. I'm going to go home now." The crew left with her. Desi could have fired us all for going against him, but he didn't. When people write about Desi being an alcoholic, they seem to do it with venom. He had a disease, and he couldn't help himself. Whatever he did, underneath it all he was a genius, a talented, lovely man. But no one ever prints the nice things I say about him. Now Kaye Ballard I had a real problem with. She didn't seem to want to take direction. Now it is true, a lot of things we did on that show were very* Lucyesque. *Eve knew it, but she didn't mind. Kaye didn't want to go along with it. She would purposely mess up a scene so we couldn't use it. I must say, though, that Eve and Kaye worked very well together, and Kaye was a pretty funny broad. Lucille loved her.*

Dann Cahn
(FILM EDITOR)

I came back into the fold for a few of these, but you can never go home again. It was a difficult show because the man in charge had a problem. If this show had been done by Desi on CBS in his heyday, it would have run five or six years. Eve and Kaye were great together.

Kaye Ballard

(ACTOR/SINGER)

It was Lucy who got me this job. I had originally met her at the Blue Angel [nightclub] in New York when she was with Gary Morton. She told Desi about me, and he sent [scripters] Bob [Carroll Jr.] and Madelyn [Davis] to see me in Detroit. Eve and I went all the way back to 1947, when I was playing the Trocadero with Spike Jones and she came to see us. Many years later, Vivian Vance came to see me in Ben Bagley's Cole Porter Remembered. *She came back to my apartment, and I told her that I had signed to do this sitcom with Desi. She looked me in the eye and said, "You are going to work with the most tasteful man in show business." And he really was. He edited every script we did on this series. The weeks Desi also appeared on the show were more nerve-wracking because the boss was right there. Also, I think Desi always had Lucy in mind with all of our work. Having Desi Jr. on the show was the high point of Big Desi's life. He adored his son, and was so proud of him.*

After we shot the pilot, Lucy threw a dinner party. She invited Eve and I, Jack Carter, Milton Berle, Jack Benny—I was in big company. Then she screened the pilot, because she hadn't seen it yet. All of these great comedians, and you could hear a pin drop. Silence. Not one laugh, just a room full of comedians just shaking their heads when they thought something was funny.

Desi Jr. makes several appearances with his father on this series as Tommy, the delivery boy. In one, he plays drums while his father does a modernized rendition of his trademark song, "Cuban Pete."

THE LUCY SHOW #136: "LUCY, THE STARMAKER"

(CBS, OCTOBER 2, 1967), 30 MINUTES

WRITTEN BY: Fred S. Fox, Seaman Jacobs
GUEST CAST: Frankie Avalon, Lew Parker

Mr. Cheever's nephew Tommy (Frankie Avalon) is entrusted to Mr. Mooney and Lucy to show him the ropes around the bank. When Lucy finds out he has great singing talent, she arranges for a producer to come to the bank to discover him against Mr. Cheever's wishes.

HIGHLIGHTS & TRIVIA

Singing idol Frankie Avalon is breaking out of his teen mold at this point, trying to appeal to adult music lovers the same way Bobby Darin and Connie Francis are. While the musical numbers are unfortunately prerecorded, this is a bright, amusing offering, and a solid showcase for Avalon's boyish charms. At the time, stage veteran Lew Parker is featured on the sitcom *That Girl* (1966–71) playing Marlo Thomas' restaurateur dad.

THE LUCY SHOW #137: "LUCY GETS HER DIPLOMA"

(CBS, OCTOBER 9, 1967), 30 MINUTES

WRITTEN BY: Ray Singer, Milt Josefsberg
GUEST CAST: Robert Pine, Doris Singleton, Lucie Arnaz, Sean Morgan, Dave Willock, Don Randolph, Olive Dunbar, Barbara Babcock, Amy Appleton, Philip Vandervort, George E. Carey

A new bank policy demands that all employees be high school graduates. When Lucy reveals an illness prevented her from finishing her final term and graduating, she must go back to school. While there, she helps a troubled young man (Robert Pine) earn his diploma.

HIGHLIGHTS & TRIVIA

In the 1963–64 season (episode #41, "Lucy's College Reunion"), Lucy is shown attending her *college* reunion. Now she's a high school dropout? These sorts of inconsistencies on the series make her character less believable. If the audience doesn't suspend their disbelief, the wacky things Lucy does oncamera stop being funny. Otherwise, this is an extremely well-acted and well-written outing, a pleasant change of tempo. Lucy is once again revealed as being intelligent and caring. Lucie Arnaz does her largest TV part to date, and handles it beautifully. The theme of completing one's education is both timely and necessary given the constantly changing environment. And a future TV star (Pine) gets his first big part.

Robert Pine

(ACTOR)

I had been under contract to Universal from 1964 to 1967. This was my first job after that. It was a huge thrill to be hired by her. It was also my first time doing a three-camera show with a live audience. I was impressed with what control she took. She was a no-nonsense lady, and I mean that in the nicest way. She ran things. If she didn't like things, she changed them immediately. She was a lady who really knew what she was doing. Lucie Arnaz was also in the cast, and that added a special flavor to it. All the staff people were bending over backwards to be nice to her. Gale Gordon sent Lucie a big thing of flowers the night of the show. Lucie more than pulled her own weight. She was charming and talented, and it was nice to see the child of a star be that way.

I was already about twenty-six, so I lied to Lucy about my age so I could get the job playing a teenager. She took a liking to me and wanted me to play her oldest son in Yours, Mine and Ours *[the 1968 big-screen comedy starring Lucille and Henry Fonda]. She even arranged for an audition. Of course, it didn't work out. [Tim Matheson got the assignment.] Perhaps because Lucie was there, the mood on the set was very lighthearted. The only awkward time for me was on Wednesday, when Lucy had to pick the extras to play in the school scenes. When they were ready for her, she said, "Robert, come with me." We walk to this other stage, like she's the visiting general and I'm her toady and we're picking meat. I realize in hindsight that she probably wanted to see how I'd look with these people, but back then I was uncomfortable. I also got to see her in action as a mother. One day, Desi Jr. called to tell her he wanted to buy an expensive car. I think he was about to turn sixteen. She didn't put it off on an aide or a maid. She took the call like any mother and said, "Goddamit, I don't want you doing this, so don't do it." Then she turned to me and said, "Can you believe this kid?" It was very human.*

Desi Arnaz Jr.

The funny thing about that story, which is true, is that I was already independently wealthy from my work with Dino, Desi, and Billy. I wasn't asking her permission; I just wanted an opinion about the car.

Another important thing happens this week. Lucie Arnaz meets fledgling actor Philip Vandervort, a fellow cast member of this episode. Within a few years, they will be married.

THE LUCY SHOW #138: "LUCY GETS JACK BENNY'S ACCOUNT"

(CBS, OCTOBER 16, 1967), 30 MINUTES

WRITTEN BY: Milt Josefsberg, Ray Singer

GUEST CAST: Jack Benny, Sid Gould

Mr. Cheever is again pressuring Mr. Mooney to bring in new accounts at the bank. Lucy comes up with the idea of getting Jack Benny's business, but he is notorious for mistrusting financial institutions. After convincing Benny to give her a chance, she demonstrates the bank's idea of a foolproof vault.

HIGHLIGHTS & TRIVIA

Jack Benny, and some very expensive special effects, make this episode a classic. Scripter Milt Josefsberg wrote for Benny for many years. This might as well have been an episode of Jack's own TV sitcom. The last scene, with Lucy and Benny sinking into the quicksand just before they get to the vault, almost doesn't happen. Benny is apprehensive about being able to stay on his feet, and Lucille has an attack of claustrophobia. However, both do the scene like the thorough professionals they are.

THE LUCY SHOW #139: "LITTLE OLD LUCY"

(CBS, OCTOBER 23, 1967), 30 MINUTES

WRITTEN BY: Milt Josefsberg, Ray Singer

GUEST CAST: Dennis Day

When the president of the bank comes to town, Lucy is elected to be his date. Disguising herself as an old woman to be more appropriate for the eighty-five-year-old gentleman, Lucy is shocked to find out he is a lively "wolf."

HIGHLIGHTS & TRIVIA

Lucille trots out her old woman bit, first done in 1953 on *I Love Lucy* (episode #68, "The Girls Go into Business"). Unfortunately, the older she gets, the less funny this characterization becomes. There is a bit of stunt casting involved in this one. Rather than use an older actor, forever youthful Irish tenor Dennis Day (best known for his work on *The Jack Benny Show*) is pressed into service in an uncharacteristic portrayal.

THE LUCY SHOW #140: "LUCY AND ROBERT GOULET"

(CBS, OCTOBER 30, 1967), 30 MINUTES

WRITTEN BY: Douglas Morrow

GUEST CAST: Robert Goulet, Mary Wickes, Lucie Arnaz, Vanda Barra, Sid Gould

When a truck driver who resembles Robert Goulet comes to Mr. Mooney for a loan and is turned down, Lucy helps him by entering the teamster in a Goulet look-alike contest sponsored by a movie studio.

HIGHLIGHTS & TRIVIA

This episode is substandard. It is probably the worst TV outing Lucille has been involved with to date. Singer/actor Goulet is misused, the plot is overwritten and underdeveloped, and Lucille is annoying in her assignment. The only worthwhile moments come from Mary Wickes and Vanda Barra, the latter who steals a scene as a waitress. Sixteen year-old Lucie Arnaz plays an adult friend of her mother's and handles it very well.

Kathleen Freeman
(ACTOR)

Mary Wickes was around Lucille all the time. She was fiercely loyal to Lucille and her kids. She adored Lucie and little Desi, and was like an aunt to them. She always played a curmudgeon of sorts, for all the world to see all the time, and maybe she did that to keep people away. She never had children of her own, but boy did she love the Arnaz kids. Mary was quite special. She was a principled, ethical woman. If there was a rule to be honored or obeyed, she did. She didn't lie. And she didn't brook people being treated badly. Mary was like a rock.

THE LUCY SHOW #141: "LUCY GETS MOONEY FIRED"

(CBS, NOVEMBER 6, 1967), 30 MINUTES
WRITTEN BY: Fred S. Fox, Seaman Jacobs
GUEST CAST: Vanda Barra, Joan Swift, Irwin Sharone

There is a forty-eight-cent shortage at the bank, so Lucy puts in her own money to make the books come out even. When the real money is found, Mr. Mooney is fired for trying to cover up his mistake. To get his job back, Lucy gives Mr. Cheever the "Gaslight" treatment and makes him think he is going crazy with guilt for firing Mooney.

HIGHLIGHTS & TRIVIA

This series really rides a rollercoaster between mediocrity and excellence. This one is a classic. The final scene, with Lucy trying to convince Cheever he is nuts, is hilarious.

THE LUCY SHOW #142: "LUCY'S MYSTERY GUEST"

(CBS, NOVEMBER 13, 1967), 30 MINUTES
WRITTEN BY: Milt Josefsberg, Ray Singer
GUEST CAST: Mary Wickes

Mary Jane brings Lucy her mail. Tearing it up because she believes it's all junk mail, Lucy inadvertently destroys a letter. Piecing it together, she finds out that "somebody's coming to visit me!" The mystery visitor turns out to be her Aunt Agnes, a health nut with a *lot* of money.

HIGHLIGHTS & TRIVIA

This well-written installment has a lot of the spirit and warmth that has been mostly missing since Vivian Vance left the show. It is also a difficult shoot, because close friends Lucille and Mary get the giggles after Lucille starts to flub her lines. By the time Lucille says, "I'm a steak and potatoes man," instead of girl, they are both in hysterics. Lucille takes gaffes with good humor in the 1950s and 1960s. That will change as the 1970s roll around.

THE LUCY SHOW #143: "LUCY THE PHILANTHROPIST"

(CBS, NOVEMBER 20, 1967), 30 MINUTES
WRITTEN BY: Fred S. Fox, Seaman Jacobs
GUEST CAST: Frank McHugh

When Lucy brings home a bum to give him a hot meal, Mr. Mooney mistakes him for an eccentric millionaire who gives away fortunes to good Samaritans.

HIGHLIGHTS & TRIVIA

Notice the ice cream cones Mary Jane brings for Lucy. They have to be small enough for Frank McHugh to gobble up in a couple of bites, so special cones are made by the prop department.

THE LUCY SHOW #144: "LUCY SUES MOONEY"

(CBS, NOVEMBER 27, 1967), 30 MINUTES
WRITTEN BY: Ray Singer, Milt Josefsberg
GUEST CAST: Jack Carter, Parley Baer, Lew Parker, Vanda Barra, Sid Gould

After Lucy takes a tumble at Mr. Mooney's house while doing bank work, Mary Jane insists that Lucy consult her cousin who is an ambulance-chasing lawyer. He talks her into suing Mr. Mooney.

HIGHLIGHTS & TRIVIA

Of all the standup comedians who appear on this series, Jack Carter comes across the best. Carter is a very close friend of Lucille Ball. At the time of this show he is married to Ball's costar (Paula Stewart) in *Wildcat* (1960), and, in fact, he introduced Lucille to Gary Morton.

Jack Carter

(ACTOR/COMEDIAN)

Lucille Ball was my best friend and my worst enemy. You never knew what to expect from her. She had this episode written for me because we were so close. She knew everything about everything. It took a special director like Jack Donahue to handle her. Most of the ones who worked with her in later years (with the exception of my friend Herbert Kenwith) were patsies. Jack wouldn't take any crap from her. If she started to countermand his direction, he'd yell, "Is there someone else directing this show? Do I hear a redhead saying something to me, the director? *Do I hear another voice?" She'd back down because he'd do it in a comical way without taking away her dignity. This was a weak script, but we made a pretty good show out of it. Lucy should have had better writers, but by this time she was churning out* product. *The writers weren't doing right by her.*

THE LUCY SHOW #145: "LUCY AND THE POOL HUSTLER"

(CBS, DECEMBER 4, 1967), 30 MINUTES

WRITTEN BY: Bob O'Brien

GUEST CAST: Dick Shawn, Stanley Adams, Remo Pisani, Joan Swift, Vanda Barra, Herbie Faye

A pool hall near the bank has been redecorated to appeal to women. Lucy enters a pool contest there to win the $1,000 prize. Her biggest competition in the women-only pool tournament is Ace (Dick Shawn), a man in drag who really needs the money.

HIGHLIGHTS & TRIVIA

This is a very enjoyable entry, due mostly to Dick Shawn's clowning and a fine supporting cast. The only fly in the ointment is the totally dated way the script has the pool sharks talking, as if in a 1930s gangster movie.

THE LUCY SHOW #146: "LUCY AND CAROL BURNETT, PART ONE" A.K.A. "COFFEE, TEA OR MILK"

(CBS, DECEMBER 11, 1967), 30 MINUTES

WRITTEN BY: Bob O'Brien

GUEST CAST: Carol Burnett, Rhodes Reason, Kasey Rogers, Eric Mason, Sid Gould, Jerry Rush

Lucy temporarily quits her job at the bank and tries out as a flight attendant for Trans Global Airways. Her roommate is clunky Carol Tilford, who is terrified of heights. They almost blow their test flight, until ingenuity and imagination save the day.

HIGHLIGHTS & TRIVIA

This episode is the first of two parts. By this point, the series is developing into a skitcom, much like Jack Benny's old TV series. There is very little continuity from week to week, and no vision for the series as a whole. Part of this is due to the fact Lucille has recently sold Desilu to the huge conglomerate Gulf & Western, which also owns Paramount Studios (located next door to Desilu in Hollywood). Everyone knows this is the final season for this still very popular series. Less attention is paid to plots and details, and more effort is placed on guest stars and musical numbers. The finale of this entry has Lucy and Carol putting on an impromptu in-flight show when the scheduled film breaks. This kind of spontaneous singing and dancing had not happened since the golden days of the MGM musical films. Without the talent and energy of the two ladies involved, it would have been very corny. Notice the subtle use of flight attendant trainees of all races.

THE LUCY SHOW #147: "LUCY AND CAROL BURNETT, PART TWO" A.K.A. "LUCY AND CAROL GET THEIR WINGS"

(CBS, DECEMBER 18, 1967), 30 MINUTES

WRITTEN BY: Bob O'Brien

GUEST CAST: Carol Burnett, Buddy Rogers, Dick Arlen, Kasey Rogers

Finally getting their flight attendant wings, Lucy and Carol, along with Mr. Mooney, put on a musical featuring the original stars of the silent movie *Wings* (1927), Buddy Rogers and Richard Arlen.

HIGHLIGHTS & TRIVIA

This is the follow-up episode of the two-parter. Rogers and Arlen appear in quite a few sitcoms at this time, as the publicity for the fortieth anniversary of *Wings* (the first feature to win an Academy Award as Best Picture) puts them back into the spotlight. The musical numbers are well done, with an energetic chorus backing up the principals. After this two-part sequence, the flight attendant plot thread is dropped without explanation, and Lucy is back at the bank as Mr. Mooney's secretary!

THE LUCY SHOW #148: "LUCY AND VIV REMINISCE"

(CBS, JANUARY 1, 1968), 30 MINUTES (COLOR AND B&W, AS MANY OF THE FLASHBACK SCENES ARE NOT IN COLOR)

WRITTEN BY: Milt Josefsberg
BASED ON AN IDEA BY: Hilda Josefsberg
SEGMENTS WRITTEN BY: Madelyn Davis, Bob Carroll Jr., Bob Weiskopf, Bob Schiller, David Braverman, Bob Marcus
GUEST CAST: Vivian Vance

Lucy breaks her leg by falling out of bed after a romantic dream. Mr. Mooney arranges for her old pal Viv to come and take care of her. They reminisce about their lives together until lunchtime. Viv goes to make lunch, and falls and breaks her leg, too. Mr. Mooney is forced to play nurse to both of them.

HIGHLIGHTS & TRIVIA

This is the second of three times that Lucille trots out old clips and builds a show around them. It is already known *The Lucy Show* is coming to an end, and Lucille wants a sentimental look-back at the show's six years. She doesn't want to do a final episode, because the show is about to be rerun on CBS on weekday mornings (replacing *I Love Lucy*, which is going into syndication). Lucille feels a final episode would hurt the show later in reruns. It is then decided to involve Vivian, and to limit the clips to those involving the two of them. Vivian thinks it would be a good idea to do a retrospective of *all* their bits together, going back to 1951. Lucille immediately nixes the suggestion. It is still difficult for her to deal with the Desi years. All but one of the clips are from the first season of *The Lucy Show*.

Wraparound scenes are filmed to introduce and conclude the clips. These are done in one day, without a live studio audience. Vivian is often a whip with a quip, and isn't intimidated by Lucille. At one point, when the Lucy character says, "I've always had a sensible reason for doing things," Viv jokes back, "Sensible? Sensible *my ass*!"

THE LUCY SHOW #149: "LUCY GETS INVOLVED"

(CBS, JANUARY 15, 1968), 30 MINUTES

WRITTEN BY: Ray Singer
GUEST CAST: Jackie Coogan, Philip Vandervort, Vanda Barra, John "Red" Fox

Lucy develops terrible insomnia when her TV set breaks and she can't fall asleep without watching it. When Mr. Mooney lends her his extra set, and she breaks it, she moonlights as a car hop to pay for a replacement. The result is the expected disaster.

HIGHLIGHTS & TRIVIA

Once more, Lucy gets involved in the life of some total stranger (Philip Vandervort), trying to make life better for him. This aspect of the Lucy character gives her some needed depth and likability. Lucille and Jackie Coogan are old friends who work well together. (Coogan last appeared on December 9, 1963, in *The Lucy Show* episode #40, "Lucy and the Military Academy.") The physical comedy between them is rehearsed endlessly to make it look spontaneous, and it works. Coogan would have been a good foil for Lucille had she chosen to use him more often.

THE LUCY SHOW #150: "MOONEY'S OTHER WIFE"

(CBS, JANUARY 22, 1968), 30 MINUTES

WRITTEN BY: Bob O'Brien
GUEST CAST: Edie Adams

After Mr. Mooney and Mr. Cheever return from a bank convention where their behavior has been less than exemplary, a young woman shows up believing Mr. Mooney has proposed to her. To save his marriage, Lucy pretends to be a much abused *Mrs.* Mooney.

Edie Adams

(ACTOR/SINGER)

I was all over the place at this time in those cigar commercials. I became a type of glamorous ditzy lady, and nobody let me sing. I wanted to do some television and stretch, but this show was no different. I didn't like the script. It was obvious that she missed Desi's hand as the backbone of the show. I agreed to do the show with the proviso that I had to leave early on Wednesday for a noon appointment. Lucy seemed very sweet and considerate and agreed, not at all like she had been in 1960 [for the Lucy-Desi hour "Lucy Meets the Moustache"]. On Wednesday, she insisted that I take a tour of the studios, which of course totally ruined any chance I had of making my appointment. At the very moment I would have returned, she said to me, "Oh, you had an appointment, didn't you?" I realized that I had been had. She wouldn't come right out and tell me I couldn't go to my appointment, but she made sure I didn't *go. The set was a much happier place than it had been in 1960, but Lucy was so driven. She was very much boss-lady. Gale Gordon was a professional. He saved the humor for the stage and didn't waste it offstage. Gary Morton was able to produce later on because he had been schooled in show business. He had to have been good* at *show business or he wouldn't have lasted as long as he did. At this point, he wasn't allowed to open his mouth.*

I never understood why Lucille was so concerned about her looks. She was still a very attractive woman, but she wore so much makeup. She overpainted her lips, and was constantly sucking her cheeks in to try to look like an ingenue. Lucille's voice had gone from soprano to bass. The only thing I can imagine that would do that to a voice so fast is a little bit too much scotch.

THE LUCY SHOW #151: "LUCY AND THE STOLEN STOLE"

(CBS, JANUARY 29, 1968), 30 MINUTES

WRITTEN BY: Milt Josefsberg, Ray Singer
GUEST CAST: Buddy Hackett, John "Red" Fox, Ray Kellogg, Sid Gould, John Harmon, Roy Engel

Lucy takes Mr. Mooney to a discount store to buy a bargain-priced fur stole for Mrs. Mooney. Soon, they are falsely arrested for possession of stolen goods, and then scheme to get Mr. Mooney's money back from the crook. Unfortunately, every attempt made at making things right gets them arrested yet again.

HIGHLIGHTS & TRIVIA

Strangely enough, when the great standup comedians of the day (Jan Murray, Don Rickles, et al) are used in this TV series, the results are usually not very satisfying. This one is no exception. Buddy Hackett is miscast, and the script gives him very little with which to work.

THE LUCY SHOW #152: "LUCY AND PHIL HARRIS"

(CBS, FEBRUARY 5, 1968), 30 MINUTES

WRITTEN BY: Bob O'Brien
GUEST CAST: Phil Harris, Gerald Mohr, Kasey Rogers, Lew Parker, Tim Herbert, Carole Cook, Sid Gould, Vanda Barra, Jerry Rush

While at a cocktail lounge, Lucy runs into a talented but alcoholic pianist and songwriter. She takes him to her house, nursing him back to health while insisting he finish the song that she knows will be a big hit.

HIGHLIGHTS & TRIVIA

If Lucy charged rent to all the people she good-naturedly takes in, she wouldn't need to work at the bank. This episode is very heavy on sentiment. Phil Harris is much too mature for the part of this musician, but his showmanship and charm make up for it. Kasey Rogers is best known for playing Louise Tate on the long-running *Bewitched* (1964–72). Vanda Barra is bit actor Sid Gould's wife in real life. The song used in the plot ("But I Love You") is actually excellent. At one time, Frank Sinatra was considering recording it.

THE LUCY SHOW #153: "LUCY HELPS KEN BERRY"

(CBS, FEBRUARY 19, 1968), 30 MINUTES

WRITTEN BY: Bob O'Brien
GUEST CAST: Ken Berry, Ralph Story, Stanley Adams, Sidney Miller, Anita Mann, Orwin Harvey, George Boyce, Jimmy Casino, Jack Bernardi

Ken visits the bank to get a loan for his dance school. Mr. Mooney is resistant, because new businesses fail so often. Lucy feels that if she can get Ken onto TV's *Ralph Story's LA*, the publicity would guarantee the school's success.

HIGHLIGHTS & TRIVIA

Lucille loves doing these musical-themed shows. She rehearses tirelessly the entire week, as she always does. The dancing goes fine until the night of the filming. While Lucille has no problem with her steps, Ken Berry does. And she is so nervous about *her* dancing that she keeps flubbing her lines with Ralph Story, causing her to remark during filming, 'I'm having a helluva time tonight, aren't I, Ralph?' Story is a local L.A. newsman who has his own weekly television program spotlighting interesting aspects of the city. He will continue on station KTLA for more than twenty years. Berry had been discovered by Lucille in her Desilu Workshop in the late 1950s. He would go on to *F-Troop* (1965–67), *Mayberry, R.F.D.* (1968–71), and *Mama's Family* (1983–90).

THE LUCY SHOW #154: "LUCY AND THE LOST STAR"

(CBS, FEBRUARY 26, 1968), 30 MINUTES

WRITTEN BY: Ray Singer, Milt Josefsberg

GUEST CAST: Joan Crawford, Vivian Vance, Lew Parker

When Lucy's car breaks down, Lucy and Viv (in Hollywood on vacation) hike to the nearest house, which happens to belong to Joan Crawford. Crawford has sent all of her furniture out to be redone, which leads the girls to think she is destitute. The duo scheme with Mr. Mooney to get Joan a job in show business.

HIGHLIGHTS & TRIVIA

This is a truly top-notch excursion. To begin with, the story line that Crawford is a cleaning fanatic is taken right out of her personal life.

Second, it is a delightful romp for Ball and Vance, who fall into step a lot more easily than they had on their last reunion episode. Notice that (for reasons unknown) Vivian now speaks with a decided nasal twang. She will sound that way for the rest of her life. The finale, with the cast doing an exceptional parody of a 1930s gangster film, is almost a total disaster.

Jane Kean

(ACTOR/SINGER)

Lucy came on the set the first day of rehearsal and was looking for Joan. So she goes to Joan's dressing room to see if she's there. She finds this woman in old clothes on the floor scrubbing everything down. Lucy bent down and asked, "Have you seen Miss Crawford?" The woman looked up at her and it was Joan.

Irma Kusely

(HAIRSTYLIST)

Joan Crawford was another Tallulah Bankhead, but only worse. Lucille actually fired her at one point, and justifiably so. Joan was so drunk she couldn't rehearse, and Lucille hated working with people who weren't professional and on their toes. My pal Gertrude Wheeler (who did Donna Reed's hair on her show) did Joan's hair, but she was never credited.

Herbert Kenwith

(DIRECTOR)

I was a visitor on the set, and I was a very close friend of Joan Crawford's. Knowing that Lucille could sometimes be peculiar about certain things on her set, I warned Joan to act as if she didn't know me. Joan didn't listen, and immediately there was antipathy from Lucille. Joan was not *drunk while she rehearsed and shot this episode. But Joan was very insecure at the first reading. She needed to be coached to get the right kind of performance out of her. Lucille made Crawford's life* tough*. If I had been she, I would have quit. Joan did not have the mastery of how to defend herself with someone like Lucille. And Crawford truly admired Lucille Ball; she had no hard feelings against her. But for some reason, Lucille really got mean with her. Joan was terrified of Lucille Ball. When it came time for Joan to rehearse her dancing, Lucille watched and then stopped the rehearsal. She came over to Joan and said, "You got into the movies as a Charleston dancer and* you can't dance*! I can't believe it!" Joan tried to make an excuse that she wasn't used to dancing to the sound of only a piano player. Lucille just looked at her and said, "We'll try this one more time and if it doesn't work, it's* out*!" Joan was very upset—every Desilu secretary was sitting there in the audience* *bleachers to watch the great Joan Crawford rehearse. Lucille barked at Joan, "Come on, let's do it again," like she was talking to a dog. Joan started to dance for a minute, then Lucille tapped pianist Marl Young on the shoulder and said, "Stop. You stop, too Joan. This number is cut." Joan ran to her dressing room in tears, and threw herself down on the floor. I was very close to Lucille, but I just wasn't brave enough at the time to ask her why she was treating Crawford this way.*

Kaye Ballard
(ACTOR/SINGER)

It was Vanda Barra who got Joan Crawford to go on that night. Vanda was standing over to the side smoking, and this little old lady came over, sobbing, "I can't go on, I can't go on!" And Vanda said, "You're Joan Crawford, *you're going on! You're* Joan Crawford *and don't you forget it! There is no question, you're going on tonight!" After the shoot, Crawford was looking for Vanda saying, "Where's that woman, where's that woman? I want to thank her!"*

There are many opinions as to why Crawford's behavior is less than professional. Some say she is so intimidated by Lucille that she is nervous and shy. Others claim she is already an out-of-control alcoholic. Crawford does seem ill at ease playing herself, and has trouble projecting her voice. However, in the show-within-the-show, she is very funny and delivers her lines perfectly. When it comes time for her to do the Charleston, the camera captures her only from the waist up, and only for about ten seconds, before the scene cuts to Lucy's reaction and the line that stops the dancing.

THE LUCY SHOW #155: "LUCY AND SID CAESAR"

(CBS, March 4, 1968), 30 minutes
WRITTEN BY: Bob O'Brien
GUEST CAST: Sid Caesar, Carole Cook, Jack Collins, Irwin Charon, Tim Herbert, Ben Gage, Sid Gould, Remo Pisani, John "Red" Fox

Bank client Sid Caesar has a look-alike who is forging Caesar's checks. Lucy schemes with Sid to catch him, but the crook keeps foiling Lucy in her own traps.

HIGHLIGHTS & TRIVIA

It has been awhile since Lucille and Sid were at the top of the Golden Age of television comedy. While Ball's star still shines bright, Sid is no longer the superstar he once was. His talent is still intact, but it is dulled by the alcoholism that Sid will overcome in the 1970s. This installment is amusing, but could have been hysterical if Caesar had been up to par.

THE LUCY SHOW #156: "LUCY AND THE 'BOSS OF THE YEAR' AWARD"

(CBS, MARCH 11, 1968)
WRITTEN BY: Ray Singer
GUEST CAST: Jack Collins, Gary Morton, Sid Gould

Mr. Mooney is considered for the presidency of the San Francisco branch of the bank, and Lucy schemes to have him named Boss of the Year to ensure that he wins the position and gets out of her hair.

HIGHLIGHTS & TRIVIA

This is the last episode of the series. It is too bad no one thinks to bring back Vivian or Lucy's stage kids for a final farewell. The show must end because it is owned by Desilu, and Desilu is no longer owned by Lucille Ball. Miss Ball wants to own her own TV product, so it is decided for her to come back in the fall with a new CBS network series produced by Ball's new company, Lucille Ball Productions. The finale of the installment, a musical number by Lucy saluting Mr. Mooney, refers to Lucy having worked for Mr. Mooney for six years, totally ignoring the first three seasons of the format. Notice that this is, by comparison to other series, a short season. Lucille Ball's sitcoms will consistently have the shortest seasons of any network sitcoms on the air from this point forward.

THE ED SULLIVAN SHOW

(CBS, MARCH 17, 1968), 60 MINUTES
PRODUCED BY: Bob Precht
DIRECTED BY: Tim Kiley
CAST: Ed Sullivan (host), Lucille Ball, the Bee Gees, the Dubliners, George Hamilton, Fran Jeffries, Jackie Kahane, Sandler and Young, Stiller and Meara

This appearance is a blatant plug for Lucille's current screen comedy *Yours, Mine, and Ours.* Dressed in a black velvet-and-lace pants outfit and the wig she sports in the feature film, she joins Ed onstage and the two sit in chairs and chat as if on a talk show. Clips are shown of *The Lucy Show* dubbed into different languages. The finale features the Redhead and a gaggle of children in a choreographed number set to the theme music to her new movie. In it, Lucille puts twenty children to bed in bunks. While Sullivan had allowed Lucille to promote her media product on his shows before, this one has none of the class or entertainment value of her previous appearances. She does not perform any comedy, and the chat between Sullivan and Ball is obviously scripted.

THE JACK BENNY HOUR: CARNIVAL NIGHTS

(NBC, MARCH 20, 1968), 60 MINUTES

EXECUTIVE PRODUCED BY: Irving Fein
PRODUCED AND DIRECTED BY: Fred DeCordova
WRITTEN BY: Hal Goldman, Al Gordon, Herbert Marks
SCRIPT CONSULTANT: Milt Josefsberg
CAST: Jack Benny (host), Lucille Ball, Larry Blake, Ben Blue, George Burns, Johnny Carson, Don Drysdale, Sid Fields, Bob Hope, Dean Martin, Paul Revere and the Raiders, Benny Rubin, Almira Sessions, the Smothers Brothers, Danny Thomas, Herb Vigran

After Danny Thomas' TV specials on burlesque and Bob Hope's specials on vaudeville, it is only natural that Jack Benny do one with a carnival theme. As "Luscious Lucille," a scantily-clad and bewigged Ball sings "It's So Nice to Have a Man Around the House" to a bevy of musclemen as a nod to Helen of Troy. She then segues into a Cleopatra salute to the tune of, ironically, "Mame," the film musical (1974) in which she will star. In "Schnookie," Ball and comedian Ben Blue do a pantomime sketch about a man on a bench being annoyed by a woman in despair. Finally, Lucille and Jack play the owners of a carnival, whose son Jack Benny (Johnny Carson) wants to be a comedian. The Redhead is nothing more than a supporting player in this sketch.

THE MIKE DOUGLAS SHOW

(SYN, APRIL 13, 1968), 90 MINUTES

EXECUTIVE PRODUCED BY: Jack Reilly
PRODUCED BY: Woody Fraser
DIRECTED BY: Ernie Sherry
CAST: Mike Douglas (host), Lucille Ball, the Joe Harnell Band, Ozzie and Harriet Nelson, the Pearce Sisters, Vivian Vance

Mike's show is taped in Philadelphia. Each week he has a cohost(s) who appear on all five daily shows. Ozzie and Harriet Nelson are the cohosts this week, and are cognizant of all the planned surprises. After the Pearce Sisters (a rock act featuring girls aged two to ten) appear, Lucille walks on as a surprise to Mike. Lucille and Harriet reminisce about being contract players at RKO in the 1930s, and then Mike introduces the next act, a lady stilt-walker. The curtains part to gasps and hoots from the audience because out walks Vivian Vance (no stilts) as a surprise to both Mike and Lucille. Lucille is dressed in a black Nehru suit, and Viv in a red short-sleeved dress. Amid much hugging, the two talk about old times, look at show photos, sing, and dance with the entire cast.

THE TWENTIETH ANNUAL EMMY AWARDS

(NBC, MAY 19, 1968), 110 MINUTES

EXECUTIVE PRODUCED BY: Greg Garrison
PRODUCED BY: Perry Cross, Richard Schneider;
DIRECTED BY: Jack Shea, Richard Schneider
WRITTEN BY: Harry Crane, Rich Eustis, Al Rogers, Jerry Belson, Garry Marshall, Ed Weinberger, George Bloom
HOSTS: Frank Sinatra, Dick Van Dyke

For the second consecutive year, Lucille Ball wins an Emmy for Outstanding Continued Performance by an Actress in a Leading Role in a Comedy Series. (Her category rivals are Barbara Feldon of *Get Smart*, Elizabeth Montgomery of *Bewitched*, Paula Prentiss of *He & She*, and Marlo Thomas of *That Girl.*) This time Lucille is much more poised, wearing an expensive blue gown and a sophisticated wig. This is the last Emmy Award Ball will win for a single role, although she will receive several more accolades from the Academy in later years for her extensive body of TV work.

Chapter Twenty

1968-69 Season

HERE'S LUCY: THE FIRST SEASON

TECHNICAL REGULARS: Executive produced by Gary Morton; produced by Tommy Thompson; directed by Jack Donohue; script consultant: Milt Josefsberg; makeup by Hal King; hairstyling by Irma Kusely; music by Wilbur Hatch

CAST REGULARS: Lucille Ball (Lucy Carter); Gale Gordon (Harrison Otis Carter); Lucie Arnaz (Kim Carter); Desi Arnaz Jr. (Craig Carter); Roy Rowan (announcer)

HERE'S LUCY #1: "MOD, MOD LUCY"

(CBS, SEPTEMBER 23, 1968), 30 MINUTES

WRITTEN BY: Milt Josefsberg, Ray Singer

GUEST CAST: Doris Singleton, Nancy Roth, Lew Parker, Nancy Howard

Uncle Harry needs a cheap band for the sweet-sixteen party of a client, so Lucy offers Craig's band, featuring Kim as the vocalist. All is well until the day of the festivities, when Kim comes home with laryngitis from a day of surfing. What else can Lucy do but don a miniskirt and mod wig, and take her place?

HIGHLIGHTS & TRIVIA

This first installment of *Here's Lucy* suffers from the same over-the-top pushing Lucille gave to the first offerings of her last two series. The script reveals very little backstory about the Carters. Harry is the brother of Lucy's late husband, and she has been working for him for two years as his secretary and only employee at the Unique Employment Agency, a firm that finds unusual jobs for unusual people. It is located in a high-rise building on Wilshire Boulevard in Los Angeles, California. Lucy Carter and her kids (fifteen-year-old Craig and seventeen-year-old Kim) live in a two-story house in Encino (which is in the San Fernando Valley, twenty miles northwest of downtown Los Angeles). The script implies Lucy is love-starved, and her kids would love to see her find a man. These themes will almost never be followed up in future episodes. Uncle Harry's meanness and parsimony are never explained in the entire season. The character of Craig will never be given any depth or growth except that he is a fine drummer. It is Lucie Arnaz' character of Kim that receives most of the attention in future seasons. For the moment, the audience will know very little about either of them.

Lucille's character of Lucy Carter is not the same as Lucy Carmichael. With two teenaged children, she needs to be more responsible and is truly fearful of losing her job. She is also, if it is possible, more stupid than Mrs. Carmichael. The character of Lucy Carter will change from week to week, depending on the needs of the script. Sometimes she will have the cleverness and chutzpah of Lucy Ricardo; other times she will give the scatterbrained character of Gracie Allen a run for her money. Although there are several fine outings in this first season, it by far the weakest one of the six-year run. This is due in part to the lack of sufficient creative vision by Tommy Thompson, Gary Morton, or Milt Josefsberg. They are not certain what the junior Arnazes are capable of, so the scripts ask very little of them. The scripts also ignore the warmth or esprit de corps of the previous Ball TV series; thankfully, this situation will change as *Here's Lucy* develops.

This first offering does little more than introduce the players, then segue into the musical numbers.

Lucille's dance is spirited, but her singing voice is dubbed by Carole Cook. It is obvious that the powers-that-be trust neither Lucie nor Lucille to perform musically at this point. The familiar faces of Lew Parker and Doris Singleton are along for the ride, but their parts are too small to add any real support.

Desi Arnaz Jr.

There had already been a tremendous amount of publicity about me because of Dino, Desi, and Billy. The fan magazines in those days weren't too concerned with Craig Carter, and as the years went on they focused almost entirely on my personal life. Craig was kind of a nerd, actually. But I think there is a piece of Craig in all of us. It wasn't so much a matter of Craig being different from Desi, but that I didn't know who I was, so why not play Craig? We all put on false fronts. Perhaps that's why some of us choose to become actors.

Lucie Arnaz

Our appearing on the show was a joint decision. We picked the names Kim and Craig because we liked the way they sounded. We had absolutely no input on story lines. I was there to learn, not to tell them how to do it. My mother was in control. She did not lighten up after she sold the studios. That term did not apply to my mother. She always had a steady focus on the work that was in front of her. The only thing that got lightened up was her hair.

Desi Arnaz Jr.

The musical numbers on this episode were all prerecorded, because we only showed this trio and yet a big band chimed in. Mom's singing was prerecorded by Carole Cook, who did these things for Mom occasionally. Also, it gave Mom breath to dance without having to worry about singing.

Lucie Arnaz

Here's Lucy *was not a domestic comedy. Much more emphasis was placed on the Lucy character being a responsible working mother, as opposed to actually seeing her make dinner or do the laundry.*

Desi Arnaz Jr.

In a way, the domestic scenes were just a backdrop to the main plots with Mom and Gale. At least in the beginning. The main relationship on the show was between Lucy and Uncle Harry, not Lucy and her kids.

Lucie Arnaz

There are two people I have known who just did not have a bad bone in their body. There was never a harsh word or a rumor spread. It was like God came down and just kissed them. One was Jimmy Durante, and the other was Gale Gordon. Gale was so unique . . . so brilliant and so studied in physical comedy. Watching him get wet was an education in itself. What a delightful man!

Doris Singleton

(ACTOR)

I was supposed to have a regular role on Here's Lucy. *[Lucille] was going to be the dumb secretary, and I was going to be the smart one. It was supposedly all set. I ran into her one day and asked her what was happening. She told me they had decided to go with her children instead. Just like that.*

Gary Morton

(EXECUTIVE PRODUCER)

My title on the show was always sort of misunderstood, because in television it can mean so many things. My job was to see to it that the sets were done right, that all things pertaining to the production were done on time, and that everything was done to please Lucille Ball. If she wanted Lawrence Welk as a guest star, I got her Welk. In fact, much of the time it seemed to fall to me to arrange to get the guest stars. I was there to protect the commodity of Lucille Ball, who was as rare as the finest diamond.

HERE'S LUCY #2: "LUCY VISITS JACK BENNY"

(CBS, SEPTEMBER 30, 1968), 30 MINUTES

WRITTEN BY: Milt Josefsberg, Ray Singer
GUEST CAST: Jack Benny, Jackie Gleason, Sid Gould

Lucy and the family go to Palm Springs for a vacation, and end up renting rooms in Jack Benny's desert mansion. While the price is right, money-hungry Benny charges them for every possible extra convenience.

HIGHLIGHTS & TRIVIA

This episode is a gem. It is shown out of order of filming to give the second week a strong show as a follow-up to the series' debut. Although the opening scene displays all of the weaknesses of many first season installments (lame jokes, lack of character definitions, etc.), once the gang is at Benny's, all is wonderfully hysterical. Jack is in top form, and ex-Benny scripter Josefsberg knows exactly where to mine the jokes. Although the bit where Lucy plays the violin is unbelievable (her playing is dubbed) and out of character, one can accept it because it is so in character for a Jack Benny plot. The finale featuring Jackie Gleason in his Ralph Kramden personage is perhaps the single best cameo in sitcom history, running neck and neck with Suzanne Pleshette's appearance on the surprise series finale of *Newhart* in 1990. It is so unexpected, that when Gleason makes his entrance, he steals the entire scene.

Lucie Arnaz

Everything that everyone has ever said about Jack Benny is true. He was a dear man. I was always aware that this was an enormous talent and a legend. And I thought that Jackie Gleason was a hoot. He was this big, funny galoot. My mother always treated him like royalty. He came in on the last day, rehearsed a little, and then did the show.

THE CAROL BURNETT SHOW

(CBS, OCTOBER 4, 1968), 60 MINUTES

PRODUCED BY: Joe Hamilton
DIRECTED BY: Dave Powers
WRITTEN BY: Stan Burns, Mike Marmer, Hal Goodman, Larry Klien, Don Hinkley, Kenny Solms, Gail Parent, Bill Angelos, Buz Kohan
CAST: Carol Burnett (host), Eddie Albert, Lucille Ball, Harvey Korman, Vicki Lawrence, Lyle Waggoner, Nancy Wilson

It is curious that although Carol Burnett really strikes comedy gold as a guest with Lucille Ball, when Ball returns the favor she falls flat. It isn't that Lucille is not a facile sketch performer, as she certainly has done well in other venues. But whether it is her familiarity with Burnett, her lack of control over material, or whether she is just too overwhelmed with her own new series *(Here's Lucy)*, Ball acts as if she is just walking through this variety installment. Although she does get to wear glamorous costumes and wigs, her sketches seem unrehearsed and her musical numbers don't sparkle. Lucille will only appear with Carol three times on Burnett's variety series, although the two remain close friends.

HERE'S LUCY #3: "LUCY, THE PROCESS SERVER"

(CBS, OCTOBER 7, 1968), 30 MINUTES

WRITTEN BY: George Balzer, Phil Leslie
GUEST CAST: Reta Shaw, Jonathan Hole

Although Kim and Craig have a school holiday, Harry makes Lucy work at the employment agency anyway, ruining a planned picnic. She must make a bank deposit and deliver a summons to a woman at a department store. Naturally, she gets the two confused and manages to wreak havoc at the store.

HIGHLIGHTS & TRIVIA

It is as if writers Balzer and Leslie have screened a dozen episodes of *The Lucy Show* and decided to take plot elements from each of them and cobble together a script. Serving a summons, battling with women at a sale, searching through garbage for lost papers—all of these have been seen before on various Lucy series. To their credit, at least the story points keep the action moving.

Lucie Arnaz

By now, we were in a set pattern. Monday morning, we'd read through that week's script with the guest stars and character actors. We'd take a break, and dismiss them. Then the regular cast would read the following week's script without the guest stars, to hear how it sounded and make preliminary cuts. After lunch, we met on the set and began to block the scenes for action with scripts in our hands. Tuesday morning, we finished what we had started on Monday, but by Tuesday evening, you had to know your lines for the rehearsal that night. The sets would already have been built and pretty much dressed. Any props that were used were already available, so we had as much time as possible to get comfortable working with them. Wednesday was a day for us to do nothing but run lines in Mom's dressing room or a similar place while our stand-ins stood under the lights. This gave the camera people time to come in, get their shots set, and have everything ready technically. That evening we'd have a dress run-through of the entire show. Thursday we'd have only half a day to do another run through without costumes. Then we'd break for dinner. While we were being made up and costumed, the audience would be brought in and warmed up. Then we'd shoot the show. There was a band on the sound stage to entertain the audience, and Gary [Morton] usually did the warmup after Roy Rowan introduced him.

This is as good a place as any to give a brief description of what a *Here's Lucy* warmup is like. Roy Rowan (the announcer) introduces the cast, and then makes certain the sponsor (Lever Brothers and Kraft Foods) is spotlighted. Then, Roy explains the mechanics of filming a comedy live; then he introduces Gary Morton. There is a small house band present, who plays music for Gary's entrance. Gary talks to the audience (usually about 330 people), asks who is from out of town, and makes jokes. He then points out DeDe Ball (Lucille's mother), to enthusiastic applause. He tells the audience (still seated in bleachers as in *I Love Lucy*, but, unlike that series, now elevated off the floor) who that week's guest star is, and introduces any celebrities in the audience. If Desi Sr. is there, he calls him his "husband-in law." Occasionally Lucille yells, "Yeah, Yeah"; that is Gary's cue to get on with it. He introduces any guest actors, the cast, and then, "the most wonderful thing to ever happen in my life—Lucille Ball!" Lucille grabs a microphone, says hello to DeDe, and then usually says, "We have a lot of good friends here and a really big show tonight, so let's go to it, OK?"

The filming usually lasts about ninety minutes and is always done on Thursday, just as in season two onward of *I Love Lucy*. There are no monitor screens for the audience (such as are now frequently provided for audiences present at live tapings), as the shows are never taped, but always filmed.

HERE'S LUCY #4: "LUCY AND MISS SHELLEY WINTERS"

(CBS, OCTOBER 14, 1968), 30 MINUTES

WRITTEN BY: Ray Singer, Milt Josefsberg

GUEST CAST: Shelley Winters, Bartlett Robinson

Movie producer C. B. Wellborn hires Lucy to be a watchdog for his overweight star, Shelley Summers. The zoftig beauty must lose fifteen pounds before the start of her next picture, and Lucy is the watchdog to ensure this occurs.

HIGHLIGHTS & TRIVIA

With Harry and the kids only having tiny roles in this one, many fans think this is an episode from *The Lucy Show*. It certainly plays that way, with the theme of a self-confident Lucy moving in with someone to help the person achieve her goal. The script is funny, but would have been better motivated if Winters' dress had been padded. In the final scene, all that is done is to put the "new" Shelley in a slimming black dress. She only looks more glamorous, not thinner.

Lucie Arnaz

What always impressed me about Shelley Winters is that she is fearless. There is nothing she won't do. She has the guts that it takes to survive in show business.

Shelley Winters

(ACTOR)

We were oncamera, and we needed a certain kind of a table in a hurry. The art director said, "Well, I'll try to find one, Miss Ball, but it will take quite awhile." Lucy said, "Go down the second aisle [in the prop warehouse], in the fourth bin, up on the second shelf." She knew everything about putting on her shows.

HERE'S LUCY #5: "LUCY, THE CONCLUSION JUMPER"

(CBS, OCTOBER 21, 1968), 30 MINUTES

DIRECTED BY: Jack Donohue

WRITTEN BY: Phil Leslie, George Balzer

GUEST CAST: Don Chrichton

When Kim and her friend Don research a school paper on the impracticality of teenage marriage, Lucy jumps to the conclusion that they are eloping.

HIGHLIGHTS & TRIVIA

This topical entry scratches the surface of what this series might have been had the decision been made to allow it to go in more dimensional directions. The introduction of more mature plot elements would not have interfered with Lucille's physical comedy, nor would they have had to be executed in anything but good taste. Don Chrichton is one of the regular dancers and bit players on *The Carol Burnett Show* (1967–78). Notice that his character carries his own first name. Quite often on this series, actors' real-life first names are used as those for their characters.

HERE'S LUCY #6: "LUCY'S IMPOSSIBLE MISSION"

(CBS, OCTOBER 28, 1968), 30 MINUTES

WRITTEN BY: Bob O'Brien
GUEST CAST: Richard Derr, Jack Collins, Joseph Ruskin

Lucy inadvertently intercepts a secret, self-destructing spy message, so an undercover government agency asks her and the family to impersonate Middle Eastern potentates to trap spies.

HIGHLIGHTS & TRIVIA

Shades of Franistan! Scribe O'Brien goes all the way back to a 1951 *I Love Lucy* episode (#31, "The Publicity Agent") to lift Lucille's impersonation of Middle Eastern royalty for this one. Actually, this episode is a satire of *Mission: Impossible* (1966–73), which Desilu had originally produced. Even the agent's name (Geller) is a nod to that series' chief executive, Bruce Geller. A large budget is devoted to costuming and sets for this installment, and Ball is very funny. The chase scene is well choreographed and the physical humor is believable.

HERE'S LUCY #7: "LUCY AND EVA GABOR"

(CBS, NOVEMBER 11, 1968), 30 MINUTES

WRITTEN BY: Ray Singer, Milt Josefsberg
GUEST CAST: Eva Gabor, Robert S. Carson

Writer Eva Von Kirsten hires Harry to find her a safe haven away from fans and prying eyes to complete the screenplay of her best-selling novel *Valley of the Puppets*. He sends Eva to Lucy's San Fernando Valley house, and the Redhead takes her job as protector very seriously.

HIGHLIGHTS & TRIVIA

Gabor (of *Green Acres*, 1965–71, fame) and Ball work well together, both used to the broad style of comedy that is the hallmark of this series. The physical humor is motivated and smoothly executed. The finale is well remembered by fans for the buckets of paints that fall on Gordon and Carson (who plays Eva's agent) as they enter Lucy's house. The name of Von Kirsten's next book, *Life with Lucille*, is awfully close to the actual name of Ball's final series.

THE TENNESSEE ERNIE FORD SPECIAL

(NBC, NOVEMBER 16, 1968), 60 MINUTES

PRODUCED BY: Greg Garrison, Don Van Attan
DIRECTED BY: Robert Sidney
HEAD WRITER: Digby Wolfe
CAST: Tennessee Ernie Ford (host), Lucille Ball, the Golddiggers, Andy Griffith

Lucille's appearance is a payback for the many times Ernie had appeared with her on TV, including a *Here's Lucy* stint already filmed but not shown as of the date of this special. Ball's best sketch showcases her as a temperance leader who can't stay away from liquor. It gives her the opportunity to do her (by now) patented drunk bit, and the chance to sing "Stay Off the Whiskey." She also participates in a rural news TV roundup and the finale, which is one of Ford's famous barnstorming square dances with Ernie doing the calls. The cameramen are careful not to shoot Lucille too closely, as videotape reveals the heavy makeup and age on Miss Ball's face.

HERE'S LUCY #8: "LUCY'S BIRTHDAY"

(CBS, NOVEMBER 18, 1968), 30 MINUTES

WRITTEN BY: Milt Josefsberg, Ray Singer
GUEST CAST: Victor Sen Yung

It is Lucy's birthday, and her kids want to make it a special day. They take her out for a Chinese dinner, but Craig finds he has left his wallet at home. Financially embarrassed, Lucy feigns illness to get out of paying the check.

HIGHLIGHTS & TRIVIA

The only positive thing that can be said about this entry is at least there is some family closeness shown. The dinner sequence seemingly contains every politically incorrect Chinese joke ever created. For some reason, while Lucille is generally sensitive to other ethnicities, she allows these Asian-unfriendly scripts to air without an apparent murmur from her.

HERE'S LUCY #9: "LUCY SELLS CRAIG TO WAYNE NEWTON"

(CBS, NOVEMBER 25, 1968), 30 MINUTES

WRITTEN BY: Bob O'Brien
GUEST CAST: Wayne Newton

Lucy takes her family to a nightclub to see Wayne Newton perform. When he announces that his drummer is leaving the act for two weeks because of an Army Reserve tour, Lucy schemes to get Craig hired as the replacement.

HIGHLIGHTS & TRIVIA

There will be many such plots during the run of *Here's Lucy* where Lucy intrudes on a situation and takes over. Although this is the best of them, they are never easy to digest because Lucy's character is so insistent. Without a motivated plot and humorous writing, Lucille just pushes harder and yells a lot in an attempt to be funny.

Lucie Arnaz

Desi's best comedy suit is his dry, dry wit. At one point, the script had Mom saying something like, "Craig, play a little 'Tea for Two' for us." He looks at her and said, "On the drums?" Not that the line was that hysterical, but the way he said it . . . his dry delivery . . . was priceless.

HERE'S LUCY #10: "LUCY'S WORKING DAUGHTER"

(CBS, DECEMBER 2, 1968), 30 MINUTES

WRITTEN BY: Bob O'Brien

GUEST CAST: Barbara Morrison, Karen Norris, Joan Swift

Kim gets her first after-school job, working as a sales clerk in a dress shop. Lucy, the ever-indulgent mother, not only spends a fortune buying clothes from Kim, but stands up for her when a customer gives her offspring a hard time.

HIGHLIGHTS & TRIVIA

This is the first episode that spotlights Kim. The fashion show sequence is funny, well-written, and a reminder of the days of old. The final scene, where Lucy gives Barbara Morrison's stuffy customer a piece of her mind, is also very satisfying. This offering is a high spot of the first season.

HERE'S LUCY #11: "GUESS WHO OWES LUCY $23.50?"

(CBS, DECEMBER 9, 1968), 30 MINUTES

WRITTEN BY: Fred S. Fox, Seaman Jacobs

GUEST CAST: Van Johnson, Jeff DeBenning

A crook masquerading as Van Johnson comes to Lucy's house, pleading car trouble and asking to use her phone and borrow money. Later, one of Harry's clients wants to pay $50,000 to have a musical comedy movie star sing happy birthday to his pet cow Ethel. Lucy tries to hire her new pal Van, whom she thinks owes her a favor.

HIGHLIGHTS & TRIVIA

This episode is written for Van Johnson to work in a not-so-subtle plug for Ball's latest film *Yours, Mine and Ours*, in which he is a featured player. This celebrity double theme has already been used on the Lucy TV series with Robert Goulet, Ethel Merman, Sid Caesar, and others. It does not get funnier with each reworking. Notice the name of the cow—Ethel? I bet Vivian Vance winced at that one!

Lucie Arnaz

Van Johnson is an ageless sprite, a trouper. He can't hear three words . . . he makes you laugh because of how deaf he is. He has this wonderful self-deprecating way about him. Mom adored Van.

HERE'S LUCY #12: "LUCY THE MATCHMAKER"

(CBS, DECEMBER 16, 1968), 30 MINUTES

WRITTEN BY: Milt Josefsberg, Ray Singer

GUEST CAST: Vivian Vance, Dick Patterson, Rhodes Reason, Alice Backus

Lucy decides it is time to find a girl for Uncle Harry. She seeks the aid of a computer dating service. The computer matches Harry up with Lucy's old pal, Viv.

HIGHLIGHTS & TRIVIA

This is Vivian Vance's first guest appearance on *Here's Lucy*. Before she can even enter the scene, the audience verbally recognizes her. The ovation for her is loud and long. There is still magic seeing Lucille and Vivian together on a stage. Vivian is stockier than we have ever seen her before. This episode places Viv living in Santa Fe, New Mexico. Later shows will have her living back east. The sequined scarf Lucille wears in the dinner scene is the same one she wore in *The Lucille Ball-Desi Arnaz Show* #13, "Lucy Meets the Moustache," in 1960. It is amazing how much time has changed lifestyles since this *Here's Lucy* episode was filmed. For example, a bank of computers is shown that probably doesn't have as much memory or power as a child's personal computer today.

HERE'S LUCY #13: "LUCY AND THE GOLD RUSH"

(CBS, DECEMBER 30, 1968), 30 MINUTES
WRITTEN BY: Howard Harris, Ben Gershman
GUEST CAST: Phil Bruns, Rhodes Reason

Kim and Craig find a rock on a geology field trip, which Lucy uses as a paperweight at work. When a miner visits the office and tells Lucy that the rock contains gold, the family rushes out to find more of the rich ore.

HIGHLIGHTS & TRIVIA

This episode is nothing more than a cartoon. One of the problems with this series is that writers are often brought in who have no background writing for Lucille. It is done to save money, to balance out the year's budget against the more expensive installments. Scripters Harris and Gershman obviously have no feel at this time for what it takes to write a successful *Lucy* script, and no amount of talent can overcome that. Handsome actor Rhodes Reason is often seen on this series in small parts requiring a good looking, macho man.

HERE'S LUCY #14: "LUCY THE FIXER"

(CBS, JANUARY 6, 1969), 30 MINUTES
WRITTEN BY: Milt Josefsberg, Ray Singer

Harry has Lucy come work at his house on a Saturday to get a tax deduction for having a home office. When a lamp doesn't work properly, Lucy decides to fix Harry's electrical wiring.

HIGHLIGHTS & TRIVIA

This one is pure Laurel and Hardy. From moment to moment, the physical comedy builds on itself as Lucy manages to wreck Harry's house. The episode has no plot, just slapstick fun almost to the point of burlesque. Normally, unmotivated humor doesn't work, but in this case it is so carefully rehearsed and performed by Ball and Gordon that it is perfection.

HERE'S LUCY #15: "LUCY AND THE EX-CON"

(CBS, JANUARY 13, 1969), 30 MINUTES
WRITTEN BY: Bob O'Brien
GUEST CAST: Wally Cox, Bruce Gordon, Irving Benson, Larry Blake, Vince Howard, Don Anderson, Tony Dante

Lucy feels sorry for ex-safecracker Rocky Smith (Wally Cox) who applies for a job, so she falsifies his application to win him a job as a security guard. When the establishment at which he is working is robbed, the blame falls on him and on Lucy. Rocky has an idea who actually did commit the robbery, so he and Lucy disguise themselves as little old ladies to capture the real culprit.

HIGHLIGHTS & TRIVIA

Lucie and Desi do not appear in this episode, and Gale's part is small. Most of the show belongs to Lucille and Wally Cox, who have an excellent working relationship. Wally will be a frequent guest on this series, always playing some sort of variation on his famous lead role in TV's *Mr. Peepers* (1952–55).

HERE'S LUCY #16: "LUCY GOES ON STRIKE"

(CBS, JANUARY 20, 1969), 30 MINUTES
WRITTEN BY: Mel Diamond, Al Schwartz
GUEST CAST: Mary Wickes, Whit Bissell, John "Red" Fox

When Harry turns down Lucy's request for a salary raise, she goes on strike. When she later overhears Harry taking out an insurance policy on her life, naming himself as beneficiary, she assumes he is planning to murder her.

HIGHLIGHTS & TRIVIA

It is plots like this that give *Here's Lucy* a bad name. To begin with, what are Harry's actual feelings for his niece and nephew? He takes out an endowment policy to ensure their education, but refuses Lucy a tiny raise to help her make ends meet. The plot situation of Lucy and her kids having to do without because Uncle Harry is cheap is not funny. Second, why would Lucy assume Harry is going to kill her? Is it in his character to be so violent? Jumping to conclusions has always been a theme in *Lucy* TV shows, but the humor comes from the fact that the conclusion is a possibility given the definitions of the characters involved. The problem is, the *Here's Lucy* characters never get defined. In addition, as stated earlier, having a plethora of writers and directors working on the series only ensures it has no overall vision or continuity. This is Mary Wickes' first visit to this new series; she will appear in many future episodes.

HERE'S LUCY #17: "LUCY AND CAROL BURNETT" A.K.A. "LUCY AND THE NEW SCHOOL GYM"

(CBS, JANUARY 27, 1969), 30 MINUTES

WRITTEN BY: Bob O'Brien

GUEST CAST: Carol Burnett, Sean Morgan, Scott Perry, John Lindesmith, Carole Cook, Virginia Hawkins, Pearl Shear, Jerry Rush

Lucy and the kids get Carol Burnett to help them raise money for a new school gym.

HIGHLIGHTS & TRIVIA

The entire plot is revealed in the time it took you to read the above sentence. Most of the episode is the musical show put on as a fundraiser. It is revealed that Kim and Craig attend Angeles High School (though what grades they are attending and when they graduate are never made known). All of Lucille's singing is again dubbed by Carole Cook, and everyone's singing is prerecorded. This is the first opportunity for Lucie and Desi to display their singing and dancing talents on the series, and both do very well. Lucie especially shows a flare for the presentational, Broadway style of performing. As usual, Lucille and Carol seem to be having great fun working together. Burnett makes several appearances on this series through the years; strangely all of such entries are entitled "Lucy and Carol Burnett." This is an entertaining, energetically performed half-hour.

Lucie Arnaz

I always think of Carol Burnett as a theatre person. I mean I know my mother did Wildcat *[on Broadway in 1960], but she never really thought of herself as a theatre person. [Burnett] has a great sense of humor, and is a very nurturing person. Every time we had one of these musical shows, I sort of blossomed. When we had one of these shows, we worked for two weeks. We'd rehearse the musical numbers for the following week's shows after we rehearsed the current week's show. It was like doing summer stock. It was all about constant memorization and working very hard. You got to see professionals like Carol and how hard they would work.*

HERE'S LUCY #18: "LUCY AND THE GREAT AIRPORT CHASE"

(CBS, FEBRUARY 3, 1969), 30 MINUTES

WRITTEN BY: Tommy Thompson

GUEST CAST: Sid Haig, Larry Duran, Walter Jonowitz, Morgan Jones, Albert Reed

When Lucy and the kids take Harry to the airport, the Redhead encounters a secret agent about to be captured. He entrusts a secret formula to her and then takes his own life. Enemy agents chase Lucy and her family all over the airport in a mad scramble to grab that formula.

HIGHLIGHTS & TRIVIA

Although it has moments of great silliness, this offering is actually a wonderfully refreshing change of pace. Filmed entirely on location at Los Angeles International Airport (LAX), it is done like a movie with one camera and (obviously) no audience. Producer Thompson also writes this episode, which is planned as a test to see if the *Here's Lucy* formula can be done on location successfully. At this point in time, *Here's Lucy* is the only U.S. television sitcom currently filmed in front of a live audience. While this outing has many elements of the Beatles film *Help!* (1965), it is funny, well-paced, and well received. It is decided that several second-season entries will be filmed in just such a manner.

Desi Arnaz Jr

I enjoyed doing the location work for this very silly episode. I like it because we had never done it before, and it gave me a chance to learn something new.

HERE'S LUCY #19: "A DATE FOR LUCY"

(CBS, FEBRUARY 10, 1969), 30 MINUTES

WRITTEN BY: Fred S. Fox, Seaman Jacobs

GUEST CAST: Cesar Romero, Mary Jane Croft, Barbara Morrison, Dick Winslow

Lucy and Harry get invited to a swanky party, but Lucy can't find a date. When Kim and Craig learn of her predicament, they match her with a suave, handsome bachelor (Cesar Romero). Unfortunately, he turns out to be a jewel thief.

HIGHLIGHTS & TRIVIA

It is a pleasure to see the Lucy character finally have a romantic interest, and a real reason to get all dressed up. The theme of l'amour for the heroine is rarely used on *Here's Lucy*, which is a shame because it is almost always very successful. This is Mary Jane Croft's first *Here's Lucy*. Named Mary Jane Lewis, just as she was in *The Lucy Show*, the part is almost exactly the same. Although Mary Jane was a regular on the previous Lucy series, she will be used very infrequently for the first four seasons of *Here's Lucy*. Cesar Romero has not costarred with Lucille since the first *Lucille Ball-Desi Arnaz Show* in 1957. Age has not dulled either his good looks or his charming manner.

Lucie Arnaz

Cesar was one of the last, great gentlemen. Debonair. I was always so proud of that because he was Cuban like my father. He and Dad were great friends. He always made every woman feel like he was flirting only with her and that she was a lady, the best thing in the world.

HERE'S LUCY #20: "LUCY THE SHOPPING EXPERT"

(CBS, FEBRUARY 17, 1969), 30 MINUTES

WRITTEN BY: Milt Josefsberg, Al Schwartz
GUEST CAST: William Lanteau, Ernest Sarracino, Irwin Charone

Two important life lessons converge as Craig gets his first job (at a supermarket) and Lucy teaches Kim how to do the grocery shopping.

HIGHLIGHTS & TRIVIA

Although it doesn't sound like much on paper, this is actually a superior effort. To begin with, both interlocking plots are well motivated and grounded in reality. The scene where Kim brings home ethnic goodies because Mr. Goldapper the grocer recommended them is an inside joke, as Goldapper is Gary Morton's real last name. The moment at lunch where Gale Gordon fumbles through an explanation, literally, of the birds and the bees is very funny and expertly handled. It is not an easy scene to perform and is done as an uninterrupted monologue. The entire supermarket sequence is a scream, thanks in part to superb support by William Lanteau as the stressed-out market manager. Lanteau is a favorite of Lucille's, and he will be used extensively on *Here's Lucy*.

JACK BENNY'S BIRTHDAY SPECIAL

(NBC, FEBRUARY 17, 1969), 60 MINUTES

EXECUTIVE PRODUCED BY: Irving Fein
PRODUCED AND DIRECTED BY: Fred De Cordova
WRITTEN BY: Gerald Gardner and Dee Caruso, Hilliard Marks, Sam Perrin and George Balzer
CHOREOGRAPHY: Jack Baker
ANNOUNCER: Roy Rowan.
CAST: Jack Benny (host), Eddie "Rochester" Anderson, Ann-Margret, Lucille Ball, Dan Blocker, Dennis Day, Jerry Lewis, Rovan, Benny Rubin, Lawrence Welk, Don Wilson

Lucille joins Jack during his monologue. She wears a black velvet gown with gold sequins and brocade; her voice is very raspy and her makeup is quite heavy. She does two cameos, in a western sketch and in a birthday cake salute. Her main contribution is a flashback sequence, where she lip-synchs to Carole Cook singing "Big Spender." In a lavender-bodiced dance-hall-girl outfit with feathers and a big feather hat, she prances like the chorine she had once been, her legs still incredibly shapely.

HERE'S LUCY #21: "LUCY GETS HER MAN"

(CBS, FEBRUARY 24, 1969), 30 MINUTES

WRITTEN BY: Fred S. Fox, Seaman Jacobs
GUEST CAST: Victor Buono, Mary Wickes, Robert S. Carson

Harry's old army buddy (Victor Buono) needs a stenographer to help him catch a possible counterintelligence spy, so Lucy is recruited to help out.

HIGHLIGHTS & TRIVIA

Three spy stories in one season? Are the writers already running out of ideas? The episode is amusing in a goofy way, with Gale Gordon garnering most of the laughs in a rash of impersonations during the hotel sequence.

Lucie Arnaz

The only thing memorable about this episode is that black wig Mom wore. Victor Buono [a well-known Hollywood character actor, best known for his role in the Bette Davis-Joan Crawford 1962 horror film, What Ever Happened to Baby Jane?*] was a nice man, but just another big star. Very big!*

HERE'S LUCY #22: "LUCY'S SAFARI"

(CBS, MARCH 3, 1969), 30 MINUTES

WRITTEN BY: Bob O'Brien
GUEST CAST: Howard Keel, Janos Prohaska

Lucy, Harry, and the kids become involved with big game hunter Stanley Livingstone as they try to recapture the Gorboona, which has escaped from a local zoo.

HIGHLIGHTS & TRIVIA

This may be the single worst *Here's Lucy* episode. The plot is stupid, and the jokes are creaky. Movie star Howard Keel's musical talents are wasted. Lucille is so hoarse from rehearsing her jungle scream all week that her voice is grating and annoying, despite her efforts to be amusing. For some reason, both *The Lucy Show* and this new offshoot series are obsessed with bears, apes, and monkeys. These installments are always silly, poorly written, and usually a waste of viewers' time. However, this one is truly bad.

Desi Arnaz Jr.

I wish I could say I wasn't in this one! It was certainly my favorite fashion statement, with the boots laced up and the knee socks! I didn't get a lot of great dialog, but look at the clothes I got to wear on the show, never mind the hair styles!

Lucie Arnaz

Every time my mother did a show where she had to be screaming, she'd get terribly hoarse and lose her voice. She never learned how to use her throat. She needed to have taken some singing lessons. By Thursday, her voice would be gone. That week, she knew she couldn't do it, and because of that it wouldn't be funny. And these gorilla and bear shows weren't all that funny. It was stretching things to a point so beyond reality that we would run into these wild animals so often.

HERE'S LUCY #23: "LUCY AND TENNESSEE ERNIE'S FUN FARM"

(CBS, MARCH 10, 1969), 30 MINUTES

WRITTEN BY: Milt Josefsberg, Ray Singer
GUEST CAST: Tennessee Ernie Ford, the Backporch Majority, Rusty Richards, Jet Sharon, Kathy Beaudine, Kittie McCue, Kyra Carleton

Farmer Ernie Epperson needs help on his farm. Realizing that such outdoor work is actually a tonic for the pressures of big city life, Lucy and Harry have a brainstorm for a musical TV commercial extolling the virtues of the restful farm while getting customers to pitch in and help out with the chores.

HIGHLIGHTS & TRIVIA

While these shows with Ernie Ford have a certain inescapable bucolic charm, this is another episode too short on plot and too long on music. The performances are fine, although all of the singing and instrumentals are prerecorded. The syndicated version of this episode, like many of them, is so choppy it is almost impossible to follow the action.

Desi Arnaz Jr.

We had this whole setup in the finale with me playing all sorts of percussion instruments: congas, and bongos, and drums, and tymbalis, and all sorts of things. And I played them live. Well, I just didn't like what I had done. So we did the opposite of what is done with most musical numbers. I went back in and rerecorded my work to match the film. I should have left it alone. It was almost impossible to get it done right, and I was about a beat and a third behind the movements.

HERE'S LUCY #24: "LUCY HELPS CRAIG GET A DRIVER'S LICENSE"

(CBS, MARCH 17, 1969), 30 MINUTES

WRITTEN BY: Milt Josefsberg, Ray Singer
GUEST CAST: Jack Gilford, Herkie Styles, Sid Gould, Joseph Mell, Ray Kellogg

It is Craig's sixteenth birthday, and like many young people he wants to get his driver's license. All would be perfect if Lucy would not interfere.

HIGHLIGHTS & TRIVIA

Lucy as an interfering nudge is a theme that started back in the 1966–67 season of *The Lucy Show*. What is different here is brilliant actor Jack Gilford as the man who gives Craig his driving test. His slow burn and nervous reactions to Lucy's schtick make this outing really work. Desi is also very effective in one of the few installments that allows him an opportunity to shine.

Desi Arnaz Jr.

"Jack Gilford was great. He was like a genius. He was very personable, and that's what made that episode so good. It also helped that this was a real situation that everyone has faced, so there was a strong identification for the audience. A very funny show."

This is the last show of the season, and the last Lucy installment for long-time employee Tommy Thompson. Lucille decides that nepotism is the name of the game, and brings in her cousin Cleo Smith (who worked with Ball on her 1966 special *Lucy in London*) to produce the rest of the *Here's Lucy* series.

THE LUCY SHOW

(CBS, MARCH 24-SEPTEMBER 15, 1969), 30 MINUTES

While all of Ball's series have always gone on hiatus for the summer, this year selected reruns of *The Lucy Show* are aired in prime time instead of a summer replacement series. Only the first week features an episode from the Vivian Vance years ("Lucy and the Ceramic Cat," episode #74, aired for the first time in color). The rest are reruns from *The Lucy Show*'s last three seasons (1965–68).

A DINAH SHORE SPECIAL: "LIKE HEP"

(NBC, APRIL 13, 1969), 60 MINUTES

PRODUCED BY: Carolyn Raskin
DIRECTED BY: Marc Breaux
WRITTEN BY: Chris Bearde, Coslough Johnson
CAST: Dinah Shore (host), Lucille Ball, Victor Buono, Elisha Cook Jr., Lorne Greene, Dick Martin, Greg Morris, Della Reese, Diana Ross, Dan Rowan, the Smothers Brothers

Dinah Shore had tired of doing her long-running weekly variety show for NBC and retired in 1963. In the late 1960s, she chose an even more difficult task, hosting a morning program for the network every weekday called *Dinah's Place*. This special is part of the deal. Occasionally, Lucille wouldn't give her all to a guest performance; this show is such a case.

Dinah plays a singing detective whose foe (Lucille) literally kills her when she sings. Ball does the same off-key singing bit she'd been doing since 1951. Comedian Dick Martin portrays a show business agent who grooms three hillbilly singers (Lucille, Dinah, and Diana Ross) for stardom. Dick is fine, but the ladies just walk through their bits. "The Fairy Godmother's Revenge" features Lucille in the title role as a cigar-chomping wand carrier, with Dinah as Bo Peep and Diana as Snow White. D and D were never known for their oncamera comedy, and they telegraph every joke (something Lucille hates and would never allow on her own show) by letting the audience know that something funny is coming up. Unfortunately, nothing humorous materializes.

"Like Hep" refers to the jive talk popular when Dinah first became a star during World War II. The then-current 1960s parallel phrase was to be "hip," and the show is meant to spoof the times, but there isn't much satire. In short, this show doesn't work at all.

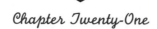

Chapter Twenty-One

1969-70 Season

HERE'S LUCY: THE SECOND SEASON

TECHNICAL REGULARS: Executive produced by Gary Morton; produced by Cleo Smith; script consultant: Milt Josefsberg; makeup by Hal King; hairstyling by Irma Kusely; music by Wilbur Hatch, Marl Young
CAST REGULARS: Lucille Ball (Lucy Carter); Gale Gordon (Harrison Otis Carter); Lucie Arnaz (Kim Carter);Desi Arnaz Jr. (Craig Carter); Roy Rowan (announcer)

HERE'S LUCY #25: "LUCY GOES TO THE AIR FORCE ACADEMY, PART ONE"

(CBS, SEPTEMBER 22, 1969), 30 MINUTES
DIRECTED BY: George Marshall
WRITTEN BY: Gene Thompson
GUEST CAST: Roy Roberts, Frank Marth, Beverly Garland

Lucy, Harry, Kim, and Craig all pile into a recreational vehicle to drive it to San Francisco for its owners. Lucy decides that a trip to Colorado to the Air Force Academy is a logical side venture, and manages to throw the rigidly controlled military institution into pandemonium.

HIGHLIGHTS & TRIVIA

This episode is the first of a four-part story sequence. Buoyed by the success of location filming in the first season of *Here's Lucy* (1968–69), Lucille Ball and company produce four episodes totally outside of studio sound stages. This episode, which was created with the cooperation of the Air Force and the states of Colorado and Arizona, is, like the other three installments, heavy on physical comedy and beautiful location photography. It is a difficult shoot, requiring all sorts of technical wonders not usually needed for a Lucy production. Lucille's wigs and makeup must be constantly changed and fixed as she faces the rigors of outdoor shooting. Practically the entire Air Force Academy appears as extras, with filming done right in the dormitories and administrative buildings. Production assistance (read that as cooperation and money) are provided by the Academy, as this is an excellent TV commercial for the Air Force at a time when the public is very down on the military due to the war in Vietnam. The scene where Lucy is dragged by a floor polisher through the halls of one of the buildings is accomplished by Lucille without a stunt double. A special dolly is placed under her body to glide her along, and the film is speeded up so she appears to be moving much faster than she actually is. Roy Roberts, a regular on *The Lucy Show*, returns here to play the Superintendent. George Marshall is a veteran director of motion pictures, making his small-screen debut here in that capacity.

Desi Arnaz Jr.

This was BIG fun for us. We had never been to the Colorado River before, and going to the Academy was a huge thrill for us. We had this genius director George Marshall working with us. He was an action director, and for Here's Lucy *these were action shows. My mother loved doing all the stunts in the wet suits. Mom liked having that kind of physicality.*

Beverly Garland
(ACTOR)

I accepted this tiny part playing a secretary just to say I had been on a show with Lucille Ball. I was already starring on My Three Sons *[1969–72], but I didn't care. Lucy asked for me because she knew my work, and that was all I had to know.*

HERE'S LUCY #26: "LUCY GOES TO THE AIR FORCE ACADEMY, PART TWO"

(CBS, SEPTEMBER 29, 1969), 30 MINUTES
DIRECTED BY: George Marshall
WRITTEN BY: Gene Thompson
GUEST CAST: Roy Roberts

This is the second entry of the four-part opening show for this season. Lucy and her family finally get things straight with the academy.

Desi Arnaz Jr.
I was always a little shy about doing shows where I had to wear shorts or bathing suits or go shirtless. I was concerned about my appearance, because in my mind I was still little dumpy Desi. I didn't see how thin I was, or that I was in good shape. I had no influence in how I was dressed . . . make sure you print it just that way! There was actually supposed to be some humor in what I wore, to make fun of my "mod" clothes. In real life, I had more of a surfer look.

HERE'S LUCY #27: "LUCY AND THE INDIAN CHIEF"

(CBS, OCTOBER 6, 1969), 30 MINUTES
DIRECTED BY: George Marshall
WRITTEN BY: Gene Thompson
GUEST CAST: Paul Fix, Mickey Manners, Iron Eyes Cody

This is part three of the four-part episode opener. Driving through Arizona on their way back to California from Colorado, Lucy stops at a quiet pool to drink some water where she meets an old Native American. Following him back to his Navajo hogan (abode), she accepts a piece of jewelry. Now the aging chief thinks they are married, and gifts her with some land: the entire state of Utah!

HIGHLIGHTS & TRIVIA
The production company decides to use authentic Navajos rather than import extras from Hollywood. They meet with the Navajo Nation Council, which gives its blessing to the endeavor. The Navajos are sticklers for authenticity, and insist that the door to the hogan be moved from north to south as is the custom. The carpenters readily comply, because the Navajos won't work until this is accomplished. The Nation also approves of the reversal of the direction of a sacred ceremonial dance, but only after Lucille convinces a dissenting medicine man that it not only will not bring them bad luck but would look better on TV.

Lucille Ball
The Navajos were fine actors, and a pleasure to deal with. Their stoic appearance belies a great sense of humor. We were very proud of this episode.

Lucie Arnaz
This was a great experience for us, because it changed everything instantaneously. We went from the three-camera theatre situation to shooting like a movie. And neither Desi nor I had done that before.

HERE'S LUCY #28: "LUCY RUNS THE RAPIDS"

(CBS, OCTOBER 13, 1969), 30 MINUTES
DIRECTED BY: George Marshall
WRITTEN BY: Gene Thompson
GUEST CAST: Rob Hughes, George Marshall

This is the final segment of the four-part opener for the season. Parking the recreational vehicle at the Grand Canyon by the Colorado River, Lucy spies a raft and is inspired to go for a ride. It turns out to be the trip of her life, as she shoots down the rapids.

HIGHLIGHTS & TRIVIA
To film this installment requires the logistical planning of an army! Schedules have to be coordinated so the crew of more than fifty are transported to the floor of the Grand Canyon safely and swiftly. Shooting time is limited, because the sheer cliffs of the canyon allow only a short time of bright sunlight to penetrate through. Coordination with the Bureau of Reclamation, operator of dams along the Colorado River, is imperative. To get the rapids for the necessary scenes, the Glen Canyon Dam has to release water. To do that, the Hoover Dam downstream has to be notified first that they could expect a certain amount of cubic feet of water. The dam has to release a certain amount of water at a preplanned moment, otherwise electricity would be generated before there is a demand for it.

Director George Marshall acts like a field marshal, commandeering a sandbar to be made into a shooting platform. The entire crew is sent to the bar in rafts, totally overtaking it. Ten disgruntled fishermen are removed to another area under protest. Lucille does almost all of her own stunts, spending hours in the freezing water. She wears a wet suit and acts like a kid!

Lucie Arnaz

My mother had a great time doing this episode. The water was so damn cold, and Desi and I were the only ones not wearing wet suits. We had to run off the dock, dive in the water, swim all around the boat, climb in and deliver two lines. George Marshall yelled "cut," and then I screamed, "Geeeezuz Keerist this water is cold." Gale Gordon used to do a hysterical impression of me cursing at the age of eighteen. We had to be in that boat for four days, sitting in several inches of water. When I get home, I was so sick with an infection that I almost had to be hospitalized. I was a very sick girl!

Desi Arnaz Jr.

I loved it that the water was cold. I was a sixteen-year-old boy, and this was fun stuff . . . diving, swimming, jumping. I had a ball!

HERE'S LUCY #29: "LUCY AND HARRY'S TONSILS"

(CBS, OCTOBER 20, 1969), 30 MINUTES

DIRECTED BY: George Marshall
WRITTEN BY: Milt Josefsberg, Ray Singer
GUEST CAST: Jack Collins, Paula Stewart, Adele Claire, Mary Wickes

Harry goes into the hospital to have his tonsils out, and is desperate to be left alone and get back home. As quickly as possible Lucy, Kim, and Craig ensure his wishes are not met, and a sexy nurse changes his mind about going home.

HIGHLIGHTS & TRIVIA

Jack Collins (seen in this installment as Harry's doctor) has become a Lucy regular. He will appear on a spate of *Here's Lucy* episodes, including the final outing. Mary Wickes (as the day nurse) is always a delight, and makes the most of her every moment oncamera. The scene where the Carter family plays charades to understand that Harry is allergic to flowers is pretty silly, but does contain one of the few pranks perpetrated by the crew. Gale expects the legs on his bed to break. Instead, the special effects crew rigs it to snap shut, forcing Gale to be folded in half. Although he masks his laughter well, careful viewing shows a very startled actor trying to cover his surprise and continue with the scene. Paula Stewart plays the sexy nurse; she was Ball's Broadway costar in *Wildcat* (1960).

HERE'S LUCY #30: "LUCY AND THE ANDREWS SISTERS"

(CBS, OCTOBER 27, 1969), 30 MINUTES

DIRECTED BY: George Marshall
WRITTEN BY: Milt Josefsberg, Ray Singer
GUEST CAST: Patty Andrews, John McLaren, Gary Morton

Patty Andrews comes to the Unique Employment Agency to hire two girls to play her sisters for an Andrews Sisters Fan Club reunion. Lucy gets the assignment for herself and Kim, but on the night of the show manages to break all the records to which the girls are to lip-synch. So, the ladies are forced to sing the songs live.

HIGHLIGHTS & TRIVIA

Although LaVerne Andrews has passed away by this point, Maxene Andrews is still very much alive but totally ignored in this episode. The surviving sisters have a love/hate relationship that will remain that way until Maxene's death many years later. All of the singing is prerecorded and lip-synched by the trio. The music (including "Bei Mir Bist Du Schoen," "Pistol Packin' Mama," and "Apple Blossom Time") is well received by the studio audience, which applauds so much between numbers that the reaction has to be cut out of the final print. This is one of the best of the second season efforts, enhanced by the excitement of working with the guest star. The character name Elroy Sherwood—the head of the fan club played by John McLaren—is an insider joke. Elroy and Sherwood are the first names of two of the Brothers Schwartz, the men behind TV's *Gilligan's Island* (1964–67) and *The Brady Bunch* (1969–74).

Lucie Arnaz

Patty Andrews is a great broad, a fabulous broad. She had a great sense of humor, and of course we got to sing all those wonderful harmonies. We had to prerecord the medley because the quality of the singing on the sound stages wasn't up to par, but it was our voices.

Patty Andrews

(SINGER)

I loved working with Lucy. And that little Lucie was so talented! This was one of my favorite television appearances, and Lucy told me it was the favorite Here's Lucy *show she'd done up to that point.*

HERE'S LUCY #31: "LUCY'S BURGLAR ALARM"

(CBS, NOVEMBER 3, 1969), 30 MINUTES

DIRECTED BY: George Marshall
WRITTEN BY: Milt Josefsberg, Ray Singer
GUEST CAST: Guy Marks, Elliot Reid, Vanda Barra

Lucy is held up at gunpoint in her home. When a handsome detective comes to visit her at work the next day advising an expensive burglar alarm, Lucy wants to borrow the needed funds from Harry. When he declines, the kids jerry-rig one of their own, which naturally traps cheap Uncle Harry.

HIGHLIGHTS & TRIVIA

Elliot Reid (the detective) has made numerous appearances with Lucille, going all the way back to radio's *My Favorite Husband* in the late 1940s. The intricate special effects for the burglar alarm (rigged by Les Warburton) make the cast tense and nervous, as a wrong cue will cost thousands of dollars in retakes. Naturally, it is all done perfectly in one take thanks to the professionalism of everyone concerned with *Here's Lucy*.

HERE'S LUCY #32: "LUCY AT THE DRIVE-IN MOVIE"

(CBS, NOVEMBER 10, 1969), 30 MINUTES

DIRECTED BY: George Marshall
WRITTEN BY: Milt Josefsberg, Ray Singer
GUEST CAST: Rob Hughes, Larry J. Blake, Jackie Joseph

When Kim starts seeing a lot of classmate Alan Stevens, Lucy gets suspicious. When the young couple go to a drive-in movie, Lucy and Harry disguise themselves as hippies to spy on them.

HIGHLIGHTS & TRIVIA

Although Ball and Gordon are very funny in their costumes, the writing in this entry is very weak. The theme of spying on someone becomes an unfortunate staple of this series, and it is never very well done. This is an expensive shoot because of all the cars needed for the drive-in scene. They are mostly older, used cars. Jackie Joseph plays a character named Jackie Berry, which is the actor's real name as she is married at the time to performer Ken Berry.

HERE'S LUCY #33: "LUCY AND THE USED CAR DEALER"

(CBS, NOVEMBER 17, 1969), 30 MINUTES

DIRECTED BY: George Marshall
WRITTEN BY: David Ketchum, Bruce Shelly
GUEST CAST: Milton Berle

Kim and Craig are bamboozled into buying a lemon from a fast-talking used car dealer. Lucy decides to teach the crook, who advertises on television, a lesson he will never forget.

HIGHLIGHTS & TRIVIA

Milton Berle has a previous professional engagement he cancels to star in this episode. This is a very funny installment, with Berle in top form as the shady car dealer. Once again, there dare not be any fluffed cues, because the rigged used car with the fireworks would take hours to re-rig. Episode cowriter David Ketchum is better known to TV fans as Agent 13 on *Get Smart* (1965–70).

Milton Berle

(PERFORMER/LEGEND)

"I was intrigued by these guys who do the commercials for used cars, especially one bald guy who shall remain nameless. I was eager to do a parody of him, and besides, playing a used car dealer gave me a chance to do all of my used material. No laugh? You try being funny as a quote in a book!"

HERE'S LUCY #34: "LUCY THE CEMENT WORKER"

(CBS, NOVEMBER 24, 1969), 30 MINUTES

DIRECTED BY: George Marshall
WRITTEN BY: George Balzer, Sam Perrin
GUEST CAST: Mary Jane Croft, Harry Hickox, Sid Gould, William Tannen, Paul Winchell

The kids need fifteen dollars. Lucy is broke, so Harry pays her to do some extra tasks, which includes taking an heirloom ring to be engraved. Guess who thinks she's lost the ring in wet cement?

HIGHLIGHTS & TRIVIA

Writers Balzer and Perrin have made a good effort and only just miss with this installment. There are several funny comedy scenes (including one that liberally borrows the knife-throwing bit from *I Love Lucy* episode #72, "Lucy Tells the Truth" of 1953) and a plausible plot. Lucy dresses in drag again, this time as a cement worker using a jackhammer. She handles it expertly. What is missing is the warmth and wit of her previous series. Ball can still handle physical comedy in genius fashion, but that was not the only thing that made her earlier work so popular. There is still no character development, nor any engaging relationships between the show's recurring characters. Paul Winchell plays a dual role here, as both the French knife thrower and the little old jeweler.

THE CAROL BURNETT SHOW

(CBS, NOVEMBER 24, 1969), 60 MINUTES

PRODUCED BY: Joe Hamilton
DIRECTED BY: Dave Powers
WRITTEN BY: Stan Burns, Mike Marmer, Hal Goodman, Larry Klien, Don Hinkley, Kenny Solms, Gail Parent, Bill Angelos, Buz Kohan
CAST: Carol Burnett (host), Lucille Ball, George Carlin, Harvey Korman, Vicki Lawrence, Lyle Waggoner

This is another payback for Carol Burnett's appearance on one of Lucille's TV shows. Ball does not do well on Carol's turf. Quite often Lucille seems as if she is walking through her part. At least, the show opens quite cleverly. Carol has been mailed an original song by a real-life amateur, Sue Vogelsanger. Burnett arranges for the composer to be in the audience the night of the taping, and has a production number mounted based on the song. The entire chorus dances around huge letters that eventually spell out Sue's name.

Lucille's contributions are not nearly as intriguing. The only skit that is truly funny has the two redheads as airline flight attendants (again) competing for a bonus award in efficiency. Harvey Korman boards the plane bound for Miami in costume as a Cuban. The obvious hijacking jokes are made, until Lucille finally asks Harvey, "Is that a Cuban accent?" Startled, he asks, "What makes you say that?" Lucille turns to him smugly and replies, "If there's one thing I know, sir, it's a Cuban accent!" This is the first public reference Lucille has made to Desi since the beginning of *The Lucy Show* back in 1962 and the audience loves it. It literally stops the show. The weakest moment in the show occurs when the cast does a *Bob & Carol & Ted & Alice* (1969) movie parody. Wearing a blond wig that does not flatter her, Our Redhead appears to read her entire part directly off the cue cards. Perhaps she is usually not allowed the same amount of rehearsal time on variety appearances as she is used to on her own show. The episode ends with a long musical take-off on the Dolly Sisters. Although Carol Burnett claims this is one of her favorite all-time sketches, it gives Lucille little chance to be humorous and runs very long.

HERE'S LUCY #35: "LUCY AND JOHNNY CARSON"

(CBS, DECEMBER 1, 1969), 30 MINUTES

DIRECTED BY: George Marshall
WRITTEN BY: Milt Josefsberg, Ray Singer
GUEST CAST: Johnny Carson, Ed McMahon, DeDe Ball, Sid Gould, Jim Henaghan, Sid Kane, Michael McClay, Mike Nicoletti, Lawrence Temple

After crashing *The Tonight Show* audience without tickets, Lucy and Harry win free meals at the Brown Derby restaurant when Lucy plays "Stump the Band." At the eatery, Lucy also crashes Johnny Carson's table.

HIGHLIGHTS & TRIVIA

Lucille is annoying throughout this episode, as her character does one pushy, stupid, or dishonest thing after another. Johnny Carson and Ed McMahon are funny and well-written for, although Carson remains too aware that he is acting for an audience. The entire Brown Derby bit, with the waiter spilling drinks on Carson, is stolen right from the 1955 *I Love Lucy* episode "L.A. at Last" (#114), although not nearly as well done here. The woman Johnny turns to in the audience in the show within a show is DeDe Ball, Lucille's mother. Two of the ushers, Michael McClay and Mike Nicoletti, are the progeny of Ball's public relations man Howard McClay and actor Louis A. Nicoletti respectively. Michael will publish a picture book about *I Love Lucy* in 1995.

Lucille Ball is not yet a regular guest on *The Tonight Show* with Johnny Carson, but will appear more frequently with him during the 1970s. Ball seems uncomfortable on these talk fests with Carson, offering a cold demeanor. Sometimes a bogus reason for appearing is offered her, such as extolling the use of jojoba root or earthworms for better health. Lucille's personal life and past are almost never discussed. In the 1980s, Lucille will prefer to share the stage with Carson's permanent guest-host Joan Rivers. These encounters take the form of hero-worship. Ball is much warmer on such occasions, discussing her grandchildren, her marriages, and her favorite recollections of *I Love Lucy*.

JACK BENNY'S NEW LOOK

(NBC, DECEMBER 3, 1969), 60 MINUTES

PRODUCED BY: Irving Fein, Norman Abbott
DIRECTED BY: Norman Abbott
WRITTEN BY: Al Gordon, Hal Goldman, Hilliard Marks, Sam Perrin, Hugh Wedlock Jr.
CAST: Jack Benny (host), Eddie "Rochester" Anderson, Lucille Ball, George Burns, Gregory Peck, Gary Puckett and the Union Gap, Nancy Sinatra

Lucille's entire contribution to the proceedings is to come out as a surprise to Jack, slap him across the face, and yell, "How dare you not invite me to be on your special!"

THE ANN-MARGRET SHOW: FROM HOLLYWOOD WITH LOVE

(CBS, DECEMBER 6, 1969), 60 MINUTES

PRODUCED BY: Burt Rosen, David Winters
DIRECTED AND STAGED BY: David Winters
WRITTEN BY: Bill Angelos, Buz Kohan, Gail Parent, Kenny Solms; music by Lenny Stack
CAST: Ann-Margret (host), Lucille Ball, Dean Martin, Larry Storch, the Watts 103rd Street Rhythm Band

Every once in awhile Lucille negotiates a TV project that really churns up her creative juices, and this is one of them. Besides having tremendous respect for Ann-Margret's talent, Ball always loves prancing and clowning in musical numbers. Not only does she get to be funny here, Lucille gets to be glamorous. This is one of Ball's best variety appearances, and again demonstrates what she could have accomplished had she had the courage to abandon her sitcom and do a TV variety show.

Ann-Margret and Lucille's duet starts with an establishing shot of the stage door at Paramount studios (formerly Desilu) where *Here's Lucy* is shot. Back at the studio, star Lucille Ball makes her exit to her enthralled fans (something which never happens in real life as the audience is escorted away from the sound stage after each filming) from the stage door, dressed in a multi-colored sheath with a chiffon print overlay. The camera cuts to Ann-Margret and Lucille as "Autograph Annie and Celebrity Lou," groupies who are there to get her autograph.

In character as "Celebrity Lou," Lucille wears a black wig with a flowered hat and a ridiculous blouse with a green pleated skirt. The two ladies sing an original number called (what else?) "Autograph Annie and Celebrity Lou." They lip-synch poorly, but at least the voice belongs to Lucille, and the choreography by David Winters is wonderful. It is obvious Ball is having a marvelous time.

HERE'S LUCY #36: "LUCY AND THE GENERATION GAP"

(CBS, DECEMBER 8, 1969), 30 MINUTES

DIRECTED BY: Jack Baker
WRITTEN BY: Fred S. Fox, Seaman Jacobs
GUEST CAST: Lesley Evans, Cecil Gold, Victor Sen Yung, Sheila Dehner, Tara Glynn, Maritz Ko, Fran Lee, Leslie McRae, Joanie Webster

Kim and Craig have written a musical for their high school that deals with the generation gap, and enlist Lucy and Harry to costar with them.

HIGHLIGHTS & TRIVIA

This is the most complex in-studio shoot of the season, requiring many changes of set, costuming, and makeup as the cast parodies intergenerational relationships in Roman times, the "Gay '90s," and the future space age. The plot is thrown away in minutes, allowing the cast to spend most of the episode performing the show within the show. Both Lucie and Desi really shine, and this makes it a most satisfying installment. The junior Arnazes are finally emerging with personalities of their own, and their musical and comedy talents are obvious. Lucie is becoming a very pretty young woman, and Desi's smoldering sexuality cannot be hidden even by the series' antiseptic scripts.

Director Jack Baker is Ball's longtime choreographer; this is one of the few times he receives TV director credit.

HERE'S LUCY #37: "LUCY AND THE BOGIE AFFAIR"

(CBS, DECEMBER 15, 1969), 30 MINUTES

DIRECTED BY: Herbert Kenwith
WRITTEN BY: Pat McCormick, Jim McGinn
GUEST CAST: Jack LaLanne, Steve March, Sherry Alberoni, Irwin Charone, Eugene Molnar, Debbie Wescott, Lord Nelson (the Dog)

Craig and Kim find a sheepdog caught in a rainstorm and bring it home with them. They call it "Bogie" after Humphrey Bogart, and the family soon learns that Bogie is decidedly female when she gives birth to a litter of pups in the Carter kitchen. The pups are soon given away, but Uncle Harry finds out that there is a reward for a lost sheepdog and her pups that sounds a lot like Bogie.

HIGHLIGHTS & TRIVIA

This is Herbert Kenwith's bow as a director of this series. He is a long-standing and close friend of Ball's, and directed her in *Dream Girl* in summer stock in 1948. Kenwith has a very strong hand as a director, and under his guidance this series gains a flair that will be lost when others take over the helm. Actor Steve March is the biological son of crooner Mel Torme and the adopted son of Arnaz family friend actor Hal March. He is a fine singer and music producer. The guest dog, Lord Nelson, is making his fourth appearance with Lucille. During rehearsal he playfully jumps at her head, missing it by inches but crashing the coffee table in the living room set.

Herbert Kenwith

(DIRECTOR)

My relationship with Lucille started in late 1947 when I had a theatre at Princeton and I blackmailed her into doing Elmer Rice's Dream Girl *for me at the theatre. She was in New York without Desi, and I went to see her at her suite at the Hampshire House Hotel. We were discussing her coming to do a play at my theatre, when she had to interrupt our conversation to do an interview. The reporter came and started inquiring as to why she was in New York, and began to push Lucille for a response. "Surely," the reporter fished at Lucille, "you must be here for a purpose. What is it?" Not knowing what to say, or maybe looking to cover up whatever her real purpose was, she answered that she was going to do a play at my theatre, and introduced me as her producer. I was astonished. The story got printed in the papers. When Lucille actually read the play, she said [the lead part] was longer than [that of] Hamlet and she didn't want to do it. So I went up to Actors' Equity [the stage actors' union] and asked if her interview constituted a contract. They said it was a thin line, but that I could prevail. Lucille did the play, and she was a huge success with sellout business.*

After that, Lucille and I were in constant contact with one another. One night many years later, I was having dinner with Lucy and her mother in Beverly Hills. DeDe [Lucille's mother] turned to me and said, "You know, Lucy is going to need a new director. What would you think of directing Lucy's show?" I told her that I had no idea that Lucille was having director trouble. Lucille then chimed in, "Herbie (and I hate being called Herbie) I'd just love it if you'd direct my show! Would you consent to directing me?" I told her that I thought it could be quite a challenge, and then DeDe interrupted me. "If you agree, " she said, "just know that Lucy is a bitch." Lucille and DeDe immediately got into it. "I'm not a bitch," she exclaimed, "I'm a perfectionist and I like things done a certain way!" I told Lucille that I didn't think we'd be in conflict, and that I accepted.

The first day of rehearsal, Gary [Morton] detained me at his office, making me late for rehearsal. I am never, ever late for anything. When I got to the rehearsal, everyone was already seated at the long, rectangular read-through table. Lucille said, "Herbert, will you sit down there?" I said, "No. I won't sit at the head of a table or the foot of a table. I want to sit on the side." "Herbert," she said, "I want you to sit down there, if you don't mind!" So we are having our first conflict right there in front of all those people. They're all watching us like a tennis match, their heads going back and forth. People reluctantly began to move their chairs and make room for me.

Lucille was in total charge. Nine times out of ten she was right about the way things were done, or at least she was right as far as her own involvement was concerned. But she needed to be stood up to. Once I had to say to her, "You do not know everything! There are some people who do know what they are doing, and I am one of them."

Gary Morton

(EXECUTIVE PRODUCER)

Lucille thought that she perhaps had made a mistake hiring Herb Kenwith to direct Here's Lucy. *He made mistakes and missed shots. He also didn't know comedy the way Lucy liked. Lucille could have directed every show herself, but it was very difficult to do the show from start to finish in four days. The smart directors learned from her, grew, and adapted. The others disappeared. Herb is a talented man, and was very close to Lucy personally, but the working relationship between them [didn't pan out].*

HERE'S LUCY #38: "LUCY PROTECTS HER JOB"

(CBS, DECEMBER 22, 1969), 30 MINUTES

DIRECTED BY: Danny Dayton
WRITTEN BY: Sam Perrin, Ralph Goodman
GUEST CAST: Mary Jane Croft, Robert S. Carson, Wanda Clark

When Harry suddenly suggests that overworked Lucy hire an assistant, she fears he is looking to replace her. So Lucy enlists the aid of Kim as the most annoying, inept secretary in history.

HIGHLIGHTS & TRIVIA

This episode is very funny, due entirely to Lucie Arnaz, who emerges here as a comedy force with which to be reckoned. Her characterization of dimwitted "Shoiley Shopenauer" is well defined and her comedy timing is impeccable. The production team wakes up after this entry, and begins to develop shows to showcase Miss Arnaz' comedy and musical abilities. Naturally, this is one of Lucie Arnaz' favorite *Here's Lucy* episodes. Notice the secretary whom Lucy interviews in the first scene. It is Lucille Ball's personal secretary Wanda Clark, who is beloved by everyone involved with Ball's TV work.

HERE'S LUCY #39: "LUCY THE HELPFUL MOTHER"

(CBS, DECEMBER 29, 1969), 30 MINUTES

DIRECTED BY: Herbert Kenwith
WRITTEN BY: Milt Josefsberg, Al Schwartz

Harry yells at Lucy because her phone is always busy, but this is due to having two teenagers who are constantly making calls. The kids persuade Lucy to get them their own phone lines if they earn the money to pay for them. Kim is hired to babysit for a pet store's inventory; Craig gets a job blowing up balloons and gluing wings on toy airplanes. Guess who ends up doing all the work?

HIGHLIGHTS & TRIVIA

There is a long scene of block comedy given to Lucille that allows her to really shine, but also points up one of the deficiencies of the show scripts now being written. Scribes Josefsberg and Schwartz build a cornucopia of objects for Lucille to play with, including glue, special effects piranhas, and a live chimp. The script sets everything up for her, but then doesn't direct Ball how to carry it out. Although director Herbert Kenwith is helpful with suggestions, Lucille Ball is not Red Skelton. She does not do improvisational work. Her best scripts give her detailed instructions not only in what but in how to do things. Given this kind of guidance, Ball may be the best comedy actor in history. Without it, she is funny but lacks direction or incisiveness.

Lucille Ball

I always loved working with animals. I think they sensed I was simpatico with them. But that chimp! It must have weighed at least twenty pounds, and by the end of the scene it felt like it gained another eighty. God, my arms were sore!

HERE'S LUCY #40: "LUCY AND LIBERACE"

(CBS, JANUARY 5, 1970), 30 MINUTES

DIRECTED BY: Jack Baker

WRITTEN BY: Fred S. Fox, Seaman Jacobs
GUEST CAST: Liberace, Paul Winchell, Ben Wrigley

Craig brings home an expensive candelabra from a scavenger hunt. When Lucy examines it and finds Liberace's name engraved on it, she is convinced Craig stole it from the pianist and schemes to return it.

HIGHLIGHTS & TRIVIA

This is a very strange episode. First of all, Craig has never exhibited any behavior that would make Lucy jump to the conclusion that he would steal under any circumstances. Second, the interaction between Liberace and Craig is a bit uncomfortable to watch.

Desi Arnaz Jr.

I liked Liberace, and I liked working with him, but that ending, with all of us doing this little time step off camera, and him screaming, "Craig, you forgot your candelabra!". . . it just didn't seem to quite jell for me. This was actually one of the biggest parts I had up to that time. When he had me try on his jacket, and fondled my lapel telling me how handsome I was . . . well, it was a bit much!

Liberace brings $50,000 worth of his spectacular wardrobe to the set, and Lucille hires a round-the-clock guard to ensure its safety. The Edwardian tuxedo jacket that lights up in the dark is debuted on this show; Liberace will use it (or others like it) in his club act for the rest of his life.

HERE'S LUCY #41: "LUCY THE LAUNDRESS"

(CBS, JANUARY 12, 1970), 30 MINUTES
DIRECTED BY: Herbert Kenwith
WRITTEN BY: Larry Rhine, Lou Derman
GUEST CAST: James Hing, Lauren Gilbert, Bee Thompkins, Rosalind Chao, Heather Lee, Romo Vincent

When Lucy accidentally backs into a Chinese laundry truck, she moonlights at the laundry to pay the owner back for the damages.

HIGHLIGHTS & TRIVIA

This is yet another of this series' Asian-themed episodes that is, in retrospect, offensive. Writers Rhine and Derman had spent years writing for *Mr. Ed* (1961-65), and their humor is hardly subtle. Lucille accidentally scalds her hand during the filming when she forgets to take her hand away when she uses the steam press. She is not badly hurt, but Desi Jr. quips, "Mom put the new crease in the wrong spot!"

THE ED SULLIVAN SHOW

(CBS, JANUARY 18, 1970), 60 MINUTES
PRODUCED BY: Bob Precht
DIRECTED BY: John Moffitt
CAST: Ed Sullivan (host)

Lucille Ball takes a bow from the audience. She is in New York for meetings with CBS executives.

HERE'S LUCY #42: "LUCY AND LAWRENCE WELK"

(CBS, JANUARY 19, 1970), 30 MINUTES
DIRECTED BY: Herbert Kenwith
WRITTEN BY: Martin A. Ragaway
GUEST CAST: Vivian Vance, Lawrence Welk, Mary Jane Croft, Nancy Howard

Lucy's old pal Viv is coming for a visit, and Lucy is in a pickle. She has written Viv telling her she is very close friends with Lawrence Welk, and now Viv is expecting to meet him.

HIGHLIGHTS & TRIVIA

This story line is an outright steal from the May 9, 1955, *I Love Lucy* episode "Harpo Marx" (#125). This time it is Viv and not Caroline who can't see without her glasses, so Lucy schemes to get them away from her. The interaction between bandleader Welk and Lucie and Desi is actually very funny. Sculptor Lowell Grant is hired to make the plaster of Paris cast bust of Welk that is used on the dummy. It is not from a mold of Welk's face but is actually sculpted. Vivian's home is now placed somewhere back east, as opposed to New Mexico, in her previous appearance. Lucy's constant "wonnerful, wonnerful" is a little silly, as is much of the episode.

Lucie Arnaz

I have very little memory of this show. You know, we had to learn these shows so quickly, and just as quickly we sort of had to forget them, to make room in your brain for the next one. Sometimes I watch old shows I did, and it's like watching someone else.

Herbert Kenwith
(DIRECTOR)

When we sat down for the first read-through of this episode, Vivian came in late. Lucille had edited out a lot of Vivian's lines. Vivian looked at the script, then said to Lucy, "I came all the way from Connecticut to do a show with you, and I'm doing every word that's in my script." Lucille said, "You can't do it, I'm cutting it." Viv said, "You can cut all you want, but I am doing every line that was written for me!" And Lucille restored all of her lines. Vivian is the only one that I ever saw stand up to Lucy.

The dinner scene was very funny, and Lucille kept cracking up while we were doing it. But it didn't really show off Lawrence Welk to any great advantage. I asked Lucille why he would agree to do a thing like this, and she whispered to me, "Well, he's not very bright." Welk read his lines so badly, so flatly, that we had to attach a musical score to his lines so that his words would go up and down with inflection. That was the only way we could make his character sound normal. After the filming, he came over to me and told me that he was very grateful for all of my help during the week, and that he had a gift for me in his dressing room. Well, I certainly didn't need to go to someone's dressing room to retrieve a gift, so I went backstage to say goodnight to Lucille. Welk caught me there, and asked me into his dressing room. He had a small object in his hand, but I couldn't see what it was. I put my hand out to shake his goodbye, and he pressed this object into my hand when he shook it. When I got outside, I saw it was a little plastic violin with a nail file inside. On the outside written in plastic was the name Lawrence Welk. I threw that thing as far away as my arm made it go!

HERE'S LUCY #43: "LUCY AND VIVIAN VANCE"

(CBS, JANUARY 26, 1970), 30 MINUTES

DIRECTED BY: Herbert Kenwith
WRITTEN BY: Milt Josefsberg, Ray Singer
GUEST CAST: Vivian Vance, Don Diamond, Don Megowan

Lucy and Viv want to go to Tijuana, Mexico, and persuade Harry to drive them (at twelve cents per mile). Harry is talked into buying two dolls for the price of one if he'll deliver a third one to the owner's niece in Los Angeles. At the border Harry is detained because the doll contains contraband, and Lucy and Viv disavow any knowledge of him to teach him a lesson.

HIGHLIGHTS & TRIVIA

Sometimes there doesn't seem to be any reason why one *Here's Lucy* episode can be mediocre and the next one excellent. This one is a winner, perhaps because Lucy and Viv scheme together instead of plotting against one another. When given half a chance, there is still magic between the two ladies. Notice the Mexican sets. Much of it is dusted off scenery and props from the 1958 Lucy-Desi hour "Lucy Goes to Mexico." For the border scene, Ball dispatches a photographer to record the changes since the first episode had been filmed. The worker inadvertently gets caught in the U.S. government's Operation Intercept, and spends hours explaining what he is doing there.

HERE'S LUCY #44: "LUCY AND ANN-MARGRET"

(CBS, FEBRUARY 2, 1970), 30 MINUTES

DIRECTED BY: Herbert Kenwith
WRITTEN BY: Milt Josefsberg, Ray Singer
GUEST CAST: Ann-Margret, John O'Neill

Craig is disappointed when he discovers that a music publicist who likes his song "Country Magic" is a charlatan. Dejection turns to thrill when he encounters Ann-Margret, who autographs the only paper he has (the song) and likes it enough to feature it and him on her next television special.

HIGHLIGHTS & TRIVIA

Another terrific episode, made so by the talents of vivacious Ann-Margret and charismatic Desi Jr. The seduction scene (with an expectant Craig waiting on the couch while Ann-Margret leaves the room to slip into something more comfortable), besides being funny and unusually adult for thi program, is kind of ironic when taken in the context of real life. Actor Desi is hardly a babe in the woods, and is already gleaning major publicity for his romances with some of Hollywood's most intriguing women. In reality, it is the girls who are looking to seduce him, not the other way around. This installment might have started an entire new story line, with Craig and his show business struggles. Instead, the fact that he has written a hit song and appears on TV with Ann-Margret is totally forgotten in later entries.

Desi Arnaz Jr.

That guitar that flew down during my number with Ann-Margret belonged to Jimmy Burton, Elvis Presley's number one guitar player. That was his pink paisley guitar; it was one of the most unusual ones ever made. Jimmy actually played the solo for me. I felt like I had died and become Elvis. I loved doing this show . . . I loved doing music. I had to learn how to dance; that was the best learning experience for me on the show. Anita Mann was the assistant choreographer . . . she later ended up doing Solid Gold *[in 1980]. Jack Baker was the choreographer, and [frequent show director] Jack Donohue was also a dancer. Ann-Margret was unbelievable. She was cute, and funny, and very nice to me. I had had a crush on her since I was ten years old. I thought she was the quintessential young woman.*

Marl Young

(PIANIST/ARRANGER)

Music director Wilbur Hatch had died just before the scoring session for this episode. He had done all of the musical scoring for Lucy since she began on television, and even before that on radio. One of Lucy's attorneys [Howard Rafiel] and I met with Gary Morton. He assumed that I had experience conducting music to what they call picture and clock [i.e., synchronizing the background music to the edited film]. He didn't ask, so I didn't tell him I'd never done that before. I had four days to learn. One cue with this episode was very difficult, in the seduction scene between Ann and Desi. I felt great the day of the recording, because Bill Magginetti and Maury Gertzman [production manager and cinematographer, respectively] came by to cheer me on. I guess I did all right, because after the next recording session, they gave me Wilbur's job.

Anonymous

The onstage chemistry between Desi and Ann was very hot. Although I don't think anything ever came of it, Ann's husband Roger Smith started coming to the set every day just to make sure nothing was going to come of it. I don't think Desi ever realized the effect he had on people. Everyone who met him fell in love with him, and loved working with him. He just oozed talent and sexuality, and he was very smart to boot."

The song "Country Magic" was written by Steve March especially for the show. Note that the robe Ann-Margret wears is the same one Vivian Vance had worn all those years earlier as Ethel Mertz.

THE KRAFT MUSIC HALL: "THE KRAFT MUSIC HALL PRESENTS DESI ARNAZ"

(NBC, FEBRUARY 4, 1970), 60 MINUTES

PRODUCED BY: Dwight Hemion and Gary Smith
DIRECTED BY: Gary Smith
WRITTEN BY: Danny Simon, Madelyn Davis, Bob Carroll Jr.
CAST: Desi Arnaz (host), Desi Arnaz Jr., Lucie Arnaz, Bernadette Peters, Vivian Vance

In what amounts to a special that could have been called Where's Lucy?, Arnaz, his children, and Miss Vance romp through an hour that has every element necessary for enjoyment except Lucille Ball. One almost expects Lucille to pop out of a closet at any moment. She and the *I Love Lucy* series are referred to so frequently that it almost seems as if she is there. The highlight of the offering is the recreation of the "We'll Build a Bungalow" number by Desi Arnaz (looking trim and sporting dyed black hair) with daughter Lucie.

Lucie Arnaz

It really is a shame that I never got to do any other performing with my Dad on television. He didn't have his own series anymore, and then I was busy with Here's Lucy, *TV movies, and stage work. I loved doing this show with my father and brother, and working with Vivian was always an inspiration for me.*

Desi Arnaz Jr.

My sister and I did other Kraft shows with other hosts, but this is the one that meant the most to us.

Desi Arnaz

It brought tears to my eyes to work with my children and see firsthand just how talented they really were. With pardonable pride, I think that when Lucie did that number with me at the end of the show, she was even better than her mother had been.

Lucille Ball

Desi and I were in complete agreement on this one. Lucie was able to do things naturally that I had to struggle with. She is so damn good as a singer and a dancer, things I was never very good at.

Lucie Arnaz

Vivian was always her own person; she did not hide in my mother's shadow. She was a theatre person, always knew her stuff, always came prepared. The only difference working with her here was that she wasn't reacting to my mother's character because Mom wasn't there. Whenever we worked with Viv, there was always this little twist between fiction and reality, because in real life we never called her Aunt Viv. But on this show, Lucie and Desi call her that. So do Kim and Craig on Here's Lucy. *I guess it was for public image.*

HERE'S LUCY #45: "LUCY AND WALLY COX"

(CBS, FEBRUARY 9, 1970), 30 MINUTES

DIRECTED BY: Jay Sandrich
WRITTEN BY: Ray Singer, Milt Josefsberg
GUEST CAST: Wally Cox, Alan Hale Jr., Gil Perkins, Boyd "Red" Morgan, Chuck Hicks, X. Brands, Harvey Stone

Mousy Wally Manley (Wally Cox) hopes to inherit his father's detective agency, but the elder Manley doesn't think his offspring is "manly" enough for the responsibility. Enter Lucy, who arranges for Wally and her to show their prowess by guarding a warehouse from phony crooks. Unfortunately, the thieves end up being real, but Wally actually does save the day.

HIGHLIGHTS & TRIVIA

Here's Lucy is finally on a roll, with several very funny entries in a row featuring solid casts. Low-keyed Wally Cox is one of Lucille's favorites and continues being a frequent guest star. Alan Hale Jr. is best remembered as the large but loving Skipper on *Gilligan's Island* (1964–67). Stuntman Chuck Hicks had originally been a part of Ball's Desilu Workshop back in the late 1950s. He found greater success as a stuntman for other actors. Director Jay Sandrich had been the assistant director in the last season (1956–57) of *I Love Lucy*. He is more famous as the director of such fine TV comedies as *The Mary Tyler Moore Show* (1970–77) and *The Cosby Show* (1984–92).

Lucie Arnaz

Wally Cox was a great actor. He had this dry, Dick Cavett sort of wit.

HERE'S LUCY #46: "LUCY AND WAYNE NEWTON"

(CBS, FEBRUARY 16, 1970), 30 MINUTES

DIRECTED BY: Danny Dayton
WRITTEN BY: Ray Singer, Milt Josefsberg
GUEST CAST: Wayne Newton, Jerry Newton, Tommy Amato

Lucy discovers a lost midget horse on the highway outside of Las Vegas, and returns it to its rightful owner—Wayne Newton. Wayne is grateful, so Lucy asks for jobs on his ranch for the entire family. When Kim and Craig display musical talents at a barbecue, Newton includes them in his show at the State Fair.

HIGHLIGHTS & TRIVIA

This is another installment filmed on location in the San Fernando Valley without a studio audience. Lucie and Desi Jr. are sent to horse trainer Glen Randall to learn dressage, the art of formal horseback riding. Although they have both been riding horses since early childhood, they spend three weeks working constantly after rehearsals for other episodes to ensure they handle Newton's prize horses perfectly.

The song "I've Got the World on a String" is recorded live on location with a synthesizer as the musical accompaniment. Once again, animals do not cooperate oncamera and the horses won't prance in time to the music. Take after take is done to get even a minute of film. Desi's good humor and ebullience is evident no matter how many times the scenes require reshooting. His sense of humor and showmanship are almost never featured onscreen.

Marl Young

(MUSICAL DIRECTOR)

Halfway through the show, there was a number, a vocal with Lucy and the whole cast. The sound quality of the song, done on location, was really awful. I decided to erase everything from the track except Wayne's vocals, brought in professional singers to double for the rest of the cast, and rerecorded the song. The day after the episode aired, I was summoned into Gary's office. I thought I was going to get a dressing-down. Instead, he told me he thought the show came out great, and wondered how I cleaned up that song. I told him the truth, and he officially gave me Wilbur Hatch's job as musical director for Here's Lucy.

HERE'S LUCY #47: "LUCY TAKES OVER"

(CBS, FEBRUARY 23, 1970), 30 MINUTES

DIRECTED BY: Jay Sandrich
WRITTEN BY: Willaim Raynor, Miles Wilder
GUEST CAST: Lyle Talbot

While cleaning the attic, Lucy and her children find a diary and a promissory note that proves one of Harry's ancestors owed one of Lucy's forebears ten dollars. When the kids figure out that the interest now makes the note worth $80,000, Lucy takes over the business from Harry.

HIGHLIGHTS & TRIVIA

I guess new writers Raynor and Wilder have not seen this show very often. Harry's ancestors are also Kim and Craig's ancestors (as are Lucy's), which means that the Carter children owe themselves $80,000. Very often there is a blurring of the actual blood relationships between the principals on this series.

HERE'S LUCY #48: "LUCY AND CAROL BURNETT" A.K.A. "SECRETARY BEAUTIFUL"

(CBS, MARCH 2, 1970), 30 MINUTES

DIRECTED BY: Jay Sandrich
WRITTEN BY: Lou Derman, Larry Rhine
GUEST CAST: Carol Burnett, Robert Alda, Buddy Lewis, Harvey Stone, Sid Gould, Francine Pyne, Lavelle Roby, Tonia Izu

When Lucy and her pal Carol Krausmeyer both enter a beauty contest for secretaries, all friendship bets are off as the two vie for the title and the attention of the judge, Robert Alda (playing himself).

HIGHLIGHTS & TRIVIA

For some reason, every episode appearance by Miss Burnett on this series has the same title. To differentiate them, it is endeavored to supply alternate titles that are actually used to refer to them when they are filmed. Lucille and Carol are always funny together on this series, and this is the best of their joint appearances. Notice the gay reference in the scene where Harry teaches Lucy how to walk more like a lady. In Burnett's hands, a line that could be offensive to gay audiences is handled so well that it only evokes laughter.

Chapter Twenty-Two

1970–71 Season

HERE'S LUCY: THE THIRD SEASON

TECHNICAL REGULARS: Executive produced by Gary Morton; produced by Cleo Smith; script consultant, Milt Josefsberg; makeup by Hal King; hairstyling by Irma Kusely; music by Marl Young
CAST REGULARS: Lucille Ball (Lucy Carter); Gale Gordon (Harrison Otis Carter); Lucie Arnaz (Kim Carter); Desi Arnaz Jr. (Craig Carter); Roy Rowan (announcer)

HERE'S LUCY #49: "LUCY MEETS THE BURTONS"

(CBS, SEPTEMBER 14, 1970), 30 MINUTES
DIRECTED BY: Jerry Paris
WRITTEN BY: Bob Carroll Jr., Madelyn Davis
GUEST CAST: Richard Burton, Elizabeth Taylor, Brooks Williams, Cliff Norton, Vanda Barra, Army Archerd, James Bacon, Marilyn Beck, Joan Crosby, Joyce Haber, Dick Kleiner, Morton Moss, Robert Rose, Vernon Scott, Cecil Smith

Movie star Richard Burton can't leave his Beverly Hills hotel because of fans mobbing him. He borrows Sam the Plumber's overalls and escapes. Lucy finds "Sam" in the crowd and hires him to fix the office plumbing. After he leaves, she finds Elizabeth Taylor's famous diamond ring in the pocket of his overalls and just has to try it on. Naturally, the ring gets stuck and she can't remove it.

HIGHLIGHTS & TRIVIA

This is the highest rated episode in *Here's Lucy* history, garnering Lucille the largest percentage of the TV viewing audience since her halcyon *I Love Lucy* days. The Burtons demand and get a special credit at the start of the show, causing an entire new opening sequence to be made featuring Richard and Elizabeth's names. Director Jerry Paris is signed to be the new director. He and Lucille do not get along at all, and after a couple of episodes he is quietly replaced by Herbert Kenwith and others. At one point during rehearsal, Richard keeps missing his position on the floor. Lucille stops rehearsal to admonish him. Burton replies, "If you'd get out of my way, I'd get to my mark." Lucille reminds him that he had to get to his mark and say his next line, because what he says brings Liz out. Liz sticks her head into the scene and yells, "The light brought me out!" At that point, a disgusted Jerry Paris said, "It's a good, honest mistake, otherwise we clear the set!"

Lucille keeps speaking very loudly during rehearsals, while the Burtons mumble. A great deal of time is spent rehearsing Taylor's pulling on Lucille's hand, trying to get the expensive ring off her finger. More than fifteen minutes are spent on a five-second bit. On filming night, all of the extras are brought onto the stage at the last minute and choreographed in front of the audience. At the end of the second hotel room scene, a photographer from *TV Guide* comes onstage and takes the famous picture of Lucille and the Burtons that will appear on the cover of an upcoming issue.

The very last line of the show is supposed to be Liz Taylor's. She says, "Verrrrry interesting . . . good night, Lucy," which is a spoof of Arte Johnson's usual good night wish on NBC's *Rowan & Martin's Laugh-In* (1968–73), which airs opposite *Here's Lucy*. CBS, not wanting any references to its rival, has the line deleted in the final print. The night of the show, the Burtons film a special message for the CBS affiliates, promoting the show. One is done straight, the other done as if drunk. After the show, champagne, caviar, and a sumptuous buffet are brought out on the set for a cast party. This installment receives tremendous publicity, not the least of which is due to the whole televised business over the sixty-carat diamond ring (for which Ball has provide insurance and security). To obtain solid press coverage, Lucille wisely uses every major columnist in town oncamera for the finale, ensuring the show will be mentioned in all of their media outlets. Columnist Cecil Smith who appears in the last scene is the husband of show producer Cleo Smith and related by marriage to Lucille.

In later years, Burton will not remember this TV experience kindly. He will characterize Lucille as a manipulative, controlling bitch. Yet, he controls his adverse feelings long enough to appear on her twenty-fifth anniversary CBS-TV special in 1975. Part of the problem lies with Lucille's nervousness. This installment is produced at the end of the season, after all of the other episodes have been done, because the Burtons only agree to appear at the last moment. It is directed by someone new (Paris), whom Lucille instantly dislikes. It is also the first installment, since 1964, written by original writers Carroll and Pugh (formerly Martin, now Davis). All of this gives Ball a bad case of nerves, which always makes her push too hard oncamera.

Lucille Ball

Richard kept throwing away comedy lines in that British "drawing room" way of his. I counted six big laughs that he wasn't getting, so I was forced to go to him and say something about it. He didn't take too kindly to it, but after the filming he came over to me and said, "There were eight!"

Gary Morton

(EXECUTIVE PRODUCER)

Gale Gordon was a rock. When we had the Burtons on, Richard turned to me one day and said that Gale was one of the finest actors around, that he should be in the Old Vic in England. I was the one who got the Burtons to do our show. We met them at the British Embassy in Los Angeles. We had to do a lot of work to get the show done because our production season was over, but we did it and got a fine show.

Irma Kusely

(HAIRSTYLIST)

I knew Elizabeth Taylor when her boobs were beestings, back when she was a girl at MGM. I did her hair for National Velvet *[1944]. I did her hair on this episode because I wasn't a stranger to her.*

Cliff Norton

(ACTOR/COMEDIAN)

I had already done some shows with Lucy. One day, Gary Morton called me and said, "We're doing a very, very special show. We finally nailed the Burtons. There is a role we think you would be good for." Needless to say, I was interested. Then he said, "The only thing is, Cliff, we are really short on money!" I said, "Fuck you, Gary, don't give me that shit. I'm gonna have to help you pay for the Burtons? Come on, you ought to be ashamed of yourself. OK, you are my friend and you've called me to do the show, but you know I won't talk money with you. You're going to have to talk to my agent, Gary. Don't even mention a figure to me, I don't want to hear it. If you're broke, take it out of your pocket. What are you asking me to do—take $100 less, or $500 less? What is that going to buy you, you're spending hundreds of thousands!? We are supposed to be friends, let's stay that way." He didn't need to save my salary, but he tried to take a shot at it, so that he could turn to Lucy and say, "Hey, we got Cliff Norton for $4.28 plus tax." But he didn't! Gary was a very nice man, but to him business was business.

These two people [Burton and Taylor] were like the king and queen of the universe without even trying. They were staying at the Beverly Hills Hotel in two bungalows, but had their food sent over from Chasen's because the hotel's food wasn't quite up to what they were used to. They had his and hers limousines, and his and hers dressing trailers, which were located on the adjoining sound stage. They managed to get a hold of Barbra Streisand's magnificent dressing trailer from Funny Girl *[1968] for Elizabeth, and something more modest (perhaps only forty feet long) for Richard. But they were gracious, professional, on time, and at their best. They were temperament-free and a delight to work with. Although there would occasionally be breaks when Lucy would huddle with Milt Josefsberg or Jerry Paris and perhaps some things changed, I never saw Lucy use excessive influence or act unprofessionally. Any changes she might have wanted she did privately and quietly. Sure she was tough, damn tough, but nobody knew her business better than Lucille Ball. She was a walking, living authority on comedy, and it showed. You had to respect her for that.*

Because of the ring, there was security at the studio that most governments don't have. I had to wear a badge except when I was actually being filmed. The party afterward was the hottest ticket in town. Everybody who was anybody was there, with lavish food and drink.

Herbert Kenwith

(DIRECTOR)

Lucille and [episode director] Jerry Paris had a huge fight on the set. She called him a horse's ass. So he turned to her and said, "Horse's asses do not direct television shows!" and walked out. Lucille ran after him, and she apologized and asked him to come back and finish directing the show. But there was no love lost between them. There was also tension between Lucy and Elizabeth Taylor. Remember, we are speaking about two very powerful women. Lucille sent Elizabeth a dozen roses the week before rehearsal. Elizabeth sent Lucy back a dozen and a half. So Lucille sent her two dozen. And back and forth they went until Lucille's dressing room looked like a funeral parlor. They were one-upping each other. Elizabeth spoke very softly during the early rehearsals, still figuring out what she could do with her part. Lucille said to her, "You sound like you're talking in a closet. You're supposed to be an actor! Speak up!" Miss Taylor referred to Lucille as "Miss Cunt" for the rest of the week, right to her face.

Lucie Arnaz

I'll never forget this week. Not because of the Burtons or that ring, but because this was the week I got engaged to Phil Vandervort. He gave me this beautiful marquis-shaped ring with a tiny little emerald and little baby diamonds all around it, which was the biggest thing that had happened to me. Little did I know that the Burtons were the biggest thing to happen to that set. I ran down there to show off the ring and tell everyone I got engaged. Mom tried to introduce me to Richard and Liz, but I just had to make my announcement. Everyone on the set applauded, and Liz came over to me, grabbing my hand. "Let me see the ring," she said. Unfortunately, she grabbed for the ring with the hand that had the ring. *I was totally upstaged. My ring was a puddle, and hers was an Olympic-size swimming pool. She was very gracious. She tried to make me feel as if I had the nicest ring in the world. She also told me to wash all my jewelry with toothpaste. I do it to this day.*

THE ED SULLIVAN SHOW: "THE GEORGIES"

(CBS, SEPTEMBER 20, 1970), 60 MINUTES

PRODUCED BY: Bob Precht
DIRECTED BY: John Moffitt
WRITTEN BY: Joe Bigelow
CAST: Ed Sullivan (host), Lucille Ball, Milton Berle, Blood Sweat and Tears, Carol Burnett, Lou Chase, Marc Copage, Jimmy Durante, the Flying Alexanders, Sergio Franchi, Peter Gennaro, James Gould, Jack Haley, Bob Hope, Tom Jones, Emmett Kelly, the Latin Rhythms, New York Mayor John V. Lindsay, Michael Link, Melba Moore, the Ousterellis Kids, the Radio City Rockettes, Penny Singleton, Tommy Smothers, Barbra Streisand, Tanya the Elephant, Danny Thomas, David Clayton Thomas, Flip Wilson

Ed Sullivan tries to add pizzazz to his variety hour by inaugurating "The Georgies," an award given out by the American Guild of Variety Artists (AGVA), the union for nightclub performers. Lucille presents Carol Burnett with the Comedienne of 1970 Award. The two Redheads do a bit where Lucille feeds Carol everything she is supposed to say, leading to Ball accepting the award herself. The prizes are named for Broadway legend (singer, dancer, actor, writer, director, producer, choreographer) George M. Cohan.

It is evenings like this that toll the death-knell for television variety. Acts like Sergio Franchi and Jimmy Durante bore young viewers, and groups like Blood Sweat and Tears and singer Melba Moore irritate the adults. Before long (1974), Ed Sullivan will be dead and music videos will all but bury the TV variety show format.

HERE'S LUCY #50: "LUCY THE SKYDIVER"

(CBS, SEPTEMBER 21, 1970), 30 MINUTES

DIRECTED BY: Herbert Kenwith
WRITTEN BY: Larry Rhine, Lou Derman
GUEST CAST: Bill Baldwin, Rhodes Reason

When Kim takes up motorcycling and Craig wants to try dangerous skin diving, Lucy attempts reverse psychology to get them to stop. She announces she is taking up skydiving, but is forced into actually doing it when the kids support her adventure.

HIGHLIGHTS & TRIVIA

To simulate Lucy skydiving, an apparatus is built outside the sound stage. Lucille is strapped by her feet onto a high platform, her lower body in a brace. The apparatus can move in any direction, making it appear as though Lucille is moving through the air. A large theatrical fan blows air at her while she lurches about as if she is falling. The camera films her from beneath, just keeping her upper body in the frame. The blue sky behind her looks as if she is in mid-air.

For the scene where she jumps out of the plane, the set piece is about a foot off the ground. A smaller wind machine and simulated fog give the appearance of movement. For the actual "landing," Lucille does a possibly dangerous stunt. She is brought up into the rafters above the stage. Crew people attach her to the phony parachute while she holds on to a stick for balance. She is put on a ledge, which is pulled out from under her on cue, allowing her to fall into the scene while suspended on wires.

Unfortunately, after Ball's spectacular entrance (which is terrific), the script gives her nothing with which to follow it.

Herbert Kenwith

(DIRECTOR)

I gave Lucille a direction about an entrance she had to make. She came over to me and got right in my face, nose to nose. She screamed in the loudest voice I have ever heard, "Why do I have to do that?" I couldn't let her get away with that, so I screamed in the loudest voice I could muster, "Because I said so!" She kept staring at me cross-eyed for about thirty seconds, then pulled away and said, "OK!" The rest of the rehearsal went fine. Afterward, she asked me to meet her and Gary [Morton] at a restaurant [in Beverly Hills] named Matteo's. I had never been there before, so when I entered the restaurant I didn't know where to look for her. She and Gary were sitting in a banquette, and from across the restaurant she yelled at me, "You've got balls!" I walked over to their table, and she repeated herself, adding, "You're the only director who has ever stood up to me and yelled at me like that!" For the next few weeks, she was like a pussycat.

HERE'S LUCY #51: "LUCY AND SAMMY DAVIS JR."

(CBS, SEPTEMBER 28, 1970), 30 MINUTES

DIRECTED BY: Herbert Kenwith
WRITTEN BY: Milt Josefsberg
BASED ON A SCRIPT BY: Sam Perrin, Ralph Goodman
GUEST CAST: Sammy Davis Jr., Irwin Sharone, Joe Jackson, Steve March, Elliot Reid, Buddy Hackett, Gary Morton, Keith Taylor

When Sammy Davis Jr. comes into Harry Carter's office because he's had a slight injury to his nose in the elevator, Harry and Lucy are sure his nose problem will probably escalate. Fearing being sued by the producers of Davis' new feature film, Lucy follows him about to treat his nose and keep him out of trouble. Naturally, she only causes more trouble.

HIGHLIGHTS & TRIVIA

This awful script is rife with topical references to the fact that Davis is Jewish, to racial equality, and to *Rowan & Martin's Laugh-In*. Although writers Perrin and Goodman do the original draft of the script, consultant Josefsberg revamps it, and it is his name that appears in the episode credits. The Lucy character is so obnoxious here that all humor is lost. Lucille is very concerned this week with lighting and camera movements. She fears that bad shadows are being cast all over the set. Lucille and Sammy are very close personal friends, and she is especially keen on making things technically perfect this time out. She engages camera coordinator Maury Gertzman in a heated discussion about how things are being done on the sound stage. Note that the door leading to the office bathroom in the Richard and Elizabeth Burton show is now a closet door. What happened to the bathroom? Buddy Hackett's cameo part is filmed on Wednesday without an audience due to a prior commitment. His part in the show will be cut out of the syndicated versions. Hackett spends most of the day telling jokes to writer Milt Josefsberg.

Desi Arnaz, his hair dyed jet black, visits the set this week. He is on the Universal lot filming an episode of the western series *The Men from Shiloh*. As he comes into view, Davis starts beating out "Babalu" on his chair. Desi joked with him, "They're giving minorities a break this week. How are you, Mother?"

Lucie Arnaz

Dad was a frequent visitor to the set. If he was in town [he had homes in Palm Springs and Baja, California] and heard that one of us was being spotlighted, or doing something special, he'd show up during the week and be there on show night. Mom and Dad had a very loving relationship. There would be this loving/kidding banter that went back and forth when he came to the set. Dad was very supportive of all of our careers, including Mom's.

Herbert Kenwith

(DIRECTOR)

Every once in awhile, we'd get in scripts that Lucille knew were inferior. There were entire scenes that she would just refuse to do because they weren't funny. [Script supervisor] Milt Josefsberg would come over to me and say, "Herbert, please make her do the scene. It'll play if she just tries it." So I would say to her, "Look, Lucy, before we throw this thing out, why don't we try it once? How can we know if this is any good on its feet until you apply your artistry to it?" So she'd try it and find something humorous to do with it, and the scene would stay in the episode. But Milt wasn't doing her any favors by giving her this material to begin with.

Desi Arnaz Jr.

Buddy helped me a lot. It was, for a drummer, like working with God. I had met him before . . . I think my friend Steve March dated his daughter. We had this big drum challenge. He stopped me during rehearsals and said, "Jeez, you're working so hard! Why are you working so hard? Relax!" In drumming, this is crucial, because if you have any tension it makes things worse. I was trying to do this whole Gene Krupa, entertaining/performing drum style, and Buddy was the King of control . . . all with the wrists and the fingers. In my rock and roll playing, I had gotten used to using my arms a lot, and really hitting the drums hard. Buddy reminded me of the technical parts of my playing, and it really helped. We both played live, and it really looked good on camera.

Buddy Rich

(DRUMMING LEGEND)

Desi had the kind of talent that could have been developed into something great had he stuck with it. But he put his acting first, and without total dedication, even wonderful talent doesn't get developed.

HERE'S LUCY #52: "LUCY AND BUDDY RICH"

(CBS, OCTOBER 5, 1970), 30 MINUTES

DIRECTED BY: Jerry Paris
WRITTEN BY: Martin A. Ragaway
GUEST CAST: Buddy Rich, Richard Yniguez, Eugene Molnar, Dick Winslow

Lucy and the family attend a Buddy Rich performance at a nightclub that is also sponsoring a drum contest. Lucy persuades percussion ace Rich to tutor Craig and the win is almost assured. However, at the last minute the sensitive young man throws the contest so an underprivileged entrant will get the prize of new drums.

HIGHLIGHTS & TRIVIA

This is one of the last episodes that spotlights Desi Jr. He will start missing several episodes to film *Red Sky at Morning* (1970), and by the end of the season will leave the series altogether. (Note: Although *Red Sky at Morning*, a nostalgic drama, opens soon after this entry airs, the installment had been filmed much earlier in the year to allow Desi the freedom to make the movie.)

HERE'S LUCY #53: "LUCY THE CRUSADER"

(CBS, OCTOBER 12, 1970), 30 MINUTES

DIRECTED BY: Herbert Kenwith
WRITTEN BY: Milt Josefsberg, Al Schwartz
GUEST CAST: Charles Nelson Reilly, John "Red" Fox, Carole Cook, Kathleen Hughes, Bob Hastings, Jerome Cowan, Donald Briggs

When the stereo Lucy buys for Craig's birthday turns out to be defective and she tries to return it, she finds out that the manufacturer (Prime Ultrasonics or PU for short) makes it almost impossible for customers to get satisfaction. With the help of the unctuous clerk (Charles Nelson Reilly) who sold her the set, and others who have been duped by the firm, Lucy leads a protest at the company's stockholders' meeting.

HIGHLIGHTS & TRIVIA

This is one of the best episodes in the ENTIRE *Here's Lucy* series. Lucy is shown as intelligent, diligent, and capable. Charles Nelson Reilly steals every scene he is in, giving perhaps the best television performance of his lengthy career. With a supporting cast that includes Bob Hastings and Carole Cook, there is not a wasted performance nor a line that is not delivered for full effect. This is a top notch production!

Desi Arnaz Jr.

I'd like to say something about Gary Morton. You know, he and Cleo really did produce the show. I don't remember Mom being in on casting, or making sure the show came in on budget. They had real jobs to do, and they did them very well. People who have written books trying to characterize Gary as less than professional, or just as Mom's consort, are looking to cash in, sensationalize, and exploit, and are looking to make money. Gary's influence was extraordinary, both on the set and off. He was a good man, and I think people have an axe to grind. My professional experience with Gary was wonderful; Here's Lucy *was film heaven compared to some sets I've worked on.*

Lucie Arnaz

Gary ran the business. About what was funny, he usually deferred to my mother. It was my mother's choice as to what story lines would fly. Gary would audition people . . . that sort of thing. A lot of people have written about how he changed the comedy on the show. That would be impossible to do. My father had great influence on my mother's comedy. After he left, Gary did not fill that spot. He would never have tried. He did not deal with the writers like my father did. That became my mother's job. And Cleo really worked hard as the line producer. She made sure everyone got paid, that all union requirements were met, and that things ran smoothly. Mom had the upper hand on the set always, but Gary and Cleo made certain Lucille Ball Productions was in good working order. Cleo is brilliant, capable, and real. She produced over 100 shows and specials.

Charles Nelson Reilly

(ACTOR/DIRECTOR)

Lucille Ball taught me one of the most important things I've ever learned about comedy when I worked on this show. We were sitting around the table, and she said, "Great joke–wrong place!" I can't tell you how many shows I've done that I have made better by remembering her wisdom.

Herbert Kenwith

(DIRECTOR)

We had a problem with that doll that squirted water. Bob Hastings [as one of the unhappy consumers] was supposed to demonstrate the doll, which would squirt water right into Gale Gordon's face. Try as he might, Bob couldn't make the water hit the exact spot on Gale's face it was supposed to. I suggested that we do an insert shot of the water hitting Gale's face after the filming. Lucille said she wanted it all done in one shot in front of the audience. Lucille got very frustrated and grabbed the doll from him and said, "Let me have it. I'll show you how to do it right!" But she couldn't do it either. Out of embarrassment, she said a few choice words to Hastings. He got so angry at the way she spoke to him that he actually started to make a lunge at her to hit her. A couple of us grabbed him and said, "If you hit her, you know you'll never work in this business again." He calmed down, and then Lucille stared him down and said, "I dare you!" Lucille was being tough with Bob, but he was way out of line. We ended up doing it as I had suggested, with an insert shot.

HERE'S LUCY #54: "LUCY THE COED"

(CBS, OCTOBER 19, 1970), 30 MINUTES

DIRECTED BY: Jack Baker
WRITTEN BY: Fred S. Fox, Seaman Jacobs
GUEST CAST: Marilyn Maxwell, Robert Alda, Cecil Gold, Kevin Edwards, Jim Bates, Judy Van Wormer, Lisa Pharren, Mickie Pollak

Harry is in charge of the musical for his class reunion at Bullwinkle University (class of 1928), but can't find any of the alumni to appear in the show. He recruits Lucy, Kim, and Craig to take the parts instead.

HIGHLIGHTS & TRIVIA

Choreographer Jack Baker once again directs, as there is little plot and lots of musical comedy. Movie star Marilyn Maxwell (1921–1972) last appeared with Lucille in the film *Forever Darling* (1956); this is one of her last television appearances. As with most of these mini-musicals, this is a superior effort. Note that Harry's graduation year of 1928 places him well into his sixties.

THE CAROL BURNETT SHOW

(CBS, OCTOBER 19, 1970), 60 MINUTES

PRODUCED BY: Joe Hamilton
DIRECTED BY: Dave Powers

WRITTEN BY: Stan Burns, Mike Marmer, Hal Goodman, Larry Klein, Don Hinkley, Kenny Solms, Gail Parent, Bill Angelos, Buz Kohan
CAST: Carol Burnett (host), Lucille Ball, Harvey Korman, Vicki Lawrence, Mel Torme, Lyle Waggoner

Lucille again pays Burnett back for her continued guest shots on *Here's Lucy* with this guest stint of her own. Lucille almost seems displeased to be there, and displays a smirking attitude throughout the hour. It is actually Mel Torme who shines this week, not only musically but in the comedy bits. It is difficult writing sketch comedy for Lucille, due to her age. She is still trying to hide how old she is, and will not do sketches in which she plays anything but "young ladies." Any suggestion that Carol might be younger than she is out. Also, Lucille needs to have physical directions written into the script. When writers leave Ball to her own devices, she is often lost. Although Lucille and Carol have the same work ethic about thorough rehearsals, Ball does not come up to the same performance standards as Burnett.

This is the last time Lucille Ball guests on the *Carol Burnett Show*. Nonetheless, it is a double whammy for Lucille, as her show *Here's Lucy* #54, "Lucy the Coed," immediately precedes the airing of Carol Burnett's show, so that this night is truly a Lucille Ball night.

HERE'S LUCY #55: "LUCY THE AMERICAN MOTHER"

(CBS, OCTOBER 26, 1970), 30 MINUTES
DIRECTED BY: Jack Donohue
WRITTEN BY: Lou Derman, Larry Rhine
GUEST CAST: Mary Jane Croft, Don Crichton, Olive Dunbar, Sid Gould, Boyd "Red" Morgan,Alma Platt, Richard Collier

For a school project, Craig films a documentary on his mother as the model American mother. Being a star affects both Lucy and Harry, as she gets haughty and he becomes warm and generous.

HIGHLIGHTS & TRIVIA

Unfortunately, most of the Derman/Rhine scripts are silly, giving Lucille little to do that has either class or intelligence.

HERE'S LUCY #56: "LUCY'S WEDDING PARTY"

(CBS, NOVEMBER 2, 1970), 30 MINUTES
DIRECTED BY: Jack Donohue
WRITTEN BY: Sam Perrin, Ralph Goodman
GUEST CAST: Bruce Gordon, Mary Jane Croft, Paul Picerni, Cynthis Hull, Sam Chew, Lyle Talbot, the Hellenic Dancers, the Mad Greeks

When Lucy finds out that a nice, young Greek couple can't get find a place to get married, she offers them Harry's house because he is away at a college reunion. Unfortunately, Harry returns early to find a houseful of Greeks, and Lucy tries to convince him that it is all a surprise birthday party for him.

HIGHLIGHTS & TRIVIA

Once again, no one is watching the script continuity. Harry just had his college reunion two weeks earlier in "Lucy the Coed" (episode #54). Both Bruce Gordon and Paul Picerni had been featured actors together in the Desilu-produced *The Untouchables* (1959–63).

HERE'S LUCY #57: "LUCY CUTS VINCENT'S PRICE"

(CBS, NOVEMBER 9, 1970), 30 MINUTES
DIRECTED BY: Herbert Kenwith
WRITTEN BY: Martin A. Ragaway
GUEST CAST: Vincent Price, Mary Jane Croft, Tol Avery, Jack Collins

Lucy buys a vintage oil painting at an auction and believes it to be valuable. She takes it to the home of actor Vincent Price, a former client and well-known art connoisseur. Unfortunately for Lucy, Price has remodeled a part of his home as a mad scientist set for his upcoming movie, and thinks Lucy is there to audition for the role of his latest victim.

HIGHLIGHTS & TRIVIA

As with many of these third season entries, the plots are improving and are much more inventive than they were earlier in the life of *Here's Lucy*. Cut out of the later syndicated print is an entire scene with Kim and Craig fretting over their mother's visit to Price's home, which takes away much of the fun in the plot for this entry.

Herbert Kenwith

(DIRECTOR)

Vincent Price was a pleasure to work with. He took direction well, and understood the style of the series. He gave Lucille and me signed copies of his cookbooks as a gift after the filming.

HERE'S LUCY #58: "LUCY AND THE DIAMOND CUTTER"

(CBS, NOVEMBER 16, 1970), 30 MINUTES

DIRECTED BY: Herbert Kenwith
WRITTEN BY: Milt Josefsberg, Al Schwartz
GUEST CAST: Wally Cox, Ruth McDevitt, Mary Wickes

Mrs. Whitmark wants a very expensive and cursed diamond split in an obscure, quiet locale, so Harry offers Lucy's house. The diamond cutter's nerves are shot by all the action he finds there, so it is left to Harry to make the unsurest cut of all.

HIGHLIGHTS & TRIVIA

Wally Cox makes his third *Here's Lucy* guest spot in three seasons. His nervous diamond cutter is very reminiscent of the type of work for which Don Knotts was known, and may have been written with Knotts in mind. This is Herbert Kenwith's final work with Lucille Ball, although episodes filmed previously will air after this one.

Herbert Kenwith

(DIRECTOR)

Ruth McDevitt [Mrs. Whitmark] was elderly by this point. She had trouble hitting her marks on the floor because she couldn't see them. Lucille got frustrated at Ruthie's inability to stand where she needed to be, so Lucille kicked her foot into the position it was supposed to be in. She did this several times, and finally Ruthie got hurt. I decided then and there that if my friendship with Lucille was going to survive, I couldn't direct her shows anymore.

JACK BENNY'S TWENTIETH ANNIVERSARY SPECIAL

(NBC, NOVEMBER 16, 1970), 60 MINUTES

PRODUCED BY: Irving Fein, Stan Harris
DIRECTED BY: Stan Harris
WRITTEN BY: Hal Goldman, Al Gordon, Hilliard Marks, Hugh Wedlock Jr.
CAST: Jack Benny (host), Eddie "Rochester" Anderson, Artie Auerbach, Lucille Ball, Mel Blanc, George Burns, Dennis Day, Phil Harris, Mary Livingstone, Frank Nelson, Dinah Shore, Frank Sinatra, Red Skelton, Don Wilson

Lucille does this show as a favor to Jack. Benny desperately wanted his real-life wife, Sadie, to appear as her character Mary Livingstone, but her intense stage fright has precluded her from any public appearances for more than ten years. Jack makes a deal with her: He will get Lucille to play her maid and literally hold her hand and be by her side the entire time she is oncamera if she will do a cameo role. Lucille (in a French maid's outfit) and Mary are oncamera for less than a minute.

A BOB HOPE SPECIAL

(NBC, NOVEMBER 16, 1970), 60 MINUTES

EXECUTIVE PRODUCED BY: Bob Hope
PRODUCED BY: Mort Lachman
DIRECTED BY: Dick McDonough
WRITTEN BY: Mort Lachman, Bill Larkin, Lester White, Mel Tolkin, Charles Lee, Gig Henry, Lloyd Turner, Gordon Mitchell, Ray Parker, Norman Sullivan
CAST: Bob Hope (host), Lucille Ball, George Burns, Tom Jones, Danny Thomas

This is a busy video night for Miss Ball; this is her third major network TV appearance in the same evening. As is becoming usual with her gigs on Hope's shows, Lucille does not shine. She loves to rehearse and work hard. The Hope show allows for almost no rehearsals; most of the program is run through quickly and read off of cue cards.

Her first sketch starts with her in the audience. Bob Hope is claiming he can demonstrate hypnotism. He goes into the audience and pulls Lucille onto the stage as a volunteer. Feigning stage fright, she tries to exit. Hope hypnotizes her into believing that she is Cleopatra and that he is Marc Antony. The sketch ends with him dragging her off the stage. Later in the proceedings, Lucille, Bob, and Danny Thomas play child actors testing for the same part. Each manages to ruin the others' audition. This sketch actually contains a few laughs.

HERE'S LUCY #59: "LUCY AND JACK BENNY'S BIOGRAPHY"

(CBS, NOVEMBER 23, 1970), 30 MINUTES
DIRECTED BY: Herbert Kenwith
WRITTEN BY: Milt Josefsberg, Ray Singer
GUEST CAST: Jack Benny, George Burns, Louis Quinn, Michael Barbera, Ben Wrigley, Florence Lake

Jack Benny hires Lucy Carter to be his confidential secretary while he dictates his autobiography. As he discusses the women he has known over the years, a series of flashbacks shows us scenes from Benny's life, with Lucy playing all the parts.

HIGHLIGHTS & TRIVIA

This is one of the best and most elaborate shows of the entire *Here's Lucy* series. It is also one of the most infamous. It is the longest shoot of any Lucille Ball show episode, ending just after two in the morning. Benny and Lucille have several costume changes, and the sets must be changed many times. Lucille rehearses the dance sequence with furor all week, refusing to stop until she feels it is done perfectly. At one point, Jack is supposed to sing a few bars of his theme song, "Love in Bloom." In rehearsal, he hits several bad notes, and quips, "I can't even hit that note on my violin!" Mary Benny's voice is recorded at her home, and Lucille lip-syncs to the recording using a "pop" sound cue when she portrays Mrs. Benny. During the vaudeville bit, Lucille breaks the heel of her shoe when she dances to "Sweet Georgia Brown." She takes them off and tries to continue with the action. Benny breaks up, and shouts, "For God's sakes, say what happened!" When Lucille finally relents and goes offstage to get the shoe repaired, Benny asides to the audience, "We're gonna have to do this goddamn thing all over again!"

According to several books dealing with Lucille Ball, she treats Benny poorly this week, berating him. Additionally, he supposedly requests a prop to use to make getting off his knees easier. She refuses it and he falls.

Lucie Arnaz

I never saw my mother treat Jack Benny the way some people have described her behavior the week this show was shot. I wasn't there on the set the whole time, so I can't swear to anything. Jack was our neighbor and a close family friend. I can't imagine she'd mistreat him. Mom might have been a little tactless sometime, but not abusive with people like Jack.

Irving Fein

(PRODUCER/MANAGER)

I was Jack's producer and manager for years, and was there with him while he did this show. Jack was a very, very big star, right up until he died [in 1974 at age eighty]. He did not need to work with Lucille Ball. He did it because he wanted to. If she had mistreated him, I would have seen it and pulled him off the set. This whole story is a gross exaggeration and misrepresentation. Lucille's [stinging] comments were made to be funny, and Jack took it that way. They were both pros.

Gary Morton

(EXECUTIVE PRODUCER)

All this stuff about Lucille mistreating Jack Benny is nonsense. I was there on the set. Jack turned to me and said, "If I worked as hard as she does, I'd still be on the air with my own show! Gary, she is the greatest female talent ever!"

Carole Cook

(ACTOR/FAMILY FRIEND)

Lucy would often talk in short hand when she was rehearsing—go here, do this, turn there, now go—and she would sometimes handle people physically, pushing them into position. She was driven. She had tunnel vision. At one point during the rehearsal week, Jack turned to me and said, "Someone ought to tell her she's got the job!" He was commenting on her intensity and inability to relax. He was making a humorous comment, although it has been written in books that he was angry. But he wasn't.

Herbert Kenwith

(DIRECTOR)

Every time we rehearsed the scene where Lucille falls to the floor and grabs Jack's pants and tears them, Jack lost his balance. After the dress rehearsal, Jack asked if a little table could be put there for him to lean on so the force of Lucille pulling on his leg wouldn't knock him over. So I had a little table brought in and had it painted white to match the couch. Lucille came in and saw [it] and inquired about it, since she had not seen it before. I told her why it was there, but Lucille insisted that it be taken away. When we filmed the scene in front of the audience, Jack lost his balance and literally fell on his face. The audience howled, because it was very funny. But Jack got hurt. We had to cut the cameras and pick him up; then I restaged the moment so that he would not fall again. That is the take we used on the final product. Jack understood Lucy. He knew she was being ambitious, and that by this point she was trying to rise above inferior scripts by controlling everything, including her guest stars.

Lucy Carter and Jack Benny actually met before in 1968 in the second episode of *Here's Lucy*, "Lucy Visits Jack Benny," when the family rented rooms from the comic legend in Palm Springs.

HERE'S LUCY #60: "LUCY AND RUDY VALLEE"

(CBS, NOVEMBER 30, 1970), 30 MINUTES

DIRECTED BY: Coby Ruskin
WRITTEN BY: David Ketchum, Bruce Shelly
GUEST CAST: Rudy Vallee, Herbie Faye, Philip Vandervort, Vanda Barra, Marnelle Wright, Gloria Wood, George Bledsoe, Thomas D. Kenny, Mack McLean, Sue Allen

Lucy and Harry find veteran singer/actor Rudy Vallee waiting tables in a restaurant. Although he is wealthy—he owns the entire block—he hopes his crooner music will become popular again. Lucy decides to modernize him and make him a star again.

HIGHLIGHTS & TRIVIA

Coby Ruskin makes his *Here's Lucy* directorial debut with this installment. His previous work had been on one camera series like *The Andy Griffith Show* (1960–68). He isn't adept at live comedy, yet he will be the program's principal director in its last three seasons.

Lucie Arnaz

I don't like to speak ill of people who are gone, but Rudy Vallee [1901–1986] was not professional. Every third word out of his mouth was an expletive. He would blame every single person around him for anything he couldn't do. If he made a mistake, it was always somebody else's fault. He was foul.

Gary Morton

(EXECUTIVE PRODUCER)

Coby Ruskin was an old vaudevillian. He would even act out the parts for Lucy. He wasn't as strong in the physical comedy as some of the other directors, but he was very well liked.

HERE'S LUCY #61: "LUCY LOSES HER COOL"

(CBS, DECEMBER 7, 1970), 30 MINUTES

DIRECTED BY: Herbert Kenwith
WRITTEN BY: Milt Josefsberg, Ray Singer
GUEST CAST: Art Linkletter, Mary Jane Croft, Vanda Barra, Richard Erdman, Scotty Garrett

As a guest on *The Art Linkletter Show*, Lucy promises not to lose her temper for at least twenty-four hours. Unbeknownst to Lucy, Harry, Mary Jane, and the kids are in on the plot and do nothing but annoy her in hopes she will lose her cool.

HIGHLIGHTS & TRIVIA

Take 1953's "Ricky Loses His Temper" from *I Love Lucy* (episode #85), shuffle it with 1966's "Lucy and Art Linkletter" from *The Lucy Show* (episode #100), and you have this installment. It is very funny, well constructed, and (thanks to Herbert Kenwith's direction) not overplayed. In actuality, Art Linkletter no longer has his own TV show, but may have still had one at the time this episode is written and filmed. An entire scene, where her kids really annoy Lucy, is later cut out of the syndication print.

Lucie Arnaz

Art Linkletter is a gentleman and a very nice man.

Desi Arnaz Jr.

This was really the only time when my drug and alcohol problem showed itself in my performance. When I was drumming, and trying to go faster, my left arm started to go slower. I covered it, but this was a sign that all was not right with my body. As far as lines go, I did pretty well. It took me awhile to get them in rehearsals, but for show night I was always right on the money. I purposely didn't learn my lines until the last moment to keep my performance fresh. Actually, this never really helped me, and I should have learned my lines early on. I never used the cue cards (although Mom did), and there weren't very many retakes. Mom had cue cards at every possible line of vision, so that no matter where she looked, the lines were available to her. They were in big, black letters, with everyone else's cues in other colors. It was a safety measure, for Mom certainly always seemed to know her lines pretty well.

Lucie Arnaz

We never, ever had a problem with Desi on the set because of his drug problems. How can I be so certain? Because it wasn't until years later that we even knew that he'd had a problem. He covered it so well, kept it so hidden, that it never showed in his work at all in all those years. Only later did we learn that he had begun drinking at eleven!

HERE'S LUCY #62: "LUCY, PART-TIME WIFE"

(CBS, DECEMBER 14, 1970), 30 MINUTES

DIRECTED BY: Ross Martin
WRITTEN BY: Larry Rhine, Lou Derman
GUEST CAST: Jean Willes, Carole Cook, Eddie Quillan, William Benedict

Harry's former college girlfriend comes to town, and he fears she still wants to marry him. To throw her off the scent, he enlists Lucy to play his pregnant wife. The girlfriend is very supportive, and wants to take care of Lucy until she delivers.

HIGHLIGHTS & TRIVIA

References to Harry's college days, and his former girlfriends, are a running theme on *Here's Lucy*. Actor Ross Martin, a close personal friend of Lucille's, makes his directorial debut with this entry. Notice that the layout of Harry's house changes from episode to episode. For some reason, a permanent set is never built.

HERE'S LUCY #63: "LUCY AND MA PARKER"

(CBS, DECEMBER 21, 1970), 30 MINUTES

DIRECTED BY: Herbert Kenwith
WRITTEN BY: Larry Rhine, Lou Derman
GUEST CAST: Carole Cook, Marc Laurence, Billy Curtis, Jerry Maren, Harry Hickox, Stafford Repp, Boyd "Red" Morgan, Orwin Harvey, Emile Autuori

A female crook and two tiny people move in next door to the Carters, claiming to be a mother and her offspring. Once Lucy realizes the truth and has them arrested, she and her children help the police by posing as the gang.

HIGHLIGHTS & TRIVIA

As with most Rhine/Derman scripts, this one is a cartoon, and a bad one at that. The Carters would have to be mentally deficient to believe those midgets are little kids, or that any children of the 1970s would be dressed in a Little Lord Fauntleroy outfit or Shirley Temple curls. The plot premise of the tiny people crooks had been used in the Lon Chaney silent movie *The Unholy Three* (1925) and Chaney's 1930 talkie remake of his 1920s classic.

Carole Cook
(ACTOR/FAMILY FRIEND)

This show featured me as the guest star, not just a supporting player. I never got guest star billing. I didn't like it, but I accepted it. She [Lucille Ball] discovered me.

Kaye Ballard
(ACTOR/SINGER)

Lucy never really helped Carole [Cook], and it broke my heart. Carole is such a talented lady, and Lucy could have done so much for her. Carole never got billing or important money. But Lucy was insecure about her own talent—Lucy, the greatest talent in the world. Carole worked too much like Lucy.

Kathleen Freeman
(ACTOR)

Would you want to see yourself walking around? Carole studied Lucille Ball, and how could she not pick up Lucy's stuff? Also, familiarity can breed two things: taking people for granted, and contempt. In Carole's case, Lucille's attitude might have been, "Well, it's just Carole."

Carole Cook
(ACTOR/FAMILY FRIEND)

I never, never, even once asked Lucille Ball to pick up a phone and make a call on my behalf. She may have done it, but it wasn't because I asked for it. Conversely, I made sure that I wasn't always at her beck and call. Powerful women like Lucille and Ethel Merman could eat you up alive. Not because they meant to, but because they were so strong and you let them.

Dick Martin
(COMEDIAN/ACTOR/DIRECTOR)

A sitcom director cannot make a show funny. He can be technically creative, but if it isn't on the paper, it won't be funny. A sitcom director doesn't even get a final cut. That's up to the producer. So it didn't really matter who was directing Lucy, or if she was doing it herself. If the scripts were inferior, the shows were inferior.

HERE'S LUCY #64: "LUCY STOPS A MARRIAGE"

(CBS, DECEMBER 28, 1970), 30 MINUTES

DIRECTED BY: Jack Donohue
WRITTEN BY: Frank Gill Jr., Vincent Bogert
GUEST CAST: Jayne Meadows, Marcel de la Brosse

A wealthy old flame from Harry's school years arrives at the office and tells him she wants to invest $100,000 in his business. Although Lucy has been turned down for a ten-dollar-a-week work raise, Harry has pledged to see to the children's education. Fearing that Harry will marry this person just to provide for her kids, Lucy does all she can to discourage the woman from marrying Harry.

HIGHLIGHTS & TRIVIA

The writers of *Here's Lucy* never seem to have a clue about what a real employment agency does. There always seem to be contracts, lawyers, investors—just like at a bank. However, this is not *The Lucy Show*, and the character of Theodore Mooney is nowhere in sight. During the filming, Lucille makes an uncharacteristic joke, which causes a retake. When Kim says she doesn't like the idea of spying on Uncle Harry, Lucy's retort is, "Why not? The audience will love it!" She is wrong. This episode is really bad, and there is no excuse for it.

Jayne Meadows
(ACTOR)

I considered Lucille a friend—a generous friend. She apologized to me because the script was so poor. She said they had to buy some cheaper scripts from lesser-known writers to balance out all the money they had spent on the Burtons. I believe I even had to wear my own clothes. Lucie Arnaz is a brilliant actor and very charming.

Miss Meadows' explanation might make some sense, except for the fact that all of the shows this season have been filmed long before the Burton episode, although that special entry is aired first.

HERE'S LUCY #65: "LUCY'S VACATION"

(CBS, JANUARY 4, 1971), 30 MINUTES

DIRECTED BY: Coby Ruskin
WRITTEN BY: Fred S. Fox, Seaman Jacobs
GUEST CAST: Parley Baer, Kimetha Laurie, Sid Gould

Lucy wants to take her two-week vacation, but hard-hearted Harry informs her she used it up on long lunches and coffee breaks. Stressed out by working with the Redhead, he has begun seeing psychiatrist Dr. Cunningham, who suggests sending Lucy away for two weeks to give Harry a much-needed break.

HIGHLIGHTS & TRIVIA

The theme of Lucy trying to get fired to take time off now becomes an overly recurring theme of *Here's Lucy*. Parley Baer, a Lucy veteran going back to the old *I Love Lucy* days, will also play Harry's shrink in several future episodes.

Lucille Ball

We had way too many of these shows where Lucy tries to get herself fired, or get herself a raise. We paid these writers a lot of money. You'd think they could have come up with something better for me than this crap all the time.

THE SUPER COMEDY BOWL I

(CBS, JANUARY 10, 1971); 60 MINUTES

PRODUCED AND DIRECTED BY: Marty Pasetta
WRITTEN BY: Saul Turteltaub, Bernie Orenstein, Gordon Farr, Arnold Kane
CAST: Lucille Ball (host), Kermit Alexander, Carol Burnett, Judy Carne, Tina Cole, Norm Crosby, Ben Davidson, Roman Gabriel, Mike Garrett, Jack Gilford, Charlton Heston, Marty Ingalls, Arte Johnson, the NFL's Deacon Jones, Alex Karras, Daryl Lamonica, Dick Le Beau, Jack Lemmon, Art Metrano, Joe Namath, Pat O'Brien, Charles Nelson Reilly, Jill St. John, O.J. Simpson, Alan Sues, Leslie Uggams, Gene Washington, John Wayne, Dave Willock

Lucille is so eager to keep working on TV it seems she will accept anything to keep busy professionally. Although she has no luck interesting the CBS network in a special from her own production company, she is happy to accept the hosting chores for this turkey. Although there is quite a bit of talent on the show, none of it is there for any special purpose. The Superbowl is only four years old at this point and its popularity is phenomenal. This special simply rips off the name and time of year to get ratings. The humor is very campy, and today would be labeled homophobic. Ball handles all of the introductions.

HERE'S LUCY #66: "LUCY AND THE 20-20 VISION"

(CBS, JANUARY 11, 1971), 30 MINUTES
DIRECTED BY: Jack Carter
WRITTEN BY: Phil Leslie, George Balzer
GUEST CAST: Jack Collins, Morreen Gemini, Colleen Gemini

Lucy wants a two-day vacation to take Kim and Craig to Mexico, but grouchy Harry won't give her the needed time off. Thinking he might be on edge because his eyes are bothering him, Lucy talks Harry into seeing an eye doctor. When he gets his glasses, Lucy's troubles really begin.

HIGHLIGHTS & TRIVIA
Another of the "Lucy wants time off" shows. This episode is interesting only for the directorial debut of comedy veteran, Jack Carter.

Jack Carter
(COMEDY LEGEND/DIRECTOR)
It was Lucy's idea that I become a director. She knew that I know comedy and timing, and that I had done hundreds of television shows in my career. We were very close friends, and it was because of her that I got my Director's Guild card. She was very gentle with me this first time. She took my direction, and supported all of my decisions.

HERE'S LUCY #67: "LUCY AND THE RAFFLE"

(CBS, JANUARY 18, 1971), 30 MINUTES
DIRECTED BY: Ross Martin
WRITTEN BY: Ray Singer, Al Schwartz
GUEST CAST: Hayden Rorke, Paul Picerni, Rhodes Reason, Robert Foulk, Sid Gould, Irwin Charone, Jody Gilbert, Larry J. Blake, Florence Lake, Emile Autori, John "Red" Fox, Vanda Barra

Kim wins an expensive sports car in a raffle, but cannot afford to pay the taxes on it. She and Lucy hold their own raffle to pay the tax and earn enough money to buy an economy car. Unfortunately, they are arrested for gambling.

HIGHLIGHTS & TRIVIA
This installment is a direct rip-off of 1955's "Ricky's European Booking" episode of *I Love Lucy* (#137). Many of the *Here's Lucy* players are trotted out for this one, but for little effect. Hayden Rorke has not worked with Ball since the first season (1951–52) of *I Love Lucy*.

MAKE ROOM FOR GRANDDADDY: "LUCY CARTER, HOUSEGUEST"

(ABC, JANUARY 21, 1971), 30 MINUTES
EXECUTIVE PRODUCED BY: Danny Thomas
PRODUCED BY: Richard Crenna
DIRECTED BY: John Rich
WRITTEN BY: Lee Erwin
CAST: Danny Thomas, Marjorie Lord, Lucille Ball, Angela Cartwright, Doris Singleton, Joe Mell

When Lucy Carter comes to New York, she is invited to stay with her old friend Kathy Williams. Danny Williams is out of town, but returns unexpectedly. He mistakes Lucy for Kathy several times, leading Lucy to believe that he has designs on her. Kathy tells Lucy that Danny likes very feminine women, so she puts on men's clothing and acts like a man to turn him off.

HIGHLIGHTS & TRIVIA
This series is a rehash of the old *The Danny Thomas Show Make Room for Daddy* (1953–64). It is unusual that Kathy Williams' character knows both Lucy Ricardo and Lucy Carter. This episode is the only oncamera time Lucy Carter ever references her late husband. Look for Doris Singleton playing Grace Munson, a character from *I Love Lucy*, although Doris had played Caroline Appleby on that series. In the credits, they carelessly give Singleton's character name as Sylvia. Although there is a live audience, the show is so humorless that they rely on

laugh track "sweetening." The canned reactions are so out of control, that there is laughter every three seconds for no reason.

Marjorie Lord
(ACTOR)

This series [Make Room for Granddaddy, *1970–71] just didn't work. The little boy playing our grandson was impossible to direct. He had done a great audition in the office, but he just couldn't cut it on the set. We began to write around him and things began to improve, but then they moved us to another night and that killed us. The other problem was that we didn't have [producer/director] Sheldon Leonard. Sheldon and Danny were a perfect comedy marriage much in the same way that Lucy and Desi were. Without Sheldon to control, Danny was left without someone to reel him in or bring him up when he needed it. Dick Crenna was producing, and is a very bright man, but he and Danny didn't have the same relationship that Danny and Sheldon did.*

I did not like the episode with Lucy. Our scenes together did not have any of the fun of our earlier work. They tried to piece together bits of I Love Lucy, Here's Lucy, *and* Make Room for Daddy *for purposes of nostalgia, but it didn't jell. Lucy's voice had gotten very deep, probably from not using her vocal chords properly when she projected. And her personality changed as she grew older; she was not as feminine as she had been. That femininity had been important to her comedy, and that changed. She got stronger in personality as the years went by. By the way, in all the years Danny and I worked together, he never patted me on the backside the way he did Lucy in two different shows. It would have been totally out of character for me.*

Angela Cartwright
(ACTOR)

From a production standpoint, the week went very much like it had been on the old show. Creatively, I think the timing was wrong. We had a writer's strike, and the scripts were rehashed old material. Additionally, television was growing up all around us, but Danny's humor had remained the same.

THE PEARL BAILEY SHOW

(ABC, JANUARY 23, 1971), 60 MINUTES
PRODUCED BY: Bob Finkel
DIRECTED BY: Dean Whitmore
WRITTEN BY: Bill Angelos, Buz Kohan, Pearl Bailey
CAST: Pearl Bailey (host), Lucille Ball

Lucille continues to keep herself busy on TV by accepting more guest shots. In this one, Lucille enters the proceedings from the audience via an elaborate Egyptian-style litter carried by musclemen. Pearlie Mae acts surprised to see her, and they exchange girl talk. Unfortunately, this variety series (which debuts with this episode) is so badly rated that few TV viewers ever see it. It is off the air by summer, 1971.

HERE'S LUCY #68: "LUCY'S HOUSE GUEST, HARRY"

(CBS, JANUARY 25, 1971), 30 MINUTES
DIRECTED BY: Charles Walters
WRITTEN BY: Fred S. Fox, Seaman Jacobs
GUEST CAST: Herbie Faye, Vince Barnett, Sid Gould, Robert Foulk, Emile Autori, Frank Scanell, Eugene Molnar

While Harry's house is being painted, he moves in with Lucy and her brood. His habits are so annoying that Lucy and the kids scheme to get rid of him—soon.

HIGHLIGHTS & TRIVIA

This is a so-so episode, with nothing much in it to recommend. It is a sad statement, for *Here's Lucy* produces many mediocre episodes during its six-year TV run. The writing, direction, and execution offer nothing fresh or crisp. If this installment was a salad, the vegetables would be wilted, and the dressing watered-down.

HERE'S LUCY #69: "LUCY AND ALADDIN'S LAMP"

(CBS, FEBRUARY 1, 1971), 30 MINUTES
DIRECTED BY: Charles Walters
WRITTEN BY: Frank Gill Jr., Vincent Bogert
GUEST CAST: Mary Jane Croft, George Neise, Robert Foulk, William Lanteau

Lucy holds a garage sale, and she comes across an old lamp she doesn't recognize. Its resemblance to "Aladdin's Lamp" moves her to clean it and make a wish—which comes true. After Kim and Harry also get their wishes fulfilled, they are certain they own the original magical lamp.

HIGHLIGHTS & TRIVIA

As bad as their prior effort was, this Gill/Bogert script is actually funny. There is also a naturalness in the performances missing in many of the *Here's Lucy* entries.

HERE'S LUCY #70: "LUCY AND CAROL BURNETT" A.K.A. "THE HOLLYWOOD UNEMPLOYMENT FOLLIES"

(CBS, FEBRUARY 8, 1971), 30 MINUTES

DIRECTED BY: Jack Carter
WRITTEN BY: Ray Singer, Al Schwartz
GUEST CAST: Carol Burnett, Jack Benny, Richard Deacon, Clarence Landry, Venord Bradley, Johnny Silver, Sid Gould, Mike Wagner, Ray Kuter, Vanda Barra, Carole Cook

Lucy runs into Carol Krausemeyer at the unemployment office after Harry fires Lucy once again. The girls decide there are so many talented people at the office, that they should put on a show to raise money.

HIGHLIGHTS & TRIVIA

This is a very pleasant outing, brightened mostly by Burnett's clowning, energy, and singing. The threadbare plot is just an excuse for an extended musical sequence, much in the style of those done on Burnett's TV variety series (1967–79). Like many of these shows, the syndicated version is so butchered and truncated that it is impossible to appreciate the musical numbers. Jack Benny appears briefly in two scenes. Carole Cook dubs all of Lucille's singing. We never learn why Harry has fired Lucy, or how she gets her job back. Comedian Jack Carter directs this one, but the experience is not as pleasant as the first time.

Jack Carter

(COMEDY LEGEND/DIRECTOR)

This was a nightmare for me. As nice as she had been the first time [the January 11, 1971 Here's Lucy *episode #66, "Lucy and the 20-20 Vision"], that's how difficult she was this time. No matter what direction I gave, Lucy countermanded it without any regard to who was listening. I spent one whole morning blocking the show, then went to lunch. When I came back, she had changed everything with no discussion or regard to the fact that I was the director. Part of the problem was that my ex-wife Paula [Stewart, who had been on Broadway in* Wildcat *(1960) with Lucille] and I were in a bitter custody battle for my son Michael. We're in court, and in walks Miss Lucille Ball, who testifies against me. Once the judge saw her, I had no chance. I think she was still angry at me for leaving Paula, and took it out on me during this episode. In retrospect, I should have stood up to her and won her respect the same way that Jack Donohue and Herbert Kenwith did. However, I was so shocked that a friend would do that to me that I just sort of let her have her way. After that, I never directed another television show, a decision I regret today.*

Carole Cook

(ACTOR/FAMILY FRIEND)

Whenever I had to dub Lucille's voice, I'd get the music ahead of time to study. Then we'd go over to Glen Glenn Sound with the band and record it the week that the episode was shot. She had to do this because although she could sing, as she got older the range of her voice narrowed. She was uncomfortable hitting high notes, or if she had to hold an extended note. Any song that had a wide range became difficult for her to sing, so I'd dub her voice instead.

HERE'S LUCY #71: "LUCY GOES HAWAIIAN, PART ONE"

(CBS, FEBRUARY 15, 1971), 30 MINUTES

DIRECTED BY: Jack Donohue
WRITTEN BY: Milt Josefsberg, Al Schwartz, Ray Singer
GUEST CAST: Vivian Vance, Robert Alda, Anita Mann, Jeanne Byron, Burt Mustin, Maurice Kelly

Harry books himself as the cruise director for a luxury liner, and brings Lucy along as his assistant so she will do all the work. Once on the ship, who does Lucy find on board but her old pal Viv. The two friends become rivals for the attention of the dashing Captain McClay.

HIGHLIGHTS & TRIVIA

First of two parts. This outing is filmed like a movie, using mostly one camera, with no audience in attendance. Originally, the shows are to be filmed on location aboard the ship, the *Lurline,* and in Hawaii. When costs prove prohibitive, Lucille has a three-quarter scale model of the ship built at the

Paramount (formerly Desilu, formerly RKO) lot. It is the second largest ship built at the studio. Ball takes up three sound stages for these two entries. Art designer Ray Beal oversees the highly accurate ship model, ensuring that it matches the pictures and diagrams supplied by the company. The Captain's surname McClay is taken from that of Howard McClay, public relations man for Lucille Ball Productions. Jeanne Byron, who plays the Captain's wife, is best known as Patty Duke's mother on her popular 1960s sitcom.

During the dress rehearsal, Lucille is concerned that someone has dropped a line of dialog during the hula lesson scene. "I think that needs a queen," she said, pointing at one of the bit players and inferring the missed piece of dialog. Vivian couldn't resist making a gay joke, "Who doesn't?"

HERE'S LUCY #72: "LUCY GOES HAWAIIAN, PART TWO"

(CBS, FEBRUARY 22, 1971), 30 MINUTES
DIRECTED BY: Jack Donohue
WRITTEN BY: Ray Singer, Al Schwartz, Milt Josefsberg
GUEST CAST: Vivian Vance, Robert Alda, Jack Donohue, Alex Plasschaert

Harry sticks Lucy with all the work aboard ship for putting on a talent show featuring the passengers. Utilizing Viv, the kids, and Harry, Lucy stages a spectacular musicale.

HIGHLIGHTS & TRIVIA

This follow-up outing is excellent. The numbers are lively, extremely well shot and choreographed, and superbly performed. It is a joy to see Lucille and Vivian having so much fun in their musical numbers. "Yellow Bird" is the last full musical solo Vivian Vance sings on a Lucy program.

Desi Arnaz Jr.

This was one of the few shows we did not do in front of a live audience. I was doing that stupid Don Ho impression and that was hard enough—I mean, who does a Don Ho impression? I must have been the first one. I actually knew Don Ho back then. I used to go onstage and perform with him. My lip-synching was terrible on that show. I think it was because I had to kiss those girls. I really liked the sequence where I wore the grass skirt and was shirtless because it showed off my body. I look back now and go, "Boy! Look how skinny I was!" I enjoyed doing the show tremendously.

Lucie Arnaz

I worked so hard on these shows. I had a friend from Immaculate Heart High named Wendy Mukai who used to be a dancer with the Don Ho show. She came over for three or four weeks prior to that episode and showed me how to do a real hula. I loved putting that show on just to prove to myself that I could do it properly.

This was Desi Arnaz Jr.'s last appearance as a regular on *Here's Lucy*.

Desi Arnaz Jr.

I had never intended to be on the show more than three years, regardless of how successful it was. I had other things I wanted to do. And I was offered a role in Red Sky at Morning *[1970]. I got that part because [producer] Hal Wallis had seen the* Here's Lucy *show with Ann-Margret. It was a thrill for me, getting to do the drama and comedy. It was such a good role. So I missed several episodes of the show to shoot the movie. And I never came back but once.*

Lucie Arnaz

Desi was right to leave. Not that it was really planned. He just kept getting job offers that he couldn't turn down. Jerry Paris was supposed to have directed these shows. Mom was upset with him because he went way over budget on the Burton/Taylor show. She accused him of nepotism and hiring too many relatives. I said, "Well, you're one to talk!"

EVERYTHING YOU ALWAYS WANTED TO KNOW ABOUT JACK BENNY BUT WERE AFRAID TO ASK

(NBC, MARCH 10, 1971), 60 MINUTES
EXECUTIVE PRODUCED BY: Irving Fein
PRODUCED AND DIRECTED BY: Norman Abbott
WRITTEN BY: Al Gordon and Hal Goldman, Hilliard Marks, Hugh Wedlock Jr., Bucky Searles
CAST: Jack Benny (host), Lucille Ball, George Burns, Phil Harris, Bob Hope, Dr. David Rubin, Dionne Warwick, John Wayne
Done on the same set as Benny's Birthday Special

(February 17, 1969), Lucille once again interrupts his monologue, this time to discuss his sex appeal. Lucille will wear the same green hostess outfit almost a year later on the *Here's Lucy* episode "Lucy's Punctured Romance" (episode #94). All of this leads to a flashback, with Lucille as a Goldwyn Girl in a 1930s wig and a loud dress with balloons attached. She breaks the other chorines' balloons with her cigarette, à la Lucy. When Benny kisses her, her balloons pop. John Wayne enters as chorus boy Marion Michael Morrison. The scene then switches to Jack's house, where he auditions, or rather tries to seduce her. The seventy-six-year-old Lothario seducing the sixty-year-old chorus girl just doesn't play, and Lucille's crying jag in the end is plain silly.

SWING OUT, SWEET LAND

(NBC, APRIL 8, 1971), 90 MINUTES

PRODUCED BY: Nick Vanoff, William O. Harbach
DIRECTED BY: Stan Harris
WRITTEN BY: Paul W. Keyes
CAST: John Wayne (host), Ann-Margret, Lucille Ball, Jack Benny, Dan Blocker, Johnny Cash, Roy Clark, Bing Crosby, Phyllis Diller, Lorne Greene, Celeste Holm, Bob Hope, Michael Landon, Dean Martin, Dick Martin, Ross Martin, Greg Morris, David Nelson, Rick Nelson, Hugh O'Brian, Dan Rowan, William Shatner, Red Skelton, Tom Smothers, Leslie Uggams, Dennis Weaver

This patriotic special features a stellar cast saluting America. Lucille does not perform any comedy, but does a serious introduction.

THE TWENTY-THIRD ANNUAL EMMY AWARDS

(NBC, MAY 9, 1971), 120 MINUTES

EXECUTIVE PRODUCED BY: Bob Finkel
PRODUCED AND DIRECTED BY: Bill Foster
WRITTEN BY: Harry Crane, George Bloom, Ann Elder, Larry Hovis, Mike Barrie, Jim Mulholland

Telecast from the Hollywood Palladium, the show is still a winner. Hosted by Johnny Carson, there is unforgivable canned laughter under his monologue. Bob Carroll Jr. and Madelyn Davis are nominated for Best Writing, Comedy, for "Lucy Meets the Burtons," but don't win.

Lucille and Jack Benny present the best supporting actor awards. They get a thirty-second ovation before they can even speak. She wears a green-and-lavender chiffon gown with an empire cut, and looks beautiful. As she ages, Lucille sometimes comes off as something of a smart-ass on these shows, but this night she is clearly happy to be onstage with Jack Benny. Gale Gordon is nominated for his role of Uncle Harry, but loses to Ed Asner of *Mary Tyler Moore* (1970–77). When Valerie Harper wins for her *Rhoda* (1974–78) portrayal, she shouts, "Lucy, remember when I was in the chorus of *Wildcat*?" In her excitement, Lucille keeps reading all of the cue cards, leaving Benny with nothing to do. Finally, he grabs one of the envelopes, yelling, "She won't let me do anything!" It is the high point of the evening.

Carol Burnett clowns with Lucille Ball during a break from taping *The Carol Burnett Show*, 1970.
COURTESY OF MICHAEL STERN.

Lucie Arnaz, Desi Arnaz Jr., and Lucille Ball in top form for "Lucy Goes Hawaiian," 1971. COURTESY OF DESILU, TOO, LLC.

Lucille Ball, Gale Gordon, Lucie Arnaz, and one of those darn chimps perform together, 1972.
COURTESY OF DESILU, TOO, LLC.

Lucille and Vivian show they enjoy working together during the filming of "With Viv as a Friend, Who Needs an Enemy?," 1972. COURTESY OF DESILU, TOO, LLC.

Lucille loved doing these musical numbers. Here she is ably abetted by Gale Gordon and daughter Lucie, 1972. COURTESY OF DESILU, TOO, LLC.

Cast members Gale Gordon and Lucie Arnaz sign Lucille's cast, 1972. Official number one fan Michael Stern *still* has that signed cast. COURTESY OF DESILU, TOO, LLC.

The ultimate guest star, "Lucy Carter Meets Lucille Ball," 1974. COURTESY OF DESILU, TOO, LLC.

Lucille Ball out on the town with daughter Lucie, 1975. COURTESY OF DESILU, TOO, LLC.

Frumpy Lucille Ball in an unhappy marriage to oncamera husband Art Carney in *Happy Anniversary and Goodbye,* 1974.
COURTESY OF DESILU, TOO, LLC.

Startled Jackie Gleason gets a kiss from brunette Lucille Ball in the disastrous special, *Three for Two,* 1975.
COURTESY OF DESILU, TOO, LLC.

Lonely Lucille Ball puts the moves on shy Art Carney in a vignette from *What Now, Catherine Curtis?,* 1976. COURTESY OF DESILU, TOO, LLC.

Vital older woman Lucille flirts with her younger stud boyfriend Joseph Bologna in the final scene from *What Now, Catherine Curtis?,* 1976. COURTESY OF DESILU, TOO, LLC.

Rare candid shot of Lucille Ball, sans makeup and wig, circa 1983. COURTESY OF MICHAEL STERN.

Lucille and Gale get into another sticky situation on "Lucy Gets Her Wires Crossed," 1986. COURTESY OF MICHAEL STERN.

Lucille poses with Rupert the Robot on the set of "Lucy Makes Curtis Byte the Dust," 1986. COURTESY OF MICHAEL STERN.

Handsome Desi Arnaz Jr, all grown up and charming. COURTESY OF DESILU, TOO, LLC.

The lovely Lucie Arnaz, as nice as she is pretty. COURTESY OF DESILU, TOO, LLC.

Chapter Twenty-Three

1971-72 Season

HERE'S LUCY: THE FOURTH SEASON

TECHNICAL REGULARS: Executive produced by Gary Morton; produced by Cleo Smith; directed by Coby Ruskin; executive consultant: Milt Josefsberg; makeup by Hal King; hairstyling by Irma Kusely; music by Marl Young

CAST REGULARS: Lucille Ball (Lucy Carter); Gale Gordon (Harrison Otis Carter); Lucie Arnaz (Kim Carter); Roy Rowan (announcer)

HERE'S LUCY #73: "LUCY AND FLIP GO LEGIT"

(CBS, SEPTEMBER 13, 1971), 30 MINUTES

WRITTEN BY: Bob Carroll Jr., Madelyn Davis

GUEST CAST: Flip Wilson, Kim Hamilton

Lucy leaves Harry's employ to work with comedian Flip Wilson, but finds herself relegated to sorting fan mail. She gets fired for trying to get Wilson's autograph, but comes back disguised to talk him into appearing as Prissy in a little-theatre production of *Gone with the Wind.*

HIGHLIGHTS & TRIVIA

If it is on the page, Lucille Ball can make it hysterical. The return of Carroll and Davis to the writing staff is a breath of fresh air desperately needed by Lucille at this juncture in her career. Although the scripts are not as funny as the ones they wrote in the past, they are not entirely to blame. They inherit empty characters and a format that they did not create. *The Wind* parody is smart, and Lucie Arnaz (as Melanie) and Flip Wilson are stand-outs. Lucille finally gets to play Scarlett O'Hara; she auditioned for the 1939 movie classic when it was originally being cast. Beginning with this episode, there are altered opening credits (deleting Desi Jr.'s name), and a new arrangement of the theme song by music director Marl Young. After several years, a Ball series has a permanent director (Coby Ruskin). With a few exceptions, he will direct every episode of *Here's Lucy* from this point forward.

Lucie Arnaz

I was very proud of this show, and my work in it. Flip was great fun to work with, and that show within the show was hysterical. . . . [He was] a great talent.

THE FLIP WILSON SHOW

(NBC, SEPTEMBER 16, 1971), 60 MINUTES

EXECUTIVE PRODUCED BY: Monte Kay

PRODUCED BY: Bob Henry

DIRECTED BY: Tim Kiley

WRITTEN BY: Herb Baker, Hal Goodman, Larry Klein, Bob Weiskopf and Bob Schiller, Flip Wilson

CAST: Flip Wilson (host), Lucille Ball, the Osmond Brothers, Ed Sullivan

This is one of Lucille's best TV variety show stints—ever. She is a huge fan of Wilson's talents, and is very pleased by his recent work on her TV series. Ball is also thrilled to be working with Ed Sullivan away from his own Sunday night variety show. Unknown to most people, Sullivan has begun to develop what would now be termed Alzheimer's Disease. Ball knows her old friend is in failing health.

The two major sketches are cleverly written by a staff that includes her old scribes Bob Schiller and Bob Weiskopf. One sketch has the entire cast doing a takeoff of the popular cartoon strip *Peanuts*, with Lucille playing (what else?) Lucy and Sullivan deadpanning his way through Snoopy. The best moments occur between Ball as a sex crazy carhop who works with Geraldine (Wilson in his famous drag characterization). Besides the fine performances, Wilson's laced shoe becomes undone during the sketch, causing much ad-libbing by Flip and breaking up by Lucille. The finale is simple, with Flip interviewing Ball and Sullivan about their lengthy TV careers.

HERE'S LUCY #74: "LUCY AND THE MOUNTAIN CLIMBER"

(CBS, SEPTEMBER 20, 1971), 30 MINUTES
WRITTEN BY: Lou Derman, Larry Rhine
GUEST CAST: Tony Randall, Morgan Jones, Sid Gould, Janos Prohaska, Roy Rowan (voice only)

Harry takes in a new business partner, Rudy Springer (Tony Randall), who wants to cut away all the dead wood at the employment agency. Lucy immediately fears for her job, and professes great athletic ability to the outdoor enthusiast. Springer makes her a deal that if she can beat him in a mountain-climbing race, she can keep her job at Carter's Unique Employment Agency.

HIGHLIGHTS & TRIVIA

This one features yet another bear in yet another silly outing.

Tony Randall
(ACTOR)

A lot of people found her [Lucille Ball] very, very tough to work with. She bossed everybody around and didn't spare anybody's feelings. But I didn't mind that because she knew what she was doing. If someone just says, "Do this!" it's awful if they are wrong. If they are right, it just saves a lot of time. And she was always right.

HERE'S LUCY #75: "LUCY AND HARRY'S ITALIAN BOMBSHELL"

(CBS, SEPTEMBER 27, 1971), 30 MINUTES
WRITTEN BY: Fred S. Fox, Seaman Jacobs
GUEST CAST: Kaye Ballard, Herbie Faye, Emile Autori, Sid Gould, Vanda Barra, Robert Foulk

Harry receives a letter from Donna, his long-lost Italian love from World War II. They had promised to remain true to one another, so when he learns she is coming to visit him, Harry starts a crash regimen to lose weight and look youthful.

HIGHLIGHTS & TRIVIA

This is a superior outing, thanks to the cast's fine, controlled performances. Herbie Faye is splendid as a burglar in a scene at the office that really has nothing to do with the plot but adds much to the show. Broadway veteran Kaye Ballard is almost unrecognizable as Donna, wearing a fat suit and upswept hair. She is one of the few people who has remained close to Lucille Ball and Desi Arnaz since their divorce, and is loyal to each of them.

The scene where Vanda Barra (as a door-to-door salesperson) arrives and Harry thinks she is Donna is a classic. After the visitor hits Harry with her purse and then leaves, Lucy says, "She swings a mean bag," and Harry is supposed to say, "She is a mean bag!" After that line, he ad libs, "Good thing she wasn't selling doorknobs," which sends Lucille into paroxysms of laughter. This breakup is wisely left in the final cut of the episode.

Lucie Arnaz

Kaye Ballard is one of my favorite people. She is almost like family. She bought my father's house in Palm Springs. She is like an Italian grandma. That scene where I am interpreting a letter for Uncle Harry is one of my favorites. And when Vanda came to the house and Gale ad-libbed, I was flabbergasted, because Gale never did that in a show. It was great to see my mother crackup like that. And Herbie Faye was so funny. What a great character actor. This was really a special show . . . great acting, a funny script, and fast-paced direction.

Kaye Ballard
(ACTOR/SINGER)

Lucy came to me and said, "You must be padded for the part!" I told her that I didn't want to be padded, but she insisted. So Gary Morton pulled me aside and said, "Do this for us, do it for Lucy. We haven't got much money in the budget for you, but just do this for Lucy and I'll have a great part written for you." Needless to say, he did not keep his word. I wore the padding, and when the show aired I got calls from all over the country asking if I was sick or maybe pregnant because I looked so bad. In the scene when I come into the office, Lucy kept breaking up at my ad libs and gestures. She cut the cameras three times and we had to go back and retake portions of the scene before she could get through it.

HERE'S LUCY #76: "LUCY AND MANNIX ARE HELD HOSTAGE"

(CBS, OCTOBER 4, 1971), 30 MINUTES

WRITTEN BY: Bob Carroll Jr., Madelyn Davis
GUEST CAST: Mike Connors, Mary Jane Croft, Marc Lawrence, John Doucette, Bob Foulk, Vince Howard

Using binoculars, Lucy inadvertently sees bank robbers counting money. Fearful the crooks will harm Lucy, Harry hires private investigator Joe Mannix (Mike Connors' character on his hit series *Mannix*, 1967–75) to protect her. Unfortunately, when Joe arrives at Lucy's house, she thinks Mannix is one of the robbers and knocks him out. The real robbers appear on the scene, and kidnap Lucy and Mannix to dispose of them.

HIGHLIGHTS & TRIVIA

The dress rehearsal is filmed for insurance, as Lucille is nervous working in a new environment. This is the first show filmed at Universal Studios. The previous summer, Ball moved her production company from Paramount to Universal. It had become too much for her to remain at her old studio and not be in total control. Also, Universal offers her a better rental deal, and builds her an area called "Lucy Lane" with special decorations that houses her own personal hair, makeup, and wardrobe departments, as well as a private dressing bungalow, and one on display for the studio tourists to see. This is the first episode aired that is shot at Universal studios that shows the Carter home. It has been redecorated, using fewer set pieces and replacing the lounges in front of the fireplace with regular chairs. Likewise, the office set is streamlined, changing the color of the chairs from dark to light and removing all of the African artifacts. This is the only time during *Here's Lucy*'s run that these sets are redressed.

Lucie Arnaz

Art Parker, our set designer, was brilliant. He did some great work for other people. But Mom liked what she liked. The same sort of stuff you saw on the set was the stuff we had at home. There was more yellow on that set than a sunflower. Mom hated change as she got older, especially in her furnishings. Other than this one time, the set never changed. In fact, in the entire six years I did the show, I never once gave the set a second thought. I did get sad moving from the lot my parents had owned to Universal Studios. Even though they built this great thing called Lucy Lane, it just wasn't the same for me.

Mike Connors

(ACTOR)

It was because of Gary Morton and Lucille that I was on Mannix. *I collected old cars in those days, and I happened to be on the Desilu lot and parked right in front of Gary's office. He, too, had an interest in old cars, and came out to see mine. While we were standing there admiring cars, he said, "You know, we just got in a script that would be perfect for you. Why don't you read it and call me back?" I took and read it and loved it. We had a meeting that led to the pilot and the show, and I look back and feel that I owe the whole thing to Gary and Lucille. When the show was floundering after the first year, Lucille went to CBS and told them she wanted the show to remain on the air, even if changes had to be made. So Joe Mannix became a private investigator, and the rest is history.*

It was such a great experience working with Lucille on her series. The thing that shocked me was how she knew every facet of show business, from the lighting to the camera to the directing to what was funny about a line. She knew just by using the wrong emphasis that it was going to kill a joke. I'll never forget the first day we walked on the set. In a moment, she realized that there was something wrong with the lighting and the camera angles. In fifteen minutes, she had totally redirected the setup to how it should be. She was sensational with how she worked with the director, making things better . . . after the first reading, I thought the script was all right, but not a wow, until we began to actually work on our feet. After she saw it, my wife thought it was one of the best comedy things I had done. Lucille told me, "You play this thing straight now. Don't think of these lines as humorous and we will get a lot of laughs. You let me do the funnies and we'll get the laughs on this thing." And she was right. I held the script the whole time we were blocking, so I could learn my lines and the moves at the same time. It was faster for me that way. Lucille was right on top of everything. They could have gotten a catering service to direct the show; she was the one in charge.

Skelton was the same way. These people knew what they were talking about.

We rehearsed the chair thing tied up on the set right from the beginning, just the way it was going to be. We were originally going to slide the chairs, but Lucille came up with the idea to bounce the chairs. It was a much funnier visual that way. There was also a great deal of experimentation to make certain that the condiment bottles worked properly. I enjoyed the live audience. In those days I had more guts than good sense. We had very few pickups, much less than the other comedy shows I did . . . Gary Morton seemed to be kept busy behind the scenes. He really had no impact with what was happening on the set.

Bob Carroll, Jr.

(WRITER)

This is one of the best of the later shows in her career. Lucy and Mike worked very well together, and that bit on the chairs came off beautifully.

Lucille Ball

I hadn't actually seen this episode for several years after it was made. When I finally sat down and watched it, I was surprised at how really funny it was, and how good Mike was in it.

HERE'S LUCY #77: "LUCY AND THE ASTRONAUTS"

(CBS, OCTOBER 11, 1971), 30 MINUTES

WRITTEN BY: Lou Derman, Larry Rhine

GUEST CAST: Hank Brandt, Hal England, Robert Hogan, Roy Roberts, Paul Picerni, Byron Morrow, Sid Gould, Hugh Douglas (voice only), Roy Rowan (voice only)

Harry's position as a Naval Reservist gets him invited to see the retrieval of three astronauts back from the moon at Cape Kennedy. Unfortunately, he makes the mistake of taking Lucy, who plants patriotic kisses on the men, forcing Lucy and Harry to go through decontamination along with the men.

HIGHLIGHTS & TRIVIA

Lucy shows more motherly affection to the astronauts than she ever does to Kim on the show. Craig is almost never mentioned anymore in the story line.

THE SULLIVAN YEARS

(CBS, OCTOBER 17, 1971), 120 MINUTES (COLOR AND B&W)

EXECUTIVE PRODUCED BY: Bob Precht

PRODUCED BY: Robert Arthur, John Moffitt

DIRECTED BY: John Moffitt

This is a compilation show of clips from Ed's hugely successful variety series (1948–71), the first of many to come through the years. A clip of Lucille and Desi from 1954 is shown.

HERE'S LUCY #78: "LUCY MAKES A FEW EXTRA DOLLARS"

(CBS, OCTOBER 18, 1971), 30 MINUTES

WRITTEN BY: Phil Leslie, Ralph Goodman

GUEST CAST: Gary Morton, Larry J. Blake

Lucy cannot get by on the salary Harry is paying her, so she and Kim make Harry feel so guilty that he'll give Lucy a raise.

HIGHLIGHTS & TRIVIA

Although director Coby Ruskin is a very congenial individual, he cannot overcome mediocre scripts like this one.

HERE'S LUCY #79: "SOMEONE'S ON THE SKI LIFT WITH DINAH"

(CBS, OCTOBER 25, 1971), 30 MINUTES

WRITTEN BY: Bob Carroll Jr., Madelyn Davis

GUEST CAST: Dinah Shore, Mike Howden

Harry takes Lucy and Kim with him to Snow Mass, Colorado, for a skiing vacation. Lucy's favorite performer, Dinah Shore, is also staying at the same lodge, and gets stuck with Lucy on a ski lift.

HIGHLIGHTS & TRIVIA

It is out of character for Harry to take Lucy anywhere, just as it is out of character for Lucy to do a good job at the office. This episode is inspired by Ball's real-life condominium in Colorado, where she often spends time skiing and relaxing. (Several months later, Ball will break her leg on the Colorado ski slopes.) Dinah is beautiful and charming on this outing, singing "Don't Let the Good Life Pass You By."

HERE'S LUCY #80: "LUCY AND HER ALL-NUN BAND"

(CBS, NOVEMBER 1, 1971), 30 MINUTES
WRITTEN BY: Bob Carroll Jr., Madelyn Davis
GUEST CAST: Mary Wickes, Lew Parker, Freddy Martin, Mrs. Freddy Martin, the Remnants

Harry's sister, who is a Catholic nun, comes to town with a problem. She needs a band for a benefit, and only has twenty-five dollars. Lucy hires an all-nun band, but has to fill in on the saxophone herself.

HIGHLIGHTS & TRIVIA

This episode is an example of the incongruities of some of the character relationships. If Sister Paula is Harry's sister, that means she is the sister of Lucy's late husband as well. That makes them sisters-in-law, and Paula the aunt of Kim and Craig. But Lucy acts as if she has never met Paula before, and the nun never inquires about her niece and nephew. It also infers that the Carters might be Catholic. It might have served this series well to have this interesting relative visit more often to add new flavor to the mix.

What the experienced scripters do add is a wonderful part for Mary Wickes as the nun, and the return of Lucy the madcap saxophonist. Freddy Martin is the real-life big band leader who discovered Merv Griffin. Although the syndicated version deletes showing how Martin comes to Lucy's house to give her a sax lesson, the lesson itself (which is retained) is classic Lucy. Even her "Oh, Fred" is reminiscent of Lucy Ricardo. As this outing proves, once again, the best *Here's Lucy* scripts are written by Bob and Madelyn.

Desi Arnaz Jr.

Mary Wickes was a highly intelligent and very spiritual woman. Her humor was so funny because it was genuine. She was a no-nonsense, New England kind of woman, not unlike my grandmother DeDe. She was very sensitive and very caring. And she never stopped working. Mary did exactly what she wanted to do. Mary Wickes [1910–1995] was a lady.

HERE'S LUCY #81: "LUCY AND THE CELEBRITIES"

(CBS, NOVEMBER 8, 1971), 30 MINUTES
WRITTEN BY: Milt Josefsberg, Al Schwartz
GUEST CAST: Rich Little, Jack Benny, Sid Gould

When a rival employment agency begins an aggressive radio campaign, Harry gives Lucy the task of finding celebrities to fight fire with fire. Coincidentally, Kim is dating impressionist Rich Little, so Lucy schemes to fool Harry into thinking Rich's impressions are the voices of actual celebrities she has commandeered.

HIGHLIGHTS & TRIVIA

Although the concept isn't bad, this story is not well written. It seems odd that Lucy has never heard of impressionist Rich Little, whose talent gets lost in the silly plot. Harry is fooled into thinking he has peeper poopers, perhaps the most ridiculous disease known to situation comedy. This is the fourth time that Lucy Carter has met Jack Benny on this series, each encounter as if for the first time.

Lucie Arnaz

Gee, Rich Little is so much older than I. How come my mother didn't mind that age difference?

HERE'S LUCY #82: "WON'T YOU CALM DOWN, DAN DAILEY?"

(CBS, NOVEMBER 15, 1971), 30 MINUTES
WRITTEN BY: Bob Carroll Jr., Madelyn Davis
GUEST CAST: Dan Dailey, Mary Jane Croft, Vanda Barra, Sid Gould

Harry fires Lucy once again, so she takes a job working for the new owner of their office building, movie star Dan Dailey. Lucy proceeds to drive Dailey crazy, so he schemes with Harry to get her to quit and take her old job back.

HIGHLIGHTS & TRIVIA

Light and fluffy, this is an entertaining half hour. It will never be anyone's favorite (except for members of the Dan Dailey Fan Club), but it is still a cut above many of the efforts not prepared by Bob and Madelyn.

HERE'S LUCY #83: "GINGER ROGERS COMES TO TEA"

(CBS, NOVEMBER 22, 1971), 30 MINUTES
WRITTEN BY: Bob Carroll Jr., Madelyn Davis
GUEST CAST: Ginger Rogers, William Lanteau

Harry takes Lucy to a Ginger Rogers Film Festival, where coincidentally Miss Rogers is in the audience incognito. Ginger gets so incensed at comments made about her screen acting that she leaves in a huff, forgetting her purse. When Lucy opens the purse and realizes who the owner really is, she arranges for Rogers to pick it up at her house.

HIGHLIGHTS & TRIVIA

This show is filmed without a studio audience after only two days of rehearsal. A technical strike is being threatened, and Lucille wants to ensure that the show gets done in time. The dance sequence had not been rehearsed the previous week and most of the lines are read from cue cards. Lucille is thrilled to be working with her old pal Ginger Rogers, harking back to their halcyon days in the 1930s at RKO.

Ginger Rogers

(FILM LEGEND)

This girl means business. She is totally focused on what she is doing. There is no horseplay with Lucille; everybody gets down to work. I was happy to be working with her after all those years. She was a tough taskmaster.

Lucie Arnaz

We had to do this one in a hurry! Ginger choreographed most of the dancing herself. I did the Black Bottom because I had just done it on a Kraft Music Hall *with Robert Young and Jane Wyatt.*

HERE'S LUCY #84: "LUCY HELPS DAVID FROST GO NIGHT-NIGHT"

(CBS, NOVEMBER 29, 1971), 30 MINUTES

WRITTEN BY: Bob Carroll Jr., Madelyn Davis

GUEST CAST: David Frost, Tommy Farrell, Sue Taylor, Rosalind Miles, Mike Howden, Ivor Barry, Sid Gould

Talk-show host David Frost hires the Unique Employment Agency to find him a traveling companion who will keep nosy fans away so he can sleep on the plane between Los Angeles and London. Unfortunately, he gets Lucy, who keeps him awake with one annoyance after another.

HIGHLIGHTS & TRIVIA

Ball has made several appearances on Frost's American talk show (1969–72), and a visit to his TV variety show (1971–73). This is his payback for Lucille's graciousness in helping him out.

THE DAVID FROST REVUE

(SYNDICATED, FIRST WEEK OF DECEMBER, 1971), 30 MINUTES

EXECUTIVE PRODUCED BY: David Frost, Marc Merson

PRODUCED BY: Allan Mannings, Mike Gargiulo

DIRECTED BY: Mike Gargiulo

WRITTEN BY: Allan Mannings, Phil Hahn, Herb Hartig, Bob Ellison

CAST: David Frost (host), Lucille Ball, Whitney Blake, Jim Catusi, Jack Gilford, George Irving, Lynn Lipton, Cleavon Little, Marcia Rodd

Capitalizing on the success of his TV talk show, David Frost provides a half-hour of satire each week for two seasons. Lucille appears in a series of blackouts that are not memorable due to the terrible writing and lackluster performing by the regulars. For trivia fans, Whitney Blake (the mother of actress Meredith Baxter), was a regular on *Hazel* (1961–66), and the co-creator of the sitcom *One Day at a Time* (1975–84).

HERE'S LUCY #85: "LUCY IN THE JUNGLE"

(CBS, DECEMBER 6, 1971), 30 MINUTES

WRITTEN BY: Larry Rhine, Lou Derman

GUEST CAST: Lola Fisher, Ben Wrigley

When Harry's doctor suggests he get away from the strains of his business, Lucy arranges for a house swap with a couple from Nairobi, Kenya. Although they have been promised all modern amenities, the Carters find nothing more than a hut, heat, animals, and insects.

HIGHLIGHTS & TRIVIA

This is truly a terrible show! Why Ball continues to approve scripts from Rhine and Derman is a complete mystery.

HERE'S LUCY #86: "LUCY AND CANDID CAMERA"

(CBS, DECEMBER 13, 1971), 30 MINUTES

WRITTEN BY: Milt Josefsberg, Al Schwartz

GUEST CAST: Allen Funt, James Millhollin, Robert S. Carson, Fred Festinger, Vanda Barra, Maurice Kelly, Peter Leeds, Paul Sorensen

An Allen Funt impersonator makes Lucy, Harry, and Kim think they are earning one hundred dollars for helping to perform a *Candid Camera* stunt, when actually they are committing robbery for a crook.

HIGHLIGHTS & TRIVIA

When Allen Funt (the creator and host of TV's *Candid Camera*, which has been on the air intermittently from 1948 until the 1990s) was a kid in the Bensonhurst section of Brooklyn, New York, he and his next-door neighbor dreamed of being famous in show business. Funt wanted to be a writer, while his pal wanted to be an actor. The pal's name was Milt Josefsberg, the scriptor of this episode.

HERE'S LUCY #87: "LUCY'S LUCKY DAY"

(CBS, DECEMBER 20, 1971), 30 MINUTES

WRITTEN BY: Fred S. Fox, Seaman Jacobs
GUEST CAST: Dick Patterson, Billy Sands

First Lucy wins the title of Dairy Mother of the Year, which gives her a prize of tickets to a game show. There she is picked as a contestant, and answers every question correctly. Her luck runs out when she finds that her prize is a chimp, and only if she can teach it a trick by the following week can she take home the real prize: $1,000!

HIGHLIGHTS & TRIVIA

Chimps, gorillas, and bears. Chimps, gorillas, and bears. No matter how many times they use them, they still aren't funny on *Here's Lucy*. This particular chimp has no personality, and the episode has no particular laughs. Even Lucy on stilts doesn't work, because the stilts are about two inches off the ground and the scene is pieced together in editing because the chimp is so uncooperative.

HERE'S LUCY #88: "LUCY'S BONUS BOUNCES"

(CBS, DECEMBER 27, 1971), 30 MINUTES

WRITTEN BY: Martin A. Ragaway
GUEST CAST: Parley Baer, Mary Jane Croft, Vanda Barra, Paul Picerni

Harry's psychiatrist suggests giving Lucy a raise so she will give him her undying loyalty. But Lucy looks askance at the raise, wondering what Harry is trying to bribe her about.

HIGHLIGHTS & TRIVIA

By this point, Mary Jane Croft and Vanda Barra are semi-regulars on *Here's Lucy*, giving the Lucy character peers to play with oncamera. Parley Baer makes another appearance as Harry's therapist, Dr. Cunningham.

Mary Jane Croft

(ACTOR)

I don't know why they didn't use me more during the first couple of years after The Lucy Show *ended. I guess the writers just didn't think of me. From this point forward, I was asked to perform much more often.*

HERE'S LUCY #89: "LUCY AND THE LITTLE OLD LADY"

(CBS, JANUARY 3, 1972), 30 MINUTES

WRITTEN BY: Fred S. Fox, Seamen Jacobs
GUEST CAST: Helen Hayes, Hank Brandt

When a little old Irish lady arrives at the employment agency, stranded with no money, Lucy takes her in. The newcomer sells property in Ireland to Uncle Harry, and Kim thinks she has swindled him. As a result, Lucy and Harry scheme to get his money back with a phony seance.

HIGHLIGHTS & TRIVIA

Broadway legend Helen Hayes brings a reality and a multi-leveled comedy performance that is rare for *Here's Lucy* by this point. As staged, the entire seance scene is ridiculous. Lucy and Harry don't even attempt to disguise their voices or Lucy's appearance, yet Mrs. Brady doesn't recognize them.

Lucille Ball

It was a privilege to have such a distinguished performer [Helen Hayes] on our show. I found myself devoting as much attention to watching her perform as to actually performing with her. She set the standard for the rest of us.

Helen Hayes

(BROADWAY LEGEND)

I had been appearing in a play in Washington, D.C., and got very ill. The doctors told me that I was allergic to all the backstage dust, and in effect, could no longer work on the stage. Miss Ball's offer came along just at the perfect time. Television gave me a new direction, and I am sure prolonged my career by many years.

HERE'S LUCY #90: "LUCY AND THE CHINESE CURSE"

(CBS, JANUARY 10, 1972), 30 MINUTES

WRITTEN BY: Martin A. Ragaway

GUEST CAST: Keye Luke, Mary Jane Croft, Tommy Farrell, Larry Blake, Sid Gould, Vanda Barra, Walter Smith

Lucy saves the life of a Chinese laundryman (Keye Luke), and he informs her that according to Chinese legend she is now responsible for his life. Lucy and Kim scheme to make the laundryman save Lucy's life, thus reversing the situation.

HIGHLIGHTS & TRIVIA

Keye Luke had come to fame playing Number One Son in several Charley Chan movies of the 1930s. He was a busy character actor for many years after that.

HERE'S LUCY #91: "LUCY'S REPLACEMENT"

(CBS, JANUARY 17, 1972), 30 MINUTES

WRITTEN BY: Fred S. Fox, Seaman Jacobs

GUEST CAST: R. G. Brown, Phil Vandervort

Harry installs a new computer in the office, and fires Lucy as being superfluous to his operation. She gets another job working in the steno pool of an insurance company. However, Lucy is miserable and wants her old job back, so she has a friend of Kim's sabotage the electronic brain in Harry's office.

HIGHLIGHTS & TRIVIA

This is a great change-of-pace episode. Ball is wonderful in the scene in the steno pool, where she cannot keep in synchronization with the rest of the regimented typists. Lucille wears a new wig with a bun that is very reminiscent of her old *I Love Lucy* look. It does make her look younger and more feminine. She never wears it again. Phil Vandervort, who plays Kim's brainy friend, is Lucille Ball's son-in-law, but not for long.

HERE'S LUCY #92: "KIM MOVES OUT"

(CBS, JANUARY 24, 1972), 30 MINUTES

WRITTEN BY: Bob Carroll Jr., Madelyn Davis

GUEST CAST: Tim Matheson

Twenty-year-old Kim, with a little persuasion from her boyfriend (Tim Matheson) decides she needs independence and wants to move out. Lucy reluctantly agrees, after finding her an apartment over a garage just one house away. However, Mother Hen won't let Kim alone, so this Hoping-to-Be-Independent Chick decides to teach her a lesson.

HIGHLIGHTS & TRIVIA

This episode is a fine showcase for Lucie Arnaz, whose talents blossom by the week. Tim Matheson had been in *Yours, Mine, and Ours* (1968) with Ball, but his future as a TV star is still many years away.

Lucie Arnaz

I've been asked why they didn't write more shows like this for me. Well, it took them a long time to figure what I could do. Remember, I started this show when I was in high school. Little by little, my talent began to show itself . . . I had to go through lots of shows where my big line was, "Oh Mother!" I was very brave to sing "I Got Love" [in this episode]. It is a song that I would not even attempt to sing today. It was written for Melba Moore, for God's sake! It was a rhythm and blues, let-it-all-out song. I had no idea how to approach it. And on top of everything else, that was done live with no prerecording, since it was just a piano.

HERE'S LUCY #93: "LUCY SUBLETS THE OFFICE"

(CBS, JANUARY 31, 1972), 30 MINUTES

WRITTEN BY: George Balzer, Sam Perrin

GUEST CAST: Wally Cox, Richard Deacon

When a Federal loan officer (Richard Deacon) inspects the employment office after Harry has applied for a $5,000 loan, he appoints Lucy as the office manager because she has raised two children on her meager salary. She immediately sublets part of the office to a toy salesman (Wally Cox), who overtakes the office with his oversized samples.

HIGHLIGHTS & TRIVIA

Although Lucille just adores working with Wally Cox, there are few permutations on his mousy character here. What makes this episode work is character actor Richard Deacon, a great scene stealer.

HERE'S LUCY #94: "LUCY'S PUNCTURED ROMANCE"

(CBS, FEBRUARY 7, 1972), 30 MINUTES

WRITTEN BY: Fred S. Fox, Seaman Jacobs

GUEST CAST: Bob Cummings, Mary Jane Croft, Billy Sands, Larry J. Blake, Sid Gould, Orwin Harvey

Lucy meets a handsome bachelor (Bob Cummings) and romance burns bright. However, the local milkman tells Kim the man drinks a lot and has a bevy of girls visiting his home. Kim and Harry scheme to save Lucy from herself by making Bob think Lucy is a deaf, alcoholic, hot-pepper-eating harlot.

HIGHLIGHTS & TRIVIA

This is the best Fox-Jacobs script for *Here's Lucy*. All of the comedy is founded in reality and builds to a logical climax. Bob Cummings was last seen with Ball in 1959 on the *Lucy-Desi hour* "Lucy Goes to Japan." His character here is clearly a rip-off of his old 1950s role from *The Bob Cummings Show* (1955–59). Billy Sands returns as the snoopy milkman, and will appear again on *Here's Lucy* in this character.

HERE'S LUCY #95: "WITH VIV AS A FRIEND, WHO NEEDS AN ENEMY?"

(CBS, FEBRUARY 14, 1972), 30 MINUTES

WRITTEN BY: Bob Carroll Jr., Madelyn Davis

GUEST CAST: Vivian Vance, Mary Jane Croft, Vanda Barra, Sid Gould

Lucy's longtime pal Viv visits, announcing that she might stay in Los Angeles permanently. Lucy is thrilled and has Viv move in with her. However, when Harry fires Lucy and hires Viv in her place, the duo quickly become enemies. Harry misses Lucy, while the Redhead wants her job back. Viv soon becomes sick of Harry, and everyone is scheming to put things back as before.

HIGHLIGHTS & TRIVIA

Although it was wonderful seeing Vivian Vance perform musical numbers in the Hawaiian show the previous season, this is Viv's best performance with Lucille since the days of *The Lucy Show*. The script is pure Lucy and Ethel, thanks to original writers Bob and Madelyn. Viv looks the best she has in years, with her hair now in a long flip and with its natural white color. Lucille seems especially pleased to be working with Vivian. In fact, they discuss the possibility of Viv returning to the fold permanently. A pilot is planned for Lucie Arnaz, and if it sells, then Lucille would need Vivian for support on the show. Unfortunately, fate is not kind. Lucie's pilot does not sell, and Vivian discovers a lump in her breast. Sixty-three-year-old Vance will undergo a mastectomy in the following months, as well as have a minor stroke. This is the last appearance by Vance on a regular Ball TV program, and the last time Viv appears on television healthy.

Lucie Arnaz

I didn't work with Viv as much as I did with my mother, but many times I was given the part of the listener, the one with whom my mother planned her schemes. So, maybe by osmosis, even before I worked with her, I learned from Viv. She changed my life. Being a theatre person herself, she's the one who reminded me that I needed to stay on the stage as much as possible. When there'd be a hiatus, she'd ask what I was doing. If my answer was a trip to Hawaii, she'd say, "What're you, nuts? You're a theatre person, you have to get back on the stage!" I think if it wasn't for her, I'd still be stuck now doing some idiotic sitcom for the rest of my life. This was the last time Vivian worked with my mother for several years. She had a stroke, and it took a long time for her to get the use of her mouth back. After that, I just don't think she wanted to come back and do that character again.

HERE'S LUCY #96: "KIM FINALLY CUTS YOU-KNOW-WHO'S APRON STRINGS"

(CBS, FEBRUARY 21, 1972), 30 MINUTES

WRITTEN BY: Bob Carroll Jr., Madelyn Davis

GUEST CAST: Susan Tolsky, Lloyd Battista, Alan Oppenheimer

Kim moves into her own apartment, in a building by the marina managed by her mother's brother Herb Hinkley. When an amorous race car driver puts the moves on her, Kim uses karate to put him in his place.

HIGHLIGHTS & TRIVIA

On paper, this is a great pilot for a TV series for Lucie Arnaz. A wacky, man-hungry friend and an over-protective uncle are sitcom staples. The script is well crafted, and Lucie is wonderful in it. What makes this show a disappointment is the casting. Susan Tolsky, who is usually a marvelous comedy actor, is too hyper here in the role of Kim's best friend, Sue. Perhaps the idea of working with Lucille Ball is too much for her. Alan Oppenheimer is dreadful as Kim's Uncle Herb. This is the first mention Lucy even has a brother; the character is quickly forgotten when the pilot doesn't sell. Lloyd Battista as the lecherous race car driver is neither particularly good looking nor charming. At times, it seems that Lucie Arnaz is performing in a different show than everyone else. Too bad the rest of the cast didn't join her. Notice that when Kim goes to unlock the front door of her apartment, the sliding latch breaks off and goes flying. Arnaz, by this time a thorough professional, just ad-libs, "Oh, fine!" and proceeds with the business at hand. Arnaz deserves much better than this, and should have become a major television comedy star on her own. She certainly has the talent and beauty for it.

Lucie Arnaz

When we first did this show I thought it was wonderful. I saw it recently and thought it was dreadful. I thought it was horrifically overacted and over-the-top. Susan's part was done so large that all of us had to match her intensity to make it look natural. Basically, I ended up being the straight man. And this is as good a time as any to take full credit for the Kim Carter look. Good, bad, or indifferent, the hairstyles and clothes were all my idea. I designed a lot of the clothes myself. Certainly, I had a lot of help. We had seamstresses at our beck and call who could make anything. They were wonderful! What a creative time in my life. So when you see me in those hot pants, that was my doing!

With the pilot's failure, Lucie Arnaz returns to the fold for a fifth season playing Kim Carter. As things worked out, Lucille Ball is going to need her daughter desperately in the next year of *Here's Lucy*.

LUCY'S TV SERIES AND THE NIELSON RATINGS

I Love Lucy *by Season*

1951–52 #3

1952–53 #1

1953–54 #1

1954–55 #1

1955–56 #2

1956–57 #1

The Lucy Show *by Season*

1962–63 #5

1963–64 #6

1964–65 #8

1965–66 #3

1966–67 #4

1967–68 #2

Here's Lucy *by Season*

1968–69 #9

1969–70 #6

1970–71 #3

1971–72 #11

1972–73 #15

1973–74 #29

Chapter Twenty-Four

1972-73 Season

HERE'S LUCY: THE FIFTH SEASON

TECHNICAL REGULARS: Executive produced by Gary Morton; produced by Cleo Smith; directed by Coby Ruskin; makeup by Hal King; hairstyling by Irma Kusely; music by Marl Young
CAST REGULARS: Lucille Ball (Lucy Carter); Gale Gordon (Harrison Otis Carter); Lucie Arnaz (Kim Carter); Mary Jane Croft (Mary Jane Lewis); Roy Rowan (announcer)

SALUTE TO TELEVISION'S TWENTY-FIFTH ANNIVERSARY

(ABC, SEPTEMBER 10, 1972), 90 MINUTES (COLOR AND B&W)
PRODUCED BY: Bob Finkel, Marty Pasetta
DIRECTED BY: Marty Pasetta
WRITTEN BY: Bob Wells, John Bradford, Lennie Weinrib
CAST: Judith Anderson, Russell Arms, James Arness, Lucille Ball, Milton Berle, Sid Caesar, George Chakiris, Jimmy Durante, Dave Garroway, Florence Henderson, Bob Hope, Snooky Lanson, Gisele MacKenzie, Harry Reasoner, George C. Scott, Rod Serling, Dinah Shore, Dick Smothers, Tom Smothers, Ed Sullivan, John Wayne, Eileen Wilson, Robert Young, Efrem Zimbalist Jr.

One of the first clip-filled salutes to television's halcyon days, with scenes from over 400 programs. Naturally, a tribute to Lucille is included, and she is presented with a TV Academy silver medallion of merit. This program airs opposite the CBS-TV special *Liza with a Z* starring recent Oscar-winner Liza Minnelli. With powerhouse Liza scheduled against it, almost no one watches this TV salute.

HERE'S LUCY #97: "LUCY'S BIG BREAK"

(CBS, SEPTEMBER 11, 1972), 30 MINUTES
WRITTEN BY: Bob Carroll Jr., Madelyn Davis
GUEST CAST: Lloyd Bridges, Mary Wickes, Vanda Barra, Sid Gould, June Whitley Taylor, Dorothy Konrad, Alan Oppenheimer

Lucy has broken her leg and is in the hospital, surrounded by her loving family and friends. The staff feels she needs rest and orders all visitors to leave her alone, which makes Lucy feel abandoned. When a handsome doctor visits the person in the next bed, Lucy schemes to have him visit her as well. The doctor catches on, and invents an imaginary illness to teach her a lesson.

HIGHLIGHTS & TRIVIA

Lucille Ball has broken her leg skiing near her condo in Aspen, Colorado, just before she is to report to work on the movie musical *Mame* (1974). The film is postponed almost a year, but Lucille Ball Productions is sent into a panic. There are deliberations about canceling the still highly rated *Here's Lucy*, but it is decided that the best thing for Lucille is to return to work. Almost all of this season's scripts must be quickly rewritten or postponed, and a rasher of new efforts must be produced immediately. In actuality, this is one of the best things that could have happened to the series at this point. Lucille's accident provides continuity and a focus that has always been missing from this program. Her inability to do physical stunts allows Lucie Arnaz and Mary Jane Croft to take over the spotlight. Because Lucy is in a wheelchair or leg cast also makes it unadvisable for Harry to scream at her, so his character becomes a lot more sympathetic. In fact, from this point forward Lucy and Harry relate as equals rather than as boss and employee. There is an affection between them that has never before been displayed. And the Lucy character is finally allowed to age. No one calls her a young lady anymore.

With the return of Bob Carroll Jr. and Madelyn Davis to part-time Lucy work, consultant Milt Josefsberg leaves the show. While the scripts improve considerably, the series no longer has a head writer.

Lucie Arnaz

The day Mom broke her leg, Liza [Minnelli], Desi [Jr., who was dating her at the time], and I followed her to the hospital off the slopes. She was screaming. Not from the pain, but because of the hundreds of people she thought would be thrown out of work because of her condition. She thought it was over. After they had meetings with the creative people, and ensured that she was not in pain, the writers began to work up plots with her in the wheelchair. The doctors' only concern was that she not hurt her leg in any way. Instead of losing months of filming time, I think we were back on the set in three weeks. For Mom, it was like doing Whose Life Is It Anyway? *(a play about an immobilized person). There is only so much acting you can do with the upper part of your body, especially comedy.*

Irma Kusely

(HAIRSTYLIST)

Lucille came to me and said she wanted to try something new with her hair. So I ordered some longer wigs, and styled them into a bouffant, not unlike Betty White's hair. It made things easier for me, because I could now do more handiwork underneath to smooth out Lucille's skin without it being detected. We had many wigs . . . sometimes as many as sixteen at one time . . . that we used. She got whatever she wanted, whatever made her feel good, unless the network for some reason objected.

HERE'S LUCY #98: "LUCY AND EVA GABOR ARE HOSPITAL ROOMIES"

(CBS, SEPTEMBER 18, 1972), 30 MINUTES

WRITTEN BY: Bob Carroll Jr., Madelyn Davis
GUEST CAST: Eva Gabor, Mary Wickes, Vanda Barra, June Whitley Taylor, R. G. Brown

Eva Gabor becomes Lucy's new hospital roommate because it is suspected she has broken her foot. The glamorous Gabor gets all the attention and special treatment, leaving Lucy feeling like an also-ran.

HIGHLIGHTS & TRIVIA

There is a static feeling to this episode that is inescapable, as both the leading lady and the guest star are immobile. Ball and Gabor have always worked well together, and it is a shame that the logistics of the situation don't allow them to do more.

HERE'S LUCY #99: "HARRISON CARTER, MALE NURSE"

(CBS, SEPTEMBER 25, 1972), 30 MINUTES

WRITTEN BY: Bob Carroll Jr., Madelyn Davis
GUEST CAST: Vanda Barra, Sid Gould

When Harry finally takes Lucy home from the hospital, he arranges for Kim and her friends to act as nurses. Unfortunately, they all flake out, forcing Harry to be at Lucy's beck and call twenty-four hours a day.

HIGHLIGHTS & TRIVIA

This is a very satisfying installment, as we see Harry getting paid back for all of his meanness to Lucy through the years. Ball's infirmity is causing the regulars to bond together like an ensemble, a concept not seen on a Ball sitcom since the vintage days of *The Lucy Show.*

HERE'S LUCY #100: "A HOME IS NOT AN OFFICE"

(CBS, OCTOBER 2, 1972), 30 MINUTES

WRITTEN BY: Fred S. Fox, Seaman Jacobs
GUEST CAST: Vanda Barra, Robert S. Carson, Susan Tolsky, Sid Gould, Phil Vandervort, Emile Autori, Gloria Wood, Peggy Clark, Gwenn Johnson

When the temporary secretaries Harry hires are even less experienced than Lucy, he simply moves the office to Lucy's house. The Redhead schemes to get rid of him, but Harry is wise to all of her plans until he finally outsmarts himself.

HIGHLIGHTS & TRIVIA

Because Lucille is wheelchair-bound, the script has a houseful of people making movement around her to compensate for it. Ball does get to do one physical bit—she closes an open file cabinet drawer with her cast-bound leg by thrusting her electric wheelchair forward.

HERE'S LUCY #101: "LUCY AND JOE NAMATH"

(CBS, OCTOBER 9, 1972), 30 MINUTES
WRITTEN BY: Bob O'Brien
GUEST CAST: Joe Namath, Desi Arnaz Jr., Dick Patterson, Kenny Endoso

Craig, home from college on a visit, is seen playing tennis by a football coach who feels he has the right stuff to be a fine quarterback. Lucy won't hear of her son playing the dangerous sport, so football great Joe Namath is dispatched to convince her otherwise.

HIGHLIGHTS & TRIVIA

Currently, Namath is a hot television property, and simply having him on *Here's Lucy* ensures high ratings. Desi Jr. is actually an excellent tennis player, and looks very natural in the tennis scene. Handsome and trim, he is hardly built like a football player, which diminishes the credibility of the story line.

Desi Arnaz Jr.

I came back to the show after not being heard from for two years. I'm sure for some of the viewers it was like, "Craig? Craig who?" I was hardly ever referred to in the show once I was gone.

HERE'S LUCY #102: "THE CASE OF THE RECKLESS WHEELCHAIR DRIVER"

(CBS, OCTOBER 16, 1972), 30 MINUTES
WRITTEN BY: Fred S. Fox, Seaman Jacobs
GUEST CAST: Jesse White, Ed Hall, Jim Bates, Harry Hickox, Robert Foulk, Rosalind Miles, Jayson William Kane, Sid Gould

A young performer is accidentally knocked down by Lucy's wheelchair. Although uninjured, his greedy manager sues Lucy for $100,000. Certain the kid is faking injuries, Kim traps him into revealing the truth.

HIGHLIGHTS & TRIVIA

In an unusual move, this episode is filmed weeks after Lucille is already ambulatory on a walking cast, and has, in fact, shot installments just that way. She is put back into the wheelchair for this one, and the entry is shown out of filming order. Although both the script and the direction are thin, Lucie Arnaz steals the show. As the one doing the scheming, the bulk of the plot falls on her shoulders and she makes the most of it. It is becoming obvious Lucie has more talent than she has ever been allowed to use on *Here's Lucy*, and she is a major asset anytime a script permits her to shine.

HERE'S LUCY #103: "LUCY, THE OTHER WOMAN"

(CBS, OCTOBER 23, 1972), 30 MINUTES
WRITTEN BY: Fred S. Fox, Seaman Jacobs
GUEST CAST: Totie Fields, Herbie Faye

Lucy receives threats from the wife of the new milkman, who thinks he is having an affair with her. Lucy makes the plump and insecure woman feel sorry for her husband and forgive him.

HIGHLIGHTS & TRIVIA

This is comedian Totie Fields' first TV sitcom role. She overpowers anyone who is in a scene with her. Ball even allows her a song at the finale to showcase her musical abilities. Fields' television work will almost always be confined to game shows, talk shows, dramas, and variety shows.

Lucie Arnaz

While we never really used canned laughter [except for editing purposes], towards the end of the run, Mom used to do what she called "sweetening." It was not nearly as heavy-handed as it is today. Today, if someone walks in the door, there is all this laughter for no reason. Some guy is putting his foot on a pedal making a machine laugh. But what Mom would do is if a joke didn't get as big a laugh as she thought it deserved, or if the audience had been momentarily preoccupied with watching something technical instead of watching the show, she would add a few chuckles from our own natural sound track for the folks at home. Mom watched the dailies as we shot, and was very involved in this sort of thing. And [maternal grandmother] DeDe was at every show, rain or shine. You can clearly hear her laughter above everyone else's. And yes, that is DeDe going "uh-oh" when Lucy got in trouble. In fact, I've heard DeDe's laugh on shows that were filmed without an audience. They used the I Love Lucy *laugh track, because it was the most natural."*

Lucille Ball

We are not in favor of canned laughter on TV. A performer in comedy comes across far better when an audience is witnessing his efforts. He comes up to an opening night tempo with a laughing, applauding audience. Canned laughter is obviously phony.

HERE'S LUCY #104: "LUCY AND PETULA CLARK"

(CBS, OCTOBER 30, 1972), 30 MINUTES

WRITTEN BY: Bob O'Brien
GUEST CAST: Petula Clark, Claude Wolff, Doris Singleton, Tommy Farrell

Pregnant singer Petula Clark wants the Unique Employment Agency to send her an assistant while she is in Los Angeles preparing for a recording session. Lucy, newly returned to work in the office, takes the assignment herself. In short order, she makes a pest of herself as she overprotects Petula from the exigencies of life.

HIGHLIGHTS & TRIVIA

This unimaginative episode is taken from any number of other *Lucy* plots where the Redhead forces her well-meaning ministrations on a poor soul. Lucille has been very loyal to writer Bob O'Brien, but his efforts repeat the same themes over and over. Rarely is the result anything more than mediocre. The only selling points to this entry are Clark's delightful singing and the always welcome presence of Doris Singleton.

HERE'S LUCY #105: "LUCY AND JIM BAILEY"

(CBS, NOVEMBER 6, 1972), 30 MINUTES

WRITTEN BY: Bob O'Brien
GUEST CAST: Jim Bailey, Los Angeles Mayor Sam Yorty, Adele Claire

Lucy books comedian Phyllis Diller to entertain at a local Chamber of Commerce charity affair. When Diller develops laryngitis at the last moment, Kim persuades impressionist Jim Bailey to fill in for her, unbeknownst to Lucy.

HIGHLIGHTS & TRIVIA

Lucille hardly appears in this one, as the episode is ably carried by the talents of Lucie Arnaz and guest star Jim Bailey. His dead-on impression of Diller is almost spooky. The musical moments between Arnaz and Bailey are very well done, and there is obvious chemistry between the two performers.

Lucie Arnaz

So much crap was written about Jim [Bailey] and me because of this show . . . that we were having this big affair. I wish! I tried! I was separated from my husband [Phil Vandervort] at the time and there he was. My mother adored Jim and never gave me a minute of trouble about him. He was gorgeous, and so talented. Show me someone who was talented, good looking, and funny, and I would always fall. The talent was what attracted me first. But nothing ever came of it.

Jim Bailey

(MASTER IMPRESSIONIST)

We almost had a disaster that week. The plot called for me to impersonate Phyllis Diller, who was supposed to be down with laryngitis. The producers decided to film the closing number with Lucie and me the night before the rest of the show was filmed in front of the live audience. After we filmed our song, Lucie and I went out for Chinese food near Universal Studios where the series was filmed. Halfway through dinner, I completely lost my voice. I had developed laryngitis. When Big Lucy was told the next day what happened, she became like a mother hen. She insisted I inhabit her luxurious and air-conditioned dressing room, held my hand during final rehearsals, read my part for me, brought in a doctor to give me cortisone shots, and continually helped build up my confidence. My voice came back and the show went on as scheduled. Lucille Ball was a very generous performer, especially to someone who was just making a name for himself at the time.

HERE'S LUCY #106: "DIRTY GERTIE"

(CBS, NOVEMBER 13, 1972), 30 MINUTES

WRITTEN BY: Bob O'Brien
GUEST CAST: Craig Stevens, Bruce Gordon

When Lucy, filthy from cleaning out her fireplace, is sent a crate of apples from her doctor, she takes some around the corner to her hairdresser. She is mistaken for an "Apple Annie" named Dirty Gertie, who is the good luck charm for a big-time crook who gives her a one hundred dollar bill for an apple. Lucy is enlisted by the police to impersonate Gertie and get the goods on the hood.

HIGHLIGHTS & TRIVIA

This is Bob O'Brien's best Lucy script, a cross between the old "Apple Annie" stories of Damon Runyon and a 1966 *The Lucy Show* episode (#109), "Lucy, the Gun Moll." Once again asked to go undercover by the authorities, Lucy Carter must have been on a CIA or FBI list, it happens so often to her. Bruce Gordon once more does a parody of the gangster role he played on the Desilu-produced *The Untouchables* (1959–63). Ball is wonderful in this one, giving one of her best *Here's Lucy* performances.

HERE'S LUCY #107: "LUCY AND DONNY OSMOND"

(CBS, NOVEMBER 20, 1972), 30 MINUTES

WRITTEN BY: Bob O'Brien

GUEST CAST: Donny Osmond, Eve Plumb, Phil Vandervort

Lucy, Kim, and twelve-year-old cousin Patricia attend Donny Osmond's nightclub show. Donny misunderstands Kim's interest in getting his autograph for Patricia, and develops a mad crush on her which Kim is forced to deal with.

HIGHLIGHTS & TRIVIA

Eve Plumb is much more recognizable to television fans as Jan Brady on *The Brady Bunch* (1969–74). Although she is now much older, her character is written for someone just entering puberty. It is never really explained whose child Patricia is, or how she is a cousin. The last name Carter means she is a relation from Harry's side of the family. It could be said that Donny Osmond having a crush on Kim is silly, except for one thing.

Lucie Arnaz

This was so many years ago that I don't think he'll mind my telling this. Donny really did have a crush on me, almost just like the one in the show. He was a joy to work with.

HERE'S LUCY #108: "LUCY AND HER PRINCE CHARMING"

(CBS, NOVEMBER 27, 1972), 30 MINUTES

WRITTEN BY: Fred S. Fox, Seaman Jacobs

GUEST CAST: Ricardo Montalban, Iggie Wolfington, Sid Gould, Gloria Wood

A handsome Prince has hired the Unique Employment Agency to find him an American wife, but upon meeting Lucy his search is over. Because Harry will get a quarter of a million dollars if a marriage occurs, he uses every method of persuasion he can think of to gain Lucy's compliance.

HIGHLIGHTS & TRIVIA

Desi Arnaz, Cesar Romero, Fernando Lamas, and now Ricardo Montalban. Lucille Ball has now done romantic scenes on TV with every big Latino star of her generation.

HERE'S LUCY #109: "MY FAIR BUZZI"

(CBS, DECEMBER 11, 1972), 30 MINUTES

WRITTEN BY: Fred S. Fox, Seaman Jacobs

GUEST CAST: Ruth Buzzi, Larry Meredith, Hal England, Michael Richardson

Kim brings her mousy friend Annie (Ruth Buzzi) home for dinner. Lucy and Kim give her a makeover so she'll have more of a chance to get a part in the local drama club's latest stage venture. She ends up looking . . . better, but it turns out the director wants Annie the way she used to look. The entire gang ends up participating in a Roaring Twenties sketch, which is pleasant entertainment but lacks any innovative sparks.

HIGHLIGHTS & TRIVIA

The name of Hal King is taken from the name of Lucille's makeup artist. Buzzi's mimicking of the time step is highly reminiscent of Lucy Ricardo in the 1951 "The Diet" episode (#2) of *I Love Lucy*. Lucie Arnaz is very funny in this show, a veritable whirling dervish in the audition scene, including doing a reprisal of her father's hit "El Cubanchero." It is easy to see why she will become a major Broadway star. The name (Dallas Noonan) of Lucille's character in the sketch is a takeoff on Texas Guinan, famed New York speakeasy hostess of the 1920s.

HERE'S LUCY #110: "LUCY AND THE GROUP ENCOUNTER"

(CBS, DECEMBER 18, 1972), 30 MINUTES
WRITTEN BY: Fred S. Fox, Seaman Jacobs
GUEST CAST: Kurt Kasznar, Reta Shaw, Romo Vincent

Lucy and Harry have been bickering so much that Mary Jane suggests they go to a group encounter and work out their problems. The psychologist advises that they switch office roles to better understand one another.

HIGHLIGHTS & TRIVIA

This is one of the *Here's Lucy* episodes that reflects such modern fads as women's liberation and group therapy encounters. Although matters are handled so broadly that any contemporary feel is diminished, this is a very funny effort.

HERE'S LUCY #111: "LUCY IS REALLY IN A PICKLE"

(CBS, JANUARY 1, 1973), 30 MINUTES
WRITTEN BY: Bob Carroll Jr., Madelyn Davis
GUEST CAST: Dick Patterson

When an ad agency wants Harry to find a young woman with an ordinary face for a commercial, Lucy gets the job. Unfortunately, the ad concept is changed to a musical one, and Lucy can't dance on her still-mending leg. All seems lost until Harry sells the agency on using both Lucy and Kim.

HIGHLIGHTS & TRIVIA

This episode is based on the 1952 *I Love Lucy* episode "Lucy Does a TV Commercial" (#30), the famous Vitameatavegamin outing. This time Lucille overreacts to the taste of sour pickles as she rehearses her lines over and over. This installment gives Ball her first block (slapstick) comedy scenes of the season, cleverly written by Bob and Madelyn so as not to put Lucille in any real danger of re-injuring her leg.

Irma Kusely

(HAIRSTYLIST)

It always bothered me that one of the shots in this show didn't match up. After Lucille was in the pickle outfit and did her stunt, her hair on top was messed up and pulled back. She stopped the scene and told me she wanted her bangs back. So I fixed the wig and they kept right on, but from one moment to the next, her bangs just pop out of nowhere. [The author] is the only other person besides myself who ever noticed.

HERE'S LUCY #112: "LUCY GOES ON HER LAST BLIND DATE"

(CBS, JANUARY 8, 1973), 30 MINUTES
WRITTEN BY: Bob Carroll Jr., Madelyn Davis
GUEST CAST: Don Knotts, Vanda Barra, Sid Gould, Ralph James

Harry's cousin Ben (Don Knotts) is in town, and he insists Lucy go out with him. When it turns out that shy Ben actually owns land in Bel Air that makes him a millionaire, Harry pushes even harder. However, Lucy is not enchanted, and schemes to turn off the nouveau riche Ben.

HIGHLIGHTS & TRIVIA

If Ben is Harry's cousin, then he is also the cousin of Lucy's late husband as well as that of Kim. Even Bob and Madelyn confuse the blood lines on this show, because they weren't clearly dealt with from the beginning. During the filming, Don Knotts keeps mixing up the names of Ben and Harry, causing several retakes. Lucille does not like wasting time and money, and "encourages" Don to get with it.

HERE'S LUCY #113: "LUCY AND HER GENUINE TWIMBY"

(CBS, JANUARY 15, 1973), 30 MINUTES
WRITTEN BY: Fred S. Fox, Seaman Jacobs
GUEST CAST: Bob Cummings, William Lanteau

Lucy buys a reproduction of an expensive chair while at an antique store. When it turns out she has been sold an original, the owner of the store dates Lucy so he can retrieve the chair.

HIGHLIGHTS & TRIVIA

It is great to see Lucy having a real romantic adventure. It is feminizing, something Lucille Ball needs at this juncture in her life. William Lanteau steals the show as the effusive store assistant. It is a shame he never gets to play a recurring character on this series, because he is always so good.

HERE'S LUCY #114: "LUCY GOES TO PRISON"

(CBS, JANUARY 22, 1973), 30 MINUTES
WRITTEN BY: Fred S. Fox, Seaman Jacobs
GUEST CAST: Elsa Lanchester, Roy Roberts, Joyce Jameson, Jody Gilbert, Queenie Smith

To collect a $30,000 reward and a $400 per-week salary, Lucy goes undercover in a prison to draw information out of an inmate. The woman can't remember the needed data, until Lucy gets her drunk.

HIGHLIGHTS & TRIVIA
This episode is a refreshing change of pace. Elsa Lanchester looks almost the same as she had in 1956 when she appeared on the *I Love Lucy* episode, "Off to Florida" (#159). Roy Roberts had been a regular (Mr. Cheever) on *The Lucy Show*. The name Warden Maginetti derives from the name of the series' associate producer William Maginetti. The name DeDe Peterson that Lucy uses in prison is the married name of Lucille's mother, after her father died and DeDe rewed.

HERE'S LUCY #115: "LUCY AND THE PROFESSOR"

(CBS, JANUARY 29, 1973), 30 MINUTES
WRITTEN BY: Bob O'Brien
GUEST CAST: John Davidson, Murray Matheson, Patti Cubbison, Mitch Carter, Irwin Charone

Not realizing that he is actually a young man, Lucy is concerned when Kim dates a college professor. While snooping on Kim, Lucy mistakes an older man for her daughter's beau, and the fireworks begin.

HIGHLIGHTS & TRIVIA
The theme of jumping to conclusions has been a staple of all Ball's TV series since day one. However, that means a lot of these plots have already been done, and new ones need fresh spins to be funny and believable. This is not one of those.

HERE'S LUCY #116: "LUCY AND THE FRANCHISE FIASCO"

(CBS, FEBRUARY 5, 1973), 30 MINUTES
WRITTEN BY: Bob Carroll Jr., Madelyn Davis
GUEST CAST: Clint Young, Sid Gould, Lola Fisher

Lucy, Mary Jane, and Harry buy a frozen custard stand. When Lucy's meddling makes all the employees leave, and Mary Jane has to go back to work, the enterprise is left in the hands of Lucy and Harry. Things couldn't get worse until Harry devises an advertising scheme Lucy can't refuse.

HIGHLIGHTS & TRIVIA
Although their writing lacks the flair of their early efforts, every script by Bob and Madelyn is head and shoulders above the rest of the *Here's Lucy* episodes. The slapstick comedy scene with the custard machine going crazy is classic Lucy. There actually is a frozen custard chain featuring a penguin that is very popular in Southern California. Great care has to be taken with the penguins, who keep fainting from the hot studio lights. This entry is based in part on *The Lucy Show* episode, "Lucy Is a Kangaroo" (#7), which was itself based in part on the unproduced 1961 special *Lucy Goes to Broadway*.

HERE'S LUCY #117: "LUCY AND UNCLE HARRY'S POT"

(CBS, FEBRUARY 12, 1973), 30 MINUTES
WRITTEN BY: Bob O'Brien
GUEST CAST: Jack Manning, Roger Twedt, Orwin Harvey

Lucy breaks a vase made for Harry by his former secretary, Miss Lindsay. She decides to take a crash course in ceramics and make him a new one.

HIGHLIGHTS & TRIVIA
The physical comedy scene with Lucille at the clay wheel has many of the elements that make for great humor. Unfortunately, it is under-rehearsed and the script doesn't give Lucille the direction with which to effectively perform the bit. The warmth between Lucy and Harry in this episode makes both characters more likeable.

HERE'S LUCY #118: "THE NOT SO POPULAR MECHANICS"

(CBS, FEBRUARY 19, 1973), 30 MINUTES
WRITTEN BY: Bob Carroll Jr., Madelyn Davis
GUEST CAST: Robert Rockwell, Leigh Adams-Bennett

Lucy and Mary Jane take a class in auto repair, so Lucy can date the handsome instructor (Robert Rockwell). Harry leaves his new acquisition, a classic Rolls-Royce, in Lucy's care when he goes out of town with the instruction to take it in for repair. When Lucy forgets, and can't get a hold of her repairman boyfriend, she and Mary Jane decide to repair the car themselves.

HIGHLIGHTS & TRIVIA

This would have been a classic Lucy-Ethel episode in the old days. Even without Vivian Vance, this is a funny installment, with the added nostalgia bonus of Robert Rockwell as Lucy's boyfriend. Rockwell is best known as Mr. Boynton on *Our Miss Brooks* (1952–56), although he made TV appearances on things as diverse as *The Adventures of Superman* (1952–57, as Superman's father on Krypton) to *Growing Pains* (1985–92, as the grandfather). In the late 1990s, Rockwell would often be seen as the loving Grandpa in a string of candy commercials.

Robert Rockwell

(ACTOR)

I didn't work for more than a year after Our Miss Brooks *went off the air because I was so strongly identified with Mr. Boynton. I hope that's because I did such a good job. I didn't take very many of these Boyntonish parts after that. Lucy was a true craftsman. She had done this work [for a long time] and she was smart. She was a little bit edgy and she wanted everything just right, which is fine because she ran the show. Lucy was very gentle with me and very kind. She suggested some line readings to me and did it in a professional manner. We got along just fine, and I think she was pleased with what I did. We didn't blow any lines, and that pleased Lucy because she ran a tight ship. Going up on your lines was frowned upon in those days. Today, everything is much looser, and if you have to shoot a scene over and over, no one seems to care.*

HERE'S LUCY #119: "GOODBYE MRS. HIPS"

(CBS, FEBRUARY 26, 1973), 30 MINUTES

WRITTEN BY: Bob Carroll Jr., Madelyn Davis

GUEST CAST: Vanda Barra, Sid Gould

Lucy talks Mary Jane and Vanda into temporarily moving in with her while they all embark on a crash diet. All is well until Harry shows up with a tray of gourmet goodies, which must be stored in Lucy's refrigerator because his is not working.

HIGHLIGHTS & TRIVIA

This is the largest part Vanda Barra will have on a Lucy episode, and it showcases her to great advantage. Under different circumstances, she might have been a good replacement for Vivian Vance. In later years, Vanda and Sid Gould divorced and she retired from acting. In the 1990s, she would become a successful restaurateur in Palm Springs, California. Sid would pass away in 1997 at the Motion Picture Home in Woodland Hills, California.

Lucie Arnaz

People don't know that Vanda Barra was a marvelous dramatic actor. She toured in Who's Afraid of Virginia Woolf? *and got rave reviews. But because of her New Yorkey kind of accent, she got comedy parts. Vanda and I became like girlfriends. I used to talk like her. She and Sid Gould could be very funny together. Sid had this thing he did to [help Gary Morton] warm up the audience. It was called the initials game. He'd ask for people in the audience to yell out initials of actors, even silent screen actors, no matter how obscure. He'd always come up with the name. The audiences loved it, especially the older folks. Or he'd play "The Flight of the Bumblebee" on this little harmonica with four holes in it, and then pretend to swallow it. He was also the very first person to say, "Bet your hippy!" Rowan and Martin admit they stole that from him. Unfortunately, Sid just could not remember his lines in front of an audience. He could only work if he could do "Sid schtick." So the parts got smaller and smaller on the show.*

Kathleen Freeman

(ACTOR)

Lucille, I am sure, gave Sid and Vanda a hard time. They were always asking to do more, to get larger parts. When you are in a position of power because you worked hard for it and you earned it, you are in a position to help other people. Now there are people (however talented they may be) who are always asking for more. Whatever they get, it's never enough. After awhile, the person in power just wants to turn to them and say, "Shut up! If you are so good, go do it yourself and leave me alone." Sid was always nipping at Lucille's heels, instead of being grateful for the work he was getting.

HERE'S LUCY #120: "LUCY AND HARRY'S MEMOIRS"

(CBS, MARCH 5, 1973), 30 MINUTES

WRAPAROUND SEGMENTS WRITTEN BY:
Bob O'Brien

Harry has sold the business. As Lucille and Harry pack up the office, they reminisce about some of their (mis)adventures together.

HIGHLIGHTS & TRIVIA

This is the third retrospective show Lucille does. It is planned to be the last show of the series. The wraparounds are filmed in one day without a live audience. Lucille wears one of her old, shorter wigs to match the look of the film clips. On Tuesday of the week this show is filmed, CBS President Fred Silverman comes to Lucille's house in Beverly Hills and talks her into doing another year of *Here's Lucy*. Rather than scrap the episode or cause costly reshooting, the script is slightly reworked so that as Lucille walks out of the office, she leaves a sign that says "closed temporarily." At one point in the filming, Gale turns to Lucille and says, "Do you remember the time you got a pickaxe up your ass?" causing the Redhead to laugh uproariously.

Around the time this episode is filmed, Lucille films several commercials for the Milton Bradley company for their games Pivot Pool and Body Language, with Mary Jane Croft appearing in the latter. Ball is paid in Milton Bradley stock as well as salary, and her likeness will appear on the covers of the game boxes. The commercials are aired all during the summer and autumn of 1973.

Chapter Twenty-Five

1973-74 Season

HERE'S LUCY: THE SIXTH SEASON

TECHNICAL REGULARS: Executive produced by Gary Morton; produced by Cleo Smith; directed by Coby Ruskin (except where otherwise noted); makeup by Fred Williams; hairstyling by Irma Kusely; music by Marl Young

CAST REGULARS: Lucille Ball (Lucy Carter); Gale Gordon (Harrison Otis Carter); Lucie Arnaz (Kim Carter); Mary Jane Croft (Mary Jane Lewis); Roy Rowan (announcer)

HERE'S LUCY #121: "LUCY AND DANNY THOMAS"

(CBS, SEPTEMBER 10, 1973), 30 MINUTES

WRITTEN BY: Bob O'Brien

GUEST CAST: Danny Thomas, Hans Conried, Sid Gould, Shirley Anthony, Bob Whitney

Lucy has taken up oil painting, and meets a talented but starving artist (Danny Thomas) who claims his work will only be worth money after he dies. Lucy gets an idea, and helps the painter fake his death to jack up the prices of his paintings.

HIGHLIGHTS & TRIVIA

This is not an original premise. Carl Reiner wrote a film called *The Art of Love* (1966, with Dick Van Dyke, James Garner, and Ethel Merman) whose plot was the same. This is the last time Danny Thomas works with Hans Conried, who portrayed Uncle Tonoose on his own series. Lucille looks good here because she is no longer shot in closeup and always filmed through a filtered lens, and partly because she has a new makeup artist. Her new look is a little more modern, but new makeup artist Fred Williams will be replaced after *Here's Lucy* ends its run.

Irma Kusely

(HAIRSTYLIST)

[Makeup artist] Hal King and Lucille had a terrific misunderstanding on the set of Mame *[1974]. She got angry at some trivial thing and swung at him. Despite what was said in other books, she never connected and never slapped him. I know, I was standing right there. He decided to retire, and they had a few months of acrimony. Later on, she would send a car for him and bring him to the house to be her guest. But he never did her makeup again. After Hal stopped working, Fred Williams started doing it. He was very good, but Hal just knew her so well. Lucille would be very impatient with Fred because his hand wasn't as light in touch as Hal's. And of course, when you have a different makeup artist, you're going to end up with a slightly different look.*

STEVE AND EYDIE . . . ON STAGE

(NBC, SEPTEMBER 16, 1973), 60 MINUTES

EXECUTIVE PRODUCED: by Steve Lawrence

PRODUCED AND DIRECTED BY: Marty Pasetta

WRITTEN BY: Frank Shaw, Ray Jessel

CAST: Steve Lawrence and Eydie Gorme (hosts), Lucille Ball, Sergio Mendez and Brazil '77

Taped on the stage of Caesar's Palace in Las Vegas, this is another of Lucille's barter appearances. It is also Steve and Eydie's least TV favorite special—ever. Lucille's main contribution is singing "Bosom Buddies" from *Mame*. She sings it off-key. Not on purpose. Her part, including inside "barbs" at Steve and Eydie, is taped in Hollywood and inserted into the program.

HERE'S LUCY #122: "THE BIG GAME"

(CBS, SEPTEMBER 17, 1973), 30 MINUTES

WRITTEN BY: Bob O'Brien

GUEST CAST: O.J. Simpson, James E. Brodhead, Tom Kelly, Cliff Norton, Al Checco, Sid Gould, Frank Coughlin, Robert Foulk, Jerry Jones, Eugene Molnar

Harry is president of the Beverly Hills Chamber of Commerce. He arranges for football star O.J. Simpson to be the guest speaker at a luncheon planned by Lucy, Mary Jane, and himself. O.J. gives Harry two hard-to-get tickets to the game, which Harry then sells for $50 to a friend. Simpson returns, and gives Lucy a parking pass and another two tickets. Harry decides he will scalp these extra tickets, and gets himself arrested.

HIGHLIGHTS & TRIVIA

If the plot doesn't sound particularly inventive, there is some humor in its delivery. Lucille, obviously reading from cue cards, gets a great deal of support from Gale and Mary Jane. More and more, Miss Croft is given a chance to be funny and create wonderful small moments for herself. The Redhead's forced laughter in the opening scene is annoying, rather than amusing. In fact, this episode would register as one of the more forgettable installments in Lucille's TV career were it not for her guest star, O.J. Simpson.

Watching this show with 20/20 hindsight makes for a spooky experience as a young O.J. Simpson, still the star tailback for the Buffalo Bills, waxes poetic about his first wife Marguerite and their children. Simpson's delivery is stiff as he still has limited acting experience before cameras and live audiences. While one would have to look hard to read menacing foreshadows into the script, seeing a young talent with promise in the security of Lucille's arena and knowing what will happen later is eerie. Lucie Arnaz does not appear in this episode as she is in New York, taping a week's worth of the syndicated version of *What's My Line?* (1968–75).

Cliff Norton

(ACTOR/COMEDIAN)

This was a fun episode to shoot. Naturally, there was nothing we could have known then about O.J. He seemed to be a great guy, and we all enjoyed being around him. He was just beginning to become known as an actor. He was pleasant, cooperative, and professional. No one was a bigger O.J. Simpson fan than my daughter Susie, who was a teenager then. I told O.J. about her, and he said, "Is she home now? Let's call her up!" So I called home, and sure enough she was there. I put O.J. on the phone, and I was afraid she was going to faint! After the shoot, O.J. and Lynn Swann (who was there to see O.J.) were wonderful to her, and gave her autographed pictures. Lucille was still queen of the roost, and she had not lost any of her control. The scripts were no longer anywhere near the standards of the original I Love Lucy *shows. The writers wrote what Lucy wanted. She was only human. She had already proven herself as the number one clown in the world. Perhaps she was in a hurry to get through things, or perhaps her creative taste buds had weakened a little bit. In these later shows, there was too much situation and not enough characterization, which [did not bring out] her talent. There wasn't enough substance and heart. Lucille had to work harder and harder to bring something to these shows, which were less respectable. I have always wondered what it would have been like to have done one of those strong, sturdy, well-built* I Love Lucy *shows.*

Gary Morton had two important functions on this series. One was to take care of the business details for Lucille Ball Productions. The other was to shop their money around on a day-to-day basis. It was not unusual back then for very wealthy people to move their money around from bank to bank, trying to get the best return available. All of the banks and investment houses wanted the kind of money Lucille and Gary had to offer, and this required daily scrutiny. Gary really excelled at this. He also kept Lucille happy, which of course was important to everyone who cared about her. One day she said to me, "You know, Gary really loves me. And he's always so clean, not like the Cuban!" Gary made Lucille feel secure as a woman, so she was free to do her work unencumbered.

HERE'S LUCY #123: "LUCY THE PEACEMAKER"

(CBS, SEPTEMBER 24, 1973), 30 MINUTES

WRITTEN BY: Bob O'Brien

GUEST CAST: Steve Lawrence, Eydie Gorme

With the agency back in business, both Steve Lawrence and Eydie Gorme come in looking for domestic help, because they have had a fight and are now separated. Lucy sees an opportunity to meddle by surreptitiously bringing the two together, but her efforts prove in vain. Steve is so angry with Eydie, he hires Lucy to replace her onstage at Caesar's Palace.

HIGHLIGHTS & TRIVIA

There is no explanation given as to why the agency is back in business, or what happened to it in the interim. Lucille takes every opportunity to plug her forthcoming film *Mame*, even though it won't open until the following spring, and sings snatches of "If He Walked into My Life" during this episode. Coincidentally, Eydie Gorme had a big hit record of that song several years earlier. Notice the "mayonnaise" that Steve scrapes off his sandwich and then eats; it is actually applesauce. Lucy's intentional massacre of "Together Wherever We Go" gets spontaneous applause from the audience. It is the only time on this series that her singing voice is ridiculed in the same way Lucy Ricardo's was.

A scene filmed for the beginning of the show is edited out because of time restraints. Rather than waste a good scene, it is restaged the night of "Lucy Gives Eddie Albert the Old Song and Dance" and used in that episode (#126).

HERE'S LUCY #124: "LUCY, THE WEALTHY WIDOW"

(CBS, OCTOBER 1, 1973), 30 MINUTES

WRITTEN BY: Bob O'Brien

GUEST CAST: Ed McMahon, Henry Beckman, Sid Gould, Tommy Farrell, Orwin Harvey, Jay Fletcher

When Lucy sees a TV commercial for a bank that lends money without a lot of hassle, she schemes to convince the banker that she is wealthy so she can borrow $10,000 to modernize the Unique Employment Agency. With the help of Kim and Harry, she becomes an affluent widow with a large staff of servants.

HIGHLIGHTS & TRIVIA

It is one of the inconsistencies of this series that Harry is portrayed as being both very wealthy and almost bankrupt, depending on the requirements of the given episode. What sort of modernization does an employment agency need—$10,000 worth of new furniture? It is becoming obvious that writer Bob O'Brien is running out of ideas for *Here's Lucy*, yet Lucille continues to order scripts from him.

HERE'S LUCY #125: "THE BOW-WOW BOUTIQUE"

(CBS, OCTOBER 8, 1973), 30 MINUTES

WRITTEN BY: Fred S. Fox, Seaman Jacobs

GUEST CAST: Bob Williams with Louie, Jonathan Hole, Sid Gould, Andy Albin, Eve McVeagh

Harry buys a pet shop as an investment, and his stingy ways soon leave him without employees. He presses Lucy into working for him on the weekend, and warns her to be especially nice to dog trainer Bob Williams, who might buy the shop. When Lucy and Kim take over washing the dogs, the suds machine goes berserk.

HIGHLIGHTS & TRIVIA

Bob Williams and his dog Louie are an unusual choice as guest stars, in that they are a variety act better suited for a nightclub. The episode is typical Lucy, with machinery going awry and pandemonium everywhere. Yet, somehow, it doesn't play as funny as it should. Eve McVeagh (as a customer) was practically a regular on *Dragnet* (1967–70), playing a variety of policewomen and bunko artists.

Lucie Arnaz

It was around this time that my mother began to rely totally on the cue cards. In the beginning of Here's Lucy, *she not only knew her lines but everybody else's. But she wanted to be able to observe what was going on in rehearsals without a script in her hand. So it became somebody else holding the script, then cue cards from the get-go. The more she used the cue cards, the less she was in the reality of the scene. It is hard to do good physical comedy when you don't know what's coming up next.*

HERE'S LUCY #126: "LUCY GIVES EDDIE ALBERT THE OLD SONG AND DANCE"

(CBS, OCTOBER 15, 1973), 30 MINUTES

WRITTEN BY: Madelyn Davis, Bob Carroll Jr.

GUEST CAST: Eddie Albert, Vanda Barra, Doris Singleton, Jerry Hausner

A woman matching Lucy's description is stalking movie stars Eddie Albert and Rock Hudson, so it is no surprise when Lucy approaches Albert to appear in a charity show, he is far from enthused.

HIGHLIGHTS & TRIVIA

While this plot is hardly novel, Ball and Albert make it pay off with a truly marvelous song and dance at the end of the episode. Lucille favors her bad right leg slightly, but is still able to successfully carry off the routine. With *I Love Lucy* alumni Singleton and Hausner on board, there is a feeling of old home week. Lucille begins wearing longer wigs (on a whim) again with this installment, after having worn shorter styles earlier in the season. Sixty-one-year-old Ball is still able to effectively entertain in a musical-comedy arena, but without the energy or sparkle of the past.

HERE'S LUCY #127: "LUCY'S TENANT"

(CBS, OCTOBER 22, 1973), 30 MINUTES

WRITTEN BY: Fred S. Fox, Seaman Jacobs
GUEST CAST: Jackie Coogan, Reta Shaw, Rhodes Reason

Lucy decides to rent out Kim's vacant room for extra spending money, but is shocked when the rental agent sends her a very eccentric man (Jackie Coogan) with a quite sour disposition. Forced to keep him because of the lease he signed, Lucy schemes to scare him away by pretending to be in love with him.

HIGHLIGHTS & TRIVIA

This is the type of simplistic plot that might have been acceptable in the first few episodes of *I Love Lucy*, but should have been unacceptable by this point. It has so many plot holes it resembles Swiss cheese, and what is there is passé. These sorts of efforts more resemble a TV variety show sketch than a situation comedy. Jackie Coogan always comes across well on a Lucy endeavor, but he works with precious little here. Lucille's voice has dropped to an even lower register this season, giving her a harder edge. Not only has it deepened, but it has lost much ability to show inflection, which gives Ball's vocal performance a flat quality. It is getting more difficult for Lucille to appear feminine oncamera.

HERE'S LUCY #128: "LUCY AND ANDY GRIFFITH"

(CBS, OCTOBER 29, 1973), 30 MINUTES

WRITTEN BY: Bob O'Brien
GUEST CAST: Andy Griffith, Sid Gould, Hank Stohl, Randall Carver, Rick Kelman, Bob Whitney, Nancy La Mar, Rosemary O'Brien, Dave Anderson Stuart, Marvin Robinson

Lucy has a huge crush on a man who says he does good work for wayward youths. Kim isn't so easily convinced, and disguises herself as an errant hippie to test just how good this man really is.

HIGHLIGHTS & TRIVIA

The program belongs to Lucie Arnaz, who shows a sensitivity and acting ability that will become even more evident in her later work. The plot is not unusual for this series, but its Christian overtones certainly are. Andy Griffith (whose sitcom was a long-time Monday night bunkmate with *The Lucy Show*) comes across very preachy in this entry, showing little of his usual light comedic touch. This is the first major exposure for young Randall Carver, who will be a first season cast member of *Taxi* (1978–83).

HERE'S LUCY #129: "LUCY AND JOAN RIVERS DO JURY DUTY"

(CBS, NOVEMBER 5, 1973),

WRITTEN BY: Madelyn Davis, Bob Carroll Jr.
GUEST CAST: Joan Rivers, Burt Mustin, James E. Brodhead, Hank Brandt, Judd Laurance, Savannah Bentley, Alice Backus, Lew Palter, Shirley Anthony, Bob Whitney, Sid Gould, Walter Smith

Lucy is on jury duty, and naturally becomes the sole dissenting voter in a trial.

HIGHLIGHTS & TRIVIA

Practically every sitcom of the 1960s had one episode that was a satire of *12 Angry Men* (1957), a classic film with Henry Fonda about a lone juror standing up for his principles. *The Dick Van Dyke Show, That Girl, The Odd Couple, All in the Family,* and others had already beaten this plot line premise to death. Despite its lack of originality, the script is well written and Lucille's scene where she discusses the trial with a fellow juror (Joan Rivers) by acting out charades is vintage Lucy. Lucille is an early booster of Joan's, and will join her several times when Rivers hosts TV talk shows.

Quite often, Ball chooses to publicly chide one of her children. Once, upon announcing Desi Jr.'s pending marriage to performer Linda Purl, Lucille tells Rivers, "I like this girl. I've told her that if he gives her any grief at all to send him to me. I'll set him straight!" On a *Tonight Show* guest-hosted by Rivers, Lucille decides to discuss her daughter's closely-timed pregnancies: "[My daughter keeps giving birth] Christmas or New Year's, Christmas or New Year's. If [Larry Luckinbill, Lucie Arnaz' husband] doesn't take a scissors . . . [referring to a vasectomy]." Lucie didn't speak to her mother for several weeks after that one.

Joan Rivers

(ACTOR/COMEDIAN/HOST)

At one point, [Lucille Ball] stopped a shot and said, "The camera angle is three inches off." [The crew] said, "Oh, no, Lucy, it's not." And she said, "Measure!" It was.

HERE'S LUCY #130: "TIPSY THROUGH THE TULIPS"

(CBS, NOVEMBER 12, 1973), 30 MINUTES

WRITTEN BY: Madelyn Davis, Bob Carroll Jr.
GUEST CAST: Foster Brooks, Jack Collins

A famous mystery writer hires Lucy to help keep him sober while he completes his latest novel. The ingenious alcoholic hides the booze everywhere, and in short order both he and Lucy are inebriated.

HIGHLIGHTS & TRIVIA

Comedian Foster Brooks is very popular at this time for his drunk bit, used on TV and in his nightclub act. The entire episode is an excuse to showcase his patented routines. Switch alcohol for food, and this episode is very similar to 1968's *Here's Lucy* episode, "Lucy and Miss Shelley Winters" (#4).

HERE'S LUCY #131: "THE CARTERS MEET FRANKIE AVALON"

(CBS, NOVEMBER 19, 1973), 30 MINUTES

WRITTEN BY: Bob O'Brien, Fred S. Fox, Seaman Jacobs
GUEST CAST: Frankie Avalon, Vic Glazer, Sid Gould, Jerry Fogel, Robert Hogan, Bill Lee, Robert Whitney

The Carters go to see Frankie Avalon perform at a nightclub, and Kim is invited on stage to do a duet with Frankie. She gets an invitation to appear in the club's amateur contest later in the week. Lucy schemes to get Avalon to play Sonny Bono to Kim's Cher for the competition.

Lucie Arnaz

If I do say so myself, I did a helluva job doing Cher on this show. And I really liked the way Frankie did Sonny. I thought he had the voice down pat. We actually went and visited their show the week before we shot ours. In fact, I copied more of Cher's mannerisms when she is offstage then when she was on. I don't think she was as animated onstage. And I copied every movement and gesture she made. Cher lent me the wig, the earrings, the eyelashes . . . we had a ball! And Frankie and I sang live to a prerecorded [music] track.

THE MERV GRIFFIN SHOW

(SYN, NOVEMBER, 1973), 90 MINUTES

EXECUTIVE PRODUCED BY: Merv Griffin
DIRECTED BY: Dick Carson
GUEST CAST: Merv Griffin (host), Desi Arnaz Jr., Lucie Arnaz, Lucille Ball, Gale Gordon, Bob Hope, Gary Morton

This is the only time Lucille appears on a TV talk show with both of her children. The biggest part of the installment features a preview screening of a musical number from her forthcoming Warner Bros. film, *Mame* (1974). Ball is highly energized, as she tapes this appearance directly after filming an episode of *Here's Lucy*. This is one of the few talk shows on which Gale Gordon appears. It is also one of Bob Hope's few unscripted TV ventures. Desi Jr., his hair dyed red for a TV movie role, looks puffy and seems fatigued. Lucille will appear with Merv several times during the 1970s and early 1980s. These appearances will usually be in the form of a salute to Ball, and will, at various times, feature Bob Carroll Jr., Madelyn Davis, Gary Morton, and Gale Gordon. There will also be a highly panned *Merv Griffin Show* taped at the Los Angeles opening of *Mame*. The entire thing is so staged, and Lucille (in a costume and wig from the film) is so haughty, that the installment is highly criticized in newspaper columns around the country.

Jack Sheldon
(ACTOR/MUSICIAN)

I first started doing Merv's show in 1970 when he came out to Los Angeles from New York. He was on CBS, and going crazy trying to compete with Johnny [Carson]. We left CBS and began to do the show for Metromedia, and that's when I met Lucille Ball. We taped at the old Hollywood Palace theatre. Merv always made everybody look good, and wanted them to have the funny lines and the spotlight. That's why he got Lucy to do things on his show that she didn't do on others. She trusted him to present her well. Merv had great show business sense.

She'd get there right before the show, all made-up and wigged and ready to go. A real pro. A pleasure to be around. Lucille was very motherly to me. She'd pull me aside and say, "You're not going to wear that on the show, are you? Go change those pants now!" If my humor on the show got a little blue, she'd say, "Now there's no reason to talk like that, Jack. It's not funny when you do that!" I felt a lot of love from her.

Lucie Arnaz was a great girl. So pretty and talented. I used to do a lot of flirting with her when she was on the show.

Lucie Arnaz
(WHILE APPEARING ON THE PROGRAM)

My mother is going to work forever. I have this nightmare that I'll be a little old lady in a wheelchair, and some nurse will come along and say, "Now Miss Arnaz, time to watch your mother's show."

HERE'S LUCY #132: "HARRY CATCHES GOLD FEVER"

(CBS, DECEMBER 3, 1973), 30 MINUTES
WRITTEN BY: Fred S. Fox, Seaman Jacobs
GUEST CAST: J. Pat O'Malley, Janos Prohaska

Claiming to be an environmentalist, Harry buys a plot of land from a recluse because he suspects there is gold to be found.

HIGHLIGHTS & TRIVIA

This episode is inferior in almost every way. Poor Janos Prohaska. Inside almost every bear or gorilla found on *The Lucy Show* and *Here's Lucy* is this tireless man, who has made a career out of playing wild animals.

A SHOW BUSINESS SALUTE TO MILTON BERLE

(NBC, DECEMBER 4, 1973), 60 MINUTES
PRODUCED BY: Bernie Kukoff, Jeff Harris
DIRECTED BY: Grey Lockwood
WRITTEN BY: Don Reo, Allan Katz, Bill Box, Stanley Davis
CAST: Sammy Davis Jr. (host), Lucille Ball, Jack Benny, Milton Berle, Kirk Douglas, Redd Foxx, Jackie Gleason, Bob Hope, Ted Kennedy, Alan King, Jack Lemmon, Walter Matthau, Jan Murray, Carroll O'Connor, Don Rickles, Archbishop Fulton J. Sheen, Henny Youngman

A salute to Mr. Television on the occasion of his sixtieth anniversary in show business. This is a roast produced by the Friars Club, one of the few that is actually telecast. The only performances are jibes at Berle, much in the style of the later *Dean Martin Celebrity Roasts.*

THE BOB HOPE CHRISTMAS SHOW

(NBC, DECEMBER 9, 1973), 60 MINUTES
EXECUTIVE PRODUCED BY: Bob Hope
PRODUCED BY: Mort Lachman
DIRECTED BY: Dick McDonough
WRITTEN BY: Lester White and Mel Tolkin, Charles Lee and Gig Henry, Mort Lachman, Raymond Silver, Steve White, Norman Sullivan
CAST: Bob Hope (host), Lucille Ball, Gary Morton, Shirley Jones, Marie Osmond, Doris Singleton

This is the only time Lucille and Gary play themselves as husband and wife within a TV sketch. Bob asks Gary to hide a necklace Hope has bought for his wife Dolores for Christmas. Lucy finds it, and thinks that Bob wants to have an affair with her. This is actually a pretty funny sketch for a Hope show, with the extra added bonus of seeing Lucille and Doris Singelton (as Lucy's friend and confidante named Doris) working together again.

HERE'S LUCY #133: "LUCY AND CHUCK CONNORS HAVE A SURPRISE SLUMBER PARTY"

(CBS, DECEMBER 17, 1973), 30 MINUTES
WRITTEN BY: Madelyn Davis, Bob Carroll Jr.
GUEST CAST: Chuck Connors, Ryan MacDonald, Sidney Clute, Sid Gould, Buddy Lewis, Bob Whitney, Walter Smith

Harry rents out Lucy's house to a production company making a movie with Chuck Connors. After being a pest, she is banished until the filming is completed. When she thinks all is clear, Lucy goes home, not knowing that Chuck Connors is sleeping in her bed.

HIGHLIGHTS & TRIVIA
The script is good and Lucille is in fine fettle, but the choice of guest star leaves something to be desired. Connors is recently in the news because he hugged and kissed Soviet Secretary Brezhnev while doing some diplomacy, so his visit is meant to be topical. But unfortunately, the Big Guy is a few bricks short of a comedy load.

Mike Connors
(ACTOR)
Chuck and I were very close friends. But when it came to comedy, he tended to go overboard. He thought he had a facility for this kind of thing, but he really didn't.

HERE'S LUCY #134: "LUCY PLAYS COPS AND ROBBERS"

(CBS, DECEMBER 31, 1973), 30 MINUTES
WRITTEN BY: Madelyn Davis, Bob Carroll Jr.
GUEST CAST: Dick Sargent, Gary Crosby, Gino Conforti, Mary Wickes, Al Lewis

A recent rash of burglaries in the area prompts Lucy to hold a neighborhood watch symposium, led by two local patrolmen. Nervous Lucy keeps phoning the cops at every suspicion, but finally gets trapped in her home by a real burglar.

HIGHLIGHTS & TRIVIA
This installment is meant to be the season opener, and is in fact one of the best episodes of the entire *Here's Lucy* series. Looking youthful in a very long wig she never wears again, Lucille is obviously invigorated by the guests on the show. Although no one person has a lot to do because there are so many characters, everyone has choice moments. Wickes and Lewis are hysterical as the overbearing wife and her henpecked husband. Conforti is winning in his turn as the crook. He is both so humorous and sympathetic, one almost wishes he wouldn't get caught. The superior script is evenly paced. All of the guest stars are very well used, and demonstrate what this series could have been if it had been focused as an ensemble comedy.

HERE'S LUCY #135: "LUCY IS A BIRD SITTER"

(CBS, JANUARY 7, 1974), 30 MINUTES
WRITTEN BY: Madelyn Davis, Bob Carroll Jr.
GUEST CAST: Arte Johnson

Harry, being a booster of the city zoo, agrees to watch a rare New Guinea Weewawk until it can be brought to its mate. It needs heat, and when Harry's furnace fails he brings it to Lucy. Naturally, she loses the bird.

HIGHLIGHTS & TRIVIA
This installment is based in part on 1964's "Lucy Gets a Bird" episode (#70) of *The Lucy Show*, although Davis and Carroll are not the original authors. This is a silly one, and its execution is hampered by Ball's flat, raspy voice. The entire last scene consists of the cast walking around and yelling "weewawk" to attract the lost bird. Had Lucille's voice been more facile, this would be a lot funnier.

HERE'S LUCY #136: "MEANWHILE, BACK AT THE OFFICE"

(CBS, JANUARY 14, 1974), 30 MINUTES
WRITTEN BY: Fred S. Fox, Seaman Jacobs
GUEST CAST: Don Porter, George Chandler, Billy Sands, John Wheeler, Dave Morick

Harry sells the agency to Mr. Richards, who hires Lucy back as his secretary. Harry is miserable without his business, so Lucy schemes to make Mr. Richards sell it back.

HIGHLIGHTS & TRIVIA
Don Porter had been Ann Sothern's foil on her two television series, both filmed at Desilu. He

understands the requirements of the broad comedy necessary for this type of series, and fits in well to the format. The theme of Harry selling his agency, or getting investors, or getting partners, has become very stale. Lucie Arnaz again steals the show, this time as a little old lady accompanied by a live lion.

Lucie Arnaz

This was the last show we shot. In those days, I had a thing for dangerous pets, like that lion. That week I had a boa constrictor. I brought it to the set, and put it on the lion. The lion just looked at it, like "so?"

HERE'S LUCY #137: "LUCY IS N.G. AS AN R.N."

(CBS, JANUARY 21, 1974), 30 MINUTES
WRITTEN BY: Madelyn Davis, Bob Carroll Jr.
GUEST CAST: Roy Roberts, Al Checco

Lucy cancels her trip to San Francisco to attend a secretarys' convention and play nursemaid when Kim gets the flu; Mary Jane breaks both of her hands; Harry gets a wrenched knee; and Kim's cat (also named Harry) has kittens.

HIGHLIGHTS & TRIVIA

An excellent installment, this one again demonstrates how good the series could have been had it been more of an ensemble comedy. Bob and Madelyn's script is crisp and extremely well paced, and all of the performers are in fine fettle. Mary Jane is especially funny, and is given more screen time than she has been afforded in some time. This is Roy Roberts' (as the doctor) last television appearance; he will pass away several months after this episode is filmed.

HERE'S LUCY #138: "LUCY THE SHERIFF"

(CBS, JANUARY 28, 1974), 30 MINUTES
DIRECTED BY: Lucille Ball, Coby Ruskin
WRITTEN BY: Fred S. Fox, Seaman Jacobs
GUEST CAST: Mary Wickes, Ross Elliott, Cliff Osmond, John Craig, Flo Halop, Boyd "Red" Morgan, Orwin Harvey, Vincent P. Deadrick, Gerald Brutsche

The town of Cartridge Belt, Montana, discovers that Lucy is the great granddaughter of their first woman sheriff, Flora Belle Orcutt. They send for Lucy to be the official sheriff and queen of a week-long festival, but Lucy ends up having to actually apprehend bank robbers.

HIGHLIGHTS & TRIVIA

Another excellent installment, with a fine cast including veteran Ross Elliott, who had played the director of the Vitameatavegamin commercial all those years ago on 1952's *I Love Lucy* (episode #30), "Lucy Does a Commercial." This is Coby Ruskin's last Lucy assignment. Lucille takes over direction during the rehearsal process and fires Ruskin. This is the only Lucy episode where Ball is actually credited as the director. From the results, she obviously does a fine job. Flora Belle was the name of Lucille's maternal grandmother; she will use the name again as the character she plays in *Stone Pillow* (1985).

Lucie Arnaz

I don't remember why my mother's name appears on this episode as a director with Coby. Maybe she fired him in midweek and just took over herself. I don't know. People have written that Mom was the real director of the show. That really isn't so. True, she did need strong directors who would stand up to her, like William Asher and Herbert Kenwith. But she wanted them to. She relied on her directors to make sure she was giving the best performance she could. It was a collaborative effort. Any director who didn't want to collaborate didn't last very long. Mom would always be thinking ahead. She knew lighting and camera movements. So if she said, "So and so needs to move here, or be shot from this angle," she was generally right. I think she got a bad rap because a lot of actors don't know those things, and didn't bother with them.

At the same time that this episode is shot, Lucille and Gale Gordon film a message for the U.S. Treasury Department promoting payroll savings at the workplace for the purchase of savings bonds.

HERE'S LUCY #139: "MILTON BERLE IS THE LIFE OF THE PARTY"

(CBS, FEBRUARY 11, 1974), 30 MINUTES
DIRECTED BY: Jack Donohue
WRITTEN BY: Madelyn Davis, Bob Carroll Jr.
GUEST CAST: Milton Berle, Elliot Reid, Sid

Gould, Vanda Barra, John Calvin, James N. Joyce, Shirley Anthony, Joyce McNeal

Milton Berle generously offers his comedy services to be auctioned off on television for charity just as Lucy's friends give her a hard time for the boring parties she throws. Lucy bids on Berle's services for her next party, and amazingly wins him for only $7.50!

HIGHLIGHTS & TRIVIA

Milton Berle, Bob and Madelyn's writing, Jack Donohue's direction, and a strong ensemble cast—it is no wonder this episode is such a winner. In fact, these last four episodes are among the best of the *Here's Lucy* series. It is not clear why Lucille does not continue to direct the series herself as there are only a handful of episodes remaining to be filmed, but she enlists the aid of old hand Jack Donohue to finish the season for her.

HERE'S LUCY #140: "MARY JANE'S BOYFRIEND"

(CBS, FEBRUARY 18, 1974), 30 MINUTES

DIRECTED BY: Jack Donohue
WRITTEN BY: Fred S. Fox, Seaman Jacobs
GUEST CAST: Cliff Norton, John Gabriel, Roy Rowan (voice only)

Mary Jane takes a charm course, and soon enough has a new boyfriend. The only fly in the ointment is that her beau falls for Lucy, who schemes to turn him off and send him away.

HIGHLIGHTS & TRIVIA

This is the only Lucy episode that centers around Mary Jane Croft. She is more than up to the task, and it is a shame that she has not been allowed to do more during her years working with Lucille Ball. She is funny, cute, charming, and endearing, sort of a middle-aged version of Georgette Baxter on Mary Tyler Moore's 1970s sitcom.

Desi Arnaz Jr.

The thing about Mary Jane is that she is very unassuming and a total professional. She is a very grounding, very leveling kind of person. She was a calming influence on the set, which was always sorely needed.

Lucie Arnaz

She looks better today than when we were doing the show. I don't know if she's been to some magician, or if she's always going to look fabulous. She is a dear, sweet lady with a delightful laugh. There was this whole gals' group on the set, with Mary Jane, Vanda, Mary Wickes, and I.

Cliff Norton

(ACTOR/COMEDIAN)

Mary Jane Croft was a strange little girl. She made strange acting choices, and they came out of her in a funny way but off-center. There was a creative insecurity about her, that I am certain had to have been encouraged by Lucy. Mary Jane was very easy to work with. We had to "cheat" to get the ladder bit done. I had to scoot down on my knees to give the appearance of climbing up to Lucy's window, using my body to pull myself "up." And there were mattresses all around, so I only fell backwards the length of my body when Lucy pushed me. It was all very safe. The tango bit actually required very little rehearsal. Lucille had been a chorus girl and I was always very light on my feet, so we worked through it in a few minutes. They added the little "bump" (when she kicks me) afterward with a sound effect.

A DEAN MARTIN ROAST: "JACK BENNY"

(NBC, FEBRUARY 22, 1974), 60 MINUTES

PRODUCED BY: Lee Hale
DIRECTED BY: Greg Garrison
CAST: Dean Martin (host), Lucille Ball, Jack Benny, George Burns, Johnny Carson, Rich Little, and others

Another in the roast series hosted by Dean Martin, this is Jack Benny's turn at receiving good-natured public put-downs. Lucille ably reads her jokes off cue-cards but does not do well with put-down humor, and her contributions to these roasts are usually edited down.

HERE'S LUCY #141: "LUCY AND PHIL HARRIS STRIKE UP THE BAND"

(CBS, FEBRUARY 25, 1974), 30 MINUTES

DIRECTED BY: Jack Donohue
WRITTEN BY: Bob O'Brien

GUEST CAST: Phil Harris, Tommy Farrell, Marl Young, Michaelani, Anthony Ortega, Henry L. Miranda

When Lucy reads that Phil Harris is forming a new orchestra and is looking for talent, she brings to him all the unemployed musical talent from the Unique Employment Agency. It so happens that most of these are minority performers, and hiring them gains Harris publicity. When the women's lib movement pickets him for not hiring a woman, Phil hires Lucy as his vocalist.

HIGHLIGHTS & TRIVIA

Marl Young plays himself as the African-American pianist Lucy brings to Harris; he is *Here's Lucy*'s musical director. This episode has the feeling of being rushed. While Lucille has always been in the forefront of integrating her casts and crew (after all, Desi Arnaz was a Cuban), this is the first time a script really makes mention of minorities.

HERE'S LUCY #142: "LUCY CARTER MEETS LUCILLE BALL"

(CBS, MARCH 4, 1974), 30 MINUTES

DIRECTED BY: Jack Donohue

WRITTEN BY: Bob O'Brien

GUEST CAST: Lucille Ball, Gary Morton, Doris Singleton, Tom Kelly, Carole Cook, Roy Rowan

Kim enters a Lucille Ball look-alike contest, but does not make the finals. Lucy brings the matter to Lucille Ball herself, who insists that she and Kim be in the contest. Both ladies end up as finalists, and not only have to look like Lucille Ball as she appears in *Mame*, but sing the jingle for the sponsor of the contest.

HIGHLIGHTS & TRIVIA

This plot had to happen sooner or later. Lucille Ball's movie musical *Mame* is just about to premiere, and the actor is becoming the most publicized woman on earth. She is appearing on magazine covers, on local television news and talk shows, and doing newspaper and magazine interviews. Ball sees no reason why she shouldn't use her own program as a vehicle for promotion. This episode is a thirty-minute commercial for *Mame*. Due to the technical constraints of the plot, there is no studio audience in attendance. The same sort of techniques that were used on *The Patty Duke Show* (1963–66) to show "twins" (as played by the same person) are used here. It is much more difficult to do this with color film, but the crew handles it in a very professional fashion. When Lucie Arnaz and Carole Cook come out to sing the "Mais Oui" jingle, they do it bumping and grinding in a lewd fashion as a joke. Lucille is not amused, and the scene is reshot.

Lucie Arnaz

Whenever we had Carole Cook on, it was like a party that week. Carole is a scream. Raunchy, very raunchy, very funny and yet very sincere underneath all that. She's a theatre person like I am . . . a real trouper. She's been married to the same man for about 182 years, and that's one of the reasons why I adore her to this day. She always had a picture of her husband Tom in a leather folder that she'd put out on her dressing table. It'd be there even if she was going to see him in twenty minutes. She wanted to keep him close.

Carole Cook

(ACTOR/FAMILY FRIEND)

Lucie and I used to do all sorts of awful, funny things to Lucille [changing lines to something off-color]. But it was very strange. Things that would have really made her laugh if we were just sitting and talking were either ignored or looked down upon on the set. She was just so focused she couldn't let the humor in.

HERE'S LUCY #143: "WHERE IS MY WANDERING MOTHER TONIGHT?"

(CBS, MARCH 11, 1974), 30 MINUTES

DIRECTED BY: Jack Donohue

WRITTEN BY: Madelyn Davis, Bob Carroll Jr.

GUEST CAST: Jack Donohue, Brian Cutler, Cindy Barnes

Lonely Lucy misses her kids, so Harry calls Kim to get her to invite Lucy over to Kim's apartment. The excited mother races over to spend the weekend, but overhears Kim tell a girlfriend that she is in the way. Lucy manufactures a phony blind date as an excuse to leave, and then seems to disappear.

HIGHLIGHTS & TRIVIA

This is probably the most realistic mother and daughter script in the series' entire six seasons. The humor is grounded in reality and is well motivated. The situation is something almost everyone can relate to. Lucille does one of her last physical bits, locking her legs into a Lotus yoga position and then not being able to undo them.

HERE'S LUCY #144: "LUCY FIGHTS THE SYSTEM"

(CBS, MARCH 18, 1974), 30 MINUTES

DIRECTED BY: Jack Donohue
WRITTEN BY: Bob O'Brien
GUEST CAST: Mary Treen, Jack Collins, Jack J. Fox, Ernest Sarracino, Sid Gould, Vanda Barra, Buddy Lewis, Harry Holcombe, Barbara Morrison, Larry Blake, Eddie Quillan

A middle-aged waitress comes to Lucy's office seeking employment because she has been fired due to her age. Seeing an opportunity to strike back at the current youth emphasis and get the woman her job back, Lucy sends Kim as the replacement. Armed with a phony degree in restaurant management and directions from her scheming mother, Kim drives the owner crazy with her wacky ideas, rudeness, and inefficiency.

HIGHLIGHTS & TRIVIA

Lucie Arnaz is savvy in her portrayal of the waitress, and, in fact, the entire episode is thrown her way. She once again proves her facility with comedy, and it is no wonder that in short order she will become a star in her own right. This is the final first-run episode of *Here's Lucy*, ending twenty-three years of Lucille Ball on weekly television. *TV Guide* calls it the end of an era. Although it is announced that Lucille is quitting to pursue her movie career, the timing and truth are not in evidence. *Mame* proves to be a disappointment at the box office (although it will later have a successful life on home video and cable television), and there will be no more theatrical movies for Ball. At the same time, CBS has canceled all of its old star vehicles to make way for the new crop on television. Only *Gunsmoke* (1955–75) will survive for one more season. Jackie Gleason, Red Skelton, Art Linkletter, Garry Moore, Jack Benny, George Burns . . . all are no longer on the network. In truth, *Here's Lucy* has been canceled. Its ratings have dipped below the top twenty for the first time in Ball's television career. Desi Jr. has already left, and Lucie Arnaz now has other plans.

Lucie Arnaz

Even if CBS had pushed more for Mom to come back another year, I don't think she would have. She had six years of shows that she wanted to put into syndication and reap some profits. I was leaving regardless to do Seesaw *[on tour]. Desi was already gone. Gale was getting older [he was sixty-eight at the time].*

Lucille Ball

What was I going to do? Start all over again with another format? Get new kids? What was I going to do, just be on the show by myself? It was time to leave.

The episode ends with poor Gale Gordon getting another pie in the face. He deadpans into the camera, "I knew it would end like this." Although this was not the last episode filmed, his words are a fine epitaph to the characters he had played all these years. From Mr. Littlefield to Mr. Mooney to Uncle Harry, Gale Gordon has been the recipient of more comedy abuse than just about any other actor in show business history.

Appearing on *The Phil Donohue Show* when it is just a local Ohio program, Ball announces that she has several exciting projects in the works, and alludes to the possibility of a new kind of series in a year or two. Lucille actually has in mind a continuing series of specials, similar in concept to the old *Desilu Playhouse* (1958–60), in which she would appear monthly doing comedy, drama, and variety. CBS will not buy that much Lucille Ball for the future, so things are taken a season at a time.

Carole Cook

(ACTOR/FAMILY FRIEND)

I don't think Lucy was ever again really happy once she wasn't working every day. She was used to arriving at the studio at ten o'clock every morning, four days a week, twenty-five weeks a year. It was a pattern for her. And although I don't think she was enjoying the work nearly as much as she had back when she worked with Viv, this had become her life.

Chapter Twenty-Six

1974-75 Season

DINAH!

(SYN, OCTOBER 15, 1974), 60 OR 90 MINUTE VERSIONS AVAILABLE TO LOCAL STATIONS
EXECUTIVE PRODUCED BY: Henry Jaffe, Carolyn Raskin
PRODUCED BY: Fred Tatashore
DIRECTED BY: Glen Swanson
WRITTEN BY: Bill Walker, Bob Shayne, Donald Ross, Norman Martin, Fred Tatashore
CAST: Dinah Shore (host), Lucille Ball

Dinah and Lucille duet on "Bosom Buddies" from Ball's current feature film *Mame*.

TIMEX PRESENTS A LUCILLE BALL SPECIAL: "HAPPY ANNIVERSARY AND GOODBYE"

(CBS, NOVEMBER 10, 1974), 60 MINUTES
EXECUTIVE PRODUCED BY: Lucille Ball
PRODUCED BY: Gary Morton
DIRECTED BY: Jack Donohue
WRITTEN BY: Arnie Rosen, Arthur Julian
CAST: Lucille Ball, Patricia Blair, Art Carney, Doria Cook, Nanette Fabray, Connie Garrison, Sid Gould, Florence Lake, Peter Marshall, Linda Todd Michaels, Louisa Moritz, Don Porter, Rhodes Reason, Arnold Schwarzenegger

Malcolm and Norma Michaels (Art Carney and Lucille Ball) finally marry off their daughter and realize that they are unhappy with themselves, each other, and their marriage. They separate, each trying to find new meaning to their lives with the help of a close friend. What they finally discover is the deep love that still exists between them.

HIGHLIGHTS & TRIVIA

This special is excellent all the way down the line. Ball is superb as the fat, frowsy put-upon wife, allowing herself to look completely unattractive and unsympathetic. Her cleverly written banter with Carney is a laugh-riot, reminiscent of the quarrels between Ralph Kramden and his wife Alice on the 1950s TV classic, *The Honeymooners* (which featured Carney as Ed Norton). The themes are much more adult than anything Lucille has done before on television, including discussions about sexuality, birth control, pre-marital sex, and alcoholism. Lucille's bass voice actually works very well in her favor, as she is not trying at all to be youthful as in most of her other TV work of this period. The rest of the cast is equally good, giving Ball the needed oncamera support she hasn't enjoyed in years. Carney, Fabray, and Marshall offer some of the best television performances of their careers. Arnold Schwarzenegger makes his American television debut as the overly muscled masseur Rico. The only real slapstick comedy is the bit where Don Porter chases Lucille across the water bed, and she springs leaks in it with her high heels. Part of the special is filmed on location in Las Vegas; Lucille must have really enjoyed it, because her next TV special is filmed entirely in the gambling capital.

Art Carney keeps flubbing his lines. Finally, in frustration, he gets up and says, "What do you expect? I'm a dentist!" Nanette Fabray also has trouble getting her words to come out right. At one point, she simply says, "Oh Shit!" After a second, she asks Lucille, "Shall I go on?" Lucille nonchalantly replies, "After 'Oh Shit,' you *can't* go on!" Ball and Carney had previously played husband and wife in 1967's risqué screen comedy *A Guide for the Married Man.*

Gary Morton

(EXECUTIVE PRODUCER)

Each special was taken one at a time, as they were made. There was no master plan. Lucy was getting *tired. The specials were a big strain on her. And CBS was looking for different types of shows. I gave Arnold Schwarzenegger his first television job on this one. We paid him $750 to play the masseur. And Lucille adored working with Art Carney.*

Jimmy Garrett
(ACTOR)

I was in the studio audience for this special. In between Art Carney's scenes, he would walk over to a piano that was on the living room set and play bawdy songs for the audience while the next scene was being set up! Gary Morton interviewed me for a small part on this special, but I wasn't cast.

Peter Marshall
(ACTOR)

When they offered me a part on this special, I initially wanted to turn it down because of the bad time I had doing The Lucy Show. *When they told me that almost all of my scenes would be with Art Carney, I said, "Yes! Great!" We used to eat at a little place just outside of Paramount Studios in Hollywood. I was at lunch with Art Carney and Nanette Fabray, and I asked them both if they had ever worked with Lucy before. They said no, and I told them that they both would quit before we were finished.*

We were doing the first read-through of the script, and Lucille Ball turns to Art Carney and says, "Have you ever done comedy before? Where did you get those line readings?" Carney quit right there and then. The next day, Nanette and I had lunch with Art at the same place and talked him out of it. Yet another day goes by, and now Nanette gets it from Lucy and she quits! It takes still another lunch to get them both to get back to work and finish the show. And yet, whatever Lucille Ball did, she was phenomenal.

In my first scene with Art in the dentists' office our characters shared, I blew a line. [Director] Jack Donohue, bless his heart, said, "Cut! One of the lights is wrong." He was trying to cover for me to keep things light. I looked up at him in the booth and said, "I love you, Jack!" Art Carney's line during the massage scene, "Et tu, Brute?," was an ad lib he did in front of the audience and they kept it in. Art was wonderful. He played piano in between scenes. Lucy, Art, Nanette, and I were photographed for a TV Guide *cover and story about the show. Something happened and we got bumped from the issue. It would have been my only* TV Guide *cover.*

A CBS BICENTENNIAL MINUTE: "LUCY'S BICENTENNIAL MINUTE"

(CBS, NOVEMBER 28, 1974), ONE MINUTE
EXECUTIVE PRODUCED BY: Lewis Freedman
PRODUCED BY: William Kayden
RESEARCHER AND ASSISTANT PRODUCER: Meryle Evans

For two years (1974–76), CBS produces 732 bicentennial minutes, sixty-second looks at the events surrounding the Revolutionary War that led up to the United States' bicentennial celebration on July 4, 1976. On October 15, 1974, Lucille Ball videotapes her segment, which deals with the history of corn husking. Ball wears a black pants outfit with a floral print jacket and a long gold medallion while standing in front of a simple, dark background.

THE SULLIVAN YEARS: A TRIBUTE TO ED

(CBS, FEBRUARY 2, 1975); 60 MINUTES (COLOR AND B&W)
PRODUCED BY: Robert Precht
DIRECTED BY: Russ Petranto
CAST: Dick Cavett (Host)

A retrospective show honoring the late Ed Sullivan (who died in 1974). Video and film clips highlight his long career on CBS, including footage of Lucille and Desi from the 1950s.

A DEAN MARTIN ROAST: "LUCILLE BALL"

(NBC, FEBRUARY 7, 1975), 60 MINUTES
PRODUCED AND DIRECTED BY: Greg Garrison
CAST: Dean Martin (host), Lucille Ball, Jack Benny, Milton Berle, Foster Brooks, Ruth Buzzi, Phyllis Diller, Totie Fields, Henry Fonda, Gale Gordon, Bob Hope, Rich Little, Gary Morton, Don Rickles, Ginger Rogers, Rowan & Martin, Nipsey Russell, Vivian Vance

What is most special about this taped roast of Lucille is that it contains the last public appearance of Jack Benny, aired six weeks after his death from stomach cancer. Dean Martin shoots a special introduction for the program honoring Jack's memory. The highlight of the roast humor is Vivian Vance's reference to Desi Arnaz being henpecked by Lucille.

TIMEX PRESENTS A LUCILLE BALL SPECIAL: "LUCY GETS LUCKY"

(CBS, MARCH 1, 1975), 60 MINUTES

EXECUTIVE PRODUCED BY: Lucille Ball
PRODUCED BY: Gary Morton
DIRECTED BY: Jack Donohue
WRITTEN BY: Bob O'Brien
MAKEUP BY: Claude Thompson
HAIRSTYLING BY: Irma Kusely
MUSIC BY: Nelson Riddle
CAST: Jane Aull, Lucille Ball, Vanda Barra, Bonnie Boland, Gino Conforti, Jackie Coogan, Lee Delano, Jack Donohue, Hal England, Joey Forman, Bruce Gordon, Sid Gould, Jay Jones, Ken Lane, Dean Martin, Gary Morton, Paul Picerni, Joan Swift, Judith Wright

Plucky Lucy Collins comes to Las Vegas on a shoestring to see the opening night of her idol, Dean Martin, at the MGM Grand Hotel. When she finds that her reservation for eight (made to ensure she gets a seat) does not entitle her to an entry for one, and that the entire engagement is sold out, she is heartbroken. Upon learning that Martin will do a special performance just for hotel employees, Lucy gets herself hired and in the process manages to upset the entire establishment.

HIGHLIGHTS & TRIVIA

This is an unusual offering. It is shot almost entirely on location at the old MGM Grand Hotel (before its tragic fire) with one camera, like a movie. There is no studio audience or laugh track used, and the silence is deafening. Lucille does many of her own stunts, and some of them are rather dangerous, like driving a car down a set of steps. The script is lame, with much of the humor (?) found in bad puns, old jokes, and stale physical comedy. The idea that sexagenarian Lucille could get a job as a cocktail waitress or a keno runner, wearing skimpy costumes, is either chivalrous or absurd. Bits of business and plots are liberally taken from the Jerry Lewis film *The Bellboy* (1960), as well as from old *The Lucy Show* and *Here's Lucy* scripts. It isn't that the special is without entertainment value; it just offers nothing fresh. Lucille's loyalty to Bob O'Brien's writing talent is unfounded; it has been years since he has offered her a fresh concept.

At one point, Dean Martin forgets the words to his signature song, "Everybody Loves Somebody Sometime." He gives Ken Lane (Martin's pianist, musical director, and the composer of the song) the finger, and then jokes, "And that don't mean you're number one!"

DINAH!

(SYN, APRIL 29, 1975), 60 OR 90 MINUTE VERSIONS AVAILABLE TO LOCAL STATIONS

EXECUTIVE PRODUCED BY: Henry Jaffe, Carolyn Raskin
PRODUCED BY: Fred Tatashore
DIRECTED BY: Glen Swanson
WRITTEN BY: Bill Walker, Bob Shayne, Donald Ross, Norman Martin, Fred Tatashore
CAST: Dinah Shore (host), Lucille Ball, Vivian Vance

In a rare talk show appearance, Viv joins Lucy to reminisce about their TV years together. Vivian, dressed in a loose-fitting tunic to cover her breast surgery totally upstages Lucille. First, she tugs on Lucille's black wig (Lucille had told Dinah she is going back to her natural color), and when Lucille reveals that it is a wig, Vivian yells, "Aha! I thought so!" Then she pulls out an old *I Love Lucy* contract from her purse and begins to read the more embarrassing codicils. "Viv, don't you dare read that," Lucille howls. "Am I lying?" Viv asks the Redhead. "Well, no . . . ," chokes Lucille as she starts to laugh. "Then allow me to continue," Viv declares triumphantly. The studio audience laughs at all of this as if they are watching an episode of *I Love Lucy*. Host Shore vacillates between shock at what is occurring on her program and belly-laughter at Vivian's performance. It is here that Viv reveals publicly for the first time that she was required to appear twenty pounds overweight as Ethel Mertz, was not allowed to wear false eyelashes, and that she insisted on using her own first name on *The Lucy Show*.

PASSWORD

(ABC, FIVE SHOWS TAPED MAY 3, 1975), 30 MINUTES

PRODUCED BY: Howard Felscher
DIRECTED BY: Stuart W. Phelps
CAST: Allen Ludden (host), Lucille Ball, Gary Morton

These five installments appear as a week's worth of daily shows on this daytime game show. Lucille and Gary had often appeared on the daytime version of *Password* during the 1960s, often inviting friends such as Carole Cook, Mary Wickes, and Gale Gordon to join them on the program. This is a sad performance by Lucille. She seems disoriented and confused, almost incapable of playing the game. Gary tries his best to make jokes and cover for her, but it is obvious that Lucille is on medication and is not feeling well.

THE TWENTY-SIXTH ANNUAL EMMY AWARDS

(ABC, MAY 19, 1975), 120 MINUTES

PRODUCED BY: Paul W. Keyes
DIRECTED BY: Tim Kiley
WRITTEN BY: Paul W. Keyes, Marc London, Bob Howard

Lucille Ball is a presenter at this year's show, and has the most embarrassing television moment of her career. While it seems to the viewing audience that their beloved Lucille is losing it, this is what really happens: Backstage at the awards, just minutes before she is supposed to go on, Ball receives a crank phone call telling her that Desi Jr. has had a terrible accident and is dead. It takes a few moments to confirm that the call is bogus, but by this time Lucille is almost in shock. She comes on stage and opens the envelope before she even announces the category. Realizing this, she drops the envelope on the podium. Unfortunately, there are about twenty other envelopes there from previous winners, and a distraught Lucille cannot tell one from another. She stalls for time by saying that she cannot see without her glasses. Milton Berle realizes she is in trouble and comes to her aid by bringing two drinking glasses on stage and makes wisecracks until he can find the correct envelope and read the winner's name. The awards show then cuts to a commercial.

Chapter Twenty-Seven

1975–76 Season

A LUCILLE BALL SPECIAL: "THREE FOR TWO"

(CBS, DECEMBER 3, 1975), 60 MINUTES

EXECUTIVE PRODUCED BY: Lucille Ball
PRODUCED BY: Gary Morton
DIRECTED BY: Charles Walters
WRITTEN BY: James Eppy
BASED ON A SCRIPT BY: Renee Taylor, Joseph Bologna
MAKEUP BY: Claude Thompson
HAIRSTYLING BY: Irma Kusley
MUSIC BY: Nelson Riddle
CAST: Lucille Ball, Jackie Gleason, Gino Conforti, Tammi Bula, Paul Linke, Vanda Barra, Irene Sale, Eddie Garrett, Mel Pape

Three short playlets starring Ball and Gleason make up this badly received special. It is shot with one camera but has a canned laugh track.

The first, *Herb and Sally*, is the story of a middle-aged couple on vacation in Rome. Lucille wears a black wig with silver highlights and looks attractive but matronly. The theme of an unloved wife begging her disinterested husband for romance and passion is hardly a laugh-fest. Ball doesn't know what to do with the material, and Gleason plays his part like a more successful Ralph Kramden. It is badly edited, completely throwing off the comedy timing of the piece.

The second vignette is entitled *Fred and Rita*. It involves two middle-aged people having an affair at a tacky, hideaway nightclub. Wearing an upswept blonde wig and feathers, Lucille looks appropriately cheap. Both Ball and Gleason are reading from cue cards unashamedly in this very short offering, lasting no more than six minutes.

The final and longest piece is *Mike and Pauline*, and has a New Year's Eve theme. Lucille wears a honey-brown wig and attractive gown as she portrays an over-emotional mother who tries to manipulate her family, including her spouse (Gleason).

HIGHLIGHTS & TRIVIA

None of this is very good. Lucille has been holding a script for several years about Diamond Jim Brady and Lillian Russell that she wants to do with Jackie Gleason. He won't do it because (supposedly) he won't fly to Hollywood for the filming. Now that she has Gleason in her clutches, it is a shame she wastes him with inferior material. Had these bits been done in front of a live audience, perhaps there might have been more of a spark. Gleason does get to do his patented shouting, but none of the material gives Lucille an even shake. The entire show is geared to Jackie, but he doesn't make the most of it. Any of the sketches might serve well as a throw-away on a variety show, but as a collection for a special it is at best sub-par. Director Chuck Walters had been a dancer and a director of musicals in the halcyon days of MGM, and directed several episodes of *Here's Lucy*.

This special is panned by the critics, and its ratings are not nearly as large as her previous two such outings. In the throws of losing its number one place after more than twenty seasons at the top, CBS is in a panic. This special pretty much spells the end of CBS' confidence in television products by Lucille Ball.

Gary Morton

(EXECUTIVE PRODUCER)

Three for Two *was a fiasco. It just didn't work. We did it without an audience, and that was a bad choice. Even with a laugh track, it didn't work.*

SHIRLEY MACLAINE: THE GYPSY IN MY SOUL

(CBS, JANUARY 10, 1976), 60 MINUTES

EXECUTIVE PRODUCED BY: William O. Harbach
CO-PRODUCED & CONCEIVED BY: Cy Coleman, Fred Ebb

DIRECTED BY: Tony Charmoli
WRITTEN BY: Fred Ebb
MUSIC BY: Donn Trenner
CAST: Shirley MacLaine, Lucille Ball

Our gal Lucy is MacLaine's only guest in this hour-long salute to the Broadway chorus people. Lucille is resplendent in a top hat, tuxedo jacket, briefs, stockings, and boots. She is musically introduced much the same way she was in 1966's "Lucy Helps Ken Berry" from *The Lucy Show* (episode #153), with a chorus of "Lucy's [Lulu's] Back in Town." Lucille is cajoled into telling a few tales from her days as a struggling actor, which leads into the song "Bouncing Back for More." The song is prerecorded, and Ball has trouble with the lip-synching. "Bring Back Those Good Old Days" is a very funny bit, with Lucille playing the big star showing Shirley how to put the "little gypsies" in their place. The extended dance finds Ball still able to kick up her heels and move well, but her bad leg keeps her from doing any real dancing.

The show is shot in New York on videotape (typical for variety shows but not Lucille's preference) with multiple cameras but with no audience, so canned applause and laughter are used. A phony audience is shot and their reactions edited into the broadcast. This is a very effective guest shot for Lucille and she enjoys the work, which shows in her performance.

NBC'S SATURDAY NIGHT

(NBC, FEBRUARY 21, 1976),
90 MINUTES (COLOR AND B&W)

PRODUCED BY: Lorne Michaels
DIRECTED BY: Dave Wilson
CAST: Dan Aykroyd, Desi Arnaz, Desi Arnaz Jr., John Belushi, Chevy Chase, Jane Curtin, Garrett Morris, Larraine Newman, Gilda Radner

This show just has to be included in this book. While Lucille is nowhere in sight in this outing, her presence is felt everywhere. Desi is promoting his autobiography *A Book* and uses this still-new program to advantage.

Desi Jr. does an almost eerie imitation of his father in a satirical salute to *I Love Lucy*. And Gilda Radner performs the first of her hysterical impressions of Lucy Ricardo. At one time, Radner was considered for the part of Lucy in a Broadway musical version of the sitcom that never materialized.

The best part of the program is an inspired send-up of *The Untouchables*. Melding that show with the *Lucy* characters is a clever way to include Gilda in the proceedings. Such moments as Desi (as Frank Nitti) phoning Gilda (as Lucy) and asking, "How is Little Nitti?" displays the perfect blending of satire, homage, comedy writing, and performing that makes *NBC's Saturday Night* (later retitled *Saturday Night Live*) so popular. Completing the circle for Desi is Tom Schiller, son of original *Lucy* scribe Bob Schiller, who is one of the writers for this hip variety series.

Desi's musical performances of "Cuban Pete" and "Babalu" are both heartwarming and a little sad. Desi Jr. accompanies him on bongos. Both numbers bring huge recognition applause from the live audience. However, it is obvious that Desi does not have the energy nor the magnetic charm of his youth. This is one of the last times Desi sings in public.

Desi Arnaz Jr.

I thought it was so cool of them to ask him to be on the show. I met Dad in New York and we both stayed at the Regency. It was written while we sat in on the show. They were receptive to anything Dad wanted to do. In the beginning, Dad was a little concerned that things would be handled properly. He was wonderful at mixing things together so that the humor did not seem contrived. In the sketch where we "show" the lost pilots, he wanted to make sure that the wraparounds he did were believable so that the bits I did playing him would be that much funnier. I Love Lucy *had never been satirized before by anyone. It was ground breaking in a strange way. Dad was worried, and so was I. I was even calling my mother and said, "Mom, we're doing so and so. What do you think?" I thought doing the impression of Dad was a good thing, especially since I wasn't trying very hard. After all, he was right there. I did the best I could with the allotted time. Dan Aykroyd was so funny playing Ness. I think he wrote Dad's Jabberwocky sketch. Nobody got some of the humor. It was just too inside. The cigar sketch [with Desi as a Cuban acupuncturist who uses cigars instead of needles] was so silly. It was funny because it didn't work. But what can you expect, putting together a ninety minute show in four days? When Dad sang, it was his first performance in years. He had just finished doing his book, and his life was very cathartic at the time. The interest in him was overwhelming. It was a fragile time for him. He was completely sober and right in the moment. As he began working that night, you can see him reacting to the audience's acceptance. He was surprised. He was also surprised that those young actors were so talented and professional, and that they cared the way that they did. And they were all so cute and young that first year.*

We were all young and healthy, and kind of naive. The drug use you've read about was real, but hadn't begun to interfere with any of us. No one knew the severity of what was going on. It hadn't started taking its toll. People thought it was going to enhance their performance. Tom Schiller blew me away about what he had learned about humor from his father, Bob. I remember when we were writing the show, there was a lot of borderline stuff that either wasn't funny or was too offensive. But they were trying everything to see what would fly.

Lucie Arnaz

I remember watching that show at my mother's condo in Aspen [Colorado] and thinking it was dreadful. I had the feeling that they were making fun of my father, but fooling him into thinking they were tributing him. It really bothered me that they never even let him finish singing "Babalu." If I had been them, I would have let my father do all the sketch material first, and then given him a few moments to be Desi Arnaz and showcase what he could really do. I really felt sad for him afterward, like he had been used.

A LUCILLE BALL SPECIAL: "WHAT NOW, CATHERINE CURTIS?"

(CBS, MARCH 30, 1976), 60 MINUTES

EXECUTIVE PRODUCED BY: Lucille Ball
PRODUCED BY: Gary Morton
DIRECTED BY: Charles Walters
WRITTEN BY: Sheldon Keller, Lynn Roth
MAKEUP BY: Claude Thompson
HAIRSTYLING BY: Irma Kusely
MUSIC BY: Nelson Riddle
CAST: Lucille Ball, Joseph Bologna, Art Carney

This is the story of Catherine Curtis, who gets a divorce after twenty-three years of marriage, and for the first time finds herself alone. She moves from her secure home in the suburbs to a luxury apartment in a fashionable Manhattan neighborhood. She has an ill-fated liaison with a handyman (Art Carney). But it is her later, unexpected love affair with a much younger man (Joseph Bologna) that finally gives Catherine the freedom and security she has been seeking.

HIGHLIGHTS & TRIVIA

The opening montage is very worthwhile because it features photographs from the life and career of Lucille Ball, including several beautiful ones of Lucie Arnaz. The first act is done entirely as a monologue by Lucille, who gives one of the most controlled, focused, and satisfying dramatic performances of her long career. Without shouting, her bass voice has the timbre and inflection missing in almost any other work she has done to this date. Lucille's dark wig suits her; it is fashionable and actually makes her look younger and more sophisticated than her *Lucy* wigs.

Like her last two specials, this one is filmed like a movie without an audience. It is the only one for which this technique actually adds anything. Normally, Lucille is always better in front of an audience. One can only surmise into what part of her heart Lucille reaches to act out this monologue; much of it has close parallels to her life with Desi Arnaz. When Lucille is called upon to slowly start crying while she talks until she is openly weeping, it is not one of *Lucy*'s crying jags but that of a character who is deeply upset.

Art Carney joins Lucille in the second act, the only actor to appear in two of Ball's specials in the 1970s. Once again, the two work very well together. In a strange way, this could almost be the real story of Lucy Ricardo. References are made to living in Westport, Connecticut, having a real charmer for a husband, and returning to life in Manhattan. With her hair pulled back, chic clothing, and an intelligence and grace missing from most of Ball's TV roles for quite some time, Catherine Curtis might be what happens to Lucy Ricardo sixteen years (of real-world life) after Lucy met Ernie Kovacs.

The last act revolves around Catherine's affair with a man years younger than she. This parallels coincidentally, the age difference between Lucille Ball and the younger Gary Morton. Catherine's indecisiveness as to how to handle the affair, discussed over a game of backgammon, might well mirror Lucille's experience in her courtship with Morton.

Ball has begun to gain weight at this time; she no longer has her chorus girl figure. With heavy makeup and Irma Kusely's wigs, she still looks beautiful, but decidedly older. Bologna's charming, Italian stud is a nice counterpoint to Lucille's portrayal. He offers her something she hasn't had since her acting days with Desi—ethnicity.

In general, this is the best non-*Lucy* project Ball does for television. It is very surprising she is not nominated for an Emmy for her performance.

Gary Morton

(EXECUTIVE PRODUCER)

With What Now, Catherine Curtis?, *we learned that it was difficult, if not impossible, to give the public a* Lucy *that they weren't used to.*

DINAH!

(SYN, JUNE 4, 1976), 60- OR 90-MINUTE VERSIONS AVAILABLE TO LOCAL STATIONS

EXECUTIVE PRODUCED BY: Henry Jaffe, Carolyn Raskin
PRODUCED BY: Fred Tatashore
DIRECTED BY: Glen Swanson
WRITTEN BY: Bill Walker, Bob Shayne, Donald Ross, Norman Martin, Fred Tatashore
CAST: Dinah Shore (host), Lucille Ball, George Segal

Movie star George Segal comes on to the show, complaining to Dinah of jet lag and hunger as he has just flown to Los Angeles from New York. Several segments go by as Segal continues to carp. Suddenly, out comes Lucille, dressed in a yellow chiffon gown and pushing a cart laden with gourmet foods. She puts a napkin under Segal's chin and begins to feed him. After the laughter dies down, she quips to Segal, "If you were on *my* show, you'd get *money*, too!" Then she exits as Segal and Dinah applaud and laugh.

Chapter Twenty-Eight

1976–77 Season

THE PRACTICE

(ABC, OCTOBER 13, 1976), 30 MINUTES

PRODUCED BY: Ron Rubin
WRITTEN BY: Sam Denoff, Dale McCraven
CAST: Danny Thomas, Lucille Ball, Dena Dietrich, Shelley Fabares, David Spielberg, Didi Conn

Lucille plays a middle-aged mystic who foresees her own diagnosis: a potentially fatal aneurysm. She refuses to take care of herself, until the good Doctor (Danny Thomas) forces her to do so.

HIGHLIGHTS & TRIVIA

This series (1976–77) is yet another unfortunate flop for veteran Thomas, who enlists Ball's aid as a ratings gimmick for the opening episode of the fall season. Thomas' characterization of an older, kindly doctor who likes to interfere in everyone's life is a pallid effort, and best left forgotten. Lucille is not shot to her advantage, and looks tired and dumpy.

Danny Thomas
(ACTOR)

I was playing the old doctor, and I had to examine her. Every time I'd move in close to examine her eyes or tonsils, she'd whisper, "You're in my shot!" She had me laughing so hard we had to stop working for an hour!

TEXACO PRESENTS BOB HOPE'S WORLD OF COMEDY

(NBC, OCTOBER 29, 1976), 60 MINUTES

EXECUTIVE PRODUCED BY: Bob Hope
PRODUCED AND DIRECTED BY: Jack Haley Jr.
WRITTEN BY: Charles Lee, Gig Henry, Jeffrey Barron, Katherine Green, Jack Haley Jr.
CAST: Bob Hope (host), Lucille Ball, Norman Lear, Don Rickles, Neil Simon

Another of the Hope prefab specials, where Lucille introduces a segment on situation comedy with Hope. Miss Ball reads jokes with Hope off cue cards and then disappears. Her entire time oncamera is no more than four minutes.

VAN DYKE AND COMPANY

(CBS, DECEMBER 9, 1976), 60 MINUTES

EXECUTIVE PRODUCED BY: Byron Paul
PRODUCED BY: Allan Blye, Bob Einstein
DIRECTED BY: John Moffitt
WRITTEN BY: Allan Blye, Bob Einstein, Dick Van Dyke, George Burditt, Paul Wayne, Mickey Ross, Ken Finkelman, Aubrey Tadman, Gary Ferrier, Pat Proft, Lennie Rips, Don Novello, Mitch Markowitz
CAST: Dick Van Dyke (host), Lucille Ball, Albert Cirimele, Andy Kaufman, Tina Lenert, the Lockers, Katee McClure, Tommy McLoughlin, Edna O'Dowl, Barry Van Dyke, John Wheeler, Mitchell Young-Evans

This is one of the last episodes of this ill-received and short-lived variety series. The opening, a mime piece where Dick Van Dyke goes to the "New You Shop" owned by Lucille to get new body parts, is silly and sets the pace for a disappointing hour. Her second sketch is called "Cancellation," where Dick plays a newly-promoted network executive who must inform a big star that her show has been axed.

This offering has a very short rehearsal schedule, and Lucille barely knows her lines or stage movements. She reads off cue cards as if she has never seen the words before. "Child Bride," about a golddigging woman who married an old man who has lived an additional forty years, has the same problems. Bad jokes and exaggerated physical comedy abound.

A short stand-up piece featuring Dick, Lucille, and Andy Kaufman fares a little better, as does another silent sketch called "The Tourists." Ball and Van Dyke seemed like a natural combination, and it's too bad they didn't have a chance to work together in the 1960s, when both were still in their prime and Carl Reiner was writing Dick's material.

CBS SALUTES LUCY— THE FIRST 25 YEARS

(CBS, NOVEMBER 28, 1976), 120 MINUTES (COLOR AND B&W)

EXECUTIVE PRODUCED BY: Gary Morton
CO-PRODUCED AND WRITTEN BY: Sheldon Keller
(Note: there is no director credited for this special)
WRAPAROUND SEGMENTS CAST: Desi Arnaz, Lucille Ball, Carol Burnett, Richard Burton, Johnny Carson, Sammy Davis Jr., Gale Gordon, Bob Hope, Danny Kaye, Dean Martin, James Stewart, Danny Thomas, Vivian Vance, Dick Van Dyke, John Wayne

This clip fest is actually produced by Lucille Ball Productions, but hides behind the CBS name so as not to appear too self-congratulatory. The clips are well-chosen for the most part, although much of the original background music is edited out and replaced by newly produced stuff created by Peter Matz.

It is the first time since 1960 that Desi Arnaz has appeared on a TV show with Lucille; it is a shame they are not seen together oncamera.

This is Vivian Vance's first *Lucy* appearance since losing a breast to cancer and she looks poorly. Strangely, neither of Lucille's and Desi's children appear, either in person or in any of the selected clips (except for very brief glimpses in the background), nor are any of her stage children from *I Love Lucy* or *The Lucy Show* represented in the special.

Although Richard Burton claimed he hated working with Lucille on *Here's Lucy* in 1970 (episode #49, "Lucy Meets the Burtons"), he swallows whatever ill feelings he has to participate in a new piece made especially for this outing. The salute's ending, with Jimmy Stewart presenting Lucille with an award (which she has previously received on *The Merv Griffin Show* some months earlier) in front of an imaginary audience is sentimental and hokey, and is badly handled.

This could have been Ball's chance to say some heartfelt words about Desi, Viv, Bill, Gale, and others she worked with through the years. However . . .

Gary Morton

(EXECUTIVE PRODUCER)

The twenty-fifth anniversary show was a joy for me to work on. I worked until three or four in the morning editing that show.

A DEAN MARTIN CELEBRITY ROAST: "DANNY THOMAS"

(NBC, DECEMBER 15, 1976), 60 MINUTES

PRODUCED AND DIRECTED BY: Greg Garrison
CAST: Dean Martin (host), Lucille Ball, Milton Berle, Red Buttons, Ruth Buzzi, Charlie Callas, Charo, Howard Cosell, Dena Dietrich, Gene Kelly, Don Knotts, Harvey Korman, Jan Murray, Jimmie Walker, Jessica Walters, Orson Welles

Another in the series of Friars Club-like roasts of celebrities. Lucille looks especially lovely, although most of what she has to say is cut out of the program to ensure that the show fits the hour format.

TEXACO PRESENTS BOB HOPE'S ALL STAR COMEDY TRIBUTE TO VAUDEVILLE

(NBC, MARCH 25, 1977), 90 MINUTES

EXECUTIVE PRODUCED BY: Bob Hope
PRODUCED BY: Sheldon Keller
DIRECTED BY: Dick McDonough
WRITTEN BY: Charles Lee and Gig Henry, Jeffrey Barron, Katherine Green, Howard Albrecht and Sol Weinstein, Sheldon Keller
CAST: Bob Hope (host), Jack Albertson, Lucille Ball, Vanda Barra, the Captain and Tenille, Chaz Chase, Sid Gould, Isobel McCloskey, Bernadette Peters, Vivian Reed, Jimmie Walker

Another cookie-cutter special, but this time Lucille shines in an impersonation of Sophie Tucker, singing "Some of These Days." Sporting a padded white dress, white wig, and an ostrich feather in her hair, Ball actually does a decent impression of Tucker, who had passed away in 1966.

DINAH!

(SYN, APRIL 15, 1977), 60- OR 90-MINUTE
VERSIONS AVAILABLE TO LOCAL STATIONS

EXECUTIVE PRODUCED BY: Henry Jaffe, Carolyn Raskin
PRODUCED BY: Fred Tatashore
DIRECTED BY: Glen Swanson
WRITTEN BY: Bill Walker, Bob Shayne, Donald Ross, Norman Martin, Fred Tatashore
CAST: Dinah Shore (host), Lucille Ball

In a rare musical moment, Lucille sings "Hey, Look Me Over," the song she introduced on Broadway in *Wildcat* (1960). Of all the talk shows Lucille does, she comes most alive on these relaxed efforts with Dinah Shore. Ball does not come on this program necessarily to plug anything, but simply to tele-visit with Dinah.

Chapter Twenty-Nine

1977–78 Season

DONNY AND MARIE

(ABC, SEPTEMBER 30, 1977), 60 MINUTES

EXECUTIVE PRODUCED BY: Raymond Katz, the Osmond Brothers
PRODUCED BY: Art Fisher, Arnie Kogen
DIRECTED BY: Art Fisher
WRITTEN BY: Arnie Kogen, Rod Warren, Mort Scharfman, Bill Dana, Paul Pumpian and Harvey Weitzman, Bruce Vilanch, Ed Hider
CAST: Donny and Marie Osmond (hosts), Lucille Ball, Ray Bolger, Paul Lynde, Paul Williams, Virginia Wood

This is one of Lucille's best variety show appearances late in her career. This slickly produced show ensures Ball is shown to her best advantage. Soft lighting, careful camera work, and new, longer wig styled by Irma Kusely make Lucille look beautiful. Appearing in a slinky, sequined pants outfit and pink boa, Lucille sings and prances to a new song, "I'm a Leading Lady." The tune leads into a fantasy sequence, as Lucille impersonates Ethel Merman in *Annie Get Your Gun*, Mae West in *My Little Chickadee*, and ends up with a whole chorus line of Lucille Balls dressed in top hat, tails, and stockings (thanks to some wonderful special effects work that replicates Lucille's image as she dances). Later in the show, ice dancers do a number to a recording of "Disco Lucy," a disco version of the *I Love Lucy* theme song that had been very popular the year before, while Lucille looks on in glee. The finale of the show is a clever spoof of *The Wizard of Oz*, with Ball playing the Tin Man while Bolger recreates his Scarecrow from the original film.

DINAH!: "THE FIRST LADIES"

(SYN, OCTOBER 5, 1977), 60- OR 90-MINUTE VERSIONS AVAILABLE TO LOCAL STATIONS

EXECUTIVE PRODUCED BY: Henry Jaffe, Carolyn Raskin
PRODUCED BY: Fred Tatashore
DIRECTED BY: Glen Swanson
WRITTEN BY: Bill Walker, Bob Shayne, Donald Ross, Norman Martin, Fred Tatashore
CAST: Dinah Shore (host), Lucille Ball, Ella Fitzgerald, Beverly Sills, Elizabeth Taylor

Elizabeth Taylor appears in a prefilmed segment. Always very at ease with Dinah, Lucille is obviously enjoying being in the company of Ella Fitzgerald. Dinah and Ella are in great voice as they sing separately and together, and Lucille is impressed. Ella's shyness inspires Lucille to encourage her to talk.

Lucille Ball

(TO ELLA FITZGERALD)

My daughter Lucie says that every time you make a mistake on a record, it sells about a million copies! You really are the best at what you do!

A LUCILLE BALL SPECIAL: "LUCY CALLS THE PRESIDENT"

(CBS, NOVEMBER 21, 1977), 60 MINUTES

EXECUTIVE PRODUCED BY: Lucille Ball
PRODUCED BY: Gary Morton
CO-PRODUCED AND WRITTEN BY: Madelyn Davis, Bob Carroll Jr.
DIRECTED BY: Marc Daniels
MAKEUP BY: Claude Thompson
HAIRSTYLING BY: Irma Kusely
MUSIC BY: Nelson Riddle
CAST: Steve Allen, Lucille Ball, James E. Brodhead, Miss Lillian Carter, Mary Jane Croft, Joey Foreman, Gale Gordon, Ed McMahon, Stack Pierce, Vivian Vance, Mary Wickes, John William Young

Lucy Whittaker decides to call President Carter during his weekly radio show and bring up a topic of local (Indiana) civic importance. He tells her he will be in her area, and will visit her to discuss the matter. Later, the plan is changed to a dinner with the President at Lucy's house, and everyone she has ever known demands to be invited.

HIGHLIGHTS & TRIVIA

This, as other "Lucy" chroniclers Bart Andrews and Tom Watson have noted, is the last hurrah. This is the last time Lucille works with Vivian, Mary Jane, or Mary Wickes. It is the first professional reunion, since 1952, between Lucille and the original director of *I Love Lucy*, Marc Daniels. This is the only "Lucy" TV show to be videotaped rather than filmed. While the process makes the show seem more intimate, the technology does not allow the cast to look their best (as they would with movie makeup and lighting). Lucille wears scarves around her neck to hide the scars from recent minor surgery, as well as wrinkles. The opening scene has to be shot twice, because Lucille is so distraught over her mother's absence (DeDe Ball has recently passed away in her mid-eighties) that she breaks down and cries. In the first take of the opening scene, Lucille is obviously distracted. Finally, she yells, "Cut! Hello Eve!" and walks over to her friend Eve Arden seated in the audience as they both dissolve in tears.

Lucille Ball

(AT THE TAPING)

Cut! I'm sorry, I got off to a bad start. My DeDe is usually in the audience, and damn it that threw me at the top. That was my Mom. She's made every show for all these years and it suddenly dawned on me as I was coming down the stairs. Forgive me! I'm glad I got that out of my system and I'm awfully glad you're here. It was maudlin, but I just couldn't help it.

Michael Stern

(LUCILLE BALL'S OFFICIAL NUMBER ONE FAN)

Eve Arden was there in the audience, as was Chuck Woolery. Lucille, Vivian, Mary Wickes, Eve Arden, and Mary Jane were awash in tears. They had all known DeDe Ball, and known how close Lucille was to her. They were all bawling their eyes out.

The producers should have kept Lucille's explanation in the show as an after-piece after the credits. Lucille is honest, touching, and charming. Now Lucille has to catch her breath and be funny. And she is! The show is actually hilarious, and the type of vehicle Lucille could have adopted if she wanted to return to television in an ongoing weekly format or as a series of specials. For the first time since her divorce from Desi in 1960, the Lucy character is given a husband, played here with enthusiasm by Ed McMahon. The interplay between Lucille, Vivian (as next-door neighbor Viv), Gale (as father-in-law Omar), and Mary (as Aunt Mary) is highly amusing, each pushing the humor as far as the envelope will go. Gale gives one of his most controlled performances, reminiscent of his early episodes as Mr. Mooney on The Lucy Show. *Mary Wickes' turn is like all her performances: perfection personified. Vivian has slight paralysis in her face from Bell's Palsy, which is a minor distraction to watch. She feels ill the night of the show and the paralysis gets worse as the taping progresses. This proves to be Vivian Vance's last public appearance.*

Irma Kusely

(HAIRSTYLIST)

This was a very sad time. It was the first show Lucille did without DeDe in the audience to cheer her on. I don't think Lucille ever really got over her death. Then Vivian, who'd had a stroke and was mostly recovered, had bad pains in her hip and leg. Lucille sent her to her doctor, and Viv came back on the set saying, "Your fucking doctor said I have cancer!" After the show, Viv was taken right back up to the San Francisco area to get treatment. She sent me some pictures, asking me to match the hairstyles with some wigs, because she knew she would lose her hair. Before they were ready, she was gone. A little more than a year after this special [actually 1979], she was dead.

Steve Allen

(MEDIA GENIUS/TV PIONEER)

I had always considered Lucille Ball to be one of the great women of beauty, not just in show business but in history. When I had worked with her back in the 1940s and 1950s, she had this cute, babydoll visage about her. I know we can't judge a person by this criterion alone, but that is how she struck me. We were social friends and both fans of one another's work, and I felt she deserved every bit of success she had. I love talent. But it came as a shock to me the Lucille I had worked with on that radio show was not cutesy or a dollbaby at all. She was strong; she was in charge. I am talking about her attitude. There was no horsing around on that show. She was open to suggestion as far as the comedy went, but we stuck to the script. There was only one week for rehearsal, and I was only there for three days. Marc Daniels seemed very competent as a director, as concerned with the comedy as he was with getting good camera shots. But he demurred to Lucy with the comedy.

She had a great sense of what was good for her comedically, although I don't think she always knew what was best for other performers. That did not, however, stop her from telling them what to do anyway. Most performers who worked with her were surprised by this aspect. Lucy's comedy also did not age well, meaning the things she did weren't as funny as she got into her late sixties and seventies. She couldn't handle the physicality or pull off being so cutesy, and like most attractive women in show business, she eventually ended up looking a little like a drag queen. She also didn't do as well without Desi. He never got enough credit for his contributions. An astute businessman, a great straight man, and funny in his own right. He knew how to set Lucy up so that a funny bit became a scream.

CIRCUS OF THE STARS

(CBS, DECEMBER 5, 1977), 120 MINUTES

EXECUTIVE PRODUCED BY: Bob Stivers
PRODUCED BY: Buddy Bregman, Bill Waters, Don Kibbee, Dominique Perrin, Bob Finkel
DIRECTED BY: Sid Smith, Tony Charmoli, Dave Hilmer, Tom Trbovitch
CAST: Lucille Ball, Telly Savalas, Cindy Williams, Michael York (ringmasters); Marty Allen, Lucie Arnaz, George Burns, Lynda Carter, Gary Collins, Robert Conrad, Lola Falana, Peter Fonda, Richard Hatch, Earl Holliman, Jack Klugman, Tony Lo Bianco, Penny Marshall, Jimmy McNichol, Kristy McNichol, Lee Meriweather, Mary Ann Mobley, David Nelson, Valerie Perrine, McKenzie Phillips, Deborah Raffin, Richard Roundtree, Susan St. James, Tom Sullivan, Abe Vigoda, Betty White, Paul Williams

There were seventeen *Circus of the Stars* specials broadcast between 1977 and 1992. Each featured popular performers acting as ringmasters, with others introducing acts and performing in the acts themselves. Lucille is resplendent in a typical ringmasters' outfit, including top hat, red jacket, and whistle. She introduces about a third of the acts on the program in the broad style of the circus.

Buddy Bregman

(PRODUCER)

I was directing from up in the booth, and asked Lucy to move a couple of feet to her right. She looked up and around, as if to figure out where the voice was coming from. Finally she said, "Oh, OK God," and sent the entire cast and crew into hysterical laughter.

A BARBARA WALTERS SPECIAL

(ABC, DECEMBER 6, 1977), 60 MINUTES

PRODUCED BY: JoAnn Goldberg, Don Mischer
DIRECTED BY: Don Mischer
CAST: Barbara Walters (host), Lucille Ball and Gary Morton, Dolly Parton, Henry Winkler, Stacy Weitzman

Lucille and Gary are interviewed in the back yard of their Beverly Hills home in one of the most unkind interviews Lucille has ever given. The entire sequence is devoted to talking of the past, and especially the differences between her two husbands. She slices and dices Desi Arnaz in a fashion that is neither considerate nor friendly. She calls Desi a loser, and blatantly infers he was a terrible husband. It is hard to believe from the way she speaks of him that they are actually still very close and talk with one another quite often.

TV—THE FABULOUS FIFTIES

(NBC, MARCH 3, 1978), 90 MINUTES (COLOR AND B&W)

PRODUCED BY: Henry Jaffe, Draper Lewis, David Lawrence
DIRECTED BY: Jonathan Lucas
WRITTEN BY: Draper Lewis, David Lawrence
HOSTS: Lucille Ball, David Janssen, Michael Landon, Mary Martin, Dinah Shore, Red Skelton

A beautifully produced tribute to the "Golden Age of Television." Lucille looks absolutely radiant in her black gown and sophisticated wig. She naturally hosts the sequence on sitcoms, and acts almost girlish when discussing the adult sitcom topics (abortion, prostitution, etc.) of the 1970s.

This show is so well done that it will be repeated later several times on the PBS TV network.

GENE KELLY . . . AN AMERICAN IN PASADENA

(CBS, MARCH 13, 1978), 60 MINUTES

PRODUCED BY: Marty Pasetta, Frank Konigsberg;
DIRECTED BY: Marty Pasetta
WRITTEN BY: Buz Kohan
MUSIC BY: Jack Elliot
CAST: Gene Kelly (host), Lucille Ball, Cyd Charisse, Gloria DeHaven, Betty Garrett, Kathryn Grayson, Janet Leigh, Liza Minnelli, Frank Sinatra, Cindy Williams

This is a musical retrospective on the women with whom Kelly has appeared in the movies. Lucille's main responsibility is to look glamorous and reminisce about making *DuBarry Was a Lady* (1943) with Kelly and Red Skelton at MGM. Lucille is given very little to say. None of the ladies on the special look particularly well, and the whole thing has an aura of being rushed and underproduced.

AFI SALUTE TO HENRY FONDA

(CBS, MARCH 15, 1978), 120 MINUTES (COLOR AND B&W)

PRODUCED BY: George Stevens Jr.
CAST: Jane Alexander, Lucille Ball, Richard Burton, Bette Davis, Kirk Douglas, Henry Fonda, Jane Fonda, Peter Fonda, James Garner, Lillian Gish, Charlton Heston, Ron Howard, Jack Lemmon, Fred MacMurray, Marsha Mason, Dorothy McGuire, Lloyd Nolan, Gregory Peck, Barbara Stanwyck, James Stewart, Richard Widmark, Billy Dee Williams

Lucille speaks briefly on her experience working with Henry Fonda on the dramatic film *The Big Street* (1942). She stands at a podium and addresses the crowd, never once actually interacting with Fonda. This is one of the few instances when Ball speaks publicly of her career in motion pictures.

A TRIBUTE TO "MR. TELEVISION," MILTON BERLE

(NBC, MARCH 26, 1978), 60 MINUTES

EXECUTIVE PRODUCED BY: Jerry Frank
PRODUCED BY: Jerry Frank, Bill Carruthers
DIRECTED BY: Bill Carruthers
WRITTEN BY: Marty Farrell
CAST: Lucille Ball, Milton Berle, Joey Bishop, George Carlin, Johnny Carson, Angie Dickinson, Kirk Douglas, Bob Hope, Gabe Kaplan, Gene Kelly, Kermit the Frog, Donny and Marie Osmond, Gregory Peck, Carl Reiner, Don Rickles, Frank Sinatra, Marlo Thomas, Flip Wilson

Yet another tribute to Uncle Miltie, this time on the occasion of his thirtieth anniversary on television. He deserves every single one of them for his contributions to early television. The show is panned, as all the stars do is enter, read a tribute to Milton from cue cards, and then exit.

CBS ON THE AIR: A CELEBRATION OF 50 YEARS

(CBS, MARCH 27, 1978), 60 MINUTES (COLOR AND B&W)

PRODUCED BY: Alexander H. Cohen, Lee Miller
DIRECTED BY: Clark Jones, Sid Smith
WRITTEN BY: Hildy Parks
MUSIC BY: Elliot Lawrence
CAST: Bea Arthur, Lucille Ball, George Burns, Arthur Godfrey

In the spring of 1978, CBS pats itself on the back for fifty years of radio and television broadcasting with a week-long, all-star salute. Each day, different people from CBS' past and present appear to introduce clips of their work and others. Although both Desi Arnaz and Vivian Vance appear for the grand collection of stars that starts the week off (and do not stand near or interact with Ball) neither is interviewed or featured as a guest. Lucille, Bea Arthur, and George Burns do a smashing production number to a specially written song, "What's So Funny about Monday?"

A DEAN MARTIN CELEBRITY ROAST: JIMMY STEWART

(NBC, MAY 10, 1978), 60 MINUTES

PRODUCED AND DIRECTED BY: Greg Garrison
CAST: Dean Martin (host), Eddie Albert, June Allyson, Lucille Ball, Milton Berle,

Foster Brooks, George Burns, Red Buttons, Ruth Buzzi, Henry Fonda, Greer Garson, Janet Leigh, Rich Little, LaWanda Page, Tony Randall, Don Rickles, Mickey Rooney, Jimmy Stewart, Orson Welles, Jesse White

Another in the series of roasts. Lucille once again has little to do, sending a few barbs Stewart's way about being a pesky neighbor in Beverly Hills. These roasts continue to use Lucille as a name draw for ratings, but, once they have her, they seem to edit her remarks considerably in the aired version. Lucille is neither a joke teller nor a punster, so perhaps this is wise.

HAPPY BIRTHDAY, BOB: A SALUTE TO BOB HOPE'S 75TH BIRTHDAY

(NBC, MAY 29, 1978), 180 MINUTES

EXECUTIVE PRODUCED BY: James Lipton, Gerald Rafshoon
PRODUCED BY: Bob Wynn, John Hamlin
DIRECTED BY: Bob Wynn
WRITTEN BY: James Lipton, Bob Arnott
CAST: Bob Hope (host), Lynn Anderson, Ann-Margret, Pearl Bailey, Lucille Ball, Johnny Carson, Charo, Bert Convy, Kathryn Crosby, Mac Davis, Sammy Davis Jr., Redd Foxx, Elliott Gould, Dolores Hope, KC and the Sunshine Band, Alan King, Dorothy Lamour, Carol Lawrence, Fred MacMurray, the Muppets, Tony Orlando, Donny and Marie Osmond, Charles Nelson Reilly, Don Rickles, Telly Savalas, Shields and Yarnell, Red Skelton, David Soul, Elizabeth Taylor, Danny Thomas, Fred Travalena, John Wayne

Lots of stars are trotted out for the first in a series of birthday salutes Hope gives himself through the years. This one is done in Washington, D.C., and sponsored by the USO. Lucille introduces a montage of Hope's leading ladies through the decades.

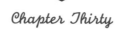

Chapter Thirty

1978–79 Season

GENERAL ELECTRIC ALL-STAR ANNIVERSARY

(CBS, SEPTEMBER 29, 1978), 120 MINUTES

PRODUCED BY: Paul W. Keyes
DIRECTED BY: Dick McDonough
WRITTEN BY: Paul W. Keyes, Bob Howard, Jeffrey Barron, Monty Aidem
CAST: John Wayne (host), Lucille Ball, Albert Brooks, Henry Fonda, Alex Haley, Pat Hingle, Bob Hope, Cheryl Ladd, Michael Landon, Penny Marshall, Donny and Marie Osmond, Charley Pride, Nelson Riddle, John Ritter, Sha Na Na, Red Skelton, Suzanne Somers, James Stewart, Elizabeth Taylor, Leslie Uggams, Jimmie Walker, James Whitmore, Cindy Williams, Henry Winkler

As TV variety shows become increasingly more passé in the 1970s, producers outdo themselves gathering huge casts and mounting outrageously overproduced production numbers to pump life back into the genre. This entry is no exception.

When Lucille joins host Wayne, she is wearing a blousy, black wrap-around dress with ruffles and gold thread. They discuss nothing that is even mildly interesting. Later, she does a speakeasy number in a pseudo Art-Deco dress and boa. She tries to prance and fake dancing, but she is obviously still favoring her bad leg. This routine would be suitable for Lola Falana, Shirley MacLaine, or even Marie Osmond, but Lucille is too unsteady on her feet to be effective. And why hire Lucille Ball to dance? Haven't the producers been watching television for the previous twenty-five years? What a waste!

A LUCILLE BALL SPECIAL: "LUCY COMES TO NASHVILLE"

(CBS, NOVEMBER 29, 1978), 60 MINUTES

EXECUTIVE PRODUCED BY: Reggie M. Churchwell
PRODUCED BY: Jack Donohue, Floyd Huddleston
DIRECTED BY: Jack Donohue
WRITTEN BY: Floyd Huddleston, Larry Markes
CAST: Lucille Ball (host), Lynn Anderson, Archie Campbell, the Fiske Jubilee Singers, Tom T. Hall, Barbara Mandrell, Ronnie Milsap, the Oak Ridge Boys, Mel Tillis

Taped on the stage of the Grand Ole Opry House in Nashville, this is the only TV variety special Lucille ever hosts that carries her name. It is not produced by Lucille Ball Productions, and, in fact, Ball is nothing more than a hired hand. Looking overweight and puffy, sixty-seven-year-old Lucille is nevertheless attractive and very gracious as a host.

The first comedy bit finds Lucille as the replacement conductor for the Nashville Philharmonic, a ragtag group of rednecks who know more about banjos than bassoons. It is taken right out of the 1963 *The Lucy Show* episode "Lucy Conducts the Symphony" (#43), although it is played more like a segment of *Hee Haw* (1969–93). The other main comedy bits include Lucille as the bitter loser in a music contest and a duel of saxophones as Barbara Mandrell and Ball struggle through Lucille's evergreen number "Glow Worm."

All of Lucille's introductions are recorded in one stretch, with the musical numbers taped separately. The music is first-rate, and takes up the bulk of the hour. There is an annoying canned laugh track throughout this special, which is unnecessary as the funny show is taped in front of an appreciative live audience. This is the only program that is also produced by Ball's longtime director, Jack Donohue.

THE MARY TYLER MOORE HOUR

(CBS, MARCH 6, 1979), 60 MINUTES

PRODUCED BY: Perry Lafferty

DIRECTED BY: Robert Scheerer
WRITTEN BY: Arnie Kogen, David Axelrod, Stan Burns, Peter Gallay, Carol Gary, Gary Jacobs, Coslough Johnson, Patricia Jones, Donald Reiker, Pat Proft, Aubrey Tadman, Gary Ferrier
CAST: Mary Tyler Moore, Lucille Ball, Mike Douglas, Joyce Van Patten, Michael Lombard, Michael Keaton, Bobby Ramsen, Ron Rifkin, Vanda Barra, Kenny Williams, Florence Halop, Wayne Devorak

What do you get when you take a cast just brimming with talent, a top director, a second-rate concept, and a rotten script? This disappointing series, which hardly lasts longer (thirteen weeks) than its predecessor *Mary* (same year, three episodes). The first problem is that the program is taped with three cameras but *without* an audience. The laugh track is always half a beat behind the comedy, as if the audience is watching the show on a delayed basis. The show-within-a-show concept wears thin, and the script is threadbare. Mary is radiant as always, but she is stuck with very unmotivated comedy.

Enter Lucille Ball, playing herself. The premise is that Mary needs a substitute guest star, so she hunts Lucy down at an exclusive Beverly Hills boutique. Both ladies get snookered on complimentary Irish coffee. This would be funny, but they get drunk almost immediately and without the slightest bit of nuance. According to the plot line, Lucy can't do Mary's show because she is booked to cohost *The Mike Douglas Show* that same week. The tipsy females decide to ask Mike for time off while on the air, so that Mike can't refuse. A segment with Lucy and Mary eating Japanese delicacies like eel and octopus is mildly humorous. The musical number, "The Girlfriend of the Whirling Dervish," is high on energy if not vocal quality, and allows Lucille to carry on like a chorus girl, something she always enjoys.

CHER AND OTHER FANTASIES

(NBC, APRIL 3, 1979), 60 MINUTES

PRODUCED BY: George Schlatter, Lee Miller
DIRECTED BY: Art Fisher
WRITTEN BY: Digby Wolfe, Don Reo
MUSIC BY: Earl Brown
CAST: Cher (host), Lucille Ball, Elliot Gould, Andy Kaufman, Bill Saluga

This quirky special features Cher living out her fantasies. Lucille appears in the guise of an old cleaning woman whom Cher encounters along the way. Our Girl looks terrible, has very few lines, and the show itself isn't very funny. The music carries the outing, and as always Cher is a trouper when it comes to performing.

Chapter Thirty-One

1979–80 Season

THE BIG EVENT: TV GUIDE, THE FIRST 25 YEARS

(CBS, OCTOBER 21, 1979), 120 MINUTES

EXECUTIVE PRODUCED BY: Robert H. Precht
ASSOCIATE PRODUCER: Tony Jordan
DIRECTED BY: Russ Petrianto
BASED ON THE BOOK COMPILED AND EDITED BY: Jay S. Harris
WRITTEN BY: Jeff Greenfield
MUSIC BY: Peter Matz
CAST: Phil Donohue (host), Lucille Ball, and a bevy of others

Every once in awhile, for no particular reason, Lucille seems to strip years off her age and looks great oncamera. This is one of those times, as she talks about TV past and present. Wearing a beige suit and her wig styled in a long bun (à la Lucy Ricardo), Lucille seems healthy and happy as she reminisces about her media roots.

SINATRA: THE FIRST 40 YEARS

(NBC, JANUARY 30, 1980), 120 MINUTES

PRODUCED AND WRITTEN BY: Paul W. Keyes
DIRECTED BY: Clark Jones
MUSIC BY: Don Costa
CAST: Frank Sinatra (host), Paul Anka, Lucille Ball, Tony Bennett, Milton Berle, Charlie Callas, Lillian Carter, Sammy Davis Jr., Glenn Ford, Cary Grant, Harry James, Gene Kelly, Rich Little, Dean Martin, Robert Merrill, Don Rickles, Frank Sinatra Jr., Nancy Sinatra, Tina Sinatra, Red Skelton, Dionne Warwick, Orson Welles, William B. Williams

A celebration of Sinatra's sixty-fourth birthday and fortieth anniversary in show business. Taped at Caesar's Palace in Las Vegas. As with many of these "salute" specials, Lucille does not perform any comedy. Her contribution is limited to a few kind words on Sinatra's behalf.

A LUCILLE BALL SPECIAL: "LUCY MOVES TO NBC"

(NBC, FEBRUARY 8, 1980), 90 MINUTES

EXECUTIVE PRODUCED BY: Lucille Ball
EXECUTIVE IN CHARGE OF PRODUCTION: Gary Morton
PRODUCED BY: Hal Kanter
DIRECTED BY: Jack Donohue
WRITTEN BY: Hal Kanter, Bob O'Brien, Paul Pumpian
CAST: Robert Alda, Lucille Ball, Johnny Carson, Gary Coleman, Gloria De Haven, Takayo Doran, Gale Gordon, Bob Hope, Gary Imhoff, Gene Kelly, Jack Klugman, Ruta Lee, Micki McKenzie, Sidney Miller, Ty Nutt, Donald O'Connor, Scotty Plummer, Doris Singleton, Ivery Wheeler

Retired superstar Lucille Ball is charged by NBC with producing a new comedy series for the network. With the help of her old TV partner Gale Gordon, she goes about lining up the proper celebrities to be in the test show, which stars Donald O'Connor and Gloria DeHaven. The two play owners of a music store and have a teenaged son devoted to rock music.

HIGHLIGHTS & TRIVIA

It is considered almost scandalous that Lucille leaves her long-standing TV home at CBS to work for rival NBC. Ball in fact still owes CBS two specials on her contract. However, they cannot agree on concepts and the "Eye" Network looks the other way. The premise for *this* special is a show-within-a-show, as the plot reveals how Lucille comes to work for NBC, and her machinations to get a sitcom produced. A wide array of current NBC stars is trotted out in presentational style, like on an old radio show. Young Gary Coleman (*Diff'rent Strokes)* is very funny, and seems extremely comfortable performing the broad comedy at hand. Bob Hope even delays his exit to wring extra applause from the studio audience. Familiar *Lucy* faces like Ruta Lee and Doris Singleton add to both the humor and the nostalgia. Notice the name of Doris' character: Wanda Clark. That actually is the name of Lucille Ball's longtime secretary.

The purpose of this special is two-fold: introduce the TV audience to the idea that Lucille is now producing comedy for NBC, and air the last half-hour as an actual pilot for a sitcom starring O'Connor.

The special is light and fluffy, fun but *not* hysterical fun. Ball is still able to greatly please an audience, and Gale seems older but full of ginger. Lucille begins to wear very heavy eye makeup here, with her eyebrows drawn well above her eyes. It is done to counteract drooping eyelids and wrinkles, but gives her eyes a racoonish look. She will wear this strange makeup for the rest of her life.

Had the special stopped at one hour, it might have been a very well received tonic for the paucity of good comedy on television at this time. Unfortunately, the sitcom-within-the-show is dreadful. O'Connor is always a delight, especially in tandem with his TV partner from the 1950s, Sid Miller. However, the plot of the pilot is so old-fashioned and corny it makes *The Brady Bunch* seem like *Caligula*. Beautiful Gloria DeHaven is miscast, and seems uncomfortable in the role of a mother. For these reasons, the sitcom does not sell as a series. This special, with major segments deleted to allow for extra commercials, will be rerun twice by NBC with no advance publicity to fill holes in its program schedule. It is of note that the opening jokes (featuring Robert Alda as Mickey Ludin, a thinly disguised version of Ball's attorney Mickey Rudin) are in bad taste, poking fun at the Asian speech patterns that pronounce *l*s as *r*s.

Irma Kusely

(HAIRSTYLIST)

Lucille adored Donald O'Connnor. He was such a nice man, and she was so pleased to put on a show featuring his talents.

Ruta Lee

(ACTOR)

Gary Morton called me and said, "We're having all these stars on the show, and we have no money. Everybody's just coming on to do it as a lark." Because it was Gary asking me, I was tempted to say no, but I did it for Lucy's sake. I kept telling him that I should have played Donald's wife in the pilot, but he said, "Get out of here! You look much too young!" Well, I think I could have been and should have been, but the series didn't go anyway. Gloria was not good in the show, and she should have been because she's a very talented lady. I don't know what went wrong there.

Lucy was very different at this point in her life. I swear the only reason she did this show was to play backgammon. Now, I didn't give a shit about backgammon, but I learned it for her. She was not her old directorial self, but very much laid back. I was sorry to see that, because it affected the quality of the show. We rehearsed at the Debbie Reynolds [dance] studios [in North Hollywood], which was like home for me. The show did have a theatre quality to it, because there were big stars, musical numbers, and a circus feeling to it.

Gary Morton

(EXECUTIVE PRODUCER)

Lucy Moves to NBC *was too much work for Lucille. She had a home, a new puppy, her children, her friends. How long could she go on working hard, clowning? She just got tired. How many new things could the* Lucy *character do?*

It has been incorrectly reported that Lucille is a guest star on a TV show called *The Music Mart* on this evening. Actually, that is the title for the projected O'Connor series, and Ball does play a cameo in the show-within-the-show, as does Gale Gordon.

Chapter Thirty-Two

1980–81 Season

THE STEVE ALLEN COMEDY HOUR

(NBC, OCTOBER 18, 1980), 60 MINUTES

PRODUCED BY: Bill Harbach, Frank Peppiatt
DIRECTED BY: Bob Bowker
WRITTEN BY: Steve Allen, Tom Moore and Jeremy Stevens, Rod Gist and Phil Killard, Tom Leopold, Catherine O'Hara, Bob Shaw, Jay Burton.
CAST: Steve Allen (host), Joe Baker, Lucille Ball, George Kennedy, Steve Landesburg, Steve Martin, Louis Nye, Catherine O'Hara

This is an hilarious comedy special. Everything about it is top notch, from the writing to the performances, especially Allen's reading of the lyrics to Donna Summer's song "Hot Stuff" as poetry. The only fly in the ointment is Lucille.

Her main contribution comes in a sketch Steve had written two decades earlier. The setting is a hospital room, and it is explained that the man in the bed (Louis Nye) has broken every bone in his body and must have absolute quiet to survive. Lucille, as the wife, enters hysterically as she touches, pulls, and yells at her husband. The short skit is not funny, having almost no motivation for the comedy. Lucille looks terrible, with heavy-lidded, baggy eyes.

Steve Allen

(MEDIA GENIUS/TV PIONEER)

I wrote that routine myself many years ago, with Gene Rayburn as the patient and [my wife] Jayne [Meadows] as the woman. Jayne got screams, doing it perfectly as she grabs at him in innocence, concern, and hysteria. We were looking for something strong for Lucy to do on this show, and we remembered the sketch. Yet, to our surprise, when she did it there were no laughs at all. We had to sweeten the laugh track later. She didn't do the right kind of hysterics. There was no believability to what she did.

BOB HOPE'S THIRTIETH ANNIVERSARY TELEVISION SPECIAL

(NBC, JANUARY 18, 1981), 120 MINUTES

EXECUTIVE PRODUCED BY: Bob Hope
PRODUCED BY: Linda Hope
DIRECTED BY: Kip Walton
WRITTEN BY: Gig Henry, Robert L. Mills, Fred S. Fox, Seaman Jacobs
CAST: Bob Hope (host), Ann-Margret, Lucille Ball, Milton Berle, George Burns, Sammy Davis Jr., Douglas Fairbanks Jr., Steve Lawrence and Eydie Gorme, Marie Osmond, Brooke Shields, Danny Thomas, Tanya Tucker, Robert Urich

In this Bob Hope retrospective outing, Lucille introduces old clips and does brief, cue-carded banter with Hope. It does take a certain type of talent to stand next to Bob Hope and laugh at his stale jokes with enthusiasm, and Lucille Ball excels at this.

THE TOMORROW SHOW

(NBC, APRIL 5, 1981), 60 MINUTES

PRODUCED BY: Joel Tator
DIRECTED BY: George Paul
CAST: Tom Snyder (host), Lucie Arnaz, Lucille Ball

Lucille rarely takes chances with her appearances on television, but decides to shed her *star* allure and appear on this Los Angeles-based show as herself. Wearing her own hair and little makeup, she hides her eyes behind sunglasses and wears an inexpensive pants suit outfit. (Lucille is not known for her sartorial splendor in private life.) She speaks candidly about not wishing to work, the loss of her mother, and wanting to play Grandma Lucy. Her remarks are sometimes curt and sharp, as she speaks of her experiences trying to travel on Amtrak from California to New York and having to get off the train because the accommodations are not to her liking. "And I'm a major stockholder!" she growls at Tom.

BUNGLE ABBEY

(NBC, MAY 31, 1981), 30 MINUTES

EXECUTIVE PRODUCED BY: Lucille Ball
PRODUCED BY: Gary Morton
WRITTEN BY: Fred S. Fox, Seaman Jacobs
DIRECTED BY: Lucille Ball
CAST: Gale Gordon, Charlie Callas, Guy Marks, Graham Jarvis, Gino Conforti, Peter Palmer, Anthony Alda, William Lanteau

This is an unsold sitcom pilot about a San Francisco monastery and the Brothers of Benevolence monks, headed by the Abbott (Gale Gordon). This show, high on energy but short on characterization, is funny but heavy on concept to the detriment of believability. This is the only TV program directed solely by Lucille Ball, and it features many of her favorite character actors.

Chapter Thirty-Three

1981–82 Season

THE THIRTY-THIRD ANNUAL EMMY AWARDS

(CBS, SEPTEMBER 13, 1981), 120 MINUTES

GUEST CAST: Lucille Ball, Ella Fitzgerald, Dinah Shore, and others

Lucille is a presenter at the prize-giving event held at the Pasadena, California, Civic Auditorium. This go-around it is Isabel Sanford of *The Jeffersons* (1975–85) who is named Outstanding Actress in a Comedy Series.

THE MAGIC OF THE STARS

(HBO, SEPTEMBER 20, 1981), 60 MINUTES

PRODUCED BY: Buddy Arnold, Bonnie Burns
DIRECTED BY: Terry Williams
CAST: Milton Berle (host), Lucille Ball, Carl Ballantine, Ruth Buzzi, Glen Campbell, Melissa Gilbert, Harvey Korman, Jack Lemmon, Walter Matthau, Dick Shawn, Tanya Tucker, Dick Van Patten

Uncle Miltie hosts this early HBO cable special in which all the guests perform magic with no tricks or electronic illusions. While this might seem a waste of high-ticket talent, the production is quite entertaining, as all those involved know how to sell their showmanship. This is Lucille's only HBO project, where once again she is being a television pioneer by appearing in a new medium. Wearing black slacks and blouse with a gold lame jacket, she makes a cane appear out of thin air. Later, she does the levitation bit, wearing a top hat, sequined outfit, and tights. Even at the age of seventy, she still looks like a million dollars in this outfit.

An interesting sidelight occurs during rehearsals of this special, as remembered by Stuart Shostak, one-time assistant to Gary Morton and a friend of Lucille's.

Stuart Shostak

(FAMILY FRIEND/VIDEOGRAPHER)

Milton was still the general in charge, towel around his neck and whistle blowing for attention. Gary turned to me as we sat in the [studio] bleachers and said, "Want to see me get Milton's goat?" He yelled at Milton, "Hey, Uncle Miltie, why don't you relax and let everyone do their jobs?" Berle saw red, and came over to where we were sitting to yell at Gary. "And what did you ever direct, you son of a bitch, that your wife didn't arrange for?" he screamed. I just shrunk in my seat as these two went at it right in my ear. I tried to sink into the floor. They continued their shouting match until Gary had enough. "Miltie, go back to yelling at everybody else," [Morton] chuckled, and as Milton walked away Gary just laughed at how he'd gotten to him.

HIGH HOPES: THE CAPRA YEARS

(NBC, DECEMBER 24, 1981), 120 MINUTES

PRODUCED BY: Carl Pingitore
SPECIAL GUEST & PRODUCER: Frank Capra Jr.
DIRECTED BY: Vincent Sherman
WRITTEN BY: Richard Schickel
MUSIC BY: Jimmy Haskell

This salute to the films of legendary filmmaker Frank Capra includes generous movie clips of his work. Introductions are made from a screening theatre by various celebrities seated alone in the audience. Lucille Ball, wearing a plain blouse and scarf around her neck, is one of these as she sits in the theatre and introduces clips from Capra's comedies.

BOB HOPE'S WOMEN I LOVE—BEAUTIFUL BUT FUNNY

(NBC, FEBRUARY 28, 1982), 90 MINUTES (COLOR AND B&W)

EXECUTIVE PRODUCED BY: Bob Hope
PRODUCED BY: Robert D. Hussey

DIRECTED BY: Kip Walton
WRITTEN BY: Gig Henry, Robert L. Mills, Fred S. Fox, Seaman Jacobs

A who's who of clips, including some with Lucille Ball from movies and TV. The Redhead *does* show up in person to trade brief quips with Hope, and she is the highlight of the program. Lucille is able to respond to Hope with such love and admiration that her appearances always stand out and look natural in the artificial environment of little-rehearsed, cue-card reading.

THE BEST OF THREE'S COMPANY

(ABC, MAY 18, 1982), 90 MINUTES

EXECUTIVE PRODUCED BY: Don Nicholl, Michael Ross, Bernie West, Budd Grossman
PRODUCED BY: Bill Richmond, Gene Perret, George Burditt, George Sunga, Joseph Staretski
DIRECTED BY: Bill Hobin, Sam Gary, Michael Ross, Jack Shea, Dave Powers
WRITTEN BY: more than forty writers
CAST: Lucille Ball (host), John Ritter

Lucille hosts this clip-filled retrospective to this still-in-production series (1977–84) because of her love for colead John Ritter's comedy work. At the end of the special, Ritter joins Ball and plants a big kiss on her cheek.

While many episode titles are self-explanatory ("Lucy and John Wayne"), fans often know a favorite Lucy TV episode by a key word or phrase rather than the actual episode title. Remember, none of Lucille Ball's television shows ever featured the name of the episode on the onscreen credits. Below are some of the most popular catch words and phrases (mostly from *I Love Lucy*), along with their corresponding title and page number:

Baby chicks	"Lucy Raises Chickens," p. 113
Carmen Miranda	"Be a Pal," p. 31
Chocolate factory	"Job Switching," p. 50
Crushing the eggs	"Lucy Does the Tango," p. 113
Ethel, let's have those biscuits	"Lucy's Schedule," p. 48
Ethel to Tillie, Ethel to Tillie	"The Seance," p. 36
Gobloots	"Lucy's Fake Illness," p. 40
Hitch in yer gitalong	"Tennessee Ernie Visits," p. 75
Jack Benny's vault	"Lucy Gets Jack Benny's Account," p. 224
Phipps is a great big bunch of gyps	"Mr. and Mrs. TV Show," p. 81
Sally Sweet	"The Diet," p. 32
Saxavibratronophonovitch	"The Audition," p. 35
The shower	"Lucy and Viv Put in a Shower," p. 160
Slowly, I turn	"The Ballet," p. 41
Starch vat	"Bonus Bucks," p. 73
The stilts	"Lucy and Her Electric Mattress," p. 156
Stomping grapes	"Lucy's Italian Movie," p. 102
Teensy and Weensy	"Tennessee Bound," p. 84
The woman is, uh, smar-ter	"Ragtime Band," p. 114
Vitameatavegamin	"Lucy Does a TV Commercial," p. 46

Chapter Thirty-Four

1982–83 Season

THE MERV GRIFFIN SHOW

(SYN, SEPTEMBER 1982), 90 MINUTES
EXECUTIVE PRODUCED BY: Merv Griffin
DIRECTED BY: Dick Carson
CAST: Merv Griffin (host), Ethel Merman, Lucille Ball, Ginger Rogers, Jerry Herman, Jule Styne, Hal David, Jack Sheldon

Merv hosts a salute to Broadway great Ethel Merman, one of the last public performances she makes before being stricken with a brain tumor. (Merman will die in early 1984.) Lucille and Ginger Rogers are surprise guests, both of them friends with The Merm since the early 1930s.

Jack Sheldon
(ACTOR/MUSICIAN)
What a thrill it was to be on the same stage with those legendary ladies. Merman was red hot. When Lucille Ball came on, it really was a surprise to her.

Stuart Shostak
(FAMILY FRIEND/VIDEOGRAPHER)
Lucy invited me to meet her backstage before the show. I knocked on the door to her dressing room, and she whispered, "Who is it?" I said it was me, and a hand came out from behind the door and pulled me in. It was Lucy. "Did anybody see you,?" she asked. I reminded her that no one knew who I was. She was very excited at surprising Ethel, and was there even though she had a cold.

ALL-STAR PARTY FOR CAROL BURNETT

(CBS, DECEMBER 12, 1982), 120 MINUTES
PRODUCED BY: Paul W. Keyes
DIRECTED BY: Dick McDonough
WRITTEN BY: Paul Keyes
MUSIC BY: Nelson Riddle
CAST: Lucille Ball (host), Tim Conway, Bette Davis, Sammy Davis Jr., Monty Hall, Glenda Jackson, Harvey Korman, Steve Lawrence, Vicki Lawrence, Jim Nabors, Jack Paar, Burt Reynolds, Beverly Sills, James Stewart

Another elaborate, black-tie party honoring a celebrity as a fund-raiser for the Variety Clubs International. The highlight of the evening is a split-screen performance of Carol's "I'm in Love with John Foster Dulles" from *The Ed Sullivan Show* while Vicki Lawrence sings the novelty song live.

FOURTH ANNUAL TV GUIDE SPECIAL

(NBC, JANUARY 24, 1983), 120 MINUTES (COLOR AND B&W)
EXECUTIVE PRODUCED BY: Ken Ehrlich, Jay S. Harris
PRODUCED AND DIRECTED BY: Stan Harris
WRITTEN BY: Neil Hickey, Stanley M. Ottenstein, Stan Harris
CAST: Michael Landon, Bryant Gumbel (co-hosts); Lucille Ball, Carol Burnett, George Burns, Joan Collins, Linda Evans, John Forsythe, Alan King

This special is a look back at the year 1982 in television. To add a nostalgic touch, clips are shown of some of the highlights in TV history. Lucille is on hand to introduce a clip from *I Love Lucy*.

BOB HOPE'S ROAD TO HOLLYWOOD

(NBC, MARCH 2, 1983) 120 MINUTES (COLOR AND B&W)
EXECUTIVE PRODUCED BY: Bob Hope
PRODUCED BY: Carolyn Raskin
DIRECTED BY: Kip Walton
WRITTEN BY: Gig Henry, Robert L. Mills, Fred S. Fox, Seaman Jacobs
CAST: Bob Hope (host), Lucille Ball, George Burns, Rosemary Clooney, Rhonda Fleming,

Dorothy Lamour, Virginia Mayo, Martha Raye, Jane Russell, Jill St. John

Another in what is becoming a staple of the Hope specials: old friends helping him introduce clips from his past movie and TV outings. Timed to coincide with the publication of his new book with the same name, this is nothing more than a glamorous commercial. Lucille's involvement is simply to appear, read a minute's worth of banter from cue cards, and then help Bob introduce clips from their movies together: *Sorrowful Jones* (1949), *Fancy Pants* (1950), *The Facts of Life* (1960), and *Critic's Choice* (1963) .

HAPPY BIRTHDAY, BOB: A SALUTE TO BOB HOPE'S EIGHTIETH BIRTHDAY

(NBC, MAY 23, 1983), 180 MINUTES

EXECUTIVE PRODUCED BY: James Lipton
PRODUCED AND DIRECTED BY: Don Mischer
WRITTEN BY: Gig Henry, Robert L. Mills, Fred S. Fox, Seaman Jacobs, James Lipton
CAST: Bob Hope (host), Lucille Ball, Christie Brinkley, George Burns, Lynda Carter, Kathryn Crosby, Phyllis Diller, Dolores Hope, Ann Jillian, Loretta Lynn, Barbara Mandrell, Dudley Moore, Ronald and Nancy Reagan, Tom Selleck, Brooke Shields, George C. Scott, Flip Wilson

An eightieth birthday celebration for Hope. These birthday extravaganzas serve two purposes: (1) they feed on the enduring public affection for Hope, and garner large ratings, and (2) they cram the show full of stars so that octogenarian Hope actually has very little performing to do.

Chapter Thirty-Five

1983–84 Season

THE TELEVISION ACADEMY HALL OF FAME

(NBC, MARCH 4, 1984), 120 MINUTES (COLOR AND B&W)
PRODUCED BY: Dwight Hemion, Gary Smith
DIRECTED BY: Dwight Hemion
WRITTEN BY: Buz Kohan
CHARTER INDUCTEES: Lucille Ball, Milton Berle, Paddy Chayefsky, Norman Lear, Edward R. Murrow, William S. Paley, David Sarnoff

A Hall of Fame is started by the organization that gives out the Emmy Awards. Each inductee is saluted by someone close to, or inspired by, that person. Lucille is inducted by Carol Burnett, after a live salute by Desi Arnaz Jr., and a musical tribute by Lucie Arnaz done on video tape from New York (where she is appearing on Broadway) called "My Mother the Star." Ball, in a formal black gown and upswept wig, looks glamorous but old. She is awash in tears as she tries to thank everyone involved. This is Lucille Ball's favorite award.

BOB HOPE IN WHO MAKES THE WORLD LAUGH? PART TWO

(NBC, APRIL 4, 1984), 60 MINUTES
(COLOR AND B&W)
EXECUTIVE PRODUCED BY: Bob Hope
PRODUCED BY: Marshall Flaum
DIRECTED BY: Tim Kiley
WRITTEN BY: Robert L. Mills, Seaman Jacobs, Fred S. Fox, Gene Perret, Marshall Flaum
CAST: Bob Hope (host), Lucille Ball, George Burns, Mickey Rooney

This is a sequel to an earlier special done in April of 1983. Much of the show is taken up with film clips. Lucille and Bob do their usual stand at center stage, reading lame jokes off cue cards while Lucille politely laughs at Bob.

THE AMERICAN PARADE

(CBS, APRIL 24, 1984), 60 MINUTES
EXECUTIVE PRODUCED BY: Russ Bensley, Perry Wolff
DIRECTED BY: Joe Carolei
WRITTEN BY: Peter Freundlich, Tom Harris
CAST: Charles Kuralt, Bill Moyers (hosts); Bill Kurtis, and others (interviewers); Lucille Ball, and others

This easy-going 1984 documentary series shares slices of American life and celebrity profiles with home viewers. In an extended interview with Bill Kurtis, Lucille provides reminiscences of working with Desi Arnaz, Vivian Vance, William Frawley, and Gale Gordon. The interview is taped in New York, as Ball is there for a tribute and symposium sponsored by the Museum of Broadcasting.

As with many interviews at this point in her career, Lucille gets choked-up and teary-eyed at the mention of the late Vivian Vance. She greatly sentimentalizes her relationship with Vance, and offers a heartfelt tribute to her.

Chapter Thirty-Six

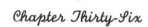

1984–85 Season

BOB HOPE'S HILARIOUS UNREHEARSED ANTICS OF THE STARS

(NBC, SEPTEMBER 28, 1984), 60 MINUTES (COLOR AND B&W)
EXECUTIVE PRODUCED BY: Bob Hope
PRODUCED BY: Elliot Kozak
DIRECTED BY: Sid Smith
WRITTEN BY: Robert L. Mills, Fred S. Fox, Seaman Jacobs, Gig Henry
CAST: Bob Hope (host), Lucille Ball, Milton Berle, Angie Dickinson, Lee Marvin

This is a special containing outtakes from various past Bob Hope TV specials, with introductions by the cast. Lucille is becoming a mainstay of Hope specials in the 1980s, much the way she was for Jack Benny in the late 1960s and early 1970s.

There is no longer a great deal of television work for Lucille Ball beyond these specials and occasional talk-show and game-show appearances. Lucille will tape ten episodes (two weeks worth) of NBC's *Body Builders* over the coming months. These stints on the game show are actually some of her best performing of this decade, as the show relies on a celebrity to guess words by acting them out without talking. Hosted by Tom Kennedy, Lucille's costars include Charles Nelson Reilly and Isabel Sanford. None of Ball's contemporaries from 1950s television comedy are still active. Eve Arden, Ann Sothern, Gale Storm, Harriet Nelson, Jane Wyatt, and others are all semi-retired, while many others have passed away. Only Donna Reed has found work this year, but not in a comedy. She replaces Barbara Bel Geddes on *Dallas* (1978–91), but only for this season. Lucille is in a class by herself.

ALL-STAR PARTY FOR LUCILLE BALL

(CBS, DECEMBER 29, 1984), 120 MINUTES
PRODUCED BY: Paul W. Keyes
DIRECTED BY: Dick McDonough
WRITTEN BY: Paul Keyes
MUSIC BY: Nelson Riddle
CAST: Monty Hall (host), Desi Arnaz Jr., Lucie Arnaz, Lucille Ball, Sid Caesar, Joan Collins, Sammy Davis Jr., Cary Grant, Shelley Long, Dean Martin, Gary Morton, Carl Reiner, Burt Reynolds, John Ritter, Frank Sinatra, James Stewart

Another in the series of salutes packaged on behalf of the Variety Clubs International charity. Lucille does not perform this evening, but instead gives a prepared speech about Variety Clubs.

There are many wonderful oncamera moments. Carl Reiner and Sid Caesar do an inspired "Professor" sketch, harking back to the TV days of the early 1950s when all of them were young and at the top of their comedic skills. Burt Reynolds is very amusing (and honest) talking about his encounter (of a dangerous kind) with Lucille in the early 1970s when he tried to date her daughter.

The highlight is Desi Jr. and a very pregnant Lucie Arnaz (who is married to actor Laurence Luckinbill) singing the song "I Love Lucy" to their mother as a ballad with special lyrics. Director Dick McDonough wisely allows the body microphones everyone wears to stay "hot" during the credits, letting the audience hear some very warm dialog between Lucy, Gary, Lucie, and Desi Jr.

NIGHT OF 100 STARS TWO

(ABC, MARCH 11, 1985), 180 MIN
PRODUCED BY: Alexander H. Cohen, Hildy Parks
DIRECTED BY: Clark Jones
WRITTEN BY: Hildy Parks
SPECIAL MUSICAL MATERIAL AND LYRICS BY: Buz Kohan

MUSIC DIRECTION BY: Elliot Lawrence
CAST: Debbie Allen, Harry Anderson, Ann-Margret, Lucie Arnaz, Edward Asner, Tracy Austin, Scott Baio, Lucille Ball, Drew Barrymore, Anne Baxter, Meredith Baxter-Birney, Shari Belafonte-Harper, Marisa Berenson, Valerie Bertinelli, David Birney, Jacqueline Bisset, Bob and Ray, Laura Brannigan, Lloyd Bridges, Morgan Brittany, Charles Bronson, Pierce Brosnan, Yul Brynner, Carol Burnett, George Burns, Ellen Burstyn, Red Buttons, Michael Caine, Dyan Cannon, Diahann Carroll, Lynda Carter, Marge Champion, Carol Channing, Dick Clark, Petula Clark, Dabney Coleman, Joan Collins, Bert Convy, Cathy Lee Crosby, Billy Crystal, Tyne Daly, William Daniels, Tony Danza, Olivia de Havilland, Robert De Niro, Colleen Dewhurst, Angie Dickinson, Richard Dreyfuss, Sandy Duncan, Charles Durning, Nancy Dussault, Linda Evans, Nanette Fabray, Morgan Fairchild, Peggy Fleming, John Forsythe, Michael J. Fox, Anthony Franciosa, David Frost, Soleil Moon Frye, Teri Garr, Lillian Gish, Linda Gray, Gene Hackman, Mark Hamill, Julie Harris, Lisa Hartman, David Hasselhoff, Florence Henderson, Dustin Hoffman, Lena Horne, Lee Horsley, Beth Howland, Kate Jackson, Van Johnson, Elaine Joyce, Danny Kaye, Linda Lavin, Michele Lee, Janet Leigh, Hal Linden, Heather Locklear, Ali MacGraw, Gavin MacLeod, Burgess Meredith, Donna Mills, Mary Tyler Moore, Melba Moore, Anne Murray, Jim Nabors, Bob Newhart, Donald O'Connor, Jennifer O'Neill, Jack Palance, Bert Parks, Bernadette Peters, Sidney Poitier, Jane Powell, Priscilla Presley, Robert Preston, Vincent Price, Juliet Prowse, Charlotte Rae, Tony Randall, Chita Rivera, Pernell Roberts, Ginger Rogers, Jill St. John, Jane Seymour, William Shatner, Brooke Shields, Dinah Shore, Jaclyn Smith, Gloria Steinhem, James Stewart, Heather Thomas, Richard Thomas, Mel Torme, Lana Turner, Leslie Uggams, Robert Urich, Joan Van Ark, Dick Van Dyke, Gwen Verdon, Robert Wagner, Raquel Welch, Billy Dee Williams, Henny Youngman, Stephanie Zimbalist

This is a sequel to *Night of 100 Stars* (1982), a benefit for the Actors Fund of America, held at Radio City Music Hall in New York City. Wearing a lot of stage makeup, Lucille does an introduction. The best moments of the show include a salute to tap dancers, with many of the names listed above joining Dick Van Dyke in a large production number, and a circus-themed segment featuring Hal Linden and Nancy Dussault. It would have been wonderful to have been a fly on the wall in *those* dressing rooms!

Chapter Thirty-Seven

1985–86 Season

BOB HOPE BUYS NBC

(NBC, SEPTEMBER 17, 1985), 120 MINUTES
EXECUTIVE PRODUCED BY: Bob Hope
PRODUCED BY: Elliot Kozak
DIRECTED BY: Walter C. Miller
WRITTEN BY: Robert L. Mills, Fred S. Fox, Seaman Jacobs, Gene Perret
CAST: Bob Hope (host), Lucille Ball, Milton Berle, George Burns, Johnny Carson, Lynda Carter, Phyllis Diller, Elvira, President Gerald R. Ford, Michael J. Fox, Dolores Hope, Michael Landon, Dean Martin, Mr. T, Tom Selleck, Danny Thomas

Hope hosts a fictional telethon to buy NBC. Lucille's contribution involves her coming on the telethon and ribbing Hope about his shortcomings. Although Bob uses Lucille repeatedly over the years, and two of her *Here's Lucy* writers are on the staff here, she is rarely given any sort of comedy to perform. It is a shame, because this is the best Hope TV special in years, with no old clips to interfere with the new presentation.

STONE PILLOW

(CBS, NOVEMBER 5, 1985), 120 MINUTES
EXECUTIVE PRODUCED BY: Merrill H. Karpf
PRODUCED AND DIRECTED BY: George Schaeffer
WRITTEN BY: Rose Leiman Goldenberg
MUSIC BY: George Delerue
CAST: Lucille Ball, Susan Batson, Imogene Bliss, Michael Champagne, William Converse-Roberts, Gloria Cromwell, Anna Marie Horsford, Patrick Kilpatrick, Stephen Lang, Matthew Locricchio, Pat MacNamara, Josephine Nichols, Patricia O'Connell, Peter Phillips, Victor Raider-Wexler, John Ramsey, Mary Lou Rosato, Stefan Schnable, Rebecca Schull, Edward Seamon, Raymond Serra, Gary Singer, Daphne Zuniga

New York City "bag lady" Flora Belle (Lucille Ball) is befriended by a neophyte social worker (Daphne Zuniga), who the elderly homeless person thinks is also living on the streets. Each woman tries to help the other in her own way, until Flora Belle learns the truth.

HIGHLIGHTS & TRIVIA

This is Lucille Ball's final TV dramatic appearance, and it almost kills her. Filmed on location on the streets of New York during a heat wave, Ball is required to wear layers of clothing to simulate the winter cold. She dehydrates and faints twice during the tough shoot. Creatively, this is a tour de force for Ball, although her performance is received with mixed reaction. Some feel she has given the best performance of her career, while others think her portrayal lacks subtlety and realism. Part of the problem is that Lucille always has to fight the stereotype of the *Lucy* character. No matter what she does or how she does it, some people always see *Lucy*.

While Lucille does make her portrayal of Flora Belle (named for her maternal grandmother, Flora Belle Hunt) come to life, she receives little support from a miscast Zuniga. Ball does all she can to shake off the shell of *Lucy*, and make her character as unglamorous as possible. She takes risks many actresses wouldn't dare, allowing herself to look bad and be seen doing things that are less than flattering. Even an outsize talent like Lucille's cannot carry an entire movie by herself. There is no one in this film whose acting ability or intensity comes anywhere near to hers.

Lucille is hospitalized after returning to Los Angeles, where she is treated for exhaustion, dehydration, and heat prostration.

Lucie Arnaz

While I don't necessarily think that this was my mother's best work, I would have loved to have played the younger woman who helps her. It kind of bothered me that nobody asked me. It would have been great to do a drama with my mother. This was a tough experience for her. She wasn't well. She kept getting these attacks where she got very hot and couldn't work. She had a bad heart. It was in the middle of summer, and here she was dressed in these layers of clothes. She had always been claustrophobic anyway. And the script was not that strong. I think at this time in her life it was almost too much for her to learn a script and create a character that was different from "Lucy." She just wasn't up to it physically.

Irma Kusely

(HAIRSTYLIST)

It bothered me terribly not to work with Lucille on this picture. It was the first major thing she had done since 1955 that I wasn't there for. But I just couldn't be away from my family that long in New York.

Rose Leiman Goldenberg

(WRITER)

We used about a dozen "actor" rats for the shoot. But Lucille didn't like them. She'd say, "These are sissy rats. I want real ones.*" She also had this idea she wanted to call a dog over and hug it, but the dog they hired didn't want to come. In the final cut, she just grabbed that dog and pulled him down. She was gonna have him whether he wanted to come or not.*

When we shot the film in Greenwich Village, people would see her and say, "Didn't that used to be Lucille Ball?" They were surprised that she was an old woman. They thought of her as being young.

Lucille Ball is just shy of seventy-four when this movie is shot in and on the streets of New York in May of 1985. After the filming, Lucille's health begins a gradual spiral of decline from which she never really recovers. When she feels better, Lucille does massive amounts of publicity for this telefilm, often doing twenty phone interviews a day. She looks thin but lovely, shedding some of the puffiness that she has displayed in recent years.

Chapter Thirty-Eight

1986–87 Season

LIFE WITH LUCY: THE FIRST SEASON

TECHNICAL REGULARS: Executive produced by Aaron Spelling, Gary Morton, Douglas S. Cramer; produced and created by Madelyn Davis, Bob Carroll Jr.; supervising producer: E. Duke Vincent; co-produced by Linda Morris, Vic Rauseo; makeup by Claude Thompson; Miss Ball's hairstyling by Irma Kusely; hairstyling by Rita Bellissimo; music by Allyn Ferguson; theme song ("Every Day") by Martin Silvestri, Jeremy Stone, Joel Higgins; theme song sung by Eydie Gorme
REGULAR CAST: Lucille Ball (Lucy Barker); Gale Gordon (Curtis MacGibbon); Ann Dusenberry (Margo MacGibbon); Larry Anderson (Ted MacGibbon); Jenny Lewis (Becky MacGibbon); Philip J. Amelio II (Kevin MacGibon); Donovan Scott (Leonard Stoner)

LIFE WITH LUCY #1: "ONE GOOD GRANDPARENT DESERVES ANOTHER"

(ABC, SEPTEMBER 20, 1986), 30 MINUTES
DIRECTED BY: Peter Baldwin
WRITTEN BY: Bob Carroll Jr., Madelyn Davis
GUEST CAST: Ruth Kobart, Gary Allen

Recently widowed Lucy Barker moves in with her married daughter Margo, son-in-law Ted (who is the son of her late husband Sam's business partner Curtis MacGibbon), and her grandchildren Becky (eight) and Kevin (six). They all live together in a three-story, clapboard house in Pasadena, California. Ted is a law student, and Curtis (and now Lucy) own M&B Hardware, a small retail store. Curtis returns from a vacation in Hawaii, and finds that Lucy has installed herself in his business *and* at his son's home. Not trusting her around the grandchildren, he decides to keep an eye on Lucy and move in to Ted and Margo's house as well.

HIGHLIGHTS & TRIVIA

There is tremendous audience reaction to Lucille's first entrance. She looks older than in her last sitcom *Here's Lucy*, but she *is* twelve years older. Her wig is almost exactly like the one she wore in that series' final episode.

Irma Kusely

(HAIRSTYLIST)

It might very well have been the same wig. It was a total coincidence that we chose that one. Perhaps we were psychologically trying to match her old look. We used a differently styled wig on almost every episode of Life with Lucy, *trying to give Lucille different looks.*

This initial effort sets up tremendous plot line tension and acrimony between Lucy and Curtis. They act as if they really dislike one another, and, in fact, have hardly spent any time together. This will be changed in future episodes, where Lucy and Curtis will be given a long history together. This series actually works best when the two characters work in harmony instead of being at odds with one another. Notice in the fire-extinguisher scene that the foam is not only being pumped from the prop machine, but is also oozing from the sides. The camera actually captures this for a few seconds. This entire scene is badly edited. Also note that the pass-through shutters in the living room set are painted off-white; these shutters will be wood-stained starting with the next installment. This entry also contains a coming attraction for the following week's offering. It is interesting to observe that the show's producers choose to use the theme music for *I Love Lucy* to underscore this piece of film instead of the theme for *Life with Lucy*. This is the only episode containing a coming attraction for the series. "

A hallmark of *Life with Lucy* is Ball's seeming problems with her lines. Even with cue cards, she sometimes stops in the middle of a sentence, searching for what to say next. This completely throws off her comedy timing. Lucy Barker is not like any of the previous *Lucy* characters. She is well-to-do financially, and not nearly as stupid as Lucy Carter (*Here's Lucy*). She is still meddlesome, but her main focus is on health and her grandchildren. Making Lucy Barker a health-food and exercise fanatic partly explains how the septuagenarian is so spry. However, this aspect of her character is written so annoyingly that it ceases to be funny after a few episodes. The grandkids seem too young for Lucille Ball's actual age (seventy-five), but they are even older than Ball's real-life grandchildren. These youngsters give typical sitcom performances, talented but without a trace of nuance.

It is never explained in the story line what Ted does for a living besides attending law school part-time, or what Margo's job is. Larry Anderson (very tall, tanned, and handsome) as Ted is a fine light comedy actor, and adds most of whatever realism can be found on *Life with Lucy*. Pretty Ann Dusenberry (as Margo) yells every line as if her life depends on it. This is partly due to Ball's insistence that everyone speak up as if in a theatre, although this is no longer necessary with 1980s technology. Sound engineer Cameron McCullough worked with Lucille all the way back in 1951 at the beginning of her sitcom career. That he now wears two hearing aids should have been a hint that his time had passed. Ann does not succeed in her role. She is not convincing as a mother or a wife, and plays her role like a cartoon.

The entire series is badly conceived. The hardware store premise ties down Lucille and Gale into the same, old, boring oncamera arguments. Besides, how many hardware store stories are there? The best scenes in every episode display the family at home, relaxing, playing, or just eating dinner. These domestic moments infuse badly needed warmth and sentimentality to the proceedings.

Stuart Shostak

(ASSISTANT TO THE PRODUCER)

Bill Cosby had just made a huge hit with his sitcom [The Cosby Show, *1984–92 on NBC*], *and ABC was having a hard time with their Saturday night schedule. They figured if they could get a powerhouse like Lucille Ball to do a show as their anchor, they could greatly improve their ratings. At the same time, they had a sitcom commitment with Aaron Spelling that was about to elapse and they wanted to take advantage of their contract. So ABC went to him and pitched the idea of him doing a Lucille Ball sitcom for the network. Spelling agreed and asked her, but the first response was no. Lucy did not want to come back and felt she had done everything she could do on television. However, she was very bored and missed working. How many games of backgammon can you play? She seemed happy in retirement, but when ABC offered Lucy an enormous amount of money plus a guarantee of twenty-two weeks whether the shows actually played or not, Gary Morton felt the time was right for her to go back to work. The continued popularity of* I Love Lucy *in reruns convinced him that the show would be well-received.*

Lucy and Gary co-owned the show with Aaron Spelling, with Spelling handling all the licensing and syndication and paperwork. This freed up Lucy and Gary to put on a show without worrying about all the business details. Lucy's only condition was that Gale Gordon appear in the show, and that Bob [Carroll Jr.] and Madelyn [Davis] come back and supervise the writing.

When the first script came in, I read it and thought it was OK until the part where Gale also moves into the house. That was Spelling's idea, and not part of Bob and Madelyn's original script. The original concept had more of a Golden Girls *[1985–92] feel to it, but the powers that be thought that the series had to be as close as possible to* I Love Lucy *to sell. So the block comedy scenes ended up being forced and unmotivated, just to have them in the show. The format was very limiting. There was talk of having Lucy and Gale play a married couple, but it was felt that the public was used to them in one kind of relationship and wouldn't accept them that way. Either way, in the intervening years since* Here's Lucy, *Lucille Ball had become revered by the public. She could do no wrong. That reverence made Gale's yelling at her not nearly as acceptable or funny. Lucy also had no contemporaries to play with. When I told Gary they should bring in a*

Mary Wickes, Doris Singleton, or Mary Jane Croft for her, his answer was, "I don't want this series to look like a rerun!" Yet, by bringing in Gale and the original writing team, that's what he got. There was a lot of politicking going on between the Life with Lucy *staff, the Spelling staff, and ABC. While the day-to-day dealings were pleasant, in hindsight we really weren't treated very well.*

They were originally going to use Frank Sinatra's recording of "Young at Heart" for the theme song, but they ran into licensing problems. So they opened it up to anyone who had ideas. They were good about that. Even the series title was up for grabs. Lucy *was one idea, as was* Lucy: the New Lucille Ball Show. *Finally, someone in the office came up with* Life with Lucy, *and they were paid $200 for it. I had worked on* Silver Spoons *(1982–86) and knew Joel Higgins from that show. He is also a composer, so when they needed a theme song, I told him. He thought he had just the thing for Lucy, and made a demo recording of it. I gave it to Gary, and they all loved it. They eventually had Eydie Gorme record it.*

Lucie Arnaz

My only real connection to this show was writing a theme song with Cy Coleman that I thought was brilliant. They bought it, and the next thing I knew, they had this other one. I'm certain that's why the show failed. But seriously, I think part of the problem was that my mother got so used to reading her lines off the cue cards that she wasn't getting behind the reality of what she was saying. I think she just couldn't do the memorization any more.

Dick Martin

(ACTOR/COMEDIAN/DIRECTOR)

This series was poorly constructed. You can't have a woman in her seventies doing dangerous physical comedy. The audience gasps instead of laughs. Had she chosen to do an ensemble comedy, like The Golden Girls, *I think she could have gone on forever."*

Ruta Lee

(ACTOR)

I don't think Lucy knew how bad this series was. Or perhaps she preferred not to think about it. The writing was so bland and silly. And her character was sad. I can't imagine why brilliant writers like Bob and Madelyn wrote something so mundane for her. I can think of a hundred situations that could have been funny for her at that age. The wonderful thing is that no one even remembers this [series].

Gale Gordon

(ACTOR)

When Lucy called me and told me she was going to go back to television, I asked her how much she wanted me *to pay* her *for me to do it. Every time we are on a stage together it is magic. By this point, we almost seemed to know when the other one is going to talk and move. It was like mental telepathy. Doing this series was a joy for me.*

LIFE WITH LUCY #2: "LUCY MAKES A HIT WITH JOHN RITTER"

(ABC, SEPTEMBER 27, 1986), 30 MINUTES

DIRECTED BY: Peter Baldwin
WRITTEN BY: Bob Carroll Jr., Madelyn Davis
GUEST CAST: John Ritter, Greg Mullavey, Ruth Buzzi, Sally Kemp

John Ritter comes into the hardware store looking for antique door knobs, and Lucy almost cripples him with a series of accidents. Lucy takes him home to help him recuperate, and gets a part in the play Ritter is doing at the Pasadena Playhouse.

HIGHLIGHTS & TRIVIA

Lucille really enjoys working with Ritter, who is one of her favorites. All week long, she refers to herself as having "Ritter-itis." During the filming of the scene where she force-feeds him a concoction of tofu, wheat germ, and sauerkraut juice because his hands are bandaged, Ritter ad-libs to her, "This is *real* sauerkraut juice!" His pained expression breaks Lucille up, and the scene had to be reshot.

Lucille Ball

This is only the third time in my entire career where I had to yell cut because I broke up laughing.

Stuart Shostak

(ASSISTANT TO THE PRODUCER)

Originally, it was supposed to be Lucy who was to swallow the harmonica in one scene, but she wouldn't do it. She felt it was like a Bugs Bunny cartoon. In reality, a person who swallows a harmonica would die or at least get their stomach pumped so, John Ritter did it.

John Ritter is superb on this entry, and his slapstick comedy scene in the hardware store is marvelous. However, the writing of the rest of the installment really lets him down.

LIFE WITH LUCY #3: "LOVE AMONG THE TWO-BY-FOURS"

(ABC, OCTOBER 4, 1986), 30 MINUTES

DIRECTED BY: Marc Daniels
WRITTEN BY: Linda Morris, Vic Rauseo
GUEST CAST: Peter Graves, Ed Bernard, Curtis Taylor

A building contractor, Ben Matthews, comes to the M&B Hardware store to talk about a contract for the store to supply plumbing fixtures. The contractor (Peter Graves) turns out to be Lucy's first love, and he wants to rekindle the flame.

HIGHLIGHTS & TRIVIA

It is learned in this entry that Leonard's last name is Stoner, and that Lucy's maiden name was Everett. Notice the improbable plot device which has a hardware store supplying a contractor with hardware, instead of the contractor going directly to a wholesaler distributor. The kid actors are so cloying and "cutesy" that they destroy any attempt at reality. Peter Graves is a fine choice as a romantic interest for Lucy, and Lucille looks stunning in her pink "date" dress. This is actually the only time on *Life with Lucy* that Lucille is not wearing slacks, a bathrobe, or a housecoat. The dress adds much-needed femininity to the character of Lucy Barker. Lucille does very well in her flirting scenes with Peter Graves. She is still able to be coquettish and make it work for her.

Larry Anderson seems to be the only one of the regular cast grounded in reality; his character of Ted acts as an anchor for the others. Curtis is obnoxious in this installment. It is as if the writers cannot decide on the proper path for Gale Gordon's character, so they try a different one in each episode. This week he is pure Mr. Mooney.

Stuart Shostak

(ASSISTANT TO THE PRODUCER)

This was a hard show to cast. Leslie Nielsen and Gary Morton were both considered for the part. Peter Graves fell during the rehearsal for this episode. It has been said that Lucy fell, but it was Peter. He leaned back and fell with this crash, and we didn't know if he would be able to make the shoot. They fixed him up and he was able to do it.

LIFE WITH LUCY #4: "LUCY GETS HER WIRES CROSSED"

(ABC, OCTOBER 18, 1986), 30 MINUTES

DIRECTED BY: Peter Baldwin
WRITTEN BY: Linda Morris, Vic Rauseo
GUEST CAST: Dick Gautier, Reva Rose, Kellie Martin, Brad Gorman, D. D. Howard

A chain hardware superstore opens nearby M&B Hardware, causing business to fall off dramatically. A local Pasadena talk-show host (Dick Gautier) visits the store, and Lucy convinces him to feature Curtis on his show as "Mr. Fixit." Now Lucy has to talk Curtis into letting her be on TV with him.

HIGHLIGHTS & TRIVIA

This entry actually has a few laughs. Dick Gautier provides his usual slick comedy turn, and the final scene on the talk show where everyone gets glued together is well executed. The only fly in the comedy ointment is the unbelievability of the situation. The most famous scene from this series has Lucy lying on an electric lounge chair that goes berserk. While Ball has little to do but ride the bucking chair, newspaper columnists chide Ball and the producers for allowing an old woman to do such a dangerous stunt. While Lucille *does* get jostled, she is hardly in danger. However, many people feel that Lucille is too old to be doing the same kind of physical comedy she used to do decades earlier.

Lucie Arnaz

Unlike someone like Katharine Hepburn, who has let the camera see her age from all angles slowly and gracefully through the years, my mother was not comfortable with looking older. For one thing, Hepburn did not have to compete with images of herself looking flawless morning, noon and night. My Mom couldn't have her face lifted because of her skin bruising easily, but she felt she was competing with herself.

LIFE WITH LUCY #5: "LUCY IS A SAX SYMBOL"

(ABC, OCTOBER 25, 1986), 30 MINUTES
DIRECTED BY: Peter Baldwin
WRITTEN BY: Arthur Marx, Robert Fisher
GUEST CAST: Brandon Call

Lucy discovers her old saxophone in a trunk in the basement. She thinks Becky has the makings of a virtuoso, but the child *loathes* the saxophone. How does the family tell over-eager Lucy without hurting her feelings?

HIGHLIGHTS & TRIVIA

Boy, did they miss the boat on this one! When Lucy pulls the saxophone from the trunk, the audience immediately gives applause from its recognition of Lucy/saxophone scenes from *I Love Lucy*. Instead of fashioning the ultimate Lucy/sax story, the writers choose to center the piece around Becky and sticky sentimentality. Scribe Arthur Marx is the son of comedy legend Groucho Marx and an award-winning writer on his own. However, like many writers through the years, Marx doesn't understand what it takes to write a successful *Lucy* script. This installment features the best performance by Jenny Lewis (Becky). Lewis will go on to appear in episodic television and TV movies.

THE LATE SHOW STARRING JOAN RIVERS

(FOX, OCTOBER 30, 1986), 60 MINUTES
EXECUTIVE PRODUCED BY: Edgar Rosenberg, Bill Sammeth
PRODUCED BY: Bruce McKay
DIRECTED BY: David Grossman
WRITING SUPERVISED BY: Hank Bradford
CAST: Joan Rivers (host), Lucille Ball, Michelle Lee, Nancy Reagan

Joan Rivers is given the Herculean task of launching an entire broadcast network with a series supervised by her husband, who is in the throws of a nervous breakdown. This ill-fated talk-fest is strongly anchored by Rivers, a major comedic talent. She has often interviewed Lucille Ball in the past as part of her guest-hosting chores for *The Tonight Show* (1983–86). Their appearances have always gone well, as Lucille feels relaxed with Joan, and Joan's respect for Ball is reflected in the topics for discussion (Lucille's grandchildren, *I Love Lucy*, looking beautiful). However, this evening something is terribly wrong, as Lucille actually cries on the air when Joan brings up *Life with Lucy*. This is Lucille's final talk-show appearance.

Michael Stern

(LUCILLE BALL'S OFFICIAL NUMBER ONE FAN)

This was probably Lucy's least favorite talk show appearance. First of all, she wasn't aware that Joan and Mrs. Reagan were dressing formally. So she wore an inexpensive purple outfit while the other ladies wore velvet, sequins, and jewels. So Lucy felt embarrassed. Then backstage, there was a knock at the door, and an aide said, "Mrs. Reagan would like to see you now." So Lucy said, "OK, send her in!" The lady had this awful expression on her face, like, "How am I going to tell Lucille Ball that she has to go see the First Lady, not the other way around." Of course, Lucy had known Mrs. Reagan for a hundred years, and also knew that she had to go see her. It was just her little joke. Lucy told me that hugging Nancy Reagan was like hugging a toothpick. Finally, Lucy got on the air, and practically dissolved in tears discussing how badly her series was doing.

LIFE WITH LUCY #6: "LUCY MAKES CURTIS BYTE THE DUST"

(ABC, NOVEMBER 1, 1986), 30 MINUTES
DIRECTED BY: Marc Daniels
WRITTEN BY: Linda Morris, Vic Rauseo
GUEST CAST: Dave Madden, Billy Van Zandt

Inventory at M&B Hardware store proves to be such a burden that Lucy leases a computer to speed up the tedious process.

HIGHLIGHTS & TRIVIA

This installment is terrible. There is not a funny moment in the entire thirty minutes. While the writers are trying to incorporate modern themes into the plots, such as computerization, they seem to have no knowledge of how retail computers actually work. Dave Madden had been a semi-regular on the Carroll-Davis produced *Alice* (1976–85) and previously was seen as talent agent Reuben Kinkard on *The Partridge Family* (1970–74).

LIFE WITH LUCY #7: "LUCY, LEGAL EAGLE"

(ABC, NOVEMBER 8, 1986), 30 MINUTES
DIRECTED BY: Marc Daniels
WRITTEN BY: Richard Albrecht, Casey Keller
GUEST CAST: Dena Dietrich, Allan Rich, Brandon Call, Eddie Carroll, Nora Boland, Charles Walker, Robin Bach, Don Diamond

Kevin's teddy bear Charley is inadvertently sold during a family yard sale. When Lucy finds the nasty woman (Mrs. Loomis) who bought it (by posting a fifty dollar reward), the individual demands five hundred dollars to return it. Lucy gets angry, and takes the greedy person to small claims court.

HIGHLIGHTS & TRIVIA

The writing in this episode is very old-fashioned, and the first half of the installment boasts of few laughs. However, the Lucille Ball of old emerges in the courtroom scene. Her timing is impeccable. While Lucille is dressed in a man's tailored suit, with suspenders and floppy bow-tie, one cannot help think of Lucy Ricardo. Marc Daniels' solid direction is evident in the blocking and Ball's physical maneuvering. The rest of the episode pales in comparison. Guest star Dena Dietrich, better known as Mother Nature on margarine commercials for more than twenty years, gives a one-note performance as Mrs. Loomis.

LIFE WITH LUCY #8: "MOTHER OF THE BRIDE"

(ABC, NOVEMBER 15, 1986), 30 MINUTES
DIRECTED BY: Bruce Bilson
WRITTEN BY: Linda Morris, Vic Rauseo
GUEST CAST: Audrey Meadows, Jim Hackett, Jacque Lynn Colton

Ted and Margo's tenth anniversary is coming up, and Lucy suggests that they renew their vows and have the wedding she had always planned for them, had they not eloped. With gentle pressure from the women in the family, Ted agrees. Just then, Lucy's sister Audrey (Audrey Meadows), the entertainment director on a cruise ship, arrives and takes charge. Audrey selfishly replaces Lucy's plans with those of her own.

HIGHLIGHTS & TRIVIA

This is the best *Life with Lucy* episode. The installment has crisp dialog, subtle direction, and Lucille gets someone worthy of her talents to play with in the person of Audrey Meadows. Such witty dialog as Audrey's, "Ah, Pasadena. 100,000 people, a dozen stories," typifies the kind of writing Lucille had been used to during her long TV career. There are tender moments, and for a change the characters of Lucy and Curtis aren't at each other's throats, which has been tiresome right from the beginning. It is learned that Curtis' late wife was named Josephine.

Lucille Ball

(IN 1984)

I'm getting too old to have Uncle Harry or Mr. Mooney yelling at me all the time.

She was right. The scene in the kitchen where Lucy and Audrey have their fight with the cake frosting is one of the only well-motivated comedy spots in the entire new series, and the two sitcom war horses really rise to the occasion. Audrey is in top form and looks beautiful. Even the duo's artificially colored hair and much-lowered voices seem a perfect match. It is reminiscent of the wonderful Lucy Ricardo/Ethel Mertz arguments, with timing that is spectacularly right.

Stuart Shostak

(ASSISTANT TO THE PRODUCER)

Audrey was going to be our ace in the hole. She was going to be a regular, to give the show a new focus and Lucy a new sparring and conspiring partner. I don't think Lucy knew how bad these shows were. And the studio audiences misled us. They laughed uproariously at everything Lucy did. If they had reacted to the comedy the way the folks did at home, everyone would have realized there was a big problem and perhaps it would have been fixed. Gary wouldn't introduce Lucy in his warmup like he used to do during Here's Lucy, *so when she made her first entrance in every episode, there was pandemonium. She had to stop to acknowledge the ovation, but that had to be cut out of the final prints. Then she was forced to follow that reception with lukewarm scripts. The comedy timing of the show was off because there was laughter that wasn't deserved. And the laughs had to be edited out for time constraints, so there was no natural flow.*

Jayne Meadows
(ACTOR)

There was something between Audrey and Lucille, something personal that I cannot go into, but Audrey will not discuss her experience working with Lucy.

[Audrey Meadows passed away in 1996 at the age of seventy-one.]

Michael Stern
(LUCILLE BALL'S OFFICIAL NUMBER ONE FAN)

I was there all day with Lucy, and the only untoward thing that occurred was at dress rehearsal. She never made up until just before the filming, but Audrey came to the set in full makeup. When they rehearsed the cake bit, Lucy smeared Audrey's face with the icing. Lucy immediately realized what she had done, and apologized profusely. It seemed that of all the weeks of Life with Lucy, *this is the one that went the smoothest and was the most professional. That was due in part to Audrey. The director [Bruce Bilson] was another story. After one lunch break, he decided that what comedy needed was a completely quiet set. So he said, "I don't care what you had for lunch, or you, or you. I want a quiet set!" About four seconds went by, and Lucy said, "I had salmon." The set exploded with laughter, and she had put him in his place. He never again had his quiet set.*

The blocking of this show proves how ridiculously the set was designed. The house has (at least) five bedrooms and two staircases but no dining room or den. The kitchen has a pass-through to the main room, which is never opened or used. Although this is the last episode aired, the following several episodes were already filmed and have never been seen by the public.

LIFE WITH LUCY: "LUCY AND THE GUARD GOOSE"

(UNAIRED), 30 MINUTES
DIRECTED BY: Peter Baldwin
WRITTEN BY: Bob Carroll Jr., Madelyn Davis
GUEST CAST: Lou Cutell, Charles Levin

When M&B Hardware is burglarized, Lucy and Curtis get a guard goose. However, the goose is on the other foot when the fowl traps Lucy and Curtis in the store.

HIGHLIGHTS & TRIVIA

It is understandable why this effort is held back. The second episode filmed, it has a very silly premise. Minutes go by when there is nothing amusing said or done. The only saving grace is Gale Gordon, who utters a string of funny one-liners. This is Gordon's best episode on *Life with Lucy*. The guest goose is very uncooperative, and its scene in the store has to be reshot.

LIFE WITH LUCY: "LUCY AND CURTIS ARE UP A TREE"

(UNAIRED), 30 MINUTES
DIRECTED BY: Marc Daniels
WRITTEN BY: Madelyn Davis, Bob Carroll Jr.
GUEST CAST: June Whitley Taylor, Tom Williams

Lucy and Curtis are spoiling the grandchildren. Lucy overhears Ted and Margo discussing this. She tells Curtis that they must move out to restore harmony. Unfortunately, she chooses to tell him in the tree house Curtis is building for Kevin, and the two get stuck up there.

HIGHLIGHTS & TRIVIA

This is the seventh episode filmed. While the theme of having two grandparents in-residence spoiling the children is a good one, nothing much comes of it in this installment. Lucille spends several minutes telling a bedtime story that is barely amusing; a laugh track has to be used because there is sparse studio audience response to it. Ball's voice is not up to the manipulations necessary to act out a children's tale, and her frequent looking at cue cards spoils her timing. The final scene, with Lucy and Curtis stuck up a tree, could have been hysterical. With five other regulars, there aren't many moments on this series for Lucille and Gale to have a scene alone together. Unfortunately, all the audience gets is the same old quarreling that had been getting stale twenty-five years earlier. The finale, with the cast all up the tree house performing "Singing in the Rain" in the rain is embarrassing!

LIFE WITH LUCY: "LUCY'S GREEN THUMB"

(UNAIRED), 30 MINUTES
DIRECTED BY: Marc Daniels

WRITTEN BY: Mark Tuttle
GUEST CAST: Jerry Prell, Doris Hess, Stuart Shostak

Lucy concocts a distasteful health drink for breakfast, which the family dumps into a dying plant before leaving the house. Upon their return, the plant is twice as tall and wide. Curtis decides to market Lucy's discovery, dubbing it "gigantagrow."

HIGHLIGHTS & TRIVIA

This is the ninth episode filmed. While in all other installments of the series the family eats in the kitchen, the opening scene to this entry has them eating in the living room using a previously unseen dining room table and chairs. The sequence at the hardware store is the only time Lucille utters her famous "spider" noise (eeeuuuu) during the course of this series. The man playing the photographer in the finale is Stuart Shostak, Ball's videographer and one-time assistant to Gary Morton.

LIFE WITH LUCY: "BREAKING UP IS HARD TO DO"

(UNAIRED), 30 MINUTES

DIRECTED BY: Marc Daniels
TELEPLAY BY: Richard Albrecht, Casey Keller
STORY BY: Laura Levine
GUEST CAST: Brad Gorman, Dick Winslow, Eddie Barth

When Lucy and Curtis have one disagreement too many, Curtis decides to retire and Lucy buys out his half of M&B Hardware.

HIGHLIGHTS & TRIVIA

This is the eleventh episode filmed. Of note is the tune Lucille hums when she is talking with Margo: "Hey Look Me Over," Ball's hit from her 1960 Broadway musical *Wildcat*. The finale features the warmest and perhaps best-acted scene Ball and Gordon ever do together. More moments like this might have made a difference in the appeal of the series.

LIFE WITH LUCY: "WORLD'S GREATEST GRANDMA"

(UNAIRED), 30 MINUTES

DIRECTED BY: Bruce Bilson
TELEPLAY BY: Bob Carroll Jr., Madelyn Davis
STORY BY: Mel Sherer, Steve Granat
GUEST CAST: Michael Zorek, Kellie Martin, Phyllis Applegate, the Dixiebelles

Everybody in the family has won a trophy except Lucy. Feeling sorry for her, Lucy's granddaughter Becky enters her in a talent contest for grandmothers at her school. The winner receives a trophy, but unfortunately Lucy has no talent.

HIGHLIGHTS & TRIVIA

This plot was fresh and new when it was done on *The Danny Thomas Show* (1953–65) and *The Brady Bunch* (1969–74). Lucille's makeup is lightened for this episode; she is at her most attractive facially. This is the final filmed installment of *Life with Lucy*. On the day of the filming of this episode Aaron Spelling receives the decree that the show is canceled. Rather than tell Lucille himself, he has an assistant telephone Gary Morton with the news, which is withheld from Lucille until after the filming. Although the premiere had a respectable twentieth top show in the ratings, the other episodes steadily decreased in viewership. This series has turned into one of the biggest disasters in sitcom history, and Lucille is devastated. She is convinced that the public no longer wants her.

Ann Sothern

(ACTOR)

She called me on the phone after the last episode. She was crying. She said, "Ann, I've been fired. ABC's let me go. They don't want to see an old grandma. They want me as the Lucy I was.*" It was hard for her not to work. She brought so much happiness to people, but I don't think she really knew how much people loved* her.

Lillian Briggs Winograd

(FAMILY FRIEND)

The failure of her last series hurt her more than anything, but not for herself. She kept saying, "My God, these people are going to be out of work!" She kept saying, "I never should have done it." The effect was awful. She couldn't understand why her comedy didn't work anymore.

Gary Morton

(EXECUTIVE PRODUCER)

Lucy couldn't do the physical comedy like she did it before. I think ABC was smart to pay us off and end it.

Lucy wanted to give TV one more shot. She said she was wrong to go back to the old creative people—that she should have hired new people and used new ideas. It was a rehash of Here's Lucy. *It would have been better if we did more believable stuff. No one goes to the studio to make a bad show. Lucy told her friend Tom Watson, "I think we're in trouble with this show!" [Producer] Aaron Spelling is a consumate pro and tried his best. Not every series can be that strong. The failure of the show really threw Lucy. She had never failed before.*

SUPER PASSWORD

(NBC, FIVE SHOWS TAPED DECEMBER 2, 1986), 30 MINUTES
EXECUTIVE PRODUCED BY: Chester Feldman, Howard Felsher, Robert Sherman
PRODUCED BY: Diane Janaver, Joe Neustein
DIRECTED BY: George Chodeker
CAST: Bert Convy (host), Lucille Ball, Betty White

In this updated version of *Password*, two celebrities work with two contestants to guess words that lead to a mystery word or phrase. Lucille and Betty White are the celebrities this day, taping five shows that cover one week. Ball is no longer as sharp as she once was playing this game. Back in the 1960s, contestants working with the Redhead generally won. Now, Lucille seems stumped to come up with good clues and frustrated by her lack of mental agility. Desi Arnaz died that morning.

Betty White

(ACTRESS/WIFE OF ORIGINAL PASSWORD HOST, ALLEN LUDDEN)

We were doing Password *the day Desi died. During a break, she turned to me and said, "You know, it's the damndest thing. Goddamn it, I didn't think I'd get this upset. There he goes." It was a funny feeling, kind of a lovely, private moment.*

ALL-STAR PARTY FOR CLINT EASTWOOD

(CBS, DECEMBER 15, 1986), 120 MINUTES
PRODUCED AND WRITTEN BY: Paul W. Keyes
DIRECTED BY: Dick McDonough
MUSIC BY: Nick Perito
CAST: Lucille Ball (host), Sammy Davis Jr., Clint Eastwood, Roberta Flack, Cary Grant, Merv Griffin, Monty Hall, Bob Hope, Marsha Mason, Don Rickles, James Stewart

Lucille hosts this salute to Eastwood, the latest in fund-raiser specials serving to honor stars while promoting the work of the Variety Clubs International. Lucille looks glamorous in a pants suit, and handles her hosting chores amiably. She does not perform any comedy. This is the last TV special hosted by Lucille Ball.

THE KENNEDY CENTER HONORS

(CBS, DECEMBER 26, 1986), 120 MINUTES (COLOR AND B&W)
PRODUCED BY: George Stevens Jr., Nick Vanoff
DIRECTED BY: Don Mischer
WRITTEN BY: George Stevens Jr., Sara Lukinson, Bob Shrum
HONOREES: Lucille Ball, Ray Charles, Hume Cronyn, Yehudi Menuhin, Jessica Tandy, Anthony Tendor
CAST: Walter Cronkite (host), Bea Arthur, Glenn Close, Pam Dawber, Agnes de Mille, Jose Ferrer, Margot Fonteyn, Valerie Harper, Rosemary Harris, Quincy Jones, Hal Linden, Walter Matthau, Robert Stack, Liv Ullmann, Peter Ustinov, Sigourney Weaver

Each year, starting in 1978, the Kennedy Center in Washington, D.C., honors individuals who throughout their lifetimes have made a significant contribution to American culture through the performing arts. The ceremonies, held at the Kennedy Center itself, cap several days in Washington for the honorees attending parties and functions, including a meeting with the President where the honorees are presented their medals.

Lucille Ball

I don't know what I would have done if I hadn't had this thing to keep me occupied. Desi died and my show got canceled. If I hadn't had this, if I hadn't this reassurance that I was still wanted, I don't think that I could have gone on.

Desi Arnaz had originally been tapped to host the segment honoring Lucille, but in his absence Robert Stack reads words written by Desi for the occasion. Then Bea Arthur, Pam Dawber, and Valerie Harper do a musical tribute to Lucille.

This is especially touching, since Valerie had got her show business start as a chorus girl in *Wildcat* (1960). Lucille looks lovely in a black and gold gown, but also appears tired and a little frail.

HAPPY BIRTHDAY, HOLLYWOOD

(ABC, MAY 18, 1987), 180 MINUTES

EXECUTIVE PRODUCED BY: Jack Haley Jr., Alexander H. Cohen
PRODUCED BY: Jeff Margolis, Hildy Parks
DIRECTED BY: Jeff Margolis
WRITTEN BY: Hildy Parks
CAST: Debbie Allen, June Allyson, Bea Arthur, Edward Asner, Lucille Ball, Gene Barry, Drew Barrymore, Hinton Battle, Shari Belafonte-Harper, Sandahl Bergman, Milton Berle, Tom Bosley, Morgan Brittany, Gregg Burge, Carol Burnett, Leslie Caron, Lynda Carter, Sid Caesar, Cyd Charisse, James Coburn, Dabney Coleman, Mike Connors, Bert Convy, Don Correia, Arlene Dahl, Tony Danza, Sammy Davis Jr., William Devane, Angie Dickinson, Nancy Dussault, Barbara Eden, Morgan Fairchild, Alice Faye, John Forsythe, Bonnie Franklin, Mary Frann, Richard Gere, Gil Gerrard, Lillian Gish, Louis Gossett Jr., Robert Goulet, Ellen Greene, Deidre Hall, Gregory Harrison, Mary Hart, Florence Henderson, Charlton Heston, Dustin Hoffman, Bob Hope, Jill Ireland, Van Johnson, Shirley Jones, Ruby Keeler, Sally Kellerman, Jayne Kennedy, Stepfanie Kramer, Patti LaBelle, Dorothy Lamour, Michele Lee, Janet Leigh, Shari Lewis, Gloria Loring, Lorna Luft, Joseph Maher, Tony Martin, Marilyn McCoo, Roddy McDowall, Ann Miller, Donna Mills, Joe Namath, Bob Newhart, Donald O'Connor, Maureen O'Sullivan, Nia Peeples, Bernadette Peters, Ali Porter, Jane Powell, Stefanie Powers, Luise Rainer, Sheryl Lee Ralph, Lou Rawls, Lee Roy Reems, Debbie Reynolds, Alfonso Ribiero, John Ritter, Ginger Rogers, Cesar Romero, Eva Marie Saint, Jill St. John, Telly Savalas, Tracy Scoggins, William Shatner, Martin Sheen, Jaclyn Smith, Robert Stack, Lionel Stander, Susan Sullivan, Loretta Swit, Alan Thicke, Lana Turner, Joan Van Ark, Dick Van Dyke, Robert Wagner, Dee Wallace-Stone, Betty White, Jesse White, Esther Williams, Treat Williams, Henry Winkler, Loretta Young

The intention of this gala is to highlight and help out the Motion Picture and TV Country House and Hospital, but it is an overproduced bomb. Stars of legendary stature are overlooked to present performers of dubious Hollywood interest such as Joe Namath. Lucille is part of the salute to television, but her appearance is brief.

BOB HOPE'S HIGH-FLYING BIRTHDAY EXTRAVAGANZA

(NBC, MAY 25, 1987), 120 MINUTES

EXECUTIVE PRODUCED BY: Bob Hope
PRODUCED BY: Linda Hope
DIRECTED BY: Walter C. Miller
WRITTEN BY: Robert L. Mills, Fred S. Fox, Seaman Jacobs, Gene Perret
CAST: Bob Hope (host), Lucille Ball, Kirk Cameron, Glen Campbell, Phyllis Diller, Dolores Hope, Don Johnson, Emmanuel Lewis, Barbara Mandrell, Phylicia Rashad, Ronald Reagan, Brooke Shields

A salute to Bob Hope's eighty-fourth birthday, taped at Pope Air Force Base in North Carolina. Lucille (beautiful in a lavender gown) and Bob duet on "I Remember It Well" from the musical film *Gigi* (1958). Lucille also does a skit, playing a gun-toting, hillbilly mother who protects the innocence of her daughters (Phyllis Diller, Brooke Shields, Barbara Mandrell) from lecherous Hope. This is the last comedy skit in which Lucille performs.

Chapter Thirty-Nine

1987–88 Season

A BEVERLY HILLS CHRISTMAS

(FOX AND SYN, NOVEMBER 1987), 60 MINUTES
PRODUCED BY: Earl Durham, Mark Shaw
DIRECTED BY: Woody Fraser
WRITTEN BY: Anita Donham
CAST: James Stewart (host), Lucille Ball, the Brown Brothers, George Burns, the Caroling Company, Lee Greenwood, Walter Matthau, Jeffrey Osborne, Alison Porter, Burt Reynolds

Lucille does this as a favor to long-time friend and Beverly Hills neighbor James Stewart. Appearing in a slacks outfit that she had worn as far back as 1967 on *The Lucy Show*, this is the only religious broadcast Ball is associated with in her long television career. Lucille reads from the Bible.

THE KENNEDY CENTER HONORS

(CBS, DECEMBER 30, 1987), 120 MINUTES
PRODUCED BY: Nick Vanoff, George Stevens Jr.
DIRECTED BY: Dwight Hemion
WRITTEN BY: George Stevens Jr., Sara Lukinson, Bob Shrum
HONOREES: Perry Como, Bette Davis, Sammy Davis Jr., Nathan Milstein, Alwain Nikolais

Lucille is on hand to host the segment honoring her close friend Sammy Davis Jr., which features uptempo performing by Ray Charles and the Nicholas Brothers.

AMERICA'S TRIBUTE TO BOB HOPE

(NBC, MARCH 5, 1988), 60 MINUTES
EXECUTIVE PRODUCED BY: Gregory H. Willenborg
PRODUCED BY: Gary Smith, Dwight Hemion
DIRECTED BY: Dwight Hemion
WRITTEN BY: Buz Kohan
MUSIC BY: Ian Fraser
CAST: Lucille Ball, Diahann Carroll, Vic Damone, John Forsythe (hosts); Ann-Margret, George Burns, Phyllis Diller, Bob Hope, Dolores Hope, Alan King, Barbara Mandrell, Donald O'Connor, Nancy Reagan, President Ronald Reagan, Dinah Shore, O.J. Simpson, Danny Thomas

Taped at the opening of the Bob Hope Cultural Center in Palm Springs, California, Lucille is lovely in a blue chiffon gown. She anchors much of the first part of the show, while the Hopes and President and Mrs. Reagan watch from a box in the theatre. Lucille does no comedy, but she is perfect as the glamorous moderator.

HAPPY BIRTHDAY, BOB

(NBC, MAY 16, 1988), 180 MINUTES
EXECUTIVE PRODUCED BY: James Lipton
PRODUCED BY: Elliot Kozak
DIRECTED BY: Tim Kiley
GUEST CAST: ALF, Steve Allen, Lucille Ball, Milton Berle, George Burns, Kirk Cameron, Diahann Carroll, Bert Convy, Sammy Davis Jr., Angie Dickinson, Phyllis Diller, John Forsythe, Dolores Hope, Ann Jillian, Jack Jones, Stepfanie Kramer, Dorothy Lamour, Michael Landon, Jay Leno, Shelley Long, Reba McEntire, Donald O'Connor, Marie Osmond, Tony Randall, Don Rickles, Brooke Shields, Dinah Shore, James Stewart, Danny Thomas, Leslie Uggams, Betty White, Jonathan Winters

This special celebrates Bob Hope's eighty-fifth birthday and his fiftieth (!) anniversary with NBC. Lucille performs a new song written especially for this occasion by Cy Coleman and James Lipton: "Comedy Is a Serious Business." Still able to wear a tuxedo jacket and briefs with no skirt (to show off her legs), Lucille performs ably but seems enervated by the process. After she finishes her number, she collapses and has to be removed from the studio. Shortly thereafter, Lucille suffers a minor stroke. This is Lucille Ball's final TV variety show appearance.

Brooke Shields

(ACTOR)

Lucy was doing a wonderful dancing and singing sketch, but there hadn't been enough time to rehearse. It was difficult for her to match her steps to the orchestration. I saw her as a little girl then—frustrated, and embarrassed that she was having trouble with the steps.

Chapter Forty

1988–89 Season

SUPER PASSWORD

(NBC, NOVEMBER 7-11, 1988), 30 MINUTES

EXECUTIVE PRODUCED BY: Chester Feldman, Howard Felsher, Robert Sherman
PRODUCED BY: Diane Janaver, Joe Neustein
DIRECTED BY: George Chodeker
CAST: Bert Convy (host), Lucille Ball, Carol Channing, Dick Martin, Betty White

In this all-celebrity version of the game show, the stars are playing for charity. Lucille does not do well here at all. Lucille suffered a stroke a few months earlier, which had briefly paralyzed her side and face. Although almost totally recovered, the effects of her stroke are obvious, as she is slightly thick of speech and seems unable to focus. At one point, Carol Channing takes Lucille's face in her hands and says, "Lucy, look at me and concentrate!" This is Lucille Ball's final game show stint.

Dick Martin

(ACTOR/COMEDIAN/DIRECTOR)

They had originally booked a fourth lady for the show, but she had to back out at the last minute. So they got me instead. We [all] made about $35,000 for the John Wayne Cancer Center [on those five shows]. Unfortunately, Lucille's mind was wandering. She had been a sharp game player, but was now very slow on the pickup. She wanted to do it so badly. But she couldn't keep up. It was kind of sad.

THE ACADEMY AWARDS SHOW

(NBC, MARCH 29, 1989), 180 MINUTES

Lucille Ball and Bob Hope appear together at the awards, introducing a group of young talent in a salute to the future of Hollywood. They are received with a standing ovation that is loud and sustaining. Ball looks beautiful in a black dress with gold trim and a sexy, slit skirt, although she actually says very few words. This is Lucille Ball's last television appearance.

Michael Stern

(LUCILLE BALL'S OFFICIAL NUMBER ONE FAN)

It was amazing being with Lucy that night. Security is very tight at these things, but because I was with Lucille Ball, it didn't matter that I had no security badges on. We were waved into any area we wanted to go. She looked great that night, but she complained that the dress was too heavy for her to wear comfortably. She gave it away the next day.

ENTERTAINMENT TONIGHT: "THE DEATH OF LUCILLE BALL"

(SYN, APRIL 26, 1989), 30 MINUTES

CAST: Mary Hart, John Tesh (hosts)

This popular program, a wrap-up of the day's events in show business, scraps its normal format and devotes its entire thirty minutes tributing Lucille Ball. Lucille has died early this morning from heart failure after being operated on several days earlier for a faulty aorta. She had been getting better after surgery and it seems she might recover, although probably forced to live in a reduced capacity physically. However, shortly after five in the morning, Lucille awakes with chest pains. Before she really knows what is happening, she is gone.

The world mourns fiercely. No one has brought the world more laughter and rest from the exigencies of everyday life than Lucille Ball.

CBS NEWS SPECIAL: LUCY

(CBS, APRIL 26, 1989), 60 MINUTES

EXECUTIVE PRODUCED BY: Lane Venardos

SENIOR PRODUCERS: Steve Jacobs, Jack Kelly, Terence Martin
DIRECTED BY: Eric Shapiro
WRITTEN BY: Jerry Cipriano, Thomas Flynn
CAST: Dan Rather (host); Charles Osgood, Mike Wallace (reporters); Oscar Katz, Jerry Lewis, William S. Paley, Ronald Reagan, Bob Schiller, Dinah Shore, Dick Van Dyke (interviewees)

Lucille's long-time network cancels regular programming to salute her on the evening of her passing. Unusually subdued with emotion, Rather hosts a loving tribute to Ball. The interviewees seem shy about speaking oncamera about her, and almost nothing of a personal nature is discussed.

1952

Best Situation Comedy: *I Love Lucy*

Best Comedienne: Lucille Ball

1953

Best Situation Comedy: *I Love Lucy*

Best Supporting Actress: Vivian Vance

1955

Best Actress (Continuing Performance): Lucille Ball

1966–67

Outstanding Continued Performance by an Actress in a Leading Role: Lucille Ball

1967–68

Outstanding Continued Performance by an Actress in a Leading Role: Lucille Ball

1988–89

Governor's Award to Lucille Ball, presented posthumously

Chapter Forty-One

Loose Change

BOB HOPE'S LOVE AFFAIR WITH LUCY

(NBC, SEPTEMBER 23, 1989), 120 MINUTES

EXECUTIVE PRODUCED BY: Bob Hope
PRODUCED BY: Linda Hope
CAST: Bob Hope (host), George Burns, Kirk Cameron, Danny Thomas, Betty White

Long-time movie and television costar Bob Hope salutes Lucille Ball in this clipfest, showing moments from their many appearances together.

I LOVE LUCY: THE VERY FIRST SHOW

(CBS, MARCH 30, 1990), 60 MINUTES

SPECIAL PRODUCED BY: Bud Grant
SPECIAL DIRECTED BY: David Steinberg
SPECIAL WRITTEN BY: Jane Milmore, Billy Van Zandt
CAST: Lucie Arnaz (host/narrator), Bob Carroll Jr., Madelyn Pugh Martin Davis

This is the first network broadcast of the original *I Love Lucy* pilot, kinescoped in March of 1951. Lucie Arnaz hosts this special from a recreation of the first Ricardo apartment. For information regarding the actual pilot, see the listing earlier in this book.

LUCY AND DESI: A HOME MOVIE

(NBC, FEBRUARY 14, 1993) 120 MINUTES

PRODUCED BY: Laurence Luckinbill, Lucie Arnaz
WRITTEN BY: Lonny Reed, Laurence Luckinbill
DIRECTED BY: Laurence Luckinbill, Lucie Arnaz
MUSIC BY: Desi Arnaz and his orchestra
CAST: Lucie Arnaz (host), Desi Arnaz Jr., Carole Cook, Marcella Rabwin, Marco Rizo, Cleo Smith, and many others.

Lucie Arnaz and husband Larry Luckinbill put together a tribute to Lucie's parents using interviews weaved through clips of home movies from the Arnaz home library. It is expertly done, heartwarming, honest, and insightful. Arnaz and Luckinbill win an Emmy for this program. It is later released on home video, with added footage and an extra video available featuring outtakes.

THE NANNY: "THE WEDDING"

(CBS, MAY 13, 1998), 60 MINUTES

CAST: Fran Drescher, Charles Shaughnessy, Lucille Ball, Renee Taylor

Via the wonders of 1990s technology, Lucy Ricardo shares the excitement of Fran the Nanny's impending marriage to upper-crust Broadway producer Maxwell Sheffield (Charles Shaughnessy). The second scene from the 1952 "Lucy Is Enciente" episode (#45) of *I Love Lucy* is misused to get Fran and Lucy in the same scene. In a dream sequence, Fran tells Lucy about her next-day nuptials, while Lucy gushes with excitement. A great idea, but it adds little to the show and is very poorly done.

LUCY'S TOP TEN TV CONTEMPORARIES BY DECADE

(RANKED IN ORDER OF IMPORTANCE BY THE AUTHOR)

The 1950s

Gracie Allen (*The George Burns and Gracie Allen Show*, 1950–55)
Joan Davis (*I Married Joan*, 1952–55)
Gale Storm (*My Little Margie; The Gale Storm Show*, 1952–55)
Eve Arden (*Our Miss Brooks*, 1952–56; *The Eve Arden Show*, 1957–58)
Spring Byington (*December Bride*, 1954–61)
Ann Sothern (*Private Secretary*, 1953–57; *The Ann Sothern Show*, 1958–61)
Audrey Meadows (*The Honeymooners*, 1955–56)
Harriet Nelson (*The Adventures of Ozzie and Harriet*, 1952–66)
Jane Wyatt (*Father Knows Best*, 1954–60)
Donna Reed (*The Donna Reed Show*, 1958–66)

The 1960s

Mary Tyler Moore (*The Dick Van Dyke Show*, 1961–66)
Marjorie Lord (*The Danny Thomas Show*, 1957–64)
Irene Ryan (*The Beverly Hillbillies*, 1962–71)
Shirley Booth (*Hazel*, 1961–66)
Bea Benaderet (*Petticoat Junction*, 1963–68)
Elizabeth Montgomery (*Bewitched*, 1964–72)
Barbara Eden (*I Dream of Jeannie*, 1965–70)
Marlo Thomas (*That Girl*, 1966–71)
Cara Williams (*Pete and Gladys*, 1960–62; *The Cara Williams Show*, 1964–65)
Doris Day (*The Doris Day Show*, 1968–73)

The 1970s

Mary Tyler Moore (*Mary Tyler Moore*, 1970–77)
Florence Henderson (*The Brady Bunch*, 1969–74)
Jean Stapleton (*All in the Family*, 1971–80)
Suzanne Pleshette (*The Bob Newhart Show*, 1972–78)
Valerie Harper (*Rhoda*, 1974–78)
Bea Arthur (*Maude*, 1972–78)
Isabel Sanford (*The Jeffersons*, 1975–85)
Bonnie Franklin (*One Day at a Time*, 1975–84)
Penny Marshall (*Laverne & Shirley*, 1976–83)
Esther Rolle (*Good Times*, 1974–79)

The 1980s

Linda Lavin (*Alice*, 1976–85)
Shelley Long (*Cheers*, 1982–87)
Nell Carter (*Gimme a Break*, 1981–87)
Judith Light (*Who's the Boss?*, 1984–92)
Bea Arthur (*The Golden Girls*, 1985–92)
Betty White (*The Golden Girls*, 1985–92)
Rue McClanahan (*The Golden Girls*, 1985–92)
Meredith Baxter (*Family Ties*, 1982–89)
Valerie Harper (*Valerie* [a.k.a. *The Hogan Family*], 1986–91)

Appendix One

The Lucille Ball Chronology

1911	August 6: Lucille Ball is born in Celoron, New York, the first child of Henry and DeDe Ball.
1915	February 28: Lucille's father dies of typhoid fever.
1918	September 17: Lucille's mother marries Ed Peterson.
1926	September: Lucille Ball moves to Manhattan to study acting at the Minton-Anderson School where one of her classmates is Bette Davis.
1930	September: After an extended illness, Lucille, who had been recuperating at home in Celoron, New York, returns to Manhattan and works as a model for Hattie Carnegie.
1933	Film producer Samuel Goldwyn brings Lucille to Hollywood to be a Goldwyn (chorus) Girl. Her first movie is the musical *Roman Scandals* (1933) starring Eddie Cantor.
1934	September: Lucille signs with the short subject department at Columbia Pictures. Her biggest role at the studio is in *Three Little Pigskins* (1934) starring the Three Stooges.
	November: Lucille signs a contract with RKO Pictures; she will remain at the studio until 1942.
1937	June 2: Lucille begins filming her first large part in an "A" film: RKO's *Stage Door*, also featuring Ginger Rogers, Katharine Hepburn, Eve Arden, and Ann Miller.
1940	June: Lucille, now billed over the title of her grade "B" RKO films, meets Desi Arnaz on the set of the musical comedy *Too Many Girls* (1940) in which they costar.
	November 30: Lucille Ball, age twenty-nine, and Desi Arnaz, age twenty-three, are married at the Byrum River Beagle Club in Greenwich, Connecticut.
1942	May: Lucille begins filming her best film at RKO: *The Big Street* (1942), a Damon Runyon story costarring Henry Fonda and Agnes Moorehead.
	August: Lucille signs a contract with MGM Studios; her best films are the 1943 musicals *Dubarry Was a Lady* and *Best Foot Forward.*

September: MGM hairstylist Sydney Guilaroff alters Lucille's brunette hair to its trademark orange/red color.

1944 November: Lucille divorces Desi Arnaz, but cohabitates with him before the decree can become final. They resume their marriage.

1946 July: MGM drops Lucille's contract and she begins free-lancing at other Hollywood film studios.

1947 June: Director Herbert Kenwith convinces Lucille to star in the Elmer Rice play *Dream Girl* at his theatre at Princeton, New Jersey. Lucille tours the country with it until the run ends in Los Angeles in March 1948.

1948 July: Lucille and Lee Bowman do a radio pilot for a domestic comedy series entitled *Mr. and Mrs. Cugat*.

September: Retitled *My Favorite Husband* and now costarring Richard Denning, the half hour radio show begins a three-year run on the CBS network; Lucille meets her future *I Love Lucy* TV sitcom writing team, Jess Oppenheimer, Madelyn Pugh, and Bob Carroll Jr. when they pen the scripts for this radio sitcom.

1951 March 2: Desi Arnaz and a pregnant Lucille shoot the pilot for *I Love Lucy*.

July 17: Lucie Desiree Arnaz is born.

October 15: *I Love Lucy* premieres on CBS-TV on Monday nights at nine P.M.

1953 January 15: Desi Arnaz Jr. is born in real life; Little Ricky is born on *I Love Lucy*.

June: Production begins on MGM's *The Long, Long Trailer* (1954), a romantic comedy headlining Lucille Ball and Desi Arnaz.

September: Newspaper columnist and radio/TV commentator Walter Winchell leaks a story that Lucille Ball had been a registered communist in the 1930s; the accusation is countered by Ball's camp and she is cleared quickly of all charges.

1954 July: Production begins on MGM's *Forever Darling*, a flop MGM fantasy comedy featuring Lucille Ball and Desi Arnaz. It is not released until 1956.

1957 May 6: The 180th and final new episode of *I Love Lucy* is aired.

November 6: The first *Lucille Ball-Desi Arnaz Show* is aired.

1960 March 3: Lucille Ball files for divorce from Desi Arnaz.

April 1: The thirteenth and final *Lucille Ball-Desi Arnaz Show* is aired.

December 16: Lucille opens on Broadway at the Alvin Theatre in the musical *Wildcat*.

1961 February 10: United Artists' *The Facts of Life*, a romantic screen comedy teaming Lucille and Bob Hope, is released to rave reviews.

April 20: An exhausted Lucille collapses onstage during a performance of *Wildcat* and the musical soon closes—after only 171 performances, and over $165,000 in advance ticket sales have to be refunded.

November 19: Lucille, age fifty, marries comedian Gary Morton, age forty-four, at Manhattan's Marble Collegiate Church with Reverend Norman Vincent Peale officiating.

1962 October 1: Lucille's third television series, *The Lucy Show*, debuts on CBS.

1963 January: Lucille purchases Desi Arnaz' half of Desilu Studios and becomes the first female head of a Hollywood studio in show business history.

June: Warner Bros.' *Critic's Choice*, a flop comedy costarring Lucille and Bob Hope, is released after being held back for almost a year; it's the fourth and final big screen teaming of Ball and Hope.

1965 September 13: *The Lucy Show* begins to air in color, but without Vivian Vance; the show's locale moves from Danfield, New York, to Hollywood, California.

1966 March 3: William Frawley dies – the first of the *I Love Lucy* series regulars to pass away.

1967 May: Lucille puts the wheels in motion to sell Desilu studios to Gulf & Western, owners of Paramount Studios.

1968 March 11: The 111th and final *The Lucy Show* airs.

September 23: *Here's Lucy*, a half-hour comedy series debuts on CBS with Lucie Arnaz and Desi Arnaz Jr. playing Lucille's onscreen children.

1970 September 14: "Lucy Meets the Burtons" episode of *Here's Lucy* airs, starring Elizabeth Taylor and Richard Burton. It is the highest rated entry of the series.

1974 March 11: The 144th and final first-run episode of *Here's Lucy* airs.

April: Lucille's final theatrical film, the Warner Bros. musical *Mame*, debuts to tepid reviews and disappointing box office.

1977 July 22: DeDe Ball dies.

1979 August 17: Vivian Vance dies.

1986 September 20: *Life with Lucy*, a new half-hour sitcom starring Lucille and Gale Gordon, debuts on ABC. The show is a disaster, and is taken off the air after only six weeks.

December 2: Desi Arnaz dies.

1989 April 18: Lucille suffers a serious heart attack in her Beverly Hills home. At nearby Cedar-Sinai Medical Center she undergoes eight hours of open heart surgery.

April 26: At 5:04 A.M. Lucille Ball, age seventy-eight, dies at Cedars-Sinai Medical Center. Per her wishes there is no funeral service and she is later buried at Forest Lawn-Hollywood Hills cemetery.

May 8: At eight P.M. a tri-city tribute is held for Lucille: at St. Monica's Catholic Church in Santa Monica, at New York City's St. Ignatius Loyola Catholic Church, and at Chicago's Old St. Patrick Church. Friends and fans come together to memorialize the late comedian.

September 17: At the Annual Emmy Awards at the Pasadena, California, Civic Auditorium Lucille Ball is awarded posthumously the Academy of Television Arts and Sciences Governor's Award.

1991 December: A life-size statue of Lucille Ball is unveiled at the Television Academy's Hall of Fame courtyard in North Hollywood, California.

Appendix Two

Who's Who in Lucy Land

DESI ARNAZ

(1917–1986)

It is difficult writing a biographical sketch for someone as well known as Desiderio Alberto Arnaz y de Acha III, the son of a prominent Cuban family. Born to wealth and position in Santiago de Cuba on March 2, 1917, Desi was destined for politics, medicine, or public service. Surrounded by race horses, mansions, yachts, and servants, he lived the privileged life that is unknown outside of Central American aristocracy. His father was mayor of his town, and Desi had several family members in high places in the Cuban government. One grandfather had been with the future U.S. President Teddy Roosevelt at San Juan Hill as a medical officer helping to fight malaria among the troops; the other one was a founding member of the Bacardi rum company.

All of this rich living came to an end in 1933 when the Batista revolution overturned the government. The vast Arnaz holdings were either burned or confiscated by the government; Desi and his mother hid in Havana while his father languished in prison. Using the little bit of money they had hidden, they obtained the release of the senior Arnaz, and Desi and his father fled to Miami. While Desi's mother later joined the family in Florida, the separation effectively ended the marriage of his parents. The refugees lived in a rat-infested warehouse, doing tile installations for a living. Desi attended Notre Dame High School, where his best friend was "Sonny" Capone, the son of the infamous Chicago racketeer Al Capone. Arnaz cleaned bird cages in dime stores for pocket money, but quickly found that the combination of his good looks and the strumming of a guitar were attention-getters.

Already a lothario, Desi discovered that his charm and musical skills translated well beyond female companionship to being onstage in front of an appreciative paying audience. After working with his own small groups, Arnaz was discovered by bandleader Xavier Cugat, who made the newcomer his protégé. After two years, Desi went off on his own, becoming a sensation in New York nightclubs. He became as famous for the women with whom he was seen as for his sexually charged conga beating.

Fate stepped in again when the Broadway composing team of Rodgers and Hart began looking for a Latin star for their new musical *Too Many Girls*. Desi was cast, and became the toast of Broadway. He was brought to California for the movie version (1940), where he first met colead Lucille Ball, then a contract star at RKO Pictures. After they married that same year, his film career was just beginning to advance when he was drafted for war service. After the war, his film career waned, and, instead, he organized a larger version of his band. They had several successful recordings, played top night club and theatre engagements, and were the band for Bob Hope's radio shows for a season (1949–50).

It was at this point that the idea for *I Love Lucy* began to take form. That story is told in full previously in this book, so a jump to Desi's bio in the late 1950s seems appropriate.

Arnaz did not cope well with the stresses of running a TV studio, and it began to take its toll on his body. His hair turned white; he gained weight; he developed diverticulitis (requiring his wearing of a colostomy bag for awhile); and his drinking turned into alcoholism. So much has been written about this addiction, but the fact of the matter was that Desi Arnaz was a gifted, talented man with a giving heart, who developed a substance abuse that masked many of his gifts.

After Lucille and Desi divorced in 1960, he continued to supervise the Desilu Studios, but without the same success he had enjoyed in the 1950s. The medium had changed drastically, and Desilu hadn't changed with it. It was now a huge corporation with three studios, angry stockholders, and executives wrestling for control. Desi was not physically up to the task. Lucille was brought back in 1962 for *The Lucy Show*, and, soon thereafter, she bought him out of his half of the studio.

Desi retrenched, spending his time at the racetrack, overseeing his hotels and real estate holdings, and wooing Edith Mack Hirsch, whom he married on March 2, 1964. He came back to series television in 1967 as producer and occasional director of *The Mothers-in-Law* for NBC. The sitcom, starring Eve Arden and Kaye Ballard, only lasted two seasons, after which Arnaz did occasional TV guest work on such series as *Rowan & Martin's Laugh-In*, *The Andy Williams Show*, *Ironsides*, and *Alice*. By the 1980s, Desi was becoming increasingly ill from his lung ailments. Mustering his remaining strength, he helped son Desi Jr. face *his* drug and alcohol demons, and, during the course of that treatment, found sobriety himself. Edith Arnaz died in 1985; shortly thereafter Desi was diagnosed with lung cancer. He and Lucille had maintained a loving relationship after their divorce, one that seemed to grow warmer with time and especially in his final years. Daughter Lucie was by his side when Desi finally succumbed to lung cancer on December 2, 1986.

DESI ARNAZ JR

(B. 1953)

No baby could possibly live up to the hoopla surrounding the birth of Desi Arnaz Jr. on January 15, 1953. Timed to coincide with the onscreen television birth of Little Ricky on his parents' TV series *I Love Lucy*, Desi's entry into the world made front page headlines throughout the U.S. and the world. After all the publicity died down, it is no wonder that Desi waited almost twelve years before becoming an independently wealthy rock star on his own. His group, Dino, Desi, and Billy (also featuring Dean Martin Jr. and Billy Henshe) propelled Desi into the world of 1960s bigtime show business. The youngsters had several hit records, and appeared on the biggest television variety shows. By the time he was fifteen, Desi was a show business veteran. Unfortunately, he became a star just as the sex and drugs revolution of the 1960s began in earnest.

In 1968, he was cast as Craig Carter on *Here's Lucy*, a TV series role he would play for three seasons. Desi's face was seen on every movie magazine and tabloid paper, as his social exploits made unfortunate headlines. Highly intelligent, incredibly handsome, seemingly self-assured, and brimming with talent, Desi lived the high life that included alcohol, drugs, and romances with some of the most beautiful women in Hollywood.

At the same time, Arnaz embarked on a series of commercial and critical successes on both the big screen and TV. *Red Sky at Morning* (1970) established Desi as a young leading man to be reckoned with. For his professional successes he won the Golden Globe Award as most promising male newcomer. TV movies like *Mr. and Mrs. Bo Jo Jones* (1971), *The Voyage of the Yes* (1972), *She Lives!* (1973), *Having Babies* (1976), *Flight to Holocaust* (1976), *To Kill a Cop* (1978), *Gridlock* (1980), and *The Night the Bridge Fell Down* (1983) provided Arnaz with a wide range of acting roles. Desi's only other TV series, *Automan* (1983–84) was a quirky but well-done science fiction series that cast Desi against type as a nebbish scientist. By this time, Desi's party life had developed into a compulsive disease involving drugs and alcohol.

Desi reached bottom, and sought help through twelve-step programs and the teachings of Vernon Howard, for whom he later became a spokesperson. Eventually, Arnaz retired from show business and settled in Boulder City, Nevada, with his wife Amy and daughter Haley.

LUCIE ARNAZ

(B. 1951)

Breaking the stereotype of spoiled Hollywood child, Lucie Arnaz has built a career based entirely on her own talent, charm, beauty, and drive. Born on July 17, 1951, Lucie Desiree Arnaz could have led the idle life of an offspring of wealthy and famous parents. Instead, she has carefully and slowly built a long show business career of her own. Making her TV debut on *The Lucy Show* in 1962, Arnaz immediately displayed two talents that have always served her well: a flair for comedy and a very photogenic face. After playing several parts on *The Lucy Show*, each one larger than the one before, Lucie was cast as Kim Carter on *Here's Lucy* in 1968. For six seasons, Arnaz honed her craft in front of a live audience, as both she and the production team learned where her talents lay and how to make the best use of it. By the time the program ended in 1974, Lucie was a beautiful young woman with a great future ahead of her.

Lucie realized that her talents lent themselves to musical comedy, and undertook parts in stock productions of such musicals as *Once Upon a Mattress*, *Cabaret*, *L'il Abner*, and *Bye Bye Birdie*. Concurrently, she began a series of TV movies, such as *Who Is the Black Dahlia?* (1975), *Death Scream* (1975), and *The Mating Season* (1980). In 1978, she received huge kudos for her role as Annie Oakley in *Annie Get Your Gun* at the Jones Beach Theatre on Long Island, New York. The theater world took notice and her stage career went into full gear. She wowed audiences as Gittle in the national tour of the musical *Seesaw*, and then became a Broadway star when she costarred with Robert Klein and Tony Roberts in *They're Playing Our Song* (1979).

More Broadway and touring company roles followed, including two with Tommy Tune and several with Laurence Luckinbill, who became her second husband. The Luckinbills have three children (Simon, Joseph, and Katharine), and Lucie is the stepmother of Nicholas and Ben Luckinbill. Although she has taken time out of her career from time to time to be a full-time mother, it has not stopped her from making movies (*The Jazz Singer*, 1980; *Second Thoughts*, 1983), doing stage work (*Lost in Yonkers*, *Grace and Glorie*), recording (*Just in Time*), and touring with her nightclub act (Las Vegas, Reno, Atlantic City, New York, Branson, Washington, D.C.).

Although her two television series (*The Lucie Arnaz Show*, 1982; *Sons & Daughters*, 1991) were not ratings successes, they were well received critically. It seems Lucie is good at anything she chooses to try. She has won the Carbonel Award (1978), the Los Angeles Drama Critics Award (1979), the Theatre World Award (1979), the Outer Critics' Circle Award (1979), the Sarah Siddons Award (1986), the Emmy Award (1993), and was nominated for the Golden Globe Award in 1980.

In 1990, Lucie and Larry Luckinbill formed Arluck Entertainment, and together produced the documentary *Lucy & Desi: A Home Movie* (1993). In 1997, they started Education through Entertainment, which produced two CD-ROMs: *Lucy & Desi: The Scrapbooks, Volume 1*, and *How to Save Your Family History, a 10-Step Guide by Lucie Arnaz*. Arnaz and her brother Desi helm Desilu, Too, a watchdog for the proper presentation of their parents' images and a production company. Lucie resides with her family in a beautifully redone Early American farmhouse in Katonah, New York.

MARY JANE CROFT

(B. CIRCA 1915)

The blonde face with the blonde voice, the petite actress was born in Muncie, Indiana. Mary Jane was actually a highly respected radio actress, who appeared in many shows of the 1940s and 1950s in Hollywood. She was able to play everything from lady judges and society dames to floozies and broad comedy parts. When television began to push radio out of the way, Mary Jane easily made the transition. She regularly appeared with two of Lucille Ball's comedian competitors, Joan Davis (*I Married Joan*) and Eve Arden *(Our Miss*

Brooks), before lending her voice to Cleo the Dog on *The People's Choice* (1955–58). Mary Jane even provided that voice when the dog appeared on *The Perry Como Show*.

Croft had only worked once with Ball (in a small part on radio's *My Favorite Husband*) when she was tapped to play her first part on an *I Love Lucy* episode. Lucille liked her professionalism, and before long Mary Jane found herself playing a recurring role during the last season (1956–57) of the classic sitcom, that of neighbor Betty Ramsey. When Lucille moved on to other things, Croft (who had by this time married director/producer Elliot Lewis) became a regular on *The Adventures of Ozzie and Harriet*. There she played Harriet's friend Clara Bagley. Concurrent with her Nelson chores, Mary Jane again joined Ball on *The Lucy Show*, and then on *Here's Lucy*, each time playing kooky, shrill-voiced dames named Mary Jane. Croft did one more special with Lucille, "Lucy Calls the President" (1977). She retired from performing after her husband Elliot passed away in the early 1990s. Still beautiful at this writing, she resides in Century City, California.

WILLIAM FRAWLEY

(1887–1966)

The man Ethel loved to hate on *I Love Lucy* had an extremely long career in show business. Born on February 26, 1887 in Burlington, Iowa, Frawley got into the only area of show business that existed in the Midwest of his youth: vaudeville. He was a song and dance man as well as a comedian, and was considered quite handsome in his day. His flashing blue eyes and courtly Irish manner quickly made him an audience favorite. He married Edna Louise Broedt in 1914, and soon thereafter introduced the standard "My Melancholy Baby" in vaudeville. The song lasted but the marriage did not; Bill and Louise were divorced in 1927.

By this point, Bill was losing his charm as fast as he was losing his hair. At the age of forty, he looked considerably older. A drinking problem developed into alcoholism, which effectively ended his stage career. Frawley wound up in Hollywood in 1933, and for the next eighteen years made a nice living playing small parts in dozens of films. The only interest he had outside of show business was sports, and Bill was an avid baseball and prize fight fan. Socially, he only saw his Irish cronies, as his failed marriage left him bitter toward women. By the early 1950s, his career had fizzled. He took a chance and contacted Desi Arnaz, swallowing his own prejudices against Latinos to get a job. Arnaz kept Frawley employed for the next nine years.

When the *I Love Lucy* format ran its course in 1960, Bill still had a long-term exclusive contract with Desilu Studios. Ignoring it, he immediately signed with TV producer Don Fedderson to costar with Fred MacMurray in the new sitcom *My Three Sons*. The slower pace of this show, shot like a film without a studio audience, enabled him to work another five years. In early 1965, Bill had a mild stroke, and was written off the program. He did film one more episode, which showed a very ill "Bub" going off to Ireland. Frawley knew his acting days were over, but he wanted to work one more time. He contacted Lucille Ball, and a cameo appearance was arranged for him on *The Lucy Show.* After the filming, Frawley retired to his apartment hotel, living with a male nurse in attendance. He had several months of relative happiness, until March 3, 1966, when a massive stroke killed him while on a stroll down Hollywood Boulevard.

GALE GORDON

(1906–1995)

The king of the slow burn, Gale was born Charles Aldrich Jr. on February 2, 1906 in New York City and raised in England. His theatrical parents pushed him into show business to help him overcome being born with a cleft palate. His distinct manner of speaking, with long open vowels and crisp syllables, was originally developed in speech therapy. He made his Broadway debut in *The Dancers* in the 1920s, but soon moved over to the then new medium of radio. Gale became one of the busiest radio actors around, sometimes appearing in as many as twenty or thirty different shows a week. Along the way, he worked with many of the talents he would later encounter on television, including Doris Singleton, Shirley Mitchell, Frank Nelson, Mary Jane Croft, Jimmy Durante, and Dennis Day. He was loved by almost everyone he encountered, except for a strange antipathy he had toward Mel Blanc (the latter famous as the voice of Bugs Bunny and other cartoon characters). Perhaps it was because they were often competitors for the same types of acting jobs, but the two men just did not get along.

During World War II, Gordon served with distinction as a Coast Guard skipper, where he commanded a war-zone landing craft off the coast of California. Shortly after the war, he met his wife, actress Virginia Curley, while doing an episode of radio's *Death Valley Days.* Their marriage was a good luck omen for Gordon's radio career, as he soon began playing lead roles such as Mayor LaTrivia on the classic *Fibber McGee and Molly* (1945). That kind of exposure brought him to the attention of producer Jess Oppenheimer, who cast him as Mr. Atterbury on the radio comedy *My Favorite Husband* (1948–51) starring Lucille Ball.

Lucille adored his style of comedy delivery, and, forever after, she was fiercely loyal to Gale. Gordon soon started doubling up in starring radio appearances when he was cast as Osgood Conklin in *Our Miss Brooks* (1949–56). Although budgetary constraints kept Gale from becoming Fred Mertz on *I Love Lucy*, by the time Desilu brought *Brooks* to television, there was enough money to pay him to give up radio and play Conklin. Gale made two *I Love Lucy* guest appearances, as well as one with the Arnazes in 1958 on one of their hour-long shows. Thereafter, Gale was never out of TV work unless by choice. When *Brooks* finally went off the air (on radio and television), Gale and Bob Sweeney went on to star in *The Brothers* for one season (1956–57), followed by *Sally* (1958). When that ended,

Gale moved to another Desilu sound stage or two, when he played regular parts in both *The Danny Thomas Show* (1953–64) and *Pete and Gladys* (1960–62) simultaneously. When Joseph Kearns passed away during the filming of *Dennis the Menace*, Gale stepped in to become another Mr. Wilson (1962–63). It was his obligation to *Dennis* that kept him from once again starting a TV series with Lucille Ball, this time *The Lucy Show*.

After *Dennis'* demise, Ball snatched him up and never let him go again. In the second season of *The Lucy Show*, he was introduced as Lucy Carmichael's long-suffering banker Theodore J. Mooney. In 1965, the series altered its format so Lucy worked for Mr. Mooney after both characters moved to Los Angeles. Now Gale was billed just under Miss Ball. Lucille kept him employed for an additional six seasons when *Here's Lucy* (1968–74) came to CBS. This time, Gale was Harrison Otis Carter, Lucy Carter's beleaguered and somewhat mean brother-in-law and boss.

After Ball ended her twenty-three-year reign as Queen of TV, Gale returned to his first love: theatre. He spent his summers taking plays all over Canada, while relaxing in the winters at his 150-acre ranch near Borrego Springs, California. There were other television guest spots, including two reunion specials with Lucille. However, no one was more surprised than Gale when he received the call to come back to TV series work when Ball launched *Life with Lucy* in 1986. After that disaster, Gale retired from show business except for a cameo appearance on the TV sitcom *Hi Honey, I'm Home* in 1991, once again playing Mr. Mooney. Both Gale and Virginia were active in community projects. Gale was named honorary mayor of Borrego Springs and served as the president of its Chamber of Commerce. When Virginia became ill and was put in a nursing home, Gale soon followed. He passed away from cancer on June 30, 1995, at the Redwood Terrace Health Center in Escondido, California.

CHARLES LANE

(B. 1899)

The thin, bespectacled, and always sour-faced character actor was born Charles Levison in San Francisco in 1899. (Some sources say 1905.) After struggling to be a stage actor, Lane's movie career started in 1931 at Warner Bros., where he played in a spate of films as desk clerks, reporters, doctors, and other stuffy types. His incredible career in films lasted more than six decades until 1987, when he played a priest in *Date with an Angel*. Charley's first television appearance was, in fact, on *I Love Lucy*. He was a regular on *Dear Phoebe* (1954–55), *Petticoat Junction* (1963–69), *The Beverly Hillbillies* (1971), and *Karen* (1975), but appeared on literally hundreds of episodes of other series. Among the best of these were *Dennis the Menace* (1961) and *Bewitched* (1967). Although Lane was signed to be a regular (Mr. Bardsdahl, the banker) on *The Lucy Show* (1962–68), he was quietly replaced after several episodes because he had trouble with his lines in front of the live audiences.

DICK MARTIN

(B. 1922)

Best known as the other comedic half of Dan Rowan, Dick was born in Detroit, Michigan, on January 30, 1922. Respected as one of the nicest men in show business, Martin is a talented actor, comedian, and director. With partner Dan Rowan, he has appeared on such television series as *The Chevy Show* (1958) and *The Dean Martin Show* (1966) before becoming a sensation on *Rowan & Martin's Laugh-In* (1968–73). As a single performer, he frequented many of the game and variety shows of the 1960s and 1970s before becoming a top television director of such programs as *The Bob Newhart Show* (1977–78). Dick played neighbor Harry Connors during the first season (1962–63) of *The Lucy Show*, but his character was phased out after six months.

ROY ROBERTS

(1900–1975)

Born in Tampa, Florida, on March 19, 1900, Roy got started in show business very late in life. He didn't begin appearing in films until 1951, and started his television career a few years later while in his middle fifties. A regular on such series as *The Gale Storm Show* (1956–60), *The Beverly Hillbillies* (1964–67), and *Gunsmoke* (1965–70), he is also fondly remembered as witchly Elizabeth Montgomery's father-in-law on *Bewitched* (1964–70). Roberts became a regular on *The Lucy Show* in 1966, when he began portraying Mr. Cheever, the boss of banker Theodore J. Mooney. His final television stint was, ironically enough, on *Here's Lucy* in 1974. Roberts died in 1975.

ROY ROWAN

(1920–1998)

Born in Paw Paw, Michigan, Rowan attended Western Michigan University in Kalamazoo. There, he began working with such other future broadcasters as Ralph Story, Paul Harvey, and Harry Carry. After years of toiling at local radio stations, Roy moved to Los Angeles and began working as a staff announcer for CBS. Besides announcing all of Lucille Ball's television series, he was also heard on *People Are Funny*, *Cheyenne*, *I Married Joan*, *Rawhide*, *Simon and Simon*, *Magnum P.I.*, and *Dallas*. In later years, Rowan also brokered the sales of radio and television stations. He died May 10, 1998, from heart failure.

DORIS SINGLETON

(B. CIRCA 1920)

One of the busiest actresses in radio and television history, Doris has been active in show business since the 1940s. Her distinctive speaking voice made her a radio favorite, and she made many appearances with Lucille Ball on radio's *My Favorite Husband*. Television soon beckoned, and Doris' pretty face and trim figure made her a frequent visitor to the tube. She was a regular on three series (*I Love Lucy*, *The*

Great Gildersleeve, and *Angel*), but Doris is also remembered for gracing such classics as *The Jack Benny Show*, *Perry Mason*, *The Adventures of Superman*, *Mr. Lucky*, *The Dick Van Dyke Show*, *The Jimmy Durante Show*, *The Lucy Show*, *My Three Sons*, *Hogan's Heroes*, *Here's Lucy*, and many others. She will always be remembered as Lucy Ricardo's friend and nemesis Caroline Appleby on *I Love Lucy*. Still beautiful, she resides in Los Angeles and occasionally accepts a guest role assignment on TV to keep active.

KEITH THIBODEAUX

(B. 1950)

The boy, who will forever be identified as Little Ricky, has traveled a long road to successful adulthood. Born in Louisiana on December 1, 1950, Keith was discovered at the age of three by bandleader Horace Heidt. After two years in bigtime show business, Keith's name and future were changed when he was cast as Little Ricky on *I Love Lucy* in 1956. His professional name became Richard Keith, and he appeared with Lucille and Desi on all of their TV shows until 1960, when the couple divorced.

Keith grew very close to Desi Arnaz Jr. and Lucie Arnaz, but relations with the Arnazes became strained in the early 1960s. Desilu Studios had no regular work for Keith, who was relegated to playing small parts on sitcoms filmed on the Desilu lot. When Keith's father had a disagreement with Lucille Ball, she fired him from his position at Desilu. This forced Thibodeaux and his family to move back to their native Louisiana, as they could no longer afford to live in California. Like many baby boomers, Keith sought solace in alcohol and drugs and followed the same downward spiral that happened to many other former child actors. In 1974, Keith accepted Jesus Christ as his personal savior, and life for him was forever changed. He married a ballet dancer, Kathy, and they have a daughter, Tara. They run the largest Christian ballet company in the world, Ballet Magnificat, and tour all over the world. Keith's memoir was published in 1993.

VIVIAN VANCE

(1909–1979)

Vivian Roberta Jones was born on July 26, 1912, in Cherryvale, Kansas. Although she always claimed to be younger than Lucille Ball, she was indeed two years older. Vivian had a very unhappy childhood, living with a disapproving and unloving mother. In her late teens, Vivian moved to Albuquerque, New Mexico, where she showed a talent for singing and displaying shapely legs. She became a local celebrity and the star of the community playhouse. The town thought so much of her that they paid her way to New York and gave her a stake to get started in big-time show business. Although she never became a star of the first magnitude, Vivian did appear in many Broadway productions. She was Ethel Merman's understudy in *Anything Goes* (1934), and later headlined in plays and musicals under the power of her own name.

Vance suffered a nervous breakdown in the mid-1940s, due to the emotional baggage of her unloving childhood, the wild sexual and emotional behavior of her youth, which gave her tremendous guilt feelings, and her unhappy marriage to abusive Phil Ober, her third husband. By 1951, she was feeling better and appeared in a stock company version of the comedy in which she had been featured when she had her breakdown, *The Voice of the Turtle*. It was there that she was discovered for *I Love Lucy*.

Vivian divorced Ober in 1959, and married book editor John Dobbs in 1960. She had made a new life for herself in Connecticut when she was summoned back to California for *The Lucy Show*. After she quit the show in 1965, Vance thought her role in *The Great Race* (1965) would jump-start her movie career, but it did not. Vivian appeared fairly frequently on television thereafter. She did as many game shows as possible, which were mostly located on the East Coast in those days, as well as yearly appearances with Ball on Lucille's CBS sitcoms. In 1973, it was discovered she had breast cancer. A stroke felled her in 1976, temporarily paralyzing one side of her body. While rehearsing the 1977 TV special *Lucy Calls the President*, Vivian was told that her cancer had spread, and she simultaneously came down with Bell's Palsy. Vivian passed away on August 17, 1979.

MARY WICKES

(1916–1995)

One of the most beloved character actresses in show business, Mary Isabelle Wickenhauser was born June 13, 1916, in St. Louis, Missouri. Sharp-featured Mary was a stage actress in New York, with over twenty Broadway credits, when she came to Hollywood in 1941. Never under contract to any one studio, Wickes mixed roles in such prestige movies as *Now, Voyager* (1942) with Bette Davis, *On Moonlight Bay* (1951) with Doris Day, *White Christmas* (1954) with Bing Crosby, *The Music Man* (1962) with Robert Preston, *Postcards from the Edge* (1990) with Meryl Streep, and Whoopi Goldberg's two *Sister Act* films (1992; 1993) with potboilers like *Blondie's Blessed Event* (1942) and *Ma and Pa Kettle at Home* (1954). Mary entered television almost at its inception, doing live work from New York. It was there that she met Lucille Ball, beginning a lifelong friendship. Mary was the first video *Mary Poppins*, beating out Julie Andrews by more than a decade. She is remembered for classic appearances on such series as *I Love Lucy*, *Make Room for Daddy*, *Bonino*, *Dennis the Menace*, *The Lucy Show*, *Julia*, *Here's Lucy*, *Doc*, and many others. Her career never seemed to wane, and, in fact, Mary was as busy as ever when she died on October 22, 1995, from complications following surgery.

Appendix Three

The Lucy *Shows Quiz*

This is not a quiz for wimps. Here are fifty, *very* difficult questions on the television career of Lucille Ball. They come from all areas of her work, and are NOT in chronological order. Some are fill in the blank, some are multiple choice, and some are a little tricky, so watch out! If you can answer even thirty out of these fifty questions, you are indeed a *Lucyphile* and can consider yourself among the few and the proud. Take a deep breath, and good luck!

1. How did Lucy's TV protégée Carole Cook get her name?
2. When did Hans Conried first work with Lucille Ball?
3. Kathryn Card played two roles on *I Love Lucy*; what were they?
4. On all of her television series over the decades, only two people were Lucille Ball's hairstylists. Who were they?
5. What country song did Tennessee Ernie Ford incessantly sing in the Ricardos' apartment?
6. True or False: Vivian Vance was born in Albuquerque, New Mexico.
7. How many children did Theodore J. Mooney of *The Lucy Show* have?
8. What product did Lucille and Desi plug weekly on *I Love Lucy* during its first four years?
9. Which of the following Hooterville actors never guest-starred on a Lucille Ball TV series: Eddie Albert, Eva Gabor, Edgar Buchanan, Bea Benaderet?
10. Who wrote the lyrics to the *I Love Lucy* theme song?
11. Two famous situation comedy characters, played by the same person, met Lucy Ricardo. Who were they?
12. One famous sitcom character met both Lucy Ricardo *and* Lucy Carter. Who was it?
13. True or False: Bob Hope appeared on *Here's Lucy*.
14. What was Desi Arnaz' full real-life name?

15. Which famous comedy star directed two episodes of *Here's Lucy*?

16. Which *My Three Sons* actors did not appear on one of Lucille Ball's TV series: Fred MacMurray, Beverly Garland, Don Grady, Tina Cole, Stanley Livingston, Barry Livingston?

17. Fill in the blank: "___________ is a great big bunch of gyps," as sung by Lucille Ball on *I Love Lucy*.

18. Which classic TV panel show lady also appeared as a guest on one of Lucille Ball's series: Kitty Carlisle, Jayne Meadows, Arlene Francis, Faye Emerson, or Betty White?

19. Two men named Thompson worked for Lucille Ball for many years. What are their first names?

20. Only one actor appeared on two Lucille Ball TV specials in the 1970s. Who was he?

21. True or false: Every episode of *I Love Lucy* was filmed in front of a studio audience.

22. Of such *I Love Lucy* competitors as *My Little Margie*, *I Married Joan*, and *Our Miss Brooks*, which TV series ran the longest?

23. Which of the following talk show hosts did *not* do a comedy scene on TV with Lucille: Merv Griffin, Johnny Carson, David Frost, Mike Douglas, or Joan Rivers?

24. Which of the following *Laugh-In* stars never appeared with Lucille: Dan Rowan, Dick Martin, Goldie Hawn, Arte Johnson, or Ruth Buzzi?

25. List all of the last names that the *Lucy* TV character was known by through the years.

26. Of "Cuban Pete," "Si Mi Lo," "Down Mexico Way," "The Lady in Red," "Guadelajara," and "Mama Inez," which was the one not sung by Desi Arnaz?

27. What is the significance of "Vance with Dance" on the *I Love Lucy* series?

28. Jimmy Garrett's character on *The Lucy Show* was called Jerry Carmichael. By what other name was he once referred to, and why?

29. Eva Gabor guest starred on *Here's Lucy* as a famous novelist. What book had her character supposedly written?

30. Of Andy Griffith, Danny Thomas, Don Knotts, Dick Van Dyke, Sheldon Leonard, and Richard Crenna, which one did *not* guest star on one of Lucille's shows?

31. Ethel Merman, Mary Martin, and Carol Channing: Which one did Lucille *not* do an impression of on her TV show?

32. What was actually in the bottle of Vitameatavegamin in one of the most famous of episodes from *I Love Lucy*?
33. What was Mrs. Trumbull's first name on *I Love Lucy*?
34. What two adjectives does Lucy Ricardo use to describe the kind of name she wants to give her baby?
35. The Lucy character on TV has spoken to two presidents on the telephone. Who were they?
36. What was Uncle Harry's full name on *Here's Lucy*?
37. Name the sisters who portrayed Teensy and Weensy on *I Love Lucy*.
38. Of Helen Hayes, Ethel Merman, Tallulah Bankhead, Bette Davis, Ginger Rogers, and Joan Crawford, which one of these legendary ladies did *not* appear with Lucille on television?
39. Sid Gould played countless character parts for Lucille during the years. What other *Lucy* acting favorite was he married to?
40. On her first appearance with Lucille, what was the name of the character Mary Jane Croft played?
41. What popular rock group of the 1960s appeared on the special *Lucy in London*?
42. What item did Lucy make Ricky destroy by fire when they married?
43. From 1951 until 1969, who was the musical director for Lucille Ball's shows?
44. Of *Password*, *To Tell the Truth*, *I've Got a Secret*, and *What's My Line?*, on which TV panel show did Lucille Ball not appear?
45. What is Lucy Ricardo's middle name?
46. What school did Marion Strong, a member of the Wednesday Afternoon Fine Arts League, attend?
47. What is the name of Little Ricky's dog?
48. Of Milton Berle, Jack Benny, and Bob Hope, with whom did Lucille make the most television appearances over the decades?
49. What was the highest rated *Here's Lucy* episode?
50. In what year did CBS begin broadcasting Miss Ball's TV shows in color?

Appendix Four

I Recommend

BIBLIOGRAPHY

There are several books I used as sources of information for this project. Listed below are the ones I feel have the best information, include the best photographs, and can provide interested fans with a picture of the personal and business lives of Lucille Ball and friends:

A Book by Desi Arnaz (New York: William Morrow and Co., 1976) This was the first attempt at anyone chronicling the life of Desi Arnaz. Although Desi did have a hand in its creation, much of the book was ghostwritten for him by ex-brother-in-law Kenny Morgan. It contains the usual glaring errors and fictions contained in most celebrity autobiographies, the most contentious of which are Desi's claims concerning the creation of *I Love Lucy*. It is, however, fascinating reading. Desi's story is compelling, and (like Lucille's autobiography) gives the best impression of what Desi thought about life, his family, and his career. This book is highly recommended, although it contains language and sexual situations that may be inappropriate for children under ten.

Desilu, The Story of Lucille Ball and Desi Arnaz by Coyne Steven Sanders and Tom Gilbert (New York: William Morrow and Co., 1993) This book is a must-own. Just about anything you'd want to know about the lives and business dealings of Lucille and Desi can be found here. As a whole, this is a fascinating and well-written book. The authors are not only talented writers and historians, but love the subject matter at hand (and it shows). Readers should be warned: There are some not very complimentary stories told in this book, and although they may very well be true, some die-hard fans may be offended by the content. Due to strong language and sexual content, this book is not recommended for children under thirteen.

For the Love of Lucy by Ric B. Wyman (New York: Abbeville Press, 1995) The success of the careers of Lucille Ball and Desi Arnaz produced a phantasmagoria of promotional products over a fifty-year history. This book chronicles them all, from lunchboxes and board games to clothing and furniture. There is no real career information presented, but for the serious fan or collector this book is like a box of chocolates: tempting, delicious, a little sticky sometimes, many empty calories, but a lot of fun!

The I Love Lucy Book by Bart Andrews (New York: Dolphin/Doubleday, 1985) An entire industry was born when Bart Andrews first wrote this book in 1976. No one had ever taken a scholarly look at a TV series before. All of us who write about pop culture owe Bart a debt of gratitude for paving the way. Completely updated and rewritten in 1985, this exhaustive tome unfortunately contains dozens of pieces of misinformation and errors. However, Bart used the best information available at the time, and what is correct is excellent.

Laughs, Luck . . . and Lucy by Jess Oppenheimer and Greg Oppenheimer (Syracuse, NY: Syracuse University Press, 1996) This one is a must for any lover of *I Love Lucy*! Told from the perspective of that show's creator and headwriter, this book clarifies a good deal of misinformation about the creation of *I Love Lucy* and the decisions that went into making it the most beloved show in television history. Included is a CD of soundtracks from both *I Love Lucy* and its radio predecessor, *My Favorite Husband*. This is the only book on Lucille Ball I have read to date that contains no blatant factual errors.

Life After Lucy by Keith Thibodeaux and Audrey T. Hingley (Green Forest, AK: New Leaf Press, 1993) This is the story of *I Love Lucy*'s most famous Little Ricky, Keith Thibodeaux. It features stories told from a perspective not shared before, as Keith was a frequent visitor to the Arnaz home in the late 1950s and early 1960s. The book goes on to discuss Keith's troubles with drugs, and how he came to find fulfillment through his belief in Jesus. While some non-Christian (or even Christian) readers may be put off by the strong religious content, I cannot imagine any young person not benefiting from reading about Keith's struggles with fame, drugs, alcohol, and spirituality. Best of all, the book has a happy ending!

Love, Lucy by Lucille Ball with Betty Hannah Hoffman New York: G.P. Putnam's Sons, 1996) While not every piece of information included in this book is fully accurate, nowhere else will you find a better portrait of how Lucille Ball actually thought and felt about her life. It is a shame that Lucille did not update this book before she passed away in 1989, as the story ends just after the beginning of *The Lucy Show* in the early 1960s. This is an excellent book for younger readers.

Loving Lucy by Bart Andrews and Thomas J. Watson (New York: St. Martin's Press, 1980) If you appreciate beautiful, glamorous pictures of lovely Lucille Ball, this is the coffee table book for you. While the text is slight, the illustrations are breathtaking. Collectors, you must own this one!

Lucille, the Life of Lucille Ball by Kathleen Brady (New York: Hyperion, 1994) This book gives the best accounting of the early life of Lucille Ball, piecing together the chronicle of her childhood and early adult life. There has been much misinformation about the first twenty years of Lucille's life published through the years (much of it proffered by Ball herself). While other tomes have tried to make sense of this time period, Kathleen does the best job of putting the truth into its proper perspective and sequence of events. The later sections of this volume, mostly, just retell the same stories found in other books. Due to strong language, this book is not recommended for children under thirteen.

The Other Side of Ethel Mertz, The Life Story of Vivian Vance by Frank Castelluccio and Alvin Walker (Manchester, CT: Knowledge, Ideas & Trends, Inc., 1998) This biography of Vivian Vance paints a sad picture of everybody's best pal. Insecure, unloved as a child, morally loose as a young woman, involved in three failed marriages, and feeling trapped by her Ethel Mertz personna, Vance is portrayed as having had a very unhappy life. While this book presents the most new information about Vivian Vance ever published (including the fact that she was *indeed* older than Lucille Ball), one cannot hope but wish that it was written more compellingly and with a little more love. However, it stands as *the* guide to the hard times of Vivian Vance. Due to sexual content, not recommended for children under ten.

LUCY ON THE WEB

This is the easiest piece of information to share with you. There is a Web site called *Lucy Links* (http://www.members.aol.com/BVD1043/index1.html) that lists and links more than sixty Web sites dealing with the life and career of Lucille Ball. You can take your pick of which you like best. Many of them share the same information. Be aware that there is much misinformation about Lucille Ball on the web!

LUCY'S TV CAREER ON VIDEO

Episodes of *I Love Lucy*, *The Lucy-Desi Comedy Hour*, and *The Lucy Show* are available from Columbia House Video. The prints are all digitally enhanced, with superior sound and picture quality.

Shokus Video carries many classic public domain television shows on videotape, including several non-*Lucy* performances by Lucille Ball. They can be reached at www.Shokus.com. For a complete catalogue, send $3 to Shokus Video, P.O. Box 3125, Chatsworth, CA 91313. The catalogue comes with a $5 discount coupon.

There are several bootleg video tapes available in stores all over the world. They contain copyrighted material, and I will not be a party to promoting products that are illegal, and rob both the copyright holders and the estates of Lucille Ball and Desi Arnaz of their rightful profits.

Quiz Answers

1. Lucille named her after Carole Lombard when she joined the Desilu Workshop.
2. On *Pantomime Quiz* in 1947
3. Minnie Finch and Mrs. McGillicuddy
4. Bert French and Irma Kusely
5. "Wabash Cannonball"
6. False, she was born in Cherryvale, Kansas, but was raised in Albuquerque.
7. Three: a grown daughter, a teenaged son, and a little boy
8. Philip Morris cigarettes (Desi died of lung cancer and Lucille of heart failure.)
9. Edgar Buchanan
10. Harold Adamson
11. Suzie McNamara and Katie O'Connor
12. Kathy Williams of *The Danny Thomas Show*
13. False
14. Desiderio Alberto Arnaz y de Acha
15. Jack Carter
16. Stanley Livingston
17. Phipps
18. Jayne Meadows
19. Maury and Tommy
20. Art Carney
21. False
22. *Our Miss Brooks*
23. Merv Griffin
24. Goldie Hawn
25. Ricardo, Carmichael, Carter, Collins, Whittaker, and Barker (OK, and McGillicuddy)
26. "Down Mexico Way"
27. A flub that was kept in an episode of *I Love Lucy* guest-starring Van Johnson.
28. Jimmy. Lucille confused the name of the actor with that of his character, and insisted that the wrong name be used the night of the filming.
29. "Valley of the Puppets"
30. Dick Van Dyke
31. She did impressions of all of them.
32. Apple Pectin
33. Mathilda

34. Unique and euphonious
35. John F. Kennedy on *The Lucy Show* and Jimmy Carter on *Here's Lucy*
36. Harrison Otis Carter
37. The Borden Twins
38. Bette Davis
39. Vanda Barra
40. Cynthia Harcourt
41. The Dave Clark Five
42. His "little black book"
43. Wilbur Hatch
44. *To Tell the Truth*
45. Esmeralda
46. The Rappahonic School for Girls
47. Fred
48. By far, Bob Hope
49. "Lucy Meets the Burtons"
50. 1965

Index

Please note that for regular cast and crew members of Miss Ball's various TV series (as well as the shows' titles), only the first page number of each TV season for that series is listed.

About the Author

Courtesy of Don Dockerdorf

Critics have called Geoffrey Mark Fidelman a walking encyclopedia of pop culture. As a former child actor, he was seen in several productions in New York as well as in summer stock and dinner theatres all over America. By the age of eighteen, he was playing major nightclubs in New York with his own jazz trio. As a freelancer, Mr. Fidelman is a Grammy-nominated writer. His first book, *First Lady of Song: Ella Fitzgerald for the Record* has been published in hardcover (Birch Lane Press, 1995), softcover (Citadel Press, 1997), and on audiotape (Blackstone Audiobooks, 1999). He is a lecturer on the history of television, jazz, and Broadway, and has been seen and heard on television and radio talk shows all over the country. Along with Paul Petersen, he has been the co-host of a talk show on the Recovery Talk Radio Network called *Taking the High Road.* Geoffrey is on the board of directors of *A Minor Consideration*, a non-profit organization that is an advocate for and helps current and former child actors, child sports participants, and the children of famous people. His current projects include a stage play he has written which will be produced in Los Angeles, a sitcom pilot he has written called *Little Ricky*, and co-authoring the autobiographies of Jack Carter, Mike Connors, Jay North, and Brandon Cruz. Mr. Fidelman resides in Sherman Oaks, California.